UNIVERSITY OF
WOLVERHAMPTON
KNOWLEDGE • INNOVATION • ENTERPRISE

Corporate Insolvency Law
Perspectives and Principles

In this volume Vanessa Finch provides a new way of looking at
corporate insolvency laws and processes. She adopts an
interdisciplinary approach in placing two questions at the
centre of her discussion. Are current English laws and
procedures efficient, expert, accountable and fair? Are
fundamentally revised conceptions of insolvency law needed if
it is to develop in a way that serves corporate as well as broader
social ends?

Topics considered in this wide-ranging study include the
different ways of financing companies, the causes of corporate
failure and the prospects of designing processes that are rescue
friendly. Alternative ways of distributing the assets of failed
companies are also examined as are allocations of insolvency
risks and the effects of insolvency on a company's directors
and employees.

Finch argues that changes of approach are needed if
insolvency law is to develop with coherence and purpose.
Corporate Insolvency Law: Perspectives and Principles offers a
framework for such an approach. This book has relevance
across the common law world and will appeal to academics,
insolvency professionals and students at advanced
undergraduate as well as graduate level.

VANESSA FINCH is a Reader in Law at the London School of
Economics and Political Science where she teaches corporate
law and insolvency law. She has published numerous articles
in these fields and she is a member of the Insolvency Lawyers'
Association Academic Advisory Group.

Corporate Insolvency Law

Perspectives and Principles

Vanessa Finch

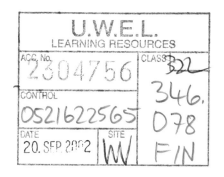

CAMBRIDGE
UNIVERSITY PRESS

PUBLISHED BY THE PRESS SYNDICATE OF THE UNIVERSITY OF CAMBRIDGE
The Pitt Building, Trumpington Street, Cambridge, United Kingdom

CAMBRIDGE UNIVERSITY PRESS
The Edinburgh Building, Cambridge CB2 2RU, UK
40 West 20th Street, New York, NY 10011-4211, USA
477 Williamstown Road, Port Melbourne, VIC 3207, Australia
Ruiz de Alarcón 13, 28014 Madrid, Spain
Dock House, The Waterfront, Cape Town 8001, South Africa

http://www.cambridge.org

First published 2002

Printed in the United Kingdom at the University Press, Cambridge

Typefaces Lexicon No. 2 9/13 pt. and Lexicon No. 1   *System* LATEX 2$_\varepsilon$ [TB]

A catalogue record for this book is available from the British Library

Library of Congress Cataloguing in Publication data

Finch, Vanessa.
Corporate insolvency law: perspectives and principles / Vanessa Finch.
    p.   cm.
Includes bibliographical references and index.
ISBN 0 521 62256 5 (hardback) – ISBN 0 521 62685 4 (pbk.)
1. Bankruptcy – Great Britain.   2. Business failures – Law and legislation –
Great Britain.   I. Title.

KD2139.F558   2002
346.4107′8 – dc21   2002070893

ISBN 0 521 62256 5 hardback
ISBN 0 521 62685 4 paperback

To Rob
and in memory of D.F.G. and M.A.G.

Contents

Acknowledgements

I would like to thank all my colleagues at the London School of Economics who have helped me with this book and who have made the Law Department such a stimulating environment in which to research law in its broader contexts.

Particular thanks go to those who have read and commented on drafts: Rob Baldwin, Hugh Collins LSE and David Milman of the University of Manchester. I owe a special debt to Judith Freedman of the University of Oxford for her all-round encouragement and support, and Susan Hunt must also be singled out for her superbly efficient work with the manuscript. I am grateful for research assistance to Opeyemi Atawo and Luke Finch. Finally, I thank Olivia, Luke and Nat for their help and forbearance during the gestation of this work.

Table of cases

Table of statutes and other instruments

Abbreviations

ACCA	Association of Chartered Certified Accountants
AR	administrative receiver
BCCI	Bank of Credit and Commerce International
CBI	Confederation of British Industry
CDDA	Company Directors' Disqualification Act 1986
CLRSG	Company Law Review Steering Group
CVA	company voluntary arrangement
DIP	debtor in possession
DTI	Department of Trade and Industry
EAT	Employment Appeal Tribunal
ECHR	European Court of Human Rights
ECJ	European Court of Justice
EEC	European Economic Community
EIB	European Investment Bank
ERA	Employment Rights Act 1996
ESRC	Economic and Social Research Council
ETO	economic, technical or organisational
FIRS	Forensic Insolvency Recovery Service
FSB	Federation of Small Businesses
HP	hire purchase
HRA	Human Rights Act 1998
ICAEW	Institute of Chartered Accountants of England and Wales
ICAI	Institute of Chartered Accountants in Ireland
ICAS	Institute of Chartered Accountants in Scotland
ILA	Insolvency Lawyers' Association
IOD	Institute of Directors
IP	insolvency practitioner

IPA	Insolvency Practitioners Association
IPC	Insolvency Practices Council
IR	Inland Revenue
IRWP	Insolvency Review Working Party
IS	Insolvency Service
ISA	Insolvency Services Account
IVA	Individual Voluntary Arrangement
JIEB	Joint Insolvency Examining Board
LS	Law Society
LSS	Law Society of Scotland
MBO	management buyout
NAO	National Audit Office
NBAN	National Business Angel Network
NIF	National Insurance Fund
OFT	Office of Fair Trading
OR	Official Receiver
PCA	Parliamentary Commissioner for Administration
PMSI	purchase money security interest
RBS	Royal Bank of Scotland
ROT	retention of title
RPB	recognised professional body
R3	Association of Business Recovery Professionals
SBS	Small Business Service
SFLGS	Small Firms Loan Guarantee Scheme
SMEs	small and medium enterprises
SPI	Society of Practitioners in Insolvency
SSP	statutory super-priority
TUPE	Transfer of Undertakings (Protection of Employment)
UCC	Uniform Commercial Code
VAS	Voluntary Arrangements Service

Introduction

This book sets out to offer a critical appraisal of modern corporate insolvency law rather than a description of existing statutory rules and case law on the subject. It will nevertheless attempt to set out rules and procedures of corporate insolvency law in sufficient detail to facilitate understanding of the framework and operation of this area of law.

A critical approach is seen as essential here on the grounds that it is impossible to evaluate areas of the law, suggest reforms or develop the law with a sense of purpose unless there is clarity concerning the objectives and values sought to be furthered, the feasibility of operating certain procedures and the efficiency with which given rules or processes can be applied on the ground.

Insolvency is an area of law of increasing importance not merely in its own right but because it impinges on a host of other sectors such as company, employment, tort, environmental, pension and banking law. It is essential, therefore, that the development of insolvency law proceeds with a sense of purpose. If this is lacking, this area of law is liable to be marked by inconsistencies of reasoning and failures of policy, with the result that related legal sectors will also be adversely affected.

The book's aims are threefold. The first is to outline the law on corporate insolvency (as at November 2001) and the procedures and enforcement mechanisms used in giving effect to that law. Corporate insolvency law will be seen as raising important social, political and moral issues rather than viewed merely as a device for maximising returns for creditors. Questions of stakeholding, community interests and the concerns of employees and the public as well as creditors will thus be discussed.

The second aim is to set out a theoretical framework for corporate insolvency law that will establish benchmarks for evaluating that law and any proposed reforms. Those benchmarks will be applied throughout the volume. It will be consistently asked whether the laws and processes under discussion will serve the variety of values and ends suggested at the start of the book.

A third objective is to move beyond an appraisal of current laws and processes and to consider whether new approaches to insolvency institutions and rules are called for: in other words, to see whether improvements have to be sought by adopting new perspectives and by challenging the assumptions that underpin present corporate insolvency regimes. The focus here is on domestic corporate insolvency law. Space does not allow an appraisal of the European Council Regulation on Insolvency Proceedings[1] or of international and cross-border issues as individual topics (these are areas that have been dealt with specifically by others[2]), though mention will be made of non-UK or international insolvency laws and processes that are of relevance to questions under discussion.

The structure of the volume is as follows. Part I deals with agendas and objectives. Chapter 1 discusses the principal concerns of corporate insolvency law and considers the set of major issues that confront corporate insolvency law. Chapter 2 examines the values and aims sought to be furthered in this area. It is chapter 2 that identifies the benchmarks already referred to.

Part II is concerned with the financial and institutional context within which corporate insolvency laws and processes play a role. The problems with which corporate insolvency law has to come to grips cannot be fully understood without an appreciation of the legal regimes that govern corporate structures and borrowing. Chapter 3, accordingly, examines corporate borrowing, its development, the nature of security interests, fixed and floating charges and different types of creditor. Chapter 4

---

1. Council Regulation (EC) 1346/2000 of 29 May 2000, OJ 2000 No. L160/1, 30 June 2000, pp. 0001–0013. See further P. J. Omar, 'The Wider European Framework for Insolvency' [2001] 17 IL&P 135; Editorial, 'Insolvency: The European Dimension' [2001] 17 IL&P 81; J. Chuah, 'EC Regulation on Insolvency Proceedings' (2000) *Finance and Credit Law* 6 (November/December); R. Obank, 'European Recovery Practice and Reform: Part I' [2000] Ins. Law. 149; P. J. Omar, 'New Initiatives on Cross-Border Insolvency in Europe' [2000] Ins. Law. 211; I. Fletcher, 'The European Union Convention on Bankruptcy Proceedings: An Overview and Comment with US Interests in Mind' (1997) 23 BJIL 25.

2. See, for example, I. F. Fletcher, *Insolvency Law in Private International Law* (Clarendon Press, Oxford, 1999); Fletcher, 'A New Age of International Insolvency: The Countdown Has Begun – Parts I and II' (2000) *Insolvency Intelligence* 1; J. L. Westbrook, 'Global Insolvencies in a World of Nation States' in A. Clarke (ed.), *Current Issues in Insolvency Law* (Stevens & Sons, London, 1991) pp. 27–56; Westbrook, 'Universal Participation in Transnational Bankruptcies' in R. Cranston (ed.), *Making Commercial Law: Essays in Honour of Roy Goode* (Clarendon Press, Oxford, 1997) pp. 419–37; P. Wood, *Principles of International Insolvency* (Sweet & Maxwell, London, 1995).

looks at the nature and causes of corporate failure and the ways in which the law decides that a company is 'insolvent', and chapter 5 moves to the administrative framework and the role of insolvency practitioners and the Insolvency Service.

Corporate insolvency law is not merely concerned with the death and burial of companies. Important issues are whether corporate difficulties should be treated as terminal and whether it is feasible to mount rescue operations. Part III reviews processes for attempting to avert corporate death and liquidation. Chapter 6 looks at the challenge of corporate rescue and at rescue proceedings and approaches in other jurisdictions (including the US Chapter 11 strategy). Chapter 7 deals with rescue mechanisms (such as negotiated settlements) that avoid resort to formal insolvency procedures as provided under insolvency legislation. Chapters 8, 9 and 10 consider different aspects of the formal rescue procedures: administrative receivership, administration and company voluntary arrangements and schemes of arrangement. Chapter 11 offers an overview and evaluation of rescue procedures and reviews proposed improvements.

Part IV is concerned with the process of liquidating companies. Chapter 12 deals with gathering in the assets of an insolvent company, the nature and scope of the winding-up process, the liquidator's role, the special issues raised by corporate groups and the parts played by the courts, directors and creditors in liquidation. Chapter 13 focuses on the *pari passu* principle and its place in the process of distributing assets. Chapter 14 discusses devices that are intended to, or have the effect of, removing assets from the liquidator's grasp.

When a corporate failure occurs this may have a dramatic impact on the lives, interests and employment prospects of a number of parties. It is important to understand the nature of these potential effects in considering how corporate insolvency law should be developed. Part V thus looks at the repercussions of insolvency. Chapter 15 reviews the implications of a corporate collapse for company directors, considers the incentives under which directors operate in times of crisis and also assesses rationales underpinning the law's treatment of directors in this context. Chapter 16 looks to employees and asks how and why their interests should be considered when companies are in mortal peril. Further issues are whether employees should be seen as having interests other than financial ones and the extent to which efficiency considerations should be tempered with reference to other objectives, such as security of employment. Finally, the Conclusion offers more general observations.

Part I

Agendas and objectives

1

The roots of corporate insolvency law

In a society that facilitates the use of credit by companies[1] there is a degree of risk that those who are owed money by a firm will suffer because the firm has become unable to pay its debts on the due date. If a number of creditors were owed money and all pursued the rights and remedies available to them (for example, contractual rights; rights to enforce security interests; rights to set off the debt against other obligations; proceedings for delivery, foreclosure or sale) a chaotic race to protect interests would take place and this might produce inefficiencies and unfairness. Huge costs would be incurred in pursuing individual creditors' claims competitively[2] and (since in an insolvency there are insufficient assets to go round) those creditors who enforced their claim with most vigour and expertise would be paid but naïve latecomers would not.

A main aim of insolvency law is to replace this free-for-all with a legal regime in which creditors' rights and remedies are suspended and a process established for the orderly collection and realisation of the debtors' assets and the fair distribution of these according to creditors' claims. Part of the drama of insolvency law flows, accordingly, from its potentially having to unpack and reassemble what were seemingly concrete and clear legal rights.

Corporate insolvency law, with which this book is concerned, is now a quite separate body of law from personal bankruptcy law although these have shared historical roots. Those roots should be noted, since the shape of modern corporate insolvency law is as much a product of past history and accidents of development as of design.

---

1. See Cork Report: *Report of the Review Committee on Insolvency Law and Practice* (Cmnd 8558, 1982) ch. 1; see ch. 3 below.
2. T. H. Jackson, *The Logic and Limits of Bankruptcy Law* (Harvard University Press, Cambridge, Mass., 1986) chs. 1, 2; see ch. 2 below.

Development and structure

The earliest insolvency laws in England and Wales were concerned with individual insolvency (bankruptcy) and date back to medieval times.[3] Early common law offered no collective procedure for administering an insolvent's estate but a creditor could seize either the body of a debtor or his effects – but not both. Creditors, moreover, had to act individually, there being no machinery for sharing expenses. When the person of the debtor was seized, detention in person at the creditor's pleasure was provided for. Insolvency was thus seen as an offence little less criminal than a felony. From Tudor times onwards, insolvency has been driven by three distinct forces: impulsions to punish bankrupts; wishes to organise administration of their assets so that competing creditors are treated fairly and efficiently; and the hope that the bankrupt would be allowed to rehabilitate himself.[4] Early insolvency law was dominated by punitive approaches and it was not until the early eighteenth century that notions of rehabilitation gained force. The idea that creditors might act collectively was recognised in 1542 with the enactment of the first English Bankruptcy Act which dealt with absconding debtors and empowered any aggrieved party to procure seizure of the debtor's property, its sale and distribution to creditors 'according to the quantity of their debts'.[5] This statute did not, however, provide for rehabilitation in so far as it did not discharge the bankrupt's liability for claims that were not fully paid.

Elizabethan legislation of 1570 then drew an important distinction between traders and others, including within the definition of a bankrupt only traders and merchants: those who earned their living by 'buying and selling'.[6] Non-traders could thus not be declared bankrupt. As for distribution, this statute again provided for equal distribution of assets among creditors.

---

3. On the history of insolvency law see Cork Report ch. 2, paras. 26–34; W. R. Cornish and G. de N. Clark, *Law and Society in England 1750–1950* (Sweet & Maxwell, London, 1989) ch. 3, part II; B. G. Carruthers and T. C. Halliday, *Rescuing Business: The Making of Corporate Bankruptcy Law in England and the United States* (Clarendon Press, Oxford, 1998); G. R. Rubin and D. Sugarman (eds.), *Law, Economy and Society: Essays in the History of English Law* (Professional Books, Abingdon, 1984) pp. 43–7; I. F. Fletcher, *The Law of Insolvency* (2nd edn, Sweet & Maxwell, London, 1996) pp. 6 ff.; V. M. Lester, *Victorian Insolvency* (Oxford University Press, Oxford, 1996).

4. See Cornish and Clark, *Law and Society*, p. 231.

5. Stat. 34 & 35 Hen. 8, c. 4, s. 1; see Fletcher, *Law of Insolvency*, p. 7; W. J. Jones, 'The Foundations of English Bankruptcy: Statutes and Commissions in the Early Modern Period' (1979) 69(3) *Transactions of American Philosophical Society* 69.

6. J. Cohen, 'History of Imprisonment for Debt and its Relation to the Development of Discharge in Bankruptcy' (1982) 3 *Journal of Legal History* 153–6.

Discharge of a bankrupt's existing liabilities came into the law in the early eighteenth century when a 1705 statute relieved traders of liability for existing debts. This restriction of discharge to traders prompted a good deal of litigation throughout the eighteenth and early nineteenth centuries and an expansion of the definition of a trader. On why bankruptcy should have been restricted to the trader, contemporary and modern commentators[7] have followed Blackstone[8] in referring to the risks that traders run of becoming unable to pay debts without any fault of their own and to the trading necessity of allowing merchants to discharge debts. It can be pointed out that long before a general law of incorporation arrived (in the mid-nineteenth century), bankruptcy served as almost a surrogate form of limited liability which needed to be restricted to those undertaking mercantile endeavours and risks. The bankruptcy legislation, moreover, provided the only means by which eighteenth- and early nineteenth-century traders might limit their liabilities.

The state of the law was, however, deficient in many respects. Non-traders were still subject to the severities of common law enforcement procedures by means of seizures and impoundings of property and persons. These processes were non-collective and debtors might be imprisoned at the behest of single creditors without regard to the interests of others. An important difference between the bankruptcy laws available to traders and the insolvency schemes for non-traders was that whereas the bankrupt's liabilities to creditors could be discharged on surrender of available assets (even if these assets were insufficient to satisfy his entire debt), the insolvent non-trader was still obliged to repay the remainder of his judgment debt even though he had suffered seizure of his goods or served his term of imprisonment. Even traders could not apply of their own accord to be made bankrupt and, although discharge was possible after 1705, the law criminalised bankrupt traders and punished them severely, with the death penalty available in cases of fraud.[9] The bankruptcy system, moreover, was liable to manipulation by creditors and laid open to the 'eighteenth century penchant for malign administration'.[10] Nor was it the case that all traders were in practice brought within bankruptcy proceedings.

7. Crompton, *Practice Common-placed: Or, the Rules and Cases of the Practice in the Courts of King's Bench and Common Pleas*, LXVII (3rd edn, 1786); Dunscombe, Jr, 'Bankruptcy: A Study in Comparative Legislation' (1893) 2 *Columbia University Studies in Political Science* 17–18.

8. W. Blackstone, *Commentaries on the Laws of England* (8th edn, Clarendon Press, Oxford, 1765–9) vol. II, no. 5: Cohen, 'History of Imprisonment', pp. 160–2; Cornish and Clark, *Law and Society*, p. 232; Cork Report, p. 33.

9. See Cork Report, paras. 37–8; Fletcher, *Law of Insolvency*, pp. 8–9.

10. Cornish and Clark, *Law and Society*, p. 232.

The Erskine Commission of 1840 noted that the common law insolvency processes were frequently being used for small traders whose creditors were owed too little to justify bankruptcy proceedings (two-thirds of those before the Insolvent Debtors Court in 1839 were traders).[11]

Pressure for reform grew alongside dissatisfaction with the confinement of bankruptcy to traders. During the nineteenth century attitudes towards trade credit and risk of default changed. A depersonalisation of business and credit was encouraged by Parliament's enactment of the Joint Stock Companies Act 1844 together with notions that credit might be raised on an institutional basis and capital through stocks rather than both of these dealt with as matters of individual standing.[12] Such changed attitudes rendered increasingly questionable Blackstone's view that it was not justifiable for any person other than a trader to 'encumber himself with debts of any considerable value'.[13] The distinction between traders and non-traders was finally abolished in 1861 when bankruptcy proceedings became available for non-traders. Soon afterwards the Debtors Act 1869 abolished imprisonment for debt.

The origins of corporate insolvency law are to be found in the nineteenth-century development of the company. The key statute was the Joint Stock Companies Act 1844 which established the company as a distinct legal entity, although it retained unlimited liability for the shareholders. From 1844 onwards corporate insolvency was dealt with by means of special statutory provisions[14] and the modern limited liability company emerged in 1855 to be followed seven years later by the first modern company law statute containing detailed winding-up provisions.[15] Only from 1855 onwards, therefore, was the concept of the limited liability of members for the debts incurred by the company established in law. Members of incorporated companies could limit their personal liability, thus creating a distinction between corporate and individual insolvency. The House of Lords in *Salomon's* case[16] confirmed that a duly formed company was a separate legal person from its members and that consequently even a one-man company's debts were self-contained and distinct. The growth of a specialised corpus of law and procedures dealing with corporate insolvency

11. Ibid., p. 234.
12. On depersonalisation of business and credit in the USA, see Rubin and Sugarman, *Law, Economy and Society*, pp. 43–4.
13. Blackstone, vol. II, no. 5, p. 473.
14. See e.g. Companies Winding Up Act 1844; Joint Stock Companies Act 1856; Companies Act 1862; Companies (Consolidation) Act 1908; Companies Acts of 1929, 1948 and 1985.
15. Limited Liability Act 1855; Companies Act 1862.
16. *Salomon v. A. Salomon & Co. Ltd* [1897] AC 22.

was manifest in the dedicated statutes already noted but it was also encouraged when issues relating to such matters became the exclusive jurisdiction of the Chancery Court in 1862.[17]

Thus the law dealing with company insolvencies developed independently from the law on the bankruptcy of individuals. By the late nineteenth century two separate bodies of law governed individual and corporate insolvency matters and these were dealt with by different courts, under different procedural rules[18] and offering different substantive remedies. A degree of cross-influence between personal bankruptcy and corporate insolvency is discernible, however, and a number of principles and provisions of personal bankruptcy have been made applicable to company liquidation.[19]

Such a bifurcation of approaches produced, during the first half of the twentieth century, a confused tangle of insolvency laws that was both difficult to operate and prone to manipulation by the unscrupulous. Various committees were set up to look at particular aspects of the law dealing with credit, security and debt[20] but it was the mid-1970s before the deficiencies in insolvency law were attended to at the governmental level. In 1975 Justice issued a report[21] pointing to a number of serious deficiencies in the law of bankruptcy and making a number of reform proposals, some of which were adopted in the Insolvency Act of 1976, a short piece of legislation that was passed to remedy a number of the most serious defects pending broader review. Further pressure to reassess insolvency law flowed from the UK's accession to membership of the EEC. This demanded that the UK negotiate with other Member States concerning a draft EEC Bankruptcy Convention. In order to secure advice for the Department of Trade, an advisory committee was appointed in 1973 under the chairmanship of Mr Kenneth Cork, as he then was. The resultant report[22] stressed that a comprehensive review of insolvency was required, not only in order to participate in negotiations with other EEC Member States, but also because the state of the law demanded this. Thus prompted, Edmund Dell MP, the Labour Government's Secretary of State for Trade, appointed a Review Committee on Insolvency Law and Practice in January 1977 with

17. Companies Act 1862 s. 81.   18. See Fletcher, *Law of Insolvency*, p. 12.
19. See H. Rajak, *Insolvency Law: Theory and Practice* (Sweet & Maxwell, London, 1993) p. 3 (citing as examples Companies Act 1985 ss. 612–13, 615).
20. See the Crowther Committee (Cmnd 4596, 1968–71) and the Payne Committee (Cmnd 3909, 1965–9).
21. Justice, *Bankruptcy* (London, 1975).
22. Report of the Cork Advisory Committee (Cmnd 6602, 1976).

Kenneth Cork again serving as chairman. The Committee was asked to review, examine and make recommendations on: the law and practice relating to 'insolvency, bankruptcy, liquidation and receiverships';[23] the possibility of formulating a comprehensive insolvency system; the extent to which existing procedures should be harmonised and integrated; and less formal procedures as alternatives to bankruptcy and company winding-up proceedings. The Cork Committee was not, however, asked to conduct a review of credit and security laws or remedies for debt enforcement, nor was provision made for the Committee to undertake an extended programme of research into the causes of company failure.[24]

The Cork Report[25] in final form was published in June 1982 at a time when the rate of business failures was at a record level.[26] The 460-page document provided a sustained critique of contemporary law and practice and a set of recommendations constituting the foundations of modern insolvency law. The report argued for fundamental reforms, and central recommendations were, *inter alia*: that a unified insolvency code replace the array of statutes that made up two distinct branches of the law; that a unified system of insolvency courts be created to administer the law; and that a range of new procedures be introduced as alternatives to outright bankruptcy or winding up, which would deal with individual cases on their merits. On particular matters of substance concerning corporate insolvency, the Cork Committee's key recommendations included steps to deal with abusive practices. These involved recommendations that private insolvency practitioners should be professionally regulated to ensure adequate standards of competence and integrity; that creditors be given a greater voice in the choice of the liquidator; and that new penalties and constraints be placed on errant directors. Cork also proposed reforms designed to increase the survival chances of firms in difficulties. He had informed the press, on the establishment of his committee, that many more companies could be saved if outside administrators could be brought into

23. Cork Report, p. 3. On the background to, and implementation of, Cork see Carruthers and Halliday, *Rescuing Business*, pp. 112–23.
24. For criticism on this point, see J. H. Farrar, 'Company Insolvency and the Cork Recommendations' (1983) 4 Co. Law. 20.
25. Cork Report. In 1979 the Cork Committee issued an interim report to the Minister, published in July 1980 as *Bankruptcy: Interim Report of the Insolvency Law Review Committee* (Cmnd 7968, 1980). The Government also produced a Green Paper: *Bankruptcy: A Consultative Document* (Cmnd 7967, 1980). This contained proposals for the privatisation of insolvency procedures which were attacked by commentators (see I. F. Fletcher (1981) 44 MLR 77) and subsequently dropped.
26. The rate of failure increased by over 35 per cent: see D. Hare and D. Milman, 'Corporate Insolvency: The Cork Committee Proposals I' (1983) 127 Sol. Jo. 230.

companies before the time when a bank would formally appoint a receiver and in circumstances when the company lacked a loan structure allowing the appointment of receivers.[27] The Cork Report, in due course, introduced the concept of the 'administrator' into corporate insolvency procedures with the function of managing a company's business during a period of grace in the hope of reorganising the company and restoring it to profitability. The report, furthermore, favoured a movement towards greater creditor participation with an increased role for creditor committees and strengthened access to information for such committees.

A special concern of Cork was the plight of the unsecured creditor, who generally received nothing at the end of the day. This concern was reflected in the recommendations that virtually all preferential claims[28] be abolished and that funding representing 10 per cent of all net realisations of assets subject to a floating charge be made available for distribution among ordinary unsecured creditors. This fund was also designed to be utilised to provide liquidators with the financial resources to investigate company affairs and to take the actions that Cork proposed should be taken against delinquent directors.

The broad philosophy of Cork – as far as it related to corporate insolvency – represented a movement towards stricter control of errant directors but also in favour of an increasing emphasis on rehabilitation of the company. Cork might have thought that existing law dealt with individual bankrupts (perhaps sole traders) in an excessively punitive and stigmatic manner,[29] but the Committee was determined to remedy the law's perceived leniency in dealing with directors who abused the privilege of limited liability. In doing so, Cork aimed to bolster standards of commercial morality and to encourage the fulfilment of financial obligations.

As for rehabilitation, the Cork Committee aimed to devise an insolvency regime that would facilitate rescues rather than just process failures.[30] Sir Kenneth Cork was to reflect on this philosophy in the autobiography he published six years after his seminal report. He wrote:

> through publication of the Cork Report, I have ... put forward our principle that business is a national asset and, that being so, all insolvency schemes must be aimed at saving businesses. I have been at pains to stress that when a business becomes insolvent it provides

---

27. See K. Cork, *Cork on Cork: Sir Kenneth Cork Takes Stock* (Macmillan, London, 1988) ch. 10, pp. 184–203.
28. See p. 425 below.   29. See Cork, *Cork on Cork*, ch. 10.
30. See Cork Report, para. 1502.

an occasion for a change of ownership from incompetent hands to people who not only have the wherewithal but also hopefully the competence, the imagination and the energy to save the business. Before the 1985 Act every insolvent business went into liquidation or receivership automatically. It was the kiss of death for them and the creator of unemployment ... [W]ith the concept of the administrator and voluntary arrangements taking its place in Britain's insolvency law, the chances look bright for more and more businesses being saved in the years that lie ahead ... [31]

The Cork Report thus provided not merely the most comprehensive and rational review of English company insolvency rules ever undertaken but it also flagged a historic movement away from punitive towards rehabilitative objectives.

The Report was not, however, to be instantly transposed into legislative form. It was not even made the subject of a formal debate in either House of Parliament.[32] Four years passed before legislation delivered the unified code of insolvency law that Cork had advocated. This came with the Insolvency Act 1986. That statute was preceded by a 1984 White Paper[33] and the Insolvency Act 1985, which together dealt with a variety of important aspects of insolvency but neither implemented the main body of Cork nor brought together in one Act all the statutory provisions relating to bankruptcy and those dealing with corporate insolvency. The Insolvency Act 1986 offered such an aggregation of measures dealing with the bankruptcy of individuals and the insolvency of companies. It consolidated the Insolvency Act 1985 and the insolvency provisions of the Companies Act 1985 (except in relation to the disqualification of directors).[34]

The Cork Report recommendations produced a sea change in English corporate insolvency and, as noted, can be seen as the foundations of modern corporate insolvency regimes. The Cork Committee had been established by a Labour Government but its recommendations were given legislative effect by Margaret Thatcher's Conservative administration. The membership of the committee was, however, characterised by strong professional and practitioner rather than political representation.[35] The Cork

---

31. Cork, *Cork on Cork*, ch. 10, pp. 202–3.
32. For an account of governmental and legislative developments in the wake of the Cork Report, see Fletcher, *Law of Insolvency*, pp. 16–20.
33. *A Revised Framework of Insolvency Law* (Cmnd 9175, 1984).
34. See Company Directors' Disqualification Act 1986. A few provisions of the Companies Act 1985 are relevant to insolvency and survive the Insolvency Act 1986 ss. 196, 425–7, 458 (see chs. 10 and 15 below).
35. See Carruthers and Halliday, *Rescuing Business*, pp. 124–5.

Report set out to be systematic, pragmatic and balanced: as seen in its efforts to recognise the interests of secured creditors (especially banks) and those of unsecured, trade creditors. The Cork approach to floating charges, for instance, was to acknowledge their effect in prejudicing weaker creditors' interests but to stop short of alienating the banks by proposing abolition of such charges.[36] As for the Insolvency Act 1986, this can be seen as strongly shaped by both professional and political factors. As Carruthers and Halliday put it:

> [I]t is inconceivable that the [1986 Act] can be understood without comprehension of the powerful ideological undercurrents that variously sought to champion reorganisation, privatise bankruptcy administration, professionalise insolvency practice and discipline company directors. While professionals and their technical interests were persuasive in the English reforms, the particular cost of the insolvency reforms, and the very fact of the parliamentary passage, testified to the affinity between professional agendas and wider party ideology.[37]

As will be seen in subsequent chapters, however, the Cork Report was not implemented to the letter by the 1986 Act and, although the different branches of insolvency law were harmonised to a degree, the long-established distinction between corporate insolvency and personal bankruptcy law and procedures survived the passing of the Act. Sir Kenneth, moreover, was to be deeply concerned that the Government was selective in its approach to his recommendations, saying in his autobiography: 'They ended up by doing the very thing we asked them not to. They picked bits and pieces out of it so that they finished with a mish-mash of old and new.'[38]

What was reflected in the 1986 Act, however, was the (already noted) aim of Cork to produce a set of rules capable of practical implementation. Thus, in the Act there can be seen two strong threads of concern: to establish formal legal procedures for business rescue and the orderly realisation and distribution of assets and to erect a regulatory framework that would prevent commercial malpractice and abuse of the insolvency procedures themselves.

The operation of the Insolvency Act 1986 is a central concern of the chapters that follow. This piece of legislation has been through the fire

---

36. See chs. 3 and 14 below.
37. Carruthers and Halliday, *Rescuing Business*, p. 148. On the politics of Cork and the committee's membership see ibid., pp. 124–49.
38. Cork, *Cork on Cork*, p. 197; White Paper, *A Revised Framework for Insolvency Law* (1984).

of the 1989–93 economic recession and has already been subject to review in a number of respects.[39] It has left on the corporate insolvency stage a number of actors operating a variety of procedures in carrying out certain key tasks. To provide a basis for further discussion it may be helpful to outline these procedures and players.

Corporate insolvency procedures

There are five main statutory procedures that may come into play when a company is in trouble. Four of these are provided for in the Insolvency Act 1986, the fifth by the Companies Act 1985.

Administrative receivership

If a creditor has lent money to a company and secured this by means of a floating charge over the whole or substantially the whole of the company's assets,[40] that creditor may, in certain circumstances, appoint an administrative receiver (AR). This individual must be an insolvency practitioner (IP)[41] and will take control of all assets subject to the security, so that he will effectively control the company. His primary duty is to realise the security[42] and, after deducting his remuneration and expenses and paying prior-ranking creditors, he pays the proceeds to his appointor up to the amount of the secured debt and pays any balance to subsequent ranking creditors, the company or its liquidator, if one has been appointed. The AR has wide powers, including the ability to manage a company's business and sell its assets. He can borrow working capital secured on the company's assets so that he can continue to run the business and sell part or all of it as a going concern. The AR's primary duty is owed to his appointor and though he *may* take a broader view and regard the interests of unsecured creditors generally he is under no direct duty to do so[43] (other than an obligation to report to them on the company's position within

---

39. See DTI/Insolvency Service, *Company Voluntary Arrangements and Administration Orders: A Consultative Document* (October 1993). See also DTI/IS, *Revised Proposals for a New Company Voluntary Arrangement Procedure* (April 1995); DTI/IS, *A Review of Company Rescue and Business Reconstruction Mechanisms* (1999); DTI/IS, *A Review of Company Rescue and Business Reconstruction Mechanisms: Report by the Review Group* (2000); Justice, *Insolvency Law: An Agenda for Reform* (London, 1994); DTI/IS, *Productivity and Enterprise: Insolvency – A Second Chance* (Cm 5234, 2001); Company Law Review Steering Group, *Modern Company Law for a Competitive Economy: Final Report* (DTI, London, 2001). Key amending legislation since 1986 has included the Insolvency Acts of 1994 and 2000.
40. See Insolvency Act 1986 s. 29(2); see also ch. 8 below.
41. See Insolvency Act 1986 s. 230(2); see also ch. 5 below.
42. On security and methods of borrowing generally, see ch. 3 below.
43. Save for preferential creditors.

three months of his appointment).[44] Ordinary unsecured creditors have few rights until the receiver completes his task and the company goes into liquidation.

The AR must be distinguished from other types of receiver appointed over a *specific* part of the company's assets.[45] Such a receiver can be removed or replaced with little formality,[46] he has no management powers and his task is to collect an income and apply it to keep down outgoings and mortgage interest.

Receivers may also be appointed by the court, although these appointments are comparatively rare. Where the option is available to them, lenders (normally banks) prefer to appoint receivers in pursuance of express powers to do so contained in their security. Indeed, receivership historically is a creation of equity and is merely a method by which a secured creditor enforces his security. Ordinary receivership is a private contractual remedy requiring no recourse to the court. Administrative receivership, however, has more of the *appearance* of a collective insolvency proceeding.[47]

Administration

This is a court-based procedure, first introduced by the Insolvency Act 1985 following the Cork Committee's recommendations and emphasis on the benefits that could flow from having a corporate insolvency procedure that was designed specifically for corporate rescue rather than asset realisation; one, moreover, that focused on the interests of unsecured creditors and of the company itself rather than those of a specific secured creditor.[48] A company may be put into administration by an order of the court instructing that an administrator should take over management and control of the company for the benefit of creditors generally. This appointee has the power on behalf of the company to do all things necessary for the management of the affairs, business and property of the company with a view to ensuring the survival of the company as a going concern, to securing a more advantageous realisation of the company's assets than would be

44. And file a report with the Companies Registrar and summon creditors' meetings to present a report.
45. E.g. Law of Property Act 1925 receivers (of income only).
46. The AR can only be removed by the court: Insolvency Act 1986 s. 45.
47. The Insolvency Act 1986 tends to treat it as such: see Insolvency Act 1986 ss. 388(1)(a), 230–7 (office holder), 42–3 and Sched. 1, 44–5; but see F. Oditah, 'Assets and the Treatment of Claims in Insolvency' (1992) 108 LQR 459 at 460–1.
48. See Cork Report, ch. 6, paras. 29–33, and ch. 9. Cork's view was that the potential benefit of rescue via a receiver/manager should also be available to cases where there was no floating charge.

effected in a winding up or to enable the company to come to an arrangement with its creditors.[49] The most significant feature of administration is that it imposes a freeze (moratorium) on all legal proceedings and creditor actions against the company, including the enforcement of security, while the administrator seeks to achieve the purpose(s) for which the administration order was granted. The position of secured creditors is thus less protected than in receivership or liquidation as the freeze includes (unless the administrator or court consents) a prohibition on any action to enforce any security or any rights under hire purchase (HP), chattel leasing, conditional sale and retention of title agreements. In addition, the administrator can sell property free of security constituted by floating charges and (with the court's consent) fixed charges and free of any rights of third parties under HP agreements or other agreements mentioned above.[50] Secured lenders with floating charges, however, effectively have the right to prevent the appointment of an administrator by appointing an administrative receiver instead.[51] Administration is, at least initially, a temporary measure and within three months of his appointment or such longer period as the court allows, the administrator must produce formal proposals for the achievement of the purposes of his appointment and submit them for approval to a creditors' meeting. Once approved, the administrator must manage the company in accordance with those proposals unless he, or any interested party, applies to the court for variation or discharge of the administration order. No winding up can take place whilst the administrator is in control, but administration is often followed by liquidation.[52]

Winding up/liquidation

Liquidation is a procedure of last resort. It involves a liquidator being appointed to take control of the company and to collect, realise and distribute its assets to creditors according to their legal priority. Once the process has been completed, the company is dissolved: liquidators have no powers to carry on the company's business except for the purpose of winding up.[53] There are two routes to liquidating an insolvent company: a creditors' voluntary liquidation and a compulsory liquidation.

---

49. Insolvency Act 1986 s. 8(3).
50. In each case the security will attach to the proceeds of sale and the administrator, when dealing with fixed charges, must account for any shortfall between those proceeds and the market value at the time of sale.
51. See Insolvency Act 1986 s. 9(2). But see p. 271 below.   52. See ch. 12 below.
53. Insolvency Act 1986 Sched. 4, para. 5.

The former process involves a resolution of the shareholders to put the company into voluntary liquidation, followed by a creditors' meeting to appoint a liquidator and establish a liquidation committee whose members are principally creditors' representatives. The liquidation committee has a supervisory role over the liquidator, while he collects in and realises the company's assets, ascertains claims, distributes dividends to creditors and investigates the causes of the company's failure. The creditors' voluntary liquidation is the most frequently used of the insolvency procedures.

Compulsory liquidation is liquidation by order of the court and is the only method by which a creditor can initiate winding up. A winding-up petition can be presented by a creditor, the directors, the company shareholders and, in certain circumstances, the Department of Trade and Industry (DTI). The petition to the court has to be based on one or more specific grounds stated in section 122 of the Insolvency Act 1986, including the inability of the company to pay its debts. If a winding-up order is made, the Official Receiver[54] (an official of the DTI) becomes liquidator, unless and until the creditors' meeting appoints an insolvency practitioner in his place (i.e. if the company's assets are sufficient to pay the liquidator's remuneration and expenses). Generally compulsory liquidation is subjected to a greater degree of court control than a creditors' voluntary liquidation, but in both methods interested parties can apply to the court to determine questions arising in the winding up or to confirm, reverse or nullify the liquidator's decisions.

Formal arrangements with creditors

Companies in distress may be able to negotiate settlements on a variety of terms and such agreements may operate within a statutory format or informally and contractually between the company, its lenders and possibly even general creditors.[55] These agreements may defer payments or postpone collection (a moratorium); they may agree to pay sums less than those due (a composition); or to pay a designated sum where there is doubt about the quantum or enforceability of a claim (a compromise). Formal, statutory arrangements or compromises may be made principally under section 425 of the Companies Act 1985 and 'compositions in satisfaction of [the company's] debts or a scheme of arrangement of its affairs', termed 'company voluntary arrangements' (CVAs), can be made under section 2 of the

---

54. The Official Receiver is not to be confused with a receiver or administrative receiver appointed by a secured creditor.
55. See ch. 7 below.

Insolvency Act 1986. (Arrangements by way of reconstruction can be undertaken by liquidators in a voluntary winding up under section 110 of the Insolvency Act 1986, while sections 165–7 and Schedule 4 of the Insolvency Act 1986 allow liquidators with the appropriate sanction to make compromises or arrangements with creditors but only according to creditors' strict legal rights.)

Small and medium-sized companies may find a CVA useful, since it is generally less complex, time-consuming and costly than alternative procedures. CVAs under section 1 of the Insolvency Act 1986 cannot, however, be undertaken when the company is in winding up and, indeed, do not even require a company to be insolvent. The use of this option will depend on the company's precise position and the attitude of its creditors. The use of a CVA allows a company to reach an arrangement with its creditors under the supervision of an insolvency practitioner. The CVA must, however, be approved by requisite majorities at shareholder (50 per cent by value) and creditors' (75 per cent by value) meetings and it does not bind creditors without notice of the meetings nor those with unliquidated/unascertained claims nor secured or preferential creditors without their agreement. The Insolvency Act 2000 introduced a moratorium of twenty-eight days into a CVA procedure for small companies.[56] The effect of the moratorium is *inter alia* to offer a company protection against petitions for winding up or administration orders, winding-up resolutions, appointments of receivers and other steps to enforce security or repossess goods – though a moratorium cannot be filed for if an administration order is already in force, the company is being wound up or a receiver has been appointed.

Schemes of arrangement under the Companies Act 1985 s. 425 are an alternative formal method. Here the court sanctions a scheme duly approved by the requisite majority of creditors of each class at separately convened meetings, and once the scheme has been so approved, *all* the creditors are bound. The section 425 scheme is, however, more cumbersome than a CVA and the latter process is, therefore, likely to be used in preference.

The players

The insolvency procedures described above involve a number of institutions or actors and these can be outlined as follows:

---

56. See ch. 10 below.

Administrators

Administrators carry out administration orders under the Insolvency Act 1986[57] and must be qualified insolvency practitioners.[58] An administrator possesses a wide range of powers,[59] including the power to sell company property, is an officer of the court and can apply to the court for directions.

Administrative receivers

Administrative receivers are usually appointed out of court by debenture holders under an express power contained in the debenture. Such a receiver is defined by section 29(2) of the Insolvency Act 1986 as 'a receiver or manager of the whole (or substantially the whole) of a company's property appointed by and on behalf of the holders of any debentures of the company, secured by a charge, which, as created, was a floating charge, or by such charge and one or more other securities'. The administrative receiver is the company's agent and must be a qualified insolvency practitioner;[60] he is an office holder;[61] he has broader statutory powers than an ordinary receiver;[62] and he enjoys the protection of section 44 of the Insolvency Act 1986 (as amended by the Insolvency Act 1994) concerning liability in respect of new contracts and contracts of employment which he adopts.[63]

Receivers

Receivers are appointed by creditors with a charge over particular assets or assets given in security pursuant to powers in a debenture and the Law of Property Act 1925. They may also (more rarely) be appointed by the court and, as such, are officers of the court and accountable to it rather than subject to the directions of the creditor in whose interest they have been appointed. Receivers are always in practice made agents of the company. A number of provisions of the Insolvency Act 1986 apply to receivership generally: for example, prohibiting the appointment of bodies corporate or undischarged bankrupts as receivers.[64]

Liquidators

Liquidators differ from receivers in so far as they act primarily in the interest of unsecured creditors and members whereas receivers look to the

---

57. Insolvency Act 1986 Part II, Insolvency Rules 1986 Part 2.
58. See ch. 9 below.   59. Insolvency Act 1986 s. 14(1).   60. Ibid., ss. 45(2), 230(2).
61. Ibid., ss. 230–7.   62. Ibid., ss. 42, 43 and Sched. 1.   63. See ch. 8 below.
64. Insolvency Act 1986 ss. 30, 32.

interests of the secured creditor who appointed them.[65] Liquidators are statutory creatures and are appointed by the company or by the court, usually on an unsecured creditor's petition. Like administrative receivers, liquidators must be qualified insolvency practitioners.

Company voluntary arrangement (CVA) supervisors

As previously noted, Part I of the Insolvency Act 1986 and Part I of the Insolvency Rules 1986 provide a statutory framework for voluntary arrangements between companies and their creditors. Central to the CVA is the issuing of a directors' written proposal to creditors. This should identify the insolvency practitioner[66] who has agreed to take responsibility for the CVA ('the nominee'). The nominee will obtain statements of affairs from the directors, require further information from company officers and report to the court. The nominee will summon a meeting of the company and all known creditors to gain approval of the scheme. If obtained, it is the responsibility of the nominee, who becomes now 'the supervisor', to see that the CVA is put into effect. The supervisor can apply to the court for directions;[67] petition for a winding up; or ask for administration of the company. On completing the CVA the supervisor must make a final report within twenty-eight days to creditors and members.

The tasks of corporate insolvency law

Corporate insolvency law has a number of key tasks to perform (for example, to distribute the assets). In outlining these we should distinguish between descriptions of core jobs and statements of the broader objectives or values that a set of insolvency laws and procedures might seek to further (for example, fairness and efficiency). To list tasks provides very limited assistance in deciding what corporate insolvency laws should seek to achieve through carrying them out, just as composing a list of garden tasks for the autumn tells us little about *why* we are gardening. Selecting 'key' tasks does, moreover, make certain assumptions about the appropriate purposes of corporate insolvency law. It is useful, nevertheless, to note the key tasks that are frequently referred to in practice and in

---

65. See Hoffmann J in *Re Potters Oils Ltd (No. 2)* [1986] 1 WLR 201. See ch. 12 below.
66. In the CVA procedure for small companies introduced by the Insolvency Act 2000 there is no requirement that a nominee/supervisor be an IP: see Insolvency Act 2000 s. 4(4) introducing a new section 389(A) to the Insolvency Act 1986 to allow persons to act if authorised by a body recognised by the Secretary of State.
67. Insolvency Act 1986 s. 7(4).

commentaries so that an image of the corporate insolvency law agenda can be conveyed. Chapter 2 will return to the theme of objectives and values to be furthered in carrying out (and in rethinking) such tasks.

The tasks can be set out thus:

- to lay down rules governing the distribution of the assets of an insolvent company, including rules protecting the pool of assets available to creditors
- to provide for management of companies in times of crisis
- to facilitate the recovery of companies in times of financial crisis and to stimulate the rehabilitation of insolvent companies and businesses as going concerns
- to balance the interests of different groupings and to protect the interests of the public and of employees in the face of financial failures or management malpractices
- to encourage good management of companies by sanctioning directors who are responsible for financial collapses where there has been malpractice and by providing for the investigation of the causes of corporate failure
- to dissolve companies when necessary.

Conclusions

Corporate insolvency law has developed enormously during the last century and the Cork Report is a conspicuous highlight in that development. Cork and its statutory aftermath, however, have not supplied complete answers. In one sense this is inevitable since laws have to develop and adapt to social and economic changes. In another sense, however, current approaches to corporate insolvency law have failed to come to grips with certain challenges that have to be faced if corporate insolvency law is to develop in a manner that contributes appropriately to the (business) life of the nation. Two challenges are of central importance. The first is to see corporate insolvency law as a complete process: not merely as a set of rules but as a system of institutions, rules, procedures, implementation processes and practical effects. This demands that, in developing corporate insolvency law, there is an awareness of implications on the ground and of impacts on the resilience of enterprises as well as on credit and employment relationships. The second challenge is to develop clarity in setting out the general purposes of corporate insolvency law and in effecting balances between different competing interests.

Cork, in many ways, did not meet these challenges directly in so far as the Committee collected limited research and evidence on the effects of different insolvency procedures and in that Cork offered a start but not a finish in outlining the objectives of insolvency law. This book seeks to take matters further in responding to these challenges: by taking on board the available research evidence on the workings of insolvency procedures; by looking to objectives and values; and by continuing to examine how corporate insolvency processes, seen as a whole, can meet those objectives.

2

Aims, objectives and benchmarks

Openness concerning the aims and objectives of corporate insolvency law is necessary if evaluations of proposals, or even existing regimes, are to be made. Without such transparency it is possible only to describe legal states of affairs or to make prescriptions on the basis of unstated premises. As will be argued in this chapter, however, it may not be possible to set down in convincing fashion a single rationale or end for corporate insolvency law. A number of objectives can be identified and these may have to be traded off against each other. It is, nevertheless, feasible to view legal developments with these objectives in mind and to argue about trade-offs once the natures of these objectives have been stipulated.

This chapter will suggest an approach that allows and explains such trade-offs but it begins by reviewing a number of competing visions of the insolvency process that are to be found in the legal literature. A starting point in looking for the objectives of modern English corporate insolvency law is the statement of aims contained in the Cork Committee Report of 1982.[1]

Cork on principles

The Cork Committee produced a set of 'aims of a good modern insolvency law'.[2] It is necessary, however, to draw from a number of areas of the Cork Report in order to produce a combined statement of objectives relevant to

---

1. *Report of the Review Committee on Insolvency Law and Practice* (Cmnd 8558, 1982). This chapter builds on V. Finch, 'The Measures of Insolvency Law' (1997) 17 OJLS 227.
2. Para. 198.

corporate insolvency.[3] Drawing thus, and paraphrasing, produces the following exposition of aims:

(a) to underpin the credit system and cope with its casualties;

(b) to diagnose and treat an imminent insolvency at an early, rather than a late, stage;

(c) to prevent conflicts between individual creditors;

(d) to realise the assets of the insolvent which should properly be taken to satisfy debts with the minimum of delay and expense;

(e) to distribute the proceeds of realisations amongst creditors fairly and equitably, returning any surplus to the debtor;[4]

(f) to ensure that the processes of realisation and distribution are administered honestly and competently;

(g) to ascertain the causes of the insolvent's failure and, if conduct merits criticism or punishment, to decide what measures, if any, require to be taken; to establish an investigative process sufficiently full and competent to discourage undesirable conduct by creditors and debtors; to encourage settlement of debts; to uphold business standards and commercial morality; and to sustain confidence in insolvency law by effectively uncovering assets concealed from creditors, ascertaining the validity of creditors' claims and exposing the circumstances attending failure;[5]

(h) to recognise and safeguard the interests not merely of insolvents and their creditors but those of society and other groups in society who are affected by the insolvency, for instance not only the interests of directors, shareholders and employees but also those of suppliers, those whose livelihoods depend on the enterprise and the community;[6]

(i) to preserve viable commercial enterprises capable of contributing usefully to national economic life;[7]

(j) to offer a framework of insolvency law commanding respect and observance, yet sufficiently flexible to cope with change, and which is also:

   (i) seen to produce practical solutions to commercial and financial problems

   (ii) simple and easily understood

   (iii) free from anomalies and inconsistencies

---

3. See paras. 191–8, 203–4, 232, 235, 238–9. See also R. M. Goode, *Principles of Corporate Insolvency Law* (2nd edn, Sweet & Maxwell, London, 1997) pp. 29–34.

4. On the importance of fairness to creditors given the mandatory, collective nature of proceedings, see also para. 232.

5. See para. 198(h) and amplification in paras. 235 and 238.

6. See para. 198(i) and amplification in paras. 203–4.

7. See para. 198(j) and amplification in para. 204.

(iv) capable of being administered efficiently and economically
(k) to ensure due recognition and respect abroad for English insolvency proceedings.

Cork's statement of aims was largely endorsed in the subsequent 1984 Government White Paper.[8] It is noteworthy, however, that the DTI objectives for insolvency legislation, as stated in the White Paper, expanded on Cork by stressing the need to provide a statutory framework to encourage companies to pay careful attention to their financial circumstances so as to recognise difficulties at an early stage and before the prejudicing of creditor interests. The White Paper, moreover, differs in emphasis from Cork in so far as its statement of objectives focuses on the interests of creditors and express mention is not made of broader, non-creditor concerns.[9]

Subsequent legislation[10] gave substantial but not complete effect to Cork's recommendations and, notably, reflected two major strands of Cork's corporate insolvency law reform policy: namely those of providing a regulatory framework to prevent commercial malpractice or the abuse of insolvency procedures themselves,[11] and of providing a formal legal procedure for business rescue.[12] What that legislation (and subsequent legislation) did not do, however, was to lay down a formal statement of the purposes of insolvency law or a set of objectives.[13]

Does Cork's expression of aims offer a sustainable and useful statement of objectives for a modern insolvency law? It has not been beyond criticism. The Justice Report of 1994[14] noted that Cork had failed to formulate a limited number of core principles to which others might be treated as subservient and that, as a result, no sense of direction could be discerned.[15]

Some notable attempts have been made to provide single or dominant rationales for corporate insolvency processes and a variety of visions will now be reviewed before an alternative approach is suggested.

---

8. *A Revised Framework for Insolvency Law* (Cmnd 9175, 1984).

9. Ibid., para. 2.

10. Insolvency Acts 1985 and 1986; Company Directors' Disqualification Act 1986. See further I. F. Fletcher, 'Genesis of Modern Insolvency Law: An Odyssey of Law Reform' [1989] JBL 365; J. H. Farrar, 'Company Insolvency and the Cork Recommendations' (1983) 4 Co. Law. 20.

11. See e.g. Company Directors' Disqualification Act 1986 ss. 2–12; Insolvency Act 1986 ss. 214, 238–41, 230(2), 390–2; Insolvency Practitioners (Recognised Professional Bodies) Order 1986 (SI 1986 No. 1764).

12. See Insolvency Act 1986 ss. 8–27 (Administration).

13. Insolvency legislation thus differs materially from typical regulatory statutes which tend to lay down objectives: see e.g. the Telecommunications Act 1984; Gas Act 1986; Electricity Act 1989; Water Act 1989; Environment Act 1995.

14. Justice, *Insolvency Law: An Agenda for Reform* (London, 1994).

15. Ibid., paras. 3.7–3.8.

Visions of corporate insolvency law

Creditor wealth maximisation and the creditors' bargain

A number of US commentators, inspired by the law and economics move-ment,[16] have argued that the proper function of insolvency law can be seen in terms of a single objective: to maximise the collective return to creditors.[17] Thus, according to Jackson,[18] insolvency law is best seen as a 'collectivized debt collection device' and as a response to the 'common pool' problem created when diverse 'co-owners' assert rights against a common pool of assets. Jackson, moreover, has stated that insolvency law should be seen as a system designed to mirror the agreements one would expect creditors to arrive at were they able to negotiate such agree-ments ex ante from behind a Rawlsian 'veil of ignorance'.[19] This 'creditors' bargain' theory is argued to justify the compulsory, collectivist regime of insolvency law on the grounds that were company creditors free to agree forms of enforcement of their claims on insolvency they would agree to collectivist arrangements rather than procedures of individual action or partial collectivism. Jackson sees the collectivist, compulsory system as at-tractive to creditors in reducing strategic costs, increasing the aggregate pool of assets, and as administratively efficient. It follows from the above argument that the protection of the non-creditor interests of other victims of corporate decline, such as employees, managers and members of the community, is not the role of insolvency law.[20] Keeping firms in operation is thus not seen as an independent goal of insolvency law.

In the creditor wealth maximisation approach all policies and rules are designed to ensure that the return to creditors as a group is maximised. Insolvency law is thus concerned with maximising the value of a given pool of assets, not with how the law should allocate entitlements to the pool. Accordingly effect should only be given to existing pre-insolvency

16. See e.g. T. H. Jackson, *The Logic and Limits of Bankruptcy Law* (Harvard University Press, Cambridge, Mass., 1986); D. G. Baird, 'The Uneasy Case for Corporate Reorganisations' (1986) 15 *Journal of Legal Studies* 127. For a refined creditors' bargain theory see T. H. Jackson and R. Scott, 'On the Nature of Bankruptcy: An Essay on Bankruptcy Sharing and the Creditors' Bargain' (1989) 75 Va. L Rev. 155. For an extensive collection of key law and economics readings see J. S. Bhandari and L. A. Weiss (eds.), *Corporate Bankruptcy: Economic and Legal Perspectives* (Cambridge University Press, Cambridge, 1996).
17. See e.g. Jackson, *Logic and Limits of Bankruptcy Law*; D. G. Baird and T. Jackson, 'Corporate Reorganisations and the Treatment of Diverse Ownership Interests: A Comment on Adequate Protection of Secured Creditors in Bankruptcy' (1984) 51 U Chic. L Rev. 97.
18. See Jackson, *Logic and Limits of Bankruptcy Law*, chs. 1 and 2.
19. Ibid., p. 17; J. Rawls, *A Theory of Justice* (Harvard University Press, Cambridge, Mass., 1971); J. Rawls, *The Liberal Theory of Justice: A Critical Examination of the Principal Doctrines in 'A Theory of Justice'* (Clarendon Press, Oxford, 1973). For further discussion see pp. 34–5 below.
20. See Jackson, *Logic and Limits of Bankruptcy Law*, p. 25.

rights, and new rights should not be created. Variation of existing rights is only justified when those rights interfere with group advantages associated with creditors acting in concert.

The creditor wealth maximisation vision has been highly influential and has been put into legislative effect in some jurisdictions. Thus the German Bankruptcy Code of 1994 (*Insolvenzordnung*)[21] aims to establish a system that will enhance market exchange processes and rationalise debt collection rather than supersede market processes.[22] It is a vision, however, that has been subject to extensive criticism, some of which has been phrased in the strongest terms.[23] Major concerns have focused, firstly, on insolvency being seen as a debt collection process for the benefit of creditors. This, it has been said,[24] fails to recognise the legitimate interests of many who are not defined as contract creditors: for instance, managers, suppliers, employees, their dependants and the community at large.[25] To see insolvency as in essence a sale of assets for creditors (what might be termed a 'car-boot sale' image), moreover, fails both to treat insolvency as a problem of business failure and to place value on assisting firms to stay in business. Thus, it has been argued that to explain why the law might give firms breathing space or reorganise them in order to preserve jobs requires resort to other values in addition to economic ones. The economic approach, as exemplified by Jackson, is alleged to demonstrate only that its own economic value is incapable of recognising non-economic values, such as moral, political, social and personal considerations.[26]

---

21. *Insolvenzordnung* v. 5.10.1994 (*Bundesgesetzblatt*, BGBI, IS2866).

22. See M. Balz, 'Market Conformity of Insolvency Proceedings: Policy Issues of the German Insolvency Law' (1997) 23 *Brooklyn Journal of International Law* 167, 170–1.

23. See e.g. D. G. Carlson, 'Thomas Jackson has written an unremittingly dreadful book' in 'Philosophy in Bankruptcy (Book Review)' (1987) 85 Mich. L Rev. 1341; see also V. Countryman, 'The Concept of a Voidable Preference in Bankruptcy' (1985) 38 Vand. L Rev. 713, 823–5, 827; J. L. Westbrook, 'A Functional Analysis of Executory Contracts' (1989) 74 Minn. L Rev. 227, 251 n. 114, 337; T. A. Sullivan, E. Warren and J. L. Westbrook, *As We Forgive Our Debtors: Bankruptcy and Consumer Credit in America* (Oxford University Press, New York, 1989) p. 256.

24. See D. R. Korobkin, 'Contractarianism and the Normative Foundations of Bankruptcy Law' (1993) 71 Texas L Rev. 541, 555; E. Warren, 'Bankruptcy Policy' (1987) 54 U Chic. L Rev. 775, 787–8.

25. See K. Gross, 'Taking Community Interests into Account in Bankruptcy: An Essay' (1994) 72 Wash. ULQ 1031.

26. See D. R. Korobkin, 'Rehabilitating Values: A Jurisprudence of Bankruptcy' (1991) 91 Colum. L Rev. 717, 762. Certain economic approaches may, of course, favour a particular corporate reorganisation and job preservation arrangement because this maximises social wealth: though in other circumstances there may, on this basis, be arguments for allowing jobs to move into new, more efficient and profitable contexts. (Jackson, in contrast, seeks to maximise creditor wealth.) On wealth maximisation as an ethical basis see generally R. Posner, 'Utilitarianism, Economics and Legal Theory' (1979) 8 *Journal of Legal Studies* 103, but cf. R. M. Dworkin, 'Is Wealth a Value?' (1980) 17 *Journal of Legal Studies* 191; Dworkin, *A Matter of Principle* (Clarendon Press, Oxford, 1986) chs. 12, 13.

The idea, moreover, that a troubled company constitutes a mere pool of assets can also be criticised. Such a firm can be seen not purely as a lost cause but as an organic enterprise with a degree of residual potential: 'Unlike mere property, a corporation, whether in or out of bankruptcy, has potential. A corporation can continue as an enterprise: as an enterprise, it can change its personality and, perhaps more importantly, whether the corporation continues and how it changes its personality affects people in ways that are not only economic.'[27] Insolvency law, indeed, has for some time on both sides of the Atlantic recognised that the rehabilitation of the firm is a legitimate factor to take on board in insolvency decision-making.[28]

Does it make sense, in any event, to point to a common pool of assets to which creditors have a claim before insolvency? Unless credit is secured, it is arguably extended on the basis that repayments will be made from income and not from a sale of fixed assets. Income, moreover, cannot be said normally to be produced by the assets themselves but, in the case of an enterprise, from 'an organisational set-up consisting of owners, management, employees plus a functioning network of relations with the outside world, particularly with customers, suppliers and, under modern conditions, with various government agencies'.[29] It is, indeed, insolvency law itself that creates an estate or pool of assets and this undermines any assertion that insolvency processes should maximise the value of a pre-existing pool of assets and should not disturb pre-insolvency entitlements.

The idea that insolvency law can be justified in a contractarian fashion with reference to a creditors' bargain has also come under heavy fire.[30] The creditors' bargain restricts participation to contract creditors. In this sense the veil of ignorance used by Jackson is transparent since the agreeing parties know their status in insolvency. It is not surprising that in an ex-ante position such creditors would agree to maximise the value of assets

---

27. Korobkin, 'Rehabilitating Values', p. 745. See also Warren, 'Bankruptcy Policy', p. 798.
28. See Korobkin, 'Rehabilitating Values', pp. 749 and 751. On the UK, see S. Hill, 'Company Voluntary Arrangements' (1990) 6 IL&P 47; Cork Report, paras. 29–33 (re administration); H. Rajak 'Company Rescue' (1993) 4 IL&P 111; Insolvency Service, *Company Voluntary Arrangements and Administration Orders: A Consultative Document* (DTI, 1993); *Revised Proposals for a New Company Voluntary Arrangement Procedure* (DTI, 1995); *A Review of Company Rescue and Business Reconstruction Mechanisms* (DTI, 1999); *A Review of Company Rescue and Business Reconstruction Mechanisms: Report by the Review Group* (DTI, 2000).
29. See A. Flessner, 'Philosophies of Business Bankruptcy Law: An International Overview' in J. S. Ziegel (ed.), *Current Developments in International and Comparative Corporate Insolvency Law* (Clarendon Press, Oxford, 1994) p. 19.
30. See Carlson, 'Philosophy in Bankruptcy', p. 1355: 'even less than a hollow tautology'.

available for distribution to themselves.[31] Jackson, moreover, focuses exclusively on voluntary and bargaining creditors, while assuming a perfect market, and leaves out of account other types of creditor, for whom there is no market at all.

The circular nature of the bargain has been exposed by critics. Creditors in the bargain are assumed to be de-historicised and equal. The creditors' bargain model explains the rule of creditor equality only by presupposing what it sets out to prove.[32] In real life, in contrast, creditors differ in their knowledge, skill, leverage and costs of litigating. The assumption that powerful creditors (e.g. secured creditors) would agree to collectivise their claims to the pool alongside their weaker brethren is highly questionable. It is more likely that what parties will agree to will inevitably mirror those disparities in rights, authority and practical leverage that shape their perspectives.[33] Jackson's solution to this problem is to suggest that secured creditors should receive from the pool no less than what they would be entitled to outside insolvency. This is the equality of *Animal Farm*, though, and is inconsistent with the homogeneity of creditors originally posited. To assume, moreover, that all creditors have purely economic interests is also questionable. Thus, for instance, employee creditors who face displacement costs that are separate from their claims for back wages might not agree to creditor equality because they could well consider that such costs should be reflected in a higher priority for their back-wages claims. They might, additionally, consider that their claims on assets morally outrank those of secured creditors and for this reason also insist on priority for wage claims.[34]

A further major weakness of the creditor wealth maximisation vision is its alleged lack of honesty on distributional issues.[35] The collectivism advocated by Jackson is treated as neutral but it begs distributional

---

31. See Korobkin, 'Contractarianism and the Normative Foundations', p. 555. See also Gross, 'Community Interests', p. 1044.
32. See Carlson, 'Philosophy in Bankruptcy', pp. 1348–9; Korobkin, 'Rehabilitating Values', pp. 736–7.
33. See Korobkin, 'Contractarianism and the Normative Foundations', p. 552.
34. See Carlson, 'Philosophy in Bankruptcy', p. 1353. It might be argued from an economic perspective that employees could be expected to compensate for employment insecurities by demanding that these be reflected in higher wage packets. Inequalities of employer/employee bargaining positions and information levels are factors, *inter alia*, however that make such expectations unrealistic: see e.g. A. I. Ogus, *Regulation: Legal Form and Economic Theory* (Oxford University Press, Oxford, 1994) pp. 38–41; S. Breyer, *Regulation and Its Reform* (Harvard University Press, Cambridge, Mass., 1982); K. Van Wezel Stone, 'Policing Employment Contracts Within the Nexus-of-Contracts Firm' (1993) 43 U Toronto LJ 353.
35. See Warren, 'Bankruptcy Policy', esp. pp. 790, 802, 808.

questions. By purporting merely to enforce pre-insolvency rights Jackson presupposes the defensibility of the state-determined collection scheme without further argument; by this process distributive elements are worked into his theory via the back door. The inappropriateness of transplanting the system of state allocation of rights becomes clearer on noting the very different functions of the respective bodies of law. Whereas pre-insolvency state entitlements are designed with an eye to ongoing contractual relationships, it is arguably the very purpose of a (federal) insolvency system to apportion the losses of a debtor's default in a new and different situation when a variety of factors impinge on decisions as to where losses should fall.

If, indeed, it is proper for insolvency law to look beyond pre-insolvency rights, this again strikes at the heart of the creditors' bargain thesis. It can be said, in the first instance, that insolvency does and should recognise the interests of parties who lack formal legal rights in the pre-insolvency scenario,[36] not least because parties with formal legal rights never bear the complete costs of a business failure. Thus, creditors may suffer in an insolvency but those without formal legal rights may also be prejudiced: not only, as already noted, employees who will lose jobs and suppliers who will lose customers, but also tax authorities whose prospective entitlements may be diminished and neighbouring traders whose business environments may be devalued. A danger of the creditor wealth maximisation vision is that it fails adequately to value the continuation of business relationships that have not been formalised in contracts and may, indeed, omit from consideration those who suffer the greatest hardships in the context of financial distress.[37]

A second point concerns those parties with various pre-insolvency legal rights. The argument that insolvency law should only give effect to these pre-insolvency rights can be countered by asserting that a core and proper function of insolvency law is to pursue different distributional objectives than are implied in the body of pre-insolvency rights; that insolvency law does so by adopting a base-line rule on equality – *pari passu* – and by then making considered exceptions to that rule. It is insolvency law's application to the turbulence of financial crisis, as distinct from the calm waters that mark pre-insolvency contracts, that can be said to justify the

---

36. See E. Warren, 'Bankruptcy Policymaking in an Imperfect World' (1993) 92 Mich. L Rev. 336 at 356.
37. See Korobkin, 'Contractarianism and the Normative Foundations', p. 581.

intrusion of a number of value judgments concerning relative priorities of various liabilities and the order in which groups of liabilities should be discharged.[38]

A broad-based contractarian approach

A vision of insolvency law that attempts to overcome the restrictions of creditor wealth maximisation is a broader contractarianism. The version discussed here is the Rawlsian scheme of Donald Korobkin.[39] Whereas Jackson seeks to justify insolvency law with reference to the rules that contract creditors would agree to from behind the veil of ignorance, Korobkin places behind the veil not merely contract creditors but representatives of all those persons who are potentially affected by a company's decline, including employees, managers, owners, tort claimants, members of the community, etc. These people chose the principles of insolvency law from behind a strict veil, ignorant of their legal status, position within the company or other factors that might lead them to advance personal interests. They would, however, foresee that the financial distress of companies would affect a wide variety of individuals and groups occupying various positions and differing in their ability to affect the actions and decisions of the companies in distress.

Korobkin argues that the parties in such a position of choice would opt for two principles to govern insolvencies.[40] First, a 'principle of inclusion' would provide that all parties affected by financial distress would be eligible to press their demands. Second, a principle of 'rational planning' would determine whether and to what extent persons would be able to enforce legal rights and exert leverage. It would seek to promote the greatest part of the most important aims (the 'maximisation of aims') and would involve formulating the most rational, long-term plan as a means of realising the 'good' for the business enterprise. It would require an outcome

38. See Warren, 'Bankruptcy Policy', p. 778; Warren, 'Bankruptcy Policymaking', pp. 353–4. On preferential status generally see Cork Report, chs. 32, 33; D. Milman, 'Priority Rights on Corporate Insolvency' in A. Clarke (ed.), *Current Issues in Insolvency Law* (Stevens & Sons, London, 1991) p. 57; S. S. Cantlie, 'Preferred Priority in Bankruptcy' in J. Ziegel (ed.), *Current Developments in International and Comparative Corporate Insolvency Law* (Clarendon Press, Oxford, 1994) p. 413.

39. See Korobkin, 'Contractarianism and the Normative Foundations'. See also Rawls, *A Theory of Justice*. For an argument that the economic approach is compatible with Rawlsian social justice see R. Rasmussen, 'An Essay on Optimal Bankruptcy Rules and Social Justice' (1994) U Illinois L Rev. 1 (an approach perhaps throwing light on the distributional limitations of Rawls' theory of justice). See also R. Mokal, 'The Authentic Consent Model: Contractarianism, Creditors' Bargain and Corporate Liquidation' (2001) 21 *Legal Studies* 400.

40. Korobkin, 'Contractarianism and the Normative Foundations', pp. 575–89.

that would 'maximumly satisfy the aims' but, in reflection of Rawls' difference principle, would mandate that persons in the worst-off positions in the context of financial distress should be protected over those occupying better-off positions. For such purposes persons in worst-off positions would be those relatively powerless to promote their aims, yet with the most to lose on the frustration of those aims.

Korobkin argues that application of his contractarian approach would produce laws corresponding in fundamental ways to the kind of insolvency system encountered in the USA. His approach, like that of Rawls,[41] however, is open to question on a number of fronts. First, the particular choices of principle made from behind the veil of ignorance depend on a particular concept of the person: it is not possible to strip the individual completely yet conclude that he or she would choose, for instance, the difference principle.[42] Risk-averse and risk-neutral individuals might produce very different principles of justice. It is not clear why an individual behind the veil might not prefer a regime marked by low-cost credit and low protection for vulnerable parties to one with high costs of credit and high levels of protection.

This introduces a second difficulty as encountered in Rawls: the extent to which diminutions in justice may be traded off against gains on other fronts, such as in wealth. Advocates of creditor wealth maximisation might object to Korobkin's scheme on the grounds that principles of insolvency law designed by a veiled and highly inclusive group are liable to be so protective of so many interests, and as a result so uncertain, that the effects on the cost of credit would be catastrophic. Korobkin's answer would be that such effects would be anticipated by those behind the veil.[43] The device of the veil, however, does not in itself explain, in a convincing fashion, important distributional issues, such as how to judge trade-offs between fairness or justice and wealth creation. Such matters are governed

---

41. On Rawls see e.g. N. Daniels (ed.), *Reading Rawls: Critical Studies on Rawls' 'A Theory of Justice'* (Stanford University Press, Stanford, 1989); R. Nozick, *Anarchy, State and Utopia* (Blackwell, Oxford, 1974) pp. 183–231; R. Wolff, *Understanding Rawls* (Princeton University Press, Princeton, N.J., 1977).

42. In F. H. Bradley's words, 'a theoretical attempt to isolate what cannot be isolated', quoted in M. Loughlin, *Public Law and Political Theory* (Clarendon Press, Oxford, 1992) p. 96. See also M. J. Sandel, *Liberalism and the Limits of Justice* (Cambridge University Press, Cambridge, 1982) pp. 93–4.

43. My acknowledgement of Korobkin's answer (Finch, 'Measures of Insolvency Law', p. 235) seems to have been lost on at least one commentator (Mokal, 'Authentic Consent Model', p. 424, n. 83)! Korobkin ('Contractarianism and the Normative Foundations', pp. 583–4) notes that parties in a bankruptcy choice situation (behind the veil) are aware of the 'difficulty of actual decision-making' and would be attracted to a rational plan based on Rawls' difference principle for this reason.

by the concept of human nature built into the system rather than the veil.[44] If such trade-offs are ruled out it can be objected that the protection offered by a just rule is of very limited value if individuals lack the resources required to take advantage of that rule. The distinction, moreover, between principles of fairness or justice and principles governing the allocation of other goods such as wealth is also problematic.[45]

It might be further objected that the contractarian approach fails to explain how agreements can be reached behind the veil as to who in a potential insolvency is most vulnerable and thus should enjoy priority of protection over those occupying less threatened positions. Korobkin acknowledges the difficulties of comparing positions in terms of vulnerability, and these are indeed real.[46] He suggests that vulnerability be measured in terms of the product of the potential loss to, and the degree of influence exercised by, an individual. There is no reason, however, why such an approach would be accepted by all parties behind the veil. Many may think that such benchmarking distorts the system in favour of those who already possess advantages and so have much to lose. A final difficulty is whether agreement could be expected on the relative valuations of, say, rights to secure or continued employment, as opposed to particular sums of money owed by parties to others. As a guide to the practical development of insolvency law contractarianism may indeed be considerably flawed by its indeterminacy.

The communitarian vision

In contrast with the emphasis on private rights contained within the creditor wealth maximisation approach, the communitarian counter-vision sees insolvency processes as weighing the interests of a broad range of different constituents. It accordingly countenances the redistribution of values so that, on insolvency, high-priority claimants may to some extent give way to others, including the community at large, in sharing the value of an insolvent firm.[47] A concern to protect community interests

---

44. Notably the concept of human nature that is assumed to attract parties behind the veil of ignorance to Rawls' difference principle rather than to more high-risk principles that are less protective of the most vulnerable.

45. See P. P. Craig, *Public Law and Democracy in the United Kingdom and the United States of America* (Clarendon Press, Oxford, 1990) pp. 262–3.

46. Korobkin, 'Contractarianism and the Normative Foundations', p. 584 and his n. 198.

47. See Warren, 'Bankruptcy Policy' and 'Bankruptcy Policymaking'; Gross, 'Community Interests'. See also *Report of the Commission on the Bankruptcy Laws of the US*, Pt 1, HR Doc. No. 137, 93d Cong., 1st Sess. 85 (1973), discussing the 'overriding community goals and values' of bankruptcy.

may, furthermore, militate in favour of insolvency laws that compel companies and their creditors to bear the costs of financial failure (for example, environmental cleaning costs) rather than shift those to third parties or taxpayers.[48]

Communitarianism thus challenges the premise that serves as the basis for the traditional economic model, namely that individuals should be seen as selfish, rational calculators. An important aspect of communitarianism is the centrality that is given to distributional concerns.[49] Redistribution is seen, not as an aberration from the protection of creditors' rights, but as a core and unavoidable function of insolvency law: 'bankruptcy is simply a…scheme designed to distribute the costs amongst those at risk'.[50]

It follows from the concerns of communitarianism that insolvency law should look to the survival of organisations as well as to their orderly liquidation. In this respect the Cork Committee's[51] statement of aims incorporates aspects of communitarianism in stressing not merely that insolvency affects interests in society beyond insolvents and their creditors, but that the insolvency process should provide means to preserve viable commercial enterprises capable of contributing to the economic life of the country.[52] To creditor wealth maximisers the communitarian vision is objectionable in so far as it clouds insolvency law by departing from creditor right enforcement and taking on issues – for example, protections for workers – which more properly should be dealt with by allocating pre-insolvency rights – for example, rights to employment security, fair dismissal and compensation on redundancy.[53] In response, communitarians might urge, first, that there is no reason why issues arising in insolvency should be governed by rules or agreements formulated without regard to insolvency and, second, that it is perfectly proper to

---

48. See e.g. K. R. Heidt, 'The Automatic Stay in Environmental Bankruptcies' (1993) 67 *American Bankruptcy Law Journal* 69; L. Manolopoulos, 'Note – A Congressional Choice: The Question of Environmental Priority in Bankrupt Estates' (1990) 9 *UCLA Journal of Environmental Law and Policy* 73. But see C. S. Lavargna, 'Government-Sponsored Enterprises are "Too Big to Fail": Balancing Public and Private Interests' (1993) 44(5) Hastings LJ 991.
49. See Warren, 'Bankruptcy Policy'. See also E. Warren and J. L. Westbrook, *The Law of Debtors and Creditors: Text, Cases and Problems* (Little, Brown, Boston, 1986) pp. 3–7, 219–26.
50. Warren, 'Bankruptcy Policy', p. 790.
51. See Cork Report, paras. 191–8, 203–4, 232, 235, 238–9.
52. Ibid., para. 198(i) and (j).
53. B. Adler, 'A World Without Debt' (1994) 72 Wash. ULQ 811 at 826; compare D. G. Baird, 'Loss Distribution, Forum Shopping and Bankruptcy: A Reply to Warren' (1987) 54 U Chic. L Rev. 815 with Warren, 'Bankruptcy Policy'.

advert to communitarian issues in both pre-insolvency and insolvency law.[54]

The breadth of concerns encompassed within communitarianism gives rise in itself to problems of indeterminacy. It may be objected that corporatist visions of the company have difficulty in defining the public good and offer 'simply a mask behind which corporate managers exercise unrestrained social and economic power'.[55] Similarly, communitarianism can be said to lack the degree of focus necessary for the design of insolvency law because of the breadth of interests to which it refers. As Schermer has argued, 'it is impossible to delineate the community…There are an infinite number of community interests at stake in each bankruptcy and their boundaries are limitless…[A]lmost anyone, from local employee to a distant supplier, can claim some remote loss to the failure of a once viable local business.'[56]

The problem is not so much that community interests cannot be identified but that there are so many potential interests in every insolvency and that selection of interests worthy of legal protection is liable to give rise to considerable contention. How, moreover, can selected interests be weighed? How might a court balance the community's interest in maintaining employment against potential environmental damage? Doubts, furthermore, have been expressed about the feasibility of redistributing funds in an insolvency.[57] Insolvency law might be designed in order to dilute the legal rights of secured creditors and redistribute the associated wealth to other parties, but (transaction costs permitting) prospective secured lenders may well alter the terms and tariffs of their respective deals so as to contract around the legal alterations. There is some evidence from US studies that such circumvention has been encountered.[58]

---

54. To argue that it is proper for insolvency law in some circumstances to look to communitarian issues and, if necessary, to adjust some prior rights is not, of course, to adopt an imperialist approach to insolvency law or to declare open season on adjusting any laws or rights that happen to arise in an insolvency, however tangentially. Nor is it to claim that communitarian issues should not be adverted to in areas of law beyond insolvency. For failure to take this point and an isolationist view of insolvency law see Mokal, 'Authentic Consent Model', pp. 419–20.

55. M. Stokes, 'Company Law and Legal Theory' in W. Twining (ed.), *Legal Theory and Common Law* (Blackwell, Oxford, 1986) pp. 155–83 at p. 180.

56. B. S. Schermer, 'Response to Professor Gross: Taking the Interests of the Community into Account in Bankruptcy' (1994) 72 Wash. ULQ 1049 at 1051.

57. W. Bowers, 'Rehabilitation, Redistribution or Dissipation: The Evidence of Choosing Among Bankruptcy Hypotheses' (1994) 72 Wash. ULQ 955 at 964.

58. See citation in ibid., p. 959.

A final objection to communitarianism urges that insolvency judges are not necessarily well placed to decide what should, or should not, be deemed a community problem, or what should be in the community's best interest,[59] and that this involves judges in politically fraught decision-making and encourages policy ad hocery. In defence, however, communitarians might respond that judges inevitably and in all sectors of the law advert to public and community interests, that an insolvency law solely for creditor protection is objectionably narrow and that if community interests impinge on judicial decisions they should be dealt with openly and fully.

The forum vision

Rather than seeing the insolvency process in terms of substantive objectives it may be conceptualised in procedural terms, its essence being to establish a forum within which all interests affected by business failure, whether directly monetary or not, can be voiced.[60] The enterprise is seen as comprising not merely the physical assets and stock of business but the focus of interests and concerns of all participants in the company's financial distress. The law's function, in turn, is seen as establishing space. It 'creates conditions for an ongoing debate in which, by expressing…conflicting and incommensurable values, participants work towards defining and re-defining the fundamental aims of the enterprise. Through the medium of bankruptcy discourse, the enterprise realises its potential as a fully dimensional personality.'[61] Not only interested parties can engage in this discourse. To some it, most significantly, allows extra-legal resources and expertise to be brought into play so as to construct the domain to be legally regulated. Thus accountants play an important part in defining the onset of insolvency and in advising on responses: 'Before corporate failure can be internalised within the legal system, it has first to be represented and calculated as an economic event by means of the calculative technologies of accountancy.'[62]

Such a vision may throw light on an important role to be played by insolvency law but it necessarily falls short of offering guidance on matters of substance. As, moreover, with other theories of legitimation through

---

59. Schermers, 'Response to Professor Gross', p. 1051.
60. See Flessner, 'Philosophies of Business Bankruptcy Law'.
61. Korobkin, 'Rehabilitating Values', p. 772.
62. P. Miller and M. Power, 'Calculating Corporate Failure' in Y. Dezalay and D. Sugarman (eds.), *Professional Competition and Professional Power: Lawyers, Accountants and the Social Construction of Markets* (Routledge, London, 1995).

providing means of representation,[63] difficult issues remain concerning the amount of representation to be offered to different parties; the 'right' balance between provisions for representation and efficiency in decision- and policy-making; and the extent to which representation should be re-inforced with legal rights.

The ethical vision

According to Philip Shuchman, insolvency laws fail to rest on an adequate philosophical foundation in so far as the formal rules of insolvency disre-gard issues of greatest moral concern.[64] He argues that the situation of the debtor, the moral worthiness of the debt and the size, situation and intent of the creditor should be taken into account in laying the foundations for insolvency law. Judgments in such matters would not be based upon intu-itions but on utilitarian principles. Thus the criteria to be employed would be 'present and prospective need, desert and the moral and philanthropic worth, and the importance of the underlying transaction...[I]n the context of bankruptcy it is assumed that inter-personal comparisons of utility are significant and that social states can be ordered according to the sum of utilities of individuals; further, that the choice of any given ar-rangement ordinarily ought to be some sort of aggregation of individual preferences.'[65]

Shuchman, therefore, argues that a distinction should be drawn be-tween debts that have arisen out of contracts that personally benefit the creditor and debts flowing from involuntary acts or loans between friends. He would, accordingly, have judges or administrators base decisions on such matters as priorities on ethically relevant realities. He would resist blind acceptance of pre-petition creditors being equal.

Whether it is realistic to expect to find ethical principles to underpin all insolvency law can be questioned,[66] as indeed might the possibility of any group of individuals or judges coming to agree on the substance of such principles.[67] The boundaries, moreover, of relevant ethical principles (and

63. See R. B. Stewart, 'The Reformation of American Administrative Law' (1975) 99(2) Harv. L Rev. 1667 and, generally, C. Pateman, *Participation and Democratic Theory* (Cambridge University Press, London, 1970).

64. P. Shuchman, 'An Attempt at a "Philosophy of Bankruptcy"'(1973) 21 UCLA L Rev. 403. See also J. Kilpi, *The Ethics of Bankruptcy* (Routledge, London, 1998).

65. Shuchman, 'An Attempt', p. 447.

66. See Carlson, 'Philosophy in Bankruptcy', p. 1389.

67. See the exchange between H. L. A. Hart, *Law, Liberty and Morality* (Oxford University Press, Oxford, 1963) and P. Devlin, *The Enforcement of Morals* (Oxford University Press, London, 1965).

the border between ethical principle and prejudice, distaste or disgust[68])
cannot be established uncontentiously. To rely upon the judiciary to evaluate the moral needs and deserts of creditors and the moral worthiness of
debts, and to incorporate such evaluations within insolvency law, places
a large degree of faith in their own moral judgment (not to say the existence of an identifiable and agreed set of moral predicates) and their determination and ability to develop a consistent and coherent body of law
on this basis. Such a system might also have considerable and detrimental
effects on the availability and cost of credit in so far as creditors' bargains
would be placed in the shadow of legal uncertainty. Creditor wealth maximisers might, finally, add that questions of consistency between bodies of
law arise, and argue that if non-insolvency law generally declines to take
on board the virtuous (or disreputable) motives of those involved in legal
transactions then insolvency law should do likewise.[69]

The multiple values/eclectic approach

In stark contrast to approaches offering a single, economic rationale, as exemplified by the creditor wealth maximisation vision, is the notion that
insolvency law serves a series of values that cannot be organised into neat
priorities. Thus Warren offers what she calls a 'dirty, complex, elastic,
inter-connected' view of insolvency law from which neither outcomes can
be predicted nor all the factors relevant to a policy decision can necessarily be fully articulated.[70] Whereas the economic account can explain
insolvency law only as a device to maximise creditor wealth, not distribute fairly, a value-based account is said to understand insolvency law's
'economic and non-economic dimensions and the principle of fairness as
a moral, political, personal and social value'.[71]

Multiple values/eclectic approaches as exemplified by Warren and
Korobkin see insolvency processes as attempting to achieve such ends as
distributing the consequences of financial failure amongst a wide range of
actors; establishing priorities between creditors; protecting the interests
of future claimants; offering opportunities for continuation, reorganisation, rehabilitation; providing time for adjustments; serving the interests
of those who are not technically creditors but who have an interest
in continuation of the business (e.g. employees with scant prospect of
re-employment, customers, suppliers, neighbouring property owners

---

68. See R. M. Dworkin, *Taking Rights Seriously* (Duckworths, London, 1977) ch. 10.
69. See Jackson, *Logic and Limits of Bankruptcy Law*, ch. 1.
70. Warren, 'Bankruptcy Policy', p. 811.   71. Korobkin, 'Rehabilitating Values', p. 781.

and state tax authorities); and protecting the investing public, jobs, the public and community interests. Such approaches incorporate communitarian philosophies and take on board distributive rationales, placing value, for instance, on relative ability to bear costs; the incentive effect on pre-insolvency transactions; the need to treat like creditors alike; and the aim of compelling shareholders to bear the lion's share of the costs of failure.

Further goals can be added by making reference to the Cork Committee's own statement of aims – a clear example of the multiple values approach.[72] Thus, as already noted, Cork emphasised the role of insolvency law in reinforcing the demands of commercial morality and encouraging debt settlement,[73] and also stressed deterrent and distributive ends in urging that insolvency should seek to ascertain the causes of failure and consider whether conduct merited punishment.

The multiple values approach, moreover, is broad enough to encompass the forum vision. Thus, in putting forward his own value-based approach, Korobkin posits the worth, *inter alia*, of insolvency law's providing a forum for the representation of views: 'under the value-based account, bankruptcy law has the distinct function of creating conditions for a discourse in which values of participants may be rehabilitated into an informed and coherent vision of what the estate as enterprise shall exist to do'.[74]

What is the case for a multiple values approach? Warren argues that a policy focusing on the values to be protected in an insolvency distribution and on the effective implementation of those values assists decision-makers even if it does not dictate specific answers. It illuminates the critical, normative and empirical questions and involves inquiries into the range of relevant issues such as who may be hurt by a business failure; how they may be hurt; whether the hurt can be avoided and at what cost; who is helped by the failure; whether aid to those helped offsets the injury to those hurt; who can effectively evaluate the risks of failure; who may have

---

72. See Cork Report, para. 198. For an overview of multiple aims and essential features of an insolvency system see E. Flaschen and T. DeSieno, 'The Development of Insolvency Law as Part of the Transition from a Centrally Planned to a Market Economy' (1992) 26 *International Lawyer* 667 at 668–71.

73. See also G. Triantis, 'Mitigating the Collective Action Problem of Debt Enforcement through Bankruptcy Law: Bill C-22 and its Shadow' (1992) 20 Canadian Bus. LJ 242, who argues that while bankruptcy law may be valuable to resolve the collective action problem and to secure efficiency, an additional objective should be to promote efficient 'private workouts' in the shadow of bankruptcy law. (See also Baird's reply, pp. 261–8.)

74. Korobkin, 'Rehabilitating Values', p. 781.

contributed to the failure and how; whether the contribution to failure serves useful goals; and who can best bear the costs of failure and who expected to bear those costs.[75]

Such an approach is thus said to highlight the empirical assumptions underlying insolvency decisions to ask tough and specific questions by coming to grips with the 'difficult and complex tapestry' of empirical presumptions and normative concerns.[76] It honestly acknowledges that judgments are made in balancing numbers of values in insolvency decision-making. Answers may not be complete but are said to be more fully reasoned than those resulting from single rationale approaches.[77]

Eclecticism, nevertheless, gives rise to not inconsiderable problems. In the first instance, little assistance is offered to decision-makers on the management of tensions and contradictions between different values or on the way that trade-offs between various ends should be effected. Questions, moreover, are easily begged in choosing which values to invoke or emphasise.[78] Nor do core principles emerge to guide decisions on such trade-offs or to establish weightings: this, as noted, was a concern that the 1994 Justice Report expressed with regard to the Cork statement of aims.[79]

The open-textured nature of eclecticism can be a problem in some multi-value schemes. Unless particular values are identified with precision, appeals can be made to an open-ended menu[80] of purposes and it is difficult to decide when to rule out appeals on the basis that they invoke irrelevant values or aims. (Cork, it should be conceded, does offer a list, as we have seen.) Eclecticism runs the danger of seeing all arguments as valid and, as a result, guidance for practical decision-making is lacking and confusion results. If an identification of the objectives of insolvency law is desired so as to provide a framework within which judges and legislators can act, then the multi-value/eclectic, even more than the communitarian, approach is guilty of settling untrammelled discretions on such individuals and allowing them freely to choose from and combine an indeterminately long list of vaguely stated ingredients.

75. Warren, 'Bankruptcy Policy', p. 796.   76. Ibid., p. 797.
77. Korobkin, 'Rehabilitating Values', p. 787.
78. See G. E. Frug, 'The Ideology of Bureaucracy in American Law' (1984) 97 Harv. L Rev. 1277 at 1379.
79. *Insolvency Law: An Agenda for Reform* (Justice, London, 1994) paras. 3.7–3.8.
80. For a view that insolvency law should offer a 'menu of options' and allow firms to choose the optimal rules for their own, perhaps idiosyncratic, requirements, see R. Rasmussen, 'Debtor's Choice: A Menu Approach to Corporate Bankruptcy' (1992) 71 Texas L Rev. 51, and Rasmussen, 'The Ex Ante Effects of Bankruptcy Reform on Investment Incentives' (1994) 72 Wash. ULQ 1159.

The nature of measuring

The above visions or approaches to insolvency emphasise different facets of corporate insolvency law's role. What fails to emerge from the review undertaken, however, is any complete view of the appropriate measures of insolvency law. Creditor wealth maximisation was narrow in its exclusive concerns with creditors' interests and pre-insolvency rights and in its conception of the insolvent company as a pool of assets. The broad-based contractarian approach begged questions concerning the nature of persons behind the veil of ignorance and failed to explain trade-offs of fairness or justice versus efficiency or between different kinds of interests worthy of protection. The communitarian vision escaped the narrowness of creditor wealth maximisation but encountered problems of indeterminacy. The forum vision made much of procedural concerns but shed little light on the substantive ends to be pursued by insolvency law or processes. The ethical vision gave rise to difficulties concerning the possibility of locating agreement as to ethical content and to establishing the boundaries of relevant ethical concerns. How ethical aspects of decisions on insolvency interacted with other, say legal, principles remained in doubt. Finally, the eclectic approach, again, gave rise to problems of indeterminacy and of contradictions and tensions between different ends.

To advance the search for measures in the light of such competing, yet contestable, visions, it is necessary to examine further the purpose of a quest for benchmarks and in doing so to answer two questions. What precisely is being measured? Is it possible to justify insolvency law or processes given present approaches? A response to these issues can be made by examining a well-known treatment of justification in company law and by suggesting that it can be built upon to develop an approach that has relevance for the insolvency arena.

A framework for analysing the fundamental rules of company law has been offered by focusing on the question of how corporate managerial power is legitimated. This issue is said to be a 'unifying theme of company law'.[81] Mary Stokes' argument, in brief, is as follows. If economic power, derived from private property, is to be legitimated within the framework of a liberal society, it is necessary to show that there are restraints preventing it from becoming a threat to liberty or a challenge to state power. Two strategies are contained within the fabric of the law to attempt this demonstration: first, it is posited that the economic power at issue is not

---

81. Stokes, 'Company Law and Legal Theory', p. 155.

sufficiently concentrated to be a threat; second, such economic power is seen as subject to constraints imposed by the competitive market. Unfortunately both strands of argument are afflicted with deficiencies. The growth of the corporate enterprise has allowed concentrations of economic power and the separation of ownership from control has produced managers' powers that are unrestrained by the market (much economic power indeed has come to be exercised not within markets but within corporate bureaucracies).

Company law can be said to have offered a response to the problem of corporate managerial power by explaining why discretion was conferred on corporate managers and by demonstrating that such discretionary power was subject to checks and controls. The justification for discretion was based by some on a contractual view of the company.[82] Thus, the owners might legitimately contract with managers to establish the latter as agents. The problem of using a contractual conception to legitimate managerial power was that this view conflicted with the case law theory of the company as a body distinct and separate from its shareholders. As companies grew, moreover, the artificiality of a contractarian analysis became apparent. A 'natural entity' view of the corporation was seen by others to be more appropriate.[83] This saw the company as a living organism with the managers as the brain and the shareholders as passive suppliers of capital. The natural entity view gave rise to a further way of justifying the vesting of discretionary power in managers: it was the expertise and competence of managers that legitimated their discretion. The boundaries of such expertise and appropriate deference to it were nevertheless difficult to delineate.

As for legitimation through checks on arbitrariness, the traditional legal model offered two mechanisms: accountability to shareholders

---

82. On the contractual view see J. E. Parkinson, *Corporate Power and Responsibility: Issues in the Theory of Company Law* (Clarendon Press, Oxford, 1993) pp. 25–32 and Parkinson, 'The Contractual Theory of the Company and the Protection of Non-Shareholder Interests' in D. Feldman and F. Meisel (eds.), *Corporate and Commercial Law: Modern Developments* (Lloyd's of London Press, London, 1996); W. W. Bratton, 'The "Nexus of Contracts Corporation": A Critical Appraisal' (1989) 74 Cornell L Rev. 408 at 415–23; M. C. Jensen and W. H. Meckling, 'Theory of the Firm: Managerial Behaviour, Agency Costs and Ownership Structure' (1976) 3 *Journal of Financial Economics* 305; F. H. Easterbrook and D. R. Fischel, 'The Corporate Contract' (1989) 89 Colum. L Rev. 1416; E. F. Fama, 'Agency Problems and the Theory of the Firm' (1980) 88(1) *Journal of Political Economy* 288; Symposium, 'Contractual Freedoms in Corporate Law' (1988) 89 Colum. L Rev. 1385; H. Butler, 'The Contractual Theory of the Corporation' (1989) 11 Geo. Mason UL Rev. 99.

83. See Stokes, 'Company Law and Legal Theory', p. 164. See also further discussion in S. W. Mayson, D. French and C. L. Ryan, *Mayson, French and Ryan on Company Law* (18th edn, Blackstone Press, London, 2001) ch. 5.

through internal company controls and directorial duties to act in the best interest of shareholders. (The latter duties legitimated discretions by compelling directors to aim at profit maximisation.)

Both mechanisms proved flawed. In large public companies the dispersion of shareholding undermined shareholder control and managers, in reality, wielded power free from shareholder constraint. Fiduciary duties failed to constrain directors because the courts allowed the latter wide discretions in defining the interests of shareholders. Judicial deference to managerial expertise did not, moreover, legitimate managerial power because it was impossible to draw a line between decisions meriting deference on the basis of expertise and decisions owing more to the pursuit of personal or non-corporate ends. Dispersed shareholding, again, produced a lack of control over managers because of low information levels and low incentives to enforce duties against directors.[84] In short, the law's quest to legitimate the power of corporate management failed.

In response to this failure two strategies might be advocated within the traditional approach: either managers could be made more responsible to the market or new legal steps could be taken to ensure management in the interest of shareholders. Both of these strategies would constitute tinkering. It would be better, argued Stokes, to recognise the misguided nature of attempts to control through markets or the ordering of power in the company and to adopt a new perspective on legitimating managerial power.[85] This new approach would accept the separation of ownership and control and break free from the contractual conception of the company. It might build on a corporatist model of the company and see its interests not merely as those of shareholders but as involving both public and private dimensions; see directors as expert public servants balancing a variety of claims by various groups in the community and doing so with reference to public policy not private cupidity; and see the company as an organic body unifying the interests of participants in harmonious purpose. Managerial power would be legitimated as giving expression to the common purposes of shareholders, creditors, employees and the community.

The corporatist vision might give rise to concerns that corporate managers would enjoy unrestrained discretions in resolving interests and defining public benefits. In response to such worries, a democratic ideal might be introduced into corporate life in order to legitimate corporate

84. See V. Finch, 'Company Directors: Who Cares About Skill and Care?' (1992) 55 MLR 179.
85. Stokes, 'Company Law and Legal Theory', pp. 173–7.

power. This ideal would demand that all those substantively affected by decisions should be involved in making those decisions.

Stokes' argument, in short, is thus that current strategies for legitimating managerial power should be seen as unnecessarily tied to traditional contractarian views of the company and as inadequate; and that the values involved in the corporatist and democratic ideals of the company should be embraced in rethinking rationales for legitimation.

The importance of the argument outlined lies in its critique of the assumptions that underpin traditionalist approaches to the legitimation of managerial power and in its stressing that the public dimension of corporate power demands measures reflecting community and democratic rather than simply private values. Against Stokes it can be countered, however, that reservations about narrow contractarianism and endorsement of the communitarian/democratic approach do not necessarily mean that arguments for legitimation based on contractarian assumptions lack all validity. Here the question is whether traditionalist arguments for legitimation are 'fundamentally misguided'[86] in the sense that they are positive deceptions or whether they are criticisable as telling only part of the story. The communitarian/democratic vision may be completely at odds with the contractarian vision but it may be that legitimating arguments from both camps may cumulate: that adding a communitarian perspective means that corporate managerial power is capable of legitimation to some degree with reference both to controls exercised over managers by the market and to controls operating through representative arrangements corresponding to the democratic ideal. Legitimating arguments such as those based on expertise and accountability can thus be seen as having cumulative force in spite of being flawed in various ways. Indeed, arguments derived from the communitarian/democratic vision are themselves not problem-free. (How much representation of which interests is appropriate? How should such representation best be achieved?)

To consider a series of legitimating arguments and point serially to the limitations of each one and to conclude that legitimation cannot result may be to misportray legitimation as a chain of arguments as strong as its weakest link rather than as a cable able to exert force according to the collective power of its (albeit imperfect) strands.[87]

---

86. Ibid., p. 174.

87. It might be argued that the strands analogy breaks down where individual strands oppose rather than lie parallel (e.g. employee versus creditor interests). The point, however, is that values may be placed on items in spite of such tensions. Employee and creditor interests are thus valued in spite of the trade-offs which often have to be made between them.

A further problem may arise if legitimation is seen exclusively as restraint, as all about the limitation of discretionary powers. Subjection to control and accountability may be necessary for legitimation but these factors may themselves be insufficient to guarantee it. Those attributing legitimacy may also demand that the system enables and encourages the protection of substantive outcomes effectively and they may also recognise the legitimacy of genuinely expert management.[88]

What lessons can be learned by those seeking measures and benchmarks for insolvency law? Indeed, whereabouts in the insolvency sphere is the power requiring legitimation? Company law was said to be about the legitimation of corporate managerial power in the hands of directors. Insolvency is more complex because it is the tendency of English insolvency law to take power out of the hands of management and place it, according to various circumstances, with different parties such as creditors, insolvency practitioners[89] and the courts themselves. It is thus the broad insolvency process in all its dimensions and with its variety of actors that requires legitimation.

A second issue concerns the basis for requiring legitimation. It cannot be assumed that since corporate managerial power in a going concern requires legitimation, insolvency regimes and powers automatically require legitimation. Insolvency processes do, however, impinge strongly upon the public interest in so far as decisions are made about the lives or deaths of enterprises and those decisions affect livelihoods and communities. Insolvency processes also have dramatic import for private rights in so far as, for instance, pre-insolvency property rights and securities can be frozen and individual efforts to enforce other legal rights constrained. On both public and private interest grounds, accordingly, the powers involved in insolvency processes can be seen as calling for strong justification. This, in turn, means that justifications should have aspects which can be democratically secured (as is appropriate in so far as the public interest is involved) and also which can be based on respect for individual

---

88. On restraint versus enabling models of influence ('red light v. green light' approaches) see C. Harlow and R. Rawlings, *Law and Administration* (2nd edn, Butterworths, London, 1997) chs. 2 and 3. On legitimation in general see D. Beetham, *The Legitimation of Power* (Macmillan, London, 1991); Frug, 'Ideology of Bureaucracy'; R. Baldwin and C. McCrudden, *Regulation and Public Law* (Weidenfeld & Nicolson, London, 1987) ch. 3; R. Baldwin, *Rules and Government* (Oxford University Press, Oxford, 1995) ch. 3.

89. For example, as administrative receivers, administrators and liquidators. Contrast the US concept of 'debtor in possession' in Chapter 11 of the Uniform Commercial Code: see J. L. Westbrook, 'A Comparison of Bankruptcy Reorganisation in the US with Administration Procedure in the UK' (1990) 6 IL&P 86; Bank of England Occasional Paper, 'Company Reorganisation: A Comparison of Practice in the US and the UK' (1983).

rights (since private interests are at issue).[90] The attribution of legitimacy should accordingly be seen against a vision of the insolvency process that is broad enough to encompass legitimating arguments that are based on communitarian approaches as well as expressive of concerns that creditors' interests be protected. How tensions and trade-offs between different legitimating rationales can be resolved remains, of course, an issue to which we shall return below.

To argue thus, it may be responded, is all very well where insolvency processes have both public and private dimensions, but in relation to some aspects of insolvency there are real disputes as to whether arrangements should be seen as an integral part of the insolvency process and not just as a matter of private debt collection or contracting. (Administrative receivership and types of 'contractual' arrangements such as *ipso facto* clauses in contracts give rise to such issues.[91]) Private contracting, indeed, can be seen as shading into the province of insolvency law so that clear boundaries do not exist.

Such a lack of clear boundaries should not, however, be seen as fatal to the enterprise of measuring insolvency processes. Persons of different political persuasions might be expected to disagree as to the aspects of insolvency processes that require legitimation by democratically secured rather than private rights based arguments. The point is that if legitimation is seen in terms of rationales that reflect both democratic (public) and private rights roots, clarity will be given to evaluations and the extent to which, for example, present arrangements in an area depend on contractarian justifications will be manifest. To explore modes of measuring or legitimating insolvency law is not to suppose homogeneity of political philosophies.

As for the array of rationales that can be used to legitimate powers impinging upon public interests and private rights, these have been identified by Stokes, Frug and others[92] and, moreover, are limited in number.

---

90. Actors in insolvency processes may, of course, carry out some functions that are oriented towards private interests and some that look to public considerations: thus liquidators both collect and realise assets for distribution to creditors and report directorial 'unfitness' to the Disqualification Unit of the Insolvency Service as part of the disqualification process. See further S. Wheeler, 'Directors' Disqualification: Insolvency Practitioners and the Decision-making Process' (1995) 15 *Legal Studies* 283.
91. E.g. hire purchase agreements made to terminate on the insolvency of the hirer: see further D. Prentice, 'Contracts and Corporate Insolvency Proceedings', paper given at SPTL Seminar on Insolvency Proceedings, Oxford, September 1995. For US treatment of agreements designed to operate only on bankruptcy see Bankruptcy Code 1978 (as amended) ss. 365(a)(1) and (b)(1).
92. See Stokes, 'Company Law and Legal Theory'; Frug, 'Ideology of Bureaucracy'. See also B. Sutton (ed.), *The Legitimate Corporation* (Blackwell, Oxford, 1993).

As Frug has commented: 'we have adopted only a limited number of ways to reassure ourselves'[93] about the exercise of powers. The rationales can be described as: firstly, formalist, which justifies with reference to the efficient implementation of a statutory or shareholders' mandate; secondly, expertise-based, which sees managers as worthy of trust due to their expertise and professionalism; thirdly, control-based, which looks to the restrictions imposed on discretions by courts, markets and others; and, fourthly, pluralist, which adverts to the degree of amenability of processes to representations from the public about how corporate affairs should be conducted.[94]

The justifications of insolvency processes can similarly be seen as dependent not merely on the adequacy of control and accountability schemes and the representation of interests, but also on the effectiveness of processes in both procedural and substantive aspects, and the degree of expertise exercised by relevant parties.

A final message to be drawn from a discussion of corporate power and its legitimation is that individual justificatory arguments may prove contentious and possess limitations (for example, the proper boundaries for expertise cannot be set without argument) but they may nevertheless possess force and may be combined with other arguments.

To argue thus, it should be clear, is at odds with Frug's well-known attack on the traditional bases for legitimating corporate or bureaucratic power. Frug identifies the four models of legitimation already noted but argues that these fail to legitimate corporate power and stresses that combining them together 'only shifts the problem of making a subjective/objective distinction away from any particular model and locates it, instead, in the boundaries between different models'.[95] For Frug each model fails to provide an objective justification for corporate/bureaucratic power, one free from contention. Linking the different models 'allows people to believe that although the device they are considering at any particular moment is empty, one of the others surely is better [and] helps theorists convince themselves (and us) that the internal difficulties of each particular story of bureaucratic legitimacy are unimportant'.[96]

---

93. Frug, 'Ideology of Bureaucracy', p. 1281. The description of rationales that follows in the text paraphrases and reorganises Frug in so far as judicial review is joined with market and other forms of control.

94. See also Baldwin and McCrudden, *Regulation and Public Law*, ch. 3, who, in the public law context, employ the headings: legislative mandate; accountability; due process; expertise; and efficiency.

95. Frug, 'Ideology of Bureaucracy', p. 1378.   96. Ibid., p. 1379.

The limitation of Frug's argument, however, lies in his fundamental idea of justification: in the notion that, without a basis in some objectivity, legitimating arguments lack force. If, as I have already contended, legitimation can be argued for cumulatively so that the justificatory cable has force in spite of its flawed strands, there is far less of a problem in combining rationales of legitimation. The exercise of power can thus be seen as capable of being rendered acceptable not on the grounds that it is 'objective in some way'[97] but because it is supportable by a thread of different arguments based on a limited number of identifiable rationales that are invoked on a collective basis.

Measuring the legitimacy of an insolvency process, decision or law, it should be made clear, differs from merely expressing a political opinion on the topic. Persons of opposing political persuasions might differ radically in their views on dealing with a troubled enterprise. One individual might favour immediate closure, payment of creditors and reliance on reinvestment to create jobs. Another might stress the importance of allowing time for reorganisation because of the high premium he or she places on continuity of employment and avoidance of the external costs that closure might occasion. An exchange of such political views would not, however, amount to a discussion of the legitimacy of the proposed move. To debate legitimacy involves a stepping back and reference, not to personal preferences, but to criteria enjoying broad acceptance as relevant. An analysis of legitimacy, accordingly, would take on board the propensity of a move to serve creditor interests as well as its communitarian effects and its efficiency, expertise, accountability and fairness implications.[98]

What, though, of the difficulty, noted above, of tensions and trade-offs between different legitimating rationales? Surely some such rationales will pull in opposite directions? How, moreover, will the above justificatory principles influence concrete decisions facing insolvency law, for example whether English insolvency law might introduce some variant of debtor in possession?

The answer to these questions is that clarity concerning the measures of insolvency law brings clarity concerning the values that can be invoked in justifying such laws. It does not produce cut and dried answers on whether

97. Ibid., p. 1380.
98. These four headings build on, but repackage, Frug: thus 'efficiency' looks to the securing of mandated ends at lowest cost; 'expertise' refers to the proper exercise of judgment by specialists; 'accountability' looks to the control of insolvency participants by democratic bodies or courts or through the openness of processes and their amenability to representations; and 'fairness' considers issues of substantive justice and distribution.

particular trade-offs between, for instance, protections for secured creditors and for employees are desirable or not. The rightness or wrongness of particular trade-offs can only be argued for by giving weightings or priorities to the protection of different interests. Such weightings and priorities presuppose substantive visions of the just society and, accordingly, persons of different political persuasions might be expected to differ on the 'right' balancing of different interests in insolvency.

The approach to evaluation offered here may produce no fine-tuned answers on substantive issues (to demand such answers would be to ask for conversion to a particular ethical or political vision). The approach, nevertheless, does have force in identifying the values and rationales that have currency in debates on insolvency law. It can, accordingly, be termed an 'explicit value' rather than a multiple value vision of insolvency processes. The explicit value perspective brings the advantage of making clear the need for and nature of trade-offs. Thus, in discussing whether a variant of debtor in possession ought to be introduced into English insolvency law, an assessment would be made of the support that such a measure would merit under the various legitimating headings made explicit above. Although the issue of trade-offs would remain, final political judgments would be made with a transparency that would be lacking were reference not made to the array of rationales described here.

Assessing the legitimacy of insolvency processes or decisions is not, however, the same thing as assessing the formal legitimacy of an insolvency law or statute. As noted, one benchmark for processes or decisions is the extent to which a statutory mandate is efficiently implemented. Where a clear mandate exists this, indeed, provides a very compelling yardstick for measuring an insolvency decision or process, and some aspects of insolvency processes do involve agents in implementing quite clear, almost mechanical, tasks as set down in statutes: for example, the liquidator's statutory duty in voluntary winding up to distribute *pari passu*.[99] To the extent that such clear mandates are lacking – and it is not always possible to produce a clear prescription as opposed to a conferring of discretions, or a listing of factors to be taken into account or proper purposes for action[100] – there is all the more need to legitimate with reference to the expertise, accountability and fairness justifications.

---

99. See Insolvency Act 1986 s. 107.
100. See e.g. the discretion conferred by the Insolvency Act 1986 s. 8(3) which lays down proper purposes for making an administration order. On strong versus weak discretions see Dworkin, *Taking Rights Seriously*, pp. 31–9, 68–71. On discretion in fact finding see D. J. Galligan, *Discretionary Powers: A Legal Study of Official Discretion* (Clarendon Press, Oxford, 1986) pp. 34–7.

Would it not be circular, however, to evaluate an insolvency law by asking (*inter alia*) whether it implements a statutory mandate? If a judicial application of a statute is at issue then circularity is avoided since it makes sense to ask if, in a particular instance, a judge's ruling involves a high degree of discretion or derives legitimacy from its clear implementation of Parliament's will as expressed in a statute (again there may or may not be a clear expression of the mandate available). What of an actual or proposed statutory provision? Does reference to the implementation of a statutory mandate involve circularity? This may not necessarily be the case. Where there is a clear policy or practice laid down then it may be claimed that Parliament's will is being effected and there is a high degree of legitimacy involved, though it will still be possible to consider whether a reform of the provision would be supportable on grounds other than mandate implementation. If, however, the provision at issue merely confers discretion (while, perhaps, laying down factors for consideration) it can be contended that there is not so much an expression of Parliament's voice as a delegation on the substantive issue. The legitimacy of any decision or act taken in implementation of such a provision would accordingly fall to be judged with reference to a series of rationales since the mandate justification only renders the others irrelevant where there is absolute clarity of the mandate.

Does this mean that an insolvency law is worthy of support provided that it has proper statutory form? Again this is not necessarily the case. It means that a very high level of democratic legitimacy is assured to a statutory insolvency provision provided that the statutory mandate is absolutely clear (a rare event). Where it is not possible to lay down a statutory provision that dictates a result with clarity, the other benchmarks come into play and reference can be made to expertise, accountability and fairness considerations in evaluating the provision and its anticipated effects.

The implication of this argument, it might be contended, is that if Parliament decrees something (anything) on insolvency with a clear voice then this is hardly challengeable. The response is that it is difficult to deny the democratic authority of our democracy's most authoritative voice but that evaluation by the hypothetical or proposed reform method noted above is still possible. In the vast majority of instances, where Parliament does not dictate a result but leaves issues and discretions open (or indeed in debating proposed legislation), evaluations may be made with reference to the array of legitimating rationales: asking, for example, of a proposed insolvency provision, whether it will produce results supportable according to expertise, accountability and fairness as well as the mandate rationales. Such evaluations may be made of and by the various actors involved in the insolvency processes: for example, judges, administrators, nominees under voluntary arrangements and liquidators.[101]

Where, though, does this leave economic efficiency in the wealth maximisation sense as a benchmark for insolvency regimes?[102] The wealth maximisation argument was criticised above as offering little assistance on distributional matters. We have seen that clear mandates are rare in the insolvency field and it is not advisable, in the absence of clear mandates, to leap to wealth maximisation itself as the next best statement of substantive objectives. Silence on distributional matters is too serious a matter to be overlooked by those concerned with fairness and justice. What is possible, however, is to take economists' concerns with economic efficiency and technical efficiency and to make these ancillary to discussions of democratically legitimate objectives (or mandates) and questions of expertise, accountability and fairness.[103] This can be done, when responding to economists' views on insolvency law, in two ways: first, by considering such views on whether the processes involved are economically efficient and conducive to wealth maximisation and whether unnecessary transaction costs are avoided; and second, by bearing in mind not only that certain

101. Liquidators may implement statutory mandates mechanically in distributing assets *pari passu*, but discretion is involved in their 'policing' functions (e.g. whether to initiate proceedings under *inter alia* the Insolvency Act 1986 ss. 214, 238 or 239) and in their reporting 'unfit' directorial conduct to the Disqualification Unit: see Wheeler, 'Directors' Disqualification', pp. 300–1.

102. Economists use 'efficiency' in a number of senses and it is as well to be clear about these. The notion of *allocative efficiency* is commonly used in two ways. A situation is *Pareto efficient* if the welfare of one individual cannot be improved without reducing the welfare of any other member of society. In contrast, a situation is *Kaldor–Hicks efficient* if those who gain could in principle compensate those who have been harmed by a position and still be better off. (This efficiency can also be referred to as cost–benefit analysis, wealth maximisation, allocative efficiency or simply efficiency.) *Technical efficiency* is concerned with achieving desired results with the minimal use of resources and costs and the minimal wastage of effort. *Dynamic efficiency* refers to the capacity of a given system to innovate and survive in a changing and uncertain environment. In this book the word 'efficiency' will be used to denote technical efficiency, and 'economic efficiency' will refer to efficiency in the Kaldor–Hicks/wealth maximisation/cost–benefit sense. On efficiency, concepts and corporate law see A. Ogus and C. Veljanovski, *Readings in the Economics of Law and Regulation* (Oxford University Press, Oxford, 1984), pp. 19–20; Ogus, *Regulation*, pp. 23–5; Law Commission, *Company Directors: Regulating Conflicts of Interests and Formulating a Statement of Duties*, LCCP 153, SLCDP 105 (TSO, London, 1998) part III; S. Deakin and A. Hughes, 'Economics and Company Law Reform: A Fruitful Analysis?' (1999) 20 Co. Law. 212; Deakin and Hughes, 'Economic Efficiency and the Proceduralisation of Company Law' [1999] CfiLR 169; J. Armour, 'Share Capital and Creditor Protection: Efficient Rules for a Modern Company Law' (2000) 63 MLR 355.

103. On efficiency as a guide to law reform, as informing rather than directing, see Deakin and Hughes, 'Economics and Company Law Reform', p. 217: 'To say that a particular arrangement is "efficient" tells us nothing at all about the value which society may place on efficiency . . . nor does it tell us anything about the weight to be attached to other values.'

economic 'inefficiencies' may be desired in society for reasons of distributional justice (for example, we may desire to protect certain economically
weak parties where this leads to non-maximisation of wealth) but also that
we value factors other than economic efficiency – not merely Parliament's
expressed will and distributional fairness but also accountability and the
need, on occasion, to allow experts to make judgments on our behalf.

Conclusions

In looking for the measures of insolvency law a series of different visions
of insolvency is encountered and, although these visions may be flawed,
they can be seen as incorporating a number of important legitimating rationales for insolvency processes. There is more to measuring such processes, it has been noted, than stipulating a series of substantive outcomes
(e.g. preserving viable enterprises). Procedural concerns are relevant also.
Measuring thus looks to the whole breadth of insolvency processes and the
cumulative force of arguments deriving from a variety of visions: making
reference, for instance, to economic or technical efficiency *in producing appropriate outcomes*; expertise; accountability; and fairness.

How does this advance matters beyond the substantive and procedural
aims set down, for instance, by Cork?[104] First, the approach arrived at here
offers an explanation of what is involved in assessing insolvency processes
and, in addition, throws light on the different kinds of legitimating argument that are contained within such lists of aims as Cork offers. Second,
it might be complained that the present approach is as lacking in precise
benchmarks as the eclectic or communitarian visions, but it has been possible to identify and make explicit a number of different rationales for justifying insolvency processes: namely efficiency, expertise, accountability
and fairness. Trade-offs between different rationales do remain a problem
but, unless single rationale explanations are accepted (and, for reasons discussed, these seem excessively narrow), the absence of easy answers has to
be accepted when dealing with processes whose essence is the balancing of
multiple objectives.

What has been offered here has been an approach to measuring that
takes on board the public and private, the procedural and substantive,
and the contractarian and democratic dimensions of insolvency. As already noted, acceptance that both the public and private dimensions of

---

104. Cork Report, paras. 191–8, 203–4, 232, 238–9.

insolvency law are to be reflected in legitimation involves an acceptance, in turn, that legitimation may be derived from both the propensity of insolvency laws and decisions to further communitarian interests and the potential of such laws and decisions to protect pre-existing rights. The vision offered in this book – the explicit values approach – holds that an identifiable list of justifications has relevance in assessing the legitimacy of insolvency processes. The list is limited rather than open-ended (as was a problem with eclectic and communitarian visions) in so far as relevant legitimating arguments are organised under the four headings noted and arguments not falling under such headings are accordingly not to be treated as relevant for purposes of legitimation.

Such a vision, in turn, implies a particular approach to insolvency procedures. Dealing with explicit values in the above manner means that trade-offs between these values have to be made throughout insolvency processes. A variety of interests will accordingly have to enter consideration in a host of procedures. Such processes must respect the interests of, and the role to be played in, insolvency by a range of parties: not merely creditors (secured and unsecured) but employees, company directors, shareholders, suppliers, customers and other 'commercial dependants' of the company. The broad public interest must also enter deliberations as a valid concern and procedural inclusivity should be seen in access to information, broad inputs into key decisions and in holding parties to account. This is not to argue that customers, for instance, should have the same access to information and processes as creditors; it is to suggest that reasonable access for customers should not be denied in insolvency procedures on the grounds that customers have no recognisable interest in insolvency. The interests of affected or potentially affected parties should be procedurally recognised where the costs of doing so are reasonable. In some particular contexts, of course, rights of reasonable access may involve excessive costs through creating legal uncertainties that cannot be resolved and in those contexts restrictions will be appropriate. Such matters will be considered in the chapters that follow.

Does an explicit values approach supply the 'fundamental or core principles' that the 1994 Justice Report advocated as guides to the 'true essence of the insolvency process'? It does not offer a series of primary principles to which others can be seen as subservient. The list of values set out here does, however, provide a core in the sense of a framework offering guidance in the development of insolvency rules and arrangements. It adds, for instance, to the arrangements of objectives set down by the Cork Committee by placing those objectives within a frame of concerns established according to the four particular rationales serving to justify insolvency rules. Those rationales provide a context for Cork's objectives rather than leave them as aims apparently plucked from the sky. The linking or cumulation of rationales also reminds us that objectives, such as are set out by Cork, do have to be weighed and traded against each other.

An explicit list of rationales, furthermore, offers a checklist to be dealt with by judges and decision-makers when dealing with insolvency issues. These actors may thus be invited not to reason with reference to a single or dominant vision of insolvency but to deal with points relevant to each of the four kinds of justificatory argument noted. Trade-offs between different ends and justifications are thus to be argued for in particular contexts and cannot be preordained according to set rules. Such argumentation should, however, be carried out explicitly and it is this structured transparency that will be the best guarantee of insolvency laws and processes that display a sense of direction.

For the purposes of this book, the rationales of *efficiency, expertise, accountability* and *fairness* provide benchmarks with which to evaluate both current and proposed arrangements. Such benchmarks can be applied not merely to substantive laws and informal rules but also to institutional structures and to those processes that are used to apply insolvency laws and rules on the ground. Throughout the chapters that follow, these benchmarks will be applied and, in particular contexts, attempts will be made to explain the balances and trade-offs that are involved between particular values or rationales. This book, however, sets out not merely to evaluate laws, processes and reforms. As indicated in the Introduction, it also aims to rethink perspectives. The ensuing chapters will, accordingly, apply the above benchmarks but will also consider whether improvements in corporate insolvency laws and processes have to come through new approaches and by adopting perspectives that challenge the underpinning assumptions of current corporate insolvency systems.

Part II

The context of corporate insolvency law: financial and institutional

3
Insolvency and corporate borrowing

The issues attending corporate insolvency law are closely linked to those surrounding corporate borrowing. It is the creation of credit that gives rise to the debtor–creditor relationship and makes insolvency possible in the first place.[1] Credit can be obtained by companies in a variety of ways, as we will see in this chapter, and the various modes of obtaining debt bring with them different arrangements for dealing with repayments. These arrangements will be relevant when dealing with companies that can no longer repay all their creditors.

To ask whether the legal framework of corporate insolvency law is acceptable involves, accordingly, some examination of the arrangements that the law recognises for obtaining credit and for raising corporate capital. If corporations or creditors in an insolvency face problems that arise from the multiplicity and complexity of arrangements for obtaining credit and the ensuing difficulty of resolving the respective claims of different types of creditor, the best way to reform insolvency arrangements might well be to rationalise the legal methods available for raising capital and obtaining credit rather than to tinker with the insolvency rules that apply to the various credit devices.[2]

Insolvency arrangements can be assessed with reference to the factors outlined in chapter 2 but the link with credit should always be borne in mind and companies should be seen in both their healthy and their troubled contexts. It would be undesirable, for instance, to reform and improve insolvency arrangements if the result was to prejudice mechanisms

1. See *Report of the Review Committee on Insolvency Law and Practice* (Cmnd 8558, 1982) ('Cork Report') ch. 1, especially para. 10, on credit as the 'lifeblood of the modern industrialised economy' and 'the cornerstone of the trading community'.
2. See Cork Report, para. 1628 for acknowledgement of this connection.

for providing healthy companies with the credit arrangements that they need for effective action in the marketplace. The arrangements that best meet the needs of healthy, trading companies, it should be recognised, are not those that necessarily produce the smoothest-operating insolvency regimes and, in designing credit arrangements (with their attendant insolvency implications), the objective should be to maximise the sum of benefits to those involved with both healthy and troubled companies. (Here 'benefits' refers to procedural and democratic as well as financial advantages.) It may be the case that companies need a wide range of flexible credit arrangements and insolvency law has to cope accordingly.

This chapter will consider the main methods by which companies can raise money and will explore the insolvency law implications of different credit arrangements. The emphasis of the chapter will rest on the benchmark of efficiency since it is necessary to respond to a considerable body of debate on credit arrangements which has focused heavily on that yardstick. As was noted in chapter 2, however, it is essential to place efficiency debates in their proper, limited, context by considering questions of expertise, accountability and distributional fairness. These matters, accordingly, will be returned to in parts III and IV of the book. The discussion here asks how the legal structure of each mode of obtaining finance or credit contributes to the supply of funds for a healthy company and whether that structure allows insolvencies to be dealt with efficiently. (The needs of healthy, trading companies will be dealt with briefly since this is not a book dealing centrally with corporate financing.) At this stage, it should be noted, it is the formal legal structure of financing arrangements that is the primary object of attention. Later chapters will broaden the discussion to consider in more detail how such arrangements are put into effect.

Financing and credit arrangements will be examined individually but it will then be necessary to consider whether, as a package, the available legal arrangements perform well in relation to both healthy and troubled companies. It is conceivable, after all, that each device may perform adequately in its own right but that collectively they may prove inefficient because they give rise to legal confusions and uncertainties. We begin by looking at the parties involved in, and the incidence of, borrowing before considering in more detail the particular routes available for the financing of corporate activity.

Creditors, borrowing and debtors

Creditors

Companies in England are able to borrow from a wide variety of individuals and institutions.[3] A first kind of creditor is the institutional lender. This is exemplified by the high street clearing bank that plays an important role in offering companies not merely loans but flexible finance in the form of overdrafts. Other types of institution are the accepting houses: a number of merchant banks which usually offer term loans for periods of five years or more. The merchant banks have traditionally been associated with the supply of venture capital: money used in relation to high-risk activities, for example to start up ventures or to effect rescues and, in reflection of higher than average risks, tending to be accompanied by demands for higher than average returns or shares in the enterprise, or both.

A second kind of commonly encountered lender is the trade creditor,[4] the individual or firm who supplies goods or services to the company but who does not require immediate payment. Such creditors will often transfer goods to a company and await payment at a later date but they may also offer goods in return for a bill of exchange (in the form, for example, of a post-dated cheque) or in accordance with leasing or hire purchase terms. These latter arrangements allow companies to spread the costs of purchasing an item (for example, a new piece of machinery) over a proportion, or all, of the asset's lifetime.[5]

A third type of creditor is the wealthy individual who may be persuaded to put money into a venture. The term 'business angel' has developed to refer to individuals who perform venture capital roles, usually offering loans and, in return for these, combining repayment conditions with the taking of an equity stake in the debtor company.[6]

Governmental agencies comprise a fourth group of creditors. Those concerned with development are exemplified by the British Technology

---

3. See generally Bank of England, *Finance for Small Firms*, Eighth Report (Bank of England, March 2001) ('Bank of England 2001'), and A. Cosh and A. Hughes, *British Enterprise in Transition* (ESRC Centre for Business Research, Cambridge, 2000) ('Cosh and Hughes 2000'), especially ch. 5.

4. Though note that sale credit does not in law constitute a loan (in the sense of providing free funds to conduct business). In legal terms it is seen as the contractual deferment of a price obligation: see p. 66 below; R. M. Goode, *Commercial Law* (2nd edn, Penguin Books, London, 1995) pp. 637–9.

5. Other (unsecured) creditors include landlords (rent arrears), utility suppliers and those with provable debts against a company in liquidation.

6. See further p. 72 below.

Group, which was formed in 1981 and, *inter alia*, assists in the financing of research ideas and inventions. Its returns come by way of a percentage of royalty payments on product sales. Agencies such as the regional development agencies provide funds with a particular focus on small businesses[7] and a number of local authorities also provide venture capital to businesses. In 2000 the Government set up the Small Business Service (SBS) and this body administers the Enterprise Fund, with over £180 million made available over three years to stimulate the provision of both debt and equity finance to UK small or medium-sized enterprises (SMEs). The fund is used to lever in private sector funding and has four main elements: the UK High-Tech Venture Capital Fund; regional Venture Capital Funds; the Small Firms Loan Guarantee Scheme (SFLGS) and the National Business Angel Network (NBAN).[8]

At the European level, the European Investment Bank (EIB) operates as a non-profit-making body and is a source of venture capital as well as medium- and long-term loans to companies of all sizes.[9] The Inland Revenue also constitutes a creditor (often an involuntary one) in so far as companies may owe tax payments, though in some cases they may have negotiated schedules for such payments.[10]

A further type of creditor is the holder of a document issued by the company which acknowledges indebtedness and which usually (but not necessarily) involves a charge on the assets of the company. Under the Companies Act 1985 a 'debenture' includes debenture stock and bonds[11] and company debentures can also be referred to as 'loan stock'. A debenture is a document given in exchange for money lent to the company and

---

7. See Bank of England, *Finance for Small Firms*, Fifth Report (Bank of England, 1998) ('Bank of England 1998') para. 7.11, and Bank of England 2001, pp. 59–62.

8. See Bank of England 2001, p. 60. The SBS also operates the SFLGS which was established by the DTI in 1981. During 1999–2000 4,279 loans were guaranteed with a cumulative value of £206 million: see Bank of England 2001, p. 28. The Bank of England report also discusses a series of tax measures designed to encourage investment in small companies: for example, the Venture Capital Trusts established by the Finance Act 1995 and the tapering system of Capital Gains Tax introduced in April 1998.

9. The European Commission has decided to adopt a Fourth Multinational Programme for SMEs for the five years from January 2001 with a budget of €450 million. The Bank of England has commented, however: 'EU schemes can provide a useful range of funds for SMEs. However, some funds can prove very difficult to access, and in some cases the costs of advice and time required to put forward a satisfactory proposal can outweigh the benefits.' (Bank of England 2001, p. 62.)

10. Local authorities can also be (unsecured) creditors for rate arrears and council taxes: see further D. Milman and C. Durrant, *Corporate Insolvency: Law and Practice* (3rd edn, Sweet & Maxwell, London, 1999) ch. 10.

11. Companies Act 1985 s. 744.

debentures and debenture stock can be offered for sale to the public.[12] The debenture holder is a creditor of the company and the latter agrees to repay the holder the principal sum by a future date and to pay, each year, a stated rate of interest in return for use of the funds.

Another major category of corporate creditor is the employee. In so far as employees have carried out work and are entitled contractually to wages and other benefits as yet unpaid, they constitute creditors of the firm. Shareholders, moreover, may also be creditors in that they may be owed money in their capacity as shareholders (such as dividends). Similarly, consumers of the company's products and other corporate customers may provide credit to the company where they pay in advance for goods or services – practices common in the mail-order, travel, furniture retail and building sectors.[13] Those who prepay are almost invariably unsecured creditors where the supplying company becomes insolvent before delivery. They are, however, important creditors for many firms.[14] Cork noted that 'In many cases, advance payments are an essential part of the trader's working capital.'[15]

Finally, there is a class of involuntary creditor that should not be forgotten. This is the individual or firm who is owed money because they are entitled to payment from the company in accordance with a court order. Thus victims of corporate torts may be treated as corporate creditors and will have participatory rights in an insolvency.

How to borrow

Credit arrangements are complex and it is, therefore, useful before proceeding further to map out the main legal methods of borrowing. This will give a picture of the array of options that are open to companies seeking funds. It should be noted first, however, that not all ways of raising money involve credit. As we will see below, companies can raise finance through the sale of equity shares – a process in which money is put into the company in return for dividends and a hoped-for increase in share value. These

---

12. See J. H. Farrar and B. M. Hannigan, with contributions by N. E. Furey and P. Wylie, *Farrar's Company Law* (4th edn, Butterworths, London, 1998) ch. 20.
13. See Office of Fair Trading (OFT), *The Protection of Consumer Prepayments: A Discussion Paper* (1984); Cork Report, para. 1052: 'the customer who pays in advance for goods or services to be supplied later extends credit just as surely as the trader who supplies in advance goods or services to be paid for later. There is no essential difference.' See chs. 13 and 14 below.
14. The OFT has estimated there to be at least 15 million prepayment transactions each year (OFT, *Protection of Consumer Prepayments*, para. 2.12).
15. Cork Report, para. 1050.

shareholders are not creditors of the company, who have rights *against* the company, but owners of the company with rights *in* it.[16]

Credit can be obtained in four main ways: by offering security; by seeking an unsecured loan; by using a sale as a *de facto* security arrangement; and by resort to a third-party guarantee.

Security

When borrowing companies offer security to lenders this may prove attractive to the latter because, *inter alia*, it reduces their loan risks by giving them privileged claims to repayment in the event of the borrowing company's insolvency.[17] The normal rule in a corporate insolvency is supposedly that all unsecured creditors are treated on an equal footing – *pari passu* – and share in insolvency assets pro rata according to their pre-insolvency entitlements or sums they are owed.[18] Security avoids the effect of *pari passu* distribution by creating rights that have priority over the claims of unsecured creditors.[19]

Security can arise either consensually or through operation of the law. There are four forms of consensual security in English law: the pledge; the contractual lien; the mortgage; and the equitable charge. Pledges involve the creditor taking possession of the debtor's assets (goods or documents of title to goods) and retaining these as security until payment of the debt. The early common law demanded actual transfer of possession to the creditor but the development of the doctrine of constructive possession obviated the need for this.[20] Where a contractual lien is used to obtain credit, the borrower gives the creditor, by contract, a power to detain goods already in the creditor's possession for non-security reasons and to use these as security for payment. This position might arise, for instance, where the

---

16. See *Farrar's Company Law*, ch. 14, p. 157: 'Capital in modern company law is used to cover not only share capital provided by the proprietors but also the loan capital provided by the creditors.' On shareholders viewed as owners of the company see, for example, H. Butler, 'The Contractual Theory of the Corporation' (1989) 11 Geo. Mason UL Rev. 99. On different characterisations of the nature of a shareholder's interest see E. Ferran, *Company Law and Corporate Finance* (Oxford University Press, Oxford, 1999) pp. 131–3.

17. See A. L. Diamond, *A Review of Security Interests in Property* (DTI, HMSO, London, 1989) ('Diamond Report'); I. Snaith, with assistance of F. Cownie, *The Law of Corporate Insolvency* (Waterlow, London, 1990) chs. 1–9. Note the lack of rationality in the use of the term 'security' in England, i.e. the lack of distinction between the security agreement which creates the security and the property securing the obligation: see R. Cranston, *Principles of Banking Law* (Oxford University Press, Oxford, 1997) p. 435. On the effect of security in general see Cork Report, p. 12.

18. On *pari passu*, see chs. 13 and 14 below; D. Milman, 'Priority Rights on Corporate Insolvency' in A. Clarke (ed.), *Current Issues in Insolvency Law* (Stevens & Sons, London, 1991).

19. See Cork Report, ch. 35, paras. 149–97; Goode, *Commercial Law*, part IV; Snaith, *Law of Corporate Insolvency*, ch. 1.

20. See Snaith, *Law of Corporate Insolvency*, pp. 12–13, 24–8.

creditor possesses an item of machinery in order to carry out maintenance work. A lien differs from a pledge in conveying a power to detain the goods rather than sell them on default by the borrower.[21]

A mortgage of chattels transfers ownership to the creditor as security on a condition (express or implied) that there shall be reconveyance to the debtor once the secured sum has been repaid. In the case of land, however, a mortgage interest can be hived off from a fee simple so that land mortgages do not involve complete transfers of ownership and both mortgagor and mortgagee have concurrent legal estates (fee simple and a term of years absolute, respectively).[22] Mortgages do not require transfers of possession and they can be applied to all classes of asset, tangible and intangible. They are, accordingly, of enormous utility to borrowers.

The use of an equitable charge allows debtors to agree that certain specific items of their property will be available as security for loans. Such a charge does not involve a transfer of ownership or possession; instead it gives the creditor a right to have the designated asset sold to discharge the debt. The equitable charge may be fixed on a particular asset or may be floating. With fixed charges the debtor may dispose of the asset only with the creditor's consent (or by repaying the debt). The floating charge hovers over a stipulated class of assets in which the debtor has present or future interest. The debtor is, however, free to deal with particular assets within the class while the charge remains floating, that is until the point when the charge crystallises and fixes on all the assets then in the fund.[23]

As for security arising through operation of the law ('non-consensual security'), this may be anticipated by the potential corporate debtor and used as a way of establishing a credit arrangement. The main forms of security thus arising are the lien, the statutory charge, the non-contractual right of set-off, the equitable right to trace and procedural securities.[24]

Liens, as noted, give persons in possession of the property of others for the purposes of work a right of retention until the work at issue has been

---

21. See Goode, *Commercial Law*, p. 644; but see *Re Hamlet International Plc* [1998] 2 BCLC 164, where a contractual possessory lien over goods, granted by a customer to a company, coupled with a contractual right entitling the company to sell such goods to pay sums owed to it by the customer, did *not* constitute a charge registrable under the Companies Act 1985 s. 395.

22. Goode, *Commercial Law*, pp. 38, 644–5.

23. Or on assets of the specified description subsequently acquired by the debtor: see Goode, *Commercial Law*, p. 646; Snaith, *Law of Corporate Insolvency*, ch. 5. (Crystallisation arises on the occurrence of a number of events, e.g. the commencement of the winding up of the company, the chargee appointing a receiver under the terms of the charging document or the chargee taking possession of the assets.)

24. See generally Snaith, *Law of Corporate Insolvency*, ch. 6; Goode, *Commercial Law*, p. 668.

paid for. Liens may arise through the operation of the common law,[25] equity[26] or statute.[27] A statutory charge gives the chargee a right to apply to the court for an order of sale where a debt has not been paid.[28] Both law and equity allow mutual debts between parties to be set off.[29] Equitable tracing allows a person whose asset has been wrongfully disposed of by another to assert a claim to the proceeds received in exchange for it. Finally, procedural securities may operate at law so that a company making a claim through the legal process can apply to have certain of its opponent's assets taken into the custody of the court as security for satisfaction of the claim at issue or, *inter alia*, an order for costs.[30]

Unsecured loans

A company can seek a loan without offering security but in such an arrangement the lender bears the risk that if the debtor company becomes insolvent its own debt will be satisfied after the secured creditors have been paid. The unsecured creditor, moreover, has no enforceable interest in the debtor's property prior to bankruptcy or winding up, only a right to sue for money owed and to enforce a court judgment against the debtor.

Like a secured loan, an unsecured loan may constitute 'loan credit' – the loan of money – or it may be 'sale credit' – where goods or services are supplied to the debtor but payment of the price for these is allowed to be delayed. In practice, however, sale credit in the normal course of trade is more likely to be unsecured than secured. Companies, moreover, may seek either fixed-sum or running account credit.[31] With the former the debtor takes a fixed amount for a stated period but in a running account there is an ongoing facility to draw varying sums within agreed limits.

Quasi-security

Companies can enter into a number of legal relationships that, on their face, appear to be sale arrangements but which operate in practice as

---

25. Some general liens may extend to all goods in the lienee's possession whether the sum payable relates to work done on those goods or other work. Thus solicitors, bankers and others enjoy these liens: see Goode, *Commercial Law*, p. 668.

26. Which does not require possession, as with the vendor of land's lien to secure the purchase price.

27. See also the maritime lien: W. Tetley, *Maritime Liens and Claims: Chorley and Giles' Shipping Law* (7th edn, BLAIS, Montreal, 1989) pp. 33 ff.; Goode, *Commercial Law*, p. 670; D. Jackson, 'Foreign Maritime Liens in English Courts: Principle and Policy' [1981] 3 LMCLQ 335.

28. E.g. the Legal Aid Act 1988 s. 16(6) gave the Law Society a charge on money and property recovered in proceedings by a legally aided litigant to secure payment of Law Society costs.

29. See Goode, *Commercial Law*, pp. 657–9 and ch. 13 below.

30. See Goode, *Commercial Law*, pp. 671–2; D. Milman, 'Security for Costs: Principles and Pragmatism in Corporate Litigation' in B. Rider (ed.), *The Realm of Company Law* (Kluwer, London, 1998). See also ch. 12 below.

31. See Goode, *Commercial Law*, p. 639; Consumer Credit Act 1974 s. 10(1).

security devices.[32] These arrangements may merit the close attention of insolvency lawyers since they can be seen as having roles both in supplementing and in circumventing legal rules and principles covering corporate insolvency. They may, for example, not require registration and the assets involved may not be caught in the insolvency net. The main devices are reservations of title;[33] hire purchase agreements; sale and lease back; sale and repurchase; and discounting of receivables.[34] The key aspect of these agreements is that the debtor company is able to raise funds by allowing ownership to rest with the 'creditor' rather than offering security, and the 'creditor' avoids having to compete for insolvency assets with other creditors because he or she holds title or has not passed title in the assets at issue to the insolvent company.

With reservations of title, for instance, the goods will be sent to the 'debtor' company by the seller, 'creditor' A, but ownership, it will be stipulated, will not pass until the full price has been paid. If the debtor company becomes insolvent, the goods, whose title remained with A, do not form part of the insolvency assets.[35] In a sale and lease back a similar effect is achieved by the debtor selling an asset to the creditor in return for a sum of money and continuing to use the asset (for example, the warehouse) by leasing it back under a hire or hire purchase agreement.[36] The creditor retains the title throughout and the warehouse does not form part of the insolvency assets or estate. Sale and repurchase offers another variation in which the company sells goods to the debtor company for a price to be paid in instalments. The agreement states that where the debtor defaults, A may repurchase the goods after deducting the amount outstanding

---

32. See F. Oditah, *Legal Aspects of Receivables Financing* (Sweet & Maxwell, London, 1991) p. 11: M. G. Bridge, 'Form, Substance and Innovation in Personal Property Security Law' [1992] JBL 1.

33. Surveys reveal that the majority of suppliers employ retention of title clauses in their conditions of sale. J. Spencer, 'The Commercial Realities of Reservation of Title Clauses' [1989] JBL 220, 221 surveyed fifty suppliers and 59 per cent of respondents said they used such clauses. Wheeler examined fifteen receiverships and liquidations and found that 92 per cent of supplies of goods had 'some sort of reservation of title provision': see S. Wheeler, *Reservation of Title Clauses* (Oxford University Press, Oxford, 1991) p. 5.

34. See Goode, *Commercial Law*, p. 656; Oditah, *Legal Aspects*, pp. 32–5, 50–5. See also Goode, *Commercial Law*, pp. 646 ff. on the imposition of conditions on the right to withdraw a deposit and contractual set-off. On charges over credit balances see *Re BCCI (No. 8)* [1997] 3 WLR 909; R. M. Goode, 'Charge-Backs and Legal Fictions' (1998) 114 LQR 178; G. McCormack, 'Charge-Backs and Commercial Certainty in the House of Lords' [1998] CfiLR 111; E. Mujih, 'Legitimising Charge-Backs' [2001] Ins. Law. 3.

35. See generally Wheeler, *Reservation of Title Clauses*; I. Davies, *Effective Retention of Title* (Fourmat, London, 1991); G. McCormack, *Reservation of Title* (2nd edn, Sweet & Maxwell, London, 1995).

36. See J. Ulph, 'Sale and Lease-Back Agreements in a World of Title Relativity: *Michael Gerson (Leasing) Ltd v. Wilkinson and State Securities Ltd*' (2001) 64 MLR 481.

from the purchase price. Finally, discounting of receivables (or factoring) involves the purchase of invoiced receivables (sums due under outstanding invoices) at less than their face value. The assignor whose receivables are so discounted receives immediate cash to the extent of the purchase price. The financier deducts an administration charge in addition to the 'discount', which, by being calculated on a daily yield basis, produces a sum equivalent to interest on the amount advanced to the assignor.[37] The company thus receives a cash sum earlier than would have been the case had it waited for its debtors to settle their accounts.

As will be discussed below, however, it is not easy to characterise many quasi-security arrangements and the courts may face difficulties in deciding whether a transaction is, for legal and insolvency purposes, a loan secured by a mortgage or charge, a sale or an outright assignment.[38]

Third party guarantees

Often a loan from a creditor such as a bank will be 'guaranteed'[39] by a third party – which may be an individual director of the debtor company but could also be a parent or subsidiary company within a group. The Government itself may also act as a guarantor and the UK offers a good deal of credit insurance to exporters through the Export Credits Guarantee Department[40] which, *inter alia*, guarantees bills of exchange purchased by banks. Guarantees may relate to specific transactions or operate on a continuing basis and relate to a flow of transactions.

The guarantor undertakes to answer for the default of the principal but guarantors can only be sued after the principal debtor's default. Usually the undertaking of the guarantor is to meet the monetary liability arising out of the default, but a guarantor may also assume a secondary liability for performance as stipulated in the contract agreed by the principal. The guarantor is not liable for any amount in excess of that recoverable from the principal debtor and, if the guarantee is given at the request of the debtor, the guarantor has an implied contractual right to be indemnified by the debtor against all liabilities incurred.[41]

37. See Oditah, *Legal Aspects*, p. 34. See further pp. 71–2, 112–13 below.
38. See Oditah, *Legal Aspects*, pp. 35–40.
39. If A owes B a financial obligation, then instead of, or in addition to, taking a charge on A's property, B may take a contract with a third party, C, under which C promises to meet A's obligation to B if A fails to do so (C being the 'guarantor'). See further R. M. Goode, *Legal Problems of Credit and Security* (2nd edn, Sweet & Maxwell, London, 1988).
40. See Goode, *Commercial Law*, ch. 30.
41. In an insurance arrangement, in contrast, the insurer protects the covered party and there is no right of indemnity against the defaulter: see R. M. Goode, 'Surety and On-Demand Performance Bonds' [1988] JBL 87.

Debtors and patterns of borrowing

The above discussion gives an idea of the main sources and credit devices available to borrowers but not of the patterns of borrowing that tend to be encountered in companies. Such patterns are liable to vary according to a number of factors such as the company's needs, size, commercial sector and plans but, bearing this in mind, some generalisations can be made. In doing so it is helpful to distinguish the practices of SMEs from those of larger companies.

Recent research on SMEs[42] reveals that small businesses tend to rely heavily on internal funds both for operating and investment purposes, with just over a third having no borrowings.[43] Internal sources of finance thus seem to be more attractive than the costs of borrowing. Around 39 per cent of SMEs would appear to seek external finance in a given two-year period, however,[44] with a greater proportion of borrowing by firms of below- rather than above-average profitability.[45] Of the SMEs surveyed by Cosh and Hughes for 1997–9, 84 per cent of those who had sought finance externally went to their bank;[46] 46 per cent had sought credit from hire purchase or leasing businesses; 10 per cent approached factoring businesses; 10 per cent looked to working shareholders or partners and less than 10 per cent had sought to raise funds by other routes (namely through venture capitalists; suppliers or customers; private individuals; or other

42. See Cosh and Hughes 2000; A. Cosh and A. Hughes, *Enterprise Britain: Growth, Innovation and Public Policy in the Small and Medium Enterprise Sector* (ESRC Centre for Business Research, Cambridge, 1998) ch. 7 ('Cosh and Hughes 1998'); Bank of England 2001; *Finance for Small Firms,* Sixth Report (Bank of England, 1999) ('Bank of England 1999'), Seventh Report (Bank of England, 2000); Institute of Directors, *Business Finance* (IOD, 1999) ('IOD 1999'). See also J. Freedman and M. Godwin, 'Incorporating the Micro Business: Perceptions and Misperceptions' in A. Hughes and D. Storey (eds.), *Finance and the Small Firm* (Routledge, London, 1994); J. Bates, *The Financing of Small Businesses* (3rd edn, Sweet & Maxwell, London, 1982); M. Chesterman, *Small Businesses* (2nd edn, Sweet & Maxwell, London, 1982) ch. 4.
43. See Cosh and Hughes 1998, p. 74; figures for the first half of 1997 indicate that total bank deposits held by the small business sector totalled £28.7 billion. Of responses to the 1999 IOD survey of firms (IOD 1999) over 90 per cent were from micro- (under nine employees), small (10–49 employees) or medium (50–249 employees) firms and respondents stated that retained profits and investments by owners/directors/shareholders were their most commonly utilised sources of finance.
44. Cosh and Hughes 1998, p. 67; Cosh and Hughes 2000 (for years 1997–9).
45. See Cosh and Hughes 2000, p. 54. In recent years SMEs have become less reliant on external finance: according to the Bank of England 2001 (p. 23) only 40 per cent of SMEs sought external finance in 1997–9 compared with 65 per cent in 1987–90.
46. In the case of 22 per cent of firms surveyed for 1995–7, overdrafts from banks represented their total use of interest-paying external finance: see Cosh and Hughes 1998, p. 74. On the advantages of borrowing from banks (expertise, purity of interests, access to advice, interests in stable markets and resources etc.) see B. G. Carruthers and T. C. Halliday, *Rescuing Business: The Making of Corporate Bankruptcy Law in England and the United States* (Clarendon Press, Oxford, 1998) ch. 4.

sources).[47] As for the amount of finance raised by SMEs, the same survey revealed that banks provided 61.2 per cent of this; hire purchase/leasing firms, 22.7 per cent; partners and shareholders, 4.4 per cent; factoring businesses, 2.6 per cent; other sources, 4.9 per cent; other private individuals, 2.1 per cent; venture capitalists, 1.3 per cent and trade customers, 0.8 per cent. These figures show a rise in bank finance compared to a similar 1995–7 analysis (from 47.4 per cent to 61.2 per cent) and a drop in hire purchase/leasing sources (from 27.1 per cent to 22.7 per cent). The Bank of England has reported an increasing use of credit cards to finance business expenditure, with 23.9 per cent of surveyed businesses using credit cards in 1998 for financing.[48]

Banks thus remain the main providers of credit for SMEs, with more borrowing by term lending than through overdrafts. In the early 1990s the Bank of England expressed concern at the dependence of small businesses on overdraft facilities for purposes other than working capital: for example, to finance long-term business expansion.[49] There has since then, indeed, been a drift away from overdraft borrowing in favour of term loans. Term lending in 2000 amounted to over £30 billion and borrowing on overdrafts was around £12 billion. The ratio of term loans to overdrafts shifted from the 1993 figures of 44:56 to 72:28 in 2000.[50] The Bank of England has, nevertheless, acknowledged that the overdraft will 'always be important to small businessmen as a flexible source of working capital'.[51]

Certain kinds of borrowing seem, additionally, to be size dependent. The Institute of Directors' (IOD's) 1999 survey did not reveal any significant differences between respondents from different industries but firm size did produce variations in certain financing modes. Micro-firms (of under nine employees) appeared to rely far more on investments of capital by owners, directors or shareholders than large firms of 250 employees or more (74 per cent of micro firms used such financing, compared to

47. Cosh and Hughes 2000, pp. 48–9. The trend noted by Cosh and Hughes when comparing results with the 1995–7 survey was a 'return to the dominance of the banks, with a decline in approaches to all other sources of finance': Cosh and Hughes 2000, p. 48. Different findings emerged from the 1,223 replies to the IOD's 1999 survey (IOD 1999). When asked how their firm had financed its activities over the preceding five years, 74 per cent said retained profits; 63 per cent investment of capital by owners/directors/shareholders; 54 per cent bank overdrafts; 47 per cent revenue from sales; 35 per cent bank term loan; 28 per cent loan by owners/directors; 20 per cent leasing; 18 per cent trade creditors; 7 per cent factoring.
48. Bank of England 2001, p. 23.   49. See Bank of England 1999, p. 17.
50. Bank of England 2001, pp. 24–5.
51. Bank of England 1999, p. 18. In 1999–2000 the overall level of overdraft lending rose after a number of years of decline: see Bank of England 2001, p. 25.

47 per cent of large firms).[52] On revenue from sales as a source of finance, the respective figures were 50 per cent for micro-firm respondents and 37 per cent for large companies. Conversely, 81 per cent of large firms used retained profits as a source of finance compared to 63 per cent of micro-firms, and while 68 per cent of large companies had used bank overdrafts, only 42 per cent of micro-firms had. Contrary to the view of the Bank of England,[53] the IOD survey suggested that the tendency to use term loans was more closely associated with larger companies than smaller ones.[54] (The IOD survey suggested that the primary determinant of choice of external finance was cost, followed by prior good experience, absence of personal collateral, maintenance of business control and speed of obtaining funds.)

Findings reported in 1997 suggested that smaller companies were more heavily dependent on asset-based financing (notably operating leases and hire purchase arrangements) than larger firms, with 50 per cent of SMEs using leasing (amounting to 19 per cent of their total debt) compared to only 7 per cent of companies of all sizes.[55] Motives for employing leasing were also found to vary, with smaller businesses tending to use leasing to finance their survival and growth while larger firms used leasing in order to reap tax advantages. Within the group of SMEs itself, it tended to be growing companies that made the greatest use of asset financing. These figures from City University Business School contrast, however, with those of the ESRC Centre for Business Research which show that between 1997 and 1999 23 per cent of SME external finance was asset-based (compared with 27 per cent between 1995 and 1997).[56]

A significant source of SME working capital has been factoring and invoice discounting.[57] A British Chamber of Commerce survey of 1996

52. See also Cosh and Hughes 2000, p. 52 who report that micro-firms use banks, venture capitalists, HP/leasing finance and factoring significantly less frequently than larger SMEs.
53. Bank of England 1999.
54. The IOD (IOD 1999, p. 6) suggested a 'pronounced tendency' for the use of loans to increase with firm size, with 31 per cent of small firms using bank loan finance compared to 46 per cent of medium-sized enterprises.
55. City University Business School, *The Role of Leasing in the Financing of Small and Medium Sized Companies* (London, 1997).
56. See the summaries in Bank of England 2001, p. 35 and Cosh and Hughes 2000, p. 52.
57. Cosh and Hughes 2000, p. 52, however, report that funding by factoring dropped from 6 per cent of external finance in 1995–7 to 2.6 per cent in 1997–9. Factoring, as noted above, is the purchase by the factor and the sale by a company of book debts on a continuing basis, usually for immediate cash. The sales accounting functions are then provided by the factor who manages the sales ledger and the collection of accounts under the terms agreed by the seller. The factor may assume the credit risk for accounts within agreed limits (non-recourse) or this risk may be retained by the seller. Invoice discounting is the purchase by the discounter and the sale by the company of book debts on a continuing basis (usually selectively) for immediate cash. The sales accounting functions are retained by the seller and the arranged facility is usually provided on a confidential basis.

reported that 11 per cent of respondents used receivables financing. An area of low uptake from SMEs, however, is equity financing, where the evidence is that only 3 per cent of external financing to small businesses in the nineties was in the form of equity[58] and only a third of businesses were even prepared to consider equity financing.[59]

Funding by the venture capital industry grew by 54 per cent between 1995 and 1996 but between 1995 and 1999 the percentage of total SME finance that was obtained through venture capital dropped to 1.3 per cent. Of total informal venture capital investment, business angel activity, on official figures, makes up only a small proportion.[60] Raising funds through the provision of venture capital often involves investments in high-risk ventures (typically with new companies) and the investor will usually demand a significant equity stake in the enterprise. The expected return is accordingly of capital gain rather than merely income from dividends. Venture capital is frequently used as a source of finance for management buyouts (MBOs) and may well involve the supply of business skills as well as funds.[61] In a 1998 White Paper the Government recognised that relatively little UK venture capital is used to fund early-stage and technology-based investments in small businesses and it urged institutional investors to consider devoting more funds to venture capital to stimulate the emergence and development of businesses with high-growth potential.[62]

---

58. Bank of England 2001, p. 43.

59. British Chamber of Commerce, *Small Firm Survey No. 24: Finance* (July 1997). On reasons for the low value of equity financing see p. 74 below.

60. In 1998–9 around £20 million was invested by business angels in UK companies: Bank of England 2001, p. 5. In February 1999 the National Business Angels Network was set up. The aim of this national network (supported by the DTI and sponsored by the clearing banks, the Corporation of London and others) is to connect companies seeking equity capital with business angels: see further 'DTI Supports Launch of Business "Angels" Network', *Financial Times*, 10 February 1999. The amount of informal lending by business angels is, however, difficult to quantify since most such angels act anonymously. One estimate is that the UK has 18,000 business angels investing around £500 million annually: see C. Mason and R. Harrison, 'Public Policy and the Development of the Informal Venture Capital Market' in K. Cowling (ed.), *Industrial Policy in Europe: Theoretical Perspectives and Practical Proposals* (Routledge, London, 1999). See also A. Belcher, *Corporate Rescue* (Sweet & Maxwell, London, 1997) pp. 133–4.

61. See Belcher, *Corporate Rescue*, pp. 131–3.

62. DTI, *Our Competitive Future: Building the Knowledge Driven Economy* (Cm 4176, December 1998) paras. 2.20, 2.24. In 2001 the Small Business Service (SBS) linked up with the National Business Angels Network in a £1.5 million scheme involving the creation of a new division of the SBS dedicated to helping small companies to link to larger investors: see *Financial Times*, 27 June 2001.

Modes of financing corporate activity

Bearing in mind the above patterns of borrowing, it is time to consider in more detail how corporate activities can be financed by either equity or credit means and to explore the efficiency with which different devices serve the needs of healthy and of troubled companies.

Equity shares

Companies can raise funds through the sale of shares either on a flotation or by a subsequent issue. The purchasers of shares have interests in the company and the money they put into the company can be used to buy assets with which to earn profits. If shareholders wish to take their money out of the company, they must sell their shares or force the company into liquidation. The former course of action is more common and relatively easy when the shares are quoted on a stock exchange. If the company is liquidated, the assets of the company are sold, liabilities and insolvency claims are met and the remaining funds are paid out to equity shareholders. These shareholders, as a group, are the last to have their claims met (all other interested parties, be they debenture holders, unsecured creditors or employees, have priority). The ordinary shareholders in a company thus take the greatest risks but they benefit from profits when the firm is successful and if, as is usual, the company is a limited liability company, in times of trouble they are liable only to the amount unpaid on their shares.

The rationale for financing through share capital is that this provides a financial basis for corporate activity: one that, on establishing the company, provides a platform for both commencing operations and seeking funds through non-equity routes such as loans. Whether a going concern raises funds through equity capital or, say, bank borrowing depends on the relative costs. In the case of equity capital, the company management must offer investors at least the annual rate of return that those investors would expect to earn in the market on a share bearing the equivalent level of risk. If a company cannot earn this rate of return it will find it difficult to attract new funds because potential investors will look elsewhere in the marketplace.

If it is assumed that markets are competitive and that a company is able to offer a competitive rate of return to investors, there should be no difficulty in raising equity capital through share sales. This, however, demands such conditions as frictionless exchanges (without transaction costs, taxes or entry/exit constraints); rational behaviour by all players in the market; many buyers and sellers; and a free flow of full, costless information to all parties.

It has been asserted that some institutions, such as the Bank of England, view the equity route as an effective way to raise finance.[63] This may be true in the case of large, established companies, but when firms are new, the market may prefer to look to those with a known record and reputation. There are thus informational deficiencies which may hinder the raising of equity capital, especially for new ventures.

Taxation regimes may also make financing through equity shares less attractive than through loans.[64] If funds are raised through borrowing, the interest paid on a loan can be deducted before payable corporation tax is calculated. Such a deduction will not apply in the case of the rate of return that has to be earned in order to satisfy investors. Loan capital may, as a result, prove cheaper than equity financing and there may accordingly be a bias towards borrowing rather than equity financing. In the case of small businesses, in particular, equity financing may play a very limited role in practice.[65] As noted already, only 1.3 per cent of external financing to small businesses in 1997–9 was in the form of equity[66] and in 1997 only a third of businesses were prepared to consider equity finance as a way of expanding their businesses.[67] Three reasons mooted for such low uptake are the lack of understanding of equity finance among small businesses, the desire of many UK entrepreneurs to avoid sacrificing any degree of ownership, independence or control, even if this could produce higher profits,[68] and a set of cultural factors found in the UK. On the last point, the Bank of

63. W. Hutton, *The State We're In* (Vintage, London, 1996) p. 145.

64. For discussion see J. Samuels, F. Wilkes and R. Brayshaw, *Management of Company Finance* (6th edn, International Thompson Business Press, London, 1995) pp. 443, 540–9.

65. See Bank of England 1999, pp. 28–9.   66. Cosh and Hughes 2000, p. 52.

67. British Chamber of Commerce, *Small Firm Survey No. 24*. The IOD survey produced a higher figure: of 1,295 members who discussed equity finance, 51 per cent said that in principle they would consider such financing in order to expand their enterprise (IOD 1999, p. 16).

68. See Bank of England 2001, p. 44; DTI, *Our Competitive Future* (1998) para. 2.27. Of those IOD respondents who stated that they were not prepared to consider equity financing, 91 per cent cited potential loss of control as a reason for their reluctance (IOD 1999). See also P. Poutziouris, F. Chittenden and N. Michaelas, *The Financial Development of Smaller Private and Public SMEs* (Manchester Business School, Manchester, 1999) who reported that only 25 per cent of private companies said that they would consider a flotation on the stock exchange as a way of raising funds for expansion. On the reluctance of US owner-managers to relinquish control see R. Scott, 'A Relational Theory of Secured Financing' (1986) 86 Colum. L Rev. 901, 914; M. C. Jenson and W. H. Meckling, 'Theory of the Firm: Managerial Behaviour, Agency Costs and Ownership Structure' (1976) 3 *Journal of Financial Economics* 305.

England has suggested that a 'fear of failure' may deter business owners from seeking venture capital.[69] The Bank has, however, noted that recent Budgets have emphasised the value of entrepreneurship and that these may combine with a less stigmatic governmental approach to business failure so as to encourage use of venture capital. To these reasons may be added a fourth: the failure of banks to offer competitively priced equity financing. The Cruickshank review[70] of March 2000 highlighted a number of key barriers to entry in the SME equity markets (including asymmetric information), confirmed the existence of an equity gap for firms which aim to raise between £100,000 and £500,000, and criticised the Small Firms Loan Guarantee Scheme for not addressing these market imperfections. The evidence nevertheless indicates that small businesses will only consider equity finance after internal sources and debt finance have been exhausted. Equity finance, in any event, is seldom used for raising sums of less than £30,000.[71]

From the above there emerge two messages for insolvency lawyers: first, that how shareholders are dealt with in an insolvency will depend very much on the efficiency with which creditors' interests are processed within an insolvency and, second, that there are scant grounds for assuming that corporate financing through the equity route does or will ever do away with a system of credit that can deal efficiently with the needs of both going concerns and companies in trouble.

Secured loan financing

Companies can borrow funds by offering security or by seeking an unsecured loan. The essence of a security interest is that it gives the holder a proprietary claim over assets in order to secure payment of a debt. In contrast, the unsecured creditor will have lent to the debtor but has a personal claim to sue for payment of the debt and the power to use legal processes to enforce any judgment against the debtor. A security interest may, as noted above, be consensual – where it results from the agreement of the parties – or non-consensual – where it arises through the operation of law. Consensual securities include pledges, mortgages, charges and liens. Non-consensual securities can be divided into liens, statutory charges,

---

69. Bank of England 2001, p. 44.

70. D. Cruickshank, *Competition in UK Banking: A Report to the Chancellor of the Exchequer* (HMSO, London, 2000), discussed in Bank of England 2001, p. 16.

71. There may, however, be substantial barriers to entry into the public equity markets in the form of fees charged by investment bankers, securities buyers and accountants, and these costs may not be justified where financing needs are modest: see Scott, 'Relational Theory', p. 916.

equitable rights of set-off, equitable rights to trace and procedural securities.[72] It should be emphasised that charges can be equitable or legal. Equitable charges do not involve the transfer of possession or ownership that gives creditors the right to have a designated asset appropriated to discharge their debt. An equitable charge is thus a mere encumbrance and does not involve any conveyance or assignment at law: it can exist only in equity or by statute.

Security may involve establishing real rights over one, some or all of the debtor's assets (a real security) or rights of recourse from a third party who has guaranteed payment to the lender in the event of the debtor's default (a personal security).[73] In this section we consider why security is asked for by creditors and the extent to which the existing legal framework for security serves the needs of healthy and of troubled companies.

Creditors are interested in security as a means of reducing the default risks they face. They will be concerned about their position in insolvency and more particularly about the ways in which the shareholders and managers of the company may transfer wealth away from lenders and dilute their potential claims. A number of fears may loom large in their minds.[74] A first worry is that excessive dividend payments may be made, thereby reducing the value of the firm.[75] Second, excessive borrowing may occur when new debt is raised – which may affect the claims of prior debt or, if subordinate, may increase the insolvency risk of all creditors by changing the level of gearing and thus the risks associated with capital structure.[76] Third, assets may be taken outside the company and out of the

---

72. See further Ferran, *Company Law and Corporate Finance*, ch. 15; Goode, *Commercial Law*, pp. 668–73; Snaith, *Law of Corporate Insolvency*, ch. 6.

73. See further Snaith, *Law of Corporate Insolvency*, chs. 2–6. Since 1981 the UK Government has, as noted, operated a government-guaranteed loan scheme designed to encourage bankers to lend to small and medium-sized companies that have exhausted normal financing channels. The Government guarantees the banker that, in the event of a default, the Government will repay 70 per cent of outstanding sums. Personal security from the borrower will not be taken but business assets will be expected to be offered as security. The guarantor may or may not go beyond guaranteeing payments and undertake liability for performance of non-monetary obligations. See generally Goode, *Commercial Law*, ch. 30.

74. See J. Day and P. Taylor, 'The Role of Debt Contracts in UK Corporate Governance' (1998) *Journal of Management and Governance* 171; C. Smith and J. Warner, 'On Financial Contracting: An Analysis of Bond Covenants' (1979) 7 *Journal of Financial Economics* 117. On agency costs generally see Jensen and Meckling, 'Theory of the Firm'.

75. I.e. if cash flows are directed to dividends rather than investment or the repayment of debt or if assets are sold (for example, by sale and lease-back arrangements) and the proceeds paid in dividends thereby reducing the value of assets available to creditors on break up: see Day and Taylor, 'Role of Debt Contracts', p. 176.

76. Ibid., pp. 176–7.

reach of creditors in an insolvency.[77] Fourth, asset substitutions may occur in a way that alters the risk profile of the firm and disadvantages the creditor (for example, where a move from tangible fixed assets to intangibles takes place).[78] Fifth, underinvestment may occur where managers forgo investments that would benefit lenders[79] (they may, alternatively, engage in inefficient strategies because their central aim is to preserve managerial jobs). Finally, managers may engage in excessive risk taking.[80] They may borrow money for stated purposes but divert those funds towards use on projects presenting higher financial risks – projects the creditor would not have funded at the given interest rates or perhaps at all.

In responding to these potential problems, creditors can seek security; obtain price protection by trading debts, where possible; spread risks by diversifying; shorten repayment periods;[81] and use covenants in debt contracts.[82] The clauses of the latter can, for instance, be used to restrict levels of dividends or asset disposals or levels of debt.

A major reason for taking security,[83] in this risk-laden context, is thus to establish claims that, on distribution of the insolvent company's assets, will rank above the claims of unsecured creditors. Creditors may also take security in order to gain access to information. This can be achieved by using the threat of realising the security to obtain access to company decision-making. The creditor can thus become privy to managerial decisions, may even be represented on the board[84] and may engage in informed

---

77. On asset dilution see Smith and Warner, 'On Financial Contracting', p. 118; G. Triantis, 'Secured Debt Under Conditions of Imperfect Information' (1992) 21 *Journal of Legal Studies* 225, 235.

78. See R. Green and E. Talmor, 'Asset Substitution and the Agency Costs of Debt Financing' (1986) 10 *Journal of Banking Law* 391; M. Miller, 'Wealth Transfers in Bankruptcy: Some Illustrative Examples' (1977) 41 *Law and Contemporary Problems* 39.

79. See S. Myers, 'Determinants of Corporate Borrowing' (1977) 5 *Journal of Financial Economics* 147.

80. See L. Bebchuk and J. Fried, 'The Uneasy Case for the Priority of Secured Claims in Bankruptcy' (1996) 105 Yale LJ 857, 873–5; Triantis, 'Secured Debt Under Conditions of Imperfect Information', 237–8.

81. See B. Cheffins, *Company Law: Theory, Structure and Operation* (Clarendon Press, Oxford, 1997) p. 74.

82. See Day and Taylor, 'Role of Debt Contracts'.

83. See R. M. Goode, 'Is the Law Too Favourable to Secured Creditors?' (1983–4) 8 Canadian Bus. LJ 53. See also Diamond Report (1989). Security may also be attractive to creditors because it gives powers of enforcement (fear of which often leads debtors to give priority of performance to secured creditors); it allows the secured creditor to prevent seizure of secured assets by other creditors; and it may also allow pursuit where the secured assets are sold to another party. See Diamond Report, pp. 9–10.

84. See further V. Finch, 'Company Directors: Who Cares About Skill and Care?' (1992) 55 MLR 179, 189–95.

monitoring in order to protect their security.[85] Security may, in addition, give the creditor a right of pursuit so that where the debtor disposes of property that is subject to a charge, a claim may be advanced against the proceeds of that disposition. The creditor may also seek security in order to increase their influence over the market behaviour of the debtor. A charge, for instance, may be so all-embracing as to give the charge holder what amounts in practice to an exclusive right to supply the debtor with credit in that potential second financiers will be deterred from lending by the breadth of the existing charge. A creditor may, furthermore, take security as an alternative to expending resources on gaining such information as will allow him or her to quantify the financial risk involved in lending. Both the taking of security and the collection and analysis of information provide ways to limit and calculate risks, but in some circumstances the former route may be preferred to the latter on the grounds that it involves lower immediate costs and greater certainty. Finally, a creditor (A) may fear that if it is unsecured, some other, more aggressive, unsecured creditors will act too quickly against the debtor company when it faces hard times and that this may prejudice the company's survival and the repayment of the debt owed to creditor A. Creditor A may thus be motivated to seek security in order to discourage or protect against such precipitate action by unsecured creditors.

Bearing in mind the above attractions of security, it might be asked: why do not all creditors always demand security when advancing goods or money?[86] A first reason is that the costs of negotiating security may be excessive given the financial risk involved. Thus, where a trade creditor advances, say, a small stock of timber to a building firm for later payment, the sums involved may not justify the costs of drawing up a security agreement.[87] Other reasons for not taking security may be the unfamiliarity of the small trade creditor with legal arrangements; the custom of informality within trading relationships; the time scales being worked to (with a large number of items being supplied at a high frequency); and the anticipated high costs of monitoring security arrangements.[88]

Finally, the relative bargaining positions of the debtor and creditor may come into play and large corporate debtors with unimpeachable

---

85. On monitoring see pp. 83–6, 89–92 below.
86. See Carruthers and Halliday, *Rescuing Business*, p. 163.
87. Supplies may, however, be delivered under retention of title clauses: see pp. 110–11, 114, below and ch. 14.
88. See Carruthers and Halliday, *Rescuing Business*, pp. 305–6; Cheffins, *Company Law*, p. 82.

creditworthiness may insist on loans without security. If both parties are rational and informed, however, even the most powerful debtor is likely to be presented with a choice by the creditor: between a certain interest rate in combination with security and a higher interest rate without security. The rational creditor will set the difference in rates after calculating the extra risks of non-repayment that a lack of security brings. In choosing which of the options to accept, the debtor will calculate whether the extra interest attending the unsecured loan is a greater cost than is involved in negotiating security and implementing a security agreement. The interest difference will tend to be smaller with a large, reputable firm and a short-term loan than with a small, newly established firm seeking a long-term loan. (The extra risk to the unsecured creditor is smaller and more easily calculated in the former instance.) The costs of the interest difference will, in all cases, rise with the size of the loan. The expenses to the debtor of negotiating and implementing the security will perhaps vary to a lesser degree according to the size and reputation of the firm and would be unlikely to rise in a manner directly proportional to the size of the loan or security (the costs of drawing up the legal documents will seldom vary directly with the sum at issue). Overall, then, one would expect security to be demanded most often by creditors who are dealing with small firms with poor or non-assessable reputations and who seek large sums over long terms.

Fixed charge financing

A fixed charge attaches, as soon as it is created, to a particular property and the holder of the charge has an immediate security over that property. In a corporate insolvency the holders of fixed charges are the first to be paid out of the insolvency estate. A company that raises money by offering the security of a fixed charge may, moreover, not sell or otherwise deal with the property at issue without the consent of the charge holder. The floating charge, in contrast, attaches to a designated class of assets in which the debtor has, or may have in the future, an interest.[89] The debtor, in the case of a floating charge, may deal with any of the property subject to the charge in the ordinary course of business.

The most common fixed charge securities created by companies are legal mortgages over land. Equitable mortgages can also be given over land or equitable interests in land and a fixed charge on chattels can be made

---

89. See pp. 80, 82, 101–5 below and ch. 14; Goode, *Commercial Law*, ch. 25.

by a company but this has to be registered in the Companies Registry. Intangible property, such as shares in another company, can also be the subject of a fixed charge.

Floating charges

The floating charge, as noted, attaches to a class of a company's assets, both present and future, rather than to a stipulated item of property.[90] The assets covered are of a kind that in the ordinary course of business are changing from time to time and it is contemplated that until some step is taken by those interested in the charge, the company may carry on business in the ordinary way and dispose of all or any of those assets in the course of that business. Central to the floating charge, accordingly, is the notion of crystallisation. The company is free to deal with the property charged until an event occurs that converts the charge into a fixed charge over the relevant assets in the hands of the company at the time. The events that the law treats as crystallising the floating charge are the winding up of the company, the appointment of a receiver and the cessation of the company's business.[91] Parties to a charge can, on some authorities, also agree contractually that a floating charge created by a debenture may be crystallised automatically on the occurrence of an expressly stated crystallising event.[92]

Floating charges are commonly given over the whole of the undertaking of the borrowing company but the company, nevertheless, may deal with or dispose of such property without the approval of, or even consultation with, the charge holder. The floating charge, as a device, raises serious issues of fairness, notably as regards the balance between the protection it offers to secured creditors and the resultant exposure of the ordinary, unsecured creditor. Such matters, however, will be returned to in chapter 14; here the focal question is efficiency.

---

90. See *Illingworth* v. *Houldsworth* [1904] AC 355; *Robson* v. *Smith* [1895] 2 Ch 118; *Re Yorkshire Ltd Woolcombers Association* [1903] 2 Ch 284; Cork Report, paras. 102–10. See generally W. Gough, *Company Charges* (2nd edn, Butterworths, London, 1991); Gough, 'The Floating Charge: Traditional Themes and New Directions' in P. Finn (ed.), *Equity and Commercial Relationships* (Law Book Co., Sydney, 1987); D. Everett, *The Nature of Fixed and Floating Charges as Security Devices* (Monash University, Victoria, 1988); S. Worthington, *Proprietary Interests in Commercial Transactions* (Oxford University Press, Oxford, 1996) ch. 4; E. Ferran, 'Floating Charges: The Nature of the Security' [1988] CLJ 213; Ferran, *Company Law and Corporate Finance*, 507–17; R. Grantham, 'Refloating a Floating Charge' [1997] CfiLR 53. See also D. Milman and D. Mond, *Security and Corporate Rescue* (Hodgsons, Manchester, 1999) pp. 50–2; Carruthers and Halliday, *Rescuing Business*, pp. 195–210.
91. See *Farrar's Company Law*, pp. 635–6.
92. Ibid., pp. 637–8; Snaith, *Law of Corporate Insolvency*, p. 69; *Re Brightlife Ltd* [1987] Ch 200; Cork Report, paras. 1575–80.

Why security? The efficiency case

Does the law's providing for security lead to an efficient use of resources?[93] Here again it is necessary to consider the position in relation to both healthy and troubled companies. In answering the question it will be assumed, in the first instance, that security is offered under a system of full priority – in which security interests prevail over unsecured claims in insolvency. An extended debate has been carried out in the USA on the efficiency case for security[94] and a number of commentators from a law and economics background have pointed to a series of advantages of security, notably that it helps companies to raise new capital and it is conducive to efficient lending by reducing creditors' investigation and monitoring costs.

Security facilitates the raising of capital A system of security, with priority, is frequently said to permit the financing of desirable activities that otherwise would not be funded.[95] Thus, where a firm has a low credit rating but the opportunity to enter into a profitable activity subject to moderate levels of risk, it may be able to obtain funds by granting security when it would be unable to obtain unsecured loans. From the creditor's point of view, the gaining of a security with priority reduces the risks of lending and such risk reduction will be reflected in a lower interest rate. A strong priority system, furthermore, assures the creditor that the security enjoyed will not be diluted by the debtor's obtaining more loans by offering further security.[96]

The fixed charge may encourage institutions such as banks to advance funds to companies but the disadvantage of such a charge, in efficiency terms, is that it restricts the freedom of management to deal with the assets charged in the ordinary course of business. This might not present great

---

93. This discussion draws on V. Finch, 'Security, Insolvency and Risk: Who Pays the Price?' (1999) 62 MLR 633.

94. See, for example, T. H. Jackson and A. T. Kronman, 'Secured Financing and Priorities Among Creditors' (1979) 88 Yale LJ 1143; R. Barnes, 'The Efficiency Justification for Secured Transactions: Foxes with Soxes and Other Fanciful Stuff' (1993) 42 Kans. L Rev. 13; J. White, 'Efficiency Justifications for Personal Property Security' (1984) 37 Vand. L Rev. 473; W. Bowers, 'Whither What Hits the Fan? Murphy's Law, Bankruptcy Theory and the Elementary Economics of Loss Distribution' (1991) 26 Ga. L Rev. 27; F. Buckley, 'The Bankruptcy Priority Puzzle' (1986) 72 Va. L Rev. 1393; S. Schwarcz, 'The Easy Case for the Priority of Secured Claims in Bankruptcy' (1997) 47 Duke LJ 425.

95. See, for example, S. Harris and C. Mooney, 'A Property Based Theory of Security Interests: Taking Debtors' Choices Seriously' (1994) 80 Va. L. Rev. 2021 at 2033, 2037; R. Stulz and H. Johnson, 'An Analysis of Secured Debt' (1985) 14 *Journal of Financial Economics* 501, 515–20.

96. Priority assured by registration: see Companies Act 1985 ss. 395–6, 400–1; *Farrar's Company Law*, ch. 38. In the USA priority is secured under Article 9 UCC by filing: see Bridge, 'Form, Substance and Innovation'.

difficulty where the company's main asset is land, but where the bulk of
assets is represented by machinery, equipment, trading stock and receivables[97] such constraints might inhibit business flexibility at some cost.
As for the fixed charge and insolvencies, enforcement issues are relatively
simple, assisted by the requirement that such charges be registered.[98]

Turning to the floating charge, the efficiency rationale is that it allows
the creation of security on the entire property of the borrowing company
and so provides companies with an easy and effective way to raise money
by offering considerable security to the lender. At the same time it involves minimum interference in company operations and management.
For bankers, the floating charge offers an attractive way to secure loans.
It gives them a broad spread of security together with priority over unsecured creditors of the company (commonly trade creditors or customers).
Any provider of finance to a company may ask for the security of a floating charge but such charges are normally encountered in the case of banks
lending by overdraft or term loan and the purchasers of debentures in the
loan stock market. (Such lenders will usually combine fixed charge security over stipulated assets such as land or buildings with a floating charge
over the rest of the company's assets and undertaking.)[99]

The Cork Report noted[100] in 1982 that the use of the floating charge was
so widespread that the greater part of the loan finance obtained by companies, particularly finance obtained from banks, involved floating charge
security and that the majority of materials and stock in trade of the corporate sector was subject to such charges.[101]

As indicated, security offers a way to reduce loan costs by reducing the
risks faced by lenders: if the company does meet trouble, the lender with
security has a better chance of recovery than would be the case if all creditors drew from the same pool.[102] Such considerations are at their strongest

---

97. See pp. 112–13 below; Oditah, *Legal Aspects*.

98. On enforcement see Snaith, *Law of Corporate Insolvency*, ch. 7. On registration see ibid.,
ch. 8.

99. The fixed charge will give priority over preferential creditors: see ch. 13 below.

100. Cork Report, para. 104.

101. In the three banks studied by Franks and Sussman more than 80 per cent of all client
companies involved in the rescue study had a floating charge held by the bank and the overall
security value over the main bank debt averaged 99 per cent: see J. Franks and O. Sussman,
'The Cycle of Corporate Distress, Rescue and Dissolution: A Study of Small and Medium Size
UK Companies', IFA Working Paper 306 (2000) p. 3.

102. The SPI's Eighth Survey, *Company Insolvency in the United Kingdom* (SPI, London, 1999),
indicated that in 1998–9 the overall returns from liquidations and receiverships to
preferential and secured creditors were 37 per cent and those to unsecured creditors were
7 per cent. Franks and Sussman ('Cycle of Corporate Distress') report that recovery rates for
banks are 77 per cent compared with 'close to zero' for trade creditors and 27 per cent for
preferential creditors.

where the form of security offers a level of risk reduction that is quantifiable. In the case of the floating charge there are, however, uncertainties inherent in the device and the relevant law (to be discussed below) which reduce the degree to which such quantification is possible.[103]

   Security reduces investigation and monitoring costs A further reason why security may both encourage lending and produce efficient lending is, as noted, that it can offer the creditor a far more economical means of managing the risks of lending than is potentially provided by an investigation into the creditworthiness of the debtor.[104] The creditor granted a security that covers the amount of the loan is thus well positioned to extend credit at an appropriate interest rate (one that reflects the costs of lending and the risks attached) but is not obliged to calculate the probability of default or the expected value of its share of the borrower's assets in insolvency. The protection offered by the security rules out the need to calculate the extent or risk of any probable loss. What the taking of security does not rule out, however, is the need to calculate the probability that corporate managers will devalue that security by such practices as asset substitution.

   Security can also be said to reduce the risks of lending by assisting creditors to take appropriate monitoring and preventative actions to deter such misbehaviour by the debtor as will reduce the probability that sums owed will not be recovered. An overall efficiency loss may occur if a firm's shareholders and managers pursue certain activities in an attempt to maximise shareholder returns but in doing so increase the expected losses to creditors by a greater amount than the expected shareholder gains.[105] Without monitoring, a firm may act in those ways prejudicial to creditor interests that were noted above. Monitoring provides a response to such risks. Thus the creditor can seek to acquire information from the company in order to determine the probability of default or in order to bring pressure on the company to encourage fiscally prudent behaviour.[106] The creditor may accordingly demand the production of periodic financial statements and

---

103. See pp. 101–5 below.
104. See Bebchuk and Fried, 'Uneasy Case', p. 914; Buckley, 'Bankruptcy Priority Puzzle', pp. 1421–2.
105. Bebchuk and Fried, 'Uneasy Case', p. 874.
106. On security being taken for 'active' rather than 'passive' reasons see R. Scott, 'Relational Theory', p. 950: 'the function of secured credit is conceived within the industry as enabling the creditor to influence debtor actions prior to the onset of business failure. This conception is markedly different in effect from the traditional vision of collateral as a residual asset claim upon default and insolvency.'

may go so far as to place a representative on the debtor company's board.[107] A creditor may react to such information by adjusting its estimation of risk and changing the interest rate charged or even adjusting the period of the loan to demand early repayment.[108] In more interventionist mode, a creditor may take the additional precaution of imposing contractual limitations on the kinds of conduct that the debtor may engage in. Such restrictions can, as noted, deal with limits on dividend payments, the maximum gearing of the company and the disposition of assets. Such clauses, however, can only offer incomplete protection for creditors since anticipating the kind of conduct that may prejudice their interests can be extremely difficult and it may be costly to draft such terms and to monitor and enforce compliance.[109] Competition in the loan market may, furthermore, limit the creditors' ability to impose such constraints: the average trade creditor, for instance, does not normally attempt to draft contracts on a transaction-specific basis. Normal trading arrangements may involve sums of money that are too small and time scales that are too short to justify extensive contractual stipulations.[110] The dilution of assets may also be subject to legal restriction[111] but those in control of a firm may still enjoy considerable discretion in deciding whether to transfer assets to shareholders and, without the probability of sustained monitoring and enforcement, legal restrictions may offer only weak deterrence.

At this point it is worth considering when a creditor will possess an incentive to monitor a debtor's behaviour.[112] Here the key is the balance between monitoring costs and the size of the loan. Monitoring will be worthwhile if it costs less than the anticipated gain in risk reduction where the latter is calculated by multiplying the diminution in the probability of non-payment that monitoring will produce and the size of the potential

---

107. See Finch, 'Company Directors', pp. 189–95. On creditor monitoring and corporate governance see G. Triantis and R. Daniels, 'The Role of Debt in Interactive Corporate Governance' (1995) 83 Calif. L Rev. 1073. On creditor control over financially embarrassed corporations see S. Gilson and M. Vetsuypens, 'Creditor Control in Financially Distressed Firms: Empirical Evidence' (1994) 72 Wash. ULQ 1005.

108. Another option may be to purchase insurance to cover losses arising from default: see Cheffins, *Company Law*, p. 75. Yet a further strategy for the creditor is to reduce risks by diversification in the lending portfolio. As noted, however, a creditor's incentive to monitor will reduce as the number of its debtors increases and the average loan sum diminishes.

109. See generally Day and Taylor, 'Role of Debt Contracts'; Smith and Warner, 'On Financial Contracting'.

110. See V. Finch, 'Creditors' Interests and Directors' Obligations' in S. Sheikh and W. Rees (eds.), *Corporate Governance and Corporate Control* (Cavendish, London, 1995) pp. 133–4; Bebchuk and Fried, 'Uneasy Case', pp. 886–7.

111. See Companies Act 1985 ss. 135–41; Second Council Directive 77/91/EEC of 13 December 1976, OJ 1997, No. L26/1; Insolvency Act 1986 ss. 238, 239, 423. See P. L. Davies, 'Legal Capital in Private Companies in Great Britain' (1998) 8 *Die Aktien Gesellschaft* 346.

112. See Jackson and Kronman, 'Secured Financing', 1160–1.

non-payment. It follows that small loans will justify only modest levels of monitoring.

Security is said to be liable to reduce the overall costs of creditor monitoring where a number of creditors have different levels of pre-existing information and monitoring costs.[113] Some creditors (for example, trade creditors) with continuing and day-to-day relationships with their debtors may enjoy low monitoring costs and may reduce their lending risks by utilising their stock of knowledge on debtor credit worthiness. Where such monitoring serves to encourage financially prudent management this will benefit the whole body of creditors.[114] Other creditors, such as banks, may not possess such bodies of information and it may be cheaper for them to reduce risks by taking security than by detailed monitoring.[115] Providing potential creditors with the choice of secured or unsecured loans thus may encourage efficient lending by allowing creditors to choose the lowest-cost ways of reducing risks and so of lending. The end result, it is suggested by proponents of security, will be a reduction of total monitoring and lending costs.[116]

A further suggested efficiency offered by security is the opportunity for creditors to develop an expertise in monitoring a particular asset or type of asset and, accordingly, to limit monitoring costs by avoiding the need to monitor the total array of the company's financial activities.[117] Finally, it can be argued that, at least in some circumstances, the granting of security can serve to demarcate monitoring functions in a manner that proves more efficient than regimes in which many creditors all replicate monitoring efforts. Thus, where security is fixed over a key asset and control of this will benefit all creditors by fostering prudent management more broadly, there is an avoidance of duplicated monitoring and the markets will reward monitors and non-monitors appropriately by compensating secured monitors with prior interests in the debtor's assets and by allowing unsecured non-monitors to charge low interest rates that do not have to reflect monitoring costs. The overall efficiency arises because even if such 'key asset' arrangements are not the norm, the opportunity of offering security allows the market to choose such arrangements where they lower costs all round.

113. Ibid.; R. Scott, 'Relational Theory', pp. 930–1.
114. See Triantis and Daniels, 'Role of Debt', p. 1080.
115. See, however, ibid., pp. 1082–8, where banks are seen as playing the 'principal role in controlling managerial slack'; R. Scott, 'Relational Theory'.
116. See, for example, Jackson and Kronman, 'Secured Financing'.
117. See D. G. Baird and T. Jackson, *Cases, Problems and Materials on Security Interests in Personal Property* (Foundation Press, Mineola, N.Y., 1987) pp. 324–8; White, 'Efficiency Justifications'.

Would such monitoring efficiencies not be achieved in the absence of security? Would the parties involved not simply negotiate the contractual arrangements that best allow them to reduce risks?[118] The argument for security here is that it provides lower transaction costs than other arrangements.[119] This is argued to be the case not least because any attempts by creditors to negotiate priority relationships between themselves would be beset by free-rider and hold-out problems, especially where a firm's creditors are numerous.[120]

The efficiency case against security

The incentive to finance efficiently The core objection to the provision of security is that when corporate debtor A arranges a secured loan with creditor B this may prejudice the interests of non-involved third parties C, D and E and may create incentives to corporate inefficiency. Such an arrangement has the effect of transferring insolvency value from C, D and E to B because C, D and E are not in a position to adjust their claims against A or the interest rates they charge.[121] This inability to adjust may occur for a number of reasons. The creditor may be involuntary, as where a party is injured by the company and is a tort claimant with an unsecured claim against the company. Such involuntary creditors cannot adjust their claims to reflect the creation of a security interest.[122]

The inability to adjust may also be a practical rather than a legal matter. Thus, voluntary creditors with small claims against the firm (for example, trade creditors, employees and customers) may not have interests of a size that would justify the expenses involved in adjusting the terms of their loans with the company and in negotiating these changes with the company. Such expenses, indeed, might be considerable and would involve expenditure on gaining information on the company's level of secured debt, its likelihood of insolvency, its expected insolvency value and the extent of its own unsecured loan.[123] In practice, small creditors may suffer from a degree of competition in the marketplace that rules out the negotiation

---

118. See Jackson and Kronman, 'Secured Financing', p. 115; Day and Taylor, 'The Role of Debt Contracts'.

119. Compare with A. Schwartz, 'A Theory of Loan Priorities' (1989) 18 *Journal of Legal Studies* 209.

120. See S. Levmore, 'Monitors and Freeriders in Commercial and Corporate Settings' (1982) 92 Yale LJ 49, 53–5; R. Scott, 'A Relational Theory', pp. 909–11.

121. See Bebchuk and Fried, 'Uneasy Case', pp. 882–7.

122. See L. LoPucki, 'The Unsecured Creditor's Bargain' (1994) 80 Va. L Rev. 1887, 1898–9; J. Scott, 'Bankruptcy, Secured Debt and Optimal Capital Structure' (1977) 32 *Journal of Financial Law* 2–3; P. Shupack, 'Solving the Puzzle of Secured Transactions' (1989) 41 Rutgers L Rev. 1067, 1094–5.

123. Bebchuk and Fried, 'Uneasy Case', p. 885.

of arrangements that adequately reflect risks.[124] If a small supplier of, say, tiles for roofing work is considering adjusting the terms on which credit is offered, that supplier may anticipate that competing small tile firms, who are ill-informed and cavalier concerning risks, may be willing to offer terms that undercut it in the market. The supplier will, accordingly, feel that it cannot adjust and, indeed, that resources spent on evaluating the need for adjustment (and its rational extent) would be wasted.

Trade creditors tend not to look to the risks posed by individual debtors but will charge uniform interest rates to their customers. It could be argued, nevertheless, that those trade creditors who are successful are those who build into their prices an interest rate element that, in a broad-brush manner, reflects averaged-out insolvency risks. They may, for instance, adjust their prices periodically until they produce an acceptable return on investment.[125] The effect is to compensate, at least over a period of time, for difficulties of adjustment. This, it could be contended, is efficient because, within reasonable bounds, even small, unsecured creditors manage to attune rates to reflect average risks.

A first difficulty with this argument, however, is that it assumes a level of stability in the trade sector and leaves out of account those trade creditors who have gone out of business through their failures to adjust, perhaps in their early weeks and years. These lost enterprises involve costs to society. The argument also leaves out of account those ill-informed and involuntary parties who cannot adjust by averaging processes or by learning from the market. Many trade creditors, for example, will operate in dispersed, changing markets in which learning is difficult, the process of matching prices to risks may take a long time and may be delayed, distorted or prevented by changes of actors and the arrival in the market of numbers of unsophisticated operators who fail adequately to consider risks. As LoPucki concludes: 'With a constant flow of new suckers and poor information flows, there is no *a priori* reason why the markets for unsecured credit cannot persistently underestimate the risk, resulting in a permanent subsidy to borrowers.'[126]

Second, those who do adjust by 'averaging' approaches to pricing credit may be adjusting to inefficient distributions of risk. Thus, if risks are placed disproportionately on the shoulders of those who can only adjust

124. See J. Hudson, 'The Case Against Secured Lending' (1995) 15 *International Review of Law and Economics* 47.
125. See Buckley, 'Bankruptcy Priority Puzzle', pp. 1410–11 and cf. LoPucki, 'Unsecured Creditor's Bargain', pp. 1955–8.
126. LoPucki, 'Unsecured Creditor's Bargain', p. 1956.

by averaging methods, the heavy risk bearers are liable to be the unsecured creditors who are least able to manage, absorb and survive financial risks and shocks. Even if rough adjustment by averaging was able to compensate for the sum, in pounds sterling, of the expected insolvency losses, small trade creditors would be unlikely to take on board the potential shock effect on their company of a debtor's insolvency. They are like ships' officers who can calculate the expected size of a hull fracture but not whether it will be above or below the waterline. There is an efficiency case for placing risks on those best able to calculate their precise extent, best able to survive them and most likely to avoid the further costs of shock: in short to place risks where they can be managed at lowest cost. The loading of risks on 'averaging' adjusters is not consistent with that approach.

Finally, the loading of risks onto small, unsecured creditors may cause competitive distortions that are socially inefficient. To give a simplified example, suppose a debtor company is in the house construction business and is considering whether to fit traditional timber or aluminium double-glazed windows in its new houses. It may buy timber windows on credit from a small, efficient carpentry company that does not demand security or aluminium frames from a multinational double-glazing firm whose lawyers insist on security. If the carpentry company adjusts its prices to reflect its high default risks (by a rule of thumb method) and *by virtue of so doing* charges more for windows than the multinational firm, the contractor will obtain the window frames on account from the multinational firm, in spite of the carpentry company having been the more efficient manufacturer. The allocation of risks has produced the distorted, and inefficient, purchasing decision.

Creditors, similarly, who grant unsecured loans on fixed interest rates will be in no position to adjust to the creation of new security interests by corporate debtor A. The resultant effect of such non-adjustment is that debtor A, in deciding to encumber further assets, knows that a group of creditors will not adjust their terms or rates. It is thus in a position to 'sell' some of its insolvency value to the secured creditor in return for a reduced interest rate.[127]

Such a favouring of the secured creditor will prove inefficient in so far as corporate decision-makers will have incentives to act so as to increase value to shareholders and secured creditors even if such increases are less than the losses to non-adjusting creditors in the form of diminutions in their

---

127. Bebchuk and Fried, 'Uneasy Case', p. 887.

expectations on insolvency.[128] A system of full priority, moreover, will give debtor company A an incentive to create a security so as to transfer value away from non-adjusting creditors in circumstances where the effect is to reduce the total value to be captured by all creditors on an insolvency.

As for the decision-making incentives of corporate managers, a further inefficiency may arise in so far as biases in favour of secured creditors may lead both to an excessive resort to secured loans (a resort encouraged by the 'subsidy' from non-adjusting creditors) and also to excessively risky decision-taking. Excessive risk-taking is liable to occur because a corporate manager, in calculating the risks attaching to any decision, will give insufficient weight to the interests of unsecured creditors. Thus, in balancing the company's potential gains versus losses in any given transaction, the prospect of having to repay non-adjusting creditors less than the full sum borrowed will distort the decision.[129] In social terms, the bearing of excessive risks by unsecured creditors may be especially undesirable since these creditors are frequently small and less able to survive losses than larger creditors, such as banks, who tend to be secured.[130]

Investigation and monitoring The argument that security encourages efficiency in information gathering can be pressed too far. It has been contended that security benefits all creditors in so far as the ability to gain credit on the basis of security evidences in itself a degree of creditworthiness.[131] A major proponent of this signalling theory has, however, himself come to question it on the grounds that bad debtors may be both willing and able to mimic the signals of good debtors.[132] Other counter-arguments to the signalling hypothesis are that the security interest may not in reality offer a clear signal since borrowing on a secured, rather than on an unsecured, basis is usually the preference (sometimes the insistence) of the creditor rather than the debtor company, and that the offering of security

---

128. On the extent to which different non-adjusting creditors are hurt by the creation of a new security interest see ibid., pp. 894–5; LoPucki, 'Unsecured Creditor's Bargain', pp. 1896–1916.

129. Bebchuk and Fried, 'Uneasy Case', p. 934; M. White, 'Public Policy Toward Bankruptcy' (1980) 11 *Bell Journal of Economics* 550. Security with priority thus exacerbates those distortions associated with limited liability: see Bebchuk and Fried, 'Uneasy Case', pp. 899–90; H. Hansman and R. Krackman, 'Towards Unlimited Shareholder Liability for Corporate Torts' (1991) 100 Yale LJ 1879; D. Leebron, 'Limited Liability, Tort Victims and Creditors' (1991) 91 Colum. L Rev. 1565.

130. See Hudson, 'Case Against Secured Lending', p. 61.

131. A. Schwartz, 'Security Interests and Bankruptcy Priorities: A Review of Current Theories' (1981) 10 *Journal of Legal Studies* 1.

132. Schwartz, 'Theory of Loan Priorities', 244.

signals not so much the creditworthiness of the debtor as the nervousness of the relevant lender.[133] It is also doubtful whether any signalling gains outweigh the costs of secured lending.[134] Other commentators, moreover, have questioned the value of signalling on the grounds that firms may seek credit as much to help with short-term cash flow problems as to finance programmes of capital expansion. Signals relating to the former, rather than the latter, may be of little value to the array of prospective creditors.[135]

The claim that security leads to efficient monitoring can also be treated with some caution. The notion that monitoring by a secured creditor will bring spill-over benefits to the advantage of creditors as a whole can be responded to by noting that those benefits are liable to be insignificant where creditors are concerned to ensure that there is no dilution of their particular security rather than to encourage good decision-making generally in relation to the company's affairs. This point can be deployed, indeed, to turn the monitoring argument on its head. If security fixes on particular assets it may offer a disincentive to monitor generally and, even where a specific item of equipment is monitored, the creditor may not examine whether it is being used productively. If, moreover, most small to medium-sized firms possess only one creditor who is sufficiently sophisticated to be able to monitor efficiently (as US evidence suggests[136]), the tendency for that creditor to be the secured creditor means that any inclination to monitor may be easily exaggerated. It can further be objected that it is rash to assume that those in possession of security are well positioned to monitor management behaviour. There may, indeed, be circumstances in which unsecured, but well-informed, trade creditors may be better placed to monitor.[137]

Other factors may also militate against monitoring by secured creditors. They may have little interest in improving the profitability of their

---

133. H. Kripke, 'Law and Economics: Measuring the Economic Efficiency of Commercial Law in a Vacuum of Fact' (1985) 133 U Pa. L Rev. 929, 969–70; M. G. Bridge, 'The *Quistclose* Trust in a World of Secured Transactions' (1992) 12 OJLS 33, 37.

134. R. Scott, 'Relational Theory', p. 907, urges that proponents of security have not offered convincing reasons why security offers a means of overcoming informational barriers that is preferable to other mechanisms, such as the development of commercial reputations or long-term financial relationships. See also C. J. Goetz and R. E. Scott, 'Principles of Relational Contracts' (1981) 67 Va. L Rev. 1089, 1099–1111.

135. See Hudson, 'Case Against Secured Lending', p. 54.

136. See M. Peterson and R. Rajan, 'The Benefits of Lending Relationships: Evidence from Small Business Data' (1994) 49 *Journal of Finance* 3, 16.

137. Bridge, '*Quistclose* Trust', p. 339; cf. Triantis and Daniels, 'Role of Debt'; R. Scott, 'Relational Theory'. Nor should it be assumed that monitoring is inevitably beneficial: this will not be the case where the negative effects of monitoring activity (for example, interference and managerial resources expended on responding to monitors) exceed positive effects as exemplified by increased pressures to act prudently.

debtor company, since, unlike shareholders, they will not enjoy a proportion of profits but face a fixed rate of return.[138] Creditors who lend to a large number of debtors may be reluctant to devote resources to detailed monitoring of each of their debtor companies, and lending institutions may lack the expertise and specialised trade knowledge necessary for assessing managerial performance effectively.[139] Creditors, moreover, may be ill-disposed to monitor because they may consider that a corporate insolvency may result from causes other than mismanagement[140] and that monitoring at best offers only partial protection against insolvency. The creditor may be interested in security principally as a means of limiting the financial consequences to them of insolvency rather than as a mechanism allowing them to intervene in order to prevent corporate disaster.

Close inspection should also be made of the argument that security provides an efficient way for different creditors to co-ordinate their monitoring activities and avoid inefficient duplications of effort. If, as noted, small and medium-sized firms tend not to borrow from more than one creditor who is capable of monitoring, there is little need for such co-ordination and its value, accordingly, may be easily overstated.[141] The notion, moreover, that one creditor will benefit from the monitoring signals sent out by another creditor has to be treated with care.[142] Thus, a large creditor such as a bank may end a relationship with a debtor and so may send out a signal, but the action may have been taken for reasons unrelated to any assessment of managerial performance (the bank may have negotiated an unfavourable agreement). A bank may, in another context, appear to be happy with management but in reality it is content with its security; it may give distorted signals because it has taken discreet steps to increase its security or shift risks; or a bank may have negotiated policy concessions with the debtor that, again, are unknown to other creditors. Nor can it be assumed that different classes of creditors have common interests that lend harmony to their monitoring efforts. When the debtor company is healthy there may be a degree of commonality in their desires to reduce managerial slackness but when the debtor firm approaches troubled times the different classes of creditors will have divergent interests and misinformation and concealment may infect the monitoring and signalling processes.[143]

138. F. H. Easterbrook and D. Fischel, 'Voting in Corporate Law' (1983) 26 *Journal of Law and Economics* 395, 403.
139. See Finch, 'Company Directors'; Cheffins, *Company Law*, pp. 75–6.
140. See discussion in ch. 4 below.   **141.** See Bebchuk and Fried, 'Uneasy Case', p. 917.
142. See Triantis and Daniels, 'Role of Debt', pp. 1090–1103.
143. Ibid., p. 1111.

Incentives to monitor may, moreover, be undermined by free-rider and uncertainty problems.[144] Thus, in the case of the floating charge, monitoring is liable to be expensive because such a charge commonly covers the entire undertaking of the debtor and this may mean that monitoring in order to detect misbehaviour or calculate risks could involve scrutinising the whole business. It is not possible, as with a fixed charge, to keep an eye on the stipulated asset alone. The competitors of a creditor who spends time and money on monitoring will be able, at little cost, to benefit from such scrutinising and any resultant signalling (for example, through observed adjustments in the interest rates charged by the monitoring creditor). The competitors, accordingly, will be able to undercut the creditor on, for example, the pricing of loans.[145] This free-rider problem gives the initial creditor a disincentive to monitor the debtor's misbehaviour and to compensate for the higher risks that non-monitoring brings by imposing higher rates of interest. The overall effect is that the floating charge may offer a relatively expensive method of securing finance.

Legal difficulties may also compound the problems of those creditors who are secured by floating charges and who wish to lower risks (and interest rates) by monitoring. Close monitoring may render the creditor liable to a wrongful trading charge on the basis of their operating as a shadow director.[146] The legal uncertainty attending this issue will again operate as a disincentive to keep rates down by monitoring.

Improving on security and full priority

The above discussion reveals that it is not possible to state in general terms whether the law's providing security will ensure efficient outcomes. The key issue is whether the distortions and incentives to inefficiency that are caused by security and priority will, in the specific context, be outweighed by the resultant gains. Individual circumstances, accordingly, have to be considered and the case for security may differ greatly according to variations in such matters as the balance between sophisticated and non-expert creditors; the duration and sizes of loans; the types of companies seeking loans; the numbers of non-adjusting creditors; and the transaction costs involved in negotiating unsecured loans and contractual schemes of priority.

144. See generally Levmore, 'Monitors and Freeriders', pp. 53–5; R. Scott, 'Relational Theory'.
145. See Levmore, 'Monitors and Freeriders', pp. 53–5; R. Scott, 'Relational Theory'.
146. See Oditah, *Legal Aspects*, p. 17; Insolvency Act 1986 ss. 214, 217(7), 251; *Ex parte Copp* [1989] BCLC 13; *Re PFTZM Ltd* [1995] BCC 280; *Secretary of State for Trade and Industry* v. *Deverell* [2000] 2 WLR 907. On shadow directors see ch. 15 below.

At this point it is necessary to consider whether arrangements other than security and full priority are likely, in some circumstances, to involve a more efficient use of resources. A host of suggestions has been put forward[147] but here attention will focus on the most prominently advocated proposals.

Abolition of security   Abolishing security would place all creditors on an equal footing in relation to the post-insolvency distribution of assets and no secured creditor advantages would be provided for.[148] It is to be expected, however, that powerful lenders, such as banks, would collaborate with corporate debtors to circumvent the abolition of security by devising arrangements that would offer them *de facto* priority over less sophisticated lenders. The company seeking finance would have an incentive to enter into such arrangements for the same reason that it would grant security, namely to transfer insolvency value from unsecured creditors to the major lender in order to obtain a loan or a better rate of interest. Firms might thus 'sell' fixed assets to the banks in lease-back arrangements incorporating options to buy the assets back for a very low price when the lease terminates.[149]

Systems of security with priority may, however, provide a lower-cost method of achieving such priority regimes than arrangements depending on the negotiation of ad hoc contracts.[150] This is because, with the former, the legal system is providing ready-made, 'off the shelf' contract rules based on common assumptions about the parties' motives. Transaction costs are reduced because these ready-made arrangements specify the legal consequences of typical bargains.[151] Lower transaction costs in this context can, however, be said to encourage the offering of security and this may increase the extent to which certain creditors suffer from the negative consequences of priority regimes (for example, transfers of insolvency value from non-adjusting, unsecured creditors; biases in investment; excessive risk-taking; reduced monitoring incentives). Again the key balance

---

147. LoPucki, 'Unsecured Creditor's Bargain'; S. Knippenberg, 'The Unsecured Creditor's Bargain: An Essay in Reply, Reprisal or Support' (1994) 80 Va. L Rev. 1967; Bebchuk and Fried, 'Uneasy Case'; Hudson, 'Case Against Secured Lending'.
148. Hudson, 'Case Against Secured Lending', pp. 57–8.
149. Ibid., p. 58; F. Black, 'Bank Funds in an Efficient Market' (1975) *Journal of Financial Economics* 323.
150. Jackson and Kronman, 'Secured Financing', p. 1157; J. White, 'Efficiency Justifications'.
151. See C. J. Goetz and R. E. Scott, 'Liquidated Damages, Penalties and the Just Compensation Principle: Some Notes on an Enforcement Model and a Theory of Efficient Breach' (1977) 77(4) Colum. L Rev. 554, 588; G. Calabresi and A. Melamed, 'Property Rules, Liability Rules and Inalienability: One View of the Cathedral' (1972) 85 Harv. L Rev. 1089.

is between the efficiency gains flowing from lower transaction costs versus the efficiency losses from the negative consequences listed.

Fixed fraction regimes Transfers of value from non-adjusting creditors can be limited by legal stipulations that a given percentage of secured creditors' claims shall be treated as unsecured[152] or that a percentage of the security's net realisable assets shall be made available for distribution among the ordinary unsecured creditors.[153] The Cork Committee proposed a 10 per cent fund in 1982 but that, as yet unimplemented,[154] recommendation appears to have been motivated by considerations of distributional justice and fairness rather than efficiency.[155] Since 1 January 1999, German insolvency law has echoed Cork in providing that 25 per cent of the proceeds of realised chattel assets subject to liens and mortgages shall be reserved for the benefit of the general insolvency estate.[156] More recently the UK Government has indicated that it will 'ring fence' a proportion of the funds generated by the floating charge and use these to benefit unsecured creditors.[157]

The extent to which the fixed fraction rule avoids the problems associated with transfers from non-adjusting, unsecured creditors depends on the percentage of the secured claim that is treated as unsecured. The larger the percentage the more the problems are avoided, but the less the value of any security taken, the greater the risk that powerful creditors will 'write around' such a rule and resort to 'alternative' modes of achieving the effects of security. A fixed fraction rule, moreover, benefits the group of unsecured creditors as a whole, not merely non-adjusters. This means that unsecured creditors who are able to adjust terms and rates will enjoy a

---

152. In which case the secured creditors participate *pari passu* with unsecured creditors in the fund available to unsecured parties: see Bebchuk and Fried, 'Uneasy Case', pp. 909–11.

153. See Cork Report, paras. 1538–41. Cork's 10 per cent fund applied to floating charges only, not fixed, and an upper limit was to be applied so that unsecured creditors would not receive a greater percentage of debts than the holders of floating charges.

154. On the concerted opposition of the Committee of London Clearing Banks (CLCB) to the 10 per cent fund proposal see Carruthers and Halliday, *Rescuing Business*, chs. 4 and 7. See also D. Milman, 'The Ten Per Cent Fund' [1999] Ins. Law. 47.

155. Note that the 10 per cent fund needs to be set in the context of a package of revisions proposed by the Cork Committee, i.e. the abolition of preferences, restrictions on ROTs and a moratorium on the enforcement of fixed charges for twelve months after a receiver's appointment: see chs. 8, 12 and 14 below.

156. This provision does not extend to real estate mortgages or other rights over real estate. For discussion see J. Drukwczyk, 'Secured Debt, Bankruptcy and the Creditors' Bargain Model' (1991) 11 *International Review of Law and Economics* 201, 208. See further M. Balz, 'Market Conformity of Insolvency Proceedings: Policy Issues of the German Insolvency Law' (1997) 23 *Brooklyn Journal of International Law* 167.

157. See DTI White Paper, *Productivity and Enterprise: Insolvency – A Second Chance* (Cm 5234, 2001) ('White Paper, 2001') para. 2.19.

windfall benefit from the 10 per cent fund and that not all of the 10 per cent fund will be available for non-adjusters. A virtue of the fixed fraction rule does, however, reside in its certainty. The creditor who takes security knows, when making an advance, that the security is only worth a set percentage of what would otherwise be its expected value. This is unlikely to reduce their willingness to lend significantly (at least where percentages allocated to the unsecured creditors' fund are modest) since interest rates can be adjusted accordingly.[158] If the negative effects of a fixed-percentage regime on secured lending are likely to be less than the positive gains to unsecured creditors, the case for the device is strong.

A 10 per cent fund might also conduce to efficiency through more rigorous enforcement against corporate managers and the insolvency estate. This is the 'fighting fund' vision of the 10 per cent rule which sees its significance in terms of providing financial resources to insolvency practitioners so as to allow their 'hot pursuit' of debtors attempting to hide monies or creditors trying to smuggle out assets before they enter into the estate.[159] The overall effect of pursuit, and its possibility, would be greater deterrence of aberrant behaviour by corporate directors, a likely increase in the fund of assets available for all creditors and, as a result, a greater chance of unsecured creditors gaining some real return. Inefficient insolvency wealth transfers might, accordingly, be reduced as well as insolvency procedures rendered more effective generally.

Insurance requirements Fixed fraction regimes, as noted, look to unsecured creditors as a group and avoid distinguishing between adjusters and non-adjusters within that group. Where, however, classes of non-adjusters can be identified, it is possible to compensate these through insurance. It has been argued that companies ought to be compelled to purchase liability insurance against tort claims to the extent that these claims cannot be met from assets.[160] This would control adverse effects of limited liability: its restricting the compensation available for tort victims, its externalising risks to those victims and its extracting a subsidy from them.[161] Damage

---

158. The Cork Report took the view that a reduction in willingness to lend could be discounted as a real possibility (ch. 36, paras. 1534–49); Goode, 'Is the Law Too Favourable to Secured Creditors?', p. 67.

159. See Carruthers and Halliday, *Rescuing Business*, pp. 341–2. See also debates in Standing Committee E, HC, vol. 78, 30 April 1985, cols. 156–8. On problems of funding litigation see ch. 12 below.

160. See B. Pettet, 'Limited Liability: A Principle for the 21st Century?' in M. Freeman and R. Halson (eds.) (1995) 48 *Current Legal Problems* 125.

161. Ibid., pp. 147–8; Hansmann and Krackman, 'Towards Unlimited Shareholder Liability'; P. Halpern, M. Trebilcock and M. Turnbull, 'An Economic Analysis of Limited Liability in Corporation Law' (1980) 30 U Toronto LJ 128; F. H. Easterbrook and D. Fischel, *The Economic*

awards, in such a scheme, would be met, first, out of any normal liability insurance possessed by the company. To the extent that such insurance proved inadequate, the claim would be made on the assets of the company in the normal way and, finally, if the assets were exhausted and the claim remained, the 'overtop insurance' would cut in and provide funds.[162] Such an insurance regime would not only offer a response to the problems of limited liability, it would also cover the claims of unpaid tort creditors in corporate insolvencies. This insurance route possesses an important advantage over proposals to defer other creditors (including secured creditors) to tort claimants in insolvency.[163] Giving tort victims higher priority in insolvency would act as a considerable deterrent to those institutions considering offering secured loans to a company since they would be faced with the risk of giving way to huge tort claims in the queue for insolvency pay-outs. In contrast, an insurance requirement would constitute a general business expense that would prove unthreatening to potential creditors. Such a requirement might operate concurrently with a 10 per cent fund and tort victims could be excluded from participation in that fund.

The problems of moral hazard that are often linked to insurance would be controlled not merely by the usual premium adjustments that would follow claims but also by the requirement that 'overtop insurance' would come into play only after corporate assets were exhausted.[164] It should be noted, however, that although insurance would provide compensation to tort victims, it would control, not eliminate, moral hazards. Corporate managers would not be fully deterred from tortious actions since risks would be shifted through the insurance mechanisms: in 'overtop' cases the insurer would meet a proportion of the tort costs. Nor can it be assumed that insurers will monitor managerial performance and act in ways that will ensure non-tortious conduct. The extent to which they will do this is liable to turn on such factors as the particular market's propensity to reward a strategy of monitoring.[165] The costs of monitoring have to

Structure of Corporate Law (Harvard University Press, Cambridge, Mass., 1991) p. 113; C. D. Stone, 'The Place of Enterprise Liability in the Control of Corporate Conduct' (1980) 90 Yale LJ 1.

162. Pettet, 'Limited Liability', p. 157.

163. See, for example, Leebron, 'Limited Liability', pp. 1643–50.

164. On insurance and moral hazard see S. Shavell, 'On Liability and Insurance' (1982) 13 *Bell Journal of Economics* 120; Shavell, *Economic Analysis of Accident Law* (Harvard University Press, Cambridge, Mass., 1987); R. Rabin, 'Deterrence and the Tort System' in M. Friedman (ed.), *Sanctions and Rewards in the Legal System* (University of Toronto Press, Toronto, 1989).

165. See V. Finch, 'Personal Accountability and Corporate Control: The Role of Directors' and Officers' Liability Insurance' (1994) 57 MLR 880; C. Holderness, 'Liability Insurers as Corporate Monitors' (1990) 10 *International Review of Law and Economics* 115; P. Cane (ed.), *Atiyah's Accidents, Compensation and the Law* (5th edn, Weidenfeld & Nicolson, London, 1993) pp. 500–36.

be reflected in premium adjustments but competitors may undercut the monitor's prices and so deter such watchfulness.

The insurance 'solution' would also be limited in a number of other respects. Insurance cover will not always be available to any given company or operation. Where, for instance, companies are small and high risk, and where moral hazard problems are severe, there may be an absence of willing insurers.[166] Insurance policies, moreover, will have ceilings on the quantum of cover together with a variety of clauses excluding liability on different grounds or allowing policies to be terminated on short notice. It cannot, accordingly, be assumed that all tort victims will be fully compensated for losses.[167]

These cautions concerning insurance do not mean that this is a device of insignificant utility in dealing with tort victims. They do, however, suggest that reforms of this kind should be treated as partial, not complete, answers.

Information requirements Transfers of insolvency wealth from non-adjusting to secured creditors would be avoided, it could be argued, if unsecured creditors were given such information concerning a debtor as would allow them to fix interest rates and loan terms in a manner truly reflecting risks.[168] One option, accordingly, is to oblige companies seeking credit to identify, when contracting with any potential creditor, any security then operating.[169] Relevant details of such securities might also be demanded: for example, information on whether they cover genuine new value or whether they are to provide current working capital.[170] In the USA it has been proposed that secured creditors who seek to place unsecured creditors in a subordinate position would have to take reasonable steps to convey their intentions to the unsecured creditors. To this end, the suggestion is that the Article 9 filing system be modified to serve the information needs of all creditors affected by the terms of a security agreement.[171]

166. See Halpern, Trebilcock and Turnbull, 'An Economic Analysis'; Finch, 'Personal Accountability and Corporate Control', pp. 892–4.
167. See G. Huberman, D. Mayers and C. Smith, 'Optimal Insurance Policy Indemnity Schedules' (1983) 14 *Bell Journal of Economics* 415.
168. See Diamond Report, para. 8.1.5: 'My general approach is based on the notion that the law should make it easier rather than harder for parties to a security agreement … to achieve their objective and the interests of third parties are best served not by prohibiting others from doing what they seek to do but by making information on what has been done readily available and affording them protection against risks that they should not have to face.'
169. Actual information rather than making creditors rely on the constructive notice of the charges registered in the register of charges as per Companies Act 1985 ss. 395–6.
170. See Hudson, 'Case Against Secured Lending', p. 58.
171. See LoPucki, 'Unsecured Creditor's Bargain', p. 1948; S. Block-Lieb, 'The Unsecured Creditor's Bargain: A Reply' (1994) 80 Va. L Rev. 1989, 2013.

There are limitations, however, to the informational solution. Any regime requiring 'reasonable' information-giving would prompt a good deal of litigation and the legal uncertainties involved in reasonableness testing would increase overall credit costs. The supply of information might assist those unsecured creditors who are currently ill-informed and, as a result, are unable to adjust terms and interest rates to cope with securities granted to others; it would not, however, assist creditors who cannot adjust because they are involuntary. (It has been suggested that in the USA at least a quarter of the debt of financially distressed companies is owed to reluctant creditors: tort and product liability victims, government agencies, tax authorities and parties not in the business of extending credit or seeking credit relationships.[172])

Another limitation of the information approach is that it does little, without further stipulation, to prevent future transfers of value from current unsecured creditors to new secured creditors. When prospective unsecured creditors are given notice of present securities they may adjust accordingly but once the adjustment is made there is vulnerability to any future granting of security.

A further shortcoming of the information approach is that unsecured creditors have to be able to use the information they receive. As already noted, however, the financial sums involved in many loans may, individually, be too small to justify the time and money expended in adjusting loan terms, the constraints of time, contractual terms and competition may rule out adjustment, and the expertise of the unsecured creditor may be insufficient for such purposes.[173] It has been suggested that competent unsecured creditors may well use the information on security that is made available and the less competent will free ride in a manner that allows the price of credit to reflect the existence of security.[174] This, however, is an 'optimistic' view[175] and it cannot be assumed that unsophisticated

172. See LoPucki, 'Unsecured Creditor's Bargain', pp. 1896–7; T. A. Sullivan, E. Warren and J. L. Westbrook, *As We Forgive Our Debtors: Bankruptcy and Consumer Credit in America* (Oxford University Press, New York, 1989) pp. 18, 294. On protecting involuntary creditors see also B. Adler, 'Financial and Political Theories of American Corporate Bankruptcy' (1993) 45 Stanford L Rev. 311; Leebron, 'Limited Liability'; M. Roe, 'Commentary on "On the Nature of Bankruptcy": Bankruptcy, Priority and Economics' (1989) 75 Va. L Rev. 219; C. Painter, 'Note: Tort Creditor Priority in the Secured Credit System: Asbestos Times, the Worst of Times' (1984) 36 Stanford L Rev. 1045.
173. See Knippenberg, 'The Unsecured Creditor's Bargain', pp. 1984–5.
174. See S. Block-Lieb, 'The Unsecured Creditor's Bargain: A Reply' (1994) 80 Va. L Rev. 1989 at 2014–15; cf. Schwartz, 'Security Interests and Bankruptcy Priorities', p. 36.
175. See Block-Lieb, 'Unsecured Creditor's Bargain: A Reply', p. 2014; Levmore, 'Monitors and Freeriders'; R. Scott, 'Relational Theory'. Free riding may, of course, reduce the incentive of the competent creditor to spend resources on processing information.

creditors will find a more streetwise creditor to free ride on, that the un-
tutored will be justified in spending resources researching the existence
of the more knowledgeable, or that there will be markets that will provide
such tutoring and guidance on appropriate levels of credit pricing.

No secured lending on existing assets Unsecured creditors would be
protected from dilution of their interests in insolvency if the law provided
for security only on non-corporate assets (for example, the houses of the
directors/shareholders of the company) or on new capital value (where the
security attaches to the new machinery or buildings that are purchased
with the loan).[176] In such cases there would be no depletion of the company's assets to the detriment of unsecured creditors in an insolvency and
unsecured creditors would be protected even against the granting of new
securities. Companies would still be able to raise capital for new projects
but such a legal regime would not allow corporate managers to use corporate assets to secure short-term working capital or loans necessary for
tiding the company over lean times and cash flow problems. A serious
concern, accordingly, might be that any restriction on the capacity of firms
to survive difficult times might lead to more frequent insolvencies and
overall inefficiency.

An adjustable priority rule An adjustable priority rule would limit inefficient transfers of insolvency value by not making the claims of non-
adjusting creditors subordinate to secured claims. Secured claims would,
in insolvency, be treated as unsecured to the extent that other creditors'
claims are non-adjusting and the extra amount received by non-adjusting
creditors would come at the expense of the secured claims. Adjusting unsecured creditors would receive what they would have received under a
rule of full priority.[177] It would not be feasible to implement such a regime
by seeking to identify in particular instances which creditors had in fact
adjusted to each security interest, but it has been suggested that a number of classes of non-adjusting creditor can be identified and reference
could be made to these in fixing priorities.[178] The main classes of non-
adjusting creditors to be protected might thus include: creditors who extended credit before the creation of the security interest and who lack
an adjustment mechanism in their loan contract; and creditors such as

---

176. See Hudson, 'Case Against Secured Lending', p. 60. On purchase money security
interests see the discussion in ch. 14 below.
177. See Bebchuk and Fried, 'Uneasy Case', pp. 905–8.   178. Ibid., p. 908.

employees and customers who are not in the loan business, were not able to consider the security interest when contracting and did not negotiate credit terms with the debtor.[179]

An adjustable priority rule might be less certain than a fixed fraction rule but it would offer superior protection to non-adjusters. Compared to full priority the adjustable priority rule increases the secured creditor's exposure to risk (security would only offer incomplete protection) and transaction costs would increase in so far as secured creditors would have an incentive to acquire such information about the borrower as would allow them to set interest rates at levels reflecting the more complex and greater risks faced.

Would incentives to offer secured loans be diminished? In relation to tort creditors it has been argued that the prospect of adjusted priorities might alarm prospective creditors considerably because of their potential exposure to risk and the difficulty of quantifying it. Tort creditors may for these reasons best be dealt with through insurance mechanisms as discussed. The tax authorities might also be left out of account in an adjusted priority regime since the Inland Revenue is well positioned to spread its risks of non-payment across the taxation system and it may be appropriate to cost a proportion of failed collections into that system. The remaining non-adjusters might be included in an adjustable priority mechanism, however, since they are not unduly threatening to secured lenders. Such a mechanism does weaken security protections but if those giving loans and taking security are sophisticated creditors they will adjust their interest rates, or amounts of security taken, to reflect the increased risks they face and, accordingly, incentives to lend on security may not be reduced materially. The cost of secured credit may increase but this is the effect of restricting the inefficient transfer of insolvency wealth from non-adjusting to secured creditors. The reduction of such transfers that would result from an adjustable priority rule might, indeed, be expected to limit the incidence of overinvestment in risky activities that is a shortcoming associated with the full priority rule.[180]

Would efficient activities be impeded by an adjustable priority rule? This might happen when the efficiency gains of the activity (for example,

179. Not included in the list of non-adjusters are tort victims and governmental creditors such as tax authorities. The former might be dealt with by insurance as considered above. On tax authorities, see p. 109 below. On the present preferential status of some government taxes in England, see ch. 13 below.
180. See Bebchuk and Fried, 'Uneasy Case', pp. 918–19.

the increases in wealth produced by an investment in new machinery) are less than the transfer of value to non-adjusting creditors (that is the boost to the value of non-adjusting claims that flows from the new secured investment). Such circumstances, it has been suggested, will be encountered only rarely and, in any event, may be countered by non-adjusting creditors agreeing mutually beneficial compromises with secured creditors to allow efficient investments and activities to take place.[181]

Secured creditors might pursue another course, however, which would weaken the role of an adjustable priority rule. They might enter into sale and lease-back arrangements so as to achieve the effects of security but escape the contribution to non-adjusting creditors involved in the adjustable priority rule. The assets at issue would be sold to the 'creditor' and leased back by the 'debtor'. On the debtor's insolvency the assets would not form part of the insolvency assets and, accordingly, would not be covered by the adjustable priority rule. Such a strategy, it has been said, would be resisted by the courts in the USA, who might consider an arrangement a secured loan even if labelled a 'lease', and would look for a real economic difference between a lease arrangement and a secured loan if it was to be acknowledged as a lease for insolvency purposes.[182] The English courts may be somewhat behind those in the USA in looking to the substance and function of arrangements rather than their form, but it can be argued that they are moving in this direction[183] and are increasingly likely to resist the use of sale-based devices that are designed to avoid the rules governing security.[184]

Rethinking the floating charge The floating charge gives a creditor security over present and future assets and commonly covers the entire undertaking of the borrowing company. Its usefulness to companies seeking funds and its attractiveness to creditors has been noted above but attention must be turned to the floating charge's overall efficiency effects. A first matter is the value of a charge that, whatever its label or details, allows companies to trade freely but gives security over all their present

181. Ibid., p. 920; Triantis, 'Secured Debt Under Conditions of Imperfect Information', 248–9.
182. See Bebchuk and Fried, 'Uneasy Case', p. 927; J. White, 'The Recent Erosion of the Secured Creditor's Rights Through Cases, Rules and Statutory Changes in Bankruptcy Law' (1983) 53 Miss. LJ 389, 420; F. Oditah and A. Zacaroli, 'Chattel Leases and Insolvency' [1997] CfiLR 29.
183. See Bridge, 'Form, Substance and Innovation'.
184. On the use of other 'devices' to jump the priority queue see ch. 14 below.

and future assets. (The usefulness of such a charge to companies seeking funds has been noted, as has its attractiveness to creditors.) The Cork Committee found the floating charge to be too much a part of the UK financial structure, and too useful, to consider its abolition.[185] The Crowther and Diamond Reports also favoured the availability of such a charge,[186] and the benefits of such charges to companies are so large that abolition is unlikely to enter the policy agenda of a UK government.[187]

The floating charge type of device does, however, give grounds for concern for another reason. It is a mechanism peculiarly conducive to the transfer of insolvency value from unsecured to secured creditors. The charge floats over the assets of the company and, accordingly, its existence ensures to a greater extent than would otherwise be the case that, on insolvency, unsecured creditors are paid out of working capital. The floating charge is an arrangement that might have been designed to allow large lenders to exploit their dominant bargaining positions and to work with the debtor companies so as to transfer wealth from unsecured creditors. The value of the charge to companies and lenders has thus to be weighed against its negative effects on unsecured creditors, and all possible steps have to be taken to reduce such effects or their consequences.[188]

A second worry is that the floating charge, as presently established in English law, is not the most efficient mechanism that can be devised to allow companies to combine borrowing on shifting assets with unrestricted commercial operation. A particular difficulty is, as noted above, the uncertainty of the unsystematised law governing its use. As Goode has argued:

> principles and rules extracted with effort from a huge body of case law are no substitute for a modern personal property security statute in which all transactions intended to serve a security function are brought together in a uniform system of regulation with rules of attachment,

---

185. See Cork Report, ch. 36, para. 1531; ch. 2, para. 110. In 2001, however, the DTI White Paper (on *Productivity and Enterprise*) proposed measures to ensure the use of collective insolvency procedures instead of administrative receivership, including restriction of the floating charge holder's right to appoint a receiver (White Paper, 2001): see ch. 8 below.
186. See *Report of the Committee on Consumer Credit* (Lord Crowther, Chair) (Cmnd 4596, HMSO, 1971) ('Crowther Report') para. 5.7.77; Diamond Report, para. 8.1.5.
187. Some commentators, though, have questioned the need for a device unreplicated in a number of jurisdictions: see Hudson, 'Case Against Secured Lending', p. 61; R. M. Goode, 'The Exodus of the Floating Charge' in D. Feldman and F. Meisel (eds.), *Corporate and Commercial Law: Modern Developments* (Lloyd's of London Press, London, 1996); Cranston, *Principles of Banking Law*, p. 441.
188. See the discussion of fixed fraction regimes, information requirements and adjustable priority rules above.

perfection and priorities being determined by legislative policy rather than by conceptual reasoning.[189]

Uncertainty attends such matters as the criteria applicable in distinguishing between fixed and floating charges (which are subject to different priority rules in relation to preferential claims on a winding up or the appointment of a receiver). On this distinction legal confusion has resulted, *inter alia*, from a good deal of litigation on the validity of claims to proceeds on the buyer's liquidation and from confusion on such points as whether charges on book debts and their proceeds are to be treated as fixed or floating.[190]

Such legal complexities and uncertainties impose considerable transaction costs on debtor companies and creditors and, in turn, lead to inefficiently high credit costs and business expenses.[191] Further uncertainties compound the position. A key weakness of the floating charge, from the holder's perspective, is that there is a risk of subordination to subsequent secured and execution creditors.[192] This means that the security offered by the floating charge is exposed to potential dilution and risks accordingly cannot be assessed. Certain devices (such as negative pledge clauses) can offer floating charge holders some protection against dilution but that protection is not complete.[193] Quasi-security arrangements such as hire purchase contracts may also dilute the value of the floating charge.

Other ways of classifying securities, might, it is arguable, prove more efficient. Thus it has been suggested that a classification of security might be based on differences in purpose and function, as in Article 9 of the USA's

---

189. Goode, 'Exodus of the Floating Charge', p. 201. See also Cranston, *Principles of Banking Law*, pp. 434–5.

190. See, for example, R. M. Goode, 'Charges Over Book Debts: A Missed Opportunity' (1994) 110 LQR 592; A. Zacoroli, 'Fixed Charges on Book Debts' (1997) 10 *Insolvency Intelligence* 41; R. Gregory and P. Walton, 'Book Debt Charges – The Saga Goes On' (1999) 115 LQR 14; F. Oditah, 'Fixed Charges over Book Debts after *Brumark*' (2001) 14 *Insolvency Intelligence* 49. See further discussion in ch. 9 below. On uncertainties attending automatic crystallisation clauses see *Farrar's Company Law*, pp. 637–8.

191. See Diamond Report, para. 1.8.

192. A floating charge will be deferred to any subsequent fixed legal or equitable charge created by the company over its assets: *Wheatley* v. *Silkstone and Haigh Moor Coal Co.* (1885) 29 Ch D 715; *Robson* v. *Smith* [1895] 2 Ch 118; and if debts due to the company are subject to a floating charge, the interest of the floating charge holder will be subject to any lien or set-off that the company creates with respect to the charged assets prior to crystallisation. If a creditor has levied and completed execution the debenture holders cannot compel him to restore the money, nor, until the charge has crystallised, can he be restrained from levying execution: *Evans* v. *Rival Granite Quarries* [1910] 2 KB 979.

193. *Brunton* v. *Electrical Engineering Corp.* [1892] 1 Ch 434; *Robson* v. *Smith* [1895] 2 Ch 118; *English & Scottish Mercantile Investment Co. Ltd* v. *Brunton* [1892] 2 QB 700; *Re Castell & Brown Ltd* [1898] 1 Ch 315; *Re Valletort Sanitary Steam Laundry* [1903] 2 Ch 654.

Uniform Commercial Code, rather than the particular form of transaction selected or the location of the legal title.[194] Creditors would be able to take security over all or any part of the debtors' existing or future property, and such issues as perfection requirements (filing or possession) and priority rules would be laid down as matters of legislative policy.

The main advantages of such an approach are said to include its eradication of the uncertainties that arise from the need to distinguish floating from fixed charges.[195] The Article 9 approach still allows debtor companies to deal with assets in the ordinary course of business while permitting immediate attachment of the security interest. Priority rules established in legislation would determine the circumstances in which such interests will be overreached by subsequent dealings. The argument thus goes beyond a call to rationalise case law; it urges that the fixed–floating distinction has involved a huge waste of time and expense and that this can be avoided by a unified concept of security.

The counter-argument is that much might be done to clarify the law on floating charges and, in any event, it is easy to exaggerate the extent to which a purposive approach to classifying security will produce a case law that is more predictable and rational than one that emphasises formal origins.[196] Closer attention might, in a purposive approach, be paid to issues of fairness between creditors but that is not to say that efficiency and certainty would necessarily be increased by assessing priority on the basis of broad considerations of function, fairness and practicality. Article 9 jurisdictions have encountered particular difficulties, for instance in separating functional securities from short-term rentals.[197] On balance it can be concluded that there are strong arguments for removing unnecessary uncertainties from the English floating charge framework but it would be

194. See Goode, 'Exodus of the Floating Charge'; Bridge, 'Form, Substance and Innovation'; R. M. Goode and L. Gower, 'Is Article 9 of the Uniform Commercial Code Exportable? An English Reaction' in J. Ziegel and W. Foster (eds.), *Aspects of Comparative Commercial Law* (Oceana, Montreal, 1969); R. Cuming, 'The Internationalization of Secured Financing Law: The Spreading Influence of the Concepts UCC, Article 9 and its Progeny' in R. Cranston (ed.), *Making Commercial Law: Essays in Honour of Roy Goode* (Clarendon Press, Oxford, 1997); Cuning, 'Canadian Bankruptcy Law: A Secured Creditor's Haven' in J. Ziegel (ed.), *Current Developments in International and Comparative Corporate Insolvency Law* (Clarendon Press, Oxford, 1994). For a view that urges caution in adopting the Article 9 approach see G. McCormack, 'Personal Property Security Law Reform in England and Canada' [2002] JBL 113.
195. See Goode, 'Exodus of the Floating Charge'.
196. On formative versus purposive judicial approaches in the competition field see P. P. Craig, 'The Monopolies and Mergers Commission, Competition and Administrative Rationality' in R. Baldwin and C. McCrudden (eds.), *Regulation and Public Law* (Weidenfeld & Nicolson, London, 1987), esp. pp. 210–14 (Article 85 demands a purposive approach).
197. See Bridge, 'Form, Substance and Innovation'; on fairness issues see ch. 14 below.

rash to assume that alternative approaches as seen in the USA will produce dramatically lower levels of legal contention.

Unsecured loan financing

Companies in the UK tend to rely heavily on short-term financing, far more so than companies in continental Europe, for instance, who make more use of longer-term loans. This short-term financing is usually provided by way of unsecured loans in the form of bank overdrafts, trade credit, bills of exchange, acceptance credits and deferred tax payments.[198]

As noted above, efficiency may not always demand that security be taken for a loan. The costs of creating a security arrangement may not be justified by the sums or risks involved in a transaction and a series of transactions may be progressing with such frequency that there is no opportunity or interval for the negotiation of security.[199]

Flexibility of financing may also be required for maximising wealth creation and this may be catered for by such unsecured borrowing as is offered by clearing bank overdrafts. When sums borrowed are no longer required, the overdraft regime allows them to be repaid quickly. Overdrafts are, moreover, comparatively cheap because the risks to the lender are less than are involved with term loans (advances on overdraft are legally repayable on demand, though banks usually undertake notice periods of, say, six or twelve months) and the loan interest is a tax deductible expense.[200] The ongoing nature of corporate overdrafts may, moreover, lead to continuing relationships between a company and its bank. This relationship will often place the bank in a good position to monitor the company's general strategy, to gain information on managerial decision-making and to assess risks of default. The bank can accordingly request forecasts, monitor financial statements on a monthly basis and watch movements in the overdraft balance on a day-to-day basis.[201] This monitoring and informational position may offer the bank a more efficient means of limiting risks than is achievable through the process of negotiating security.

For the company, the downside of the overdraft is that if an overdraft loan is recalled (as it may be on short notice) the firm has to be in a position to repay. This can be difficult where, for instance, the money has been used to purchase fixed assets and the company may be forced to dispose of such

198. On trade finance and unsecured loans see Cranston, *Principles of Banking Law*, ch. 14.
199. See Cheffins, *Company Law*, p. 82; Bebchuk and Fried, 'Uneasy Case', pp. 886–7.
200. Samuels *et al.*, *Management of Company Finance*.   201. Cheffins, *Company Law*, p. 70.

assets quickly and for considerable loss if it is to make repayment. Overdraft lending, moreover, may be vulnerable to broad political changes or currents of financial thought. Thus, when governments require banks to restrict lending, overdrafts may be a primary target and companies may face swift curtailments in the availability or extent of their overdrafts.[202]

From the early 1990s onwards the major clearing banks and the Bank of England were, as noted, concerned at the reliance of small companies on overdraft facilities for the purposes of financing long-term business expansion.[203] These worries were prompted by feelings that such use of overdrafts evidenced both a lack of financial planning and an excessive reliance on funds liable to be subject to recall at short notice. The banks were also attempting to come to grips with the high levels of bad debts experienced at the end of the 1980s, with Third World debt problems and with a recession in industrialised countries. The banks' response was to seek to move debtor companies away from overdraft borrowing and into term loans. This policy succeeded so that, as noted above, the ratio of fixed loans to overdrafts changed between 1993 and 2000 from 44:56 to 72:28.

The unsecured overdraft is likely, however, to remain the first choice mode of raising short-term flexible finance for most companies. Its flexibility brings a considerable efficiency for the borrower because interest is charged only on the outstanding balance. Any cash flowing into the company will reduce almost instantly the balance of the advance and so the interest that has to be paid.[204] Alternative sources of finance, in contrast, usually involve a fixed sum to be repaid over a fixed term and interest has to be paid on the full sum for the full term.

Other forms of unsecured credit, such as those mentioned above, bring benefits that can be similar to those offered with overdrafts. Thus, the unsecured loans involved in trade credit arrangements offer low transaction costs, they allow credit agreements to be tailored to the particular transacting parties and they make use of information derived from trade relationships (on, for example, creditworthiness) as a way of reducing risks in a manner that is swifter and more efficient than resort to security.[205] It should not be assumed, however, that a trade creditor will always be well

---

202. Triantis and Daniels, 'Role of Debt'; R. Scott, 'Relational Theory'; Cheffins, *Company Law*, p. 75.

203. See Bank of England 1998, p. 17.

204. Samuels *et al.*, *Management of Company Finance*, p. 561.

205. J. MacNeil, 'Economic Analysis of Contractual Relations' in P. Burrows and C. Veljanovski (eds.), *The Economic Approach to Law* (Butterworths, London, 1981); B. Klein, 'Vertical Integration, Appropriable Rents and the Competitive Contracting Process' (1978) 21 *Journal of Law and Economics* 297.

positioned to assess the broad competence of their debtor's management. A trade creditor's expertise in a specific sector may, for instance, be of limited value in assessing corporate debtor performance in a completely different sphere of operation.[206] Where, of course, the value of a transaction is so small that a trade creditor would not rationally engage in the expense of monitoring the debtor,[207] the unsecured loan may still prove more efficient than taking security: the trade creditor may simply charge an interest rate that they hope will cover the risks of default.

Unsecured loans can assist wealth creation in another way, by assisting in the flow of money. To take an example, a supplier of machinery, in sending goods to a customer overseas, may accept a bill of exchange in the form of a cheque post-dated to a time after the arrival of the goods at their destination. The buyer of the goods can thus delay payment of the bill until the goods arrive but the seller can obtain cash immediately after dispatch by discounting the bill of exchange, by presenting it to a bank which buys it while charging a percentage discount. Use of the bill of exchange thus assists both the buyer and the seller and avoids delays in the use of funds.

For healthy companies, accordingly, unsecured loans provide a valuable means of acting efficiently in the marketplace. This efficiency derives not merely from the low transaction costs involved but also from utilising the monitoring and information-collecting capacities of creditors for the purposes of risk reduction and, in turn, for lowering the cost of credit.

All is not rosy in the garden, however, since a lack of security can lead to inefficiencies in the flow of cash between traders. Without security trade creditors are poorly placed to demand payments of outstanding debts. A secured creditor faced with non-payment has recourse to the charged assets and has rights to appoint a receiver or can apply to court for orders of foreclosure or sale.[208] Such a response is not open to the unsecured trade creditor, and late payment of debts was seen as a major problem in the 1990s.[209] As a *Financial Times* editorial put it in 1994:

> delays in settling invoices have become endemic. The practice plays havoc with cash flows, kills off thousands of smaller enterprises every

---

206. See Finch, 'Company Directors', p. 191.
207. See, however, the discussion at pp. 87–9 above relating to non-adjusting unsecured creditors.
208. Usually the debenture contains provisions enabling the loan creditor or trustee to appoint an administrative receiver without resort to the court and in practice this is the most common remedy: see *Farrar's Company Law*, pp. 662, 665.
209. See ch. 4 below.

year and wastes immense amounts of time in chasing unpaid bills...
UK companies have to wait on average 20 days longer beyond the due
date than their French counterparts, the next-worst payers in Europe.
The CBI says that late payment threatens the survival of one in five
companies.[210]

This is a problem that impacts most severely on small companies which
tend to be ill-equipped to absorb financial shocks[211] and which may not be
well positioned to be able to chase large debtors. The evidence, moreover,
suggests that the problem of late payment is predominantly one of larger
debtor companies failing to pay smaller suppliers.[212]

It may, however, be that late payment inefficiencies can be responded to
by statutory means. The Late Payment of Commercial Debts (Interest) Act
came into force in 1998 and allows companies employing fewer than fifty
persons to claim interest (at base rate plus 8 per cent) on payments more
than thirty days late.[213] A right of pursuit in the courts is given to
claimants, but the Act allows collection agents to be used or the sale of
interest to a third party such as a factoring firm. Such a statute may assist in changing the commercial culture that endorses late payment as
a means of obtaining credit from companies in weak bargaining positions, but certain realities have to be borne in mind in assessing the 1998
Act. The bargaining power of large companies may still be used to discourage small companies from availing themselves of the Act's assistance.
Large operators, for instance, may indicate to suppliers that business may
be withdrawn if proceedings for the recovery of interest are brought. In the
alternative, those in the strongest bargaining positions may insert long
credit periods into their contracts. The legal costs, moreover, of recovering
interest may deter small enterprises from pursuing actions, in the absence
of a right of recovery for those costs. What small creditors really need, it

210. *Financial Times*, 28 March 1994. The credit market quarterly review for January–March
1999 suggested that firms of under £1 million turnover met with average payment delays of
twenty days: *Guardian*, 6 July 1999.
211. The Federation of Small Businesses reported that 13 per cent of failures were caused by
late payment and at any time £17 billion is owed by larger companies to smaller suppliers:
Guardian, 15 December 1998. The high street banks themselves have been accused of being the
worst late payers: *Guardian*, 15 December 1998. See now Companies Act 1985 (Directors'
Report) (Statement of Payment Practice) Regulations 1997 (SI 1997 No. 571) regarding PLCs
and their large private subsidiaries' mandatory statements of payment practice.
212. See DTI Consultation Paper, *Improving the Payment Culture* (DTI, July 1997) p. 11.
213. The right to claim has been phased in and from 1 November 2000 small businesses have
also been able to claim from other small businesses as well as from large businesses and the
public sector. From 1 November 2002 all businesses and the public sector will be able to claim
on debts incurred after that date. See also the Council Directive on Late Payment of
Commercial Debts (2000/35, 29 June 2000) published OJ 2000 No. L2000/35. G. McCormack,
'Retention of Title and the EC Late Payment Directive' (2001) 1 JCLS 501.

can be argued, is a Swedish-style cheap, summary procedure for collecting payments without having to employ lawyers.[214]

Do unsecured loan arrangements, as they stand, however, conduce to efficient insolvency procedures? Here attention must be paid to the position of unsecured creditors in an insolvency and the way that this may affect their behaviour and expenses of doing business. When there is a corporate insolvency, secured creditors can remove their secured assets at will, via receivership, free from any notion of *pari passu*.[215] Other suppliers of credit can also prevent their 'debts' from falling into the fund of corporate assets available for distribution: noteworthy here are 'creditors' who have used 'self-help' devices such as retention of title clauses or trust mechanisms.[216] Unsecured creditors will see such 'creditors' escape the insolvency net but, in addition, the unsecured creditors must join the back of the queue for payment from the corpus of assets, a queue headed by the holders of fixed charges, followed by insolvency practitioners who incur expenses acting as office holders, then those with preferential debts (for example, sums owed to the Inland Revenue and Customs and Excise, sums due to employees for remuneration[217]) and then holders of floating charges. Only shareholders and certain deferred debts[218] come after the unsecured creditors. Satisfaction of such prior claims means that unsecured creditors' hopes of recovering anything of substance in the winding-up process are usually dashed.[219] Nor, furthermore, can the unsecured creditor expect any assistance in the form of altruism from receivers who collect from the company's assets for fixed and floating charge holders.[220] The receiver is appointed by debenture holders and has a principal duty to further the interests of those secured creditors. Thus, receivers are primarily concerned with generating funds for their debenture holders and this obligation takes precedence even over possible damage to the company's and unsecured creditors' interests.[221]

---

214. See discussion in ch. 4 below.

215. Note this is not the case with administration: Insolvency Act 1986 ss. 10, 11. On the *pari passu* principle of distribution see chs. 13 and 14 below.

216. See ch. 14 below.   217. But see ch. 13 below.   218. See Insolvency Act 1986 s. 74(1)(f).

219. See Cork Report, paras. 1480 ff.: for unsecured creditors corporate liquidation is usually 'an empty formality' because 'in all too many cases insolvency results in the distribution of the proceeds among the preferential and secured creditors, with little, or nothing, for the ordinary unsecured creditors'.

220. See ch. 8 below. See V. Finch, 'Directors' Duties: Insolvency and the Unsecured Creditor' in A. Clarke (ed.), *Current Issues in Insolvency Law* (Stevens, London, 1991).

221. *Gomba Holdings UK Ltd and Others v. Homan and Bird* [1986] 1 WLR 1301 at 1305; *Downsview Nominees Ltd v. First City Corporation Ltd* [1993] 2 WLR 86. Unsecured creditors *per se* are owed no duty by the receiver: *Lathia v. Dronsfield Bros. Ltd* [1987] BCLC 321. See ch. 8 below.

Such a regime may be unfair to the unsecured creditor (a matter to be considered in chapter 14) but why may inefficiency be produced? A first inefficiency may arise where there are unnecessary transaction costs: where, for instance, the legal costs faced by the unsecured creditors and creditors overall are higher than they should be because the relevant law is subject to avoidable and unnecessary uncertainties. (This is a matter to be returned to below when the processes for managing insolvency have been explored further.)

The second inefficiency of concern here takes us back to the balance between secured and unsecured creditors that was discussed above. Where unsecured creditors are unable to adjust to the granting of security there is liable to be a transfer of insolvency wealth to the secured creditor and unsecured creditors will bear excessive amounts of risk.[222] This leads to the inefficiencies noted above, which need not be reviewed again here.

Ownership-based (quasi-security) financing

As already noted, companies can raise funds or gain the use of goods by using sale arrangements in a manner that substitutes for security. Since the celebrated *Romalpa* decision,[223] trade suppliers of goods on credit have frequently used 'retention of title' clauses to stipulate that ownership of the goods shall not pass until payment for the goods has been received.[224] Surveys suggest that the majority of suppliers employ such clauses in their conditions of sale.[225] Retention of ownership operates in substance as security, but' 'simple' retention of title arrangement is not treated by English law as a security arrangement and, accordingly, there is no requirement of registration, as with a company charge or a bill of sale, in order for such a clause to be valid against third parties.[226]

---

222. See LoPucki, 'Unsecured Creditor's Bargain', p. 1899; Hudson, 'Case Against Secured Lending'; Leebron, 'Limited Liability'.

223. *Aluminium Industrie Vaassen BV* v. *Romalpa Aluminium Ltd* [1976] 1 WLR 676. Note that prior to this decision, although title retention clauses were common on the continent, they were rare in the UK. (The plaintiff in the *Romalpa* case was a Dutch company, using its standard terms of supply.)

224. Or, indeed, until all sums due from the purchasing company (e.g. in respect of previous supplies) have been satisfied: *Armour* v. *Thyssen Edelstahlwerke AG* [1990] 3 WLR 810. See further Snaith, *Law of Corporate Insolvency*, pp. 198–214.

225. Spencer, 'Commercial Realities of Reservation of Title Clauses' (p. 221), surveyed fifty suppliers and found 59 per cent of respondents used such clauses; Wheeler, *Reservation of Title Clauses*, examined fifteen receiverships and liquidations and found 92 per cent of suppliers of goods had 'some sort of reservation of title provision' (p. 5).

226. In a 'simple' retention of title clause the 'security' applies to the goods as supplied but a 'complex' retention of title clause seeks to apply to goods even when they have been altered or changed. The thrust of case law is that whereas simple clauses do not constitute charges,

The value to the creditor/owner of retention of title is that on the insolvency of the debtor company the assets at issue do not belong at law to the company, cannot be claimed by the insolvency practitioner and are not available for distribution among the creditors. The creditors of an insolvent company cannot make any claim against goods that are owned by others but are in the possession, control or custody of the company.[227] Powerful trade suppliers of goods are thus well placed to use their bargaining power to avoid the severe consequences, on a corporate insolvency, of status as unsecured creditors.

For a trade creditor, such as a supplier of goods and materials, a retention of title clause may prove more attractive than the taking of security (for example, a floating charge) because the latter may be seen as an expensive and cumbersome resort to a legal framework; because retaining title, in comparison, involves a simple standard contractual term not requiring general disclosure; because the customer, when approached for security, might refuse and look elsewhere for supply (fearing that offering security signals a lack of creditworthiness or financial instability to others in the market); and because requests for security might drive customers away, in so far as such requests are seen as hostile actions evidencing a lack of goodwill and trust.[228]

A hire purchase agreement keeps the title to the relevant asset with the seller until the end of the stipulated hire period and is often used as a source of medium-term credit for the purchase of plant and equipment. The hire purchase company supplies the equipment which can be used immediately by the hiree who will make a series of regular payments (including an interest charge) and, after repayment, will become the owner by exercising a right to purchase for a nominal sum. Legal title does not pass to the hiree until payments under the agreement have been completed. The

complex ones are regarded as charges and are registrable. The Company Law Review Steering Group (CLRSG) issued a consultation document, *Modern Company Law for a Competitive Economy: Registration of Company Charges* (DTI, London, October 2000), which (at p. 26) considered the simple/complex distinction to be 'sensible and workable' but asked for views on whether there should be a statutory definition of those retention of title clauses that are to be registrable. For discussion of the case for such definition see J. de Lacy 'Corporate Insolvency and Retention of Title Clauses: Developments in Australia' [2001] Ins. Law. 64. The CLRSG document, *Modern Company Law for a Competitive Economy: Final Report* (DTI, London, 2001) ('CLRSG, *Final Report*, 2001') ch. 12, advocates a regime of notice-filing which would link priority to the relative timing of registration. Simple retention of title clauses would not be registrable (para. 12.60). See further D. Milman, 'Company Law Review: Company Charges' [2001] Ins. Law. 180. See also McCormack, 'Retention of Title' on the EC Late Payment Directive's obligation on Member States to recognise contractually agreed-upon 'simple' ROT clauses in contracts for the sale of goods. See pp. 114–16 below.
227. See Snaith, *Law of Corporate Insolvency*, p. 197.
228. See Wheeler, *Reservation of Title Clauses*, pp. 38–9.

hirer, again, retains a secure position regarding any insolvency of the hiree, provided that the value of the asset at issue remains higher than the re-payment sum outstanding and does so for the duration of the agreement. The hiree, in turn, enjoys the use of the equipment and only has to make an initial payment rather than the full purchase price. Hire purchase tends to be an expensive form of finance but the hiree company can claim tax relief on the interest element in the payments made and in regard to any invest-ment allowances.

Leasing operates like hire purchase but at the end of the period of the lease the ownership of the asset still remains with the lessor. It is an ar-rangement that has grown in popularity for four reasons.[229] First, the com-pany may not have the funds to purchase a large asset, or, if it does, it may have a more profitable use for the cash. Second, leasing may provide tax advantages where investment allowances can be secured or where the lessor pays a higher marginal tax rate than the lessee (less tax will be col-lectable than would have been the case with a purchase). Third, leasing al-lows equipment to be updated flexibly and transfers the risks associated with technologically advanced fields to the lessor. Similarly, where a com-pany is ill-positioned to calculate asset depreciation rates it can transfer risks to the lessor. Finally, if leased assets can be kept off the balance sheet (for example, by classification as operating leases) a company can show a higher return on assets in its accounts than would have been possible had the asset been purchased.

Factoring and invoice discounting involve a company raising funds by selling receivables, such as debts owed to the company, to a financial in-termediary who will offer the company a cash percentage of their face value.[230] (Factoring, in the alternative, may operate by the advance of a sum on the security of the receivables.) The company will obtain funds more rapidly than would have been the case had payment from the customer been awaited.

Factoring and invoice discounting have become increasingly impor-tant to UK companies. From 1999 to 2000 there was an 8 per cent increase in funds advanced through factoring (to £16 billion). The increase in fund-ing through invoice discounting was 21 per cent (to £57.2 billion).[231] It is, indeed, the need for finance that leads companies to use factors and invoice discounters. These are devices of particular value to small, fast-growing

229. Samuels *et al.*, *Management of Company Finance*, pp. 586–7.
230. Factors in general will advance up to 80 per cent of invoice value: see Bank of England 1998, p. 28.
231. Bank of England 2001, p. 32

companies who experience late payment problems and wish to release funds tied up with debtors for use as working capital. Factoring and invoice discounting tend to prove more expensive than bank financing but they allow businesses to grow in line with their sales and can also be especially useful when a company has exhausted its overdraft facilities and is not in a position to raise new equity. Sales of receivables, moreover, do not have to be registered and borrowing ratios are unaffected.[232]

Sale and lease-back allows funds to be raised by a company selling assets to a financial intermediary but it also allows the company to continue using the assets by leasing them back. The company thus secures funds and only has to pay out rental charges (which are tax deductible) and the purchaser is protected against loss by the transfer of ownership. A sale and lease-back may be preferred by a company to a mortgage because the latter will adversely affect the debt to equity ratio of the company since it appears as a debt on the balance sheet.[233]

The broad efficiency case for the above quasi-security devices is that they provide ways to supply the financing that healthy trading companies need during their various stages of development. They are part of the flexible menu of financial devices that the market provides to trading companies and which help to increase cash flows. It could thus be argued that the growing use of financing methods such as factoring is strong evidence of their utility.

When attention is turned to the insolvency context, however, there are a number of efficiency concerns to be noted.[234] A first caution is that quasi-security devices may produce transfers of insolvency wealth away from those unsecured creditors who cannot adjust to the use by others of such devices. The result may be the production of those inefficiencies that were discussed above in relation to security: thus, for instance, companies may have an excessive incentive to rely on unsecured credit and their managers may be under-deterred from making high-risk decisions that affect the interests of unsecured creditors. Many submissions to the Cork Committee, furthermore, argued that on the continent of Europe the wide use of

---

232. See Snaith, *Law of Corporate Insolvency*, p. 220. See generally Oditah, *Legal Aspects*.

233. See Samuels *et al.*, *Management of Company Finance*, p. 584; Goode, *Commercial Law*, pp. 652–3. Variants on sale and lease-back are sale of stock/inventory or assignments of work in progress, where the company, in the former case, sells its stock, e.g. of bonded whisky, to a bank, receives funds and has an option to repurchase on maturation (of the whisky) at a price reflecting the initial sale price plus interest. During the period of maturation the bank owns the whisky and the company has funds for investment in further projects: see further Samuels *et al.*, *Management of Company Finance*, pp. 452–3.

234. See Diamond Report; Crowther Report. On the use of other 'devices' to jump the priority queue, see ch. 14 below.

reservation of title clauses had 'virtually emasculated' insolvency procedures as an effective remedy for unsecured creditors since there was generally nothing left in the estate for them.[235] Quasi-security devices tend to
be contracted for by the larger, better-placed companies who would otherwise be unsecured, and the effect is to exploit this superior positioning and
produce distortions in the pricing of credit. This last point can, perhaps,
be overstated because the costs of inserting a retention of title clause into
a supply contract may be small (standardised contracting reduces costs in
this respect), but there are, nevertheless, suppliers of certain types of goods
who cannot retain title effectively and who may, as a result, have to bear
undue expected insolvency costs. As the Cork Committee noted in relation to retention of title clauses: 'Fuel supplied to heat furnaces or fodder supplied for livestock disappears on consumption and paint applied
to the fabric of a factory becomes attached to the realty; the supplier of
credit is necessarily left with an unsecured claim in the insolvency of the
customer.'[236]

A second objection to the use of quasi-security is that it undermines
many of the efficiencies that are associated with the system of secured priorities. Security, with priority, can be said to reduce the price of credit by
reducing risks to lenders. They anticipate, when they are given security,
that the protection they enjoy will not be diluted in value by subsequent
actions of the debtor.[237] If, however, the debtor looks to quasi-security and
shifts its asset pattern so as to rely more heavily on the use of assets that are
leased or subject to hire purchase agreements, retentions of title or other
sale-based security devices, the protection offered to the secured creditor

---

235. Cork Report, para. 1624.

236. Ibid., para. 1619. On the English courts' reluctance to recognise extensions of ROTs into
the manufactured product or its proceeds (i.e. without its being registered as a charge) see
ch. 14 below. See also *Chaigley Farms Ltd* v. *Crawford, Kaye & Greyshire Ltd* [1996] BCC 957 but cf.
Armour v. *Thyssen* [1991] 2 AC 339. See further J. de Lacy, 'Processed Goods and Retention of
Title Clauses' [1997] 10 *Palmer's In Company*; de Lacy, 'Corporate Insolvency and Retention of
Title Clauses'.

237. As the essence of a floating charge is that the company is free to deal with its assets in the
ordinary course of business, it has been held that this includes being able to create fixed
charges on assets within the class covered by the floating charge, having priority over the
floating charge, in order to secure borrowing in the ordinary course of the company's
business: see *Wheatley* v. *Silkstone & Haigh Moor Coal Co.* (1885) 29 Ch D 715. In view of the court's
recognition (in *Re Automatic Bottle Makers Ltd* [1926] Ch 412) of the possibility of creating a
second floating charge over a *part* of the assets covered by a first floating charge and with
priority over the first charge, it has now become standard practice to include in a contract of
floating charge a 'negative pledge' clause, prohibiting the company from creating any charge
over the assets covered by the floating charge with priority over the floating charge. On the
question of establishing knowledge or notice of such a clause (thereby depriving a
subsequent chargee of protection), see *Farrar's Company Law*, p. 640.

will be diminished. Fewer assets within the new pattern will enter the insolvent estate and the holder of, say, a floating charge will have a call on a slimmer body of assets. The efficiency loss is caused by the uncertainty faced by the secured creditors: if they cannot assess the level of protection that their security will offer they either will not lend or will cost into the price of credit the increased level of risk that they face. Uncertainty thus increases credit costs.

A third objection continues the theme of uncertainty. In so far as quasi-securities do not have to be registered, there is a lack of information available to creditors, secured and unsecured, concerning the position of a company's indebtedness. The trade creditor, for instance, may deal with a customer who displays large warehouses with stocked shelves to the world but the title to these assets and stock may belong to a third party and the information relating to this position may well be unavailable to that trade creditor. This possibility will be anticipated by the rational trade creditor who will increase the cost of supply to reflect the unknown risks faced; but, again, uncertainty increases credit costs inefficiently.

The need for more information on quasi-security was recognised by the Crowther and Diamond Committees which both argued in favour of a new register of 'security interests' which, for Diamond, would include 'not only mortgages, charges and security in the strict sense but also any other transfer or retention of any interest in or rights over property other than land which secures the payment of money or the performance of any other obligation'.[238] The Company Law Review Steering Group advocated a system of notice-filing in 2001.[239] Registrable charges would include floating charges, all charges on goods and complex retention of title clauses (where the title protecting the indebtedness shifts from one good to another on transformation), but not simple retention of title clauses where the seller merely retains title on transfer.

The above problems are compounded by legal uncertainties. Insolvency lawyers, like any others, will always succeed to an extent in rendering the application of laws uncertain: if necessary they will argue about

---

238. Diamond Report, para. 9.3.2 (proposals that, *inter alia*, would cover retentions of title and hire purchase agreements and certain leasing arrangements). See Cork Report, para. 1639, which also argues that clauses reserving title that were not duly registered should be void against a liquidator, trustee, administrator or any other creditor. For support of the Diamond approach and a comparative view see de Lacy, 'Corporate Insolvency and Retention of Title Clauses'.

239. CLRSG, *Final Report*, 2001, ch. 12, para. 12.12. See further Milman, 'Company Law Review'.

the relevant facts as much as the applicable laws.[240] There are degrees of uncertainty, however, and costs to companies will increase where the law is excessively complex or uncertain. The problem associated with quasi-security is that the law is fragmented, it treats essentially similar transactions in very different ways and causes unnecessary legal complications.[241] As Diamond concluded: 'The complexity and uncertainty of the law leads to expense and delay and hinders legitimate business activities… The variations in the different legal rules cause problems in determining priorities between competing interests and give rise to fortuitous differences in insolvency.'[242] On reservations of title in particular, another commentator suggested that the formal law was 'uncertain in its application in almost every area. The most basic level of law in simple reservation of title clauses is open to differing interpretations.'[243]

Finally, it could be cautioned that quasi-securities not only queer the pitch for security mechanisms but they may also fail to work well themselves. In the case of retention of title clauses, it has been suggested that even claimants with the strongest cases face a formidable series of obstacles to recovery, that those insolvency practitioners who act as administrative receivers or liquidators enjoy huge expertise and 'repeat player' advantages over claimants and that the overall result is that only 15 per cent of claimants succeed in recovery.[244] It is, accordingly, conceivable that, as presently operated, a device such as the retention of title clause achieves the worst of both worlds: it is perceived (wrongly) as a huge threat by holders of floating charges and this escalates credit costs, but the device fails, at the end of the long and legally uncertain day, to deliver real protection to the quasi-secured creditor.

240. See Wheeler, *Retention of Title Clauses*, pp. 34–6.

241. The finding of the Diamond Report, para. 1.8(c), and the Cork Report, para. 1627, noted how consultee after consultee had made a 'cry for certainty' to avoid the prospect of 'interminable and expensive litigation'. Note, also, Cork's response that, given *inter alia* the 'illogical and complex' law relating to security in respect of goods, 'nothing that we propose in relation to insolvency law can prevent this': para. 1628.

242. Diamond Report, paras. 1.8(d)–(e). On the solution to these difficulties and Diamond's proposals for a 'new law on security interests to replace the multitude of different rules we have now', see ch. 14 below.

243. Wheeler, *Retention of Title Clauses*, p. 34. It is now, as noted, accepted that a simple retention of title (as opposed to a complex one) is effective: see A. Hicks, 'Retention of Title: Latest Developments' [1992] JBL 398.

244. Wheeler, *Retention of Title Clauses*, p. 178. See also Spencer, 'The Commercial Realities of Retention of Title Clauses', in whose survey half of respondents said that their clauses had been challenged by receivers or liquidators. In practice the insolvency practitioner not only will consider whether the wording of the ROT clause establishes a prima facie claim but will also be influenced by the bargaining position of the supplier: see *Leyland DAF Ltd* v. *Automotive Products plc* [1993] BCC 389; A. Belcher and W. Beglan, 'Jumping the Queue' [1997] JBL 1 at 17–19.

Conclusions

The above discussion has reviewed the main mechanisms by which companies can finance their operations. Even a non-exhaustive view, however, indicates the range of legal instruments that are available for the financing of companies. Also made clear is the complexity of the trade-offs that have to be borne in mind in assessing the legal structures of financing. The needs of healthy companies as well as troubled companies have to be considered; the balance between credit and other financing arrangements has to be evaluated; and the needs of companies of different sizes and profiles have to enter the analysis. The purpose of this chapter has not been to evaluate the UK banking system and its ability to service industry.[245] It has been to map out the legal framework of borrowing and to consider whether this is, in structural terms, conducive to the efficient meeting of healthy and troubled companies' needs.

A number of general conclusions can be drawn at this stage. First, it is clear that, at least in some contexts, there may be significant dangers of inefficient transfers of insolvency wealth from unsecured creditors to secured creditors or to those availing themselves of quasi-security devices. The nature of any efficiency loss will, as noted, depend on a number of context-specific factors: for instance, the number of different kinds of creditors that supply financing to a firm; the levels of risks being run by the company; the types of transaction being engaged in; the levels of transaction costs involved; and the nature of the competition in the various credit markets to which the company can turn. Where such transfers of insolvency wealth occur, they may prejudice healthy companies' needs (corporate decisions on financial risks may, for example, be taken with distorted weightings being given to the interests of different creditors). Transfers of this kind may also affect the needs of troubled companies in so far as decisions as to the lives or deaths of troubled companies – decisions which affect different creditor groups in different ways – may also be made with unbalanced views of the interests of different creditor classes. Not only that, but corporate managers may possess incentives to subsidise their company's secured loans by taking their unsecured credit from those unsecured creditors who are least well informed about risks, least able to adjust loan terms, least protected in insolvency and least likely to be capable of absorbing financial shocks.

---

245. For an outspoken view see Hutton, *The State We're In*. See also the White Paper, *Our Competitive Future*, para. 2.21; Bank of England 2001; Cruickshank, *Competition in UK Banking*.

It may also be concluded that certain courses of action have the potential to reduce inefficient insolvency wealth transfers. Procedures could be adopted so as to allow unsecured creditors to become more fully informed about the risks they are running. The value of informational steps should not, however, be exaggerated. They do not assist unsecured creditors who are involuntary or cannot adjust because of lack of resources, paucity of time or expertise, competitive pressures or other reasons. This does not mean, however, that there is no case for assisting those who can be put in a position to adjust and for adopting measures such as the registration of quasi-securities. Similarly, measures designed to increase information flows and transparency in credit arrangements will reduce inefficient wealth transfers but may also assist creditors in their monitoring of debtors and the encouragement of efficiency in decision-making. This will be of value to healthy as well as troubled companies.

As for involuntary, unsecured creditors who cannot adjust, other steps might be taken to reduce wealth transfers away from such a group. A fixed fraction rule, as proposed by the Cork Committee, is a blunt instrument (it benefits all unsecured creditors) but it is a known quantity that allows attendant risks to be calculated and which is unlikely to reduce the availability of secured credit. It would accordingly not impede trading materially but would provide funds of assistance in capturing insolvency assets and would reduce insolvency-driven inefficiencies. Compulsory insurance against tort liabilities could reduce inefficient subsidies from a particular group of involuntary, non-adjusting unsecured creditors.

The above review also suggests that the collectivity of financing arrangements and the array of legal devices encountered in England is likely, in its present form, to impose unnecessary costs on both healthy and troubled companies. Where the financial markets supply a wide range of devices for obtaining finance and credit this might be thought to be consistent with the needs of healthy companies. Companies presented with such wide choices are thus able to select the types of, say, credit which will prove least costly to them given their size, profile, sector, financial plans, transaction patterns and so on. It is one thing, however, to provide a range of clearly identifiable modes of acquiring funds and another to present companies with a patchwork of legal devices that is so confused that they may have difficulty in identifying the kinds of borrowing relationships that they are considering or even have entered into. Where the legal gateways to borrowing are unnecessarily confused and uncertain, unnecessary transaction costs are again produced for both healthy and troubled companies.

We have seen, moreover, that just as confusion attends the legal categories of borrowing, it also permeates the system of priorities, so that the benefits of clear ranking are undermined by the capacity of 'creditors' to employ such quasi-security devices as retention of title clauses and thereby to bypass priority mechanisms. The costs of credit will inevitably rise as such uncertainties increase risks.

Addressing the confusions that are found in the range of credit arrangements demands that attention be given to the legal frameworks that establish the different credit devices. It also demands that thought be given to the application of these frameworks on the ground and the possibility of devising credit arrangements that not only are set up with clear legal frameworks but are operated in the business world in an efficient, fair, accountable and transparent manner. During the rest of this book such matters will be a central concern.

4

Corporate failure

This chapter looks at what constitutes corporate failure, who decides that a company has failed and why some companies fail. From the insolvency lawyer's point of view it is important to understand the nature and causes of corporate decline so that the potential of insolvency law to prevent or process failure can be assessed and so that insolvency law can be shaped in a way that, so far as possible, does not contribute to undesirable failures or prove deficient (substantively or procedurally) in processing failed companies.

The purpose of insolvency law is not, however, to save all companies from failure.[1] The economy is made up of a vast number of firms, each engaged in marketing and product innovations that are designed to improve competitive positions and each being challenged in the market by other firms. Business life involves taking risks and dealing with crises, and the price of progress is that only those able to compete successfully for custom will survive.[2] An efficient, competitive marketplace will thus drive some companies to the wall because those companies should not be in business: they may be operated in a lazy, uncompetitive manner, their products may no longer be wanted by consumers and managerial weaknesses may be placing their creditors' interests at unacceptable risk. The role of insolvency law in such cases is not to take the place of the market's selective

---

1. Where rescue professionals were appointed in formal insolvency proceedings the overall business preservation rate fell from 30 per cent to 20 per cent in the years 1996/7 to 1997/8: see the Society of Practitioners of Insolvency's Eighth Survey, *Company Insolvency in the United Kingdom* (SPI, London, 1999) ('SPI Eighth Survey') p. 14. The R3 Ninth Survey of Business Recovery in the UK (2001) ('R3 Ninth Survey') put the overall survival rate at 18 per cent (R3 is the successor title for the SPI). Smaller companies were revealed as having a modest survival rate (15 per cent) compared to 32 per cent for companies in the £1m to £5m turnover band.
2. See M. White, 'The Corporate Bankruptcy Decision' (1989) 3 *Journal of Economic Perspectives* 129.

functions but to give troubled companies the opportunity to turn their affairs around where it is probable that this will produce overall benefits or, where this is not probable, to end the life of the company efficiently, expertly, accountably and fairly.

It can also be argued, however, that insolvency laws and processes should be able to look beyond the immediate position of the company and should be sufficiently accessible to democratic influence to allow consideration of factors beyond the narrow confines of the firm or the strictly economic. Corporate failures may lead to the breaking up of teams with experience and expertise; to wasted resources and to run-on effects such as the unemployment of staff; harm to customers and suppliers; general impoverishment of communities and losses of confidence in commercial, financial, banking and political systems. A large corporate insolvency may, for instance, produce not merely job losses and harm to the community, but it may prejudice the availability of commercial credit as banks are shocked into newly restrictive lending policies. An insolvency often spreads ripples that extend considerably beyond the troubled firm.

What is failure?

Companies routinely encounter difficult times and survive them. Some firms, however, undergo formal or informal rescue procedures before regaining health and others may end up in liquidation. R3 reported in 2001 that 18 per cent of businesses survived insolvency and continued to operate in one form or another and nearly one in five jobs were preserved.[3] In 1998 the number of companies liquidated was 13,204.[4] To talk of 'troubled' or 'failing' companies is accordingly to refer in a broad brush fashion to companies encountering a variety of problems and in different stages of decline or regeneration. More precision can be brought to such discussions by distinguishing between companies that are in distress and companies that are insolvent.

Distressed companies are those that encounter financial crises that cannot be resolved without a sizeable recasting of the firm's operations or

3. R3 Ninth Survey, p. 1.
4. DTI figures. The total for all types of liquidations in 1996–7 was 16,082: CSO Annual Abstract of Statistics, DTI, 1996–7. Insolvencies in the recession of the early nineties peaked at just under 25,000 in 1992. In 1999 the Annual Report of the Insolvency Service reported 5,209 compulsory liquidations and 9,071 creditors' voluntary liquidations for the year reviewed.

structures.[5] Such distress may be seen in terms of default, where the company has failed to make a significant payment of principal or interest to a creditor.[6] Alternatively, distress can be seen in terms of financial ratios. Thus, calculations based on a company's accounts can be used to reveal profitability ratios, liquidity ratios and longer-term solvency ratios.[7] Assessing whether a company is in distress may involve reference to these ratios individually or collectively, but the central issue is whether the company is revealed to be in such a state of crisis that drastic action is required.[8]

A company is insolvent for the purpose of the law if it is unable to pay its debts.[9] No legal consequences attach to a firm, however, simply by virtue of its insolvent state. Such consequences only follow the institution of a formal proceeding such as a winding up or the appointment of an administrator or administrative receiver. There is, moreover, no single legal definition of inability to pay debts. Within the Insolvency Act 1986 and other insolvency-related statutes there are a number of tests of insolvency and these relate to the purposes of different legislative provisions. The two main reference points regarding the inability to pay debts are the 'cash flow' and the 'balance sheet' tests.[10] The cash flow test is set out in

---

5. C. Foster, *Financial Statement Analysis* (2nd edn, Prentice-Hall, Englewood Cliffs, N.J., 1986) p. 61; A. Belcher, *Corporate Rescue* (Sweet & Maxwell, London, 1997) ch. 3. The SPI Eighth Survey revealed that 71 per cent of businesses in its sample of formal insolvency cases experienced a break-up sale of assets. For a spectrum of potential indicators of distress see R. Morris, *Early Warning Indicators of Corporate Failure* (Ashgate/ICCA, London 1997); see also J. Day and P. Taylor, 'Financial Distress in Small Firms: The Role Played by Debt Covenants and Other Monitoring Devices' [2001] Ins. Law. 97.

6. In Belcher's terms a 'default proper' as opposed to a 'technical default' of a loan term, which relates to principal and interest payments but to other issues, e.g. retention by the firm of a minimum level of net worth.

7. Profitability ratios address the firm's effectiveness using available resources, liquidity ratios speak to its capacity to pay its debts in the short term and longer term, solvency ratios consider the firm's capital structure and its ability to meet longer-term financial commitments (see Belcher, *Corporate Rescue*, p. 40). Ratios are often used in attempts to predict insolvency: on which see Belcher, *Corporate Rescue*, ch. 4; E. I. Altman, 'Financial Ratios, Discriminant Analysis and the Prediction of Corporate Failure' (1968) 23 *Journal of Finance* 589; J. Pesse and D. Wood, 'Issues in Assessing MDA Models of Corporate Failure: A Research Note' (1992) 24 *British Accounting Review* 33; R. Taffler, 'Forecasting Company Failure in the UK Using Discriminant Analysis and Financial Ratio Data' (1982) *Journal of Royal Statistical Society*, Series A, 342.

8. Wruck defines financial distress as 'a situation where cash flow is insufficient to cover current obligations. These obligations can include unpaid debts to suppliers and employees, actual or potential damages from litigation and missed principal or interest payments': K. Wruck, 'Financial Distress, Reorganisation and Organisational Efficiency' (1990) 27 *Journal of Financial Economics* 419 at 421.

9. See R. M. Goode, *Principles of Corporate Insolvency Law* (2nd edn, Sweet & Maxwell, London, 1997) ch. 4; J. Boyle, J. Birds, E. Ferran and C. Villiers, *Boyle and Birds' Company Law* (4th edn, Jordans, Bristol, 2000) pp. 638–40.

10. See Goode, *Principles of Corporate Insolvency Law*, pp. 67–70. Note that the Insolvency Act 1986 s. 123(1)(a) and (b) provides two specific alternative methods of establishing inability to pay debts to facilitate the proof of insolvency (i.e. for creditors) for the purposes of winding up or administration proceedings.

section 123(1)(e) of the Insolvency Act 1986 and, according to this, a company is insolvent when it is unable to pay its debts as they fall due. (The fact that the firm's assets exceed its liabilities is irrelevant.) The courts, moreover, will pay regard to the firm's actual conduct so that insolvency will be assumed if the company is not in fact paying its debts as they fall due.[11] Insolvency under this test is a ground for a winding-up order[12] or an administration order[13] or for setting aside transactions at undervalue, preferences and floating charges given other than for specified forms of new value.[14]

The balance sheet or asset test of section 123(2) of the Insolvency Act 1986 considers whether the company's assets are insufficient to discharge its liabilities, 'taking into account its contingent and prospective liabilities'. This may involve assessing the value of assets and judging the amount the asset would raise in the market; though a difficulty arises through the Act's failure to indicate whether valuations should be made on the basis of a 'going concern' or 'break-up' sale. Particular difficulties may arise where there is no established market value for the commodity. The test, furthermore, gives rise to potential problems in so far as there is no statutory definition of prospective liabilities. Standard accounting practice treats contingent liabilities more subtly than section 123(2) and that section does not include any particular basis for measuring assets and liabilities.[15] The balance sheet test is also one of the tests prescribed for the purpose of grounds for winding up,[16] administration[17] or the avoidance of transactions at undervalue,[18] preferences[19] and avoidance of certain floating charges.[20] It is also a test relevant in considering the disqualification of directors[21] and the one test used in identifying insolvent liquidation for the purposes of assessing directorial liabilities for wrongful trading.[22]

Defining insolvency at law is further complicated by the use of further tests in statutes other than the Insolvency Act 1986. Thus, under the Company Directors' Disqualification Act 1986 a company becomes insolvent for the purposes of potential directorial disqualification if its assets are insufficient for the payment of its debts and other liabilities together with

11. See *Cornhill Insurance plc v. Improvement Services Ltd* [1986] 1 WLR 114.
12. Insolvency Act 1986 s. 122(1)(f).   13. Ibid., s. 8(1)(a).
14. Insolvency Act 1986 ss. 238–42 and 245, especially ss. 240(2) and 245(4).
15. See Belcher, *Corporate Rescue*, pp. 46–7. Prospective and contingent liabilities must be taken into account according to *Re A Company (No. 006794 of 1983)* [1986] BCC 261.
16. Inability to pay debts for the purposes of winding-up orders can also be assessed in ways independent of insolvency: see Goode, *Principles of Corporate Insolvency Law*, pp. 71, 108–9.
17. Insolvency Act 1986 s. 8(1)(a).   18. Ibid., ss. 238, 240(2).
19. Ibid., ss. 239, 240(2).   20. Ibid., ss. 245, 245(4).
21. Company Directors' Disqualification Act (CDDA) 1986 s. 6(2).
22. Insolvency Act 1986 s. 214.

the expenses of winding up, or when it goes into liquidation or when an administration order is made or an administrative receiver is appointed.[23] Under the Employment Rights Act 1996, and for purposes concerning employee rights to payment from the National Insurance Fund on an employer's insolvency and the employee's job termination, the employer is deemed insolvent when a winding-up order or administration order has been made; a resolution for voluntary winding up has been passed with respect to the company; a receiver or manager has been appointed; possession has been taken by holders of debentures secured by floating charges; or any property that is the subject of a charge and a voluntary arrangement has been approved under Part I of the Insolvency Act 1986.[24]

Finally, for the purposes of a member's voluntary winding up under section 89 of the Insolvency Act 1986, the company's directors must make a declaration of solvency but reference is not made to the cash flow or balance sheet tests. The issue is whether the company will be able to pay its debts in full, together with interest at the official rate, within such period (not exceeding twelve months from the commencement of the winding up) to be stipulated in the declaration.

Insolvency law thus defines 'insolvency' in different ways for different purposes.[25] Legal definitions, moreover, are not the only measures for corporate failure. If economic criteria are employed, a company might be said to be failing if it cannot realise a rate of return on invested capital that, bearing in mind the risks involved, is significantly greater than prevailing market rates on similar investments. Such failure would not necessarily lead to 'legal' insolvency but, if lasting in nature, this is a possibility. Alternatively, a failure to produce appropriate financial returns might result in corporate financial distress or investor-driven changes in the company's staffing and strategies.

Who defines insolvency?

A corporate insolvency can involve a number of concerned parties. These include creditors, shareholders, group subsidiaries,[26] directors and managers of the company, employees, suppliers and customers. A host of

---

23. CDDA 1986 s. 6(2).
24. See Goode, *Principles of Corporate Insolvency Law*, pp. 73–4.
25. Thus we have seen that the Insolvency Act 1986 confines the term 'insolvency' to a formal insolvency proceeding: Insolvency Act 1986 ss. 240(3), 247(1). The phrase 'unable to pay its debts' embodies the concept of a *state* of insolvency: see Goode, *Principles of Corporate Insolvency Law*, p. 65.
26. See ch. 12 below.

professional advisers will also have a role to play and these may include financial and management consultants, lawyers, bankers and accountants.

As seen above, there is no simple objective point in corporate affairs when the law states that the company is insolvent. The law creates opportunities for action rather than laying down consequences for stipulated states of affairs. Different tests are applied for different purposes and there are judgments involved in assessing each test. Thus, the question of whether a firm fails on the cash flow test of ability to pay debts depends on a set of constructions. As Miller and Power have put it: 'Corporate failure is itself constituted out of an assemblage of calculative technologies, expert claims and modes of judgment.'[27] Not only different parties but also different professionals will possess distinctive ways of perceiving and constructing corporate events and of deciding how to respond to these. Accountants invariably have a choice of ways to portray a company's performance in both healthy and troubled times.[28] There is a variety of ways, moreover, to deal with financial challenges and distress so that insolvency becomes as much a negotiable or technical issue for the accountant as an objective one.[29] The law, on this view, can be seen as overlaid on the facts as established by the accountants, so that 'the calculative technologies of accountancy trigger legal processes and provide the knowledge of those processes that law comes to administer after the event'.[30] The accountants can thus be seen as straddling the corporate process and not only providing auditing, consultancy and other services for healthy companies, but also dominating the legally created market for insolvency administration and the extra-legal market for corporate rescue. In these roles, the accountants carry out regulatory, advisory and managerial functions. The law says little in detail about the economic substance of corporate failure (it prefers to set down procedures for dealing with vaguely defined circumstances) and, because this is the case, it creates a 'legal space in which such matters can be negotiated'.[31] The legal process thus becomes highly dependent on extra-legal expertise: on the portrayals of corporate affairs

27. P. Miller and M. Power, 'Calculating Corporate Failure' in Y. Dezalay and D. Sugarman (eds.), *Professional Competition and Professional Power: Lawyers, Accountants and the Social Construction of Markets* (Routledge, London, 1995).
28. On the weak role of accountants and auditors in securing information for assessing corporate health, from an Australian perspective, see F. Clarke, G. Dean and K. Oliver, *Corporate Collapse: Regulatory, Accounting and Ethical Failure* (Cambridge University Press, Cambridge, 1997) ch. 17.
29. Miller and Power, 'Calculating Corporate Failure', p. 54.
30. Ibid., p. 56.
31. Ibid., p. 58; though see the portrayals of insolvency practitioner work as obfuscatory rather than negotiatory in S. Wheeler, *Reservation of Title Clauses* (Oxford University Press, Oxford, 1991).

that are presented by the accountancy and economic professionals who appear before the courts and pull the triggers created by the insolvency legislation.[32] Central to such endeavours are the ratio analyses that have 'transformed the nature of corporate failure and opened it up to a new regime of judgment and assessment'.[33] The conception of economic viability, in turn, becomes a matter of debate over accountants' calculative technologies so that, at the end of the day, the accountants play as much of a role in constructing the events of insolvency as do lawyers, judges or involved parties.

The message for insolvency lawyers is that insolvency law, to be understood, has to be seen as a tool in the hands of different professionals, one that is manipulated in different ways by those groupings. The resultant processes are consequently not fully captured by images of legal definition and the mechanical transposition of insolvency law into practice.

Why companies fail

Companies can be said in the main to fail through either internal deficiencies (such as poor management) or pressures exerted by external factors (such as natural disasters).[34] This section reviews the causes of failure and the concluding section considers the potential impact of insolvency law on these respective causes.

32. On the role of insolvency professionals in shaping insolvency processes see ch. 5 below.

33. Miller and Power, 'Calculating Corporate Failure', p. 59. For a classic multi-variant analysis looking at the ratios of working capital to total assets; retained earnings to total assets; earnings before interest and losses to total assets; market value of equity to book value of long-term debts and sales to total assets, see E. I. Altman, *Corporate Bankruptcy in America* (D. C. Heath, London, 1971).

34. On corporate failure see C. F. Pratten, *Company Failure* (Institute of Chartered Accountants in England and Wales, London, 1991); C. Campbell and B. Underdown, *Corporate Insolvency in Practice: An Analytical Approach* (Chapman, London, 1991); H. D. Platt, *Why Companies Fail: Strategies for Detecting, Avoiding, and Profiting from Bankruptcy* (Lexington Books, Lexington, Mass., 1985); J. Argenti, *Corporate Collapse: The Causes and Symptoms* (McGraw-Hill, London, 1976). Insolvency practitioners tend to put most corporate failures down to mismanagement of one kind or another. A 1991 Harrison Willis survey of 200 IPs listed the top ten reasons for failure as: 1. poor management; 2. poor management information; 3. high gearing; 4. poor financial controls; 5. high interest rates; 6. poor cash flow/cash management; 7. slow response to changing markets; 8. excessive overheads/spending; 9. lack of strategic plan; 10. poor communication with banks: see Cork Gully Discussion Paper No. 1 (London, June 1991) p. 2. The SPI Eighth Survey and R3's Ninth Survey both indicated that the most frequent primary reasons for failure were managerial failings (fraud; over-optimism in planning; imprudent accounting; erosion of margins; product obsolescence/technical failure; over-gearing) and financial problems (loss of long-term finance; lack of working capital/cash flow) followed closely by loss of market and then bad debts. Bad debts increased significantly as a primary factor from 1996/7 to 1997/8 (from 8 per cent of cases to 14 per cent) but were set at 9 per cent in the R3 Ninth Survey. See also Day and Taylor, 'Financial Distress in Small Firms', p. 107 for a study of clothing companies and media/marketing companies in distress.

Internal factors
Poor financial controls[35]

The immediate cause of failure in a company is a lack of cash available to pay bills when they are due. A common cause of corporate decline, accordingly, is failure to take adequate steps to control cash flows. In the normal course of business a company's current bank account is liable to fluctuate from deficit to surplus levels as it issues funds to purchase materials, pays its work forces, produces its goods and then awaits the inflow of funds through payment of customers' bills. (Such fluctuations may be compounded where the firm's business is seasonal in nature.) Managing cash flows involves the collection of relevant information and the organisation of this: normally the charting out of anticipated cash receipts and disbursements on a weekly or monthly basis. Planning cash flows will involve consulting with lenders, negotiating appropriate credit lines and presenting potential lenders with projected cash flows, plans for product or market development and, amongst other things, programmes for cost control. Such planning has to cope with a number of situations that can decrease liquidity. These situations include: trading losses that reduce cash flows and assets relative to liabilities; bad debts or other write-offs; needed investments in expansion; and falls in the value of assets (which reduce the company's ability to raise cash by granting security).[36]

The firm's managers will aim to make arrangements with the firm's bankers and other creditors so that funds are available to bridge the gaps between deficit and surplus and to continue funding production, marketing and sales activities. At the same time, the firm has to remain able to pay its own debts as they fall due. Funds, accordingly, must be negotiated to allow such obligations to be met. Where the firm's creditors are no longer willing to lend (perhaps because they have lost confidence in the firm's management), or where loan arrangements have not been negotiated, the firm may find it difficult to keep operating or to pay its debts unless it has taken other steps to deal with cash flow problems, such as maintaining a level of cash reserves sufficient to sustain itself between the troughs and peaks.

Over-dependence on short-term financing may, in turn, lead to financial difficulties. Thus, where a firm resorts to overdraft financing in order to fund long-term investment plans, it becomes highly vulnerable. If

---

35. Poor financial controls are dealt with separately here from mismanagement but may be seen as a particular form of managerial failure: see Platt, *Why Companies Fail*.
36. See Pratten, *Company Failure*, p. 8.

the bank withdraws the overdraft facility the firm may not have time to obtain alternative funding before it enters difficulties.[37] Lack of control over current assets is a further major cause of corporate failure. When assets are purchased on credit they have to be used in a manner that allows interest payments to be paid and a profit made. If assets are unused or wasted, a company will be in financial trouble unless other activities can carry the losses. Managers must invest in assets such as equipment so as to meet market demands, but they must be wary of possible market changes that will reduce or remove the potential profitability of their equipment. Assets, accordingly, must be managed so that, overall, a firm has sufficient flexibility to cope with market changes. Attention has to be paid to the balance between long-term fixed asset costs (funds tied up with, say, machines) and variable cost items (e.g. labour and fuel costs which are more easily adjusted than fixed asset costs). Long-term assets (e.g. steel production plants) can be highly profitable but they carry greater risks than variable cost items due to their inflexibility, particularly if they are specialist in nature and there is no ready market providing a means to realise their value by sale. If the balance of a firm's investment is tilted too far in the direction of long-term fixed costs, its ability to cope with slow markets diminishes and failure may result.

Similarly, problems may arise where the company operates with 'high gearing': arrangements that involve a high proportion of fixed interest commitments or fixed interest capital in relation to the firm's total assets (i.e. all fixed and current assets). With high gearing a firm devotes a high proportion of its gross profits to the servicing of loan capital. It accordingly becomes highly vulnerable to changes in market conditions and interest rates. Poor control of gearing may thus cause firms to fail when general economic, or particular market, conditions deteriorate and there is some evidence that companies with high gearing are more likely to move into crisis than those with low gearing.[38]

Inadequate financing is a further cause of failure. This may occur when the company fails to raise sufficient funds by debt or equity means to render its operation profitable. If funds, for instance, suffice for production

---

37. The Bank of England has expressed unease at the dependence of small UK businesses (highlighted by the last recession) on overdraft facilities to finance anything from working capital to long-term investment projects: see Bank of England, *Finance for Small Firms*, Sixth Report (1999), p. 28. (Banks have now moved their emphasis to some extent away from the use of overdrafts and towards term lending: ibid. See ch. 3 above.)

38. See R. Hamilton, B. Halcroft, K. Pond and Z. Liew, 'Back from the Dead: Survival Potential in Administrative Receiverships' (1997) 13 IL&P 78, 80.

purposes but do not provide adequately for marketing and sales activities, the company is unlikely to make ends meet. Over-expansion and over-trading may also produce severe problems when a firm increases its volume of business more quickly than it is able to raise the funds necessary to finance such operations properly.[39]

Mismanagement

Most English company directors are untrained and unqualified.[40] Poor management, moreover, has been said to account for around a quarter of recent company insolvencies.[41] One survey has suggested that in 46 per cent of cases companies fail because of matters primarily in the control of the management and that in almost a quarter of cases businesses would have been rescuable if directors had sought the right advice earlier.[42] Some commentators have cautioned, however, that mismanagement often provides a more convincing explanation of which firms in a trade fail than of the number of firms that fail (which may be dictated by the nature of the market, the product and the role of available economies of scale).[43] One

---

39. Over-expansion is the most frequent corporate weakness identified by J. Stein, 'Rescue Operations in Business Crises' in K. J. Hopt and G. Teubner (eds.), *Corporate Governance and Directors' Liabilities: Legal, Economic, and Sociological Analyses on Corporate Social Responsibility* (De Gruyter, Berlin, 1985).

40. The Institute of Directors (IOD) revealed in 1990 that: less than 10 per cent of directors had received any training; less than a quarter possessed professional or managerial qualification; and only 24 per cent of survey respondents considered training 'very important': IOD, *Professional Development of and for the Board* (January 1990); see also V. Finch, 'Company Directors: Who Cares About Skill and Care?' (1992) 55 MLR 179, 210. A further IOD report published in 1998 indicated that directors had become more professional since the beginning of the decade but that there were still 'shortcomings' in their behaviour (65 per cent of respondents had 'prepared themselves' for their boardroom role compared with just 10 per cent in 1990; the proportion of respondents taking training courses had also increased from 8 per cent to 27 per cent; but while 61 per cent of respondents – mainly senior directors of small to medium-sized companies – said directors should have a formal induction to the board, only 6 per cent had such an induction themselves: IOD, *Sign of the Times* (1998)).

41. The SPI Eighth Survey reported that 26 per cent of company collapses in 1996/7 could be put down primarily to bad management and that in 36 per cent of cases mismanagement was a secondary cause of failure: p. 5. The figure for primary cause changed slightly in the R3 Ninth Survey to 25 per cent. The notion of mismanagement can, however, be drawn sufficiently widely to produce far higher figures. See, for example, Campbell and Underdown, *Corporate Insolvency*, pp. 1–3: 'Companies become insolvent when their management fails to develop adequate long term strategic plans to deal with problems of profitability and cash flow.' (The most frequent managerial failings noted in the SPI Eighth Survey were lack of information, over-optimism in planning and erosion of margins.) The R3 Ninth Survey indicated that reasons for failure were cited in order of prominence as: management failings (25 per cent), financial (21 per cent), loss of market (20 per cent) and bad debts (9 per cent).

42. See R3 Ninth Survey, p. 2. In the case of larger companies with over £5 million turnover R3 suggested that nearly half could have been rescued if the right advice had been sought (R3 Ninth Survey, p. 3).

43. See Platt, *Why Companies Fail*, p. 6.

aspect of poor management already discussed is an inability to establish adequate financial controls, and poor information collection and use is very often associated with poor financial controls. Lack of cost information is a major failing since successful corporate operation demands that managers possess knowledge concerning the profitability of the firm's different activities. It is essential to know, for instance, if the price at which a product is being sold is producing profits for the company. Selling at a price below cost will soon lead to failure. Other informational deficiencies may involve the lack of cash flow forecasts, the absence of budgetary control data and the non-availability of figures on the values of company assets.[44] Information, moreover, must flow properly through the firm and poor lines of communication have been said to be one of the main causes of failure.[45] 'Creative accounting' techniques can disguise the true state of financial affairs in a company or can delay the emergence of accurate information about the firm. Such techniques, accordingly, can contribute to mismanagement generally and can reduce the company's ability to respond successfully to market and other pressures.[46] They can also lead managers, investors and bankers to expand corporate operations more rapidly, and at higher risk, than the true state of affairs merits. Creative accounting techniques may also camouflage the firm's true levels of debt or inflate profit and asset figures and, as a result, managers may be led to raise the gearing of the company in a dangerous manner.

It has been suggested that accountants in auditing and advisory roles might play a stronger role in ensuring that accurate information is available on a company's financial position and in warning of dangers.[47] Moves on two fronts might thus be considered: methods of reporting to management and shareholders could be rethought; and accountants' training might be revised so as to improve their managerial advisory role.[48] On the first front, however, it should not be assumed that auditing strategies and assumptions can be revised to reveal the 'true position'

---

44. Argenti, *Corporate Collapse*, pp. 26–7, 30–3, 94–5.
45. Ibid., p. 30 (reporting the assessment of Mr Kenneth Cork, as he then was).
46. On creative accounting and whether auditors should control this more rigorously, see Pratten, *Company Failure*, pp. 50–1; Clarke, Dean and Oliver, *Corporate Collapse*, ch. 2. On auditing as a preoccupation and an end in itself rather than an effective management tool see M. Power, *The Audit Society* (Oxford University Press, Oxford, 1998) ch. 6.
47. See, for example, Pratten, *Company Failure*, p. 48 and references to press reports therein. See R. Taffler and D. Citron's 1995 Study (City University) on auditors' qualification of accounts: only one in seven companies surveyed which failed between 1987 and 1994 carried a warning from auditors in its last set of accounts about its status as a 'going concern'.
48. Pratten, *Company Failure*, p. 50.

of a company. Uncertainties in markets and future prospects will always mean that such items as asset valuations contain similar elements of uncertainty. What can, perhaps, be done is to map out the location and extent of uncertainties in as clear a way as possible.[49] A further key issue is whether auditors can make reliable assessments of the degree to which a company is at risk.[50] Auditors suffer from a number of limitations in judging corporate prospects, not least their restricted knowledge of managers' forthcoming strategies and decisions in a changing marketplace. There are dangers, moreover, that overt auditors' warnings of risk might themselves contribute to corporate troubles.

As for training and advice, accountants might focus more on such topics as the causes of corporate failure, the requirements of success and the economics of pricing. They might, accordingly, strengthen their roles in advising corporate managers during the ongoing process of corporate decision-making. This, in turn, might be expected to improve information use and managerial decision-making more generally. The result could, for instance, be greater managerial awareness of the dangers involved in creative accounting or in failing to develop accurate costing figures.

Managers may also prove deficient by failing to respond to changes in the company's environment.[51] Thus, when key personnel depart from a company or markets or technologies move in new directions, a company's managers must be capable of developing new staffing arrangements and new products and strategies to keep the firm competitive. Appropriate information and research and development systems are likely to be necessary if such lack of responsiveness is to be avoided. A further managerial failing may involve leaving the company particularly vulnerable to changes in the market or the broader environment: as where an excessive dependence on a particular supplier contract or customer is allowed to build up and inadequate provision is made for the departure of that supplier or customer.

49. See, for example, Power, *Audit Society*, p. 144: 'The issue is rather a question of organisational design capable of building in "moral competence" and of providing regulated fora of openness around these competences.'
50. Pratten, *Company Failure*, p. 57. On the accountancy profession's concern at the 'expectations gap' – the difference between what audits do achieve and what it is thought they achieve, or should achieve – see the *Report of the Committee on the Financial Aspects of Corporate Governance* (Cadbury Committee) (December 1992) paras. 2.1 and 5.4; J. Freedman, 'Accountants and Corporate Governance: Filling a Legal Vacuum?' (1993) *Political Quarterly* 285.
51. Campbell and Underdown, *Corporate Insolvency*, p. 18.

Managers may fail simply because they lack appropriate skills. They may be brilliant engineers but poor financial directors. Lack of identification with the company's interests may be another managerial failing. This may range from a targeting of personal rather than corporate objectives through to practices of defrauding the company for the purpose of making illegal personal gains.[52] Fraudsters may, for example, forge cheques in their own favour or steal the stock of the company. Directors may engage in extravagant lifestyles at the firm's expense, employees may turn their backs on corporate interests and parent or associate companies may milk successful businesses of their profits, put no investment back into those businesses but use the proceeds to fund other operations within a group. All of these forms of conduct, illegal and legitimate, may drive a firm into failure.

In the case of small businesses, it has been suggested that a fifth of all failures are attributable to marketing errors.[53] A company's managers may have conducted inadequate research into markets and competitors, they may have failed to set up effective organisations for marketing or may have adopted weak sales strategies. Managers of small firms may, indeed, have a general tendency to focus on product development and give too little attention to marketing.[54]

Managers may perform their own tasks competently but they may prove to be poor leaders. Poor management may thus lead to inadequacies of supervision, morale and productivity. As a result, the company may operate with high costs, low productivity and diminishing levels of profit. The governance structure of a company may also prove conducive to mismanagement.[55] This may be the case with notable frequency in certain circumstances: where, for instance, a single individual dominates a company;[56] where there is an imbalance on the board (between, for example, financial and technical experts); or where there is a lack of representation on the board (e.g. of accountants). Where procedures for briefing managers and board members are inadequate this, again, may lead to defective control mechanisms and poor decision-making in the company.

52. For a view that fraud-induced failures are, in fact, rare, see Pratten, *Company Failure*, p. 6; K. Cork, *Cork on Cork: Sir Kenneth Cork Takes Stock* (Macmillan, London, 1988).
53. See M. Gaffney, 'Small Firms Really Can Be Helped' (1983) *Management Accounting* (February).
54. See Campbell and Underdown, *Corporate Insolvency*, p. 21.
55. See C. Daley and C. Dalton, 'Bankruptcy and Corporate Governance: The Impact of Board Composition and Structure' (1994) 37 *Academy of Management Journal* 1603.
56. See Argenti's discussion of Rolls Royce's troubles in the early 1970s: *Corporate Collapse*, ch. 5.

As for the characteristics of those managers that are associated with corporate failure, Stein has suggested that the following traits tend to be exhibited by insolvency-prone managers.[57] First, all bad managers tend to be 'out of touch with reality', a condition in which they possess little consciousness of risks. This propensity tends to be found together with high levels of technical knowledge and a willingness to learn on the technological front, or else with high ability in marketing and sales. The area of risk tending to be neglected by such managers is that associated with growth and over-expansion. Second, bad managers tend to be very strong willed, autocratic, unwilling to delegate and able to impose themselves on their business partners and co-workers. Such dominance tends to be underpinned by their high abilities with regard to technical or sales issues and their uncritical attitude to growth. Almost all such individuals possess 'remarkable stress tolerance'[58] and the high level of their assertiveness often translates into ambitious plans for corporate dominance of the market. In around half of such individuals there is a tendency to personal high living.

A different sort of manager is, according to Stein, also associated with corporate failure and this is labelled the 'improvident' manager. This individual tends to act in an ill-informed, 'blind' fashion in pursuit of favourable opportunities to advance in the market and tends not to carry out the necessary studies on the sustainability of an expansion or the financial underpinnings required for such a development.

Mismanagement, moreover, may be seen in the shape of single aberrant acts as well as in ongoing weaknesses. Corporate managers may make catastrophic mistakes or fail to deal with particular problems and, in doing so, may place the company in peril. A decision, for instance, may be taken to move the firm's business into a market sector in which the firm is unable to compete, or a huge investment may be put into the production of a poor product. Corporate managers may also embark on a project so large that its failure will place the survival of the company at risk.[59] Such managers may err, again, by buying other companies that are weak,

---

57. Stein, 'Rescue Operations in Business Crises'. In 1996 the business information group, CN, published research indicating that nearly 4,000 company directors (four times as many as had previously been thought) had been associated with more than ten company failures: *Financial Times*, 28 October 1996. (CN reported that of the 2.6 million UK company directors on its database, 952,432 (or 37 per cent) had been associated with one or more failures in the previous seven years and one in twelve directors was a 'serial failure' associated with at least two collapses.)

58. Stein, 'Rescue Operations in Business Crises', p. 390.

59. See the discussion of the Rolls Royce RB211 project in Argenti, *Corporate Collapse*, ch. 5.

over-priced and whose acquisition cannot be turned to advantage.[60] Failure to deal with a key technological change may also constitute a managerial error that renders the firm's survival uncertain. Most products become obsolete as technologies advance, substitutes come on the scene or consumers' tastes change, and companies that fail to adapt in a suitable manner may go out of business.

External factors

External pressures routinely place companies under stress. Astute managerial teams tend to cope with such stresses and their companies usually survive. Such pressures, however, can lead lesser managers to fail. In the extreme, some external shocks may be so severe that even the most skilled managers cannot save the company.

Changing markets and economic conditions are factors that almost invariably impinge on corporate activities.[61] A business may fail because a demand swing is too severe for it to respond successfully: where, for example, consumers change a preference rapidly from one fashion design to another. The prices of raw materials may escalate in an unpredictable manner and to a degree that makes a company's product or price unattractive to consumers. A major competitor may attack the company's market with a level of commitment and aggression that pulls the financial carpet from beneath the company's feet, and economic cycles (often compounded by drops in investor confidence) may produce slumps that are so severe and sustained that the company fails. Since 1970 the economy has been subjected to a series of shocks which have caused problems for many companies. These shocks have included the oil price rises of 1973–4 and 1979–81, the wage explosions of 1973–4 and 1978–80[62] and the credit squeeze of the early 1990s.

Some trade sectors (notably manufacturing and construction) are more prone to failure and insolvency than others and the seasonality encountered in some sectors can place severe stresses on corporate solvency.[63] The

---

60. An example of this was British and Commonwealth's acquisition of Atlantic Computers in the 1980s: see Pratten, *Company Failure*, p. 34. See also Campbell and Underdown, *Corporate Insolvency*, p. 23. See also the 1997 University of Exeter study of domestic takeovers in 1984–92 (A. Gregory).

61. On international market shifts and recessions as causes of corporate failure see K. Dyson and S. Wilks, 'The Character and Economic Content of Industrial Crisis' in Dyson and Wilks (eds.), *Industrial Crisis: A Comparative Study of the State and Industry* (Blackwell, Oxford, 1985).

62. Pratten, *Company Failure*, p. 4.

63. The SPI Eighth Survey, p. 7 and the R3 Ninth Survey suggest that, in declining order, the sectors most prone to insolvency are manufacturing; construction; retailing; wholesaling and distribution; transport and communications; hotel and catering; finance and property (categories of 'other services' and 'other sectors' are left out of account).

seasonality of the toy industry, with its focus on Christmas sales and discounting at other times of the year, has been said to explain the sector's
long history of corporate failures.[64]

Overseas producers can provide severe price competition and this has
been identified as the probable cause of decline in UK manufacturing industries in such sectors as cars, motor cycles, machine tools, paper and
textiles.[65] Nor do pressures come only from markets. Governments and
regulatory bodies may take actions that precipitate failures. The British
Government's high interest rate policy produced a surge of company failures in the second half of 1990, so that the number of companies entering receivership during those six months matched the figure for the whole
of the preceding year. Companies also suffered shocks from high sterling
exchange rates in 1980–1 and 1990–1, as well as from credit explosions in
1972–3 and 1986–9.[66] Rapid inflation made matters worse for companies
during the 1970s, early 1980s and in 1990. Recessions resulted in 1974–
5, 1980–1 and 1990–1.[67] Adapting to such changes is particularly difficult
for companies when the shocks cannot be predicted. Firms that relied on
long-term fixed price contracts during the early 1970s were especially hard
pressed by inflation.

Where companies operate with high levels of gearing and tight repayment schedules they will be particularly vulnerable to changes in overdraft costs when, as at the start and end of the 1980s, there are dramatic
increases in the minimum lending rate.[68] If governments impose squeezes
on credit, lenders will tend to ration credit and give priority to those firms
that are considered the best risks. These are unlikely to be new or small
firms or those with existing problems, and, accordingly, the proportion of
loans going to established large firms will tend to rise when money is tight.
Small firms tend to be less capable of surviving such credit shortages than
large firms. So, overall, the result tends to be a rise in the number of small
firm failures.[69] Governments may even precipitate corporate failures more
directly when, for example, they withdraw or decline further financial aid,
as occurred in January 1971 when the Government decided not to support

---

64. SPI Eighth Survey, p. 9.
65. See Slater, *Corporate Recovery*; Campbell and Underdown, *Corporate Insolvency*, p. 19.
66. In 1996/7 the strength of the pound and the impact of loss of Asian business were said to
be contributory factors in corporate failure in 20 per cent and 18 per cent of cases respectively:
see SPI Eighth Survey, p. 6.
67. Pratten, *Company Failure*, p. 4.
68. See Campbell and Underdown, *Corporate Insolvency*, p. 19.
69. The R3 Ninth Survey indicated that nearly nine out of ten insolvent companies had a
turnover of less than £5m and 80 per cent of insolvent companies employed fewer than
fourteen persons.

Rolls Royce further in the RB211 engine affair[70] and, more recently in October 2001, when anticipated state subsidies were not forthcoming and Railtrack was put into administration.

Regulators, be they agencies, government departments or European bodies, may impose critical stresses on companies by a number of routes. It is commonly complained by industry that the costs of complying with regulations are a burden (particularly for small businesses)[71] and on occasion such costs can break the camel's back.[72] In response, however, it can be said that competent managers will generally be able to cope with regulatory burdens, and that if regulation kills firms because the managers of those firms are incompetent, or because regulation outlaws a product central to the company's output, those firms should go to the wall because they are either uncompetitive or Parliament's voice demands that they cease business. If regulators, for instance, enforce statutory rules prohibiting, say, the production of eggs in battery cages, and if battery producers fail to adapt by employing other processes, the effect will be to drive those producers out of business in accordance with the legislative will.

Regulators, however, may produce unjustifiable failures where they regulate badly. They may, for example, vacillate in their demands, delay licensing approvals unnecessarily and impose excessive costs on businesses. A failure to regulate may also produce insolvencies where, for instance, effective regulation is necessary to sustain consumer confidence in a product. The BSE crisis of 1996–9 demonstrated that regulatory deficiencies relating to animal foodstuffs can produce dramatic levels of corporate failure in the farming industry. Deregulation can also precipitate failure by breaking down the entry barriers that have protected enterprises and allowed relatively inefficient operators to survive. Where, moreover, there is a rush of new entrants into a competitive industry there

---

70. On 4 February 1971 a receiver was appointed: see Argenti, *Corporate Collapse*, p. 90.

71. See Bank of England, *Finance for Small Firms*, Eighth Report (March 2001) p. 7 and CBI, *Cutting Through the Red Tape: The Impact of Employment Legislation* (November 2000). The CBI argues that the direct costs to companies of new employment rights introduced since May 1997 could be over £12 billion. A Federation of Small Businesses Report, *Barriers to Survival and Growth in UK Small Firms* (London, 2000), suggests that small firms' concerns rest on regulation.

72. On compliance costs and governmental responses see, for example, DTI, *Burdens on Business* (1985); White Papers: *Lifting the Burden* (Cmnd 9571, 1985), *Building Business, Not Barriers* (Cmnd 9794, 1986), *Releasing Enterprise* (Cm 512, 1988); DTI, *Counting the Cost to Business* (1990); DTI, *Checking the Cost to Business* (1992); DTI, *Cutting Red Tape for Business* (1991); DTI, *Cutting Red Tape* (1994); DTI, *Thinking about Regulation* (1994); HM Treasury, *Economic Appraisal in Central Government* (1991); Deregulation Unit, Cabinet Office, *Checking the Cost of Regulation: A Guide to Compliance Costs Assessment* (1996); Deregulation Unit, *Regulation in the Balance: A Guide to Regulatory Appraisal Incorporating Risk Assessment* (1998).

may naturally follow a period in which the less efficient are weeded out. Rates of failure can be expected to rise where the costs of entry and exit to a newly deregulated sector are high.

Government taxation policies can also bring marginal companies to the point of failure and industrial relations problems can break companies. If production is stopped by a prolonged strike the consequences for a firm may be severe. Where the company's own workforce are involved in an industrial dispute the firm's managers may have some control over events and may have to shoulder some blame for mismanagement. If, however, the dispute is between employers and workers at a key supplier or customer, there may be little that even the most competent managers can do.[73]

Unexpected calamities may also threaten companies. These may range from natural disasters, such as earthquakes that destroy essential firm assets, to the illegal acts of humans, for example, the criminal behaviour of a financial fraudster or an arsonist who burns down a firm's premises. Devastating losses may also result from new legal liabilities: thus a court decision rendering tobacco companies liable to governmental bodies for the cost of treating lung cancer sufferers might precipitate a series of corporate failures. Penalty clauses in contracts may produce similar effects where companies fail to deliver finished products on time.[74]

The behaviour of other companies may also constitute an external cause of corporate failure. Many large firms use the process of delaying settling the invoices of small suppliers as a means of extracting credit from those suppliers. Late payments of this kind may present small firms with considerable cash flow problems yet they may be in too weak a position to negotiate a solution with a large customer.[75] The Blair Government recognised this problem and has passed the Late Payment of Commercial Debts (Interest) Act 1998 which came into force on 1 November 1998.[76] This

---

73. See J. R. Lingard, *Corporate Rescues and Insolvencies* (2nd edn, Butterworths, London, 1989) p. 3.

74. See Argenti, *Corporate Collapse*, p. 91 on the role of penalty clauses in the Rolls Royce failure of 1971; Cork, *Cork on Cork*.

75. Lloyds TSB figures released in 1998 suggested that delay in receiving payment was the single biggest worry for small businesses: *Guardian,* 27 October 1998. The Federation of Small Businesses suggested in 1997 that late payment accounted for 5,000 of the 40,000 small UK company failures of 1995 (*Financial Times,* 29 January 1997).

76. From 1 November 2000 small businesses have had the additional right to claim interest on the late payment of commercial debts from other small businesses. On 12 July 2000 the Government launched the Business Debtline – a telephone helpline aimed at helping small businesses with debt problems – and in September 2000 the Minister for Small Businesses announced the setting up of a new advisory service for small firms encountering financial problems: see DTI Press Notice P/2000/482.

allows small businesses (with fewer than fifty employees) to claim interest (at base rate plus 8 per cent[77]) from large companies, the public sector and other small businesses if payments for the supply of goods and services are late.[78] Where no date for payment is contractually stipulated, claims arise thirty days from the date of delivery of goods or of the invoice for payment.[79] Such legislation cannot, however, be assumed to provide complete protection for small firms. As noted in chapter 3, the bargaining power of large customers may still be wielded to threaten withdrawals of business where small firms use the Act,[80] and small firms still face the legal costs of pursuing late payers.[81]

Where a company trades with other companies the latter may cause failure involuntarily: where, for example, they owe debts and fail to settle these before or after their own failures. Finally, the actions of a firm's creditors or investors may bring about downfall. Mention has already been made of the effects that a bank's withdrawal of an overdraft facility may have. Lenders may withdraw credit through lack of confidence in a firm's management, or as a result of government action (a credit squeeze), or for reasons internal to the creditor itself, such as a new policy of shifting from overdraft to fixed-term lending. Similarly, investors in a company may take precipitate action for a number of reasons. They may lose confidence in the firm's business or its management and the shares may drop to a point that triggers a crisis of confidence in the company's creditors who

77. Late Payment of Commercial Debts (Rate of Interest) (No. 2) Order 1998 (SI 1998 No. 2765). On the 1998 Act see S. Baister, 'Late Interest on Debts' (1999) *Insolvency Bulletin* 5.
78. From 1 November 2002 all businesses and the public sector will be able to claim on debts incurred after that date.
79. The average payment period in the UK is fifty days, higher than that encountered in Finland, Denmark, Sweden, Germany, Austria and the Netherlands: *Financial Times*, 29 January 1997. Firms with under £1m turnover met with average payment delays of twenty days according to the Credit Management Review for the first quarter of 1999: see *Guardian*, 6 July 1999.
80. On 6 July 1999 the *Guardian* ran a story on the June 1999 Credit Management Review which suggested that small firms were reluctant to use the new Act for fear of antagonising customers on whom they were reliant and that firms with a turnover of less than £1m were still waiting more than twice as long for payment than firms with turnovers of over £50m. An Association of Chartered Certified Accountants (ACCA) survey of 1999 suggested that 92 per cent of small businesses had experienced no reduction in payment times since the 1998 Act: see *Company Lawyer* August/September News Digest (1999).
81. It has been suggested that companies should have the right to compensation for the costs incurred in chasing up late payments, which would strengthen deterrence; that statutory interest should be automatically applicable without going to court (as in Sweden); or that what is needed is a fast, cheap, summary legal procedure for creditors to collect late payments without having to use a lawyer: the Fair Payment Group and *Intrum Justitia* (see *Financial Times*, 3 October 1997). See also the Council Directive on Late Payment of Commercial Debts (2000/35, 29 June 2000) published OJ 2000 No. L2000/35; G. McCormack, 'Retention of Title and the EC Late Payment Directive' [2001] JCLS 501.

then start pressing their claims. This process may spiral and bring about a company's collapse.[82]

In concluding on the internal and external causes of corporate failure, it should not be assumed that single causes or single patterns of causes are to be encountered when numbers of failures are analysed. Collapses generally result from the operation of a number of causes, and involve both external pressures and various internal failings. Argenti has suggested that three prevalent types of corporate failure are encountered in the business world.[83] These types or 'trajectories' of failure are those associated with small companies, the 'high rollers' and the large companies. For small companies the typical failure involves never rising above a poor level of performance and surviving only for a short period.[84] In such companies the proprietor often possesses great determination and knowledge of a trade but lacks basic financial and business skills and is managerially incapable of leading the firm through troubled times. Where the company is new, moreover, it is vulnerable to recessions, high interest rates and other pressures because it has had little time to establish accumulated profits or secure contracts with customers and suppliers.[85] High rollers make up only a small percentage of companies and tend to be led by colourful, flamboyant characters who are attractive to investors. As with small firms that fail, however, the leaders of high rolling firms tend to lack managerial skills. There is a propensity to allow enthusiasm to produce over-trading

---

82. Pratten, *Company Failure*, p. 11.

83. Argenti, *Corporate Collapse*, ch. 8. In 1844 the Select Committee on Joint Stock Companies divided 'bubble companies' into three categories: those founded on unsound calculations and which could not succeed; those so ill-constituted as to render mismanagement probable; and those faulty or fraudulent in their object: see *Farrar's Company Law* (4th edn, Butterworths, London, 1998) p. 622; Campbell and Underdown, *Corporate Insolvency*, pp. 23–5.

84. The SPI Eighth Survey suggests that 28 per cent of insolvent companies fail between the ages of five and ten years; 22 per cent between three and four years; 19 per cent between one and two years and 5 per cent after less than one year (SPI Eighth Survey, p. 8). The R3 Ninth Survey revealed an increase in the age of failed businesses, with 18 per cent aged two years or less and 43 per cent four years old (figures for the previous survey were 24 per cent and 46 per cent respectively). The first year failure rate had dropped from 5 per cent to 3 per cent between the Eighth and Ninth Surveys. According to P. Ganguly and G. Bannock (eds.), *UK Small Business Statistics and International Comparisons* (published on behalf of the Small Business Research Trust, Harper & Row, London, 1985), up to 60 per cent of business failures in any one year occur in those firms less than three years old. New companies exploiting new products seem to be particularly prone to failure: see Pratten, *Company Failure*, p. 3; MERA, *An Evaluation of the Loan Guarantee Scheme*, Department of Employment Research Paper No. 74 (1990).

85. See J. Hudson, 'Characteristics of Liquidated Companies' (Mimeo, University of Bath, 1982). Hudson's study found that the most dangerous period for companies involved in creditors' voluntary liquidations and compulsory liquidation lay between their second and ninth years.

which, when manifest, leads the firm's bankers to refuse advances and precipitates failure.

With large companies that collapse, the management teams involved are usually professional but the long-established companies that encounter trouble tend to lose touch with their markets or grow slow and inefficient. *En route* to failure, such companies tend to experience an initial downturn, a plateau and then a collapse. Large companies, however, will tend to possess greater resilience than small firms because they have larger reserves of assets that can be used to reorganise and they have greater negotiating power when approaching bankers and governments for assistance in attempting a turnaround.[86]

Conclusions: failures and corporate insolvency law

Can corporate insolvency law contribute to the avoidance of undesirable corporate failures and the unwanted consequences of failure? In some respects, the law can be seen as largely irrelevant. It can offer very little assistance where external factors such as new foreign competitors, catastrophic trade disputes or natural disasters drive companies out of business. In other regards, however, the nature of insolvency law can impinge on corporate failure or success. First, it can do so in relation to the costs that such laws impose on healthy and on troubled companies. If, for instance, uncertainties attend the security and priority systems established by law, credit costs will be unnecessarily high, international competitiveness will be prejudiced and companies will face undesirable financial turbulence and stresses. If transaction costs are higher than they should be (because firms have to spend large sums on advisers in order to organise their credit and priority arrangements) then, again, unwarranted pressure is placed on companies and this may in some cases produce failure.

Insolvency law can also impact on the main internal causes of failure that have been discussed above: deficiencies of financial control and management. The extent of this impact should not be exaggerated, however. Corporate managers cannot be assumed to be wholly rational and mechanical followers of legal rules.[87] A host of legal processes and rules nevertheless provides a framework of incentives for company managers.

---

86. See ch. 7 below and the 'London Approach'.
87. For an argument that corporate insolvency law can make only a marginal contribution to the efficiency of corporate management, see 'The Fourth Annual Leonard Sainer Lecture – The Rt Hon. Lord Hoffmann', reprinted in (1997) 18 Co. Law. 194. See also Finch, 'Company Directors'.

Deficiencies of financial control are discouraged by the law in so far as failure to keep adequate records may be grounds for disqualifying a person from holding office as a company director on the basis that there has been general misconduct in the affairs of the company or unfitness on the part of the director.[88] The rules on directorial disqualification and the system of DTI investigation[89] may also affect corporate failures in another way. A number of individuals, if unregulated, are likely to operate numbers of companies in cynical anticipation of their failure and employ phoenix operations to enrich themselves at the cost of creditors. The success with which insolvency law controls such phoenix operations may affect the incidence of corporate failure.[90]

Managerial standards in companies may also be influenced by the regimes of monitoring that the law establishes and encourages.[91] The provisions of insolvency law are relevant here in so far as these establish the regimes of security and priority that offer creditors specific sets of incentives to review the actions of corporate managers. Thus, for instance, the strong position in which current insolvency law places secured creditors gives creditors with fixed charges very few incentives to monitor corporate affairs beyond looking to see that the assets that are the subjects of their charges are not alienated or wasted.[92] The amount of information that creditors may possess, and which allows them to monitor corporate behaviour, is again dictated in large part by insolvency law. When, for example, administrative receivers (ARs) are appointed by debenture holders,

---

88. See Company Directors' Disqualification Act 1986 ss. 2–3, 6–9. On disqualification see ch. 15 below; S. Griffin, *Personal Liability and Disqualification of Company Directors* (Hart, Oxford, 1999); A. Mithani and S. Wheeler, *Disqualification of Company Directors* (Butterworths, London, 1996); L. S. Sealy, *Disqualification and Personal Liability of Directors: A Guide to the Changes made by the Insolvency Legislation of 1985 and 1986* (5th edn, CCH New Law, Kingston upon Thames, 2000); V. Finch, 'Disqualifying Directors: Issues of Rights, Privileges and Employment' (1993) ILJ 35; Finch, 'Disqualification of Directors: A Plea for Competence' (1990) 53 MLR 385; D. Milman, 'Personal Liability and Disqualification of Directors: Something Old, Something New' [1992] 43 NILQ 1.

89. See P. L. Davies with contributions from D. D. Prentice (ed.), *Gower's Principles of Modern Company Law* (6th edn, Sweet & Maxwell, London, 1997) ch. 25; Finch, 'Company Directors', pp. 195–7.

90. See Insolvency Act 1986 s. 216, the purpose of which is to contribute towards the eradication of the 'phoenix syndrome', whereby companies are successively allowed to run down to the point of winding up, only to rise phoenix-like from the ashes as a new company formed and managed by an almost identical group of persons and utilising a company name similar to that under which the former company was trading. See further I. F. Fletcher, *The Law of Insolvency* (2nd edn, Sweet & Maxwell, London, 1996) pp. 500–1, 664–7; Company Law Review Steering Group (CLRSG), *Modern Company Law for a Competitive Economy: Completing the Structure* (November 2000) ch. 13; CLRSG, *Modern Company Law for a Competitive Economy: Final Report* (2001) ch. 15.

91. See generally Finch, 'Company Directors'.

92. See Stein, 'Rescue Operations in Business Crisis', p. 394.

the information to be supplied to the ARs by company officers and the arrangements for reporting to creditors and creditors' meetings are governed by the Insolvency Act.[93]

The regimes of personal liability for directors that are established at law may, again, create incentives to manage in a particular way. The rules on wrongful trading, for instance, and the possibilities of actions for misfeasance may provide deterrents to errant directors.[94] In the case of misfeasance actions, these may be brought by shareholders or creditors against past or present company officers who breach any fiduciary or other duty owed to the company,[95] and insolvency law's priority regimes dictate shareholders' and creditors' own incentives to pursue directors. Shareholders are unlikely to act if they will not recover sufficient funds from a director to pay creditors in full before taking their own share, and unsecured creditors are unlikely to pursue actions unless the company's available funds will pay the creditors in full before them.

Insolvency law may also affect the levels of skill that corporate managers have to exhibit and this will have an effect on failure levels. The relatively low standard expected from directors' duties of skill and care could be raised if the objective criteria of the 'wrongful trading' section of the Insolvency Act 1986 (s. 214) were to be adopted.[96] The deterrence element in the wrongful trading provisions is provided by requirements of reasonable diligence and the courts' capacity to order personal contributions to corporate assets where directors fail to show they have taken proper care.[97] Company law may, furthermore, choose to require a variety of different levels of competence, training and professionalism from directors and this is likely to bear on the propensity of a given company to fail.[98]

If it is accepted that one cause of corporate failure is the taking of unjustifiable risks by directors then insolvency law has relevance beyond the imposition of duties of care and personal liabilities for breach of these. Insolvency law affects the balance of risk bearing in the company. If, as

---

93. Insolvency Act 1986 ss. 47(1), 48(1)–(2). See ch. 8 below. The terms of debentures routinely give creditors rights to consultation and information on such matters as the value of assets subject to floating charges and borrowing levels: see ch. 3 above.

94. Under Insolvency Act 1986 ss. 214 and 212. On the effectiveness of s. 214 as, *inter alia*, a deterrent, see ch. 15 below.

95. See F. Oditah, 'Misfeasance Proceedings against Company Directors' [1992] LMCLQ 207; L. Doyle (1994) 7 *Insolvency Intelligence* 25, 35. See ch. 15 below.

96. See Finch, 'Company Directors'; *Norman* v. *Theodore Goddard* [1991] BCLC 1028; *Re D'Jan of London Ltd* [1994] 1 BCLC 561; CLRSG, *Modern Company Law for a Competitive Economy* (March 2000) ch. 3, (November 2000) ch. 13, *Final Report* (July 2001) pp. 42–5. See further ch. 15 below.

97. See *Re Produce Marketing Consortium Ltd* [1989] 5 BCC 569; D. Prentice, 'Creditors' Interest and Directors' Duties' (1990) 10 OJLS 265; Finch, 'Company Directors'; see also ch. 15 below.

98. On directorial levels of care and professionalism, see Finch, 'Company Directors'.

suggested in chapter 3, unsecured creditor interests and risks are under-represented in corporate affairs because of the present framework of insolvency law, it follows that corporate decisions are liable to undervalue such interests, that excessively risk-laden decisions will be taken and that an unjustifiable number of failures will occur. The expected costs to unsecured creditors are not internalised by the company or fully recognised by corporate managers.

Corporate failure through excessively high gearing may again be influenced by the insolvency/corporate law regime. Thus, it might be argued that the law places many creditors in a position from which they are not able to judge with accuracy the financial position of a prospective borrower and the risks involved in a loan. Company law, for instance, does not at present demand that retentions of title be registered and lenders who are ignorant of a debt applicant's true position may be inclined to grant credit in circumstances that would not have prompted a loan if relevant knowledge had been to hand. The overall effect of poor information may be that firms find it too easy to operate with high gearing. Excessive gearing will also tend to be accompanied by high levels of interest because creditors will demand high returns in order to reflect the high risks that poor information imposes on them. This combination of high gearing and high interest payment levels leads, in turn, to high prospects of corporate failure.

Finally, insolvency law affects levels of corporate failure because it creates the set of incentives that holds sway in the processes for ending corporate lives. Undesirable failures may be caused where certain parties possess incentives to call a halt to corporate activity at times when this is not in the general interest of involved parties. If, for example, the law on wrongful trading operates with a particular level of severity it will give directors of troubled companies a particular motivation to cease business operations at any given time in the process of corporate difficulties.[99] An excessively severe wrongful trading law could thus lead to premature closures of companies which might have revived but have not been given a chance of turnaround because the directors have been fearful of the consequences to them of trading on. Similarly, the regime of priorities gives certain creditors incentives to act where this is in their own interests but not those of others. A bank secured with a floating charge under the present insolvency law regime may thus be inclined to appoint a receiver

---

99. But see A. Walters, 'Enforcing Wrongful Trading: Substantive Problems and Practical Disincentives' in B. Rider (ed.), *The Corporate Dimension: An Exploration of Developing Areas of Company and Commercial Law: Published in Honour of Professor A. J. Boyle* (Jordans, Bristol, 1998) and discussion in ch. 15 below.

in circumstances where it would overwhelmingly serve the interests of unsecured creditors and shareholders to have an administrator appointed specifically to promote the survival of the company and its undertaking.[100]

Nor do all dangers stem from premature curtailments of corporate activity. When the company faces insolvency and when creditors' interests would best be served by an orderly running down of a business, it may be the case that directors will be pulled in the direction of continued trading by their interest in preserving their employment and business standing. Wherever directors do continue to trade in these circumstances, there is a prospect that the company will descend into a more damaging failure than would otherwise have been the case and the additional loss will fall not on the directors but on the company's creditors.[101]

Insolvency law also sets out time scales and procedures to be adopted when companies are in trouble. Levels of corporate failures can be affected by the use or non-use of cooling off periods and moratoria, as encountered in the Chapter 11 procedures found in the USA.[102] The variety of rehabilitation procedures offered by insolvency law can also affect the possibilities of failures and recoveries.

In the above, and other, respects then, insolvency law, like company law, can affect a company's chances of survival or failure in difficult times. Insolvency law can also impinge on overall levels of success or failure. It is important, accordingly, to bear in mind the reasons why companies do fail when the challenges facing insolvency law are considered. Attention should be paid, for instance, to those areas of greatest contribution to failure, of greatest imposition of transaction costs and greatest impediment to recovery programmes. What insolvency law (and indeed company law) should, as a general rule, seek to avoid is loading risks and stresses on those points in corporate life where companies are at their most vulnerable.

---

100. See Insolvency Act 1986 ss. 9(2), 8(3)(a); ch. 8 below; DTI/Insolvency Service White Paper, *Productivity and Enterprise: Insolvency – A Second Chance* (Cm 5234, 2001), ch. 2 of which proposes to limit the power to appoint an AR to certain capital market transactions.
101. See P. L. Davies, 'Legal Capital in Private Companies in Great Britain' (1998) 8 *Die Aktien Gesellschaft* 346.
102. See ch. 6 below.

5

Insolvency practitioners

Corporate insolvency processes are not mere bodies of rules: they are elaborate procedures in which legal and administrative, formal and informal rules, policies and practices are put into effect by different actors. Those actors, in turn, have cultural, institutional, disciplinary and professional backgrounds which influence their work.[1] They also operate under the influence of a variety of economic, career and other incentives and are subject to a host of constraints ranging from legal duties and professional obligations to client and own-firm expectations. The Cork Report, in an oft-quoted statement, urged that the success of any insolvency system is very largely dependent upon those who administer it,[2] and socio-legal scholars have emphasised how insolvency law is not applied in a mechanical way but is manoeuvred around or manipulated by means of administrative structures 'designed and imposed by dominant actors'.[3]

This chapter looks at how insolvency law is made operational by those actors who dominate insolvency processes: the insolvency practitioners (IPs). In accordance with the discussion in chapter 2, it will be asked whether present practitioner structures and modes of operation can be

---

1. On the roles of accountants and lawyers in insolvency see J. Flood and E. Skordaki, *Insolvency Practitioners and Big Corporate Insolvencies*, ACCA Research Report 43 (ACCA, London, 1995).

2. See *Report of the Review Committee on Insolvency Law and Practice on* (Cmnd 8558, 1982) ('Cork Report') para. 732. The Government, moreover, saw insolvency practice as a key to the entire Cork reforms: see the account in B. G. Carruthers and T. C. Halliday, *Rescuing Business: The Making of Corporate Bankruptcy Law in England and the United States* (Clarendon Press, Oxford, 1998) p. 437. On the emergence of the insolvency practitioner profession see Carruthers and Halliday, *Rescuing Business*, chs. 8–11 and Flood and Skordaki, *Insolvency Practitioners*, ch. 3.

3. See S. Wheeler, 'Capital Fractionalised: The Role of Insolvency Practitioners in Asset Distribution' in M. Cain and C. B. Harrington (eds.), *Lawyers in a Post Modern World: Translation and Transgression* (Open University Press, Buckingham, 1994) pp. 85–104; Wheeler, *Reservation of Title Clauses* (Oxford University Press, Oxford, 1991).

supported as productive of insolvency regimes that are efficient, expert, fair and accountable. This will demand examinations of both the way that IPs carry out their tasks and the way that IPs are regulated.[4]

The chapter commences by outlining the development of the current administrative structure of insolvency law; it then examines IP structures and performance with reference to the above criteria; and finally it considers alternative ways of administering insolvency regimes. Before proceeding further, however, it should be emphasised that corporate insolvency involves not a single process but a number of processes. Four separate insolvency procedures for companies all involve IPs: company voluntary arrangements (CVAs); administration orders; administrative receiverships; and liquidations. These all differ markedly in their characteristics and in their approaches to the balancing of interests.

CVAs are in essence agreements between companies, their shareholders and their creditors for the satisfaction of corporate debts or for schemes of arrangement of the companies' affairs. Subject to protection for secured creditors[5] and preferential creditors,[6] the parties to the agreement are free to agree almost any terms. Party involvement in the agreement is, moreover, governed by statute: thus a proposal for a CVA needs the approval of 75 per cent of the company's unsecured creditors and over 50 per cent of its shareholders.[7] The CVA, if approved, is binding on all those who had notice of the meeting, and the company may continue to trade. An IP will be involved in giving effect to the terms of the CVA[8] but in doing so he or she can be seen to be implementing what is in essence a private contractual agreement insulated from public interest concerns.

---

4. See Insolvency Regulation Working Party (IRWP), *Insolvency Practitioner Regulation – Ten Years On* (DTI, 1998) ('IRWP Consultation Document'); IRWP, *A Review of Insolvency Practitioner Regulation* (DTI, 1999) ('IRWP Review'). The IRWP had, as members, representatives of each of the professional bodies that authorise insolvency practitioners, as well as the DTI Insolvency Service, with the Society of Practitioners of Insolvency (now renamed R3) in attendance. See further V. Finch, 'Insolvency Practitioners: Regulation and Reform' [1998] JBL 334.

5. See Insolvency Act 1986 s. 4(3).   6. Ibid., s. 4(4).

7. Both percentages calculated in value. See Insolvency Rules 1986 rr. 1.17–1.20. On CVAs under the Insolvency Act 2000 and generally see ch. 10 below; S. Hill, 'Company Voluntary Arrangements' (1990) 6 IL&P 47; Insolvency Service, *Company Voluntary Arrangements and Administration Orders: A Consultative Document* (1993); Insolvency Service, *Revised Proposals for a New Company Voluntary Arrangement Procedure* (1995); J. Flood, R. Abbey, E. Skordaki and P. Aber, *The Professional Restructuring of Corporate Rescue: Company Voluntary Arrangements and the London Approach*, ACCA Research Report (ACCA, London, 1995).

8. The IP will in practice usually have been involved in the drawing up of the proposals. On the significance attached by major creditors to the professional reputation of the IP involved see D. Milman and F. Chittenden, *Corporate Rescue: CVAs and the Challenge of Small Companies*, ACCA Research Report 44 (ACCA, London, 1995).

Administration was provided for by the Insolvency Act 1986[9] but it is a formal procedure and requires a court order. Such an order is granted on the petition of a company, its directors or one or more of its creditors[10] and results in the appointment of an administrator. One of the aims of an administration order is to sustain a business while plans are made for its future.[11] The administrator is thus involved in the day-to-day management of the company as well as in formulating rescue plans. When under an administration order, a company is protected from creditors' demands[12] and it can continue to trade, but proposals for rescue have to be agreed by creditors.

The Cork Report[13] anticipated that in rescue operations an administrator might take on board society's interests and employment considerations when deciding whether to sustain a business. The Insolvency Act 1986, however, makes no mention of such factors and the administrator looks no further than to the interests of creditors viewed solely as creditors.

Administrative receivers (ARs) are appointed without court involvement by debenture holders who hold security over the whole (or substantially the whole) of the company's assets.[14] The IP acting as an AR has a central function of realising company assets in order to meet the claims of the debenture holder and, in so doing, he or she can continue the business and can sell it as a going concern. On such a sale the AR distributes funds received to the creditors in due order of priority. The responsibility of the

---

9. See Insolvency Act 1986 ss. 8–27. CVAs were also introduced by the Insolvency Act 1986 ss. 1–7.

10. Insolvency Act 1986 s. 9. On administration generally see ch. 9 below; D. Milman, 'The Administration Order Regime and the Courts' in H. Rajak (ed.), *Insolvency Law: Theory and Practice* (Sweet & Maxwell, London, 1993) pp. 369–83; I. Dawson, 'The Administrator, Morality and the Court' [1996] JBL 437; H. Rajak, 'The Challenges of Commercial Reorganisation in Insolvency: Empirical Evidence from England' in J. S. Ziegel (ed.), *Current Developments in International and Comparative Corporate Insolvency Law* (Clarendon Press, Oxford, 1994); J. L. Westbrook, 'A Comparison of Bankruptcy Reorganisation in the US with Administration Procedure in the UK' (1990) 6 IL&P 86.

11. See Insolvency Act 1986 s. 8(3) for the specific purposes for which an administration order can be made.

12. On the moratorium see Insolvency Act 1986 ss. 10, 11; M. G. Bridge, 'Company Administrators and Secured Creditors' (1991) 107 LQR 394; A. Bacon and R. Cowper, 'The Moratorium Emasculated: Another Blow for Corporate Recovery?' (1997) 10 *Insolvency Intelligence* 73. See also ch. 9 below.

13. Para. 498.

14. See Insolvency Act 1986 s. 29(2). See further ch. 8 below. On receivers generally see I. F. Fletcher, *The Law of Insolvency* (2nd edn, Sweet & Maxwell, London, 1996) ch. 14; Cork Report, ch. 8; R. M. Goode, *Principles of Corporate Insolvency Law* (2nd edn, Sweet & Maxwell, London, 1997) ch. 9; J. S. Ziegel, 'The Privately Appointed Receiver and the Enforcement of Security Interests: Anomaly or Superior Solution?' in Ziegel (ed.), *Current Developments in International and Comparative Corporate Insolvency Law* (Clarendon Press, Oxford, 1994).

receiver is to the creditor who requested the appointment and not to the company or other creditors.[15] In essence this is, accordingly, a creditors' remedy that does not demand that the AR pay any heed to the wishes or interests of the company or to its directors, shareholders, other creditors (other than minimal obligations to report) or the interests of employees or the broader public.

Liquidators are appointed in signification of the end of a company and are responsible for collecting in the company's assets, realising them and distributing the proceeds to the company's creditors. If there is a surplus this can go to the shareholders. In compulsory liquidation a winding-up petition is made to the court and, if granted, the court orders that the company be wound up. In creditors' voluntary liquidation the shareholders resolve initially to put the company into liquidation, the creditors effectively taking control away from the shareholders at the subsequent creditors' meeting when they appoint a liquidator.[16] The IP, acting in both types of liquidation, looks to the interests of all creditors but also acts in the public interest in so far as he is under a duty to report directorial unfitness to the Disqualification Unit of the DTI's Insolvency Service as part of the disqualification process of the Company Directors' Disqualification Act (CDDA) 1986.[17]

IPs may be involved in the above four procedures[18] but other actors also have roles to play. Thus the Official Receiver (OR), an appointee of the Secretary of State, has important investigatory functions to perform when acting in cases of liquidation.[19]

The evolution of the administrative structure

Over the last two centuries accountants have sought to dominate insolvency work and have striven with some success.[20] For most of the second

---

15. See *Lathia v. Dronsfield Bros. Ltd* [1987] BCLC 321.
16. Insolvency Act 1986 ss. 99, 100, 166. On liquidation generally see ch. 12 below.
17. See S. Wheeler, 'Directors' Disqualification: Insolvency Practitioners and the Decision-making Process' (1995) 15 *Legal Studies* 283. On directors' disqualification generally see ch. 15 below; V. Finch, 'Disqualifying Directors: Issues of Rights, Privileges and Employment' (1993) ILJ 35; Finch, 'Disqualification of Directors: A Plea for Competence' (1990) 53 MLR 385.
18. Corporate insolvency procedures do not, of course, exhaust the work of IPs. They are also involved in the personal side of insolvency (bankruptcy) as nominees and supervisors of IVAs and as trustees in bankruptcy. See Finch, 'Insolvency Practitioners', pp. 353–4; Fletcher, *Law of Insolvency*, chs. 3, 4, 7.
19. Especially in compulsory liquidation: Insolvency Act 1986 s. 136. The OR is a civil servant and officer of the court. There are currently forty OR offices in England and Wales: see IS Annual Report 2000–1, p. 13.
20. See Flood and Skordaki, *Insolvency Practitioners*, ch. 3; C. Napier and C. Noke, 'Accounting and Law: An Historical Overview of an Uneasy Relationship' in M. Bromwich and A. G.

half of the nineteenth century many accountancy firms earned the vast majority of their fees from insolvency work and it was, indeed, this work that boosted not only accountants' incomes but also their professional organisation.[21] Accountants throughout this period have consistently emphasised their superior professional expertise to lawyers in the insolvency field. By the time that the Cork Committee deliberated, however, a number of worries had arisen, notably regarding the qualifications of those persons engaged in insolvency work.[22] The Cork Report itself was concerned that arrangements prior to the date of its inquiry were open to abuse and did not command public confidence.[23] The Report accepted the case for a scheme of IP regulation operating under ministerial control and covering all persons, other than the OR, who hold office as liquidators, trustees in bankruptcy, administrative receivers, administrators or supervisors of voluntary arrangements. The regime envisaged by Cork anticipated that IPs would be provided by the private sector but would be required to be members of an officially recognised and regulated professional body capable of exercising disciplinary supervision over an individual acting as an IP. In the case of IPs who did not belong to a recognised professional body (RPB), these would be licensed individually by the Department of Trade with a view to ensuring proper levels of competence, skill and integrity.

The Insolvency Act 1986 gives legislative effect to the Cork vision and restricts action as an office holder in any designated insolvency proceeding to persons qualified under the 1986 Act.[24] Qualification is achieved by the methods advocated by the Cork Report, namely membership of, and authorisation by, an RPB or licensing directly by the Secretary of State. Acting as an IP in any designated proceeding when not qualified to do so constitutes a criminal offence.[25]

There are now seven RPBs which may grant authorisation.[26] This will only be forthcoming for individuals, not firms, and only on demonstrating, through professional examinations, a prescribed level of technical knowledge and expertise in accountancy and law. Since 1990 all applicants

---

Hopwood (eds.), *Accounting and the Law* (Institute of Chartered Accountants in England and Wales, London, 1992).

21. Flood and Skordaki, *Insolvency Practitioners*, p. 10.

22. Cork Report, ch. 15.

23. See generally Fletcher, *Law of Insolvency*, ch. 2; I. Snaith with assistance of F. Cownie, *The Law of Corporate Insolvency* (Waterlow, London, 1990) ch. 10; Cork Report, para. 756.

24. Insolvency Act 1986 s. 230. Excluded from the qualification requirement are ORs and receivers appointed by the court or holders of fixed charges.

25. Insolvency Act 1986 s. 389.

26. The ACCA, ICAEW, ICAS, ICAI, LS, LSS and IPA. For the Secretary of State's authorising of RPBs see Insolvency Act 1986 s. 391 and the Insolvency Practitioners (Recognised Professional Bodies) Order 1986 (SI 1986 No. 1764).

to become qualified IPs have been required to pass an examination organised centrally by the Joint Insolvency Examining Board (JIEB), whichever RPB they belong to. They must also be able to demonstrate a minimum level of appropriate experience. Those who apply for qualification to the Secretary of State rather than to an RPB must generally pass the JIEB examination, though a discretion to make exceptions exists.[27] There are now just over 1,800 IPs in the UK who are authorised and regulated by the Secretary of State directly or by an RPB.[28]

On insolvency matters the Secretary of State's functions are exercised through the Insolvency Service (IS) which is an executive agency of the DTI. It is headed by a chief executive, the Inspector General, and employs around 1,550 staff. The IS is responsible for, amongst other things, advising on the form and effectiveness of insolvency legislation, ensuring that the RPBs regulate their members properly with suitable rules that are effectively enforced and authorising and regulating Secretary of State authorised IPs.[29] The Secretary of State issues a Framework Document setting down objectives for the IS and, as well as monitoring the RPBs, the IS runs a twice-yearly 'licensing forum' for discussion of authorisation and regulatory issues with the RPBs.

The bulk of RPB-authorised IPs are accountants. The Institute of Chartered Accountants of England and Wales (ICAEW) has the largest number of IPs (834 on 1 January 1997). Many of these are not full-time IPs but are general accountancy practitioners, some with audit and investment business clients. Around 16 per cent of its IPs generate insolvency fee income of under £50,000 per annum and around 20 per cent are full-time IPs from the Big Five accountancy firms.[30]

The RPBs act as self-regulators in so far as they exercise control over their own qualified members, but the system constitutes governmentally monitored self-regulation since the IS supervises the regulatory process,

---

27. See IRWP Consultation Document pp. 13–14.
28. In 2000 there were 124 IPs who were authorised by the Secretary of State: see IS Annual Report 2000–1, p. 28.
29. The IS's Control Unit conducted monitoring visits to three RPBs in 2000–1 and to twenty-nine practitioners authorised by the Secretary of State. The IS also takes, *inter alia*, disqualification proceedings against unfit directors and carries out, through its ORs, the functions of liquidators in compulsory liquidations and trustees in bankruptcy. The IS also monitors, on a day-to-day basis, those IPs directly authorised by the Secretary of State. The IRWP Review (p. 22) recommends that this monitoring function ought to be contracted out to a professional body so as to leave the IS to concentrate on its functions as a regulator of the RPBs' regulatory activities.
30. IRWP Consultation Document p. 44. On the historical evolution of the dominance of the accountancy profession over insolvency work see Flood and Skordaki, *Insolvency Practitioners*, ch. 3.

conducts regular visits to each of the RPBs and seeks to ensure that standards are maintained. For their part, the RPBs operate a variety of control measures designed to control and correct misconduct. A range of disciplinary penalties applies to members and includes the sanction of expulsion from membership – which, for an RPB authorised practitioner, will produce automatic revocation of authorisation.

The RPBs have, since 1994, carried out monitoring visits to all IPs and some co-operate in carrying out such functions, notably by using the services of the Joint Insolvency Monitoring Unit. There are differences in style and form of regulation among the seven RPBs (each, for instance, has its own complaints mechanism) and these reflect variations in traditions as well as powers of intervention. A degree of consistency of approach derives, however, from the RPBs' common subjection to a memorandum of understanding with the Secretary of State[31] and to monitoring by reference to common standards required and approved by the IS.

Establishment of the Society for Practitioners in Insolvency (SPI), a multi-disciplinary trade association, paved the way for lawyers and accountants to develop a shared professional perspective on insolvency work.[32] Around 80 per cent of all IPs belong to this body, now known as R3,[33] and its activities include assisting with training, continuing professional education and ethical issues as well as the issuing of guidance notes.

Harmonisation of the RPBs' approaches is assisted, in particular, by the RPBs' system of best practice guidance. Statements of Insolvency Practice are adopted by the RPBs. These are drafted by R3 after consultation with the RPBs and the IS and are absorbed within each of the RPBs' own regulatory regimes.[34] They have persuasive rather than mandatory force. Differences of regulation do, nevertheless, remain within the overall system. The IS, working within a statutory framework, has, for instance, no sanction against its IPs other than removal of authorisation. The seven RPBs can make their own regulations and impose their own penalties and the RPBs responsible for solicitors have statutory powers of intervention.

---

31. The memorandum covers authorisation, handling of complaints, monitoring activities, best practice and exchange of information between RPBs.

32. See Flood and Skordaki, *Insolvency Practitioners*, p. 37.

33. On 28 January 2000 the SPI renamed itself R3: the Association of Business Recovery Professionals.

34. Statements of Insolvency Practice (SIPs) have been issued on a number of topics including liquidators' investigations into the affairs of an insolvent company, records of meetings in formal insolvency proceedings and remuneration of insolvency office holders. On remuneration see SIP 9, 1996 and p. 153 below. The Best Practice Liaison Committee, attended by the IS, RPBs and R3, meets a number of times a year to monitor progress on preparing SIPs.

Evaluating the structure

Efficiency

Criticisms of IP performance in recent years have focused on the charges made for services rendered and the value for money that has been supplied.[35] Matters came to a head in 1997 when, in three large insolvencies, accountants acting as IPs charged huge fees but recovered little for creditors. The three accounting firms handling the administration of the Maxwell empire reported fees of nearly £35 million and the receivers to the Robert Maxwell estate, accountants Buchler Phillips, recovered £1.672 million but their bills, together with those of solicitors Nabarro Nathanson, came to £1.628 million, leaving only £44,000 for creditors.[36] In *Mirror Group Newspapers plc* v. *Maxwell*[37] Ferris J described the fee claim as 'profoundly shocking', adding: 'If the amounts claimed are allowed in full, this receivership will have produced substantial rewards for the receivers and their lawyers and nothing at all for the creditors of the estate. I find it shameful that a court receivership should produce this result in relation to an order of more than £1.5 million.'[38]

Mr Justice Ferris noted increased concern at the generally perceived high level of costs in insolvency cases and other judges had already spoken out on the subject. Mr Justice Lightman expressed concern in a November 1995 lecture to the Insolvency Lawyers' Association[39] and, returning to the topic in 1998, he noted the 'visceral disquiet' in the press on the subject.[40]

How then should charging levels be approached? At present, those who have power to fix the remuneration of office holders fall into two

35. Press comments on IPs' fees have used terms such as 'obscene', 'vultures' and 'vampires': see Flood and Skordaki, *Insolvency Practitioners*, p. 23.

36. See 'Insolvency Experts in Firing Line over Fees', *Financial Times*, 1 August 1997. The collapse of the Bank of Credit and Commerce International (BCCI) yielded fees of over $169.2m for Touche Ross, and the administrators of Polly Peck International charged (with legal fees) nearly £25m.

37. [1998] BCC 324.

38. Mr Justice Ferris passed the issue to a taxing officer, Master Hurst, whose judgment was delivered in April 1999: see *Mirror Group Newspapers* v. *Maxwell and Others* [1999] BCC 684. Buchler Phillips was awarded 99 per cent of its claim and no wrongdoing was found in its conduct. Blame was laid on the way Maxwell had organised his business: 'Many assets which on the face of it appeared to be the personal property of Mr Maxwell were either worthless or, because of the immensely complex financial labyrinth which he had constructed, could not ultimately be recovered as personal property.' See J. Kelly, 'The Recovery Position', *Financial Times*, 22 April 1999.

39. See Mr Justice Lightman, 'The Challenges Ahead' [1996] JBL 113.

40. See Mr Justice Lightman, 'Office Holders' Charges: Cost, Control and Transparency' (1998) 11 *Insolvency Intelligence* 1. See also Mr Justice Lightman, 'Office Holders: Evidence, Security and Independence' [1997] CfiLR 145.

categories. In the first, there are liquidation committees, creditors' committees, general bodies of creditors, or (in some cases) those persons appointing the office holder. In the second, there is the court, which may act in exercise of an original jurisdiction or in an appellate capacity.[41] In the case of most IPs who act as receivers, their fees are fixed by the debenture holders (usually the banks) and are based on time and expenses. In liquidations, IPs may charge a percentage of the value of assets realised or distributed, or they may bill by time, bearing in mind also any complexities, exceptional responsibilities and so forth. The creditors' committees authorise remuneration. This has given rise to the criticism that, in a professionally comfortable arrangement, accountants, sitting in creditors' committees, are left to authorise the payment levels of their fellow accountants.[42] The criteria governing remuneration levels set by courts are set out in a number of items of primary or secondary legislation[43] but diverse approaches are contained in these rules and, except in relation to provisional liquidators, the rules fail to lay down criteria for use by the court in fixing remuneration.

In July 1998 Mr Justice Ferris delivered a report on office-holder[44] remuneration to the Lord Chancellor.[45] The Ferris Report urged that all parties (courts or other bodies) should look to the same criteria when fixing remuneration and that the aim should be to provide IPs with 'reasonable', not 'minimal', remuneration. Ferris argued that the system of setting rewards should be predictable, transparent and proportional and

---

41. See Report of Mr Justice Ferris' Working Party on *The Remuneration of Office Holders and Certain Related Matters* (London, 1998) ('Ferris Report').

42. See Flood and Skordaki, *Insolvency Practitioners*, p. 23. For details of an R3-funded study of IP remuneration see D. Milman, 'Remuneration: Researching the Fourth R' (2000) *Recovery* (August) 18.

43. The following office holders have remuneration fixed pursuant to the following rules: court-appointed receiver, RSC, Ord. 30, rr. 3 and 5; receiver and manager of a company's property appointed under an instrument, Insolvency Act 1986 s. 36; administrator appointed under Part II of the Insolvency Act 1986, Insolvency Rules 1986 r. 2.47(6); provisional liquidator, Insolvency Rules 1986 r. 4.30; liquidator, Insolvency Rules 1986 rr. 4.130 and 4.148A; special manager under Insolvency Act 1986 s. 177, Insolvency Rules 1986 r. 4.206(5); trustees in bankruptcy, Insolvency Rules 1986 rr. 6.138, 6.141 and 6.142.

44. The term 'office holder' was introduced by the Insolvency Act 1986 ss. 230–46. These sections, however, show that the 'office holder' is not a definite class of IP but more of a 'drafting expedient' in that the expression is differently defined for the purposes of different sections and 'simply means the class of IP to which the particular section or group of sections is intended to apply': see D. Milman and C. Durrant, *Corporate Insolvency: Law and Practice* (3rd edn, Sweet & Maxwell, London, 1999) p. 17.

45. Ferris Report. For comments see K. Theobold, 'The Ferris Report' (1998) 14 IL&P 300; Lightman, 'Office Holders' Charges'; the Hon. Mr Justice Ferris, 'Insolvency Remuneration: Translating Adjectives into Action' [1999] Ins. Law. 48.

that two bases of remuneration should be adopted. In smaller cases, a new scale of charging (to be further considered) would replace the OR's scale[46] as a basis for remunerating office holders in private practice. The aim here was to reduce transaction costs and unduly high fees. The OR's scale applies in relation to a diversity of offices and is used in default of some other rate of remuneration being agreed. Many IPs, however, consider that the OR's scale is unrealistically low. This leads them to negotiate fees and often they gain inappropriately high fees due to 'ignorance or idleness on the part of the creditors' committees'.[47] The Ferris proposal for more generous scale fees was designed to encourage reference to the scale (a relatively cheap process for setting fees) and to produce fewer negotiations of excessive remuneration. In all cases where a scale or percentage was not appropriate, Ferris urged that reference should be made not simply to time spent but to value provided. In assessing the latter, the criteria deemed relevant should be those presently governing provisional liquidators,[48] namely: the time properly given to the company's affairs; the complexity of the case; any responsibility of an exceptional kind; the effectiveness with which the duties have been carried out; and the value and nature of the property that had to be dealt with.[49]

A strong theme in the Ferris Report was the office-holder's need to justify claims to remuneration with proper recording mechanisms that go beyond mere time records but justify the carrying out of the work at issue. Thus, within proportionate bounds, the office holder, said Ferris, should explain the nature of the main tasks undertaken; the reasons for carrying out, or persevering with, that work; and the time spent on those tasks. The test of whether an office holder acted properly in undertaking particular tasks at a particular cost was whether a reasonably prudent man would expend money on such actions,[50] and the charging rate should be the

---

46. Set out in Insolvency Regulations 1994 regs. 33–6 and Sched. 2.

47. See Ferris, 'Insolvency Remuneration', p. 50. In 1996, the SPI sought to respond to criticisms of IP fee levels by issuing guidelines (Statement of Insolvency Practice) requiring IPs to explain to creditors their rights if they are dissatisfied with fees or costs as well as the bases of remuneration. The rules state that they must be made available to 'every identifiable creditor' before any resolution is passed to fix fees for insolvency office holders.

48. Insolvency Rules 1986 r. 4.30.

49. The Ferris Report, para. 6.6, considered that the criteria noted embraced a number of other criteria that had been put to the Committee as relevant, viz: the need for investigatory work leading to additional realisations; the commercial and/or personal risks involved; the current time rates generally adopted by IPs for the type of work; any antisocial hours involved; and any international aspects involved.

50. See the judgment of Mr Justice Ferris in the *Maxwell* case.

broad average or general rate charged by persons of the relevant status and qualifications who carry out this work.[51]

The costs of the IS have also been the subject of criticism. In 1996–7 the total expenditure of the IS was £76 million but the net cost to the taxpayer was £9 million. This result has been achieved by a 'combination of fixed fees and draconian percentage charges'.[52] Thus, the fee scales provide for the OR acting as liquidator to charge 20 per cent on the first tranche of realisations and 10 per cent on the first tranche of distributions. At the same time, creditors' money, as realised by trustees in bankruptcy and liquidators, is paid into the Insolvency Services Account (ISA), where in 1996–7 it generated banking fees of £16 million and a £37 million surplus investment income, but did not pay more than a low rate of interest (subject to tax) to creditors.[53] The overall effect, say critics, is to penalise creditors – most strikingly in those years when the investment account produces a surplus.[54]

The Cork Committee received strong and widespread criticism of the ISA regime,[55] particularly in regard to the low rate of return on compulsory deposits. The requirement that an IP deposit surplus funds in the ISA was also attacked as providing an incentive for liquidators to protract proceedings and delay the submission of accounts. Cork urged that the administration of insolvency was a public service and should be paid for out of general taxation rather than funded by creditors. The existing system, said Cork, was costly, time-consuming and unfair[56] and, instead, liquidators should be obliged to deposit funds in an interest-bearing account. As an alternative to public funding of the IS, Cork recommended that there should be a levy on the registration of new companies.[57] The rationale for use of the ISA has, moreover, been undermined by the 1986 Insolvency Act.

---

51. In relation to solicitors' charges see *Jones* v. *Secretary of State for Wales* [1997] 1 WLR 1008. It should be noted that such a notion of the 'going' or 'market' rate may prove generous where the market is organised by a profession that influences standard charges and so is not fully competitive.

52. See H. Anderson, 'A Fair Share of the Company Failures Cake', *Financial Times*, 7 April 1998.

53. Ibid.

54. See Justice, *Insolvency Law: An Agenda for Reform* (Justice, London, 1994) paras. 5.7–5.11; Cork Report, ch. 17, paras. 847–55. In 1991–2 the IS paid a surplus of £5 million to the DTI (*Financial Times*, 2 September 1992) and in 1992–3 the surplus was £9 million: Justice, *Insolvency Law*. Net income from the Insolvency Services Investment Account in the years 1995–6 and 1996–7 was £45 million and £31.4 million respectively.

55. Cork Report, paras. 847–55.

56. Ibid., p. 201. For further criticism see Justice, *Insolvency Law*.

57. Cork Report, p.201.

Historically the ISA was used to prevent unscrupulous practitioners misappropriating funds but the 1986 Act set up a licensing and bonding system[58] that offers protection from, and compensation for, such abuse. The Government has now taken in these points and in its 2001 White Paper[59] argued that the ISA regime produced revenues for the Government but did not enable income from the insolvency fund to be used in order to deal with cases properly. The White Paper concluded that paying the bulk of the interest generated on insolvency funds into government coffers could no longer be justified and this position should be redressed legislatively.[60]

Expertise

When the Cork Committee considered the qualifications of IPs, it noted that the absence of some 'minimal qualification' was much criticised.[61] The Committee then stressed that 'a certain degree of knowledge and experience' was essential for the IPs to discharge their functions adequately. They needed to be familiar with the relevant law on: debtor–creditor relations; the organisation and proceedings of courts dealing with insolvency; the investigation of business dealings and transactions of insolvent debtors; the pursuit and recovery of assets fraudulently disposed of; voidable preferences; and the distribution of assets to creditors. The IP, moreover, had to be capable of taking complete control of a business of some size and complexity and of carrying it on to sell as a going concern or to make other proposals for its continuance as an economic unit.

The Cork Report, as noted, served as a foundation for the systems of entry screening, qualification and monitoring that have been described above. It can be argued that the current regime's reliance on professional control through different 'home' RPBs encourages a breadth of expertise in IPs.[62] Thus, accountancy and lawyer-based IPs are required to display qualities of general professional expertise in a manner that would, perhaps, not be the case if IPs were regulated as a discrete, more narrowly defined, profession.

---

58. IPs must obtain and deposit with their authorising RPB (or the Secretary of State) a bond issued by an insurance company by which it makes itself jointly and severally liable with the IP for the proper performance of his duties: Insolvency Act 1986 s. 390(3); IP Regulations 1990 regs. 11 and 12(1) and Sched. 2, Part 11 (as amended by the IP (Amendment) Regulations 1993). The bond must be for the general sum of £250,000 and for additional specific sums in accordance with the prescribed limit applicable to particular cases in which the IP is to act. (The amount of required cover is calculated by reference to the value of the assets of the insolvent with a minimum of £5,000 and a maximum of £5 million.)

59. DTI/Insolvency Service, *Productivity and Enterprise: Insolvency – A Second Chance* (Cm 5234, 2001).

60. Ibid., para. 1.51.   61. Cork Report, para. 735.   62. See IRWP Review, pp. 35–6.

Questions can still be raised, however, about the scope of IPs' skills. A 1995 analysis of CVAs asked whether IPs are the right people to carry these arrangements out since, by training, they know best 'how to kill companies'.[63] IPs have, in addition, been found to possess a limited knowledge of CVAs,[64] and it has been suggested that the 'going concern' departments of the Big Five accountancy firms might be better equipped to engage in corporate rescues than the IPs who are actually involved with insolvencies.[65] The statistics reveal that receiverships and liquidations are popular in comparison with administrations and CVAs, and Flood *et al.* argue that a senior accountant captured the essence of the IP vision of insolvency work in saying 'We are debt collectors.'[66] This line of analysis suggests that the training, expertise and approach of IPs is not sufficiently grounded in managerial skills to encourage them to give proper weight to rescue in reviewing options for troubled companies. The law may set up a variety of insolvency procedures but here we see that the machineries of implementation may have a very considerable role in shaping insolvency processes on the ground.

A concern voiced in recent years is not so much that IPs lack skills but that, within the insolvency process, there is often an imbalance of skills in favour of IPs. This topic, however, will be considered in dealing with fairness.

Fairness

Does the present regime of implementing insolvency processes ensure fairness to affected parties?[67] If IPs are allowed to act where conflicts of interest arise there is a potential for unfairness or bias, and insolvency processes have the capacity to throw up a plethora of conflicts of interests for IPs. The latter, and their firms, for instance, may have ongoing links with different companies or creditors who are involved in various ways in an insolvency; relationships with the directors of individual companies may create conflicts; personal interests and other appointments held may be relevant; the IP's firm may have financial interests present or future that

---

63. See Flood *et al.*, *Professional Restructuring*, p. 17. R3 has, however, now established a Society of Turnaround Professionals, which held its first AGM in 2001, and it is to be expected that such an organisation will contribute to the development of a rescue culture: see 'Turnaround Talk' (2001) *Recovery* (September).

64. See L. Gee, *How Effective are Voluntary Arrangements?* (Levy Gee, London, 1994).

65. Flood *et al.*, *Professional Restructuring*, p. 17.   66. Ibid.

67. This section of the chapter builds on V. Finch, 'Controlling the Insolvency Professionals' [1999] Ins. Law. 228.

are potentially affected by advice or decisions relating to a troubled company; and the quantity of work or remuneration that an IP receives may be affected by actions or recommendations made.

It is, accordingly, necessary to consider how the present system controls such conflicts. The Insolvency Act 1986 does not expressly prevent an IP from acting where there is a conflict, but in considering whether a person is fit and proper to act as an IP, the Secretary of State[68] must take into account whether, in any case, the applicant has acted as an IP but has failed fully to disclose to persons who might reasonably be expected to be affected that there is, or appears to be, a conflict of interest between his so acting and any interest of his own (personal, financial or otherwise). The Secretary of State must also consider whether the insolvency practice of the applicant is, has been, or will be carried on with the independence, integrity and professional skills appropriate.[69]

These provisions do not apply to the RPBs who also authorise persons to act as IPs, but the RPBs and the DTI do issue guidance on conflicts of interest.[70] The Secretary of State's 'Code of Conduct' warns practitioners to be vigilant about potential conflicts of interest between their IP work and any personal, professional or financial commitments which might impair their objectivity or appear to do so. Specifically prohibited in the Code is acting as a liquidator after having acted as an administrative receiver, and the appointment of auditors as liquidators or administrative receivers, except in the case of a members' voluntary liquidation, where it is beyond reasonable doubt that the company is solvent and that all debts can be satisfied within a twelve-month period. Similar rules are issued by the accountancy bodies in a combined approach through the ICAEW, but the ICAEW's Statement on Insolvency Practice[71] expresses rules on accepting appointments in greater detail than the Secretary of State's Code of Conduct. A key notion is that of the 'material professional relationship'.

---

68. The Insolvency Practitioner Regulations 1990 specify the matters to be taken into account by the Secretary of State in determining whether a person is fit and proper to hold an IP licence. Section 419 of the Insolvency Act 1986 empowers the Secretary of State to make regulations prohibiting persons from acting as IPs where conflicts of interest may arise. No such regulations have been made.
69. See Insolvency Practitioner Regulations 1990 reg. 4(1).
70. See generally H. Anderson, 'Insolvency Practitioners: Professional Independence and Conflict of Interest' in A. Clarke (ed.), *Current Issues in Insolvency Law* (Stevens, London, 1991) pp. 1–25.
71. ICAEW, Guide to Professional Ethics, Statement on Insolvency Practice, September 1998. Solicitors are regulated in accordance with the Solicitors Practice Rules 1990, as amended. (See *The Guide to the Professional Conduct of Solicitors* (8th edn, Law Society, 1999), Insolvency Practice.)

This arises where 'material'[72] work is being carried out, or has been carried out, during the previous three years, and means that an IP who is a member of a recognised accountancy body should not act as an IP in relation to a company if they, or their partners, have been auditors to that company or if they have carried out one or more 'significant'[73] assignments within three years of the onset of the company's insolvency. (Such requirements do not, however, rule out an IP acting in a members' voluntary liquidation as long as he has given 'careful consideration' to all the implications of acceptance in the particular case and is satisfied that the directors' declaration of solvency is likely to be substantiated by events.[74])

The courts, for their part, have stressed that IPs must consider not only their own personal or professional interests and connections but also whether persons with whom they are associated have held appointments that would lead to a lack of independence. Harman J has stated that it would be most unlikely (but not totally impossible) that a director could ever be a proper liquidator of a company.[75] In *Re Lowestoft Traffic Services Co. Ltd*[76] Hoffmann J stated that the public interest required that a liquidator should not only be independent, but should be seen to be independent, and he displaced a liquidator from office following considerable creditor disquiet at the appointment.[77] Conflicts of interest, moreover, arise where an IP holds a number of appointments and acts for more than one company involved in an insolvency: where, for example, a group is liquidated and the IP acts as liquidator for the parent company and the subsidiary companies. The courts have, however, tended to adopt an accepting attitude to such conflicts, seeing them as inevitable and routinely handled by experienced IPs.[78] The ICAEW Statement on Insolvency Practice acknowledges the possibility of conflicts but states that it would be 'impracticable' for a series of different IPs to act.[79] Where a direct conflict may arise, the courts may work around this by allowing IPs to secure the appointment

---

72. As defined in ICAEW, Insolvency Practice, paras 7.0 and 7.1.

73. See ICAEW, Insolvency Practice, para. 7.0 (ii) 'where a practice or person has carried out one or more assignments, whether of a continuing nature or not, of such overall significance or in such circumstances that a member's objectivity in carrying out a subsequent insolvency appointment might or reasonably could be seen to be prejudiced'.

74. See ICAEW, Insolvency Practice, para. 10.0.

75. See *Re Corbenstoke Ltd (No. 2)* [1989] 5 BCC 767.

76. [1986] BCLC 81; [1986] 2 BCC 98.

77. The liquidator had been appointed at a creditors' meeting where the chairman (a director) had used proxy voting to outvote the creditors, who favoured another IP. See also *Re Rhine Film Corporation (UK) Ltd* [1986] 2 BCC 98.

78. See Dillon LJ in the Court of Appeal in *Re Esal (Commodities) Ltd* [1988] 4 BCC 475.

79. See ICAEW, Insolvency Practice, para. 22.0; Anderson, 'Insolvency Practitioners', p. 14.

of independent persons to deal with specific issues of conflict. Thus, in *Re Maxwell Communications Corp*.[80] Hoffmann J declined to appoint an additional administrator where the existing administrators had acted for Robert Maxwell personally. He considered the conflicts to be only distant possibilities and able to be dealt with by allowing the existing administrators an area of discretion.

As for powers of control, the courts may remove liquidators,[81] administrative receivers,[82] administrators,[83] supervisors of CVAs[84] and voluntary liquidators.[85] Parties aggrieved by the acts of liquidators may apply to the courts to reverse or modify these,[86] although the courts are generally reluctant to interfere in the administration of insolvency.[87] Creditors, or members of the company, who are aggrieved by the actions of an administrator may similarly apply to the court under the 1986 Act.[88] IPs also owe common law duties of care and good faith to the company,[89] and liquidators in compulsory windings up and administrators are considered to be officers of the court and obliged to act honourably.[90] It should not be forgotten, furthermore, that under the Human Rights Act 1998 and Article 6 of the Convention, there is a right, *inter alia*, to an independent and impartial tribunal. Where, accordingly, IPs act as office holders and determine rights, conflicts of interests may be pointed to and human rights issues raised.[91]

The above controls have not, however, removed fears that harmful conflicts of interest are involved when investigating accountants are

80. [1992] BCLC 465, 469.   **81.** Insolvency Act 1986 s. 172.   **82.** Ibid., s. 45.
83. Ibid., s. 19(1).   **84.** Ibid., s. 7(5).
85. Ibid., s. 108. See *Re Keypack Homecare Ltd* [1987] BCLC 409. Liquidators may still be removed in some cases without the court being involved: see Insolvency Act 1986 ss. 171–2.
86. Insolvency Act 1986 ss. 168(5), 112(1).
87. See *Re Hans Place Ltd* [1993] BCLC 768; *Re Edennote Ltd* [1996] 2 BCLC 389. The passing of the Human Rights Act 1998 may give rise to incidences of judicial oversight. It will cover the actions of ORs and is likely also to apply to IPs carrying out functions of a public nature. Challenges based on the protection of property rights (Article 1 of First Protocol) or privacy (Article 8 of Convention) may, for example, be made in the courts: see A. Arora, 'The Human Rights Act 1998: Some Implications for Commercial Law and Practice' (2001) 3 *Finance and Credit Law* 1; R. Tateossian, 'Briefing' (2000) 2 *Finance and Credit Law* 5; N. Pike, 'The Human Rights Act 1998 and its Impact on Insolvency Practitioners' [2001] Ins. Law. 25.
88. Insolvency Act 1986 s. 27, arguing that the company's affairs etc. are being or have been managed by the administrator in a manner which is unfairly prejudicial to their interests: see ch. 9 below. On liquidation, liquidators, administrative receivers and administrators can be found liable for breaches of duty (or 'misfeasance') under Insolvency Act 1986 s. 212; see chs. 8, 9 and 12 below.
89. *Re AMF International Ltd (No. 2)* [1996] 2 BCLC 9; *Re Home and Colonial Insurance Co. Ltd* [1930] 1 Ch 102; *Re Windsor Steam Coal Co. (1901) Ltd* [1929] 1 Ch 151; *Pulsford* v. *Devenish* [1903] 2 Ch 625.
90. They are therefore subject to the rule in *Ex parte James, Re Condon* (1874) 9 Ch App 609. See further I. Dawson, 'Administrator, Morality and the Court'.
91. See W. Trower, 'Human Rights: Article 6: The Reality and the Myth' [2001] Ins. Law. 48; see also n. 87 above.

appointed as receivers.[92] A common business occurrence is that a bank, with concerns about the viability of a debtor company, will appoint accountants, often IPs, to investigate and report on the company's financial situation and prospects. (Such investigating accountants may also be called in by directors of the company who seek reassurance that it is proper to continue trading.[93]) If these investigators report that it is possible to save the company, and devise an action plan for the bank accordingly, they will receive fees for the investigation and planning. If, on the other hand, the investigators advise the bank that the safest way to secure repayment of funds is to appoint a receiver, there is a high probability that the investigating firm of accountants will pick up the lucrative receivership work that ensues.[94] This is because they can argue that the investigating accountants are already familiar with the company's books, figures and position and because the bank is usually the largest secured creditor and is likely to be well placed to insist on the appointment of the receiver of its choice. As for other affected parties such as unsecured creditors, employees, customers of the company and shareholders, they are poorly placed to contest the investigator's findings because they do not have the information that would be necessary to make authoritative claims concerning the company's prospects of viability.

The investigators are subject to real conflicts of interests: they are in a position to report on the company's viability but have a chance of privileged access to work and to assets. They are likely to ensure that the bank (which is effectively the investigating firm's real client) obtains as much of the insolvency assets as possible. It has also been alleged that: 'Certain IPs, in their guise as receivers, gorge themselves on the cash and assets at the expense of the main body of ordinary unsecured creditors and shareholders...the receivers' fees are, of course, preferred and secured over all others.'[95] The real danger is that such conflicts can produce biased advice to creditors and may exacerbate the existing propensity of large secured creditors to look to their own, not the company's or

---

92. See Flood and Skordaki, *Insolvency Practitioners*, pp. 16–17. Note, of course, that only *administrative* receivers have to be IPs: Insolvency Act 1986 s. 388(1).

93. The directors may be concerned about future liability under the Insolvency Act 1986 s. 214, 'wrongful' trading: see ch. 15 below.

94. Conflicts of interest appear stark where the investigation has been carried out for no fee and the only way the accountant can recover costs is by appointment as receiver: see J. Wilding, 'Instructing Investigating Accountants' (1994) 7 *Insolvency Intelligence* 3 (who states that 'in nearly all cases if the bank decides to appoint a receiver subsequent to an investigation, then it is the investigating accountant who will be appointed').

95. See Lord Evans of Watford in HL Debates, vol. 596, cols. 432–3, 26 January 1999.

body of creditors' interests, and to end the lives of companies before they have been given a reasonable opportunity of recovery. No independent ombudsman reviews complaints on these matters and there is no compensation scheme. The regime has been characterised as 'the Chaps regulating the Chaps'.[96]

Concerns at these potential conflicts of interest were voiced in a House of Lords debate in January 1999, a debate marked by a unanimity of view on the need to control such conflicts.[97] Note was taken of evidence suggesting that existing arrangements did tend to produce an investigators' bias in favour of receivership rather than continuity of corporate operations. Attention was drawn to a 1993 change of policy by the Royal Bank of Scotland (RBS) when it decided to stop the practice of appointing a company's investigating accountants as its receivers. The RBS also adopted a policy of 'rescue' rather than 'burial' as a first response to corporate problems. Over a subsequent four-year period the RBS's share of receiverships fell from 11 per cent to 5 per cent and in 1996 the number of the bank's receiverships was 82 per cent lower than in 1992.[98] The RBS calculated that if it had not changed its policy, 279 more companies would have gone out of business and some 56,000 jobs would have been lost. Extrapolating to the UK as a whole, this implied that in the given period 2,200 companies and 44,700 jobs could have been saved by a generalised change of policy of the kind adopted by the RBS.[99] On the propensity of investigators to favour receiverships, researchers at Warwick University found in 1992 that 97.5 per cent of investigating accountants were subsequently appointed receivers to the company they investigated initially.[100] The SPI conducted a survey of its membership in 1994 and found that in 35 per cent of cases investigating accountants recommended receivership.

96. See G. McCormack, 'Receiverships and the Rescue Culture' [2000] 2 CFILR 229, 245; P. Sikka, 'Turkeys Don't Vote for Christmas, Do They?' (1999) Insolvency Bulletin 5 (June); J. Cousins, A. Mitchell, P. Sikka, C. Cooper and P. Arnold, Insolvency Abuse: Regulating the Insolvency Service (Association for Accounting and Business Affairs, 2000).

97. Lord McIntosh of Haringey noted that 'every single speaker' had supported Baroness Dean of Thornton-le-Fylde in her call to end the practice of investigators being appointed as receivers: HL Debates, vol. 596, col. 947, 26 January 1999.

98. See T. Kennedy, 'Rescue Culture: The Royal Bank of Scotland's Approach' (1997) Insolvency Bulletin (September); Baroness Dean of Thornton-le-Fylde, HL Debates, vol. 596, col. 937, 26 January 1999; R. Newton, 'Insolvency Bar Reaps Results at Royal Bank' (1994) Accountancy Age, 10 February.

99. What was not mentioned in the debate, however, was the point that the number and proportion of receiverships had fallen in the economy as a whole, over the same reporting period. See further D. Finn, 'Conflict of Interest' (1999) Insolvency Bulletin (March).

100. Referred to at HL Debates, vol. 596, col. 937; but see the counter-evidence of A. Katz and M. Mumford in their ICAEW/ICRA sponsored research project 'Should Investigating Accountants be Allowed to Become Receivers? The Question of Continuity', ICAEW Discussion Document, September 1999 (see also the version at (2000) Recovery 20).

The relevant professional ethics do not prohibit investigators from taking subsequent appointments as receivers but hold that if open discussions of the financial affairs of the company are thereby prevented, then the propriety of a subsequent appointment as receiver might have to be justified by an investigating member or other principal in the relevant practice. In short, transparency is seen as the control over the potential conflict. Banks and IPs tend to oppose a prohibition on subsequent appointment as receivers and do so on efficiency grounds, arguing that a fresh IP would have to undertake the expense of coming up to speed on the firm's position (work already carried out by the investigator) and that such additional costs would be burdens on the creditors.

In the January 1999 House of Lords debate, Baroness Dean called on the Government to ask the ICAEW and other bodies to change their rules to stop investigating firms becoming receivers and drew attention to a 1992 finding by the Ethics Committee of the ICAEW that some 30 per cent of accountants believed there to be an 'actual, not just perceived, conflict of interest' here.[101] In February 1999 Richard Page MP introduced a Ten Minute Bill proposing an amendment to the Insolvency Act 1986 which would preclude an investigating accountant from being appointed as a receiver of the firm under review.[102] Parliamentary time was not made available for the Bill and it did not proceed to second reading.[103] As for the Government's position on investigators' conflicts of interest, this was, in so far as represented by Lord McIntosh of Haringey,[104] that the appointment of investigators as receivers was plausible but only subject to two conditions: a demonstration that a prohibition on subsequent appointment would really increase costs and disruptions (a contention that RBS experience cast doubt upon); and the insolvency profession demonstrating that it enforces the highest standards of professional conduct in this area. The Government undertook to re-examine the issues[105] and the matter was put out to consultation by the IS[106] whose paper noted that, although appointing an investigator as a receiver often involved efficiencies, it could also produce a conflict of interest. The same paper also made the point that precluding investigating accountants from acting as receivers might give

---

101. HL Debates, vol. 596, col. 937, quoted in McCormack, 'Receiverships and the Rescue Culture', p. 244.
102. See HC Debates, vol. 324, col. 933, 3 February 1999.
103. See McCormack, 'Receiverships and the Rescue Culture', pp. 243–5.
104. HL Debates, vol. 596, col. 950, 26 January 1999.
105. White Paper, DTI, *Our Competitive Future: Building the Knowledge Driven Economy* (Cm 4176, December 1998).
106. Insolvency Service, *A Review of Company Rescue and Business Reconstruction Mechanisms* (DTI, September 1999) pp. 16–17.

rise to a danger of their extending monitoring or workout procedures or recommending inappropriate insolvency mechanisms.

Post-consultation, the IS Review Group was not persuaded that a legislative prohibition would be appropriate.[107] A research study had revealed no significant differences in the recommendations made by IPs acting as investigating accountants with no expectation of receivership appointments and those made by IPs who might have had such expectations.[108] Efficiency considerations favoured continuity of appointment and perceptions of conflicts of interest might be met, said the Review Group, by amendments to the Bankers' Code and the Insolvency Practitioners' Ethical Guidance.

It remains to be seen whether the Review Group line will reassure the public. What may be required is a provision in the Bankers' Code that allows directors to contest receivership appointments and which requires investigators, when proposed as receivers, to issue a Statement of Cause that requires directorial approval. Such a Statement might be expected to present evidence of an exceptional case for continuity based on factors such as the complexity of the company's affairs, the need for urgency and the IP's familiarity with the corporate position. The newly formed Insolvency Practices Council provides here the potential for a degree of informed public interest input[109] but suspicion of self-regulation is strong and responses via codes of practice may be perceived as too predictable and too weak to create lasting confidence.

A further conflict of interest may affect decision-making when IPs stand to receive different fees for carrying out different insolvency procedures. In seeking to explain the low commitment of IPs to CVAs Flood *et al.* state:

> One reason for the reluctance shown by the corporate hemisphere to specialise in CVAs is the matter of fees. Receiverships attract higher fees than CVAs...An IP who specialised in CVAs commented: 'I get £25,000 over two years for a CVA, whereas in receiverships you can get £75,000 over six months'...Only three of the Big Six accountancy firms had completed CVAs for the first eight months of 1993.[110]

---

107. Insolvency Service, *A Review of Company Rescue and Business Reconstruction Mechanisms*, Report by the Review Group (DTI, 2000) ('IS 2000') pp. 31–2.
108. I.e. under a Royal Bank of Scotland policy: see Katz and Mumford, 'Should Investigating Accountants'; IS 2000, p. 31.
109. IS 2000, p. 32. The first IPC Chair, Mr Graham Kentfield, was appointed on 21 December 1999. For a discussion of the IPC and its role see pp. 178–80 below.
110. Flood *et al.*, *Professional Restructuring*, p. 25.

If private practitioners are provided with economic disincentives to engage in some rescue procedures there is, accordingly, a danger that certain interests, for example those of employees, will be unfairly dealt with and too little stress placed upon keeping the company as a going concern.

Conflicts of interest may not, however, be the only sources of unfairness within the administration of insolvency regimes. Unfairness may arise where the parties involved in transactions are ill-matched in terms of information, expertise or power. Such inequalities may mean that the interests of certain parties are not fairly represented in the procedures or in the outcomes of insolvency processes. Socio-legal commentators on insolvency have thus emphasised the extent to which the rules on insolvency, which may speak loudly of fairness, are manipulated by experts to the advantage of their clients, or even themselves.[111] Wheeler's examination of the enforcement of retention of title clauses reveals that small trade creditors, who seek the protection of such clauses, are confronted in the enforcement process by the IPs who tend to act for large, secured creditors (in receiverships) or for the body of creditors (in liquidations) and who constitute the 'dominant actors' in the process. This domination flows from their *de facto* positions as the possessors of the assets at issue; their superior knowledge concerning the assets and their utility to the company; their superior financial capacity and legal competence; and the familiarity with insolvency processes that flows from their status as repeat players in the insolvency game. On this account, the IPs use this superiority to protect the source of their fee income – the insolvency estate – from diminution by, amongst others, the holders of retention of title clauses. The procedures that are encountered are not properly 'negotiations': they are 'defence strategies' put up by the IPs.[112] What the IPs do is erect barrier upon barrier so as to defeat claims on the estate. They will thus 'fob-off' claimants; insert delays into processes; demand answers to never-ending lists of questions; employ bluffing; and confront the claimant with a mass of legal and administrative technicalities.[113] The overall picture is neither of negotiations between matched parties, nor of independent fair-minded officials holding the ring between different interests. It is of highly trained practitioners acting for the economically powerful and gaining the advantage over less well-resourced parties.

111. See Wheeler, 'Capital Fractionalised'; Wheeler, *Reservation of Title Clauses*; Carruthers and Halliday, *Rescuing Business*.
112. Wheeler, *Reservation of Title Clauses*, p. 96.
113. Only 24 per cent of suppliers used lawyers in the study discussed in ibid., p. 101.

What can be done to reduce such unfairness? In relation to conflicts of interest it has been suggested that concerned parties should be able to have recourse to a professional tribunal or an arbitration body.[114] There might, accordingly, be an appeal body established by the licensing bodies of IPs, and directors, creditors, employees or others aggrieved at the appointment of, say, a receiver, might put their case to such a body without recourse to the courts. The basis for complaint would be that the relevant provision of the professional code of conduct had not been followed and the arbitrator would be able to rule on compliance with the code. An ombudsman could also be established[115] by the profession and investigatory as well as reporting powers might be exercised by such a person. The case for such an arrangement is considered in the next section.

Accountability

The accountability of IPs is provided for, in the main, by the self-regulatory regimes outlined above.[116] Attention should be paid to those concerns that are traditionally expressed in relation to self-regulatory mechanisms.[117] These include the tendency of such mechanisms to exclude 'outsiders' from policy- and rule-making processes; the lack of accountability of self-regulators to the public rather than to members;[118] the tendency of self-regulators to favour members' interests rather than those of the public; their generally poor record of rule enforcement; their anti-competitive effects (for example, through the imposition of excessive restrictions on access); their low levels of procedural transparency,

114. See Lord Montague of Oxford in HL Debates, vol. 596, col. 940, 26 January 1999.
115. See Justice, *Insolvency Law*, para. 5.19.
116. As noted, IPs are held accountable in some respects by statute: see Insolvency Act 1986 s. 212 (misfeasance); statutory obligations to file periodic returns at the Companies Registry, Insolvency Regulations 1986 (SI 1986 No. 1994) and the Insolvency Practitioners Regulations 1986 (SI 1986 No. 1995). For a review of IP regulation by the IP regulators see IRWP Review. (This section of the chapter builds on Finch, 'Controlling the Insolvency Professionals' and 'Insolvency Practitioners'.)
117. See generally R. Baldwin and M. Cave, *Understanding Regulation* (Oxford University Press, Oxford, 1999) ch. 10; J. Black, 'Constitutionalising Self-Regulation' (1996) 59 MLR 24; A. Ogus, *Regulation: Legal Form and Economic Theory* (Oxford University Press, Oxford, 1994) pp. 107–11; C. Graham, 'Self- Regulation' in G. Richardson and H. Genn (eds.), *Administrative Law and Government Action* (Clarendon Press, Oxford, 1994); A. C. Page, 'Self-Regulation: The Constitutional Dimension' (1986) 49 MLR 141; R. Baggott and L. Harrison, 'The Politics of Self-Regulation' (1986) 14 *Policy and Politics* 143; V. Finch, 'Corporate Governance and Cadbury: Self-Regulation and Alternatives' [1994] JBL 51. For critiques of particular self-regulatory regimes see R. B. Ferguson, 'Self-Regulation at Lloyds' (1983) 46 MLR 56; C. Scott and J. Black, *Cranston's Consumers and the Law* (3rd edn, Butterworths, London, 2000); L. C. B. Gower, *Review of Investor Protection* (Cmnd 9125, 1984); R. B. Ferguson and A. C. Page, 'The Development of Investor Protection in Britain' (1984) 12 *International Journal of Sociology of Law* 287; J. Black, *Rules and Regulators* (Clarendon Press, Oxford, 1997).
118. See Justice, *Insolvency Law*, p. 27.

information disclosure and reason giving; and the failure of voluntary schemes of self-regulation to control those persons who are both most likely to cause mischief and least likely to participate in such schemes.[119]

Criticisms of IP regulation echo the above points in some respects, with advocates of independent regulation stressing the protectionism and lack of objectivity of self-regulation.[120] The quality of RPB monitoring and enforcement has also, in the past, been brought into serious question. In 1993 the IS conducted an inspection of around 55 IPs and found that half of these were failing seriously to meet their statutory requirements. Ten per cent of those inspected generated very serious disciplinary problems which led to the withdrawal of licences and criminal prosecutions.[121] Pressure from the DTI led, as a result, to the establishment of the Joint Insolvency Monitoring Unit by the RPBs and to the current regime of regular, random inspections. To conclude that the above problems stemmed from self-regulation might, however, be unfounded. The DTI, in the same period, found many serious regulatory breaches among the 150 IPs that it regulated directly and disciplinary action (including deregulation) also resulted.

Ten years into the current IP regulatory regime, the Insolvency Review Working Party (IRWP) began its work, and its resulting Consultation Document noted a series of potential concerns. Major worries were the absence of systematic external review of the IS as an authorising body[122] and the absence of a greater degree of external involvement both in the writing and enforcement of rules and in monitoring the degree to which the authorising bodies act in the public interest. Other issues were the lack of flexibility, particularly on sanctioning techniques, found in the IS authorisation regime[123] and the scope of the work covered by the regulatory regime. (The IRWP noted that questions had arisen concerning both the need for an IP to be in control of some matters that are regulated but are not insolvency matters and also whether some activities currently carried out by unregulated individuals – for example, non-administrative receivers – should be incorporated into the insolvency regime.) A further problem was said to be posed by unscrupulous 'ambulance chasers' who targeted persons in

---

119. On the 'consensual paradox' and the tendency of voluntary mechanisms to regulate those least in need of regulating while failing to control those who most need to be restrained, see R. Baldwin, 'Health and Safety at Work: Consensus and Self-Regulation' in R. Baldwin and C. McCrudden (eds.), *Regulation and Public Law* (Weidenfeld & Nicolson, London, 1987) p. 153.

120. See H. Anderson, 'The Case for a Profession', *Financial Times*, 17 February 1998.

121. A. Jack, 'Insolvency Regime to be Tightened', *Financial Times*, 22 January 1993.

122. Ibid., p. 15.   123. Ibid., p. 15.

financial distress and provided them with poor advice at an extortionate price. The complex, fragmentary nature of the regulatory regime for IPs was also a concern as was absence of a single regulator for an insolvency profession. A plurality of regulators leads, on some accounts, to confusion when members of the public seek the relevant complaints authority, to duplication of resources and to unnecessarily high costs as well as differences in regulatory style and inconsistencies of regulatory response. The 'part-time' nature of much IP work was another worry with the absence of a dedicated regulatory system under which only full-time professionals would be allowed to act. Final problem areas were identified in the liability of IPs to disciplinary action under two regimes – for example, as solicitor as well as IP – and the 'practitioner-led' nature of insolvency regulation.

Reforming IP regulation

Proposals for reforming IP regulation have ranged from the radical to the modest, from abandoning 'practitioner-led' regulation in favour of control by a new independent agency to fine-tuning the current system.[124] The options can be dealt with under four headings: insolvency as a discrete profession; an independent regulatory agency; departmental regulation; and fine-tuning professional-led regulation.

Insolvency as a discrete profession

It might be argued that many IPs engage in insolvency work as their primary role and that they should be controlled by a single self-regulatory professional body. Against such a suggestion, however, it can be said that the majority of IPs are in general practice as either accountants or lawyers and that there is benefit in having the relevant RPBs monitoring and regulating the full range of their members' activities, not just insolvency; that the inter-weaving of insolvency and general practice work, notably the use, in insolvency work, of general practice infrastructures and staff support mechanisms, calls for such 'full-range' control.[125] In order to establish a discrete insolvency profession it would, moreover, be difficult to avoid demanding that all IPs be full-time insolvency workers. Such a requirement, it could be cautioned, would lead to a thinning of the ranks

---

124. For proposals see IRWP Consultation Document; Justice, *Insolvency Law*; IRWP Review. Not under discussion here is a return to the pre-Cork world that placed unqualified debtor/creditor appointees in charge of insolvency processes, a position that the Cork Committee viewed as incapable of sustaining public confidence.

125. The IRWP Review (p. 35) contends that co-operation with regulators is likely to be higher where regulation is by professional peer group rather than a body distanced from the home profession and that more rigorous regulation is likely to be provided by a peer group 'with its own reputation and self-interest at stake'.

of IPs, a reduction in the breadth of experience of the average IP and an undesirable narrowing of the range of practitioners available to debtors, creditors or others. It is the part-time nature of much IP work, it can be said, that ensures that there are sufficient IPs in practice to meet demand when insolvency peaks and to offer choice to the public.[126]

Establishing an insolvency profession might thus enhance accountability in one respect and diminish it in another. It would provide one body to be held responsible for regulation in the sector and would offer a focus for public attention. It would, on the other hand, offer little assurance that the public interest was being considered more properly in self-regulatory decision- or policy-making than under the present system. It would, moreover, replace dual scrutiny (as IP and as accountant or lawyer) with single scrutiny by the insolvency regulatory agency. If there is seen to be value in having specialist scrutiny of work done *qua* accountant or lawyer during insolvency processes then abandoning dual scrutiny may materially weaken accountability in spite of the capacity of a specialised profession to develop particular expertise in insolvency work. Transparency of regulation might be expected to be unaffected by professionalising insolvency practice in itself though the consistency brought by a move to a single professional body could have some enhancing effect. As for efficiency and effectiveness, the move to a less flexible single profession might prove detrimental if a move to full-time professionalisation prejudiced the production of a cadre of qualified IPs from which clients could choose.

On balance, the enhanced focus offered by a single profession does not seem to compensate for the losses involved in such a reform, notably the ensuing narrowing of experience that would be offered by the average IP, the shrinking of the body of IPs and the loss of dual scrutiny.[127]

An independent regulatory agency

Allocating IP regulation to a new independent agency established on a statutory basis would improve on present arrangements in some respects. Instead of the confusion of seven RPBs and the IS there would be a single regulator. This, it could be argued, would increase consistency and the co-ordination of regulation, it would encourage certainty in so far as one agency might publish, and work in a settled manner to, a single set of objectives for regulation, it would allow expertise to be pooled and high levels of competence to be developed. Above all, however, it would reassure the public that regulation was being carried out impartially, that

---

126. See IRWP Consultation Document, p. 27.
127. The IRWP Review (not unsurprisingly) also concluded that regulation through the present professional RPB should be retained (p. 36).

the public interest was being properly considered in decision- and policy-making and that the concerns of private professionals were not being allowed to dominate proceedings.

Accountability, or the lack of it, is, however, the other side of the independence coin. As commentators have noted,[128] the agency approach would involve the creation of an unelected quango. Accountability through the usual agency routes of published objectives, ministerial appointments, Annual Reports and subjection to Select Committee and National Audit Office scrutiny might not satisfy critics, although the use of ministerial guidelines that have been approved by Parliament[129] might provide a higher level of democratic control.

It has also been alleged that an independent agency would involve higher regulatory costs than the present regime, that it would be unrealistic to expect the public purse to bear these and that, if funds were obtained by a levy on practitioners, this would be passed on in charges to creditors and, in the process, some smaller practices would be driven out of the market. The anticipated effect would be an increasing domination of insolvency work by large firms and an unfortunate reduction in diversity of choice within the IP market.

Here the key issues are whether costs would really increase and who would bear the costs. A point made by the IRWP is that the RPBs provide regulatory services in a manner that is cost free to those involved in insolvencies.[130] Professionals volunteer their free services to RPBs for the good of their professions, though costs can be seen as borne at the end of the day by the broad array of users of professional accountancy or legal services (many of whom will not be involved in insolvencies and so are subsidising insolvency regulatory work). A move to agency regulation would mean that users of insolvency services would pay for the regulation of IPs. This might constitute a fairer arrangement than the system now in operation but it might be expected to meet opposition from those involved in the insolvency sector.

An independent agency, it has been said, might tend to regulate in an excessively restrictive manner.[131] Under the present system the RPBs exert control with reference to the standards of acceptable professional

---

128. Anderson, 'Case for a Profession'.
129. A practice advocated for the utilities: see P. Hain, *Regulating for the Common Good* (GMB Communications, London, 1994) p. 22; T. Prosser, *Law and the Regulators* (Oxford University Press, Oxford, 1997) p. 294.
130. IRWP Consultation Document, p. 29.
131. See generally E. Bardach and R. A. Kagan, *Going by the Book: The Problem of Regulatory Unreasonableness* (Temple University Press, Philadelphia, 1982).

conduct. These may be formulated in broad terms, non-legalistically.[132] An independent regulator, exerting control not through professional codes and standards but through enforceable rules, is more likely to become enmeshed in legalism and the minutiae of compliance.[133] This would, again, tend to increase costs, would demand that IPs devote more time to compliance work and would be likely to reduce the general efficiency of insolvency regimes.

The responding argument is that a move from control by professional standards to control via rules will lead to greater transparency and assurance to the public and that this more than justifies the modest increase in costs that may be involved. It might also be contended that a dedicated agency would be better positioned to keep its eye on how IPs perform in relation to insolvency matters than would be the case with a professional body concerned also with a host of other affairs.

A complication that independent regulators would have to face is that, as already noted, most current IPs are part-time and combine insolvency work with other work as an accountant or lawyer and that even 'full-time' RPB-authorised IPs are controlled simultaneously as IPs and as professional lawyers or accountants.[134] Were regulation by an independent agency to be introduced this would mean, first, that an IP would be subject to regulation by two different organisations, the agency and the professional body; second, that drawing a line between matters of professional concern and issues within agency jurisdiction would be difficult; and, third, that the possibility of 'double jeopardy' might arise were failings of performance to come to the attention of, and be subjected to political sanctioning by, two different bodies.

On the last point it could be contended that a single professional body is better able to co-ordinate two regulatory functions and avoid the double jeopardy that is possible with separate bodies. The first point – concerning regulation by two professions – returns to the issue of costs. If the majority of IPs will, as at present, be individuals who are regulated by their home professional bodies, a move to independent agency regulation is liable to increase costs since the regulatory infrastructure of the home professional body will remain and the expenses of agency regulation, when added to these, will produce higher costs than current arrangements in which the RPBs cover insolvency as well as home professional matters. A duplication of regulatory expenses might also be involved in independent insolvency

132. See Black, *Rules and Regulators*, ch. 1.   133. Ibid.; Ogus, *Regulation*, p. 107.
134. See IRWP Consultation Document, pp. 27, 44 (20 per cent of RPB-authorised IPs from the Big Five accountancy firms are full-time).

regulation in so far as when an accountant/lawyer acts as an IP (using his firm's resources and infrastructure) it will often be difficult to tease apart the respects in which he acts as a professional accountant/lawyer or an IP or both. As already suggested, however, the public may be reassured by dual regulation, seeing it as a belt and braces approach that prevents errant behaviour from escaping the regulatory net. Whether such reassurance justifies the extra costs involved is a matter for political judgment after the figures have been investigated in full.

Departmental regulation

The regulation of IPs might be given over completely to the IS of the DTI with the RPBs relinquishing their supervisory role.[135] In terms of accountability, this could be claimed to offer an improved arrangement. At present, the chief executive of the IS (the Inspector General) is responsible for the day-to-day operations of the service. The Secretary of State is answerable to Parliament for the framework documents to which the chief executive works and for broad policy issues, but not for day-to-day management matters. Members of Parliament can write to the Inspector General of the IS on operational issues and the Inspector General is accountable to, and reports to, the DTI Ministers on progress and performance of the IS and implementation of its five-yearly Corporate Plan. This plan contains performance targets[136] and the IS, in addition, acts in pursuit of the standards set down under the Citizens' Charter.[137] Work targets, and figures representing the extent to which these are achieved, are published by the IS in its Annual Reports.[138] The Parliamentary Commissioner for Administration (PCA) also has the right to investigate and report on the actions of the IS (though functions of Official Receivers as officers of the court are beyond PCA jurisdiction). Such mechanisms might not offer an unquestionably satisfactory regime of accountability[139] but they offer more

---

135. Not under discussion here is a system in which all IPs would be civil servants provided and authorised by the DTI. Such a regime would constitute nationalisation of the private practitioner-led machinery now encountered and is unlikely to appeal to the major political parties. Departmental provision of all IPs would give rise to difficulties (notably the DTI's ability to meet variation in demand for such services – a capacity offered by the private marketplace that would be hard to match) even if costs were passed onto users of insolvency services.

136. See IS Framework Document 1990 (DTI, 1990).

137. Cabinet Office, *The Citizens' Charter: Five Years On* (London, 1996).

138. See, for example, the Annual Report 2000–1, Annex C.

139. For discussion see N. Lewis, 'The Citizens' Charter and Next Steps: A New Way of Governing?' (1993) *Political Quarterly* 316; R. Baldwin, 'The Next Steps: Ministerial Responsibility and Government by Agency' (1988) 51 MLR 622; G. Drewry, 'Forward from FMI: The Next Steps' (1988) PL 505; Drewry, 'Next Steps: The Pace Falters' (1990) PL 322.

democratic input (via ministers) than is available with RPBs and they manifest a commitment to the public interest.

Like the proposal for independent agency regulation, departmental control offers a unified scheme able to formulate, and work to, a single set of objectives but it is open to the same objections concerning duplications of jurisdictions, costs and jeopardy. As for expertise, the IS, unlike a new agency, would be able to draw on over a decade of experience in the field (though both would be able to buy in expertise from the body of existing specialists).

Departmental regulation may address public interest concerns more openly than resort to a mixture of private RPBs but a departmental system does not offer the same impartiality as an independent agency. The bias that outsiders may fear when viewing a departmental regime is that of leaning towards the preferences of the Government in power. In some regulated sectors where valuable franchises or contracts are handed out this may be a special concern.[140] Insolvency regulation involves no allocation of such valuables but it usually demands that assets be distributed and government departments, moreover, may be involved as creditors of firms or individuals involved in an insolvency or bankruptcy. It is important, therefore, that IPs should be seen to be acting in a professionally independent manner, free from conflicts of interest.[141] Overall, then, departmental regulation rates generally lower than independent regulation as far as perceived fairness is concerned.

Fine-tuning practitioner-led regulation

The IP regulatory regime now in operation incorporates a large element of self-regulation in so far as most IPs are members of the RPB that supervises them (albeit under IS oversight). Self-regulatory regimes, in general, are said to possess a number of virtues:[142] those regulating tend to be specialists in the relevant area; they have excellent access to information at low cost and are in constant touch with developments in the profession; they know which regulatory demands will be seen as reasonable and liable to be complied with readily; they can monitor behaviour easily and in a variety of ways; they tend to know 'where the bodies are buried'; and they can investigate matters in a less formal way than external regulators. They can, furthermore, employ general professional standards and requirements

---

140. As, for example, in the television, radio or rail sectors.
141. See Anderson, 'Insolvency Practitioners'; Lightman, 'Office Holders'.
142. See the references at n. 117 above.

to achieve results and influence cultures rather than rely on enforcing detailed rules;[143] they are financed by practitioners; and they are highly adaptable to changes in the economic, legal and social environments.

Such claims can be made in various forms and with different degrees of conviction for the current IP regulation regime and, rather than move to radical change, it may be preferable to fine-tune that regime. It is worth considering four main suggestions. The first of these is that the existing regulatory bodies should be further co-ordinated, rationalised or amalgamated.

On co-ordination it has been noted above that the RPBs already do co-ordinate in a number of respects. They are bound, for example, by a memorandum of understanding with the Secretary of State; they are monitored by reference to common standards; they operate with a Joint Insolvency Monitoring Unit and Joint Insolvency Examination Board. To continue with the present regime and encourage further emphasis on co-operation and consistency (for instance, by making joint insolvency monitoring mandatory across RPB- and IS-authorised IPs) would require no new structures and would offer dual control by ensuring that lawyer and accountant IPs would remain regulated both as IPs and as lawyers or accountants (such control being beneficial where it is difficult to tease apart IP and home professional work).

It may be argued that co-ordination would still leave too many authorising bodies for under 2,000 IPs; that this would be both inefficient and confusing to the general public or affected parties who may have a complaint about an IP and who would be uncertain about where to pursue this. The inefficiency point, as already noted, however, may be overstated, since it may be efficient to build on existing professional mechanisms for such a small number of IPs rather than to set up new regimes. Complaints issues, moreover, may be addressed by combining a co-ordination strategy for regulation with a unification policy for complaints: by establishing, for example, an Insolvency Ombudsman (a proposal returned to below).

Rationalisations and amalgamations might be employed to reduce the number of RPBs or to create a unified system without resort to an independent regulatory agency. The broad difficulty with both strategies

---

143. On 'interpretive communities' and the way that shared interpretations can be achieved without resort to further, detailed, specifications by means of rules see Black, *Rules and Regulators*, pp. 30–7; S. Fish, *Doing What Comes Naturally: Change, Rhetoric and the Practice of Theory in Literary and Legal Studies* (Clarendon Press, Oxford, 1989).

is that, whereas control via existing professional bodies reduces potential 'problems' of dual discipline and double jeopardy, strategies of rational-isation and amalgamation introduce this issue in a new form. This point is, however, turned on its head if dual discipline is seen as a virtue. Less contentious is the suggestion that dealing with questions of dual control is liable to increase overall regulatory costs.

One means of amalgamating would be to establish a single sub-contracted body by agreement between the authorising bodies and to del-egate functions of monitoring to this while retaining the responsibility for disciplining and sanctioning IPs in the home professions. As the Consulta-tion Document notes, however,[144] such an agreement would give rise to po-tential confusions and conflicts of functions and responsibilities. It would also court the danger of confusing lines of accountability. At present the RPBs are overseen by the Secretary of State. Establishing a sub-contracted body under the umbrella of the authorising bodies would mean that indi-vidual RPBs would not exercise control over it and the Secretary of State's monitoring would be placed at a further distance.

A second way to improve the current regime would be to harness the monitoring capacity of the accountancy or solicitors' firm and to authorise firms as well as individuals as IPs. One advantage would be that transfers of work between different IPs might be made administratively simpler and cheaper. It could also be said that clients tend to see themselves as dealing with firms, not individuals, and to see responsibility for good or poor per-formance as attaching to the firm. The reality of much IP work, moreover, is that the IP uses the resources of the home firm, that the efficiency or oth-erwise of the insolvency work done may depend as much on the general professional performance of the firm and its employees as on the activities of the relevant individual. Regulating the firm would make it explicit that the support structure and internal controls of the firm are essential to the work of the IP and themselves require regulation.[145]

To regulate firms expressly would give them an incentive to ensure that their IPs operate to high standards. The firms, moreover, are far better placed than the RPBs or any external regulators to gain information on how IPs are doing their job, to review performance periodically and to rem-edy or sanction instances of under-performance. To attach IP functions to firms would mean that any qualified IP within the firms might carry out insolvency functions. This might involve some loss of personalisation

---

144. IRWP Consultation Document, p. 29.   145. Ibid., p. 19.

within insolvency processes, since there would be no guarantee that individual X (rather than firm Y) would carry out the functions at issue. A move to regulate at firm level would, however, improve scrutiny of the context within which IPs operate and would do so without removing responsibility from the individual IP.

A third proposed improvement to the present machinery involves the establishment of an Insolvency Ombudsman. This idea has been put forward by a number of parties, including the Cork Committee and Justice.[146] An Ombudsman would handle complaints relating to individual cases rather than deal with general issues and the ombudsman process would only come into play after other alternative routes were exhausted (at present each RPB has its own complaints procedure). The Ombudsman might take a variety of different actions, including requiring organisations to correct matters, referring issues back to an organisation for reconsideration, facilitating conciliation between parties and making awards.

Creating an Ombudsman would offer a central location for complaints and a better and simpler public profile for insolvency complaints mechanisms. Establishing such a post has, however, been opposed by the IRWP on the grounds that it is doubtful whether an extra tier of complaints procedure is needed when, at present, all RPBs already operate mechanisms; that the extra costs involved might be considerable and would have to be borne by those affected by insolvency; that delays could be caused since such an Ombudsman might have a heavy workload and office holders might not be able to complete the insolvency procedure until the complaint was finally resolved; and finally that an 'expectations gap'[147] might be created in so far as affected parties might anticipate the provision of effective remedies and do so in an unrealistic manner.[148] The IRWP also doubted whether the Ombudsman device could readily be applied in the insolvency area where there was the absence of a customer or client relationship.[149]

---

146. See Cork Report, paras. 1772–3; Justice, *Insolvency Law*, p. 25. Ombudsmen are now found in other professional fields. Thus there is a Legal Services Ombudsman as well as Ombudsmen in the insurance/unit trust, banking, building society and pension sectors. See R. James, *Private Ombudsmen and Public Law* (Ashgate, Dartmouth, 1997).

147. On the 'expectations gap' in the accountancy sector see J. Freedman, 'Accountants and Corporate Governance: Filling a Legal Vacuum?' (1993) *Political Quarterly* 285. See also *Report of the Committee on the Financial Aspects of Corporate Governance* (Cadbury Committee) (December 1992) paras. 2.1 and 5.4; V. Finch, 'Board Performance and Cadbury on Corporate Governance' [1992] JBL 581.

148. See IRWP Consultation Document, ch. 5.   149. See IRWP Review, p. 37.

The last two of the above arguments may be the weakest: the possibility of an expectations gap would, on such an approach, remove the case for most systems of scrutiny, review or appeal yet there may be real value in many instances in providing a means of scrutinising the propriety and efficiency of administrative processes, especially where there are likely to be parties dissatisfied with the substantive outcomes of decisions. Nor is it clear why the value of an Ombudsman depends on the existence of a client relationship. Provided that aggrieved parties can be identified, the Ombudsman will have a role in investigating maladministration.

The value of a new complaints system would lie in the handling of complaints outside the RPBs. At present some RPB complaints mechanisms involve reference to independent assessors who scrutinise the handling and determination of complaints, but not all do so. (Even if a separate Ombudsman is not established, each authorising body should be compelled to operate a mechanism in which either complaints are decided by independent assessors or complaints decisions are reviewed by such assessors.[150]) An Ombudsman might also, however, take a broader view of the insolvency process than a body focusing on the behaviour of a particular member practitioner. In insolvency proceedings there is a lack of a speedy and cheap way for a creditor or group of creditors to challenge the conduct of an IP, and the position of a debtor is even weaker.[151] Matters can be raised by a multiplicity of routes: through the courts under the Insolvency Act 1986[152] or by resort to the relevant professional body. A host of parties may also be involved: solicitors, estate agents, accountants and other advisers. To make the services of an Ombudsman available to creditors and debtors or other aggrieved parties would provide a mechanism for cutting through such complexities and for appraising the respective responsibilities and performances of a range of professionals in a way not linked to a particular RPB's perspective. Such an Ombudsman might also be given a general power to make (non-binding) recommendations to the Secretary of State on issues relating to insolvency processes.

Ombudsmen, however, react to instances of alleged maladministration rather than monitor general practice or act to forestall errant behaviour. A fourth proposal for reform is more precautionary. This stems from the Select Committee on Social Security's report of 1993 on the work of the

---

150. See IRWP Consultation Document, p. 33.   151. See Justice, *Insolvency Law*, p. 25.
152. See *inter alia* Insolvency Act 1986 ss. 6, 27.

Maxwell insolvency practitioners.[153] The suggestion is that there should be a system of independent monitoring of the progress of all insolvencies over a certain value. When originally made, the proposal met with a cool response from the Conservative Government[154] which argued that the task of monitoring insolvency processes should be left with creditors since it was their interests that were paramount; that it was unclear that independent monitoring would add significantly to creditors' efforts; and that the Government was not disposed to increase the costs associated with insolvency by instituting additional regulation. The counter-view, however, is that creditors cannot be assumed always to be sufficiently well informed, expert and well placed to be entrusted with protecting public and private interests in insolvency processes and that, even if creditors were well informed, expert and well placed, their commitment to protecting the broad public, as opposed to their own private, interests could by no means be taken for granted. Such involvement of the public interest is likely to occur in very large cases of insolvency – as the Maxwell episode demonstrated – and there seems a strong case for allocating a monitoring task in these cases to an Insolvency Ombudsman or an Insolvency Review Board, as discussed below.

The flagship proposal of the IRWP was to introduce a new mechanism for public interest concerns to feed into the devising of regulatory standards. The IRWP was aware of criticisms that the existing IP regulation regime provided insufficient input for the public interest since the authorising bodies set agendas and write rules as well as enforce them. It proposed the establishment of a new Insolvency Practices Council (IPC) with a majority of lay members which would: keep under review the appropriateness of IPs' professional and ethical standards; put proposals to the bodies devising professional and ethical standards for IPs; recommend issues to those bodies for consideration; and consider whether standards, once adopted, were observed and enforced.

The IPC's first chair was appointed in December 1999 and it came into being in the spring of 2000.[155] The IPC is not designed to operate independently of the existing regulatory regime but to be a body linked to present mechanisms.[156] The IRWP Review rejected the notion of setting up

153. See Justice, *Insolvency Law*, p. 8.
154. For the Government response to the Report see Cm 2415, 1993.
155. The IPC is made up of an independent chairman with five lay members to provide a majority and three IPs to provide expertise. Mr Graham Kentfield, former Chief Cashier of the Bank of England, chairs the IPC.
156. IRWP Review, pp. 45–6.

an 'overriding body' to oversee current structures. It did so on the grounds that the IS offers public accountability through its link to the Secretary of State and through its role in overseeing the RPBs: 'it would not be a sensible task for any new body, set up to reflect the public interest in insolvency regulation, to second guess what the DTI and the IS are already doing'.[157] The Review also recommended that the IS should be released, so far as possible, from the duty it has to monitor practitioners directly authorised by the Secretary of State 'so that it can concentrate wholly on its high level function as a regulator of regulators'.[158]

Such proposals, however, seem strongly to have reflected the hold that current institutional arrangements had on IRWP affections and, again, fail wholly to convince. At the end of the day, the public input being proposed is as modest as it is possible to imagine. The IPC does not draft standards, it merely makes suggestions to R3, which will continue with the drafting of standards. Little has emerged to date on how the IPC will consider 'whether professional and ethical standards are satisfactorily enforced and observed'.[159] Indeed, the Review specified that the IPC's remit 'would not extend to the operational activities or responsibilities' of RPBs or the IS.[160] The IRWP's opposition to a more powerful, more independent insolvency oversight board was based on the view that such an accountability mechanism would 'obscure'[161] the ministerial accountability to Parliament that operated *via* the IS. The Review did, however, concede that the (proposed) IPC

> would be a more appropriate forum for continuing interface with the general public than the Service can be...At present when the IS reacts to concerns from the general public...[i]t does so as part of what might be termed the 'ministerial post bag' process. The new Council, by contrast, would provide a dedicated (and a visible) contact point for raising such concerns.[162]

---

157. Ibid., p. 43.   158. IRWP Review, p. 7.

159. Ibid., p. 7; recommendation 2(c), a phrase repeated in the IPC's Annual Report 2000, p. 1.

160. IRWP Review, p. 48. See Sikka, 'Turkeys Don't Vote for Christmas', p. 7, who comments: 'The IPC will, however, be a toothless tiger unable to intervene in any specific or live case...[T]he IRWP proposals would not dampen down public anxieties about self regulation, insolvency practices, the absence of an-Ombudsman or a compensation scheme.' There is evidence, however, that the IPC will go public in attacking malpractice. On 9 May 2001, for instance, the *Financial Times* reported that the IPC was 'demanding' that the insolvency profession crack down on members who offer bad advice and, in particular, earn large fees for supervising repayment schemes of an unsuitable nature for debtors: see M. Peel, 'Watchdog Cracks Down on Insolvency Advice to Bad Debtors', *Financial Times*, 9 May 2001. The IPC's Annual Report 2000 stated that the IPC was 'not an-Ombudsman', it could not adjudicate on individual cases, but it was 'anxious to learn about general areas of concern' (p. 2).

161. IRWP Review, p. 50.   162. Ibid., p. 49.

Such an awareness of the failings of accountability through the IS and the minister might have led the IRWP to the view that a focused, independent oversight board might have a role to play in supplementing any accountability through the IS, but unfortunately it did not.

There is, it seems, a case for an independent Insolvency Review Board that would exercise oversight of the overarching kind that the IRWP rejected. Such a board would be independent of the RPBs and the IS and would: identify areas where, in the public interest, standards and guidance should be produced, modified or enhanced; provide an interface with the public; publish an Annual Report to the Secretary of State and the RPBs; and be a forum for constant review of the insolvency regulatory system. The Board would not become involved in complaints handling in relation to individual cases. It would be IP-funded and its members might come from consumer groups, professional organisations, employee, business and management groups and the judiciary. They should have an understanding of insolvency but only a small minority (if any) should be IPs.

A special reason for establishing such a board is the fragmented nature of existing responsibility for insolvency procedures.[163] The DTI has the major responsibility now but that Department is ill-positioned to take a detached view of the area since it is routinely involved in many aspects of procedures. There is also some diffusion of responsibility between the DTI, the Lord Chancellor's Department and other government departments (for example, where particular issues such as the family home or the employment implications of insolvency processes are raised). An Insolvency Review Board would have broad strategic relevance and offer a level of policy co-ordination that is at present lacking. Insolvency is an area peculiarly marked out by fragmented responsibility and diversity of inputs: therein lies the special case for a co-ordinating body. The argument for such an institution seems strong in all scenarios of reform, except, perhaps, those involving the setting up of an independent regulatory agency for insolvency which could carry out such functions as might be allocated to an Insolvency Review Board.[164]

To summarise, there are a number of ways in which the accountability of IPs might be improved. Persuasive arguments, for instance, point towards the increased external scrutiny that an Ombudsman or Insolvency Review Board would bring. The case for radical institutional reform in the

163. See Justice, *Insolvency Law*, p. 28.
164. On the case for an independent regulatory agency to replace the RPBs and the IS, see Finch, 'Insolvency Practitioners', pp. 343–4.

shape of a new regulatory agency, a new discrete profession or an expanded and exclusive role for the IS, seems, in contrast, not to be made out.

Accountability can also be developed through accessible processes. An important question, therefore, is whether the procedures adopted by IPs are transparent and amenable to inputs from affected parties. Those procedures will be dealt with in later chapters and, accordingly, will not be reviewed here. What should be considered at this point, however, is whether IPs are, because of their institutional make-up, predisposed to encourage or obstruct accessibility and transparency. On this point it can be argued that professionals, at least when they act for a client, tend to put client interests before accessibility or transparency, and, in doing so, will rapidly take refuge behind professional status, knowledge and expertise. When IPs act as receivers for debenture holders, for instance, there is evidence that they are slow to volunteer information to other parties (who might reduce the insolvency fund available for the client or for fee payment) and that they may exploit their positions or expertise and knowledge by deliberately 'muddying the waters'.[165] Within the different context of liquidation – where the IP owes duties to all creditors – there tends to be a relatively greater degree of openness and willingness to impart information.[166] Even in liquidation procedures, however, institutional factors may lead to a lack of transparency and poor access. Thus, it has been argued that IPs have been strongly concerned, in the 1980s and 1990s, to build up their professional status and that, if creditors' meetings in insolvent liquidation are observed: 'What is revealed is that IPs, as an emerging professional group, use the meeting space to establish, within their own group, power and territory and that creditors, in whose interests the meeting is being held are, in fact, marginalised and relegated to the role of audience.'[167] Trade creditors, it is argued, are likely to be particularly disadvantaged as IPs tend, at such meetings, to direct their comments towards fellow professionals (often IPs representing large creditors). The trade creditors become 'largely a silent observing body only' and cannot participate in any active sense.[168] Overall the creditors' meeting can be seen as a series of 'almost private exchanges between the dominant professional actors'.[169] The tendency to exclude 'outsiders' was noted above in outlining common

---

165. See Wheeler, *Reservation of Title Clauses*, p. 107; see also ibid., pp. 65, 89–90.
166. Ibid., p. 76.
167. S. Wheeler, 'Empty Rhetoric and Empty Promises: The Creditors' Meeting' (1994) 21 *Journal of Law and Society* 350, 351.
168. Ibid., p. 367.   169. Ibid., p. 369.

criticism of self-regulatory mechanisms, and here we find echoes in Wheeler's account of the IPs' work at the creditors' meeting. It reinforces the fear that where professionals are involved with non-experts and non-repeat players, there is unlikely to be transparency and wide accessibility.

Conclusions

Could greater efficiency, expertise, fairness and accountability be achieved by turning away from professional self-regulation and implementing insolvency laws through other mechanisms? Few would argue for a move back to the pre-Cork era in which any person, whether qualified or not, could be appointed as a receiver or liquidator.[170] Implementation through a cadre of court officials or specialist civil servants might, however, be considered.[171] It should be borne in mind that:

> The institutional locus of (insolvency) work has substantial concern for all parties. It determines the relative weight of public and private interests. It affects what motivations underlie the behaviour of professionals…how insulated will be the market from governmental intervention and what mechanisms, such as inspection or self-regulation, governments will initiate or support in order to ensure a public or political interest is served.[172]

The professional or disciplinary bases of those applying insolvency laws can, in turn, shape processes so that different knowledge bases, perceptual frameworks and bodies of expertise define and construct the issues and machineries of insolvency in different ways. They also 'locate the solution to the problem in different institutional sites'.[173] If, for example, lawyers play a central role in insolvency processes, proceedings are likely to take place in judicial or quasi-judicial settings in an adversarial fashion.[174] Such processes may place a strong emphasis on fairness but they are likely to be expensive and time-consuming. In contrast, less adversarial procedures conducted by specialist civil servants may be cheaper and swifter but are more likely to be tainted by perceptions that political influences, biases or unfairnesses have intruded.

It has been seen above that present arrangements are open to attack on a number of fronts but resort to court officials or civil servants would bring difficulties too. In both cases it would be necessary to use bodies

---

170. See Cork Report, ch. 15.
171. See Carruthers and Halliday, *Rescuing Business*, pp. 31, 375.
172. Ibid., pp. 375–6.   173. Ibid., p. 23.   174. Ibid., p. 31.

of highly specialised officials and these 'quasi-professionals' might be as prone to exclude outsiders from insolvency processes as any current professionals. Court servants would be reached through judicial processes and dangers of legalism might attach to their use. Civil servants within a specialised unit might well be thought by the public to be susceptible to governmental influence unless their unit or agency was placed at remove from the minister. Lack of accountability would then be a charge liable to be made. In the case of both sets of public officials, there would be concerns about their lack of business experience and their narrowness of professional background. In the case of current private practitioner IPs it can be argued, first, that they offer a choice of professional background and, second, that there is value in having IPs with the breadth of training and experience in the private business sector that use of private professionals brings.

In conclusion, then, there seems to be no strong case for replacing private, professional IPs with public officials, of one kind or another, as the main implementers of insolvency procedures. There are, however, good reasons for tightening the mechanisms whereby IPs are regulated, and a number of valuable reforms have been considered above. Not least of these are the proposals to rethink the duties of IPs to the broad array of interests involved in insolvencies and to subject the current IP regulatory regime to more stringently independent oversight. The framework of laws that governs insolvency is of considerable importance but equal attention should be paid to those who shape the application of those laws.

Part III

The quest for turnaround

6

Rescue

This part of the book assesses the role of rescue procedures in insolvency. We begin by considering what rescue involves, the reasons why rescue may be worth attempting and the array of devices that can be employed in seeking to turn corporate affairs around.

What is rescue?

Rescue procedures involve going beyond the normal managerial responses to corporate troubles. They may operate through informal mechanisms as well as formal legal processes. It is useful, therefore, to see rescue as 'a major intervention necessary to avert eventual failure of the company'.[1] This allows the exceptional nature of rescue action to be captured and it takes on board both informal and formal rescue strategies.

Central to the notion of rescue is, accordingly, the idea that drastic remedial action is taken at a time of corporate crisis.[2] The company, at such a point, may be in a state of distress[3] or it may have entered a formal insolvency procedure. Whether or not a rescue can be deemed a success raises a further set of issues. Complete success might be thought to involve a restoration of the company to its former healthy state but in practice this scenario is unlikely. The drastic actions that rescue necessarily involves

---

1. See A. Belcher, *Corporate Rescue* (Sweet & Maxwell, London, 1997) p. 12; Belcher, 'The Economic Implications of Attempting to Rescue Companies' in H. Rajak (ed.), *Insolvency Law: Theory and Practice* (Sweet & Maxwell, London, 1993). See also D. Brown, *Corporate Rescue: Insolvency Law in Practice* (John Wiley & Sons, Chichester, 1996) ch. 1; M. Hunter, 'The Nature and Functions of a Rescue Culture' [1999] JBL 491; R. Harmer, 'Comparison of Trends in National Law: The Pacific Rim' (1997) 1 *Brooklyn Journal of International Law* 139 at 143–8.
2. Belcher, *Corporate Rescue*, p. 12; Harmer, 'Comparison of Trends'.
3. See ch. 4 above, pp. 121–2.

will almost inevitably entail changes in the management, financing, staffing or *modus operandi* of the company and there are likely to be winners and losers in this process. As Belcher observes: 'All rescues can be seen as, in some sense, partial.'[4] This observation also serves to point out that a rescue may be 'successful' from the point of view of some parties (for example, shareholders or employees) but not from the perspective of others (for example, managers or creditors). Assessments of rescues may accordingly have to be qualified in order to reflect these different points of view.

A distinction can also be made between the company and the business. Thus, even where a company is liquidated, successful steps may be taken to retain aspects of the business as operational enterprises, to sustain the employment of groups of workers and to ensure the survival of some economic activity. Similarly, successful results may be obtained where the company is taken over and loses its individual identity accordingly.

The time scales used to judge a rescue may also affect judgments as to its success or failure. Some rescues may produce a short-lived survival of the company or the business and, before success is deemed to have been achieved, it may be necessary to consider whether the rescue efforts have produced sustained results.

As for the end products of rescues, these may be various.[5] The company may be restored to its former state, as noted, but it is more likely to be reorganised (where, for example, managerial reforms are instituted), restructured (where, perhaps, closures of elements of the business are involved), refinanced (as where new capital is injected or debts are rescheduled), downsized (where operations may be cut back, workforces reduced or activities rationalised), subjected to sell-offs (where parts of the business are sold to other firms or even to managers in management buyouts (MBOs)) or taken over (as where the market for corporate control operates with regard to a troubled company and a takeover prompts drastic managerial changes[6]).

---

4. Belcher, *Corporate Rescue*, p. 23; Harmer, 'Comparison of Trends'.
5. See Belcher, *Corporate Rescue*, pp. 24–34; Brown, *Corporate Rescue*, pp. 6–8; R3's Ninth Survey of Business Recovery (2001) suggests that nearly one in five businesses survive insolvency and continue in business in one form or another.
6. On the market for corporate control see J. Franks and C. Mayer, 'Capital Markets and Corporate Control: A Study of France, Germany and the UK' (1990) 10 *Economic Policy* 191–231; C. Bradley, 'Corporate Control: Markets and Rules' (1990) 53 MLR 170; J. Fairburn and J. Kay (eds.), *Introduction to Mergers and Merger Policy* (Oxford University Press, Oxford, 1989).

Why rescue?

Some visions of insolvency processes and laws are highly unsympathetic to the whole notion of corporate rescue. As was seen in chapter 2, the 'creditor wealth maximisation' vision, which sees insolvency as a process of collecting debts for creditors and as a response to the 'common pool' problem, is at tension with the notion that keeping firms in operation (and protecting interests beyond those of creditors) is an independent goal of insolvency law.[8] It may be the case, in some circumstances, that maximising potential returns to creditors will demand some sort of rescue activity but this will not always be the case and a failed rescue may reduce creditors' returns materially.[9] On most occasions, those economic theories that focus on creditor interests will hold that the collective actions of liquidation will reduce transaction costs for individual creditors and make for administratively efficient processes.[10] It is efficient, on such a view, to decline to save 'hopeless' companies and to allow the market to redeploy resources swiftly, and at least cost, to more productive uses.[11]

In chapter 2 it was argued, however, that the creditor wealth maximisation vision was excessively narrow and that, in looking at insolvency processes, attention should be paid to interests beyond those of creditors: to social and distributional goals; to public as well as private interests; and to values such as expertise, fairness and accountability. Whether existing English rescue procedures perform adequately with regard to these factors is best considered when the details of different procedures are examined in the chapters below. At this stage it is worth noting that an approach going beyond creditor wealth maximisation – in short a 'social' as opposed to an

---

7. If regimes are largely creditor-driven it is likely that prospects for rescue will be less than where regimes are debtor-driven: see Harmer, 'Comparison of Trends', pp. 147–8. On classifying jurisdictions as pro-creditor or pro-debtor regarding, *inter alia*, the general position on insolvency, see P. Wood, *Allen & Overy Global Law Maps: World Financial Law* (3rd edn, Allen & Overy, London, 1997).

8. See the discussion at pp.28–33 above. T. H. Jackson, *The Logic and Limits of Bankruptcy Law* (Harvard University Press, Cambridge, Mass., 1986) ch. 9; D. G. Baird, 'The Uneasy Case for Corporate Reorganisations' (1986) 15 *Journal of Legal Studies* 127.

9. Rescue is likely to increase returns to creditors where there is a good prospect of turning corporate fortunes around (for example, by coping with a short-term dip in the market) or where the company is worth more as a going concern than as assets sold off piecemeal.

10. See G. Dal Pont and L. Griggs, 'A Principled Justification for Business Rescue Laws: A Comparative Perspective, Part II' (1996) 5 *International Insolvency Review* 47 at 62; G. Lightman, 'Voluntary Administration: The New Wave or the New Waif in Insolvency Law?' (1994) 2 *Insolvency Law Journal* 59 at 62.

11. See Lightman, 'Voluntary Administration'; M. White, 'The Corporate Bankruptcy Decision' (1989) 3 *Journal of Economic Perspectives* 129.

'economic' approach – leaves open the scope for rescue and justifies rescue activity with reference to a number of objectives and values. In relation to the technically efficient[12] achievement of social and distributional goals, regard can thus be had to the potential of a rescue procedure to achieve a number of results. These may include the preservation of a business that, in the longer term, is worth saving or is worth more as a going concern than if sold piecemeal; the protection of the jobs of a workforce; the avoidance of harms to suppliers, customers and state tax collectors; and the prevention of damage to the general economy or to business confidence in a sector.[13]

For its part, the Cork Committee[14] laid the foundations for a 'rescue culture' and was clear on the legitimacy of considering the broader picture. A good, modern system of insolvency law, said Cork, should provide a means for preserving viable commercial enterprises capable of making a useful contribution to the economic life of the country:

> We believe that a concern for the livelihood and well-being of those dependent upon an enterprise which may well be the lifeblood of a whole town or even a region is a legitimate factor to which a modern law of insolvency must have regard. The chain reaction consequences upon any given failure can potentially be so disastrous to creditors, employees and the community that it must not be overlooked.[15]

In the period since the Cork Report the rescue culture has strengthened and been endorsed by the judiciary as well as bankers and politicians.[16] In *Powdrill* v. *Watson*[17] Lord Browne-Wilkinson stated in the House of Lords:

---

12. 'Technically efficient' in the sense that whatever social and distributional goals are set by society, the aim should be to produce these at minimal cost and without waste.

13. On the social costs of corporate failure see B. G. Carruthers and T. C. Halliday, *Rescuing Business: The Making of Corporate Bankruptcy Law in England and the United States* (Clarendon Press, Oxford, 1998) pp. 69–71; E. Warren, 'Bankruptcy Policy' (1987) 54 U Chic. L Rev. 775 and the reply, D. G. Baird, 'Loss Distribution, Forum Shopping and Bankruptcy: A Reply to Warren' (1987) 54 U Chic. L Rev. 815.

14. *Report of the Review Committee on Insolvency Law and Practice* (Cmnd 8558, 1982) ('Cork Report').

15. Cork Report, para. 204. See also paras. 203 and 198(j). When read together these paragraphs indicate that, in the Cork Committee's view, insolvency law should provide mechanisms not only to rescue potentially profitable organisations but also to ensure that a commercial enterprise can survive *even* if there is no immediate prospect of a return to profitability, if it is in the economic interests of the community. See also Hunter, 'Nature and Functions of a Rescue Culture', pp. 497–9; and on the social costs of failure see Carruthers and Halliday, *Rescuing Business*, pp. 69–70.

16. On the development of the rescue culture see Insolvency Service, *A Review of Company Rescue and Business Reconstruction Mechanisms*, Report by the Review Group (DTI, 2000) ('IS 2000') pp. 12–23.

17. *Re Paramount Airways Ltd (No. 3) sub nom. Powdrill* v. *Watson* [1995] 2 AC 394, [1995] 2 WLR 312, [1995] 2 All ER 65.

The rescue culture which seeks to preserve viable businesses was and is fundamental to much of the Act of 1986. Its significance in the present case is that, given the importance attached to receivers and administrators being able to continue to run a business, it is unlikely that Parliament would have intended to produce a regime as to employees' rights which renders any attempt at such rescue either extremely hazardous or impossible.[18]

The British Bankers' Association publicly endorsed a rescue culture in its 1997 paper, *Banks and Businesses Working Together*.[19] The Blair governments have also sought to encourage a movement towards a more US-style philosophy of enterprise that is less censorious of business failures and more encouraging of rescue. Peter Mandelson, when Trade Secretary in 1998, made a number of speeches that advocated a reassessment of attitudes to business failure and a need to encourage entrepreneurs to take risks.[20] He announced the need to reconsider the position of the Crown as preferential creditor[21] so that hard-pressed companies were not driven into insolvency by demands relating to tax debts. The 1998 White Paper, *Our Competitive Future: Building the Knowledge Driven Economy*,[22] echoed such sentiments and, in 1999, a joint DTI and Treasury initiative was mounted in order to further the rescue culture and examine how it could be made to work more efficiently. This initiative resulted in a September 1999 Consultation Document and a May 2000 Report[23] which included a series of rescue-orientated proposals that are discussed in the chapters that follow. More recently, the Chancellor, Gordon Brown, announced in June 2001 that a White Paper would be produced in order to 'reduce the penalties for honest failure and to create a modern and fair commercial system'.[24] The promised White Paper[25] proposed removing the Crown's preferential rights to recover unpaid taxes ahead of other creditors and reducing the role of administrative receivership.[26]

18. [1995] 2 AC 394 at 442 (quoted in Hunter, 'Nature and Functions of a Rescue Culture', p. 511).
19. British Bankers' Association, *Banks and Business Working Together* (London, 1997) para. 3: 'Banks have long supported a rescue culture and thousands of customers are in business today because of the support of their bank through difficult times.'
20. See Hunter, 'Nature and Functions of a Rescue Culture', p. 519.
21. See ch. 13 below.
22. Cm 4176, December 1998, paras. 2.12–2.14.
23. Insolvency Service, *A Review of Company Rescue and Business Reconstruction Mechanisms*, Interim Report (DTI, September 1999); IS 2000.
24. See HM Treasury Press Release, 8 June 2001.
25. DTI/Insolvency Service, *Productivity and Enterprise: Insolvency – A Second Chance* (Cm 5234, 2001).
26. Ibid. On the merits of floating charges see ch. 3 above and ch. 14 below. On administrative receivership see ch. 8 below. On preferential status see ch. 13 below.

A key issue in any process that purports to be rescue-orientated is whether it provides for intervention at a sufficiently early stage in proceedings and action of a sufficiently speedy nature to allow the above ends to be achieved. In R3's Survey of Business Recovery of 2001, the rescue professionals who responded indicated that in 77 per cent of cases there was, by the time they were appointed, no possible action that could be taken to avert company failure.[27]

The trade-offs between achieving 'social' ends and the costs imposed on various parties have, moreover, to be taken into account.[28] Many rescue activities will involve the forestalling of enforcement actions by certain parties and the use of periods of grace in which realignment efforts are made. During these periods certain interests will suffer. Creditors, for example, may be prevented from realising their securities. Distributional and social goals may demand that creditors make certain concessions for the purposes of rescue but considerations of both efficiency and fairness impose limits on the sacrifices that can be justified.[29] In assessing such trade-offs, balances have to be drawn between the probabilities of achieving certain desirable ends and the (usually far higher) probabilities of imposing costs on parties who are asked to make sacrifices.[30]

To move to another benchmark of chapter 2, attention should also be paid to the propensity of any given rescue procedure to allow business judgments to be taken by experts.[31] The argument for expert decision-making may, like those for fairness and accountability, be the more important where democratically established goals for rescue are difficult to identify.) Where, for instance, a rescue procedure involves a handover of control from a specialist insider (for example, a director) to a generalist outsider (for example, an insolvency practitioner), this may involve the expenses of parties coming up to speed with the particular company's financial, operational and market positions but also dangers that judgments will be made by persons who are not fully familiar with the relevant

---

27. R3 Ninth Survey. Business preservation rates were, overall, 18 per cent, with hotel and catering having the highest preservation rate (28 per cent).
28. On the political consequences of such choices see Carruthers and Halliday, *Rescuing Business*, p. 155.
29. See Dal Pont and Griggs, 'Principled Justification', p. 47.
30. Ibid., pp. 61–71 and see the discussion of the policies of (1) redistribution determined by relative ability to bear costs and (2) allocating the costs of business failure to those who stand to benefit most from business success.
31. On the tendency of US rescue processes to place more faith in management than the English system, see Carruthers and Halliday, *Rescuing Business*, pp. 509–10. See pp. 197, 202–4 below.

market sectors and business circumstances.[32] Experts should also be allowed to *exercise* their expertise. A consideration in judging a rescue regime is, accordingly, whether it gives the expert sufficient information and time to be able to effect a rational, balanced judgment. 'Expert' decisions may amount to little if those taking them are, by force of circumstances, ill-informed and subjected to unduly tight deadlines.[33]

Rescue procedures also stand to be judged according to their fairness. Issues here are whether those processes allow equal weight to be given to the voices of various affected parties; whether the processes are open to self-interested manipulation by certain individuals or groups; and whether those administering the processes are (and can be seen to be) operating even-handedly.

Finally, considerations of accountability are relevant. Acceptable levels of supervision and approval should be instituted so that opportunities for opportunistic behaviour are curtailed and regimes are not only fair but also capable of generating the degree of consent that is necessary for effective rescues to be achieved. This, in turn, demands that supervisory functions are not allocated in a way that itself allows manipulation. The transparency and accessibility of processes must also be sufficient to allow affected parties to apprise themselves of relevant facts and to ensure that such parties' representations are considered. Again, however, the costs of supervision and access have to be borne in mind and the pitfalls of excessively legalistic procedures and undue levels of court supervision should be avoided.[34]

In relation to issues of both fairness and accountability it should be emphasised that different groupings may possess widely divergent interests and incentives when the company meets troubled times.[35] Shareholders and directors will tend to favour ensuring that the company continues to operate for as long as possible. The former are residual claimants in insolvency and have little to lose by trading on. The directors may wish to prolong operations in order to eke out or stabilise their employment.[36] Both

32. See M. Phillips, *The Administration Procedure and Creditors' Voluntary Arrangements* (Centre for Commercial Law Studies, QMW, London, 1996); N. Segal, 'An Overview of Recent Developments and Future Prospects in the UK' in J. Ziegel (ed.), *Current Developments in International and Comparative Corporate Insolvency Law* (Clarendon Press, Oxford, 1994) p. 10.

33. See Belcher, *Corporate Rescue*, pp. 240–1.

34. See Phillips, *Administration Procedure*, pp. 11–12.

35. See Carruthers and Halliday, *Rescuing Business*, pp. 48–51.

36. Directors may not bear the financial risks of continued trading but their inclination to trade on should be constrained by fears of personal liability for wrongful trading, fraudulent trading, breach of duty or of disqualification: see ch. 15 below.

shareholders and directors will thus tend to gamble on further business activity since they will enjoy whatever gains result. Corporate creditors, in contrast, will tend to favour ceasing operations sooner rather than later since they will bear the losses that result from any continued trading.[37] Employees, again, will tend to favour continuing trading in the hope of securing their jobs and in the knowledge that further losses will be borne by other parties. Insolvency practitioners, as noted in chapter 5, may possess incentives to encourage companies to move towards formal insolvency procedures because these are likely to generate fee income. Such acute divergences of interest make it especially important that rescue regimes are not only fair and accountable but seen to be so.

Approaches to rescue

In analysing English rescue procedures it is helpful to consider how other jurisdictions deal with the central challenges of rescue.[38] The purpose of such comparisons is not to argue that English law should follow other countries but to set out key choices with clarity and to show that there may be a wide variety of ways to achieve rescue objectives.

What then are the important issues to consider in such a comparison? A first must be the priority that an insolvency regime gives to rescue. Is, for instance, insolvency law seen merely as a means of debt collection for creditors or does it place importance on rescue to the extent that creditors' rights are placed on the procedural back burner or even modified? Can the regime be said to be creditor or debtor friendly? Does it, for instance, involve a moratorium on the enforcement of creditors' rights and does it allow broad access to the rescue process? A second issue is whether the regime is fault-based. Does it, for instance, treat the directors as responsible for corporate troubles to the extent that they are seen as blameworthy and in need of tight regulation and monitoring?[39] Does it give priority to setting down heavy penalties for directors who misbehave?

37. Carruthers and Halliday, *Rescuing Business*, p. 244.
38. For comparative analyses of rescue, see L. S. Sealy, 'Corporate Rescue Procedures: Some Overseas Comparisons' in F. Macmillan (ed.), *Perspectives in Company Law* (Kluwer, London, 1995); IS 2000, Annex A; Brown, *Corporate Rescue*, chs. 24 and 25.
39. Hunter contrasts a 'rescue culture' – marked by a bias in favour of preserving businesses – with old notions 'that the insolvent trader should be regarded as morally defective, and that individuals, partnerships and corporations who or which cannot pay their debts must, as part of the settled scheme of things, be made bankrupt or wound up': Hunter, 'Nature and Functions of a Rescue Culture', p. 499.

A third key consideration relates to the managerial and oversight functions within rescue processes and to whom these are allocated. Regimes may be placed under the control of the courts, the directors, independent professionals or even the market, and they will have quite different characteristics. A court-driven rescue approach, for instance, will tend to be characterised by formality but alternative rescue regimes will rely more heavily on contractual or negotiated forms of dealing.

A fourth issue is whether the rescue process as a whole is focused or diverse. A focused process will rely on a small number of procedures and gateways to rescue whereas the diverse system of rescue may involve a host of different processes and philosophies.

Finally, an important comparative dimension is the financial context within which rescues operate. Rescue opportunities and processes may be heavily influenced by the structures that are available in a jurisdiction for raising corporate finances. Here the informal conventions governing such matters as banking arrangements may be as important as formal statutory structures. A further issue is how the law of a country or its bankers makes provision for funding within the rescue context: is, indeed, any special regime available for rescue purposes?

We will see, in the chapters that follow, that present English rescue procedures might be portrayed as giving strong priority to the protection of creditor interests and limited priority to rescue; as quite heavily fault based and oriented to the control of errant directorial conduct; and as reliant on strong supervision of directors by independent insolvency practitioners and the courts. The English system is also quite diverse in so far as a number of rescue processes and gateways (informal and formal) may have relevance to a troubled company and it is set within a financial system that strongly favours the secured creditor.

The corporate insolvency regime encountered in the USA offers a set of contrasting characteristics and it is worth outlining these, as well as noting the alleged strengths and weaknesses of the US approach.[40] Chapter 11 of the United States Bankruptcy Code (dating from the Bankruptcy Reform Act 1978) is a 'reorganisation' procedure whose policy objective is strongly oriented to the avoidance of the social costs of liquidation and the retention of the corporate operation as a going

---

40. Chapter 7 of the US Bankruptcy Code is the most common form of bankruptcy. It is a liquidation proceeding in which the debtor's non-exempt assets are sold by the Chapter 7 trustee and the proceeds distributed according to the Code's priorities. It is available for individuals, couples, partnerships and corporations.

concern.[41] There is no requirement that the debtor be insolvent or near insolvent in order to apply for Chapter 11 protection: the process is an instrument for debtor relief, not a remedy for creditors. As in England, a central purpose of the process is to preserve the value of the enterprise where this is likely to be greater than the liquidation value. Chapter 11 is, however, to English eyes highly sympathetic to the debtor, almost always started by a voluntary petition by the debtor and marked by the following characteristics.

There is an automatic moratorium or stay on enforcement of claims against the company and its property. This is triggered by the filing of a Chapter 11 petition. Secured creditors and landlords will usually initiate court action to seek to lift the stay but the moratorium will be upheld if the court finds that the debtor has provided the creditor with 'adequate protection' of their property interests. (This usually consists of periodic payments.) The debtor, in turn, must seek court permission to use cash as he is subject to a lien. Such issues, however, are often resolved by the parties by means of an agreement that is approved by the court. There is provision in Chapter 11 for 'cramdown' whereby a plan that is confirmed by the court may be imposed on a class of objecting creditors. (Generally a secured class may be crammed down if it receives the value of its collateral plus interest.) Objecting creditors are shielded by the 'best interest' test under which the court must be satisfied that each objecting creditor will receive under the plan as much as they would in liquidation. There is, in addition, a 'feasibility' test under which the court must find that the debtor is reasonably likely to be able to perform the promises it makes in the plan. It is nevertheless the case that in US law prior legal rights may be more dramatically affected than in England in order to effect a reorganisation and a new start for the company. Even unliquidated and unaccrued liabilities, for instance, can be restructured and constrained in Chapter 11.[42] In English administration there is no division of creditors into classes and there is nothing equivalent to the US notion of class cramdown.

41. For comparison of Chapter 11 with the UK law, see J. L. Westbrook, 'A Comparison of Bankruptcy Reorganisation in the US with Administration Procedure in the UK' (1990) 6 IL&P 86; G. Moss, 'Chapter 11: An English Lawyer's Critique' (1998) 11 *Insolvency Intelligence* 17; Moss, 'Comparative Bankruptcy Cultures: Rescue or Liquidations? Comparisons of Trends in National Law – England' (1997) 23 *Brooklyn Journal of International Law* 115; R. Connell, 'Chapter 11: The UK Dimension' (1990) 6 IL&P 90; Carruthers and Halliday, *Rescuing Business*, ch. 11; J. Franks and W. Torous, 'Lessons from a Comparison of US and UK Insolvency Codes' in J. S. Bhandari and L. A. Weiss (eds.), *Corporate Bankruptcy: Economic and Legal Perspectives* (Cambridge University Press, Cambridge, 1996); R. Broude, 'How the Rescue Culture Came to the United States and the Myths that Surround Chapter 11' (2001) 16 IL&P 194.
42. Westbrook, 'Comparison of Bankruptcy', p. 89.

An important cultural difference between England and the USA concerns the issue of fault, as Moss has observed:

> In England insolvency, including corporate insolvency, is regarded as a disgrace. The stigma has to some extent worn off but it is nevertheless still there as a reality. In the United States business failure is very often thought of as a misfortune rather than wrongdoing. In England the judicial bias towards creditors reflects a general social attitude which is inclined to punish risk takers when the risks go wrong and side with creditors who lose out. The United States is still in spirit a pioneering country where the taking of risks is thought to be a good thing and creditors are perceived as being greedy.[43]

This cultural difference is reflected in the allocation of managerial and control functions. Under Chapter 11 the pre-petition management may remain in control throughout the proceedings,[44] though in law the bankruptcy estate vests not in the debtor company but in a separate conceptual entity: the debtor in possession (DIP).[45] The DIP is akin to a trustee. An examiner or trustee can be appointed under Chapter 11 if the creditors convince the court that investigation of the directors is necessary[46] but the DIP is in virtually the same position as the trustee except for the latter's powers of investigation and entitlement to compensation.

---

43. Moss, 'Chapter 11', p. 18; see also Carruthers and Halliday, *Rescuing Business*, p. 246; Westbrook, 'Comparison of Bankruptcy', p. 143, who argues that in the USA business failure is more readily seen as 'the inevitable downside of entrepreneurship and risk'. See also M. Draper, 'Taking a Leaf out of Chapter 11?' (1991) 17 *Law Society Gazette* 28.

44. The debtor in possession can, however, be a team of corporate salvage experts employed to reorganise the company or a new management team appointed after the financial troubles have started. In practice figures suggest that considerably more than half of US managers lose their jobs within two years of filing for Chapter 11, a stark contrast with the normal turnover figure of around 6–10 per cent per two years: see Broude, 'How the Rescue Culture Came to the United States'; E. Warren, 'The Untenable Case for Repeal of Chapter 11' (1992) 102 Yale LJ 437 at 449; L. LoPucki and W. Whitford, 'Corporate Governance in the Bankruptcy Reorganisation of Large, Publicly Held Companies' (1993) 141 U Pa. L Rev. 669. Stuart Gilson of Harvard Business School has been quoted as stating that around 80 per cent of chief executives and a high proportion of senior managers lose their jobs in a Chapter 11 restructuring: *Financial Times*, 3 October 2001. But see S. Gilson, 'Bankruptcy, Boards, Banks and Blockholders' (1990) 27 *Journal of Financial Economics* 355; Franks and Torous, 'Lessons from a Comparison', pp. 459–60.

45. See Brown, *Corporate Rescue*, pp. 753–5.

46. Creditors can now appoint their own trustee after the Official Manager is appointed: US Bankruptcy Code (Title 11) s. 11, as amended by the Bankruptcy Reform Act 1994. The court can also oust the DIP at any time 'for cause', although this is rare: see J. Ayer, 'Goodbye to Chapter 11: The End of Business Bankruptcy as we Know It' (Mimeo, Institute of Advanced Legal Studies, 2001). In public companies the appointment of a disinterested trustee is mandatory within ten days of order for relief. If no trustee is appointed, the court can appoint an examiner to investigate the debtor regarding, for example, allegations of fraud, mismanagement, etc.

It is, however, in the position of the secured creditor that the most dramatic contrast between the USA and England is encountered. In England there is the concept of a floating security that hovers over the company's assets and crystallises into a fixed security when financial disasters happen. There is no equivalent in the USA and receivership on the English model is unknown there. The security holder in England has a level of control over rescue procedures that a US banker could only dream of. (Westbrook has quipped that 'if an American banker is very very good, when he dies he will go to the United Kingdom'.[47] In England the floating security holder is able, when affairs go wrong, to appoint a receiver and manager of the entire business – an 'administrative receiver' – whose task is to obtain the best realisation for the secured creditor that is reasonably practicable. The floating charge holder in England can veto an informal rescue or an administration by inserting a receiver.[48] This is unthinkable in the USA. An underpinning English assumption here is that banks will do everything possible to save a company prior to inserting a receiver. In contrast, it has been argued that US businesses regard banks as 'uncertain and fickle business allies at best'.[49]

The part to be played by a company's shareholders also differs in the USA and England, and again reflects differing attitudes to corporate distress. In the USA, the shareholders are given an important role in rescue proceedings. This has been said to flow from a commitment to the entrepreneurial ethic and, again, a belief that financial troubles often stem from external forces. It produces an emphasis on preserving not merely the business but the troubled company itself. In England, the tendency is to view the prior shareholders as at least in part responsible for the company's troubles (along with their directors) and to have interests that can be treated as having expired once a formal legal insolvency proceeding has started. The products of rescues tend to reflect this divergence of approach. In England most insolvency practitioners look to sell the business but in the USA it is far more often the case that a rescue produces an agreed composition between the company and its creditors with the former equity owners keeping some ownership.[50]

47. Westbrook, 'Comparison of Bankruptcy', p. 87.
48. See, however, the DTI/IS White Paper, *Productivity and Enterprise*, paras. 2.5–2.18, where proposals, *inter alia*, to abolish the floating charge holder's effective right to veto are aired: see further ch. 8 below.
49. Westbrook, 'Comparison of Bankruptcy', p. 88.
50. On the evolving relationship between creditors and equity owners in Chapter 11 see Ayer, 'Goodbye to Chapter 11'.

The parts played by professionals also differ. In English administrations a key individual is the insolvency practitioner. This is the person, rather than the directors, who runs the rescue operation. Rescues under the English system tend to be dominated by a small number of London-based specialist accountants. In the US system, with its DIP, bankruptcy tends to be locally operated and involves lawyers rather than accountants.

The level of court supervision involved in the rescue process is also linked to the above factors. In English administration the central role of the independent insolvency practitioner means that little court supervision is required. In the USA the power of the DIP and the possibility of cramdown are balanced by considerable court protection for creditors in the reorganisation. In short the US regime is closely regulated by the Bankruptcy Court whereas English administration relies more heavily on the administrator's discretion and the agreement of the creditors.

In terms of legal focus, the US rescue system is concentrated on the Chapter 11 reorganisation, whereas in England a number of insolvency processes possess a rescue function: notably schemes of arrangements under ss. 425–7 of the Companies Act 1985, company voluntary arrangements under the Insolvency Act 1986, administrations and receiverships. As will be seen below, the use of a variety of procedures raises issues of consistency and coherence in the English system.

Finally, note should be taken of the different financial contexts within which the Chapter 11 and English rescue procedures operate. In England it is usual for companies to raise a good portion of their capital by resort to bank loans secured by floating charges. This is consistent with English judicial and legislative policy which encourages financing through secured loans at interest rates that are reduced by giving secured creditors high levels of protection. In the USA, financing is more often achieved through the bond market and the secured creditor 'does not enjoy the general sympathy of the public or the courts'.[51] Where credit is obtained contractually through hire purchase or retention of title arrangements, the English courts tend to approach rights issues with a high respect for the sanctity of contract, whereas US courts look more directly to the need to protect parties collectively in a rescue scenario.

Chapter 11 procedures have been criticised on a number of fronts.[52] A first concern has been the delay and expense involved. Delay is inevitable

---

51. Moss, 'Chapter 11', p. 18.

52. On Chapter 11 and its weaknesses see, for example, L. LoPucki and G. Triantis, 'A Systems Approach to Comparing US and Canadian Reorganization of Financially Distressed Companies' in J. Ziegel (ed.), *Current Developments in International and Comparative Corporate*

since Chapter 11 gives debtors 120 days after filing so as to propose a reorganisation plan. This is followed by sixty further days to obtain creditor and shareholder approval. Extensions to such periods are frequent and it is usual for creditors to be held at bay for one or more years (the average duration of Chapter 11 proceedings is one-and-a-half years). When, moreover, a firm proceeds from Chapter 11 to Chapter 7 for liquidation, the process takes an average of fourteen months.

Why do Chapter 11 cases take so long to process?[53] A major reason is that the professionals have few incentives to act quickly. Chapter 11 is based on judicial oversight and lawyers' fees accordingly tend to be very considerable. Under the old Bankruptcy Code courts linked such fees to creditors' returns, but the present regime allows market rates to be charged for services rendered and costs of $1 million a week are not unknown.[54] Professional fees, moreover, have been estimated to use up between 3 and 8 per cent of the firm's assets.[55] The expenses of litigation tend, furthermore, to be fuelled where the DIP approach leaves managers in control of a company since this may produce a lack of trust between creditors and management: a position that often gives rise to litigation that stands to be paid for out of the estate.

The US judges could refuse to extend deadlines and place Chapter 11 processes under a tighter rein, but bankruptcy judges are ill-placed to do this because of their workloads. In 1991 each bankruptcy judge faced an average of 3,244 cases. In any event, judges who are in doubt about a Chapter 11 case tend to opt for the line of least resistance, which is to give the parties more time to think. As for shareholders, their inclination will tend to be to wait rather than liquidate since they have little to lose by this.

The expenses and delays involved in Chapter 11 may explain its relatively low incidence in the USA. According to the administrative office of the US courts, for the year to 30 June 1997 there were 1,316,999 bankruptcies (individual and corporate) filed in the USA, but only 11,159 of these were Chapter 11 cases. These figures for Chapter 11 cases represented a 54 per cent drop on numbers in the early 1990s.[56] To some extent these statistics can be

Insolvency Law (Clarendon Press, Oxford, 1994); M. Bradley and M. Rosenzweig, 'The Untenable Case for Chapter 11' (1992) 101 Yale LJ 1043; D. Boshkoff and R. McKinney, 'The Future of Chapter 11' (1995) 8 Insolvency Intelligence 6; M. Galen with C. Yang, 'A New Page for Chapter 11?' Business Week, 25 January 1993, p. 2; Brown, Corporate Rescue, pp. 768–72.

53. Note, however, the new Small Business Chapter 11 established by the Bankruptcy Reform Act 1994, and Justice Small's 'Fast Track Chapter 11': see Boshkoff and McKinney, 'Future of Chapter 11'.

54. See Galen, 'A New Page for Chapter 11?', p. 3.

55. 'When Firms Go Bust', The Economist, 1 August 1992, p. 70.

56. In 1991 24,000 firms filed for Chapter 11 protection and 650,000 were liquidated under Chapter 7.

explained by legal changes and diversions to other bankruptcy processes,[57] but there is evidence that rescue rates in Chapter 11 tend to be disappointing. Statistics suggest that only 17–26 per cent of Chapter 11 plans are confirmed, only half of these produce payment of agreed sums to creditors and 80 per cent of firms in Chapter 11 are eventually liquidated.[58] As for workforces, the indications are that firms tend to have shed half of their workers before a plan is confirmed. These results have prompted some commentators to argue that the millions and millions of dollars spent on lawyers and accountants might have been better used to repay creditors through swifter liquidations.[59]

The utility of Chapter 11 for small companies has been particularly subject to question. The National Bankruptcy Review Commission argued in 2000 that for small firms Chapter 11 is too long and costly, and the Commission put forward proposals for tighter time limits. This line of argument is supported by statistics that reveal Chapter 11 to produce a far higher success rate for large firms than for small firms.[60]

Lengthy Chapter 11 proceedings give rise to further concerns. One often-voiced comment is that unhealthy distortions of competition can result in some markets. It has thus been argued that when Transworld Airlines and Continental Airlines operated from the protection of Chapter 11 they were able to keep capacity levels artificially high and slash fares to below cost levels (since their creditors could not enforce). The healthy competitors of these airlines were, as a result, placed under extreme and unfair financial pressures.[61] The effect of indefinite Chapter 11 moratoria can be said also to prevent insolvency law from fulfilling an important function:

57. For example, the debt limits for eligibility for relief under Chapter 13 were raised in 1994 from $100,000 to $250,000 (unsecured debt) and from $350,000 to $750,000 (secured debt). Chapter 13 is a repayment plan for individuals with regular income and unsecured debt of, now, less than $269,250 and secured debt of less than $807,750 (2001 figures).

58. See Fenning and Hart, 'Measuring Chapter 11: The Real World of 500 Cases' (1996) 4 *American Bankruptcy Institute Law Review* 119 at 152; 'When Firms Go Bust', *The Economist*.

59. See Bradley and Rosenzweig, 'Untenable Case for Chapter 11'.

60. In 1987 69 per cent of firms with a turnover of over $100 million survived but only 30 per cent of those with businesses of over $25 million did so. A study by Edith Hotchkiss at Boston College, Massachusetts, examined 200 public companies that emerged from Chapter 11. She found 40 per cent to suffer from operating losses for the next three years and a third of the sample had to restructure their debt a second time, often under court protection: reported in *Financial Times*, 3 October 2001.

61. See Galen, 'A New Page for Chapter 11?', p. 2. Franks and Torous also note 'serious concern' in the USA that Chapter 11 is used by some firms to secure competitive advantages: see Franks and Torous, 'Lessons from a Comparison', p. 463. Broude, however, cautions that a Chapter 11 filing may fail to produce a competitive advantage because, even when it reduces costs, it affects sales and market positions: 'you'll think twice before buying a laptop made or sold by a company that is in Chapter 11' ('How the Rescue Culture Came to the United States', p. 197). Other commentators have recounted how airlines in Chapter 11 in the early 1990s (for example, Continental, Pan American, Eastern) found that the Chapter 11 stigma discouraged passengers: 'Going Bust for Survival', *Financial Times*, 3 October 2001.

the weeding out of companies who use resources inefficiently so as to allow the redeployment of those resources for more efficient uses and to leave the field to those firms who are able to act efficiently. Here there is a contrast with the Canadian Companies' Creditors Arrangement Act (CCAA) under which the courts are more likely to terminate reorganisation proceedings at an early stage: for example, on failure to gain a creditors' vote.[62]

The DIP regime gives further grounds for concern. An important worry is that Chapter 11 allows existing managers to trigger the process. This renders Chapter 11 open to abuse as a device employed not for genuine reasons of reorganisation but in order to reap a market advantage or for another purpose. It has been suggested that Chapter 11 is open to use, *inter alia*, to settle tort liabilities or legal judgments; to reduce labour costs; to reject pensions obligations; or to resolve environmental damage liabilities.[63] The absence of an early scrutiny of the reorganisation plans by an independent professional (as in English administration) or a court (as in Canada) means, first, that 'abuses' of Chapter 11 for tactical reasons are not picked up and, second, that proposals that have no real chance of success are allowed to run. The latter scenario means that the early liquidation of non-viable companies is prevented. Where, as in Canada, there is more aggressive court screening of applications for protection, this not only brings more rapid liquidation in hopeless cases but also encourages the firm's managers to produce and disseminate, at an early date, a body of information about the financial condition of a debtor and a reasoned case for the proposal. This points to a further difficulty of DIP. It is the debtor who draws up financial statements in order to file for Chapter 11 and such a debtor may be liable to present a misleading picture of the company's profitability. Chapter 11 procedures can be criticised as not creating, as in Canada, scrutiny processes that will favour the production of early, accurate information. This, in turn, conduces to a lack of trust and to higher litigation costs.

A further worry about Chapter 11 may be exaggerated. To leave the old managers at the helm of a firm may be 'like leaving an alcoholic in charge

---

62. See G. Triantis, 'The Interplay between Liquidation and Reorganisation in Bankruptcy: The Role of Screens, Gatekeepers and Guillotines' (1996) 16 *International Review of Law and Economics* 101–19 at 112. On continuing Canadian reform of the Bankruptcy and Insolvency Act 1992 and of the Companies' Creditors Arrangement Act 1985, see R. Marantz, R. Chartrand and S. Golick, 'Canadian Bankruptcy and Insolvency Law Reform Continues: The 1996/97 Amendments' (1998) 14 IL&P 22.

63. See Carruthers and Halliday, *Rescuing Business*, p. 266, and K. Delaney, *Strategic Bankruptcy: How Corporations and Creditors Use Chapter 11 to their Advantage* (University of California Press, Berkeley, 1989).

of a pub'[64] but corporate troubles do not always stem from mismanagement and, where managers have performed poorly, creditor pressure in the USA will tend to have resulted in the introduction of new managers at an early stage of the reorganisation. The Chapter 11 process, as has been noted, tends to be associated with high managerial turnover and 'is not a safe haven for management'.[65]

In other respects, however, there may be cause for concern about the role of the managers under Chapter 11. Some commentators argue that such managers are poorly disciplined by the Chapter 11 regime.[66] A key objective of Chapter 11 is to solve problems of financial distress but the regime may be so soft on managers that it fails to correct the underlying inefficiencies of which the financial distress was a mere manifestation. If a regime gives strong rights to creditors (as English insolvency law does) those creditors will have an incentive to monitor managers and will be able to punish managerial slackness by demanding changes of underperforming staff. The same creditors will be able to prompt restructuring and asset divestments that enhance efficiency. Managers, in short, will be kept on their toes by the looming presence of the empowered creditor.[67] Chapter 11 may be said to blunt this disciplinary role of creditors by its orientation towards rescue rather than enforcement.

This point can, however, be exaggerated. As already noted, creditors in the USA can bring pressure to bear so as to institute managerial changes, and a number of other factors may give managers an incentive to act efficiently. Firms may operate salary schemes that incentivise efficiency, shareholders may monitor managers, and the market for corporate control, as well as that for managerial talent, may again create healthy incentives. In relation to one worry, though, it is less easy to find reassurance. Chapter 11 may induce even operationally efficient managers to run unjustifiably high business risks. Within Chapter 11 the managers are liable to identify their interests with those of the equity holders and may be likely to indulge in speculative business actions. If these succeed the benefits will flow to the shareholders but if they fail the creditors will bear the losses and the reorganised estate reduces in value. Managers have little to lose from such high-risk activity.

64. Moss, 'Chapter 11', p. 19.
65. Carruthers and Halliday, *Rescuing Business*, p. 265; S. Gilson, 'Management Turnover and Financial Distress' (1989) 25 *Journal of Financial Economics* 241; LoPucki and Whitford, 'Corporate Governance'; Broude, 'How the Rescue Culture Came to the United States'; see also n. 44 above.
66. See e.g. Triantis, 'Interplay between Liquidation and Reorganisation', p. 104.
67. Ibid.

In one reported US case the company officials sought to save the business by resorting to the gaming tables of Las Vegas.[68]

From an English perspective, there are perhaps three final reservations about Chapter 11.[69] The first is that the US Code gives the shareholders a significant role in the rescue process. Moss argues: 'Where in reality there is nothing properly left for shareholders this seems to enable them to use blocking tactics so as to extract value from the situation in which equitably they should receive none.'[70] It should be noted, however, that Chapter 11 is a procedure which is not triggered by insolvency or near insolvency, and it may accordingly be responded that shareholders do have a genuine interest until the point of insolvency arises. A way out of this problem would be to provide that where a Chapter 11 filing does happen to involve a company that is in insolvency or likely to become insolvent, the court should be empowered to reduce the role of the shareholders. A second reservation about Chapter 11 concerns the latter's complex system of classes: a system designed to offer protection to creditors who may suffer from cramdown. The US classes regime makes for a drawn-out process that is legalistic and does not conduce to the quick sale of a going concern: a position that sits oddly with Chapter 11's strong rescue orientation.[71]

A final 'English' worry may relate to the tension in Chapter 11 between rescue of a company and rescue of a business. Preservation of the company may reflect a US concern to encourage investment in entrepreneurial enterprises but in England more emphasis might be placed on saving the business, preserving employment and protecting the wider business community from the fallout of an insolvency. English insolvency law, faced with a conflict between risks to the company and risks to the business, will tend to opt for the route that favours the business.[72] There may, moreover, be good grounds for adopting this position, one of which may be that shareholders are liable to be lower-cost risk bearers than employees or business partners since, *inter alia*, they are liable to be able to spread risks and absorb losses more efficiently than the latter.

A look at the US position should not, however, blind us to the approaches that other jurisdictions adopt, nor should lessons be learned exclusively from the US experience. Other countries have their own special

---

68. *Re Tri-State Paving*, discussed in Boshkoff and McKinney, 'Future of Chapter 11'.
69. See Moss, 'Chapter 11'.   70. Ibid., p. 18.
71. For a view that Chapter 11 has lost its role as a device for the protection of equity, see Ayer, 'Goodbye to Chapter 11'.
72. Moss, 'Chapter 11', p. 18. See, however, the UK Insolvency Act 1986 s. 8(3); see further ch. 9 below.

characteristics.[73] The South African system, for instance, relies very heavily on judicial supervision.[74] There is no floating charge in South Africa and no receivership, but the regime of judicial management involves the court appointment of an insolvency practitioner to take control of the business with the object of paying the company's debts and restoring the company to financial success. The process involves the courts throughout, with the master supervising the judicial manager and even calling creditors' meetings. The narrowness and expertise of this process has led most lawyers and businessmen to prefer to use the scheme of arrangement procedure that resembles that set out in the English Companies Act 1985 ss. 425–7.

Many noteworthy features are, of course, shared by different regimes. The French and German systems, for instance, have a single entry point to the insolvency process and the company is then assessed for the most appropriate outcome.[75] This contrasts with the English system in which rescue procedures may be triggered by managers, floating charge holders or creditors according to a number of procedures. In some countries the rescue mechanism is triggered by petition to the court with the company having to be insolvent (for example, in France and Australia[76]) or likely to be insolvent (for example, in Germany and Ireland). In England there is a requirement of likely insolvency for some procedures, but the US Chapter 11 involves no requirement of current or near insolvency at all.[77]

Countries vary on the priority they give to rescue and the balance they effect between creditor and debtor interests. In Japan, for instance, equity and employees are a primary consideration and informal rescues rather than legal bankruptcy procedures are the norm.[78] Banks and trading partners with shares will usually attempt to effect a rescue, and commitments over a number of years are not uncommon. If, however, matters

---

73. See Sealy, 'Corporate Rescue Procedures'.

74. See further Brown, *Corporate Rescue*, pp. 819–24.

75. IS 2000, p. 39. On German insolvency reforms see M. Balz, 'Market Conformity of Insolvency Proceedings: Policy Issues of the German Insolvency Law' (1997) *Brooklyn Journal of International Law* 167. On French insolvency reforms see P. J. Omar, 'The Future of Corporate Rescue Legislation in France, Part II: Survey and Analysis' [1997] ICCLR 171; Omar 'French Insolvency Laws: An Outline of Reform Proposals' [1999] Ins. Law. 132; Omar 'The Reform of Insolvency Law in France: The 1999 Orientation Document' [2000] Ins. Law. 263.

76. On Australia see A. Keay, 'The Australian Voluntary Administration Regime' (1996) 9 *Insolvency Intelligence* 41; Keay, 'Australian Insolvency Law: The Latest Developments' (1998) 11 *Insolvency Intelligence* 57.

77. IS 2000, p. 39.

78. Brown, *Corporate Rescue*, pp. 831–2. See also H. Oda, 'Japan's Case For Reform', *Financial Times*, 6 October 1998.

are resolved in court, the legal process looks to give returns to creditors. In Germany there is also a strong emphasis on the informal resolution of problems and staying out of court by relying on support from the banks. Creditors in Germany may either opt for a straight liquidation or can reschedule debt. In the latter event, a court-appointed official will decide if the firm can be saved in a way that meets at least 75 per cent of creditor claims. Creditors can veto any plans drawn up by the court and firm, but shareholders play no part in the process.

In France the law is hard on creditors. In the *redressement judiciaire* process a court-appointed official will help managers to draw up a plan and the law is directed towards the securing of jobs by keeping troubled firms alive. Creditors have no say over which plan the court accepts and the broad body of creditors have one representative (court-appointed) during negotiations. French law thus offers a stark contrast with English law which puts creditors first.

It has been noted that as far as running the rescue process is concerned, English law places the floating charge holder in a prime position and a secured creditor is given a strong hand, whereas Chapter 11 can give the DIP a central role. Bankers, as floating charge holders, are also given leading insolvency roles in New Zealand, Australia, Ireland and Sweden. The Irish and German regimes place the insolvency practitioner at centre stage, though in the glare of a judicial spotlight, and creditors make the final decision. In France the courts make the key decisions. Voting arrangements also vary markedly across regimes.[79] In English administration a simple majority of creditors (by value of claims) is required but in a company voluntary arrangement or a scheme of arrangement a 75 per cent by value majority is required.[80] In the USA a two-thirds majority of the value and number is required, whereas in Germany it is a simple majority. In Irish examinations the majority has to be numerical representing also a 75 per cent majority by value of claims represented at the creditors' meeting. In France the court decides the final outcome, and in some countries (for example, the USA and Ireland) there is a process of cramdown, whereby the court can overturn the creditors' decision.[81]

Moratoria periods again differ. Chapter 11 involves an indefinite initial period (though creditors can apply to the court to execute their security), whereas in France the period is a maximum of six months (subject to

---

79. See Brown, *Corporate Rescue*, chs. 24 and 25.
80. A majority in number voting is also required in a CVA.
81. See IS 2000, Annex A.

review). In Australia it is twenty-eight days (extendable to sixty); in Ireland it is sixty-three days (extendable to ninety-three); in Sweden it is typically a maximum of three months (extendable three-monthly to a year); and in New Zealand it is as agreed.

Finally, mention should be made of rescue financing and the provision made for this. In Chapter 11, post-petition financing and supplies can be obtained and priority given to their lender. Super-priority financing is also available in Germany, France, Australia, Sweden and New Zealand, but it is not available in England, although it was proposed by the DTI's Insolvency Service in 1993[82] (a suggestion later dropped).

To summarise this comparative sketch, other countries display a variety of players, processes and priorities in their insolvency and rescue regimes, but in all regimes certain difficult decisions have to be made on such matters as: Who controls corporate rescue operations? What sort of oversight regimes are appropriate? How should rescue needs be balanced against creditors' rights? Should rescue processes be triggered only on insolvency or near insolvency? Whose voices shall be heard in rescue procedures? Chapters 7–10 below examine how these issues and others are dealt with in England. But first it is worth reviewing the rescue options that are open to an English company.

Rescue options

Troubled companies and their directors, creditors or shareholders are able to take a number of informal as well as formal steps in order to effect rescues. Informal actions do not demand any resort to statutory insolvency procedures but are contractually based. They are usually instituted by directors or creditors and they may involve the use of professional help: where, for instance, a 'company doctor' or firm of accountants is appointed (usually on a creditor's insistence) to investigate the company's affairs and to make recommendations. Such informal steps may result in the kinds of remedial action already referred to: changes in management, corporate reorganisations or refinancings, for example. Alternatively, under the 'London Approach', co-ordination of a creditors' agreement in accordance with informal guidelines may be achieved with the Bank of England acting as an honest broker in making efforts to persuade reluctant parties to

---

82. DTI/IS, *Company Voluntary Arrangements and Administration Orders: A Consultative Document* (October 1993). See ch. 9 below.

pursue such informal settlements.[83] Formal arrangements under which rescues may be attempted are provided for in the Insolvency Act 1986[84] and include company voluntary arrangements (CVAs),[85] receiverships and administrative receiverships[86] and administration.[87]

From the company management and shareholders' point of view, a general advantage of informal rescue is that publicity concerning corporate troubles may be minimal, the stigma of formal insolvency may be avoided and the goodwill and reputation of the company preserved. Avoiding the adverse publicity that would often follow the commencement of a formal insolvency proceeding can have a significant impact on the ability of a company to survive and on the realisable value of its assets.[88] The cost of informal procedures is also likely to be lower than where court proceedings are involved.[89] Delays and attendant costs may, furthermore, be reduced where rescues are managed without hostile litigation.[90] Informality also ensures flexibility so that terms can be adjusted and renegotiated in a way that formal procedures (such as approval processes) do not allow. From the point of view of company directors, a further considerable advantage of informality is that this avoids the intervention of an insolvency practitioner in the role of a formal scrutiniser of directorial actions. Where rescues are formal, IPs possess extensive powers to investigate corporate affairs together with a duty to report on the conduct of directors.[91] Such IPs will, moreover, assume control of the company. Informal rescues thus avoid the investigations and changes in power and control that directors may fear.[92] Another incentive for management to see that the company remains outside formal insolvency

---

83. See ch. 7 below. In 1998 the Financial Services Authority took over from the Bank of England as banking regulator.

84. See too Companies Act 1985 s. 425; chs. 9 and 10 below.

85. Insolvency Act 1986 ss. 1–7.   86. Ibid., ss. 28–69.   87. Ibid., ss. 8–27.

88. See Brown, *Corporate Rescue*, pp. 11–13; N. Segal, 'Rehabilitation and Approaches other than Formal Insolvency Procedures' in R. Cranston (ed.), *Banks and Remedies* (Oxford University Press, Oxford, 1992) p. 133.

89. But see discussion of the London Approach in ch. 7 below.

90. 'Formal insolvency not only crystallises parties' rights, but also their attitudes': Brown, *Corporate Rescue*, p. 11.

91. See Insolvency Act 1986 ss. 234–7. Once an administrative receiver has been appointed, an administration order made or the company has gone into liquidation, the relevant IP is under a duty to submit to the Secretary of State a report on the conduct of the directors of the company: Company Directors' Disqualification Act 1986 s. 7(3) and the Insolvent Companies (Reports on Conduct of Directors) No. 2 Rules 1986. This could lead to action being taken for the disqualification of those directors: see ch. 15 below.

92. Though a cessation of power would, from that point, reduce dangers of subsequent liquidator actions for fraudulent or wrongful trading under the Insolvency Act 1986 ss. 213 and 214; see ch. 15 below.

is that formal insolvency procedures carry with them the stigma of (usually culpable) failure.[93] In terms of external perceptions, particularly in employment markets, it may be 'bad news' for management to be associated with a company which has had recourse to formal insolvency procedures.[94]

From the point of view of many banks and secured lenders, informal rescue may be attractive in ways that can outweigh attendant risks. It not only offers the prospect of repayment in full, if ultimately successful, but it also provides an opportunity to acquire a fresh injection of funds from other sources (such as shareholders or other banks) and it allows such well-positioned creditors to extract enhanced or new security, or priority, as the price for supplying further funds to the company. A bank, for instance, may improve its position by taking a floating charge as security. This will give it the power to veto an administration petition[95] and, even if a rescue ultimately fails, the bank will often have improved its security position and will be able to appoint a receiver to realise its debt ahead of unsecured creditors.[96] Unsecured creditors, in the main, will remain ignorant of such informal rescues and are likely, as a result, to suffer a transfer of insolvency value in favour of the secured creditors.

This last point introduces a first disadvantage of informal rescue: its potential to prejudice the interests of less well-placed creditors. Informality may be attractive to directors, but, from the point of view of certain creditors, a deficiency of informality may be the absence of investigative powers and the lack of an inquiry into the role of directors in bringing a company to the brink of disaster. A fundamental weakness of informal rescue is, furthermore, that the agreement of all parties whose rights are affected will generally be required if the rescue is to succeed. Informal rescues demand that parties with contractual rights agree to compromise, waive or defer debts, or alter priorities. Dissenting creditors, accordingly, have the power to halt informal rescues by triggering formal insolvency procedures, including liquidation. This renders the informal rescue a fragile device that

---

93. See Segal, 'Rehabilitation and Approaches', p. 132.
94. Ibid., where the point is made that we have not yet reached the stage in England (as arguably occurs in the USA) of regarding the reorganisation of companies in difficulty through the use of court procedures as 'being an acceptable, even standard, tool of business management'.
95. If the taking of the charge results in administrative receivership being created: see Insolvency Act 1986 s. 29(2)(a); Re Croftbell [1990] BCC 781. But see ch. 8 below.
96. See Brown, Corporate Rescue, p. 12; J. R. Lingard, Corporate Rescues and Insolvencies (2nd edn, Butterworths, London, 1989) p. 37.

is dependent on a high degree of co-operation from a range of parties.[97] In contrast, a formal procedure such as administration involves a moratorium on the enforcement of a wide range of creditors' rights and so creates a more sustainable space within which a rescue can be organised.

Conclusions

Rescue procedures can be evaluated in accordance with the measures set out in chapter 2 and, in making such evaluations, interests in addition to those of creditors have to be borne in mind. Rescues involve parties acting with very divergent concerns; some participants in rescues possess conflicts of interest; and rescues often demand that important decisions be taken in the most difficult and urgent of circumstances. The procedures that are used in attempts to turn companies around might, accordingly, be expected to be open to serious question when assessments of legitimacy are made. Such assessments demand that the particulars of different rescue arrangements be dealt with and these are considered in the chapters that follow.

97. Brown, *Corporate Rescue*, p. 13. In an informal bank rescue, for example (see pp. 219–29 below), the negotiations between the banks are as intensive as, and often more difficult than, negotiations with the borrower: 'there will usually be a multiplicity of interests, and even different rights and obligations within the bank group which need to be ironed out. Some banks may start out as secured, while others start out as unsecured.' Segal, 'Rehabilitation and Approaches', p. 133.

ec chap 2

7

Informal rescue

For most troubled companies, entering into formal insolvency procedures is a course of last resort only to be pursued when informal strategies have been exhausted. These informal strategies may, as discussed above, take a variety of forms, and different modes of action are reviewed in this chapter. Before looking at particular devices, however, it is worth considering the processes that lead up to the selection of an informal rescue strategy.

Assessing the prospects

There are seldom clearly identifiable times in corporate life when rescue steps are required. As noted in chapter 4, the financial state of a company can be thought of as a portrait painted by accountants or company directors, a picture that may reflect a variety of 'calculative technologies', disciplinary perspectives and even sets of negotiations.[1] Different actors, moreover, may play key roles in setting up rescues. Often it is a firm's bank that initiates turnaround steps. When insolvency professionals are brought into a firm to carry out turnaround work such a step is instigated by a secured lender in 60 per cent of cases.[2] A firm's own directors may institute actions. They may call in firms of accountants to act as company doctors or specialist corporate troubleshooters may be consulted. Directors are responsible for appointing turnaround IPs in a fifth of cases.[3] There are

---

1. See P. Miller and M. Power, 'Calculating Corporate Failure' in Y. Dezalay and D. Sugarman (eds.), *Professional Competition and Professional Power: Lawyers, Accountants and the Social Construction of Markets* (Routledge, London, 1995).

2. See R3, Ninth Survey of Business Recovery in the UK (2001) p. 2. There is now a Society of Turnaround Professionals with fifty founding members. This body was established by R3 and held its first AGM in 2001: see 'Turnaround Talk' (2001) *Recovery* (September).

3. R3, Ninth Survey.

particular dangers to be borne in mind by directors when rescue measures are under consideration. They must look to their potential legal liabilities and must act consistently with their obligations. These are reviewed in chapter 15 but will be noted in outline here.[4]

The first of four main areas of concern is the director's potential liability for wrongful trading under section 214 of the Insolvency Act 1986, which requires directors to monitor the financial position of the company and when they conclude, or should conclude, that there is no reasonable prospect of their company avoiding insolvent liquidation they must take every step which a reasonably diligent person would take to minimise potential loss to the company's creditors. If, after a company has entered insolvent liquidation, a court considers a director has failed to discharge such a duty, it may require the director to make such contributions to the company's assets as it thinks fit.[5] What matters for such purposes is not the actual knowledge of the director but the knowledge that might reasonably be expected of a person carrying out the director's particular functions in the company. In the rescue context, directors must consider the prospects of avoiding insolvent liquidation and, if they are unsure of the position, must take heed of their duties to minimise potential losses to creditors and, when necessary, must cease trading and commence suitable insolvency procedures. A particular concern of directors will, accordingly, be whether any agreed arrangement will allow debts to be paid as they fall due and whether projected cash flows and incomes will allow rescheduled loan payments to be met.

A second area of directorial concern will be their potential liability for fraudulent trading under section 213 of the Insolvency Act 1986. Directors, under this provision, may be liable to make contributions to the company's assets where it appears, in the case of the winding up of the company, that any business has been carried on with intent to defraud creditors or for any fraudulent purpose. Criminal liability may also be involved.[6] Fraudulent trading will thus be engaged in when a director obtains credit for the company when he knows that there is no good reason for thinking that funds will be available for repayment when due or shortly thereafter.[7]

---

4. See N. Segal, 'Rehabilitation and Approaches other than Formal Insolvency Procedures' in R. Cranston (ed.), *Banks and Remedies* (Oxford University Press, Oxford, 1992).

5. See Insolvency Act 1986 s. 214(1). Such jurisdiction was deemed to be primarily compensatory in *Re Produce Marketing Consortium Ltd* [1989] 5 BCC 569; cf. discussion in ch. 15 below.

6. Companies Act 1985 s. 458; *R v. Grantham* [1984] 2 WLR 815.

7. *R v. Grantham*.

A third area of relevant directorial concern covers the general fiduciary duties of directors to act *bona fide* in the interests of the company, a duty that requires consideration of the interests of creditors as well as shareholders.[8] Where rescue arrangements are under discussion, directors must remember that their fiduciary duty relates to all creditors' interests, not merely those of the dominant creditors who may be those principally engaged in negotiating a rescue.

Finally, directors should consider whether a rescue arrangement may render them liable to disqualification from being a company director. A court must disqualify a director where it is satisfied that he was a director or shadow director of a company which has become insolvent and it is satisfied that his conduct as a director is such that he is unfit to be involved in the management of the company.[9] When companies are in trouble the real risks on this front tend to arise when directors hold creditors at bay while rescue options are reviewed or repay some debts rather than others for strategic reasons.[10] It is not, indeed, only directors who have to exercise a degree of legal caution in the rescue context. Lenders are potentially liable for wrongful trading as shadow directors where they become too closely involved with managing a company in its rescue phase and the company ends up in liquidation.[11]

As for the different processes that tend to be adopted in the progress towards a rescue, these can be thought of with reference to the following stages.

The alarm stage

First alarms are often sounded in companies when it is not possible to find the cash to pay immediate bills.[12] The company directors may then raise the issue of rescue steps or a creditor may do this: as where a bank sees that overdraft limits are being exceeded unacceptably and expresses its concerns. A meeting will usually be called at this stage and major

8. *Liquidators of West Mercia Safety Wear Ltd* v. *Dodd* [1988] 4 BCC 30. See further ch. 15 below; V. Finch, 'Directors' Duties: Insolvency and the Unsecured Creditor' in A. Clarke (ed.), *Current Issues in Insolvency Law* (Stevens, London, 1991); Finch, 'Directors' Duties Towards Creditors' (1989) 10 Co. Law. 23; Finch, 'Creditors' Interests and Directors' Obligations' in S. Sheikh and W. Rees (eds.), *Corporate Governance and Corporate Control* (Cavendish, London, 1995).

9. Company Directors' Disqualification Act 1986 s. 6. See V. Finch, 'Disqualifying Directors: Issues of Rights, Privileges and Employment' (1993) ILJ 35; and ch. 15 below.

10. See *Re Sevenoaks Stationers Retail Ltd* [1990] BCC 765.

11. See Insolvency Act 1986 s. 251; *Kuwait Asia EC Bank* v. *National Mutual Life Nominees Ltd* [1990] BCC 567; *Re Hydrodan (Corby) Ltd* [1994] BCC 161; *Re PFTZM Ltd* [1995] BCC 40; *Secretary of State for Trade and Industry* v. *Deverell* [2000] 2 WLR 907 (CA); and ch. 15 below.

12. See Segal, 'Rehabilitation and Approaches', p. 147.

creditors will discuss issues with directors. At this point the Governor of the Bank of England has suggested that three things are often evident.[13] The first is that no-one, including the company, has a sufficiently complete and robust picture of the company's financial position to make a soundly based decision on its future. Secondly, the amount of a debt, including off-balance-sheet items and the number of creditors, is usually larger than anybody supposed and, thirdly, it is far from uncommon that the creditors find they have varying interests.

The evaluation stage

When the banks have become apprised of the company's position there usually follows a period in which urgent attempts are made to identify the nature and extent of a firm's problems and to assess prospects of turnaround.[14] At this time deadlines for action vary from case to case but may be very tight, the main pressures to the company coming from cash flow problems and threats of actions by creditors. Attention will be paid to means of securing a breathing space that will allow the company to regroup and, accordingly, sources of financing to cover immediate needs must be secured and the co-operation of creditors must be sought. Here it should be emphasised that informal rescues require the unanimous consent of affected creditors[15] and that this may often be difficult to obtain. Where, for example, a good deal of debt is owed to trade creditors who are heterogeneous and not amenable to (or capable of) negotiating rescue agreements, informal solutions will be difficult to achieve.[16] Where, in contrast, debts are owed to small numbers of sophisticated lenders such as banks, the prospects of informal resolutions are brighter. To this end it is commonly necessary to bring major creditors together and to seek to

13. Ibid., quoting the Governor's *Special Report*, 25 October 1990.

14. Ibid., pp. 148–9; C. Campbell and B. Underdown, *Corporate Insolvency in Practice: An Analytical Approach* (Chapman, London, 1991) pp. 62–5. The Small Business Service set up a rescue scheme in 2001. Within the scheme business advisers go into small companies suffering from short-term difficulties and put together rescue packages on their behalf (*Financial Times*, 24 September 2001). For a review of the rescue role of the Swedish Office for Composition and Reconstruction see G. Cook and K. Pond, 'Swedish Corporate Rescue' (2001) *Recovery* (September) 27. For an analysis of other jurisdictions see, for example, S. Gilson, 'Managing Default: Some Evidence on How Firms Choose between Workouts and Chapter 11' and T. Hoshi, A. Kashyap and D. Scharfstein, 'The Role of Banks in Reducing the Costs of Financial Distress in Japan', both in J. S. Bhandari and L. A. Weiss (eds.), *Corporate Bankruptcy: Economic and Legal Perspectives* (Cambridge University Press, Cambridge, 1996). See also ch. 6 above.

15. A. Belcher, *Corporate Rescue* (Sweet & Maxwell, London, 1997) p. 116.

16. S. C. Gilson, K. John and L. H. P. Lang, 'Troubled Debt Restructurings: An Empirical Study of Private Reorganisation of Firms in Default' (1990) 27 *Journal of Financial Economics* 323.

co-ordinate actions. Where appropriate the creditors will agree to a period of grace in which existing credit lines are maintained and, if necessary, extra funds are provided for an interim period.

Analysis of the company's state will proceed apace during this period and parties will explore such issues as the reasons for the company's decline, the severity of the problems encountered, the extent of the viable core of the business, the human resources available to the company and the state of relevant markets and positions within these.[17] Financial reviews of the whole company will be undertaken, including an audit of each of the functions carried out by the company.

Such an evaluation will frequently be carried out by investigating accountants who will usually be nominated by the lead bank. The overall aim is to identify the company's potential for survival and the steps that have to be taken to produce turnaround. Company directors at such a time will not, however, be inactive. They will continue to manage the company's affairs and will usually have been asked to prepare business plans and sets of proposals for dealing with the company's difficulties. The investigating accountants have a role in considering such business plans and both the investigators and creditors will focus on whether the critical ingredients for successful turnaround are to be encountered in the company. To this end they will examine whether the managers are sufficiently able, motivated and decisive to effect a rescue, whether there is a core of business that is strong enough to found restoration of corporate fortunes and whether necessary changes can be made within the available time scales.[18]

Towards the end of the evaluation stage will come the review by the rescuing bank or banks.[19] This review will consider the report of the investigating accountants together with the managers' business plan. Discussions with investigators and managers will be conducted and the banks will attempt not only to assess the prospects for company turnaround but also to produce some consistency and co-ordination of approach between the various banks. They will thus come to terms with issues of priorities between creditors in relation to recoveries and also with the banks' collective position. Key issues in relation to the latter are whether additional security should be taken, whether new financial facilities should be provided and whether equity interests should be exchanged for debt.[20]

17. Campbell and Underdown, *Corporate Insolvency*, p. 62.
18. Ibid., p. 61. See also J. Wilding, 'Instructing Investigating Accountants' (1994) 7 *Insolvency Intelligence* 3.
19. See A. Lickorish, 'Debt Rescheduling' (1990) 6 IL&P 38, 41.
20. Ibid.

The recovery planning stage

If action at the preceding stages suggests that the prospects of recovery are good, plans for recovery will be devised. By this time the company and its banks will have agreed the terms on which finances will be made available during the support period and on which new securities will be offered. A support agreement will set out relevant provisions. The creditors will also have agreed arrangements between themselves covering, for instance, the sharing of losses and recoveries and the interest rates appropriate.

When recovery objectives and strategies are drawn up by managers and advisers, they must be supported by creditors and also by other key players beyond the company. The assent of a major customer or supplier may, for example, have to be secured if a recovery is to have prospects of success.

Implementing strategies

On completing the above preliminary stages, a number of agreed actions will be taken in an effort to achieve corporate turnaround.[21] The first of these steps may, indeed, have already commenced.

Managerial and organisational reforms

A successful rescue will almost always involve the retention or institution of an appropriate workforce and managerial team. Once the future activities of the company are settled upon, it will be necessary to see that persons with the appropriate skills are employed and that those who will no longer contribute appropriately will part ways with the company. Replacements, recruitments, promotions and staff reductions may all have to be brought about and attempts made to reduce the attendant disruptions and confusions. Changes at the top of management will often be required in order to move a company in a significant new direction out of crisis and to signal to outsiders and markets that positive remedial steps are being taken. R3's Ninth Survey of Business Recovery (2001) found that insolvency professionals considered that for companies with over

---

21. On turnaround techniques and their use, see Society of Practitioners of Insolvency Eighth Survey, *Company Insolvency in the United Kingdom* (SPI, London, 1999) pp. 12–14. The survey revealed that turnaround efforts failed (and formal insolvency ensued) in 37 per cent of cases in the manufacturing, wholesale, distribution and construction sectors. R3's Ninth Survey revealed that respondent insolvency professionals considered that in 77 per cent of cases there were, by the time they were appointed, no possible actions that might realistically have averted company failure. Nearly one in five businesses did, however, survive insolvency and continue in one form or another.

£5 million turnover a change of management could have averted company failure in 10 per cent of cases. When the SPI asked its members, in 1998, what actions companies might have taken to avoid falling into 'intensive care' scenarios, a change of management (in 28 per cent of cases) came second only to earlier actions to stem losses.[22] In more than half of SPI-studied cases inadequate management was noted as an obstacle or hindrance to obtaining a non-insolvency solution to corporate difficulties (but such difficulties were rarely so serious as to prevent turnaround).[23] As for methods of company rescue, the R3 Ninth Survey revealed that turnaround practitioners used change of management as a primary tool of rehabilitation in 20 per cent of cases.

On the organisational front, a variety of steps can be taken. The corporate governance structure of the company can be reformed so as to improve checks and balances, but the organisation of operations can also be revised in ways that may improve performance: for example, by decentralising and devolving power so as to create lower-cost modes of supervision, greater senses of responsibility, increases in morale and tighter management. Such decentralisations of operations may also lead to greater flexibility by creating identifiable free-standing parts of a business and, accordingly, greater opportunities to sell off these units as elements in asset reduction strategies.[24]

Asset reductions

A strategy designed to secure profitability is the reduction of corporate activities to a healthy core by cutting away unprofitable products, branches, customers or divisions and disposing of assets that are poorly utilised or are not needed for core profitable business operations.[25] Such reductions may include sales of subsidiaries, equipment or surplus fixed assets, closure of branches or streamlining of stocking arrangements. Asset reductions may, however, involve considerable costs. Beyond the fees payable to lawyers, accountants and other professionals there may be redundancy expenses, prices attached to contract cancellations and other divestment costs.

22. SPI Eighth Survey, p. 13. R3's Ninth Survey cited managerial failings as the most common primary reason for corporate failure (25 per cent of cases) and in nearly 50 per cent of cases insolvency was due primarily to the failings of management.
23. SPI Eighth Survey.
24. See Campbell and Underdown, *Corporate Insolvency*, p. 67.
25. Ibid., p. 66. On the use of sell-offs and management buyouts see Belcher, *Corporate Rescue*, pp. 26–31.

Cost reductions

An essential element in most rescue packages is a programme of cost reductions.[26] This will involve investigations into current costs and potential savings and will cover not merely raw materials and equipment but
also workforce expenditure.

Debt restructuring

Troubled companies are often too highly geared or have a pattern of borrowing that is inefficient. A number of steps can be taken to reorganise corporate debts but successful reorganisation depends on the ability of those
managing the company to convince financiers and other interested parties
that the appropriate rescue plan has been put into effect, that the prospects
of recovery are sound and that the proposed debt reorganisations offer a
better prospect of return to creditors than would resort to formal insolvency procedures.

If the company's main problems relate to cash flows, short-term difficulties or underinvestment, steps can be taken to inject new funds into
the company. Creditors in such circumstances will usually demand additional levels of security and may act to improve the overall security of
their position: for example, by using floating charges over the corporate
assets.[27] Co-operation from banks is most likely to be found where large
reputable companies encounter such difficulties. Banks fear bad publicity and any association with conspicuous failure or large-scale unemployment. They will accordingly tend to be most helpful to large, high-profile
and respectable firms with considerable numbers of employees.[28]

Consolidation of funding is a step that can also be taken when banks are
helpful. Substantial benefits can be obtained by reorganising a proliferation of funding agreements and bringing these together in a simple financial arrangement. This process may allow a firm to negotiate a reduction

26. The SPI Eighth Survey indicated that the most common primary turnaround techniques
were cost reductions, debt restructurings, raising new equity and negotiating with banks.
These steps were followed in (descending) frequency of use by improved financial controls,
asset reductions, changes of management, product/market changes, organisational changes
and improved marketing (SPI Eighth Survey, p. 13); the R3 Ninth Survey of 2001 indicated
that the primary method of rehabilitation used most frequently by turnaround managers
was debt restructuring, resorted to in 39 per cent of cases involving such practitioners. Cost
reduction, however, was only used as a primary method in just over 11 per cent of cases, but as
R3 noted, 'little can be read into this change due to the small sample but it will be interesting
to see next year's results'.
27. When new security is given to a creditor in a rescue operation it may be questioned
whether this constitutes a preference under the Insolvency Act 1986 s. 239; see also Insolvency
Act 1986 s. 245. See ch. 12 below.
28. See Lickorish, 'Debt Rescheduling', pp. 38, 39.

in the overall cost of borrowing or a conversion of short- to longer-term credit facilities. Other arrangements such as sales and lease-backs of property and equipment may additionally be employed.

Debts can also be rescheduled in order to ease immediate problems. This may be a useful course of action where the company's credit is supplied by a small number of banks and the company's financial problems are short term in nature.[29] Rescheduling does not, however, remove balance sheet deficits or improve gearing ratios. It involves a contract between the debtor company with all or some creditors, and this may alter obligations by deferring payments, harmonising obligations between different creditors or granting security (or additional security) to creditors.

Rescheduling may appeal to banks because, as noted already, such informality avoids the adverse publicity involved in precipitating the liquidation of a company. It may also allow securities to be adjusted and, where a number of banks are involved, rescheduling may prove far less complex and expensive than receivership. Similarly, where creditors in a variety of jurisdictions are involved with a company, it may be quicker and cheaper to respond to difficulties by negotiating new contracts than by resorting to formal proceedings. Problems with rescheduling will tend to arise when many banks are involved but some of them feel uncommitted to the company involved, lack a close relationship to it and feel no loyalty to the enterprise.[30] In these circumstances, the creditor agreement necessary to make rescheduling work will be difficult to secure.

A particular response to multi-bank support for companies with liquidity problems was developed in London in the 1970s and is now known as the 'London Approach'.[31] The Bank of England identified, at that time, a need to co-ordinate discussions among banks with loans outstanding to firms in difficulty. For broad economic reasons the Bank wanted to avoid unnecessary receiverships and liquidations and preserve viable jobs and productive capacity.[32] The principles of the London Approach were established in 1990 and the process is entirely informal and

---

29. See generally ibid.   30. Ibid., p. 40.

31. See J. Flood, R. Abbey, E. Skordaki and P. Aber, *The Professional Restructuring of Corporate Rescue: Company Voluntary Arrangements and the London Approach*, ACCA Research Report 45 (ACCA, London, 1995); J. Flood, 'Corporate Recovery: The London Approach' (1995) 11 IL&P 82; Belcher, *Corporate Rescue*, pp. 117–22; J. Armour and S. Deakin, 'Norms in Private Insolvency Procedures: The "London Approach" to the Resolution of Financial Distress', ESRC Centre for Business Research Working Paper Series No. 173, September 2000, reprinted in [2001] 1 JCLS 21; R. Obank, 'European Recovery Practice and Reform: Part I' [2000] Ins. Law. 149, 151–2.

32. Flood *et al.*, *Professional Restructuring*, p. 27.

comprises a set of principles providing a framework for bank support.[33] There is, by design, no formal code or list of rules[34] and the approach relies on consensus, persuasion and banking collegiality in order to reconcile the interests of different creditors to a company in difficulty.[35] The process involves four phases. First comes a standstill covering all debt owed and all bank lenders must give support at this stage. Second, the bank sends in an investigating accountant (who will not be the company's auditors). Third, the lead bank negotiates with the other banks in order to secure new facilities for the company (which are generally accorded priority) and, finally, where negotiations are successful, a new financing agreement for the company is put into effect and is monitored.

The London Approach has been said to have four main tenets:[36] the banks are supportive and do not rush to appoint receivers; information is shared amongst all parties to the workout; banks and other creditors work in a co-ordinated fashion to reach a collective view on whether and how a company shall be given financial support; and pain is shared on an equal basis. London Approach proposals typically provide that the banks share the benefits of the rescue and the costs of the restructuring process pro rata to their outstanding exposure at the time when the banks agree to desist from enforcement actions against the debtor company.

In favour of the London Approach, it can be said to provide an efficient means of rescue that avoids the delays and expense of formal actions. Central to the Approach has been the role of the Bank of England in facilitating the emergence of an agreed course of action by the banks. The Bank has acted as a neutral intermediary and chairman and has used its authority to push discussions through banks' hierarchies. Informal pressures can also be exerted by the Bank of England where the banks are proving difficult. Most lending agreements contain covenants that require the unanimous agreement of creditor banks to the kind of changes of repayment practice that rescues usually demand. This means that one recalcitrant bank can threaten to vote against a rescue proposal and put the company at issue

---

33. See now the guiding principles set out in the British Bankers' Association, *Description of the London Approach* (Mimeo, 1996).

34. The Bank published the approach through a number of papers by Bank officials: see P. Kent, 'The London Approach' (1993) 8 *Journal of International Banking Law* 81–4; Kent, 'The London Approach: Distressed Debt Trading' (1994) *Bank of England Quarterly Bulletin* 110; Kent, 'Corporate Workouts: A UK Perspective' (1997) 6 *International Insolvency Review* 165.

35. See C. Bird, 'The London Approach' (1996) 12 IL&P 87; R. Floyd, 'Corporate Recovery: The London Approach' (1995) 11 IL&P 82; D. Weston, 'The London Rules and Debt Restructuring' (1992) Sol. Jo. 216.

36. Belcher, *Corporate Rescue*, p. 118; Kent, 'London Approach: Distressed Debt Trading', 110.

into receivership unless the other banks repay its own loan. Such a stance would prejudice the rescue, but the Bank of England under the London Approach has been able to bring pressure on a rogue bank and encourage it to co-operate. If necessary the Bank of England has been prepared to talk to a foreign bank's national regulator in order to bring the creditor into line. It has been said that the Bank's role 'is part missionary, part peacemaker. As missionary we advocate the London Approach as a basis for constructive co-operation regarding customers' cash flow crises. As peacemaker we try to help banks resolve those difficulties which threaten to undermine an attempted workout ... Our interest is not as a supervisor or "regulator" of the market.'[37]

A number of factors may lead banks to co-operate in a London Approach rescue.[38] A first consideration has been the threat of Bank of England regulatory sanctions, which may underpin the informal pressure applied by the Bank. This may well have been the case in the 1970s and 1980s but Bank interventions in workouts were reduced from the mid-1980s onwards in favour of the Bank's encouraging the involved parties to organise workouts themselves. The Bank's supervisory role as banking regulator was, moreover, transferred to the Financial Services Authority in June 1998.[39] Other incentives to co-operate do exist, though. Individual banks may fear that if they act obstructively, the banking community will exclude them from further profitable deals or deny them future co-operation. This fear will also reduce 'hold-outs': strategies in which individual banks may attempt to extract better terms by threatening non-cooperation. Co-ordination is also encouraged by the practice whereby a 'lead bank' organises the gathering and distribution of the information relevant to the rescue. This cuts down the information asymmetries that would reduce trust and co-operation levels. It also rules out 'free riding' in the information collection process, since costs are shared.[40]

The London Approach may also offer an effective way of avoiding such publicity as would introduce unproductive disruptions of the rescue process. Where the main bank creditors adopt a low profile in the London Approach, the company's unsecured creditors may be unaware of developments and this may avoid the interference with the turnaround process

37. P. Kent, 'The London Approach: Lessons from Recent Years' (1994) *Insolvency Bulletin* 5 (February).
38. See Armour and Deakin, 'Norms in Private Insolvency Procedures'.
39. Ibid., p. 3. See the Bank of England Act 1998.
40. See generally R. Haugen and L. Senbet, 'Bankruptcy and Agency Costs' (1988) 23 *Journal of Financial and Quantitative Analysis* 27–38.

or the company's business operations. (A high profile well-publicised rescue process might in contrast be followed swiftly by refusals to supply and
customer disappearances.) Secrecy has also been said to be a precondition
of co-operative rather than competitive behaviour on the part of banks.[41]

Institutionalised norms have also been said to have a role in overcoming
co-ordination problems.[42] Armour and Deakin argue that in order for a rational creditor to renegotiate debts rather than enforce them, the prospective gains must be greater under the former strategy and the creditor must
be confident that other creditors will see the likely surpluses from renegotiation as at least matching the expected returns from insolvency proceedings. In the London Approach such confidence flows from the common
knowledge that negotiations are secret and require unanimity; that information will be shared; and that new lending will be given super-priority.
It is the emergence of these understandings as accepted norms (notwithstanding their non-legal status) that, on this account, gives the London
Approach effectiveness.

The value of the London Approach has, however, been largely confined
to very large rescue attempts and extensive borrowings.[43] One reason is
that implementation costs have been high – up to £6 million – and the
Bank of England has had to be selective in using its good offices.[44] The
fees of the lawyers and accountants who act in such rescues have been criticised as extremely high and there may be other indirect costs that are
not inconsiderable.[45] One variety of indirect costs may arise from the loss
of decision-making power that a rescue produces within a firm. With the
London Approach, a firm may remain under bank control for up to ten
years[46] and the firm's managers may lose the power to take decisions without approval. The market may also respond to rescue measures in a manner that acts to the detriment of the company. In response to these points,
however, it is worth bearing in mind that inefficiencies and losses to firms
and creditors would be considerably higher if formal processes were to be
pursued. What may remain a concern is whether the efficiency strengths of

41. Flood *et al.*, *Professional Restructuring*, p. 24.
42. See Armour and Deakin, 'Norms in Private Insolvency Procedures', pp. 30 ff. (JCLS version).
43. Only around 150 London Approach workouts were effected between the late 1980s and the 1990s: see Flood *et al.*, *Professional Restructuring*, p. ii; F. Pointon, 'London Approach: A Look at its Application and its Alternatives' (1994) *Insolvency Bulletin* 5 (March).
44. Flood *et al.*, *Professional Restructuring*.
45. See K. Wruck, 'Financial Distress, Reorganisation and Organisational Efficiency' (1990) 27 *Journal of Financial Economics* 419; Belcher, *Corporate Rescue*, p. 121.
46. Flood *et al.*, *Professional Restructuring*, p. ii.

the London Approach are undermined by the fee levels of lawyers, accountants and other professional consultants. If the market for such services is not highly competitive it is to be expected that the gains of the London Approach will be materially captured not by the companies, shareholders or creditors but by the consulting professions.

A further factor that limits the utility of the London Approach is the lack of any formal moratorium and the need for unanimity of support from relevant creditors. A company that is the subject of such a workout will be exposed to creditors' demands while the terms of the rescue are being negotiated. When a large number of banks is involved in such negotiations the complexities involved may make for extensive periods of discussion and, accordingly, exposure to demands. Whether banks will co-operate with a London Approach rescue will depend on their balancing the costs of negotiation versus the prospects of disruption and unproductive outcomes, and high numbers of banks and other creditors will militate against a successful use of the London Approach. In cross-border cases the domestic and international creditors involved may be of very many kinds. They are likely to be geographically dispersed and may have assets spread across a number of jurisdictions. They will have to work together against a background of different attitudes, procedures, expectations, regulatory regimes and laws. Languages, modes of interpretation, conceptual frameworks and insolvency law objectives may also vary.[47] Relationships of trust may also be strained by suspicions that the domestic banks are too favourably disposed towards the domestic debtor (for reasons of longer-term domestic strategy). Co-operation between the banks may, as a result, be low.[48] Where large sums are owed to numbers of trade creditors it is likely to be difficult to obtain informal agreements to a workout. The claims of trade creditors, assuming these creditors are included in deliberations, may also be highly divergent in their characteristics and this may impede negotiations. Trade creditors, moreover, may be less inclined to make informal arrangements than banks and they may be less well equipped to negotiate such deals.[49]

As for secured creditors, they are likely to see their interests as concurrent with those of unsecured creditors where the troubled company's collateral is small but if they are fully secured, their incentive to co-operate

---

47. See Obank, 'European Recovery', p. 149.
48. Ibid. The London Approach has been used as a model in other jurisdictions: see N. Segal, 'Corporate Recovery and Rescue: Mastering the Key Strategies Necessary for Successful Cross Border Workouts – Part I and Part II' (2000) 13 *Insolvency Intelligence* 17, 25.
49. See Belcher, *Corporate Rescue*, p. 116.

may be weak. In some conditions, moreover, a secured creditor may possess an incentive to move towards immediate enforcement – where, for example, delay will reduce the value of the relevant collateral[50] – and here they may prefer insolvency to renegotiation. Where, as in the UK, it is common practice for companies to raise significant sums by secured loans, this imposes limits on negotiated solutions. More optimistically, however, it can be argued that even where banks have secured loans in such circumstances they may be induced to adopt a co-operative stance because they indulge in 'mutual aid' understandings and anticipate requiring a return favour from other banks in the future, or because they want to protect their reputations.[51]

London Approach restructurings depend, as noted, upon the supply to involved parties of accurate, relevant and timely information. This is crucial to the creditor who is deciding whether restructuring offers a better option than insolvency. There are, however, a number of reasons why such information may not flow. Where cross-border issues are involved and business or banking cultures are attuned to secrecy, managers may be very slow to disclose information fully.[52] They may, moreover, contest the data produced by independent professional advisers.

A number of factors have also been identified as new strains on the London Approach.[53] The first of these is the growing body of stakeholder groups. The London Approach was attuned to the 1980s when banking creditors dominated and institutional shareholders were passive, but matters have changed in a way that makes steering a rescue operation far more difficult:

> Today could not be more different. Bond holders, secondary debt
> traders, the US private placement market, joint venture partners,
> special creditor and supplier groups and intermediate investors have
> all discovered a voice and a willingness to interfere in one way or
> another … It pushes the process to the limit and sometimes beyond the
> sphere of influence of the Bank of England.[54]

The situation nowadays, then, is that the Bank of England has a voice that is joined by others and it has retreated from its central role in influencing renegotiations for a number of reasons: as a matter of policy;

50. Armour and Deakin, 'Norms in Private Insolvency Procedures', p. 45 (JCLS version).
51. Ibid. See also R. Sugden, *The Economics of Rights, Cooperation and Welfare* (Blackwell, Oxford, 1986).
52. See Segal, 'Corporate Recovery and Rescue – Part II', p. 28.
53. See Bird, 'London Approach'.   54. Ibid., p. 87.

through reallocation of regulatory functions;[55] and because large UK companies are resorting less to bank loans and making more use of disintermediated debt finance, notably bond issues, to raise funds.[56] Creditor co-ordination is affected adversely by the increasing complexity of financial structures which often produce conflicts of interest between junior and senior creditors. The emergence of markets for distressed corporate debt and the growing practice of trading in syndicated bank loans are other factors making co-ordination difficult.[57] Trading in distressed debt, for instance, means not only that the costs of communicating with involved parties to a renegotiation are high (because the parties are changing) but there is an increase in risks of breaches of confidentiality and of unhelpful market responses to these breaches. It might be responded that players in the distressed debt market will tend to co-operate on rescues – for reasons paralleling the banks' incentives – and there is evidence that market associations for distressed debt (as formed in London and New York) may encourage co-operation. Nevertheless, the sheer involvement of a greater number and diversity of players is likely to militate against the rapid, informed and cheap negotiation of rescues by a stable group of parties. The enforcement 'club' has, in short, been destabilised.

The globalisation of the financial markets that intensified in the 1990s and the internationalisation of credit are matters that particularly strain the London Approach. Where, as is increasingly the case, companies are bound up with overseas intermediate holding companies or subsidiaries, and where foreign banks are involved as creditors, the possibilities of gaining informal agreements on reconstruction, investment and short-term cash recovery diminish. Such difficulties are compounded by the need to provide flexibility in lending in a way that a traditional bankers' steering committee finds hard, and by the impact of different national insolvency regimes.

Changes such as the globalisation of financial markets, movements in the pattern of fund raising and the trading of loans, operate to undermine the understandings or norms that are the foundations of the London

55. Richard Obank has, however, argued that transfer of banking supervision from the Bank of England to the Financial Services Authority under the Bank of England Act 1998 may not affect the London Approach significantly and 'could actually strengthen the Bank's role in work-outs by boosting its role as an independent mediator': Obank, 'European Recovery', p. 151.

56. See Armour and Deakin, 'Norms in Private Insolvency Procedures', p. 48 (JCLS version); P. Brierley, 'The Bank of England and the London Approach' (1999) *Recovery* 12 (June).

57. See Segal, 'Corporate Recovery and Rescue – Part II', p. 26. On the Barings' liquidation of 2001, the heavy involvement of 'vulture' funds and the 'lack of affinity' between fellow creditors, see M. Peel, 'Liquidators Galore', *Financial Times*, 20 September 2001.

Approach. Each of these factors tends to reduce the likelihood of repeated interaction amongst parties with claims against a distressed company. Parties buying bonds or distressed debt ('vulture investors') or parties operating from abroad are less likely to have any expectation of repeat business with the banks in question:

> This increases the likelihood that one or more such parties may incorrectly observe the conventions operating in the London Approach workouts and adopt strategies which precipitate insolvency. Simultaneously it reduces the efficiency of the sanctions which the 'club' of London banks can threaten to exert. They are unable to exclude buyers of bonds or distressed debt from participation in future loan syndication.[58]

Should the London Approach be formalised and placed on a statutory footing? This would run counter to its existing philosophy of flexibility and informality, and a regime based on shared values, understandings, moral suasion and favours might be difficult to encapsulate in statutory language. Formalisation would, however, allow steps to be taken that would potentially facilitate the production of agreements between creditors. At present if a creditor refuses to agree to a proposed arrangement this may wreck the workout (a difficulty that has led the Bank of England to consider the possibility of replacing unanimity with a qualified majority voting system[59]). Bankers, however, may be reluctant to appear uncooperative to their fellow bankers since they may be seeking co-operation from others in a future rescue. If debt trading becomes even more widespread this will undermine rescue since some smaller lenders may look to extricate themselves from a situation rather than to work towards solutions.[60] Trading in the distressed market, moreover, remains a challenge to the London Approach since the banks have successfully resisted suggestions that a code of conduct should ban debt trading at 'sensitive' times. The banks are consequently left with their powers of influence and persuasion to deter others from spoiling rescues.[61] A moratorium might, nevertheless, be provided

---

58. Armour and Deakin, 'Norms in Private Insolvency Procedures', pp. 48–9 (JCLS version).
59. See Belcher, *Corporate Rescue*, p. 119; Kent, 'London Approach: Distressed Debt Trading', p. 115.
60. See Kent, 'London Approach: Distressed Debt Trading'; Belcher, *Corporate Rescue*, p. 120.
61. See Flood *et al.*, *Professional Restructuring*, p. 32. Mr Penn Kent, an executive director of the Bank of England, mooted the idea in 1994 of adopting a code of practice requiring buyers of distressed debt to comply with the Bank of England's approach to debt restructuring. The Bank of England dropped this idea, however, after talks with bankers: J. Gapper, 'Bank Seeks Code for Debt Sales', *Financial Times*, 28 January 1994; N. Cohen, 'Debt Trading Reform Rejected in Bank U-Turn', *Financial Times*, 24 March 1994.

for and the risks of creditors 'defecting' by selling their debt into the secondary distressed debt market might be limited by statutory restrictions on such defection, at least for a stipulated period. As noted above, however, such a ban on debt trading has been opposed by British and foreign banks and legal restrictions of the kind mooted might prove too legalistic to have many supporters. What has proved more acceptable has been the use of a code of practice. In October 2000, INSOL International produced a 'Statement of Principles for a Global Approach to Multi-Creditor Workouts'.[62] This has been described as 'a rare combination of clarity and flexibility'[63] and has been endorsed by bodies such as the World Bank, the Bank of England and the British Bankers' Association. The Statement sets out eight principles[64] which are of relevance to domestic multi-bank situations, and these provide for co-operation on such matters as a 'standstill period' during which creditors should refrain from enforcing claims.

One respect in which such a statement of principles may prove to be of real value is in providing a foundation for the resolution of disputes between creditors. To this end more use might be made of arbitrators or mediators in the informal rescue process. Such persons would have the task of facilitating negotiations between different stakeholder groups and would seek to secure agreements more rapidly and cost-effectively than is otherwise possible.[65]

As already indicated, the London Approach could be said to lead to some lowering of managerial expertise in so far as supervision arrangements by the bank will detract from decision-making powers. In reply, however, the potential effects on managers of formal alternatives should be compared, and it could be asserted that improvements of expertise are to be encountered when managers who have steered the company into financial troubles are led by negotiations with bankers to see the error of their ways and to arrive at more financially sound modes of conducting business. On the question of expertise, another issue is whether modern banks, subject to severe competitive pressures, have the capacity and will

---

62. For discussion see Chief Editor, 'International Approach to Workouts' (2001) 17 IL&P 59.
63. Ibid.
64. Reproduced verbatim at (2001) 17 IL&P 59, 60. Principle 2 does countenance the disposal of debts to third parties during the standstill period.
65. A Price Waterhouse survey conducted in 1996 revealed that 53 per cent of respondents favoured the use of such mediators: see J. Kelly, 'Banks Back Plan for Rescuing Big Companies', *Financial Times*, 2 December 1996. The Vice-Chairman of the INSOL Lenders Group has suggested that it would be useful, in international cases, to have an 'honest broker' in each jurisdiction to assist in the application of the INSOL International Principles, a role that could be filled by the appropriate regulator: see (2001) 17 IL&P 59.

to devote significant resources and senior expertise to the management of a major inter-creditor rescue arrangement.[66] Professional experts can be brought in but these, as noted, tend to be highly priced. If there is, or becomes, a shortage of the kind of banking expertise that is needed to work the London Approach, it is to be expected that the regime will decline in importance.

Moving to issues of accountability and accessibility, the London Approach can be criticised for its secrecy and exclusivity. Not all creditors will have access to negotiations in the London Approach and attempts may be made to conduct operations without, say, trade creditors gaining information on developments. This may be efficient but it would not appeal to excluded creditors on accessibility grounds.

As for those creditors who are involved in negotiations, much depends on the procedures followed by the lead bank. This is the bank that co-ordinates the rescue, appoints the investigators, puts the rescue team together and manages information flows. The London Rules state that the lead bank must have sufficient resources and the necessary expertise to ensure that information is made available to all lenders participating in the rescue on a timely basis. Performance on this front varies, however. In the view of the Bank of England: 'One of the most frequent complaints we receive at the Bank of England is that a lead bank has failed to provide banks with information which they regard as essential for the decisions that they are being asked to make.'[67] Lead banks, nevertheless, are subject to a number of pressures to release information. They will work closely with the steering committee, which is a body of three or five persons elected by the creditors and which will encourage the dissemination of information. Lead banks also have an incentive to keep the other banks informed and content, for if the latter are not satisfied with their position they may withdraw their co-operation or they may sell their debts in the secondary distressed debt market.

As for fairness, it might be contended that the London Approach workouts operate for the benefit of large lenders and tend to undervalue small, especially unsecured, creditors' interests. Larger creditors might respond that their efforts benefit the broad array of corporate stakeholders and that many small creditors, who do not contribute to the costs of the rescue, are to some extent free riding on the efforts of the banks. This response might,

---

66. See Bird, 'London Approach', p. 88.
67. M. Smith, 'The London Approach', conference paper to Wilde Sapte Seminar, 1992, quoted in Flood *et al.*, *Professional Restructuring*, p. 28.

however, overlook the ability of the banks, in certain instances, to compensate themselves for their efforts by improving their security or equity position in a rescue agreement. There is evidence that during periods of rescue bank credit tends to contract but unsecured trade credit tends to expand, sometimes dramatically.[68]

In summary, then, the London Approach exemplifies a number of the virtues and vices of informal rescue activity. It tends to be practised in relation to large debtor companies only and gives grounds for concern on a number of fronts. If, however, it is placed alongside the available formal alternative procedures, its virtues appear more prominent.

Debt/equity conversions

A further mode of informal rescue and one often implemented through London Approach procedures is the conversion of debt to equity.[69] In this procedure the creditor agrees to exchange a debt for an equity share in the company and hopes that at some future date this will produce a greater return than would have been obtained in a liquidation. Recent celebrated cases of such conversions have included Eurotunnel, which in 1996 owed £9.1 billion to its 225 banks. These banks agreed to write off £4.7 billion of that debt in return for 45.5 per cent of the company's shares. Similar debt for equity conversions have been associated with the names of Saatchi and Saatchi plc (£211 million of debt); Brent Walker Group plc (£250 million of bank debt); Signet (formerly Ratners Jewellers, £460 million of debt) and Queens Moat (£200 million of debt).

From a creditor's point of view, a conversion may be attractive because it offers the prospect of a future return on investment that is potentially unlimited as the company's fortunes upturn and potentially far more valuable than the returns available on liquidation. Where banks have loaned without security – as is often the case with lending to larger quoted groups that have borrowed from many banks – there is the prospect of low recovery rates in an insolvency and debt to equity conversion can be more desirable than resort to formal insolvency procedures. In contrast, the creditor that is fully or partially secured has a far weaker incentive to support a troubled company by taking an equity position. Where the creditors,

---

68. See J. Franks and O. Sussman, 'The Cycle of Corporate Distress, Rescue and Dissolution', IFA Working Paper 306 (2000) p. 2: trade credit expansions of up to 80 per cent are noted in cases that end in a formal insolvency procedure.

69. See K. Kemp and D. Harris, 'Debt to Equity Conversions: Relieving the Interest Burden' (1993) PLC 19 (August); Belcher, *Corporate Rescue*, pp. 120–1; DTI, *Encouraging Debt/Equity Swaps* (1996).

companies and projects involved are high profile, a further advantage of the debt to equity conversion is that it brings public relations returns: the creditor is seen in the public eye to be committed to industry and loyal to its customers in their hour of need.

From the company's perspective, a conversion takes away the burden of interest repayment, it eases cash flow and working capital difficulties and it improves the appearance of the balance sheet because managerial work-force efforts will be seen as producing profits rather than as merely servicing interest burdens. The financial profile and gearing of the company will improve as debts and competitive disadvantages are removed. The company will then be better placed to seek new credit lines from creditors, to attract new business and to reassure its current customers. This, in turn, is likely to improve morale within the company and increase the prospects of turning fortunes around. For directors, particular benefits will occur as the threat of liability for wrongful trading is reduced as debts are taken off the balance sheet in a conversion.

The DTI issued a Consultation Paper in 1996 which stressed the important contribution that debt/equity swaps can make in allowing troubled companies to reorganise their affairs.[70] The DTI favoured encouraging such swaps but thought it inappropriate to require creditors at law to participate in compulsory swaps. Instead, the Department sought to raise the profile of swapping; to make involved parties more aware of the potential benefits of swaps; and to encourage the development of model debt/equity swap schemes that could be adapted to particular circumstances.[71]

Debt to equity conversions do, however, involve a number of difficulties and disadvantages. They can be time-consuming and expensive to negotiate, not least because the consent of the company's existing shareholders as well as of the main creditors will usually be required. The former will have to agree to the issue of new shares, and such shareholders may be inclined to hold out in order to improve their positions. Where there are divergences of approach or position on the part of the creditors, it may again be difficult to come to a prompt, agreed restructuring plan. These divergences may arise because exposure levels vary, the banks may be based

---

70. DTI, *Encouraging Debt/Equity Swaps.*
71. See, for example, Appendix E – The Economics of Bankruptcy Reform – in the DTI/Insolvency Service's Consultative Document, *Company Voluntary Arrangements and Administration Orders* (October 1993); P. Aghion, O. Hart and J. Moore, 'Insolvency Reform in the UK: A Revised Proposal', Special Paper No. 65 (LSE Financial Markets Group, January 1995) and in (1995) 11 IL&P 67; A. Campbell, 'The Equity for Debt Proposal: The Way Forward' (1996) 12 IL&P 14. See further ch. 9 below, pp. 312–16.

in different jurisdictions or they may work subject to different regulatory constraints and within their own business cultures.[72] Where foreign banks are involved it will be necessary to consider, for instance, whether these are subject to regulatory restrictions on the holding of equity.[73]

For creditors, a negative aspect of a conversion is that there will be a loss of priority on a subsequent liquidation in so far as they have become shareholders and as such will be eligible to receive no return until all creditors have been repaid. The financial flexibility of the creditors' operations will also be reduced by conversion since it will be more difficult to realise their investment afterwards: sale of shares after a conversion may prove difficult or unproductive. Ownership of shares may, moreover, involve a culture shock for UK banks who, unlike their German counterparts, are unused to owning material portions of industry. They may be inclined to sell any accumulated shares once the market becomes liquid but such liquidity may be a long time coming.

For these reasons there may be alternatives to either formal insolvency proceedings or debt to equity conversions that may be more attractive to creditors and debtors. Debt rescheduling may be appropriate where the number of bank creditors is small and the company's financial problems can be overcome by changing the progressive interest or principal repayments. What rescheduling will not do is remove balance sheet deficits or improve gearing ratios.

Another alternative is to convert debt to limited recourse or subordinate debt. In such a process the creditors agree either that their debts will be converted from a general corporate obligation into claims secured against specific assets or that they will rank for repayment behind other debts (but ahead of equity). This will give some protection to directors with regard to wrongful trading liabilities but again it will not remove balance sheet deficits or gearing problems.[74]

In summary, debt to equity conversions can provide an effective and efficient means of allowing troubled companies to continue operations and of avoiding formal insolvency procedures. The main effectiveness and efficiency concerns relate to the time and money that has to be expended in

72. See Kemp and Harris, 'Debt to Equity Conversions', pp. 22–3, for a discussion of UK regulatory issues that covers disclosure requirements under the Companies Act 1985 s. 198; the relevance of the Companies Act 1985 s. 204 on 'concert party' acquisitions; waivers or 'whitewashes' under the City Code on Takeovers and Mergers; insider dealing considerations; and false market avoidance.
73. Ibid., p. 25. The US Bank Holding Company Act 1956 with few exceptions generally prohibits US banks from acquiring equity securities.
74. Kemp and Harris, 'Debt to Equity Conversions', p. 22.

achieving the agreements of involved parties. Here much depends on the numbers and types of creditors involved.

The worry, in terms of expertise and the scope for exercising it, is that banks may not always be attuned to the assessment of equity risks. Some may be better placed than others. The Royal Bank of Scotland set up a unit called Specialised Lending Services in the early 1990s which specialises in helping companies by taking equity share stakes. Banks, moreover, are able to buy in expertise from accountants and other consultants in order to make equity assessments. Whether banks can operate sufficiently astutely to make equity-holding activities profitable is another issue. The National Westminster Bank was forced in 1991 to acknowledge the failure of its Growth Options equity stakeholding venture, and that bank has since conceded that it had not been able to make money out of small equity shareholdings.[75]

The accessibility and accountability of conversion processes tend to be quite high in relation to major creditors since their consent will be required for those processes to work. Similarly, the requirement of shareholder approval for new share issues will ensure that those stakeholders gain a voice in the rescue process. Minor creditors may not be offered easy access in a debt to equity conversion but their interests will not usually be affected detrimentally, and they may well benefit from the reductions of debt that follow a conversion and from the reductions in the length of the potential queue for insolvency payments that will follow a conversion that changes the status of certain creditors to shareholders. For these reasons, it is also difficult to criticise conversions on the grounds that they involve unfairness to any affected parties. A company's shareholders may suffer when a conversion takes place: Eurotunnel shareholders initially paid 350p for their shares only to see these valued at 115p during the debt to equity conversion process. Such shareholders, however, take risks openly and they suffer less in a conversion than they would in a liquidation.

Conclusions

Turning a company around by informal actions, negotiations and agreements offers a number of potential gains. It avoids the expenses of formal insolvency procedures and it offers companies new opportunities to enjoy business success. Assessing the efficiency of informal rescue procedures,

---

75. See C. Batchelor, 'From Lender to Investor', *Financial Times*, 23 March 1993.

individually or as a group, is, however, fraught with a number of diffi-culties. Informal rescue ranges from crisis management and turnaround to the use of consultancy services to improve management. It is accord-ingly almost impossible to separate out rescue activity from routine ne-gotiations with creditors and other business partners. The lack of any for-mal gateway rules out such identification. Nor will information on much turnaround work be readily available: publicity, after all, will often be highly counterproductive. What can be looked to is the success rate of forms of rescue work that involve certain parties. Thus, the figures of R3 reveal that in a small sample of cases where IPs were appointed, the ratio of turnaround projects that succeeded or were still in progress to turnaround projects that failed and resulted in a formal insolvency was 62:50.[76]

Informal action can be swifter and cheaper than formal activities but this is not always the case and it can also be more partial and less well in-formed. We have seen that informality does give grounds for concern on some fronts. The expenses of informal actions may be high. The expertise being applied at key points in informal processes may not always be appro-priate. The accessibility and accountability of some procedures may be low (secrecy may be treated as a virtue in some informal rescues) and whether all affected parties are dealt with fairly can be a matter of fortune.

The philosophy of rescuing companies, it should be emphasised, is very different in orientation from many aspects of formal liquidation in-solvency procedures. It is less strictly guided by statutory rules and its main focus is not the maximisation of returns for the various creditors in strict order of priority. It looks towards ongoing commercial viability and involves the application of skills relevant to marketing, manufacturing, product development and general management as well as the legal issues. Those practising rescue have accordingly to exercise judgment and adopt a different stance from the insolvency practitioner engaged in liquidation who is content simply to collect assets for distribution. Experience, com-petence and powers of staff motivation are all called for in the ideal res-cue professional. It is in the arena of rescue that insolvency moves furthest from the mechanical application of rules for the benefit of creditors.

76. R3's Ninth Survey.

8

Receivers and their role

The first potential rescue procedure to be considered here is receivership.[1] It follows from the above discussion that an appraisal of receivership should go further than offering an outline of powers and duties and should consider the role and conception of receivership as it operates. This chapter, accordingly, will look at receivership as a process as well as an institution. The laws, procedures and actors involved in receivership will be examined and the benchmarks of efficiency, expertise, accountability and fairness will be employed in asking whether receivership plays an acceptable role in insolvency as a whole. The part played by receivers in rescues will be a focus here, but attention will also be paid to ongoing corporate operations and the impact of receivership on these. At a more general level, questions will be asked about the way the receivership role is conceived within current insolvency law and whether an alternative approach is called for.

To set the scene for such a discussion it is necessary to outline the development of receivership, the procedures adopted in receivership and the duties and obligations that form the legal framework for receivership.

---

1. Receivership is generally regarded as a method by which a secured creditor can enforce his security rather than a true collective insolvency proceeding: see, *inter alia*, R. M. Goode, *Principles of Corporate Insolvency Law* (2nd edn, Sweet & Maxwell, London, 1997) pp. 203, 205; J. H. Farrar and B. M. Hannigan, *Farrar's Company Law* (4th edn, Butterworths, London, 1998) p. 663; Insolvency Service, *A Review of Company Rescue and Business Reconstruction Mechanisms*, Interim Report (DTI, September 1999) p. 9. On some consequences of this approach see F. Dahan, 'The European Convention on Insolvency Proceedings and the Administrative Receiver: A Missed Opportunity?' (1996) 17 Co. Law. 181. See also the distinction between insolvency proceedings and other proceedings such as receivership adopted by the amended Acquired Rights Directive 98/50: discussed in ch. 16 below, at pp. 563–4.

The development of receivership

Receivership is a long-established method by which secured creditors can enforce their security.[2] There have traditionally been two types of receiver in English law: the receiver appointed by the court[3] and the receiver appointed by a debenture holder under the terms of the debenture deed. The 'administrative receiver' is a new institution introduced by the Insolvency Act 1986 and is covered by a distinct statutory regime. The receiver is thus a person appointed to take possession of property that is the subject of a charge and he or she is authorised to deal with it primarily for the benefit of the holder of the charge. The court has an inherent jurisdiction to appoint a receiver in order to take care of property until the rights of the interested parties can be determined. This jurisdiction includes, in the case of a business, the power to appoint a manager so that courts can appoint a receiver/manager even in the absence of any express power in the relevant debenture. After the Law of Property Act 1925[4] all mortgages by deed contain an implied power to appoint a receiver.

The modern term 'administrative receiver' refers to the individual who, under the Insolvency Act 1986, is the receiver and manager of the whole (or substantially the whole) of a company's property, appointed by the holders of a debenture secured by a charge which was, as created, a floating charge.[5] This individual is typically appointed by the secured creditor under the terms of the relevant floating charge at a time of crisis in the debtor firm's affairs. He or she must be a qualified insolvency practitioner within the meaning of Part XIII of the Insolvency Act 1986.[6]

This chapter focuses on administrative receivership, the roots of which are to be found in the Cork Report[7] and the Insolvency Act 1986. The Cork Committee (Cork) saw the aims of insolvency law in terms of the dozen objectives set out in paragraph 198 of the Cork Report and discussed in

---

2. See Goode, *Principles of Corporate Insolvency Law*, ch. 9; D. Milman and C. Durrant, *Corporate Insolvency: Law and Practice* (3rd edn, Sweet & Maxwell, London, 1999) ch. 4. See also I. F. Fletcher, *The Law of Insolvency* (2nd edn, Sweet & Maxwell, London, 1996) pp. 360–1 and *Re Maskelyne British Typewriter Ltd* [1898] 1 Ch 133. On aspects of administrative receivership still left to private contract see L. Clarke and H. Rajak, '*Mann v. Secretary of State for Employment*' (2000) 63 MLR 895 at 899.

3. See further S. Fennell, 'Court-appointed Receiverships: A Missed Opportunity?' (1998) 14 IL&P 208.

4. S. 101.   5. Insolvency Act 1986 s. 29(2).

6. It is an offence under the Insolvency Act 1986 ss. 388, 389 for a person to act as an IP without being properly qualified under the Insolvency Act 1986 s. 390. The IP must be a member of a recognised professional body or obtain authorisation to act under the Insolvency Act 1986 s. 393. See ch. 5 above.

7. *Report of the Review Committee on Insolvency Law and Practice* (Cmnd 8558, 1982) ('Cork Report').

chapter 2 above Cork stressed that the public interest should be protected by corporate insolvency processes because groups in society beyond the insolvent company and creditors were affected by an insolvency. Cork also emphasised that means should be provided for preserving 'viable commercial enterprises capable of making a useful contribution to the economic life of the country'. After the enactment of the Insolvency Act 1986 four different formal insolvency procedures are available to play a part in corporate rescues and reorganisations. These are: (1) administrative receivership; (2) administration under Part II of the Insolvency Act 1986; (3) company voluntary arrangements under Part I of the Insolvency Act 1986; and (4) creditor schemes of arrangement under the Companies Act 1985. These procedures establish regimes for the management of the affairs of a business and they are binding on the managers of the business as well as on the creditors. In this sense they are 'formal' procedures to be distinguished from the informal methods that can be adopted in response to corporate troubles. It should be emphasised that companies in financial difficulties do not have to resort to formal procedures.[8] If the involved parties (directors, shareholders and creditors) can come to (and sustain) an agreement on the steps to be taken to effect a rescue then informal processes are likely to offer a far speedier and cheaper way of reversing corporate fortunes than resort to formality. Recent research suggests that there is 'an elaborate rescue process outside formal procedures' with about 75 per cent of firms emerging from rescue and avoiding formal insolvency procedures altogether by either turning around their fortunes or repaying their debts.[9]

When Cork looked at receivership, a receiver might be put in place by the traditional methods of appointment by the court or under the powers contained in an instrument such as a mortgage debenture. The latter process would be triggered by the written instigation of the debenture holder. Whether a receiver could be appointed out of court depended on the terms of the instrument creating the debt or charge and normally the receiver's duties and powers would be set out in that document. Usually the debenture holder would provide that the receiver would take into custody the property of the company (the whole property or the part charged with the instrument). The Companies Act provided specifically for receivership on behalf of a debenture holder secured by a floating charge. These provisions

---

8. See ch. 7 above.
9. See J. Franks and O. Sussman, 'The Cycle of Corporate Distress, Rescue and Dissolution: A Study of Small and Medium Size UK Companies', IFA Working Paper 306 (2000) p. 2.

were designed to ensure that members and creditors of the company, as well as debenture holders, should have sufficient information about the financial position of the company after the appointment of the receiver.[10]

The receiver was able to apply to the court for directions, carry on the company's business (if appointed also as manager), borrow money on the security of the assets, sell the assets, agree compromises with creditors and generally act as might be necessary in pursuit of the interests of those who appointed him. Normal practice involved a receiver and manager moving into the company's premises at the earliest practical opportunity after appointment. Fresh contracts might be entered into by the receiver and indemnification obtained from the company.[11]

The receiver dealt with the assets in similar fashion to a liquidator until the claims of any preferential creditors and the appointing debenture holder were satisfied. The actions of the receiver would, however, affect other parties and, in particular, the interests of unsecured creditors and shareholders would often depend on the receiver's decisions. Where the receiver realised assets these were paid out, first, to meet the receiver's own expenses and remuneration, second, to pay the costs of the debenture holder or appointer, third, to meet preferential claims such as taxes, rates and unpaid wages or salaries, and, fourth, to pay the debenture debt with appropriate interest. If there was a surplus after these payments, this had to be paid over by the receiver to the company or, if it was in liquidation, its liquidator.

Cork received numerous suggestions for reform of receivership and a number of complaints, 'mainly from or on behalf of ordinary unsecured creditors who are highly critical of the apparent lack of concern for their interest when the receiver has been appointed'.[12] Major worries noted by Cork related to the following:[13]

- The low level of distributions to unsecured creditors in a winding up where there is a floating charge.
- 'Such injustices' as the right of a receiver to retain goods for which the supplier has not been paid.
- The lack of information available once a receiver has been appointed.
- The excessive regard by receivers for the interests of the charge holder and the insufficient attention paid to the interests of creditors and shareholders.

10. See Cork Report, para. 186.   11. See now Insolvency Act 1986 s. 44(1)(b) and (c).
12. Cork Report, para. 436.   13. Ibid., paras. 437–9.

- The practice of appointing receivers who are closely connected with a company either as directors or as relatives of directors or shareholders or through its parent company.
- The lack of a receiver's duty to account for his actions to ordinary creditors.

In relation to some of the above points, Cork was unpersuaded that radical legal changes were called for.[14] The Committee took the view that it would be wrong to make the receiver specifically accountable to anyone, even the debenture holder, if that would involve a requirement to take instructions.[15] The receiver, said Cork, owes fiduciary duties to the debenture holder and duties to the charge holder and company to exercise reasonable care to obtain proper prices for property and to preserve the goodwill of the business. Statutory obligations were also owed to preferential creditors. Cork's overall view was that incidences of damage to third parties in receivership were few in number and it would be 'wrong and unhelpful' to treat receivers as merely the nominees of appointers.[16] Cork cautioned that if receivers had to have regard to a statutory list of matters and interests, 'the effectiveness of the floating charge would be seriously weakened'[17] since creditors would be driven to early enforcement of fixed securities, to greater use of hybrid forms of security (e.g. fixed charges on future book debts[18]) and to direct enforcement of the security without the appointment of a receiver. None of these steps, the Committee urged, would advance the conduct of trade generally or the interests of unsecured creditors. Such a list of matters and interests to be considered might also increase opportunities for 'expensive and delaying litigation' without benefit to unsecured creditors.

As to the proposal that statute law should make receivers accountable to all the creditors, secured and unsecured, Cork responded that this again would drive prospective lenders away from floating charges into other alternatives. If such difficulties were anticipated and receivers were bound to have regard to priorities *inter se* when looking to protected interests, this again would lead to unhelpful legal challenges, delays and expenses. Cork summarised:

---

14. On Cork's 'exaggerated representation of the virtues of receivership' see G. McCormack, 'Receiverships and the Rescue Culture' [2000] 2 CFILR 229, 236. On the efficiencies generated by receivership, however, see J. Armour and S. Frisby, 'Rethinking Receivership' (2001) 21 OJLS 73.
15. Cork Report, para. 444.   16. Ibid., para. 446.
17. Ibid., para. 447.   18. Ibid., para. 449.

It is an undoubted virtue in the eyes of those who appoint them, that receivers can act economically, swiftly and with little danger of successful challenge before the event. A statutory provision of the kind now under consideration offers potential detriment to the holders of floating charges without, it seems to us, any real advantage to anyone else.[19]

Overall, then, Cork was unwilling to introduce any fundamental reform of the law to change receivers' accountability. Recommendations were, however, made on other fronts, notably that receivers should hold suitable qualifications; liabilities on contracts and rights to bind the company by contract and entitlement to indemnity should be set in statute; and receivers appointed out of court should be deemed, until liquidation, to be agents of the company unless the charge provided otherwise. Receivers, moreover, should continue to be personally liable on contracts they enter into (but they should have a right of indemnity); there should be no personal liability for payment of rent merely because the receiver has taken possession of the premises; and, after winding up, the receiver should not have the power to bind the company to further liability (except in dealing with secured assets in accordance with due powers or if the transaction has been approved by the liquidator, provisional liquidator or court).

On procedures for carrying out receivership, a series of recommendations offered further responses to the criticisms noted above.[20] Cork thus recommended that receivers should advertise their appointments in the same way as liquidators and advise all known creditors within twenty-eight days (a notification recommendation not extended to shareholders); receivers should call a meeting of creditors within three months of appointment (an obligation that could be dispensed with by the court in appropriate circumstances); and, in relation to groups of companies, one meeting and one committee of creditors should be used (at the receiver's discretion). Receivers, Cork said, should be required to present a brief report covering such matters as events leading up to appointment; policy (in outline) on realisation and future trading and disposals; amounts due to holders of the floating charge and preferential creditors; estimates of sums likely to be available for other creditors; and a preliminary statement of affairs of the directors with receivers' comments. Cork added that there should be a statutory duty to appoint a committee of creditors and such a

---

19. Ibid., para. 451.   **20.** Ibid., para. 476.

committee should be entitled to receive information from the receiver and to make representations to court if dissatisfied. Finally, receivers should be obliged to give notice of intention to resign; removal of the receiver should only be by the court on cause shown; and the receiver should be required before ceasing to act to send all creditors a summary of receipts and payments for the whole period of the receivership.

Processes, powers and duties: the Insolvency Act 1986 onwards

The Insolvency Act 1986 established the new type of administrative receivership. The administrative receiver (hereafter 'receiver') can only be appointed by a creditor of a company who has taken security over the whole or substantially the whole of a company's property by a package of security interests that must include a floating charge.[21] This means that a floating charge holder will be entitled to appoint a receiver even if a series of fixed charges and preferential debts have priority over the floating charge. All that is necessary is that the floating charge covers a substantial part of the company's property.[22] Such a creditor will, indeed, be present in the case of most troubled companies since it is usual practice for UK companies to rely to a considerable extent on finance from banks and for the latter to take out security packages that will render them eligible to appoint a receiver to protect their loan.

It is common for debentures to set out lists of the situations entitling the debenture holder to appoint a receiver.[23] Typical events include: failures to meet demands to pay principal or interest;[24] the presentation of a winding-up petition or the passing of a resolution to liquidate the company voluntarily;[25] the presentation of a petition for administration or the initiation of a CVA; the levying of distress or execution against the Companies Act; failure to meet any obligations, or to abide by any restrictions

---

21. Insolvency Act 1986 s. 29(2). On the phrase 'substantially the whole' see Goode, *Principles of Corporate Insolvency Law*, pp. 206–7.

22. Note that where the security is composed of fixed and floating charges the AR's appointment is effected under the floating charge: see *Meadrealm Ltd* v. *Transcontinental Golf Construction Ltd* (1991, unreported).

23. See generally Milman and Durrant, *Corporate Insolvency*, pp. 55–6.

24. On the 'reasonable opportunity' pay test see ibid., p. 56 and *Bank of Baroda* v. *Panessar* [1986] BCLC 497 ('adequate time' test preferred to 'reasonable opportunity').

25. If the court has appointed a liquidator its leave is required before a receiver can be appointed, but such leave will normally be forthcoming: Insolvency Act 1986 s. 130(2); *Henry Pound and Sons Ltd* v. *Hutchins* (1889) 42 Ch D 402.

that are set out in the debenture;[26] ceasing to trade; placing the assets in jeopardy; or being unable to pay debts.

Typically a bank appoints a receiver suddenly and against the wishes of the directors: 'often the bank will have been trying for some time without success to obtain promised management information or has been driven to the conclusion that the directors are hopelessly inadequate to their task and a security may be in jeopardy. One way or another, the arrival of the receiver is likely to provoke considerable resentment.'[27]

A debenture holder who is able to appoint a receiver is also in a position to block the effective operation of other insolvency procedures. The party entitled to appoint a receiver must be given notice of a petition for administration and may then put in the receiver, a course of action that will lead to the dismissal of the petition for administration.[28] Similarly in the case of a CVA, the creditors' meeting called to consider this may not approve a proposal affecting the enforcement rights of a secured creditor without the latter's approval.[29] Nor may a liquidator take possession of assets under the control of a previously appointed receiver.[30]

It is often the case that a creditor bank will appoint a receiver on the recommendation of the accountant whom the bank has instructed to conduct a review of the company's performance and prospects. That receiver, moreover, will often be a partner of the same accountancy firm: a practice giving rise to some controversy and suggestions that unacceptable conflicts of interest are involved (these issues were discussed in chapter 5). Normal procedure will then involve the receiver in taking over the management of the company and notifying the business world of this change both through the Companies Registry[31] and by disclosing the receivership in all letters, invoices and business exchanges.[32] Creditors must be informed of the receivership within twenty-eight days[33] in stipulated form.[34] Notice of the receivership must also be given in a local press advertisement and in the *Gazette.*

26. An example would be a grant by the company of a new security interest in contravention of the terms of the debenture.

27. See Milman and Durrant, *Corporate Insolvency*, p. 54, who note also that the directors may occasionally welcome the appointment of a receiver who will be taking the difficult decisions (and being given the blame from employees for these). Receivers may also have a 'better chance of persuading creditors to be patient than the directors who have been promising a cheque for months'.

28. Insolvency Act 1986 s. 9(2)(a); s. 9(3). But see pp. 297–8 below.

29. Ibid., s. 4(3).

30. See Armour and Frisby, 'Rethinking Receivership', p. 76; *Re Crigglestone Coal Co.* [1906] 1 Ch 523.

31. Companies Act 1985 s. 405(1).   32. Insolvency Act 1986 s. 39.

33. Ibid., s. 46.   34. Insolvency Rules 1986 r. 3.2 (as amended).

Appointment of the receiver does not bring the company's trading to a halt since company contracts will generally continue to be enforceable by and against it; its assets remain in its ownership and its directors remain in office.[35] Legal control of the company, however, passes to the receiver even though factual control may seem, to an outsider, not to have changed. This legal control means that the receiver is entitled to direct the company as to the conduct of the firm's management.[36] The contracts of employment of employees are generally unaffected by the appointment of a receiver out of court, but termination of contracts will be involved if certain events take place, such as sale of the business.[37]

The powers of the receiver will be stipulated in the relevant debenture and in any subsequent orders.[38] A series of implied powers is also set out in Schedule 1 of the Insolvency Act 1986.[39] Receivers are thus equipped to take a series of actions for the enforcement of the debenture holder's rights: to manage the company's business;[40] to borrow using the company's assets as security;[41] and to take possession of a company's assets.[42] They may also institute legal proceedings,[43] go to arbitration or settle disputes,[44] and prove for debts owed to the company by insolvent debtors.[45] Cheques can be issued and documents executed in the company's name[46] and necessary payments made.[47] Once the assets are collected the receiver possesses power to sell these in order to create funds for repaying the debenture holder; subsidiary companies can be established and portions of the business transmitted to these as ongoing operations or for sale.[48]

A receiver may apply to the court for directions in relation to the performance of his or her functions and the court may give directions or make an order declaring the rights of persons (before the court or otherwise) as

---

35. See L. Doyle, 'The Residual Status of Directors in Receivership' (1996) 17 Co. Law. 131.
36. *Meigh v. Wickenden* [1941] 2 KB 160, 166; *Re Joshua Shaw & Sons Ltd* [1989] BCLC 362.
37. Also if the receiver arranges for new inconsistent employment contracts and if the continued employment of an employee is incompatible with a receiver taking over the running of the company: see Milman and Durrant, *Corporate Insolvency*, pp. 61–4.
38. Fletcher, *Law of Insolvency*, p. 365.
39. See Insolvency Act 1986 s. 42 which provides that the powers conferred on an administrative receiver by the appointing debentures shall be deemed to include the list of powers set out in Schedule 1 to the 1986 Act and these deemed powers operate 'except in so far as they are inconsistent with any of the provisions of those debentures'. The list of powers includes, *inter alia*, the power to carry on the business of the company, to sell or otherwise dispose of the property of the company by public auction or private contract and to raise and borrow money and grant security over the property of the company.
40. Insolvency Act 1986 Sched. 1, para. 14.
41. Ibid., para. 3.   42. Ibid., para. 1.   43. Ibid.
44. Ibid., paras. 6 and 18.   45. Ibid., para. 20.   46. Ibid., paras. 10 and 8.
47. Ibid., para. 13.   48. Ibid., paras. 15 and 16.

it thinks fit.[49] Receivers can thus apply to the court for directions in order to resolve disputes about entitlement to the secured property.[50] Receivers, furthermore, can dispose of property subject to a third party's security (which ranks in priority to the rights of the receiver's appointee) on an order of the court.[51]

Receivers, however, possess powers not merely to act for the debenture holder, but to act for the company. These follow from the execution of the debenture.[52] Receivers are thus placed in a strange position: they have two principals but are not subject to the control of either of them. They cannot be instructed or sacked by the company's board[53] and, as Fox LJ said in *Gomba Holdings*:[54]

> The relationship set up by the debenture and the appointment of a receiver is tripartite and involves the mortgagor, receiver and debenture holder. The receiver becomes the mortgagor's agent whether the mortgagor likes it or not. The mortgagor has to pay the receiver's fees as a matter of contract. The mortgagor cannot dismiss the receiver and cannot instruct him in the course of his receivership.

The debenture holder, in return, is largely protected from responsibility for the acts and omissions of the receiver.[55]

In summary, it has been said of the receiver: 'He can best be described as an independent contractor whose primary responsibility is to protect the interests of his appointor, but who also owes a duty to his deemed principal, the company, to refrain from conduct which needlessly damages its business or goodwill, and a separate duty, by statute, to observe the priority given to preferential creditors over claims secured by a floating charge.'[56]

When receivers agree contracts, employment or otherwise, they act as agents of the company but they may incur personal liabilities (except in

---

49. Insolvency Act 1986 s. 35.
50. See, for example, *Re Ellis, Son & Vidler Ltd* [1994] BCC 532.
51. Insolvency Act 1986 s. 43. Note that this would not cover property subject to a ROT clause: see s. 43(7). Contrast Insolvency Act 1986 s. 15 regarding administrators: see ch. 9 below.
52. See further Goode, *Principles of Corporate Insolvency Law*, pp. 215–16.
53. ARs can only be removed by an order of the court: Insolvency Act 1986 s. 45(1).
54. *Gomba Holdings UK Ltd* v. *Homan* [1986] 1 WLR 1301.
55. See Insolvency Act 1986 s. 44(1)(a).
56. Goode, *Principles of Corporate Insolvency Law*, p. 217. For a critique of the receiver as deemed agent see J. S. Ziegel, 'The Privately Appointed Receiver and the Enforcement of Security Interests: Anomaly or Superior Solution?' in Ziegel (ed.), *Current Developments in International and Comparative Corporate Insolvency Law* (Clarendon Press, Oxford, 1994). Ziegel (p. 459) asks: 'Why not reverse the statutory presumption and declare the receiver to be the secured party's agent or, alternatively, an independent functionary?'

so far as the contract provides otherwise). An important issue here concerns the circumstances under which the receiver will be deemed to have adopted an employment contract for which he or she will be personally liable. The Insolvency Act 1986 governed such issues through section 44(1)(b) which made the receiver personally liable on contracts adopted by him in carrying out these functions. Receivers have a statutory indemnity covering such liabilities[57] but until the mid-1990s receivers sought to avoid such liabilities by issuing a standardised letter informing each employee that the office holder was not adopting, and would not adopt, their contract of employment. The company, the letter went, would continue to be their employer for the time being (this became known as a *Specialised Mouldings* letter[58]). The validity of *Specialised Mouldings* letters was, however, put to the test in the *Paramount* case.[59] Lord Browne-Wilkinson, in the House of Lords, was forced to the view that such letters did not exclude adoption once the fourteen-day period of grace[60] ran out and that contracts of employment were inevitably adopted if a receiver (or administrator) caused the employment to continue beyond the fourteen days. *Paramount* thus left receivers in an awkward position since it may be difficult to form a professional judgment on the feasibility of rescue within such a short time.[61]

The deficiencies of the law in this area were partially addressed before the House of Lords decided *Paramount*, when the Insolvency Act 1994 was passed. This applied only to employment contracts adopted on or after 15 March 1994 (and thus left *Paramount* to address contracts adopted between the commencement of the Insolvency Act 1986 (January 1987) and 15 March 1994). Under the Insolvency Act 1994, where a contract of employment is adopted, a receiver will only become liable personally for 'qualifying liabilities' which are defined (for example, to pay wages or salary or pension contributions incurred when the receiver is in office) and which

---

57. Insolvency Act 1986 s. 44(1)(c). See also Fletcher, *Law of Insolvency*, p. 371 and, on employment contracts, see Milman and Durrant, *Corporate Insolvency*, p. 67; *Re Paramount Airways Ltd (No. 3)*, reported as *Powdrill v. Watson* [1995] 2 WLR 312, [1995] BCC 319, [1995] 2 All ER 65 ('*Paramount*'); Insolvency Act 1994 amendments. See further P. L. Davies, 'Employee Claims in Insolvency: Corporate Rescue and Preferential Claims' (1994) 23 ILJ 141; I. F. Fletcher, 'Adoption of Contracts of Employment by Receivers and Administrators: The *Paramount* Case' [1995] JBL 596.

58. See unreported ruling of Harman J in *Re Specialised Mouldings* (13 February 1987).

59. *Paramount*: the case that laid the foundation for this issue was *Nicol v. Cutts* [1985] 1 BCC 99.

60. Provided for in the Insolvency Act 1986 s. 44(2) which states that an AR is not taken to have adopted a contract of employment by reason of anything done or omitted within fourteen days of his/her appointment.

61. See Fletcher, 'Adoption of Contracts', p. 602; P. Mudd, 'The Insolvency Act 1994: *Paramount* Cured?' (1994) 10 IL&P 38; Mudd, '*Paramount*: The House of Lords Decision – Is There Still Hope of Avoiding Some of Those Claims?' (1995) 11 IL&P 78.

accrue and relate to services rendered only after the date when the contract was adopted. This means that where services are rendered partly before and partly after adoption of contracts, only such a sum as reflects services rendered after adoption will qualify under section 44 and will be accorded the enhanced protection that flows from the receiver's personal liability.[62] With regard to payments referable to periods pre-adoption or before the receiver's appointment, employees will thus stand as unsecured creditors with claims against the company alone.

Turning to duties of the receiver, the primary obligation is to act *bona fide* to realise the assets of the company in the interests of the debenture holder.[63] The receiver's powers of management have been said to be ancillary to that duty.[64] There is, as indicated, no duty to obey the firm or generally to provide the company with details and information concerning the conduct of the company's affairs.[65] At one time, however, the courts assumed that receivers owed a duty of care in tort to the company and subsequent encumbrancers and guarantors of the company's debt. The duty was to use care to obtain the best possible price when selling company property.[66] In the *Downsview Nominees* case[67] the Privy Council held that a receiver only owed equitable duties to non-appointing debenture holders and to the company to act in good faith. Specific equitable duties were owed to these parties to do such things as keep premises in repair and avoid waste.[68] The Privy Council accepted that a receiver was subject to a specific equitable duty to take reasonable care to obtain a proper price for assets sold, but it denied the existence of a general duty of care in tort to subsequent encumbrances or the company with regard to dealing in the secured

---

62. In administration such employees would have 'super-priority' by virtue of the Insolvency Act 1986 s. 19(4) and (5) which gives such payments priority over any charges. In receivership there is personal liability of the receiver, who is entitled to indemnity out of the company's assets: s. 44(1)(c). On the case for a 'uniform approach which transcends the differences between the various forms of insolvency proceedings' see H. Anderson, 'Insolvent Insolvencies' (2001) 17 IL&P 87.

63. *Re B. Johnson & Co. (Builders) Ltd* [1955] Ch 634, 661–2; *Downsview Nominees Ltd* v. *First City Corporation* [1993] AC 295.

64. *Gomba Holdings UK Ltd and Others* v. *Homan and Bird* [1986] 1 WLR 1301 at 1304–5 (Hoffmann J); [1986] 3 All ER 94.

65. Ibid.

66. Per Lord Denning MR in *Standard Chartered Bank Ltd* v. *Walker* [1982] 1 WLR 1410; *Cuckmere Brick Co. Ltd* v. *Mutual Finance Ltd* [1971] Ch 949; *American Express* v. *Hurley* [1986] BCLC 52. For analysis and criticism see L. Bentley, 'Mortgagee's Duties on Sale: No Place for Tort?' (1990) 54 *Conveyancer and Property Lawyer* 431. See also H. Rajak, 'Can a Receiver be Negligent?' in B. Rider (ed.), *The Corporate Dimension* (Jordans, London, 1998); *Parker-Tweedale* v. *Dunbar Bank plc* [1991] Ch 12 at 18 (Nourse LJ).

67. *Downsview Nominees Ltd* v. *First City Corporation* [1993] AC 295.

68. J. Boyle, J. Birds, E. Ferran and C. Villiers, *Boyle and Birds' Company Law* (4th edn, Jordans, Bristol, 2000) p. 334.

assets.[69] More recently, however, the Court of Appeal in *Medforth* v. *Blake*[70] reasserted that the duties of receivers are equitable rather than tortious but stated that a receiver owed a duty, if managing the mortgaged property, to do so with due diligence, which amounted to an equitable duty of care. In *Medforth* the owner–manager of a pig farm owed sums to the Midland Bank that became unacceptable to the lender. The loan terms provided for the appointment of a receiver and a receiver was appointed with power to run the business. The business was run by the receiver for four years before new terms were agreed between Medforth and the bank. During that period the receiver had not negotiated with the relevant pre-existing pig feed suppliers in order to obtain the 10 to 15 per cent discounts that Medforth had received and which Medforth had repeatedly advised the receiver to ask for. Around £200,000 of discounts had not been obtained during the receivership. The issue was whether the receiver owed Medforth a duty of care that had been breached or whether there had been a breach of good faith.

Sir Richard Scott VC delivered the sole judgment of the Court of Appeal and stated: 'The proposition that in managing and carrying on the mortgaged business the receiver owed the mortgagor no duty other than of good faith offends in my opinion commercial sense ... If [the receiver] does decide to carry on the business why should he not be expected to do so with reasonable competence?'[71] It was argued for the receiver in *Medforth* that the cases of *Re B. Johnson & Co. (Builders) Ltd*[72] and *Downsview*[73] established that receivers owed no duty to exercise skill and care and that to go beyond the duty to perform with good faith would undermine receivership by doing away with the judicially sanctioned advantages that receivership as an institution offered.[74] Scott VC's response was that the authorities cited gave non-exhaustive lists of the obligations of receivers

---

69. See further Rajak, 'Can a Receiver be Negligent?' pp. 140–3; A. Berg, 'Duties of a Mortgagee and a Receiver' [1993] JBL 213; R. Nolan, '*Downsview Nominees Ltd* v. *First City Corporation Ltd* – Good News for Receivers – In General' (1994) 15 Co. Law. 28; A. Hogan, 'Receivers Revisited' (1996) 17 Co. Law. 226; L. Doyle, 'The Receiver's Duties on a Sale of Charged Assets' (1997) 10 Insolvency Intelligence 9. See also *Huish* v. *Ellis* [1995] BCC 462; C. Pugh, 'Duties of Care Owed to Mortgagors and Guarantors: The Hidden Liability' (1995) 11 IL&P 143.

70. [1999] 3 All ER 97. See S. Bulman and L. Fitzsimons, 'To Run or Not to Run...(the Borrower's Business)' [1999] Ins. Law. 306; S. Frisby, 'Making a Silk Purse out of a Pig's Ear: *Medforth* v. *Blake and Others*' (2000) 63 MLR 413; McCormack, 'Receivership and the Rescue Culture'; L. S. Sealy, 'Mortgagees and Receivers: A Duty of Care Resurrected and Extended' [2000] CLJ 31; L. Ife, 'Liability of Receivers and Banks in Selling and Managing Mortgaged Property' (2000) 13 Insolvency Intelligence 61.

71. [1999] 3 All ER 97 at 103.   72. [1995] Ch 635.   73. [1993] AC 295.

74. See Frisby, 'Making a Silk Purse', p. 415; McCormack, 'Receivership and the Rescue Culture', pp. 238–40.

and that, since on strong authority receivers had to take reasonable steps to obtain proper prices on asset sales, it would be anomalous not to impose a corresponding duty in relation to the management of those assets. Scott VC went on to state that principle and authority supported the following seven propositions:

1. A receiver managing mortgaged property owes duties to the mortgagor and anyone else with an interest in the equity of redemption.
2. The duties include, but are not necessarily confined to, a duty of good faith.
3. The extent and scope of any duty additional to that of good faith will depend upon the facts and circumstances of the particular case.
4. In exercising his powers of management the primary duty of the receiver is to try and bring about a situation in which interest on the secured debt can be paid and the debt itself repaid.
5. Subject to that primary duty, the receiver owes a duty to manage the property with due diligence.
6. Due diligence does not oblige the receiver to carry on a business on the mortgaged premises previously carried on by the mortgagor.
7. If the receiver does carry on a business on the mortgaged premises, due diligence requires reasonable steps to be taken in order to try and do so profitably.[75]

Whether the imposition of *Medforth* duties of competence on receivers will enhance the institution of receivership or detract from it will be considered below. A final note, however, should be made on the extent of the *Medforth* duty. Scott VC stated that the extent to which this would go beyond an obligation to exercise good faith would depend on the 'facts and circumstances of the particular case'.[76] This creates a certain opacity and on the facts in *Medforth* there were, indeed, elements of recklessness that some might construe to have approximated to a lack of good faith.[77] The danger is that a degree of further litigation may be required before clarification is brought to the issue – perhaps by modelling the duty more

---

75. [1993] 3 All ER 97 at 111 G–J.
76. [1999] 3 All ER 97 at 111. In *Re TransTec Automotive (Campsie) Ltd* [2001] BCC 403 Jacob J held that the receiver's primary duty was to try to bring about a situation where the interest on secured debt can be paid and the debt itself repaid (relying on *Medforth* v. *Blake*, ibid.). The obligation to take reasonable steps to maximise realisations enabled receivers to adopt selfish bargaining techniques when dealing with commercially vulnerable customers who could not obtain the supplies elsewhere: see further D. Bayfield, 'Receiver Can Use Vulnerability of Customer' (2000) 13 *Insolvency Intelligence* 38. But see J. Guthrie, 'Group on Receiving End Fights Back', *Financial Times*, 28 January 2002 on the Land Rover/KPMG court ruling which may make it harder for receivers to use strong-arm tactics.
77. See Frisby, 'Making a Silk Purse', pp. 322–3.

precisely on the duty to obtain a reasonable price. Until then receivership as an institution will be subjected to a period of increased transactional costs.

In addition to the mixture of common law duties owed by a receiver is the set of statutory obligations imposed by the Insolvency Act 1986. Notable among these is the obligation of a receiver appointed to enforce a floating charge[78] to ensure that the regime of statutory preferential claims is correctly applied.[79] It is the receiver who is obliged to see that preferential claims are settled when receivership and liquidation coincide.[80] Provisions on disclosure of information include duties to furnish annual accounts to the company's registry, the company, the appointor and the creditors' committee;[81] a duty to prepare a report within three months of receiving a statement of affairs from the company officers;[82] and an obligation to summon a meeting for unsecured creditors to consider this report.[83] As for the enforcement of the receiver's duties, the statutory obligations are usually underpinned by criminal sanctions of fines and the common law duties can be backed up by enforcement actions taken in the ordinary courts. It is now clear that the company can bring a direct action against its receiver.[84]

Finally, as far as termination of the receivership is concerned, this may result from the receiver's death,[85] removal by court order,[86] or ceasing to be a qualified IP.[87] The usual process, however, involves the completion of duties, notably realisation of all valuable assets and the making of all possible distributions to interested parties in the order of priority fixed by the law. Notification is then given to the company and the creditors' committee and any surplus funds are passed to the company. Resignations of receivers require at least seven days' notice of intention to be given to the appointor company, any liquidator and the creditors' committee.[88] The receiver will also have to vacate office if an administrator is appointed by the court.[89] Removal of the receiver by the appointer is, after the Insolvency Act 1986

---

78. But not a fixed charge: *Re G. L. Saunders Ltd* [1986] 1 WLR 215.
79. Insolvency Act 1986 s. 40; *IRC v. Goldblatt* [1972] Ch 498; *Woods v. Winskill* [1913] 2 Ch 303. See also Statement of Insolvency Practice, SIP 14 (June 1999).
80. *Re Pearl Maintenance Services Ltd* [1995] 1 BCLC 449.
81. Insolvency Rules 1986 r. 3.32.   82. Insolvency Act 1986 ss. 47 and 48.
83. Ibid., s. 48(2); Insolvency Rules 1986 rr. 3.9–3.15; see Milman and Durrant, *Corporate Insolvency*, p. 73.
84. *Watts v. Midland Bank plc* [1986] BCLC 15.
85. The replacing includes giving notice under Insolvency Rule 3.34.
86. Insolvency Act 1986 s. 45(1).   87. Ibid., ss. 45(2), 389, 390.
88. Insolvency Rules 1986 r. 3.33.   89. Insolvency Act 1986 ss. 45(2), 11(1)(b).

s. 45(1), only possible following a successful application to the court. The purpose of this reform was to make the receiver independent of the appointing debenture holder.[90]

Efficiency and creditor considerations

In some regards the administrative receiver may be thought to be particularly well placed to secure the rescue of an ailing company. As noted, the receiver is not necessarily required to go to court in order to act and there is no need to secure the agreement of directors, shareholders or creditors before actions to protect the debenture holders' interests are taken. The company's assets can be disposed of free from security interests (apart from those of the appointor) if the court gives leave.[91] Receivers owe obligations to report to other creditors but have no duties to accede to their wishes or even to listen to their views.[92] After appointment they act in a highly independent fashion and, as noted, the debenture holder can only remove them from office by securing an order of the court.[93]

It could be contended, however, that the independent and swiftly responsive model of receivership may now have been prejudiced by the *Medforth v. Blake*[94] imposition of a duty of care on receivers.[95] In *Medforth* itself it was argued on behalf of the receivers that imposing a duty of due diligence would undermine receivership. In response, though, it has been noted:

> Scott VC was unimpressed by that submission and justifiably so. The advantages of receivership to the modern day financial institutions go far beyond the avoidance of wilful default liability. Statute has conveyed an array of powers on administrative receivers, all of which will accrue to the benefit of the appointor, so much that escaping liability as mortgagee in possession will be little more than an afterthought to the contemporary debenture holder.[96]

90. Milman and Durrant, *Corporate Insolvency*, p. 76.
91. Insolvency Act 1986 s. 43.
92. See E. Ferran, 'The Duties of an Administrative Receiver to Unsecured Creditors' (1988) 9 Co. Law. 58. Ferran suggests that the disclosure requirements may benefit unsecured creditors in an indirect way, namely by providing them with ammunition with which to persuade a liquidator that an action should be brought against the administrative receiver.
93. Insolvency Act 1986 s. 45.   94. [1999] 3 All ER 97.
95. For a review of the discussion see Frisby, 'Making a Silk Purse', pp. 420–2; Sealy, 'Mortgagees and Receivers'.
96. Frisby, 'Making a Silk Purse', p. 420.

Receivership as an institution may have powerful institutional support-ers[97] but *Medforth* could give rise to legal uncertainties that are liable to produce defensive attitudes on the part of receivers and which could de-crease the efficiency of receivership as an institution. As already noted, Scott VC's judgment left some doubt as to the scope of the equitable duty owed by the receiver.[98] In suggesting that this might 'depend on the facts and circumstances of the particular case'[99] Scott VC missed the opportu-nity to lay down a guiding rule. The facts in *Medforth* indicated a very high level of negligence in so far as the warnings concerning the pig feed dis-count were repeatedly not acted upon. The receiver's behaviour could be construed as close to a breach of good faith and this leaves open a series of questions about receiver failure, notably whether the *Medforth* type of behaviour would have involved a breach of duty in the absence of the warn-ings that were given. A number of receivers will, as a result of such uncer-tainty, be exposed to litigation and, until the law is clarified, the institu-tion of receivership will involve higher transaction costs than would be the case with a more legally definite rule.

Such a process of legal clarification may indeed take some time because Scott VC's judgment in *Medforth* contained what has been dubbed some 'fancy footwork'[100] in escaping the constraints of previous case law, in 'applying an equitable label to a common law concept'[101] and by declining to arrive at the just result by reasoning in terms of wilful default and good faith. As one critic of the decision wrote: '*Medforth* is an attempt wholly to outmanoeuvre the *Downsview* analysis by rewriting the obligations in equity of the receiver by creating an equitable duty of care which can hardly be distinguished in practice from the common law tortious duty of care so comprehensively foresworn in *Downsview*.'[102] Whatever the

---

97. See B. G. Carruthers and T. C. Halliday, *Rescuing Business: The Making of Corporate Bankruptcy Law in England and the United States* (Clarendon Press, Oxford, 1998) pp. 134–6, 197–205, 286.

98. For criticism of the *Medforth* reasoning on the equitable duty see Sealy, 'Mortgagees and Receivers'.

99. [1999] 3 All ER 97 at 111: a point taken by Nicholas Warren QC in *Hadjipanayi* v. *Yeldon et al.* [2001] BPIR 487 at 492–5, when, in reviewing the duties of a mortgagee-appointed receiver, he deemed it arguable (but no more) that receivers may owe a duty to co-operate with the mortgagor in selling the mortgaged property with its attendant business as a going concern.

100. McCormack, 'Receiverships and the Rescue Culture', p. 240.

101. See J. Anderson, 'Receivers' Duties to Mortgagors. Court of Appeal Makes a Pig's Ear of It' (1999) 37 *CCH Company Law Newsletter* 6. On the content of the equitable duty to take care, its history and its existence in other equitable relationships see R. Gregory, 'Receiver's Duty of Care Considered' (1992) *CCH Company Law Newsletter* 9.

102. J. Anderson, 'Receivers' Duties to Mortgagors', p. 7.

doctrinal rights and wrongs here, the potential for litigation on these points should not be written off. That is the danger for receivers and for all parties who see legal certainty as serving their interests.)

There is a response to such concerns, however, that may offer some reassurance to the parties just mentioned. (It can be argued, first, that *Medforth* does not add significantly to uncertainties for the receiver because the long-established obligation to secure a reasonable price is liable to overlap significantly with a *Medforth* obligation of competence: many instances of lack of competence will mean there is a failure to secure a reasonable price. They might also constitute instances of wilful default per *Downsview*.[103] Second, it can be added that receivers who are wary of *Medforth* should not find it beyond their capabilities to protect themselves from legal attack by establishing proper procedures that reflect the minimal levels of competence of a reasonable business person.[104])

(A second concern about *Medforth* might be the belief (consistent with the judgment in *Downsview*[105]) that imposing an equitable duty of care on receivers will compromise the receiver's primary obligation to act in the interests of the debenture holder.) This worry is perhaps readily responded to by stating that a duty to exercise skill and care should not impinge on such a primary obligation or place other interests on a par with those of the debenture holder in the considerations of the receiver: the requirement is merely that 'decisions be competently taken'.[106] As the IS has noted in reporting its 1999–2000 consultation exercise on rescue: 'Some respondents asserted that the effect of (*Medforth*) was to remind receivers of their wider duties and that, accordingly, this diluted the force of the criticisms that receivership was not a collective procedure. This is arguably an overstatement of the *Medforth* decision.'[107] *Medforth* does not change the balance of power so much as demand an absence of behaviour lacking in care. (This response also provides an answer to a further concern about *Medforth* – represented by Lord Templeman's view in *Downsview* – that liability in negligence would lead receivers to sell assets 'as speedily as

---

103. See also A. Walters, 'Round Up: Corporate Finance and Receivership' (1999) 20 Co. Law. 324, who argues, at p. 329, that 'Given the possible damage that an incompetent receiver could do to the equity of redemption, it is perhaps not surprising to see the Court of Appeal applying a modern form of equitable duty analogous in some respects to the old-fashioned concept of "wilful default" by a mortgagee in possession.' Walters thus equates *Medforth v. Blake* [1999] 3 All ER 97 with *Knight v. Lawrence* [1991] BCC 411.
104. See V. Swain, 'Taking Care of Business' (1999) *Insolvency Bulletin* 9.
105. See Frisby, 'Making a Silk Purse', p. 420.   106. Ibid.
107. Insolvency Service, *A Review of Company Rescue and Business Reconstruction Mechanisms*, Report by the Review Group (DTI, 2000), p. 52 ('IS 2000').

possible'.[108] If there is a clear duty to the appointor, an obligation to act competently should have, at worst, a neutral effect on speed of disposition, and in many cases it will favour a less precipitate, more deliberate, style of decision-making. Whether receivers' duties to creditors should be broadened is a matter to be returned to below in considering issues of fairness.

Note should now be taken of a number of difficulties that constitute limitations on the collectivity of receivership. Receivership involves no moratorium on the enforcement of claims against the company. This means that a receiver is powerless to stop other creditors from acting to enforce their claim and, in doing so, throwing a spanner in the works of the rescue plan. Nor is there any power in the receiver's hands to stop the company from entering into liquidation. Liquidation will not stop receivers from acting. They will continue in office, exercising powers in the interests of their appointor (acting as agent for the appointor, no longer for the company). But the chances of a successful rescue will be reduced by the advent of liquidation.[109] Once that stage is reached there is no prospect of corporate survival although the receiver may succeed in selling off some part of the business as a going concern.

Nor, as we have seen, is the receiver always obliged to attempt to rescue the business. The receiver is only obliged to pursue the rescue option if this course is in the interests of the appointing debenture holder. If the interest of the appointor is best served by a simple realisation of the assets, the administrative receiver is obliged not to attempt to rescue unless the full approval of the appointor is forthcoming. There are reasons for thinking, moreover, that receivers will tend to play safe and to favour simple realisations rather than rescues when in doubt. Receivers are private professionals not public officials and are dependent for their livelihood and appointment on a relatively small group of financial institutions, such as banks, taking floating charges. Although administrative receivers cannot be removed from office once appointed, except by order of the court, they would jeopardise future appointments if they disregarded their appointor's wishes.[110]

The statistics indicate that receivership results in rescue in fewer instances than other formal procedures: the DTI's 1993 Consultative

108. [1993] AC 295 at 316.
109. See also Re Leyland DAF Ltd [2001] 1 BCLC 419 (upheld Feb. 2002 (CA)) where Rimer J held that a liquidator could have recourse to assets covered by a crystallised floating charge to reimburse properly incurred liquidation expenses.
110. A. Clarke, 'Corporate Rescues and Reorganisations in English Law after the Insolvency Act 1986' (Mimeo, University College, London, 1993) p. 7.

Document on Company Voluntary Arrangements reported on SPI research which revealed that in 1993 50 per cent of administrative receiverships terminated with a break-up sale of the company's assets, but that 67 per cent of all administrations and 75 per cent of all CVAs achieved a complete or partial survival of the enterprise.[111] When, indeed, the Royal Bank of Scotland adopted a rescue culture it immediately cut the number of receivers appointed.[112] This is perhaps because, as has been pointed out, receivership can only be effectively used for rescue purposes if the company has a dominant creditor (perhaps a bank or consortium of banks); if that creditor is willing actively to support rescue; and if other parties refrain from spoiling actions. If such conditions exist, moreover, it may well be possible to forgo receivership and mount a rescue by means of informal agreements.

When the IS consulted on rescue mechanisms for its 2000 Review[113] it encountered very different appraisals of receivership. Most of its respondents were favourably disposed towards the institution of receivership, a situation that was not surprising given that most responses came from law firms and trade associations.[114] These respondents stressed that administrative receivership was an integral part of the rescue culture in the UK that contributed to rescue and corporate survival. They emphasised the ability of receivers to take rapid and effective actions to prevent deterioration in the viability of businesses (particularly where fraud was evident or suspected); the sizeable number of businesses that go into receivership and then are sold as going concerns; and the relatively low costs of initiating the procedure (as seen by creditors and practitioners). The 'larger professional service firms' considered that the banks took a responsible attitude towards receivership and only appointed receivers as a last resort. They conceded, however, that non-bank floating charge holders were 'more likely to act precipitately as they tended to be less focused on preserving a long term relationship with the debtor'. Research conducted by Franks and Sussman and discussed by the IS[115] gives some

111. R3's Ninth Survey of Business Recovery in the UK (2001) indicated business preservation rates associated with appointments as follows: receiverships 59 per cent; administrators 79 per cent (up from 41 per cent in a small sample); CVAs 74 per cent. Receiverships were found in the SPI's Eighth Survey, *Company Insolvency in the United Kingdom* (SPI, London, 1999), to save 31 per cent of jobs compared to 37 per cent for CVAs and 40 per cent for administrators (1997–8).

112. In 1992 the RBS appointed 418 receivers (11 per cent of the national total); in 1996 it appointed 48 (5 per cent of the national total): see M. Hunter, 'The Nature and Functions of a Rescue Culture' [1999] JBL 491 at 508, n. 66.

113. IS 2000, p. 53.   114. Ibid., pp. 15, 48.

115. Ibid., pp. 16–19; Franks and Sussman, 'The Cycle of Corporate Distress'.

support to the 'last resort' account. The IS noted the key research finding that: 'It seems clear that banks rarely petition for the liquidation of
a company and that, in recent years, they have tended to see administrative receivership as a last resort for a troubled company. Where an administrative receiver is appointed, going concern sales (of the whole of
the business or of some part of it) are achieved in about 44 per cent of
cases.'[116]

Many business people consulted by the IS were, however, concerned
about the power of the floating charge holder:

> They were very sceptical about the banks' contentions that receivers
> would only ever be appointed as a last resort and tended to be wary of
> their banks in times of difficulty. Some business people told us of
> personal experiences where the banks appeared to have acted very
> unreasonably. Many considered that banks were only adopting a more
> relationship driven style at the larger end of the market and that the
> banks did not have the same interest in the SME end of the market –
> with the result that in times of trouble, the banks would be looking to
> exit the relationship as quickly as possible, via receivership if
> necessary.[117]

Respondents who voiced reservations about the effectiveness of administrative receivership as a rescue device emphasised three points.[118] The first
was that: 'It can lead to unnecessary business failures and undermines the
rescue culture, particularly when the relationship between the floating
charge holder and the business breaks down; the floating charge holder
may then decide to withdraw support from the business and appoint an
administrative receiver when an alternative lender might have elected to
continue such support.' The second was that: 'Because the purpose of the
receivership is primarily to ensure repayment of the amount due to the
secured creditor, there is no (or there is insufficient) incentive to maximise the value of the debtor company's estate.' The third point was that
the growth of asset-backed lending, factoring and invoice discounting as
modes of corporate financing, together with a growing diversity of parties able to appoint administrative receivers, has made it more difficult
to ensure that the appointment of an administrative receiver is effectively
treated as a measure of last resort by lenders. Such diversity, in turn, makes

116. IS 2000, p. 17.
117. Ibid. See also Carruthers and Halliday, *Rescuing Business*, p. 286.
118. IS 2000, p. 15. Points relating to the consistency of administrative receivership with
international and EU requirements have been left out of account here.

it more difficult to rely on self-regulatory measures by creditors such as the British Bankers' Association's Statement of Principles.[119]

The pessimistic view of receivership, however, has to be contrasted with what has been called the 'concentrated creditor governance' theory of receivership.[120] This theory urges that the law on receivership can generate significant and worthwhile efficiencies. Two propositions lie at the heart of this argument: first, that debt finance can act as a mechanism of corporate governance, especially in small and medium-sized enterprises (SMEs) where other governance mechanisms such as hostile takeovers are less important; and second, that concentrating a firm's debt finance in the hands of a relatively small number of creditors can reduce total monitoring and decision-making costs. The suggestion here is that giving control over enforcement to a 'concentrated creditor' allows that creditor to utilise the information it has gathered during the course of its deliberations on whether or not to continue to support the debtor, and that this allows for quicker and cheaper enforcement than would take place with the collective insolvency procedure in which an outsider appointee takes over the firm. This increases expected returns from enforcement and toughens the disciplinary effect of debt finance.

This argument emphasises that a number of problems are faced in creditor collective actions. First, there is the issue of information. It will cost creditors money to gain information on whether to enforce the debt or renegotiate it, but the benefit of such information will be only a fraction of the total value at stake and so individual creditors will be notionally underinformed. They may, moreover, seek to free ride on the monitoring of others and, overall, there will be collective underinvestment in monitoring. 'Hold out' problems may also affect collective action since collective renegotiation or decisions to sell the firm as a going concern may demand that all creditors agree the course of action. Individual creditors will thus have incentives to hold out against such agreements until their co-operation is bought. If such problems are severe, a race to enforce debts may result as collectivity breaks down.[121]

The suggested solution to such problems is not to follow Jackson and argue for state-imposed collectivism: this, say Armour and Frisby, will

119. British Bankers' Association, *Voluntary Code of Practice* (1997) (the 'Bankers' Code'). See further D. Milman and D. Mond, *Security and Corporate Rescue* (Hodgsons, Manchester, 1999).
120. See Armour and Frisby, 'Rethinking Receivership'.
121. Ibid., p. 84; S. Levmore, 'Monitors and Freeriders in Commercial and Corporate Settings' (1982) 92 Yale LJ 49 at 53–4; T. Jackson, 'Bankruptcy, Non-Bankruptcy Entitlements and the Creditors' Bargain' (1982) 92 Yale LJ 857 at 859–68.

reduce enforcement costs but it will do 'nothing to ameliorate collective action problems associated with information gathering beforehand'.[122] A more comprehensive solution, in their view, is for the debtor to have one main creditor who will act as a whistle blower. This will produce savings because creditor concentration means that the main creditor has appropriate incentives to monitor the debtor for default and, also, can renegotiate swiftly and efficiently since there is only one significant creditor. It is argued that enforcement in this manner is better informed and quicker than if carried out by a state official. It is a low-cost strategy for the creditor bank and so this increases the effectiveness of debt as a disciplinary mechanism for under-performing managers. Receivership thus is a vehicle for facilitating the efficient disposal of assets by a concentrated creditor.

Empirical research was said to support the case for the creditor concentration approach. Professionals involved in receivership thought that in the majority of cases receivers were appointed by a bank that was the debtor firm's principal lender. Statistics also indicated that receivership appointments were largely confined to SMEs with annual turnovers of less than £5 million and that the majority of appointments were made by banks.[123] As for monitoring, there was evidence that clearing banks typically lend to SMEs through local business relationship managers, but that some routine monitoring of debtors is conducted and that risk evaluations are carried out. If performance dropped below a certain point, the debtor's file would be transferred to a central 'intensive care' division of the bank and into the hands of specialist staff acting with the primary objective of turning corporate affairs around. Scrutiny by the bank would then become more intensive and, if the firm's fortunes did not change, the bank might appoint an accountant to carry out an independent business review. The function of that review would be to build a bridge between the bank and the troubled company's management in order to find a solution – which might or might not be a receivership. The whole process, in terms of creditor concentration theory, amounts to an information-gathering exercise initiated by the concentrated creditor that generates benefits for other creditors in terms of improved quality decision-making.

The creditor concentration theory is, however, subject to a number of objections. Leaving aside issues of fairness to non-appointing creditors,

---

122. Armour and Frisby, 'Rethinking Receivership', p. 85.
123. Ibid., p. 92; SPI Eighth Survey, p. 11. The Price Waterhouse Coopers database of insolvency appointments lists 1,145 receiverships in 1998, of which 68 per cent (773) were made by banks.

and focusing on economic efficiency considerations, the first problem is
that concentration may produce inefficient and distorted decisions concerning the continuation of the business as a going concern. Proponents
of concentration concede that (consistently with their legal obligations)
receivers generally see their role as being to maximise recoveries for the
main creditor (hereafter 'the bank'). The danger, as summarised by one
commentator, is:

> The receivership system may lead to an equilibrium in which the
> company is prematurely and inefficiently liquidated. The problem
> stems from the feature of this system which allows creditors to act in
> individualistic self-interest. They have the right to recover the value of
> their claim without considering the overall value of the pool of assets
> upon which they draw. This may force the company to liquidate its
> assets even though on efficiency grounds it should continue
> business.[124]

Proponents of the creditor concentration theory might respond that there
is evidence that banks do not act in a precipitate fashion. Armour and
Frisby note that SPI data suggest that, overall, secured creditors receive
on average only 37 per cent of the face value of their debt and that only
18 per cent of secured creditors recover in full.[125] Such figures, however,
are not conclusive. They may, for instance, indicate that receivers act with
a short-term zeal to gain returns to banks and that this not only damages
non-appointing creditors but also fails to maximise returns to banks.

A second defence of receivership might lie in the argument that banks
will be unwilling to close marginal businesses since indirect costs will
be involved where the closed firm's customers, suppliers and employees
are also bank customers and stand to be adversely affected by closures.
It could be added that banks will not act precipitately for reputational
reasons, since closing SMEs will not sit well alongside advertising campaigns stressing the banks' caring and listening characteristics.[126] This defence, however, has limited mileage. On the bank's decision to institute a
receivership, it may well be the case that some banks, in buoyant financial conditions, will act in an understanding manner, but it would be rash

---

124. D. Webb, 'An Economic Evaluation of Insolvency Processes in the UK: Does the 1986
Insolvency Act Satisfy the Creditors' Bargain?' (1991) *Oxford Economic Papers* 144.
125. SPI Eighth Survey, pp. 14–15; Armour and Frisby, 'Rethinking Receivership', p. 96.
126. British Bankers' Association, *Banks and Business Working Together* (1997) sets out a number
of principles for dealing with SMEs, stating, *inter alia*, 'Banks have long supported a rescue
culture and thousands of customers are in business today because of the support of their bank
through difficult times': discussed in Hunter, 'Nature and Functions of a Rescue Culture'.

to design insolvency regimes by presupposing continuing general good-will in banks. Such goodwill may be sketchily distributed and short lived in hard times when insolvencies will multiply. The incentive will be for banks to put receivers into post with an eye to their own selfish interests. Some would argue, moreover, that the general UK trend is for banks to operate in an increasingly hard-nosed manner and to move away from 'gentlemen's club' altruistic stances.[127] Once the receiver is appointed, moreover, the bank is not running operations and the receiver has a legal obligation and, as seen above, an inclination to act in the bank's interests rather than broader interests.

The creditor concentration theory is also open to contest on its assumptions concerning the monitoring of corporate managers. A key assumption is that banks will possess strong incentives through concentration to monitor managerial performance. This will produce benefits to the general body of creditors. There are, however, reasons for thinking that this will not always be the case. In so far as credit is not 100 per cent concentrated in the secure loan from the bank, the bank will undermonitor since its incentive to oversee will relate to the extent of its secured loan and not the total sum owed to creditors and at risk through managerial activities. It is, moreover, the case that where the secured creditor is not first in the queue to be paid (e.g. where there are fixed charges and preferential creditors) any incentive to monitor will be reduced. Thus, if the prospect of recovery of the sum owed stands to be reduced to 25 per cent by the existence of prior claims, the inducement to monitor will be a quarter of the efficient incentive.

Attention must, in addition, be paid to the purposes to which such monitoring is put. It would be rash to assume that monitoring relates to the general health and well-being of the enterprise rather than the prospect of repayment of the loan.[128] The more modest the loan is in relation to overall corporate turnover the more likely it is that the bank will take its eye off overall business health. It may even be the case that a generally poorly performing company would, on receivership, be able to meet the sum owing to the bank on the floating charge.[129]

The monitoring of management, moreover, can be seen as merely one of a number of ways in which a creditor can deal with the risks of lending.

127. W. Hutton, *The State We're In* (Vintage, London, 1996); Carruthers and Halliday, *Rescuing Business*, pp. 197–205.
128. See V. Finch, 'Company Directors: Who Cares About Skill and Care?' (1992) 55 MLR 179 at 189–95.
129. Webb, 'An Economic Evaluation', p. 145.

Taking increased security offers an alternative way of managing developing risks as do the processes of spreading risks and of adjusting interest rates and associated charges for credit. From the point of view of a creditor, the objective in lending will be to manage risks in the most efficient manner: that is the one that allows the bank best to compete in the marketplace and best to maximise returns for its own shareholders. Such an objective is likely to be met by the bank adopting a mixture of strategies: perhaps combining some taking of security, some monitoring and some adjustment of interest rates. The problem for the creditor concentration theory is that, even if concentration is assumed, it cannot be taken for granted that the bank's incentive will be to monitor managerial practice with an eye either to ongoing corporate health or to instituting receivership at the appropriate time. Many banks will often find it cheaper to deal with risks by increasing security and by increasing charge rates.

Nor should the virtues of monitoring be accepted unquestioningly in setting these up as a justification for any unfairness in underprotecting the interests of certain classes of creditor. The notion that monitoring protects creditors assumes that there is a linkage between this and improvements in the management of the firm. It may well be the case that underperforming managers fail to deliver the goods in many instances because of irrationalities, lack of ability, failures of strategy and deficiencies of understanding. It takes a considerable leap of faith to believe that such poor performers will be highly responsive to the messages received from monitoring banks. If a typical unsecured creditor was to be offered the choice of a larger share of the insolvency estate or better monitoring of management he or she might well opt for the former. The point can also be made that even if creditor concentration is present, the bank may only possess partial control over the firm since finance may have been raised by quasi-security devices such as hire purchase or retention of title arrangements. The claims of such finance suppliers will take precedence over the floating charge and the bank will have reduced *de facto* control over the firm's assets.

A final difficulty concerns creditor concentration itself and how this is to be ensured. If levels of concentration are left to the market, it may or may not be (or remain) the case that the typical SME has only one main (bank) secured creditor. It would, accordingly, be risky to design a regime of insolvency law on that continuing assumption. If, on the other hand, insolvency law is set up to offer firms an incentive to resort to only one main secured creditor, this would not be consistent with the provision of the flexible financing opportunities that firms need in order to respond efficiently to market changes. There may also be problems of 'reverse agency costs' in so far as the main creditor bank may chill the firm's investment decisions – leading to valuable opportunities being forgone in favour of lower-risk alternatives.[130]

Expertise and the institution

The Insolvency Act 1986, as noted, provides that all receivers must be qualified insolvency practitioners within the meaning of Part XIII of the 1986 Act. The 1986 Act, in turn, responded to Cork's view that persons performing as IPs must possess some minimal professional qualifications and be subjected to control.[131] General issues relating to the expertise of IPs have been discussed in chapter 5 and will not be rehearsed here, save to note that some commentators have questioned whether the training and approach of IPs gives them a sufficient grounding in managerial skills and provides them with a proper orientation towards rescue rather than mere debt collection. Within the context of receivership it can be argued that there are particular institutional factors that militate unduly against rescue options, notably the ongoing relationship that most receivers have with the major lending banks and the primary legal obligations of receivers to act to protect the bank's interests. Receivers, even if managerially trained, would find themselves ill-positioned to put such skills into good effect for the purposes of rescue. They may be proved to be highly expert at protecting the bank's interests but this may constitute a narrower expertise than the overall public interest demands. Receivers, moreover, act with one hand tied behind their backs even if disposed to exercise their skills in favour of rescue. Receivership is not a collectivist approach proper and, accordingly, other parties cannot be bound in a manner that prevents interference with the receiver's proposed route out of corporate troubles.

As far as particular or sectoral skills are concerned, problems may arise when receivers are appointed at an early stage of corporate troubles. If those troubles are mainly to do with financial management then the IPs acting as receivers may be able to assist the company by rationalising affairs. If, however, attention to corporate problems demands detailed knowledge of a particular industry, market or mode of organising the

---

130. See G. Triantis and R. Daniels, 'The Role of Debt in Interactive Corporate Governance' (1995) 83 Calif. L Rev. 1073 at 1090–1103.
131. Cork Report, para. 756.

business, there may be a danger that the receiver is far less well equipped to effect a rescue or appropriate sale of assets than managers who are familiar with the scene. Receivers will accordingly have to rely heavily on management.

As was seen above, receivers are, at law, obliged to perform their functions with certain levels of skill. It is clear from the judgment of Scott VC in *Medforth* v. *Blake*[132] that a receiver, when managing assets, owes the mortgagor more than a duty to exercise good faith. Reasonable competence must also be displayed and an equitable duty of care is owed. As noted also, *Medforth* was adopting a policy line consistent with prior case law that demanded that a receiver must take reasonable steps to obtain a proper price from the sale of assets.

Accountability and fairness

The receiver operates at a low level of accountability. The appointing debenture holder, as noted, has no power to direct the receiver and the receiver owes the troubled company neither a duty of obedience[133] nor a duty to provide information in relation to the management and conduct of its affairs.[134] On selling assets, however, there is, as we have seen, legal accountability through the obligation to take reasonable steps to obtain a proper price and, during management again, a duty of care is owed to the debtor company – though subject to a fiduciary duty to act in the interests of the debenture holder.[135]

Just as the troubled company has little input into the receiver's decision-making, so the array of junior creditors is distanced from such processes. Cork responded to complaints on this front with proposals designed to create 'a relationship of accountability' between the receiver and the unsecured creditor.[136] It has been suggested, however, that the resultant legislative steps have done little to ensure meaningful participation rights: the requirement that there be a creditors' committee, for instance, is designed to assist the receiver in discharging his functions but it contains no power to direct the receiver in relation to the carrying out of

---

132. [1999] 3 All ER 97.   133. *Meigh* v. *Wickenden* [1942] 2 KB 160.
134. *Gomba Holdings UK* v. *Homan* [1986] 3 All ER 94.
135. Armour and Frisby, 'Rethinking Receivership', p. 77.
136. Cork Report, para. 481. See Insolvency Act 1986 s. 48(2) and Insolvency Rules 1986 rr. 3.9–3.15 on the calling of a meeting of the creditors. See further Armour and Frisby, 'Rethinking Receivership', p. 79.

these functions.[137] This contrasts with the stronger powers possessed by liquidation committees[138] and meetings of creditors in administration.[139] In any event, the Insolvency Service has noted that 'very few such committees are appointed' and has concluded that the present framework for administrative receivership does not 'provide a basis for accountability or properly aligned incentives in relation to the bulk of cases'.[140]

Turning to fairness, it can be argued that receivership operates in a manner that is procedurally and substantively unfair to non-appointing creditors and others. In substance it is a private procedure that allows enforcement of the appointor's security rights to the potential detriment of other creditors, employees, the company and a range of stakeholders including suppliers and customers. Procedurally it is unfair because the interests of these parties may be affected by the receiver's actions but there is no appropriate regime of access and input into decision-making for such potentially prejudiced parties. Indeed, in the current climate of concern with corporate governance issues and stakeholder interests,[141] the system of receivership can be said to raise serious governance considerations in that it allows a large number of large companies to be handed over and dealt with by one interested party with little or no concern for other claimants.[142]

It is clear, moreover, that there is concern about such unfairness. The IS in 2000 noted that a number of the respondents to its consultation were worried that the floating charge and administrative receivership placed too much power in the hands of one creditor and caused unfairness in so far as there was no incentive for the floating charge holder to consider the interests of any other party; the floating charge holder could take decisions having a significant impact on returns to other creditors without there being any requirement for their consent; the administrative receiver owed a duty of care to the floating charge holder and not to creditors in general; and, unlike in other procedures, the cost of administrative receivership would fall on unsecured and preferential creditors if there were surplus funds over and above those needed to discharge the secured

---

137. See Armour and Frisby, 'Rethinking Receivership'; Ferran, 'Duties of an Administrative Receiver'.

138. Armour and Frisby, 'Rethinking Receivership'; I. Grier and R. E. Floyd, *Voluntary Liquidation and Receivership* (3rd edn, Longman, London, 1991) p. 184.

139. Insolvency Act 1986 s. 24. On administration see ch. 9 below.

140. DTI/Insolvency Service, *Productivity and Enterprise: Insolvency – A Second Chance* (Cm 5234, 2001) ('White Paper, 2001') p. 9.

141. See, for example, the Company Law Review Steering Group's Consultation Documents: *Modern Company Law for a Competitive Economy* (1998), (1999) and (2000).

142. Milman and Mond, *Security and Corporate Rescue*, p. 48.

creditor's debt.[143] On the last point, research by Franks and Sussman for the IS[144] noted that the costs of receivership are significant and tend to be borne by the bank 'only in the minority of cases in which they recover less than 100 per cent', and that when the bank is paid in full 'the junior creditors are effectively paying the cost of realising the bank's security'. As for the quantum of such costs, the research suggested that for recoveries of between £100k and £500k the median percentage taken in costs tended to be between 20 per cent and 29 per cent. The White Paper of 2001 noted that 'unsecured creditors have no right to challenge the level of costs in a receivership, even though they have an identifiable financial interest where there are sufficient funds to pay the secured creditor in full'.[145]

Floating charge holders might argue that receivership is fair because they have paid for their right to appoint a receiver in so far as they have lowered interest rates in reflection of the easy enforcement and risk control that such a right gives them. The banks, furthermore, may suggest that they charge very low margins on secured loans while trade creditors' gross profit margins may be anything up to 50 per cent, 'so the latter's losses will be offset by the higher profits they made when the company was trading profitably and paying its debts'.[146] It may be responded, however, that many unsecured creditors are simply in no position to negotiate security arrangements, that typically they lack the bank's knowledge of the company's financial position, that markets often do not allow high profit margins, that the institution of receivership offers a ready means for the better placed banks to exploit their positions, and that the interest rates charged by the floating charge holders are excessively profitable because risks are loaded onto unsecured creditors.

The concerns of trade and expense creditors are reinforced by the Franks and Sussman research for the IS which found that bank rescues often led to a rise in debts due to trade and expense creditors while the indebtedness to the bank decreased:

> It is in both the bank's and the company's interests not to disclose that the company is in intensive care. The research shows that during the rescue process the debt owed to the bank tends to contract (by averages,

143. See IS 2000, p. 15. See also Davies, 'Employee Claims in Insolvency', p. 150: 'The promotion of rescues as distinct from the promotion of banks' interests in rescues, requires the decision as to the best way of realising the company's assets to be taken in the general interests of the company's creditors and not by the agent of one particular type of creditor.'

144. IS 2000, pp. 16–19.

145. White Paper, 2001 (*Productivity and Enterprise*), p. 9.

146. IS 2000, p. 18.

for the three banks involved [in the study,] of 34 per cent, 19 per cent and 45 per cent respectively where the 'rescue' is successful and the company returns to the branch and by averages of 15 per cent and 8 per cent for Banks 1 and 2 where the company moves to a debt recovery unit) whilst trade credit expands modestly.[147]

Society as a whole may also complain about the unfairness of receivership since this is a regime that does not aim to maximise overall social benefit: its purpose is merely to secure a return to the debenture holder. This would be an empty complaint if it could be argued with conviction that receivership brings overall benefits to society because, for example, debenture holder monitoring is generally effective in protecting interests across the range of corporate creditors and stakeholders. As we have seen, however, it is difficult to make out the case that such benefits are achieved. The IS made the point in 2000 that a number of problems bedevil consumers of different insolvency regimes, notably the difficulty of assessing the impact of different insolvency procedures while making allowance for other factors such as the selection that takes place before a company enters a particular procedure and the stage in corporate decline at which resort is made to a procedure.[148]

Information on the relative performance of different procedures is, moreover, thin on the ground and the IS has pointed to the need for more systemic data on such matters as: the direct costs (such as legal and professional fees) of administration, CVAs and administrative receiverships; the typical recovery rates for different classes of creditor by procedure; the survival rates for businesses under different procedures; and the respective levels of gross recoveries or realisations.[149]

Finally, an important aspect of fairness in decision-making is the disinterestedness of decision-makers. On this front there has been a good deal of concern in recent years about conflicts of interest and the frequency with which receivers are appointed from firms of accountants who have advised and advocated receivership to the major creditors of the troubled firm. As has been noted in chapter 5[150] these matters were discussed by the IS in its 1999 and 2000 Reviews of Company Rescue and Business Reconstruction Mechanisms. The IS favoured control through voluntary codes of practice rather than the introduction of a statutory prohibition

---

147. IS 2000, p. 17. 'If formal insolvency ensues the bank will recover anything between 60–80 per cent of its indebtedness whilst trade creditors will recover nothing': ibid.
148. Ibid., p. 18.   149. Ibid.   150. See pp. 163–4 above.

on such appointments but, as already argued, what may be required is a new power for directors to contest the appointment of investigators as receivers.

Revising receivership

The Government announced in the White Paper of 2001 that it believes 'that administrative receivership should cease to be a major insolvency procedure'.[151] The IS has proposed restricting the use of receivership and developing a more effective and flexible administration procedure (for discussion of which see chapter 9). The White Paper proposals are considered below but it should not be assumed that these proposals will inevitably be put into effect without amendment.[152] Receivership may survive since it has powerful institutional supporters; if it is believed that receivership in some form will survive, potential reforms should be considered.

Is it possible to retain the advantages of receivership but reduce its unfairness and lack of procedural propriety? Here, a number of proposals are worth considering. One is that the duties of receivers to parties other than the appointor should be 'clarified and upgraded'.[153] It is clear now that receivers do owe obligations to the debtor company to obtain a proper price on sale of assets and to exercise care when continuing trading (if consistent with the fiduciary duty to act in the interests of the debenture holder). Receivers could, however, be given statutory duties to consider the interests of the company and/or junior creditors when exercising their powers. New Zealand, for instance, has experience of a statute that imposes on receivers a duty to act in good faith and, in addition, an obligation to exercise the receiver's powers with responsible regard to the interests of unsecured creditors, guarantors and others claiming an interest in property through the debtor.[154] The imposition of such an obligation in England

---

151. White Paper, 2001 (*Productivity and Enterprise*), p. 10; for discussion, see pp. 269–71 below. See also R3 Ninth Survey which noted the declining use of receivership over the years surveyed. Receivership accounted for 6.6 per cent of all insolvency proceedings in the Ninth Survey, 8.8 per cent in the Eighth (SPI) Survey and 14.4 per cent in the Seventh (SPI) Survey.

152. In November 2001 Industry Secretary Patricia Hewitt stated that the Enterprise Bill (based on the 2001 White Paper – *Productivity and Enterprise*) would not abolish the right to appoint an administrative receiver for secured creditors with floating charges created before the Bill becomes law.

153. See Milman and Mond, *Security and Corporate Rescue*; McCormack, 'Receiverships and the Rescue Culture'.

154. See New Zealand Receivership Act 1993 s. 18(3); McCormack, 'Receiverships and the Rescue Culture', p. 237; Goode, *Principles of Corporate Insolvency Law*, pp. 242–3.

would mean that, provided the appointor's interests were not affected adversely,[155] the receiver would have a duty to act so as to maximise benefits to other parties. The provision would give the junior creditors, company, employees and other interested parties an increased level of protection from harms that are gratuitous in the sense that avoiding them would do no damage to the receiver's appointor.)

It has been objected that enforcing such obligations would present courts with difficult questions of assessment.[156] In the field of insolvency and corporate law generally, however, the courts have to deal with precisely such issues of judgment. A further contention may be that receivers might be led by such duties to make excessively risk averse decisions, a tendency that would reduce expected returns to all parties.[157] It can be replied, though, that there may be a trade-off worth making here on both fairness and efficiency grounds; that if receivers have to avoid 'gratuitous' damage to non-appointor interests this involves few costs to the appointor and potential gains to other parties. As for excessive risk aversion, this should not happen if the legal stipulation is clear, and a duty to advert to a range of interests and examine options that are cost free to the appointor does not seem a duty that is more onerous in kind than very many other obligations borne by IPs. Litigation is expensive and non-appointors such as unsecured creditors will tend to be parties with low inclinations to resort to law. It is unlikely, accordingly, that receivers will feel that their every judgment will be liable to second-guessing in court. The likely outcome of such an obligation is that the courts will take a procedural approach and check to see that receivers have considered non-appointors' interests in making decisions. It is far less likely that the courts will feel inclined to enter routinely into substantive issues of receiver trade-offs of different creditor group interests.

Cork, as already noted, considered but rejected such a proposed approach on the grounds that it would drive prospective lenders to the early enforcement of fixed securities, to greater use of hybrid forms of securities and to direct enforcement of their security; and that it would cause delay and expense.[158] The Cork view was that the virtues of

---

155. The New Zealand Receivership Act 1993 s. 18(2) expressly preserves the receiver's primary responsibility to protect interests of the debenture holder: see Milman and Mond, *Security and Corporate Rescue*, p. 49.

156. Armour and Frisby, 'Rethinking Receivership', p. 100.

157. B. Cheffins, *Company Law: Theory, Structure and Operation* (Clarendon Press, Oxford, 1997) pp. 543–4; Armour and Frisby, 'Rethinking Receivership', p. 100.

158. Cork Report, paras. 449–50.

receivership – economic and swift action with little opportunity for successful legal challenge before the event – would be lost by extending duties to others. Such fears, however, might have been given too much play and have built on a notion that receivers would have to balance a series of interests in acting. In fact, no such balancing act would be involved in stating that the receiver's primary duty is to the appointor but that where the appointor's interests are not prejudiced, other interests should be given weight.

One proposal that has been publicly discussed is that appointor banks should be obliged to give a fixed number of days' notice to companies before appointing a receiver.[159] This change was included in the early drafts of the Insolvency Bill 2000 and was designed to offer businesses an opportunity to win creditor support for rescue. The banks, however, opposed a notice requirement, arguing that notice would trigger a rush by stakeholders to protect their own interests rather than secure the firm's future: creditors, for instance, would act swiftly to repossess goods. A further suggested problem is that banks would anticipate such a rush to collect and would respond by introducing receivers at an earlier date than would otherwise have been the case. In any event, notice would not facilitate talks with creditors because the company's bank would be unlikely to continue to cash cheques drawn on the company's account in the interim period.[160] If, moreover, a company was on the verge of receivership it would generally be too late to start talking to creditors and the bank's decision to introduce a receiver would normally have been preceded by weeks or months of joint efforts by banks and directors to solve the problem outside insolvency – an approach reinforced by the British Bankers' Association's 1997 Statement of Principles.[161] The Trade and Industry Select Committee took the view that when secured creditors were adamant about appointing a receiver there would be few situations in which there were reasonable prospects of success for a CVA. This was because an injection of new funds by the bank

---

159. See DTI/IS, *Company Voluntary Arrangements and Administration Orders: A Consultative Document* (October 1993) ('DTI 1993') p. 11 (five days' notice unless there has been a moratorium within the previous twelve months). In Canada the Insolvency Act 1992 s. 244 requires the enforcing secured creditor to send the debtor notice, and ten days have to expire between notice and enforcement: see McCormack, 'Receiverships and the Rescue Culture', p. 248.

160. See McCormack, 'Receiverships and the Rescue Culture', pp. 229–42.

161. See the letter to the *Financial Times* of 8 October 1999, from Barclays Bank's Head of Corporate Support and Recoveries, Ivan Armstrong. The British Bankers' Association's Statement of Principles states, for example, 'Where we have requested an independent review of your business to help you solve the underlying problems, we will seek to discuss the information provided with you (and, should you request, your advisors) before taking any action.' (Principle 8.)

was usually a precondition for a CVA to work.[162] The CBI warned that a period of notice could allow unscrupulous directors to stash away assets while creditors' hands were tied. The Commons Trade and Industry Committee was not convinced of the case for notice in early 2000 and recommended that the clause in question be dropped from the Insolvency Bill.[163] The Government noted these views and consultee comments and deleted the clause from the Bill.[164]

A different proposal is designed to give notice of a decision to appoint a receiver but to ensure that the decision is justified. This would demand that a receivership should only be initiated by a court order.[165] The advantage here would be that this would control 'rogue or disputed' receiverships and allow the court to check whether other rehabilitative possibilities had been properly considered. It would also improve predictability by allowing courts to demand that receivers lodge a schedule of timetabled activities. Advocates of such change argue that administrators have to work to fixed schedules and receivers ought to be able to do so as well. As for suggestions of undesirable expenses and delays (which might precipitate rushes to collect), it is argued that experience with administration has shown that prompt court hearings and immediate orders can be obtained in pressing financial situations. There could also be a prohibition on enforcement of claims against the company which could be triggered by the lodging of an application for a receivership order.

Turning to the access of non-appointor stakeholders to receivers' decision-making, it could be said that this would automatically be improved if receivers were obliged to consider non-appointor interests along the lines discussed above. For the sake of clarity, however, it would be advisable to spell out the access rights of non-appointor stakeholders. At present, as we have seen, the receiver is obliged to furnish annual accounts to the company registry, the company, his appointor and the creditors' committee.[166] A receiver's report, together with a copy of the director's statement of affairs, has to be sent to the Companies Registry and it has to be prepared within three months of receipt of the company officer's statement of affairs.[167] Copies of the report (but not the statement of affairs) must be sent to the debenture holders, liquidators and all known

162. McCormack, 'Receiverships and the Rescue Culture', p. 242.

163. See House of Commons Trade and Industry Committee, *Fourth Special Report, Government Observations on the First and Second Reports from the Trade and Industry Committee* (session 1999–2000) HC 237, p. 7.

164. Ibid., para. 12.

165. See Milman and Mond, *Security and Corporate Rescue*, pp. 48–9.

166. Insolvency Rules 1986 r. 3.32.   167. See Insolvency Act 1986 ss. 47 and 48.

unsecured creditors. A meeting of unsecured creditors must be summoned to consider the report[168] and the receiver must comply with reasonable requests for information.

Such a regime, however, leaves out of account the interests of a number of parties who may be affected by the company's demise. Let us consider the case of a customer that makes clothing from the specialist cloth supplied by a company. Let us also assume that the customer's business and hundreds of jobs will be at risk if the cloth supplier closes down immediately and there is no opportunity to arrange another supplier. Insolvency law could set up a regime in which the clothing customer would have access to information about the receiver's actions and would be able to propose steps. The clothing customer might also be given access to procedures that allow representations to be made to the receiver, perhaps on the lines: 'If other things are equal we would be obliged if you would allow cloth supply to continue for a week as this is likely to avoid real risk to 450 jobs.' At present the clothing manufacturer would be guaranteed access to information and be given a potential voice only if coming within the category of unsecured creditors within the terms of section 48 of the Insolvency Act 1986. Unsecured creditors, however, do not exhaust the parties potentially affected by insolvency.

It might be objected that to give substantive rights to the broad array of stakeholders would remove the speed and flexibility that are the great virtues of receivership, but here the proposal involves not substantive but procedural rights – to information and access only. It can be left to the receiver to decide whether, at insignificant cost, the jobs at the clothing manufacturer can be protected. Reputational considerations can be left at this point to encourage the receiver to act in the broad social interest.

Conclusions

The DTI's 2001 White Paper[169] acknowledges concerns both with the adequacy of administrative receivership's incentives to maximise economic value and with the levels of broad stakeholder transparency and accountability provided for. The lack of fit between the collective approaches of international law and administrative receivership is also noted,[170] so that:

---

168. Insolvency Rules 1986 rr. 3.9–3.15.
169. White Paper, 2001 (*Productivity and Enterprise*), ch. 2.
170. Ibid., para. 2.3. On collectivisation improving the prospects of UK creditors in international insolvencies, see Editorial, 'A Radical New Look for Insolvency Law' (2002) 23 Co. Law. 1.

The Government's view is that, on the grounds of both equity and efficiency, the time has come to make changes which tip the balance firmly in favour of collective insolvency proceedings – proceedings in which all creditors participate, under which a duty is owed to all creditors and in which all creditors may look to an office holder for an account of his dealings with a company's assets ... [A]dministrative receivership should cease to be a major insolvency procedure.

The right to appoint a receiver, says the Government, should be restricted to the holders of floating charges granted in connection with transactions in the capital markets.[171] In order to reassure secured creditors, however, the White Paper proposes reforms to the administration process to make it more effective and accessible, to give unsecured creditors a greater say in the process and its outcome, and to reduce risks to secured creditors.[172]

The proposed improvements in administration procedure will be discussed in chapter 9 below but consideration should be given here to the position of the floating charge holder in the revised administration procedure. Under the Government's 2001 proposals, the holder of a floating charge will be 'fast tracked' into administration in so far as he or she will be entitled to an administration order on a petition to the court demonstrating: the validity of their charge; the company's being in default; and the existence of the debt. There would be no requirement of a Rule 2.2 report.[173] In cases of urgency, floating charge holders (or holders of security comprising a significant part of the company's property) would be entitled to petition for an administration order without giving notice and, again, there would be no requirement of a Rule 2.2 report. On the hearing of a without-notice petition, the court would be empowered to make an interim administration order under which the interim administrator would be required to report to court within fourteen days of appointment. At that point the court would be able to make an administration order, winding-up order

171. See White Paper, 2001, para. 2.18, which states that the right to appoint an administrative receiver will be retained for 'certain transactions in the capital markets' and that situations covered by Part VII of the Companies Act 1989 will fall outside the White Paper proposals. Consequently administrative receivership would no longer be permitted except in the case of enforcement of market charges within the context of the separate insolvency regime for capital markets inaugurated by Part VII of the Companies Act 1989. (Part VII of the Companies Act 1989 deals with transactions carried out by recognised investment exchanges and clearing houses; certain overseas exchanges and clearing houses; and certain money market institutions.) See also n. 152 above regarding the Industry Secretary's statement of 9 November 2001 that abolition of the right to appoint an AR will not apply to corporate lending agreements entered into prior to the commencement of the relevant provisions of the Enterprise Bill when enacted.
172. See White Paper, 2001, para. 2.6.   173. See Insolvency Rules 1986 r. 2.2.

or other order as it thought fit. The administrator would owe a duty of care to *all* creditors, unsecured creditors would be able to participate in the process and, consistent with the move towards collectivism, secured creditors would have no right of veto on administration.[174] There would also be court oversight in a transparent fashion. An administration order would enable the administrator to realise the security of a floating charge 'whilst taking into account as far as possible the possibility of preserving all or part of the company's business'.[175] Overall, says the White Paper, the holders of floating charges and other security would be provided with 'a procedure that is as flexible and cost-effective as administrative receivership whilst remedying the major defects of that procedure'.[176]

These proposals are consistent with this chapter's arguments in favour of broader obligations for receivers. Much, however, depends on the formulation that any legislation adopts and the way that the judges interpret the obligations of administrators who are appointed by floating charge holders. We might ask whether the 'duty of care to all creditors' will be seen as rescue-oriented, as requiring floating charge holders' interests to be compromised in any way for the greater good, or as demanding that unsecured creditors' interests are served only where this is cost free for floating charge holders.

The banks, which routinely use floating charge security, have been offered a sweetener for giving up receivership in so far as the 2001 White Paper proposes to abolish Crown preferences in all insolvencies.[177] Banks may, nevertheless, be expected to object to the proposed package and argue that financing institutions will be forced to secure their investments on fixed assets, which will raise the cost of capital and reduce its flexibility. It should be noted, however, that the Government is not proposing to end the floating charge, only the way in which it is enforced and the interests that have to be taken into account in that enforcement process.

The current legal position offers a private interest vision of receivership in which the primary focus rests on protecting the bank. After cases such as *Medforth* v. *Blake* this may be portrayed as a 'responsible' or 'competent' private interest vision but, at heart, the concept is unchanged. It might be suggested that the alternative view of receivership is a public interest notion that loses the very essence of the process: the enforcement

174. Except in certain specified circumstances in connection with certain transactions in capital markets (White Paper, 2001, para. 2.15).
175. White Paper, 2001, para. 2.14.   176. Ibid., para. 2.12.
177. White Paper, 2001, para. 2.19.

by one creditor of their secured interest. That, indeed, would be the position if reforms were to oblige receivers to balance the substantive interests of the range of stakeholders potentially affected by the corporate demise. Another approach, however, escapes this difficulty: this is the 'inclusive' model of receivership. In this vision the receiver acts to protect the bank's interest but in a procedurally inclusive manner. If it becomes a central function of the receiver to collect information about the potential effect of different courses and schedules for action and to set protection of the bank's interests within that broader frame, the receiver becomes the focal point for information-gathering rather than a blinkered pursuer of the bank's interest. In many instances such an inclusive approach might make little difference to the actions that have to be taken, but in a significant number of cases it might allow affected parties – not merely creditors – to suggest to the receiver ways of protecting their concerns at little or no cost to the bank. The end product would not be pursuit of the public's rather than the bank's private interest, but 'gratuitous' harm to the public interest would be avoided in so far as more explicit trade-offs between the bank's and other parties' interests would be involved.

In terms of efficiency, there may be fears of some loss of process speed in a move to inclusive receivership (or a version of administration that operates on such lines) but any loss should not be dramatic. The receiver will be offering opportunities of access rather than carrying burdens of active consultation and there would be little need to defend substantive trade-offs. The expertise of receivership should be enhanced in so far as a fuller picture of the company's position will be developed as a result of inclusivity and the receiver's judgment will accordingly be more broadly informed. On the accountability and fairness fronts, there are clear procedural gains to be achieved by inclusivity. For the body of banks that prefer to listen, to care and to see the wider picture, such a movement to inclusivity should be a matter to be welcomed.

9

Administration

The Cork Committee, as we have seen, placed emphasis on the value of insolvency processes in providing ways of rescuing troubled companies, as well as in realising corporate assets.[1] Its recommendations led to the procedures governing administration orders and company voluntary arrangements (CVAs) that are set out in the Insolvency Act 1986. This chapter examines the administration regime, considers how this tends to satisfy the values set out in chapter 2, assesses potential reforms and reviews the philosophy underpinning modern administration.

The rise of administration

Cork criticised the law on floating charges on a number of grounds but noted one real advantage flowing from the floating charge holder's power to appoint a receiver and manager over a company's undertaking: receivers were given extensive powers to manage and in some cases had been able to restore troubled companies to profitability and return them to their former owners. In others, the receivers had been able to dispose of all or part of the business as a going concern and, in either case, the preservation of the profitable parts of the enterprise had been 'of advantage to the employees, the commercial community and the general public'.[2]

---

1. *Report of the Review Committee on Insolvency Law and Practice* (Cmnd 8558, 1982) ('Cork Report') ch. 9. On the rescue culture see e.g. M. Hunter, 'The Nature and Functions of a Rescue Culture' [1999] JBL 491; B. G. Carruthers and T. C. Halliday, *Rescuing Business: The Making of a Corporate Bankruptcy Law in England and the United States* (Clarendon Press, Oxford, 1998); Insolvency Service, *A Review of Company Rescue and Business Reconstruction Mechanisms*, Interim Report (DTI, 1999) ('IS 1999') p. 4; Insolvency Service, *A Review of Company Rescue and Business Reconstruction Mechanisms*, Report by the Review Group (DTI, 2000) ('IS 2000') pp. 12–13; R. Gregory, *Review of Company Rescue and Business Reconstruction Mechanisms: Rescue Culture or Avoidance Culture?* (CCH, Bicester, December 1999). See also ch. 6 above.
2. Cork Report, para. 495.

In the absence of a floating charge there was no possibility of such an appointment and the choice lay between an informal moratorium and a formal scheme of arrangement under the Companies Act 1948. Neither procedure was, however, wholly satisfactory. Formal schemes of arrangement were expensive and time consuming and informal procedures were not binding on non-assenting creditors and were difficult to sustain in practice. When neither course of action was possible the directors had no option but to cease trading and the results were bleak: 'We are satisfied that in a significant number of cases, companies have been forced into liquidation and potentially viable businesses capable of being rescued have been closed down, for want of a floating charge under which a receiver and manager could have been appointed.'[3]

Cork, accordingly, proposed the institution of the administrator who would be appointed in order to consider: reorganisations with a view to restoring profitability or maintaining employment; ascertaining the chances of restoring a company of dubious solvency to profitability; developing proposals for realising assets for creditors and stockholders; and carrying on business when this would be in the public interest but where it was unlikely that the business could be continued under the existing management.[4]

Three key notions underpin Cork's vision of the administrator: that rescue opportunities should be taken sufficiently early in corporate troubles to stand a chance of success; that companies should be given a breathing space from the pressure of claims; and that consideration should be given to the interests, not merely of creditors and shareholders, but of the widest group of parties potentially affected by the insolvency. As Sir Kenneth Cork wrote in his autobiography:[5]

> We saw that if a company was to be saved, action should be initiated a
> long time *before* the time when a bank normally appointed a
> receiver ... [Companies] needed a period when the dogs were called off
> and they were able to recover a degree of equilibrium. They needed, in
> other words, a moratorium for which existing law made no
> provision ... The appointment of an administrator, we suggested,
> would not constitute an 'act of insolvency'. None of the things would
> happen which happened when a company became officially insolvent.
> For an administrator should be brought in *before* a company was

3. Ibid., para. 496.   4. Ibid., para. 498.
5. Sir Kenneth Cork, *Cork on Cork: Sir Kenneth Cork Takes Stock* (Macmillan, London, 1988) p. 195.

declared insolvent, where for instance, the directors were obviously incompetent or dishonest and the ordinary processes could not remove them, or where in the national interest the government should take a hand … He would have all the powers and more of a receiver, and he would have to realise the assets for the general good … He would be responsible to *all parties* who were interested in the particular debtor company.

The Insolvency Act 1986 provided a mechanism for appointing an administrator but, as will be seen, only partially gave effect to the Cork rescue approach. Sir Kenneth Cork, indeed, was to summarise the government's mode of legislative implementation as follows: 'They ended up by doing the very thing we asked them not to do. They picked bits and pieces out of [the Cork Report] so that they finished with a mishmash of old and new.'[6]

Under the Insolvency Act 1986 Part II, administration is effected by an order of the court that directs that the affairs, business and property of the company shall be managed by the administrator.[7] An application for an administration order is made by petition supported by affidavit[8] and such a petition can be made by the company,[9] the directors,[10] a creditor or creditors,[11] a contingent or prospective creditor,[12] the supervisor of a CVA[13] or the Bank of England.[14] In over 80 per cent of cases the application is made by the company or the directors (with debenture holders petitioning in a negligible number of cases)[15] and it is almost invariably accompanied by an independent report from the proposed administrator.[16]

---

6. Cork, *Cork on Cork*, p. 197.   **7.** Insolvency Act 1986 s. 8(2).

8. Part 2, Insolvency Rules 1986.

9. Insolvency Act 1986 s. 9(1). See generally R. M. Goode, *Principles of Corporate Insolvency Law* (2nd edn, Sweet & Maxwell, London, 1997) pp. 283–5.

10. Insolvency Act 1986 s. 9(1). A petition can only be presented if all the directors are petitioners or if the petition is consequent to a board resolution: *Re Equiticorp International plc* [1989] BCLC 317. Cork recommended that individual directors be allowed to bring petitions in an *in camera* hearing: Cork Report, para. 500. See further D. Milman and C. Durrant, *Corporate Insolvency: Law and Practice* (3rd edn, Sweet & Maxwell, London, 1999) pp. 32–3.

11. Insolvency Act 1986 s. 9(1).

12. *Re Consumer and Industrial Press Ltd* [1988] 4 BCC 68; *Re Imperial Motors (UK) Ltd* [1989] 5 BCC 214.

13. Insolvency Act 1986 s. 7(4).

14. Banks (Administration Proceedings) Order 1989 (SI 1989 No. 1276). See A. Hogan, 'Banks and Administration' (1996) 12 IL&P 90.

15. See H. Rajak, 'The Challenges of Commercial Reorganisation in Insolvency: Empirical Evidence from England' in J. S. Ziegel (ed.), *Current Developments in International and Comparative Corporate Insolvency Law* (Clarendon Press, Oxford, 1994) p. 199, table 8.1.

16. Ibid., Insolvency Rule 2.2. Reports are not mandatory but tend to be viewed as carrying considerable weight. See *Re Newport County Association Football Club Ltd* [1987] 3 BCC 635. (See also Practice Note (Administration Order Applications: Independent Reports) [1994] 1 WLR 160, [1994] 1 All ER 324, [1994] BCLC 347.) On administration petitions being dismissed despite being supported by Rule 2.2 reports, see B. Isaacs, 'The Hazards of Contested

The following conditions have to be satisfied: the company must be, or be likely to be, unable to pay its debts within the meaning of section 123 of the Insolvency Act 1986;[17] the company must not already be in liquidation;[18] an administrative receiver must not have been appointed (or, if he has, his appointor must consent to the order; or the appointing order or charge is open to challenge under sections 238–40 or 245 of the Insolvency Act 1986[19]); and the company must not be an insurance company.[20] Additionally, the court must consider that making an administration order would be likely to achieve one or more of the following purposes:[21]

    (a) the survival of the company and the whole or any part of its undertaking as a going concern;

    (b) the approval of a voluntary arrangement under Part I of the Insolvency Act;

    (c) the sanctioning, under s. 425 of the Companies Act 1985, of a compromise or arrangement between the company and its creditors or any class of them or between its members or any class of them; and

    (d) a more advantageous realisation of the assets than would be effected on a winding up.[22]

The effect of presenting a petition for an administration order is that a moratorium is triggered and a stop is imposed on the enforcement of most types of claim, secured and unsecured, against the company. The company cannot be wound up and the leave of the court is required for such actions

Administration Petitions' (2001) 14 *Insolvency Intelligence* 22. The DTI/IS White Paper, *Productivity and Enterprise: Insolvency – A Second Chance* (Cm 5234, 2001) ('White Paper 2001') proposed that where parties disagree on who should be appointed as administrator 'the court should have regard to the interests of the creditor or creditors who will be principally affected by the administration' (para. 2.11). Under the proposed 'fast track' procedures (of paras. 2.8–2.10) a floating charge holder would not have to provide a Rule 2.2 report in applying for an administration and, in cases of urgency, such a report would not be required from holders of floating charges or of other security 'comprising a significant part of the company's property'.

17. Insolvency Act 1986 s. 8(1)(b). See ch. 4 above.
18. Insolvency Act 1986 s. 8(4).   **19.** Ibid., s. 9(3).
20. See Insurance Companies Act 1982. See also G. Moss, 'Insurance Company Insolvency: A Step in the Right Direction' (1999) 12 *Insolvency Intelligence* 45.
21. Insolvency Act 1986 ss. 8(1)(b), 8(3). See *Re Harris Simons Construction Ltd* [1989] 5 BCC 11; *Re Primlaks (UK) Ltd* [1989] BCC 710. The White Paper 2001 would widen these purposes to permit an order to be made 'to enable the realisation of the security of a floating charge holder whilst taking into account, as far as possible, the possibility of preserving all or part of the company's business': para. 2.14.
22. On the administration process as a quasi-liquidation procedure see I. F. Fletcher, 'Administration as Liquidation' [1998] JBL 75. See also D. Milman, 'The Courts and the Administration Regime: Supporting Legislative Policy' [2001] Ins. Law. 208 at 209–10; S. Frieze, 'Exit from Administration' (2001) 14 *Insolvency Intelligence* 41. On liquidation see ch. 12 below.

as enforcing a security against the company, repossessing goods in the company's possession under a hire purchase agreement, or the commencement or continuation of any other legal proceedings or levying distress against the company or its property.[23] Protection also extends to property owned by the company but in the possession of third parties such as lessees.[24] Such a moratorium does not, however, stop a debenture holder from appointing an administrative receiver, nor does the presentation of a petition stop the directors from calling a meeting of members to consider voluntary liquidation or stop a creditor from presenting a winding-up petition.[25] Managerial powers are unaffected by the petition[26] and the company can create secured interests.[27]

When an administration order is made, any winding-up petition must be dismissed.[28] An administrative receiver must vacate office,[29] and during the operation of the administration order there is a stronger freeze on the enforcements of right against the company than operates on presentation of the petition. After the order is made, an administrative receiver cannot be appointed and no winding-up petition may be presented without the consent of the administrator or the leave of the court.[30] Powers of the company and its officers are not exercisable without the administrator's consent and this effectively divests the directors of their powers.[31] The directors, moreover, have a duty to co-operate with the administrator.[32]

Administration does not provide for a permanent restructuring of creditors' interests or for a distribution to unsecured creditors.[33] The

---

23. Insolvency Act 1986 s. 10(1).

24. *Re Atlantic Computer Systems plc (No. 1)* [1992] Ch 505, [1992] 2 WLR 367, [1990] BCC 859.

25. Entry into liquidation is not permitted however until the petition is heard: Insolvency Act 1986 s. 10(1)(a); Milman and Durrant, *Corporate Insolvency*, p. 37.

26. Though the court on hearing the petition may make an interim order appointing an interim manager: see D. McKenzie Skene and Y. Enoch, 'Petitions for Administration Orders – Where there is a Need for Interim Measures: A Comparative Study of the Approach of the Courts in Scotland and England' [2000] JBL 103; Milman and Durrant, *Corporate Insolvency*, p. 35; Insolvency Act 1986 s. 9(4). The CLRSG recommended that the duty on a voluntary liquidator to report offences discovered in the course of his functions (introduced in the Insolvency Act 2000 amendment of Insolvency Act 1986 s. 219) should be extended to administrators: CLRSG, *Modern Company Law for a Competitive Economy: Final Report* (July 2001) ('*Final Report*, 2001') para. 15.25.

27. *Bristol Airport plc v. Powdrill* [1990] Ch 744, 768.

28. Insolvency Act 1986 s. 11.

29. Ibid.   30. Ibid., s. 11(3)(d).   31. Ibid., s. 14(4).

32. Ibid., s. 235. Breach of this duty renders the directors liable to disqualification: see CDDA 1986 s. 9, Sched. 1, Part II, para. 10g.

33. Contrast with the US Chapter 11 procedure: see ch. 6 above.

process operates as a temporary freeze during which proposals for a permanent solution to the company's problems can be devised. These solutions will then have to be put into effect through the institution of another insolvency regime such as a CVA or liquidation or a compromise arrangement under s. 425 of the Companies Act 1985, to operate either during the currency of the administration order or after it has been brought to an end.[34]

The powers of administrators resemble those of administrative receivers. Similar managerial functions are carried out with commensurate powers, in both cases exercised as agents of the company.[35] The administrator possesses the additional power to remove and appoint directors and to call any meeting of the members or creditors of the company.[36] In a number of respects, though, administration differs from receivership.[37] First, the administrator does not owe allegiance to any particular appointing creditor, but is appointed by the court as an officer of the court to protect the interests of the company and the general body of creditors.[38] Being an officer of the court, the administrator is obliged to act fairly and honourably – a formal requirement not applicable to a receiver.[39] The administrator must manage the affairs of the business and the company's property in accordance with directions (if any) given by the court[40] or in accordance with his proposals approved by the creditors[41] (by majority vote in value). Those affected by the administrator's actions have, moreover, wide powers to contest these actions in court. Any creditor or member of a company can complain to the court about the conduct of the administration on the grounds of unfair prejudice to creditors or members generally or some part of its creditors or members or that an act or proposed act or omission would involve such prejudice.[42] The court, on such a complaint, has extremely wide powers to control the administrator's management.[43]

---

34. See Rajak, 'Challenges of Commercial Reorganisation'.
35. Insolvency Act 1986 s. 14(5). Unlike a normal agent the administrator is not subject to control and direction by the company, his principal: s. 14(4). Section 14 aims to ensure that an administrator normally incurs no personal liability on any contract or other obligation he may enter into on the company's behalf.
36. Insolvency Act 1986 s. 14, Sched. 1; see Goode, *Principles of Corporate Insolvency Law*, p. 309.
37. Goode, *Principles of Corporate Insolvency Law*, p. 310.
38. See *Re Atlantic Computer Systems plc (No. 1)* [1992] Ch 505, [1992] 2 WLR 367, [1990] BCC 859.
39. See I. Dawson, 'The Administrator, Morality and the Court' [1996] JBL 437; D. Milman, 'A Question of Honour' [2000] Ins. Law. 247.
40. Insolvency Act 1986 s. 17(2).
41. Ibid., ss. 23 and 24; see p. 279 below.
42. Insolvency Act 1986 s. 27(1).   43. *Re Charnley Davies Ltd* [1990] BCC 605.

A second difference from receivership is that rescue can be, and generally is, an objective of the administrator's appointment. This is made clear in the first basis for the court's appointment, set out in section 8(3)(a) of the 1986 Act, which requires the administrator to pursue a policy of rescuing both the company and substantially the whole of the business. Administration is, moreover, a court-driven procedure and the court exercises a close supervisory function. Administration demands the seeking of a court order whereas receivership involves no such requirement. The administrator, moreover, requires leave of the court to exercise a range of his or her powers to dispose of charged property.[44] The administrator must, like the AR, be an IP, but he or she cannot be appointed, replaced or remain without a court order. Administration also differs from administrative receivership in so far as it involves a moratorium. The procedure is attuned to rescue in so far as such protection is combined with the power to override the wishes of secured creditors. Finally, receivers are personally liable on contracts but administrators contract as the company's agent.[45]

Procedurally, the administrator must set out how the purposes of the order are to be achieved,[46] and a statement of proposals must be sent to the Registrar of Companies within three months (or such longer period as the court allows).[47] The statement must be laid before a meeting of creditors on at least fourteen days' notice and a copy sent to all members of the company or a notice published in the prescribed manner stating the address where copies can be obtained free of charge. It is an offence to fail to comply with these requirements.[48] The creditors may approve the proposals of the administrator or amend them with the latter's consent.[49] Such proposals may provide for a CVA or a scheme of arrangement under s. 425 of the Companies Act 1985 if such a scheme is a purpose specified in the administration order.[50]

---

44. Insolvency Act 1986 s. 15. But the court's consent is not needed if the security is (or was originally) a floating charge. The consent of the chargee or owner of the property is not needed re section 15.

45. Ibid., s. 14(5).   46. Ibid., s. 23(1).

47. Ibid. The White Paper 2001 (para. 2.13) would shorten the period to twenty-eight days.

48. Insolvency Act 1986 s. 23(3). On the problems that may arise for administrators regarding the commercial need for an expeditious disposal of assets and the statutory time limits and duties of consultation with the company's creditors, see *Re T & D Industries plc and T & D Automotive Ltd* [2000] 1 WLR 646; *Re Harris Bus Company Ltd* (unreported) 16 December 1999 (Rattee J); *Re Charnley Davies Ltd* [1990] BCC 605. See further A. Plainer, 'Administrators: When to Go to Court?' (2000) 2 *Finance and Credit Law* 1; Plainer, 'Challenging an Administrator' (1999) *Insolvency Bulletin* 5 (July/August); H. Roberts, '*T & D Industries plc* Revisited: Further Guidance for Administrators in Disposing of Assets' (2000) 16 IL&P 61.

49. See Insolvency Act 1986 s. 24(1) and (2).

50. On ending administration see Insolvency Act 1986 s. 19(1)(2).

Efficiency

Has the administration procedure provided a technically efficient mode of rescuing ailing companies or realising corporate assets? The evidence suggests that whatever its virtues and vices, administration has been little used as a rescue device.

Use of administration

The insolvency regime, as envisaged by Cork, was thought to offer company directors a set of incentives to opt for administration in times of trouble. It provides them, in the first instance, with protection from disqualification and wrongful trading actions: punitive prospects that Cork hoped would lead directors to seek outside help at early stages of trouble.[51] Administration also offered directors some continuing role in the management of the business and the chance of persuading creditors, within the protection of the moratorium, to accept something less than full-blown insolvency. They would, furthermore, be able to nominate a friendly IP who would sympathise with their positions. Such incentives, thought Cork, would produce effective rescue mechanisms. The committee's view was that if insolvency practitioners could become involved with companies at an early stage of their natural decline they stood a good chance of saving the business and 'four out of five never needed to have become insolvent'.[52] Not only that, but lack of legal rescue provisions at such an early stage led, according to Cork, to a series of evils. It encouraged directors to keep trading, delayed the introduction of expert reviews, and gave rogue creditors incentives to break ranks on informal moratorium debt collection, all of which factors militated against successful corporate rescues.[53]

The DTI's 1993 consultative document revealed that from 1990 to 1993 there were 88,000 corporate insolvencies in England. Of these, 21,500 had entered receivership, over 40,000 went into creditors' voluntary liquidation, and over 26,000 into compulsory liquidation. Only 296 CVAs and 447 administration orders were encountered.[54] By the time the DTI Insolvency

---

51. Carruthers and Halliday, *Rescuing Business*, p. 289.
52. Quoted in ibid., p. 286. In R3's Ninth Survey of Business Recovery in the UK (2001) rescue professional respondents indicated their belief that in 77 per cent of cases by the time they were appointed there were no possible actions that could realistically have averted company failure. In younger companies (under one year) in 90 per cent of cases there was thought to be no such rescue action possible.
53. Carruthers and Halliday, *Rescuing Business*, p. 286.
54. Rajak, 'Challenges of Commercial Reorganisation', p. 202 reported that in 1990 there were 211 administrations compared to 15,051 liquidations and 4,318 receiverships.

Service published the 1999 figures for corporate proceedings under the Insolvency Act 1986, the ratio of administration appointments to liquidations (voluntary and compulsory) was 440:14,280 (with 1,618 administrative receiverships).[55] The business preservation rate in administrations in 1998–9 was given by R3 (formerly the SPI) in 2001 as 79 per cent[56] and the job preservation rate was put at 40 per cent by the SPI in its Eighth Survey.[57]

Veto by floating charge holder

Why then has administration not operated as the popular rescue option that Cork had hoped to establish? It is possible to identify a number of factors that weaken the effectiveness of administration as a rescue device and tend to discourage its use.[58] A key consideration is that administration is a procedure that can be blocked by a floating charge holder who chooses to appoint an administrative receiver as a means of protecting his or her own interest. If, indeed, a petition for administration does not contain what amounts to the consent of any person entitled to appoint an AR, the petition will be dismissed. Administration, accordingly, is a process that can only be used if the firm has no creditor with a floating charge (an increasingly rare occurrence given the proliferation of secured lending in standard British financing arrangements and banking practice[59]) or if the floating charge holder is happy to see the company's troubles dealt with by administration rather than administrative receivership. In some circumstances the latter situation may obtain and some considerations may lead the floating charge holder to accept administration as preferable to the insertion of a receiver.[60] Factors favouring this approach include the attractiveness of the moratorium which may be seen to outweigh the disadvantages of administration: for example, where protection is needed against suppliers of goods who have retained title[61] or where a large firm has a

---

55. IS 2000, p. 14; as the Insolvency Service's 1999 Review points out, such figures do not give the whole picture of insolvency because they do not take on board all the companies that are struck off the register but do not enter any formal process.

56. R3 Ninth Survey: up from 41 per cent in the SPI's Eighth Survey of *Company Insolvency in the United Kingdom* on a small sample.

57. SPI Eighth Survey (1999): the figure had dropped from 65 per cent in the Seventh Survey.

58. See DTI/Insolvency Service, *Company Voluntary Arrangements and Administration Orders: A Consultative Document* (October 1993) ('DTI 1993') ch. 5.

59. IS 2000, p. 12, para. 36.

60. See Rajak, 'Challenges of Commercial Reorganisation' p. 206; Goode, *Principles of Corporate Insolvency Law*, p. 293.

61. Rajak, 'Challenges of Commercial Reorganisation', p. 206, who notes that ROT holders are blocked by the wide definition of hire purchase agreements in the Insolvency Act 1986 s. 10(4).

complex structure and considerable time and effort has to be put in before a way forward is arrived at.[62] Administration may also be attractive if: criticisms from creditors will be directed towards the administrator rather than the debenture holder or their receiver; the size of the sum due does not justify the appointment of a receiver; the debenture holder thinks that his or her charge is vulnerable; or the debenture holder has been given the right to nominate the administrator. Additional considerations may be that a court-appointed insolvency officer may be better placed than a receiver to recover assets from foreign jurisdictions[63] and an administrator, but not an AR, can apply to have suspect pre-insolvency transactions set aside.[64]

Surveys nevertheless suggest that in 60 per cent of cases where administration orders are made the floating charge holder will appoint a receiver.[65] In most cases of corporate decline the floating charge holder will be very aware that administrative receivers act in the interests of the appointing floating charge holder, whereas administrators act for all creditors. It is unlikely, accordingly, that the floating charge holder will, in normal cases, allow administrations to run unhindered. Floating charge holders, moreover, lose control if they allow administration to occur rather than put in a receiver. Once the administrator is appointed even fixed charge security holders cannot enforce without leave and the general creditors enjoy the income generated by the property subject to such charges.[66] Floating charge holders faced with an administration also stand to see a diminution of the value of the assets covered by the floating charge, since their debt will be satisfied after the expenses and remuneration of the administrator have been met, as well as after there has been payment of all debts and liabilities (including certain taxes) that are incurred by the administrator as a result of contracts he or she has entered into.[67] Administration also brings temporal uncertainty to the floating charge holder since the administrator has no power to make distributions and considerable time may elapse before payments are made on debts.

62. DTI 1993, p. 30.
63. Rajak, 'Challenges of Commercial Reorganisation', p. 206.
64. Ibid. See Insolvency Act 1986 ss. 238, 239, 244.
65. See M. Homan, *A Survey of Administration Under the 1986 Insolvency Act* (Institute of Chartered Accountants, London, 1989); Rajak, 'Challenges of Commercial Reorganisation', p. 205. See further H. Anderson, 'Receivers Compared with Administrators' (1996) 12 IL&P 54. On reform of the power of veto see pp. 291–2 and 297–8 below.
66. Milman and Durrant, *Corporate Insolvency*, p. 51.
67. Ibid., p. 51.

Process costs

The procedural costs of administration are also very considerable.[68] This is largely due to the high level of judicial supervision involved in administration. The court is involved in appointing the administrator and will usually be involved when the administrator is given power to interfere with private rights.[69] Nor is the judicial role confined to checking to see that the administrator has acted in good faith and *intra vires*: the court will often have to examine the issue in depth and make its own judgment. Such a process will frequently involve the use of expert evidence, and decision-making, as a result, may be slow as well as costly. The expenses of obtaining the administration order itself can be very considerable. Figures as high as £20,000 have been cited as a minimum starting cost, with the money having to be provided in advance in order to secure the services of the necessary IPs.[70] The Rule 2.2 (of the Insolvency Rules) report, which has become in practice a prerequisite[71] to the making of an order, is almost always written by an accountant and often involves the practitioner's solicitors. This tends to increase the obligations of the IP, the company and the court and so raises costs considerably and places applications beyond the reach of smaller firms.[72] Banks who instigate formal insolvency procedures may, moreover, have undesirably low incentives to control the costs of these procedures (about half of which comprise fees to IPs). This is because such costs will be borne disproportionately by unsecured creditors in a regime that distributes assets by priority.[73] Administration, accordingly, is too expensive a process to be used for the rescue of small or even medium-sized businesses.

---

68. DTI 1993, p. 29.

69. See Insolvency Act 1986 s. 15, but note s. 15(1), (3) and (4) where the court's consent is not needed.

70. DTI 1993, p. 29; Milman and Durrant, *Corporate Insolvency*, p. 51. But see C. Morris and M. Kirschner, 'Cross-border Rescues and Asset Recovery: Problems and Solutions' (1994) 10 IL&P 42–3 suggesting that in smaller cases the expense may be only £1,500–£2,000.

71. The DTI's 1993 Consultative Document described it as 'almost mandatory', DTI 1993, p. 29. The DTI White Paper of 2001 on *Productivity and Enterprise* (paras. 2.8–2.10) proposed that holders of floating charges should be able to petition for an administration order without a Rule 2.2 report, as should all security holders in cases of urgency.

72. See Justice, *Insolvency Law: An Agenda for Reform* (Justice, London, 1994) pp. 37–8; D. Brown, *Corporate Rescue: Insolvency Law in Practice* (John Wiley & Sons, Chichester, 1996) p. 656. But see Practice Note (Administration Order Applications: Independent Reports) [1994] 1 WLR 160, which encouraged brevity of such reports and dispensation with these in simple cases.

73. See J. Franks and O. Sussman, 'The Cycle of Corporate Distress, Rescue and Dissolution: A Study of Small and Medium Size UK Companies', IFA Working Paper 306 (2000).

Consultation

A further reason for the low uptake of administration is the administrator's lack of any obligation to consult creditors before taking action.[74] This means that he or she may sell the company's property before holding a creditors' meeting. Such a lack of involvement may make creditors reluctant to instigate or (in the case of floating charge holders) accede to administration. When the administration process is employed it achieves rescue in about 40 per cent of cases and liquidation occurs in around 50 per cent of instances.[75] Estimating the success of administration is, however, difficult and, as has been pointed out,[76] it is necessary to know whether net realisations after allowing for the costs of administration are greater (and more swiftly achieved) than they would have been in some other (actual or potential) procedure. Such difficulties have to be faced even if the assessing parties agree about the right balance between, for instance, the preservation of jobs and maximising the pool of assets for creditors.

The timing of administration orders

Yet another reason for the inefficiency of administration as a rescue device – and a factor tending to reduce the incidence of resort to administration[77] – is that administration orders can only be applied for at the latest stages of corporate decline, when chances of rescue have severely diminished. As noted, the court, under section 8(1)(a) of the Insolvency Act 1986, has to be satisfied that the company 'is or is likely to become unable to pay its debts' within the meaning of the Insolvency Act 1986 s. 123. This requirement of near-insolvency is starkly at odds with the Cork vision which demanded that an administrator should be appointed at an earlier stage in corporate decline. This was, as noted, a point of great disappointment to Sir Kenneth Cork, who commented on the Government's Insolvency Act 1986 approach:

> They said [an administrator] could only be appointed when a company was insolvent or was in the process of becoming insolvent which missed the whole point ... To them insolvency was insolvency; for them it was essential that a company went broke before anyone took action.

74. DTI 1993, p. 30. See further cases and articles noted under n. 48 above.
75. H. Rajak, 'Administration of Insolvent Companies in England 1987–1990: An Empirical Survey' (quoted in Goode, *Principles of Corporate Insolvency Law*, p. 322).
76. Goode, *Principles of Corporate Insolvency Law*, p. 323; Rajak, 'Administration of Insolvent Companies', pp. 211–12.
77. For a review see DTI 1993, ch. 5.

> Behind it lay the absurd theory that shareholders could always remove incompetent directors.[78]

Sir Kenneth's view of section 8(1)(a) is perhaps more pessimistic than it needs to be. It is open to the court to operate administration as a pre-insolvency rather than an insolvency procedure. To date, however, there is no case law that offers guidance on the restrictiveness with which 'likely to become unable to pay its debts' (section 8(1)(a)) will be interpreted. Some commentators have suggested that the subsection does not require insolvency to be likely in the immediate future but only 'fairly soon'.[79] If administration was seen in a pre-insolvency sense by the courts then it might serve rescue purposes if used for such objectives as: protecting the company from creditors during a period of cash flow difficulties; overcoming short-term problems more serious than cash flow difficulties but which could be survived by using CVAs or schemes of arrangements to reschedule debts; or reorganising the firm and selling unsustainable parts of the business so as to leave the company with the profitable parts under the protection of the moratorium.[80] There may, however, be difficulties in convincing courts to endorse administration at early stages in decline. This is a procedure that involves curtailment of the rights of at least some of the creditors of the company and it may prove difficult to persuade the court that such interference is merited unless insolvency is imminent.

Administration depends on an exercise of discretion by the court, and it has been argued that in the late 1980s the judiciary moved to a more sympathetic approach to the granting of orders.[81] Rajak has reported that in a studied sample, the courts of London, Leeds and Birmingham made 465 orders on 559 petitions (an 83 per cent success rate overall and 77 per cent in London).[82] Such figures, however, may indicate not so much a judicial sympathy with the use of administrations at early stages of corporate decline as a highly selective use of applications by parties who are wary of speculative approaches to the court that are expensive to mount and carry through.

---

78. Cork, *Cork on Cork*, p. 197.
79. Goode, *Principles of Corporate Insolvency Law*, p. 286. Note that Edington plc went into administration on the grounds of 'prospective insolvency': see Milman and Durrant, *Corporate Insolvency*, p. 39.
80. See M. Phillips, *The Administration Procedure and Creditors' Voluntary Arrangements* (Centre for Commercial Law Studies, QMW, London, 1996) p. 21.
81. Rajak, 'Challenges of Commercial Reorganisation', p. 203; *Re SCL Building Services Ltd* [1989] 5 BCC 746; *Re Rowbotham Baxter Ltd* [1990] BCC 113.
82. Rajak, 'Challenges of Commercial Reorganisation', p. 203.

A judicial willingness to grant administration orders on a pre-insolvency basis would not, however, ensure that parties would come forward with applications. There may be numerous reasons why such early applications tend to be few in number. Company directors often lack knowledge of the applicable insolvency procedures. They may, in addition, possess poor internal accounting and information systems and may not know that the business is approaching insolvency. They may, furthermore, be unwilling to put the company into an insolvency procedure which they see as ceding control of the business to an outside accountant.[83] The administrator has power to remove and appoint directors, and directors will tend to opt for courses of action that leave them with an assured role in the company's immediate future. Other suggested reasons for directorial slowness to resort to administration in times of trouble were put to the DTI in its 1999–2000 consultations and included: mistrust of IPs; unrealistic optimism; fear of failure; fear of the bank withdrawing support; and concern over the cost of advice.[84] Directorial fears for their own reputations and future job prospects must also constitute a reason for inaction.

Employment contracts

The courts have not always decided cases in a manner that enhances the effectiveness of administration as a rescue device. In the case of *Powdrill* v. *Watson*,[85] for instance, the Court of Appeal held that administrators who kept employees in post after the administration came into effect (and after the fourteen-day period of grace provided for in section 19(5) of the Insolvency Act 1986)[86] had adopted the relevant employment contracts. The administrators were, accordingly, liable to pay not only the wages, pension contributions and holiday pay referable to the post-administration order period, but were also obliged to pay liabilities under the adopted employment contracts out of the company assets in priority to most creditors. The effect, critics noted,[87] was to force administrators (and administrative receivers) to dismiss employees within the fourteen-day period. This contrasted with the established practice of retaining employees but making it clear to them that their contracts were not being adopted.[88]

83. I.e. as an IP: DTI 1993, p. 30.   **84.** IS 2000, pp. 54–5.   **85.** [1994] 2 BCLC 118.
86. On the 'inadequacy' of the fourteen-day period for administrators see R. Agnello, 'Administration Expenses' (2000) *Recovery* (March) 24–5; *Re Douai School Ltd*, reported as *Re a Company (No. 005174 of 1999)* [2000] BCC 698.
87. See I. F. Fletcher, 'Adoption of Contracts of Employment by Receivers and Administrators: The *Paramount* Case' [1995] JBL 596–604.
88. Brown, *Corporate Rescue*, p. 660; *Re Specialised Mouldings Ltd* (unreported) 13 February 1987 (Harman J).

The Court of Appeal's decision in *Powdrill* prompted a strong adverse reaction from the insolvency profession and others. Following energetic lobbying of the President of the Board of Trade, legislation designed to redress the effects of *Powdrill* was rushed through Parliament and became the Insolvency Act 1994. This Act had the effect on administrations of introducing a new subsection, 19(6), to the Insolvency Act 1986, to provide that sums payable in respect of liabilities incurred while the administrator was in office under contracts of employment that had been adopted by him or by any predecessor were to be paid out of the assets covered by a floating charge created as such and were to have the same priority as sums covered by section 19(5) – namely sums owed under contracts entered into by the administrator or a predecessor – to the extent that they constitute 'qualifying liabilities' as defined in the new subsections 19(7)–(9) of the Insolvency Act.[89] The effects of the 1994 Act are, however, limited. It applies only to contracts of employment entered into on, or after, 15 March 1994, and this leaves considerable potential for post-*Powdrill* claims; it does not affect the concept of 'adoption' or the issue of contracting out (though it does take away the most undesirable consequences of the 1986 provisions as interpreted in *Powdrill*). It leaves a number of questions open – such as when liabilities are incurred and whether it is possible to dismiss and re-employ workers in a manner not amounting to a sham[90] – and it is unclear on the consequences of voluntary payment by administrators.

When the House of Lords decided consolidated appeals on the meaning of 'adopt' within sections 19 and 44 of the Insolvency Act 1986, the liabilities under employment contracts of both administrators and administrative receivers were at issue.[91] Focusing here on administration,

---

89. A qualifying liability per section 19(7)–(9) is one to pay a sum by way of wages or salary or contributions to an occupational pension, which is in respect of services rendered wholly or partially after the adoption of the contract but disregarding payment for services rendered before the adoption of the contract. This includes wages or salary payable in respect of holiday, absence through sickness or other good cause. Sums payable in lieu of holiday are deemed wages or salary in respect of services rendered in the period by reference to which the holiday entitlement arose (Insolvency Act 1986 s. 19(9) and (10); Insolvency Act 1994 s. 1(6)). See *In re FJL Realisations Ltd* [2001] ICR 424 (also reported as *Inland Revenue Commissioners v. Lawrence* [2001] BCC 663) in which the Court of Appeal held that, as the administrator's liability under contracts of employment was to pay the employee the full salary *including* the statutory amounts in respect of PAYE and national insurance contributions, it was not possible for the administrator to split the contractual liability in two. Accordingly, the sums deducted to the Inland Revenue were a liability of 'any sums payable in respect of debts or liabilities incurred' for the purposes of section 19(5) and (6) and as such enjoyed special priority over any charges arising under section 19(4) of the Insolvency Act 1986.
90. See Brown, *Corporate Rescue*, p. 481.
91. *Powdrill v. Watson* (also known as *Re Paramount Airways Ltd No. 3*) [1995] 2 WLR 312, [1995] 2 All ER 65 (House of Lords). See, e.g., Fletcher, 'Adoption of Contracts', p. 474.

their Lordships were concerned with the rights of parties affected by the 1,200 or so administrations commencing between 29 December 1986 (the commencement date of the Insolvency Act 1986) and 15 March 1994 (the commencement date of the Insolvency Act 1994). The House of Lords decided unanimously that the contracts of employment in question had been adopted by the administrators. This ruling was greeted with 'shock and disappointment'[92] by the insolvency and banking community. It meant that cases involving adoption of employment contracts by administrators after 15 March 1994 would be dealt with under the Insolvency Act 1994 but that cases on adoption between 1986 and 1994 would be dealt with on the basis set out by the House of Lords in *Powdrill*. That decision, however, still leaves uncertainty on such points as whether the release of administrators by the court under section 20 of the Insolvency Act 1986 will prevent employees from asserting priority rights;[93] whether administrators are able to contract out of adoption;[94] and whether administrators are personally liable under adopted contracts after their court release.[95] As for the general efficiency implications of transferring employee contracts and protecting employees' acquired rights in the insolvency context, these are returned to in chapter 16 below.

The protection offered by the moratorium

The role of the judiciary has always been important in relation to the moratorium accompanying administration.[96] The effectiveness of the moratorium stands to be reduced by the court's exercise of a ready discretion to allow enforcement actions against the company during the moratorium, or if the courts interpret the coverage of the moratorium restrictively. Similarly, the courts can render administration prohibitively expensive if they become too deeply involved in judgments attending the moratorium.

On issues of scope and coverage, the indications are that all relevant actions and claims against the company will be within the moratorium's area of protection.[97] Sir Nicholas Browne-Wilkinson VC emphasised in *Bristol*

---

92. Brown, *Corporate Rescue*, p. 489.
93. See Lord Browne-Wilkinson at [1995] 2 WLR 312 at 344E.
94. See Brown, *Corporate Rescue*, p. 491.
95. See P. Mudd, 'The Insolvency Act 1994: *Paramount* Cured?' (1994) 10 IL&P 38; Mudd, '*Paramount*: The House of Lords Decision – Is There Still Hope of Avoiding Some of Those Claims?' (1995) 11 IL&P 78.
96. See D. Milman, 'The Administration Order Regime and the Courts' in H. Rajak (ed.), *Insolvency Law: Theory and Practice* (Sweet & Maxwell, London, 1993); Milman, 'Firming Up Moratoria' [2001] 3 *Palmer's In Company* 1; Milman, 'Courts and the Administration Regime'.
97. *Bristol Airport plc v. Powdrill* [1990] Ch 744; *Exchange Travel Agency Ltd v. Triton Property Trust plc* [1991] BCC 341; *Re Atlantic Computer Systems plc* [1990] BCC 859.

Airport plc v. *Powdrill*[98] that it was the essence of administration that businesses would be carried on by administrators who had acquired the right 'to use the property of the company free from interference by creditors and others'. The courts, however, are not content to allow the administrator to judge whether to allow a creditor to enforce a claim or to balance the interests of a single creditor against those of the company and its creditors as a whole. The judiciary, accordingly, have rejected the view that they should desist from interfering with the administrator's decision if the claimant fails to show that something in the administrator's conduct merits adverse criticism.[99] Dangers of excessive litigation expense and court involvement have been met by the courts making it clear, first, that they expect administrators themselves to consent to the enforcement of claims where there will be no attendant adverse effect on the conduct of the administration and, second, that administrators who unjustifiably refuse consent will be penalised in costs.[100] As to the criteria that are to govern decisions whether or not to permit enforcement of a particular claim, the courts have tended to balance the interests of the petitioning creditor against those of other corporate creditors.[101] They have avoided taking into account the wider public, employee or trade-dependent interests that may be affected by the potential rescue of the business. Nicolls LJ stated in *Re Atlantic Computer Systems plc*:[102]

> In carrying out the balancing exercise, great importance or weight is normally to be given to ... proprietary interests ... [T]he administration procedure is not to be used to prejudice those who were secured creditors when the administration order was made in lieu of a winding up order ... The underlying principle here is that an administration for the benefit of unsecured creditors should not be conducted at the expense of those who have proprietary rights which they are seeking to exercise, save to the extent that this may be unavoidable and even then this will usually be acceptable only to a strictly limited extent.

Such an approach may be of value to the court in imposing limits on the interests that they have to take into account when deciding enforcement issues, but it is hardly consistent with Cork's vision of administration as

---

98. [1990] Ch 744.   99. *Re Meesan Investments Ltd* [1988] 4 BCC 788.
100. *Re Atlantic Computer Systems plc* [1990] BCC 859.
101. Ibid., at 879 (Nicolls LJ). On *Re Atlantic Computer Systems* see further M. G. Bridge, 'Company Administrators and Secured Creditors' (1991) 107 LQR 394; Bridge, 'Form, Substance and Innovation in Personal Property Security Law' [1992] JBL 1 at 18–21.
102. [1990] BCC 859 at 880.

a process that takes on board the broad array of interests affected by the potential insolvency.

As for the statutory extent of the moratorium, section 11(3) of the Insolvency Act 1986 provides that on the making of an administration order: 'No other steps may be taken to enforce any security over the company's property, or to repossess goods in the company's possession under any hire purchase agreement, except with the consent of the administrator or the leave of the court and subject (where the court gives leave) to such terms as the court may impose'; and 'no other proceedings and no execution or other legal process may be commenced or continued, and no distress may be levied, against the company or its property except with the consent of the administrator or the leave of the court and subject (where the court gives leave) to such terms as aforesaid'.

What constitutes 'a security' for such purposes is defined in section 248(b)(i) as 'any mortgage, charge, lien or other security'. This reference to 'other security' both gives the court considerable discretion to determine whether certain enforcement actions are ruled out by section 11(3) and creates some uncertainty. In *Bristol Airport* v. *Powdrill* the court took a wide view of the moratorium and the airport was prevented by section 11 from asserting a statutory lien for unpaid airport charges with respect to an aircraft leased by a third party to the company. In *Re Atlantic Computer Systems plc*, items of computer equipment were leased or let under hire purchase agreements to a company which sublet them to third parties. The company went into administration and the Court of Appeal ruled that the owners of the equipment were not entitled during the administration period to receive from the administrators, as expenses of the administration,[103] the payments due under the head leases and hire purchase agreement. The equipment was held to be within the possession of the company for section 11(3) purposes and so leave was required to take steps to terminate the head agreements, repossess the equipment and enforce any security in relation to it – though leave would be granted in the circumstances.[104]

A concern in recent years has been whether the landlord of the company in administration may exercise a right of peaceable re-entry to the corporate premises or whether this is ruled out as 'enforcement of

---

103. The Court of Appeal refused to invoke an 'expenses of the administration' principle (similar to liquidation: see ch. 12 below) because administration was a novel regime and solutions to problems it posed were not to be found in settled areas of insolvency law. See further Bridge, 'Company Administrators', p. 395.
104. See Bridge, 'Company Administrators'.

security' under section 11(3).[105] The importance of this point to a troubled company is difficult to exaggerate: the protection offered by the moratorium may assist rescue efforts very little if the company is liable to lose access to its work premises. Peaceable re-entry, moreover, is a procedure allowing a landlord to forfeit a lease without having to obtain a court order and can be instigated on non-payment of rent or breaches of covenant by the tenant. All the landlord normally has to do in practice is to change the locks and exclude the tenant from the premises.

Over the last decade it had become clear that the courts were unlikely to extend the protection of the section 11 moratorium so as to stop peaceable re-entry. The case of *Exchange Travel Agency* v. *Triton plc*[106] had suggested that peaceable re-entry would be covered by the moratorium as it involved enforcement of the security interest. But matters changed with *Razzaq* v. *Pala*,[107] a decision which put forward the more recent and dominant view that the moratorium will not cover peaceable re-entry. The DTI review group was of the view in 2000 that the law should be changed to bring landlords within the ambit of the statutory moratorium.[108] This change was effected in the Insolvency Act 2000 and now the same position obtains in relation to moratoria in administration and within the CVA procedure set out in the Insolvency Act 2000. This demanded an amendment of the Insolvency Bill 2000 which, as initially drafted, echoed the moratorium terms of the Insolvency Act 1986.[109]

105. See P. McCartney, 'Insolvency Procedures and a Landlord's Right of Peaceable Re-entry' (2000) 13 *Insolvency Intelligence* 73; R. Hanson, 'Landlords' Right to Effect Peaceable Re-entry Against Tenants in Administration' (1999) *Insolvency Bulletin* 7; P. Shaw, 'Administrators: Peaceable Re-entry by a Landlord Revisited' [1999] Ins. Law. 254; J. Byrne and L. Doyle, 'Can a Landlord Forfeit a Lease by Peaceable Re-entry?' [1999] Ins. Law. 167; D. Milman, 'Landlords of Insolvency Companies' [1999] 6 *Palmer's In Company* 1; A. Bacon and R. Cowper, 'The Moratorium Emasculated: Another Blow for Corporate Recovery?' (1997) 10 *Insolvency Intelligence* 73. On the power of a landlord to distrain for unpaid rent by taking goods and, in a receivership, bypassing other unsecured creditors, see P. Walton, 'The Landlord, his Distress, the Insolvent Tenant and the Stranger' (2000) 16 IL&P 47.
106. [1991] BCC 341.
107. [1997] 1 WLR 1336 (dealing with security interests per section 383(2) of the Insolvency Act 1986); *Razzaq* dealt with bankruptcy but it is likely that the courts will take the same view in relation to corporate insolvency: see *Ezekiel* v. *Orakpo* [1976] 3 All ER 659; *Clarence Coffey* v. *Corchester Finance* (unreported) 3 November 1998; *Re Lomax Leisure Ltd* [1999] EGCS 61, discussed in Hanson, 'Landlords' Right'; *Christopher Moran Holdings Ltd* v. *Bairstow* [1999] All ER 673.
108. IS 2000, p. 37.
109. See McCartney, 'Insolvency Procedures', pp. 75–6; M. McIntosh, 'Insolvency Act 2000: Landlords' Right of Peaceable Re-entry' (2001) 17 IL&P 48. See Insolvency Act 2000 s. 9 – peaceable re-entry covered by the administration moratorium; Schedule A1, para. 12 – peaceable re-entry covered by the new CVA moratorium: see ch. 10 below. The moratorium is likely to be further strengthened if the floating charge holder's statutory power of veto under the Insolvency Act 1986 s. 9(2) is removed. Such a reform was firmly recommended in November 2000 by the Insolvency Service Review Group (see IS 2000 para. 73), and the DTI

Expertise

Turning to the issue of expertise, a number of questions are posed by the administration procedure, notably whether it allows high quality judgments to be made on rescue options; whether the appropriate information is gathered; and whether the judgments that are made are implemented.

Chapter 5 raised a number of issues concerning the orientation of IPs and whether they tend to be attuned to asset realisation rather than rescue. The concern of critics, in short, is that IPs are accountant non-specialists in the relevant field of enterprise and will thus be less capable of effecting rescue-related reorganisations than would be the case in a regime that retained more managers in place and imposed supervision over these.[110] Limitations on creditor involvement in administration may also reduce expert input into decision-making. As noted, the IP may make highly significant disposals of assets before a creditors' meeting is convened and it can be asked whether closer creditor monitoring of managerial decisions would be preferable to action by outside professionals.[111]

Expertise, it may also be objected, tends to be too narrowly channelled through the Rule 2.2 report which both increases costs and detracts from other means of informing judgments such as consulting a wide range of parties affected by the insolvency. Rule 2.2 reports, on this view, tend to become excessively elaborate and expensive without always adding a great deal to decision-making. A simpler, cheaper, more accessible regime, the criticism runs, would be likely to improve rescue decisions as well as make them more acceptable to a wide range of affected parties – on which, more below.[112]

Accountability and fairness

As for the accountability and fairness of administration, a first problem is that the administrator is not obliged or entitled to consider the public

White Paper of 2001 on *Productivity and Enterprise* proposed to end the floating charge holder's veto except in relation to certain transactions in the capital markets (para. 2.15). See also IS 2000, para. 43 for a suggestion that a moratorium could be introduced for schemes of arrangement under the Companies Act 1985 s. 425: see ch. 10 below.

110. See Phillips, 'Administration Procedure', p. 10. The Insolvency Service in its 2000 Review reported that 'many of the respondents considered that the insolvency profession took sufficient steps to assist and promote recovery' and that the SPI provide extensive training in this field: IS 2000, pp. 55–6.

111. Phillips, 'Administration Procedure', pp. 11 and 22.

112. See pp. 319–23 below; Phillips, 'Administration Procedure', p. 5; CBI submission to DTI's 1993 consultative document.

interest or the interests of all parties materially affected by the potential
insolvency. This means that customers and suppliers and employees of the
company – all of whom may have considerable stakes in its future – have no
voice in administration if they do not constitute creditors of the firm. The
company's unsecured creditors have a voice through the creditors' meeting and approval mechanism in determining the course of action taken by
the administrator, but such creditors vote according to the value of their
debts and not according to the extent of their dependence on the company's fortunes. An employee, accordingly, will only have a vote that reflects any money owed to him or her and account is not taken of their future role within the company. When, moreover, the court scrutinises, at
various points, the administrator's actions, it will look to the financial interests of creditors and members rather than broader concerns.[113] Such an
approach again is at odds with the Cork Committee's argument that the
court should appoint an administrator, *inter alia*, to restore profitability or
maintain employment; or to carry on a business 'where this is in the public
interest'.[114] Sir Kenneth Cork himself spoke of his committee's intention
that an administrator would have a role to play: '[w]here, in the national
interest, the government should take a hand as happened in the case of
Rolls Royce'.[115]

Shareholders as members of the company can, as noted, apply to the
court under section 27 of the Insolvency Act 1986 if they have a complaint
that the administrator's proposal, if implemented, will prejudice some
part of them or them generally. Such shareholders, however, are not involved in approval of the administrator's proposals, which under s. 24 is
a function given to the creditors alone. On this point it might be argued
that there is some consistency with Cork's suggestion that society's interest lies not in the preservation or rehabilitation of a company as such but in
the commercial enterprise.[116] Such an argument, however, may go too far:
even if it is accepted that society's interest lies in the enterprise and not
the company, this does not in itself mean that the interest of shareholders
should be ignored by granting shareholders no procedural rights. If there
is a prospect of rescue can shareholders be said wholly to have given over
their interests in the company to the creditors? Shareholders clearly do
have an interest in the administrator's actions. There is, indeed, no basis
for stating that Parliament established administration in pursuit of the

---

113. See, for example, Insolvency Act 1986 s. 27(1)(a).
114. Cork Report, para. 498.   115. Cork, *Cork on Cork*, p. 195.
116. Cork Report, para. 193; see Goode, *Principles of Corporate Insolvency Law*, p. 275.

survival of the enterprise and that the company's survival was not a legitimate objective in view. Section 8(3)(a) of the Act states explicitly that an administration order can be made for the purpose, *inter alia*, of 'the survival of the company and the whole or any part of its undertaking as a going concern'.[117] It seems, accordingly, hard to deny the legitimacy of shareholder interest in administration.

It may well be that society, or an administrator, will feel obliged to place the interests of shareholders in a secondary position in formulating substantive proposals to deal with the near insolvency. That, in itself, does not make it fair to decline to recognise the procedural rights that shareholders' interests give them. We see, for instance, that in the US Chapter 11 procedure,[118] shareholders have an interest which is subordinate to that of creditors but is nevertheless deemed worthy of consideration. To exclude such shareholders procedurally, moreover, may not only be unfair, it may, as indicated above, reduce that co-operation that an efficient system of administration vitally requires.[119]

To summarise the discussion thus far, administration is a procedure that is oriented towards rescue as well as asset realisation but it underperforms in a number of respects when assessed on efficiency, expertise, accountability and fairness counts. Whether changes can be made to correct such under-performance and whether administration might be reformulated in an improved configuration if seen from a more productive viewpoint are matters to which we now turn.

Ministering to administration

A number of proposals aimed at improving administration have been made in recent years and the main suggestions should be considered. They can be dealt with by looking respectively at those designed to cure ills on the efficiency, expertise and accountability and fairness fronts.[120]

---

117. See *Re Rowbotham Baxter Ltd* [1990] BCC 113.   118. See pp. 198, 204 above.
119. See Goode, *Principles of Corporate Insolvency Law*, pp. 275–6; J. L. Westbrook, 'A Comparison of Bankruptcy Reorganisation in the US with Administration Procedure in the UK' (1990) IL&P 86. (Of course, it has been noted (see ch. 6 above) that there can be a problem of shareholder access being used as a blackmailing and blocking tactic in the US Chapter 11 procedure.)
120. The 2001 White Paper's proposals on floating charge holders' access to administration have been discussed in ch. 8 and will not be dealt with here.

Efficiency

Retention of managers in post

Giving control of the company to an outside IP tends, as has been indicated, to be expensive and to discourage directors from seeking help at a date that is early enough in corporate decline to maximise opportunities for turnaround. It has been suggested, accordingly, that a new approach should be adopted, one that gives directors a greater role in rescue and which will be perceived by them as less threatening. After all, it has been argued:

> The English approach is founded upon the outdated philosophy that those who have managed the company so that it requires protection should not be allowed to continue to manage it. As a proposition it is fundamentally flawed. Not all directors of insolvent companies are unfit to continue to manage them or, indeed, to manage any other companies ... Once it is accepted that the directors of insolvent companies are competent to manage solvent companies and accept credit, why should they not be competent to manage an insolvent company? Furthermore, why should that be the position where they understand the affairs and business of that company?[121]

This argument can be pressed too far. The fact that a director's conduct has not merited disqualification does not *per se* mean that the best way to effect rescue is to give such a person a free hand. Nor will such a director be in a position to exercise a number of the administrator's powers (for example, to recover preferences or transactions at an undervalue, or to report other directors to the DTI[122]). There may, nevertheless, be a case for dividing the functions of administrators and directors so as to allow directors a continuing role in the company, albeit one played under supervision. After all, there may be, as was seen in chapter 4, a number of reasons for corporate troubles that do not imply lack of managerial competence. At present many administrators delegate much day-to-day management to the existing directors but this delegation is an exercise of discretion and such a process does little to allay directors' fears that administration is likely to bring a ceding of control to outsiders.

How might a division of functions be stipulated? One means would be to amend the law so that administrators would have to propose a division of responsibilities under section 14 of the Insolvency Act 1986 upon which

121. Phillips, 'Administration Procedure', pp. 16–17.
122. Ibid., p. 17.

the court would give directions.[123] This procedure, however, would still fail to offer the troubled director any secure ongoing role in the company: a great deal would depend on the discretion of the administrator and the courts.

The Insolvency Act 2000 and its new company voluntary arrangements procedure will be discussed in the next chapter, but it can be noted here that during the twenty-eight-day moratorium of the Insolvency Act 2000, the company's management remains in control subject to supervision and a restriction on the disposal of assets. As for the administrator's approach to retaining a company's managers in place, the Insolvency Service's 2000 Review Group Report[123] recommended that: 'the insolvency profession should consider how its practice (in regard to keeping management in place) will be developed, for example through the medium of agreed best practice'. The profession was invited, moreover, to consider *inter alia* the ways in which administration could be 'used more flexibly and at less cost to achieve the rescue of more companies (rather than businesses) with consequent benefits for all concerned in the company's affairs'.[125]

A statement of agreed best practice would still offer the directors little guarantee of a role in the company: again they would fear an adverse exercise of discretion in relation to the application of best practice requirements. There may, accordingly, be a case for a legal presumption that on day-to-day matters the directors will retain control but, in addition, there will be a statement that this (as in the CVA procedure) will be subject to legal limitations (e.g. on disposal of assets) and to powers of supervision to be exercised by the administrator. Such a presumption might be rebuttable where an administrator is able to convince the court that allowing managerial continuity would not be in the interests of affected parties on counts that, again, might be set down and could include references to the directors' competence, skill or proposed mode of running the company and turning it around.[126]

Administration as a pre-insolvency process

Attempts to encourage earlier resort to outside help might also be furthered by relaxing the criteria governing the entry of firms into administration. As the Insolvency Service said of administration: 'It could be made

---

123. Ibid., p. 18.   124. IS 2000.   125. Ibid., pp. 22–3.
126. For a description of the historical use of 'debtor in possession' and voluntary arrangement of debt in England see Gregory, *Rescue Culture or Avoidance Culture?*, pp. 6–8.

more of a reconstruction mechanism by removing the requirement that companies must be insolvent (presently or prospectively) to enter into the procedure.'[127]

Dropping the insolvency requirement might reduce the stigma attached to administration but it might be asked why a solvent company would ever opt for administration. It is possible, though, to think of circumstances in which administration is appropriate: for example, where a subsidiary company is performing badly and is only solvent through draining cash out of the group; or where a company suffers the loss of a major customer but remains solvent for the time being.[128]

To amend section 8(1)(a) of the Insolvency Act 1986 in this manner would, however, introduce the prospect of applications for administration orders being launched on the basis of simple managerial under-performance. The danger is that actions of this kind would be used as devices to be deployed in boardroom or shareholder group battles rather than as mechanisms for dealing with genuine troubles. Such a danger, nevertheless, could be reduced considerably by careful drafting, designed, for instance, only to provide for the granting of administration orders where the court is satisfied that the company, as run on present lines, is at risk of becoming insolvent in the foreseeable future. This drafting would set out to define the status of administration as a pre-insolvency as well as an insolvency process and would constitute a change from the current more restrictive approach. It would not, however, liberalise to the extent of allowing administration in an unrestricted fashion to solvent companies.

Removing the floating charge holder's veto

The Insolvency Service Review Group had, by 2000, come firmly to the view that restrictions had to be placed on the ability of the floating charge holder to put in a receiver and halt the administration process: 'Our firmest recommendation is that the law should be changed to remove the right enjoyed by the holder of the floating charge to veto the making of an administration order, thus bringing the position in administration in line with that proposed for the moratorium in a CVA.'[129] By July 2001 the Government had endorsed this proposal in its White Paper on *Productivity and Enterprise*[130] and stated that its intention was to remove the floating charge

---

127. See IS 1999, p. 17.   128. See IS 2000, pp. 58–9.
129. Ibid, p. 21.   130. White Paper 2001, para. 2.15.

holder's effective veto over the making of an administration order except in relation to certain capital market transactions.[131]

A potential problem with the proposal to abolish the veto is that abolition creates a strong incentive for floating charge holders to insert receivers at an early date in order to avoid the less favourable processes of administration. The effect of abolition might be to increase the number of instances in which premature receiverships kill off chances of rescue in relatively hopeful scenarios. The Insolvency Service anticipated this problem in 2000 and stated that if precipitate receiverships occurred systematically there would be a case for restricting the enforcement of a floating charge to a right of the secured creditor to petition for an administration order: 'This would preserve the security value of the floating charge whilst ensuring that its enforcement was undertaken collectively and in a way that maximised accountability to all interested parties.'[132] This is the route taken by the 2001 White Paper on *Productivity and Enterprise*.

At this point, the Insolvency Service and the White Paper approaches come close to advocacy of abolishing administrative receivership in favour of a 'single gateway' approach with one enforcement procedure short of liquidation.[133] The issues attending such a reform will be returned to below under the heading 'Accountability and fairness'.

Reducing the costs of administration

Numerous methods of reducing the costs of administration have been canvassed. One suggestion, noted by the DTI in 1993, is that where the result of administration is the survival of the company the administrator should be relieved of the requirement to make a report on the conduct of the directors to the DTI Disqualification Unit.[134] Such a development might,

---

131. See ch. 8 above, pp. 269–72.

132. IS 2000, p. 22. See, however, Gregory, *Rescue Culture or Avoidance Culture?*, who urges caution regarding new policy here, arguing that 'if it should be created [it should follow] from a consideration of the relative rights and interests of risk capital, debt and secured debt' and noting that the IS 1999 Report recognised that the proliferation of forms of asset financing, such as leasing and debt factoring, renders rescue more problematical. Gregory asks whether it is 'worth attacking general financing secured by fixed and floating charges'. On arguments relating to secured credit and fixed and floating charges, see further ch. 3 above and ch. 14 below.

133. The 2001 White Paper does not 'abolish' administrative receivership in so far as it retains it in connection with certain transactions in the capital markets: see White Paper 2001, paras. 2.5, 2.18, and pp. 269–72 above. In November 2001 the Industry Secretary, Patricia Hewitt, announced that the Enterprise Bill (based on the 2001 White Paper) would not abolish the right to appoint an administrative receiver for secured creditors with floating charges created before the Bill becomes law.

134. The Company Directors' Disqualification Act 1986 s. 7(3) (CDDA) imposes such a duty on office holders such as the Official Receiver, liquidator, administrator or administrative receiver.

however, have only a modest effect on the cost of administration. The administrator is not called upon by sections 7(3) and 6(1) of the CDDA 1986 routinely to report on the conduct of all directors. The obligation to report arises only where it appears to the administrator that a director's conduct makes him unfit to be concerned in the management of a company. Another argument for retaining the reporting obligations is that the skill of the administrator in effecting a rescue constitutes no good reason for overlooking the unfit conduct of a director who has brought a company to the brink of disaster. The state punishes those who are unfit to drive (e.g. through drink) even where, through good fortune, no-one is injured, and similarly directors may need to be disqualified for unfitness even where creditors have been saved from injury because fortune or a skilled administrator has intervened.[135]

A different argument favouring non-reporting may, however, have greater force. This asserts that company managers should be given all incentives to seek administration orders without undue delay and that directors must, accordingly, not be placed in fear of scrutiny by the administrator for the purposes of disqualification. Whether such an incentive effect would outweigh society's need to root out unfit directors is, however, a moot point. Further suggestions for reducing the cost of administration include providing for the greater involvement of the directors in the day-to-day running of the company (a matter already discussed) and reducing the role and complexity of the Rule 2.2 report. As noted, the Chancery Division Practice Direction issued in 1994 set out to deal with the latter problem and rigorous application of a Practice Direction backed up through rulings on costs may offer the best way forward.[136]

It might be contended that reducing the level of court supervision over administration might offer a ready way to reduce costs. Again, though, it has been argued that the courts offer responsive and flexible supervision at low cost.[137] Court guidance ex ante may, moreover, operate in a manner that reduces the dangers of expensive legal challenges to the actions of administrators after the event. In addition, the role of the court should not be underestimated in ensuring that proper checks and balances are maintained, powers are not exceeded, biases are avoided, interests are given adequate respect and procedures are properly followed. Administration,

135. On disqualification see ch. 15 below.
136. [1994] 1 WLR 160. The 2001 White Paper proposals to bypass the Rule 2.2 report (paras. 2.8–2.10) apply only to floating charge holder applications or to holders of security who apply in case of urgency.
137. Phillips, 'Administration Procedure', p. 25.

after all, demands that sensitive decisions be made between different parties, and fears that IPs are never wholly free from the influence of banks and economically powerful security holders will never be far from the surface. In this climate it is essential that the courts are there to see fair play.

A final suggestion aimed *inter alia* at lowering costs is the proposal of the DTI in 1993 that there should be an additional procedure constituting a short-term administration.[138] Costs would be lowered in such an arrangement by providing for the appointment of an administrator and for a moratorium without the need for a lengthy court application and a formal independent Rule 2.2 report. The aim of the procedure would be to give short-term relief from creditors in order to facilitate corporate survival or reorganisation. The first step would be filing in court of a notice together with an IP's consent to act, plus directors' statements that administration is expected to achieve either survival of the company (and the whole or part of the undertaking) as a going concern; the approval of a voluntary arrangement; or sanction of a scheme under section 425 of the Companies Act 1985. It would also have to be stated that no administrative receiver is in office (or such person consents to the short-term administration).

The effect of filing would be an instant twenty-eight-day moratorium during which the IP would become administrator. No court hearing would be involved but filing would be advertised. The administrator would take control of the company and assess whether a rescue plan could be put to creditors; a creditors' meeting would be called within twenty-eight days to decide whether survival or a creditors' arrangement would be achieved or whether a move should be made to liquidation, receivership or full administration. The right of a floating charge holder to appoint an AR would be suspended during the moratorium. The administrator would have the usual powers of management under s. 14 of the Insolvency Act 1986 but would not be required to report under the CDDA 1986.

Such an additional process could serve as a worthwhile low-cost addition to the array of processes available, though, as with full administration, it is arguable that interests beyond those of creditors should enter into consideration. If, however, it is accepted that the 1994 Practice Direction has done much to reduce the 'mandatory' nature and the length of

---

138. See DTI 1993, ch. 6 for an outline of the process. Compare this with the 2001 White Paper's proposal that floating charge holders petition for administration without the need for a Rule 2.2 report: White Paper 2001, para. 2.12; see ch. 8 above.

the Rule 2.2 report, it may be that not much will be gained (and, indeed, added expense may be incurred[139]) from such a new procedure.[140]

Facilitating rescue funding

Companies involved in any potential rehabilitation process face the central problem that funds must be obtained in order to allow a turnaround to be effected:[141]

> Continued trading is essential for some form of going concern to emerge at the end of the process and for a company to continue trading through an insolvency procedure, it will routinely require access to some form of external finance. Unless that finance is available the rescue will fail, the assets will have to be sold piecemeal and the company will be forced into liquidation.[142]

When a company enters a formal insolvency process the difficulties of obtaining financing may increase considerably. At such times creditors will view lending to the company on an unsecured or under-secured basis as a very risky activity in which repayment depends on the success of the proposed rescue. Few lenders, as a result, may come forward under these conditions.

In recent years, two main routes to improved rescue funding have been mooted and they should be examined here. They relate to super-priority funding and reforms of the rules on book debt security.

Super-priority funding In a super-priority regime the providers of funds during a moratorium would be given priority over all existing creditors.[143] This concept is found in the US Chapter 11 provisions and in 1993 the DTI invited comments on its suitability in the UK. Such super-priority, the DTI said, might be financed either from cash flow or (in England and Wales) by a lien over specific uncharged assets. Such funds would have to

---

139. In that two creditors' meetings may be necessary as twenty-eight days may not provide enough time to work up proposals: time for notice of the meeting must be deducted from the preparation time. See R. Gregory, 'Insolvency Law Reform', *CCH Company Law Newsletter*, 14 December 1993, pp. 12–13.

140. See Gregory, 'Insolvency Law Reform'.

141. R3's Ninth Survey of 2001 indicated that in one in five cases of failed companies with in excess of £5m turnover, the main factor preventing a positive outcome was lack of funding.

142. IS 2000, p. 33. In 1999 the Insolvency Service cited the SPI's Eighth Survey, indicating that lack of security for extra funding was cited in 51 per cent of cases as a barrier to turnaround and lack of appropriate finance in 43 per cent of cases.

143. See p. 207 above. On super-priority generally see D. Milman and D. Mond, *Security and Corporate Rescue* (Hodgsons, Manchester, 1999). The INSOL International *Statement of Principles for a Global Approach to Multi-Creditor Workouts* (October 2000) is endorsed by the Bank of England. Principle 8 states that where additional funding is provided in a standstill period, the repayment of this should 'so far as practicable, be accorded priority status'.

be used only in the ordinary course of business (e.g. to pay employees during the moratorium) and any extraordinary items would have to be authorised by the lender. One advantage of super-priority, suggested the DTI, was that where funds were provided by the main secured lender on such a basis, there would be reassurance to the lender that their security was not being dissipated during the moratorium. It had to be faced, however, that, should the company fail, the super-priority funding would operate at the expense of other creditors.

The idea of super-priority has, however, been subject to ebbs and flows of favour at the DTI. In 1995 the DTI looked at CVA procedures and rejected super-priority on the grounds that the comfort of super-priority might militate against a lender's giving proper consideration to the viability of a business. As for the earlier suggestion that super-priority loans might be repaid earlier from cash flow, or secured by a lien over specific uncharged assets, the DTI was concerned that a company contemplating a CVA would not have sufficient cash flows or uncharged assets during a moratorium. Given such worries, the DTI proposed that nominees should be required to consider the availability of funding as part of the initial assessment of the CVA's prospects of success. If the assessment was favourable, said the DTI, there was no substantial reason why funders would not support the company. In 1999 the Insolvency Service was more favourably disposed and announced that its Review of Company Rescue and Business Reconstruction Mechanisms would reconsider super-priority. Note was taken of London Business School research by Maria Carapeto which showed that of 326 firms that had filed for Chapter 11 protection in the USA, some 135 had raised super-priority (or 'debtor in possession') financing which had comprised around 19 per cent of the total debt of the company. About half of the new finance was advanced by pre-petition lenders and high levels of such lending were associated with positive effects on recovery rates.[144]

In 2000 the Insolvency Service Review Group Report noted that for most CVAs additional funding tended to be provided by owners/directors or by existing lenders, often with the benefit of existing or increased security and/or personal guarantees. New secured finance was available only to

144. The DTI 1999 makes no reference, however, to the interest rates in Chapter 11 lending. These rates are frequently at a premium. As Gregory notes, 'Some argue that the total volume of Chapter 11 financing (19 per cent of total company debt) is more of a comment on the cost of Chapter 11 procedures than a reflection of the commercial needs of the company ... Statistical comparisons here are actually misleading because like is not being compared with like': *Rescue Culture or Avoidance Culture?*, p. 21. On Chapter 11 procedure see ch. 6 above.

the extent that existing secured creditors agreed to this or if the company had uncharged assets or charged assets with surplus value that could be offered as security. The prevalence of the floating charge meant, however, that uncharged assets were rare in corporate insolvencies.

The Review Group had considered in detail the options for post-petition funding under Chapter 11 of the US Bankruptcy Code.[145] The types of funding possible in the USA were: unsecured credit (section 364(a)); indebtedness with administrative expenses status (section 363(b)); credit or indebtedness with super-priority administrative expenses status, securable by a lien (charge) on unencumbered property or a junior lien on encumbered property (section 364(c)); or credit secured by a superior or equal lien on previously unencumbered property (section 364(d)). Companies might also seek permission from a secured creditor or the court to use the 'cash collateral' (the cash equivalent in its possession) to finance continued operations.

The Review Group did not think it appropriate to attempt to replicate Chapter 11 in the different business cultural and economic environment of the UK but considered that the basic principles underlying US practice were relevant. These principles were summarised[146] as holding that:

- Making additional finance available to a business in distress could be 'value enhancing' for the business, provided that it was part of a properly considered plan for financial recovery.
- If it was value enhancing for the business in the short, medium or long term, it would also be value enhancing for creditors or it would at least not worsen their position.
- The partiality of their outlook might prevent individual creditors from seeing this potential for value creation or giving it the same value as one would in relation to the business as a whole.
- The specialist insolvency judges and courts could take a broader view and they have the power to grant security to new finance during Chapter 11 even if this displaces the security held by an existing creditor: but displacement must not diminish the expected return to that creditor. The principle is that additional finance should only be provided where it is genuinely value enhancing for all.
- There is no automatic approval for post-petition financing but practice has evolved so that in the early stages of Chapter 11 some form of such financing 'necessary to avoid immediate and irreparable harm to the company's estate' is usually approved without difficulty.

145. IS 2000, pp. 33–5.   **146.** Ibid., pp. 33–4.

The Review Group floated the idea that the law might allow the authorities supervising an insolvency procedure to have regard to similar considerations to those in the USA in assessing proposals for super-priority finance. In practice this approach would allow super-priority financing to be approved by the courts (or a subordinate tribunal) if several criteria were met. The principal criteria suggested[147] were:

- The super-priority finance could reasonably be expected to enhance the value of the enterprise as a whole and, thus, returns to all creditors.
- The position of each individual creditor would be protected and their expected return would be at least the same as if the finance were not provided.
- The courts would need to be given significant discretion and the criteria to be satisfied before super-priority finance was granted would need to be demanding. Practice would no doubt evolve over time in terms of how such provisions operated.
- Secured creditors would need to be given appropriate influence over the selection or confirmation of the insolvency practitioner.[148]

In such a regime there is an attempt to ensure that a proper judgment is made about the prospects of viability. Concerns that super-priority funders will not assess viability on a proper basis are addressed by making the court or tribunal the arbiter on such matters. It is essential, accordingly, that a properly resourced and skilled system of courts or tribunals be established and that these incorporate appropriate insolvency expertise.[149] It might be objected that such judgments will not be located in a commercial or market context but, in response, the Insolvency Service's suggestion is that an option might be to have 'a system of expert tribunals with a strong commercial flavour dealing with cases on a day to day basis and to focus on the role of the higher courts as resolving disputes as to the application of the law and reviewing the procedures followed by the expert tribunal'.[150]

In 2000 the Insolvency Service considered that there was a case for such an approach to super-priority funding but put the proposal on the agenda for 'detailed consideration and wide consultation'.[151] It remains to be seen whether implementation will result, but a central issue for debate will be

---

147. Ibid., p. 35.   148. Ibid., p. 35.
149. A point made in ibid., p. 35, para. 137.   150. Ibid.
151. Implications for Crown preferences were also signalled as an issue for discussion, ibid., p. 35. See also HM Treasury, *Enterprise for All: The Challenge for the Next Parliament* (June 2001) and the White Paper 2001, para. 2.19 proposal to remove the Crown's preferential status (see ch. 13 below).

whether it is feasible, in times of corporate trouble, to seek court approval for rescue funding, whether the expenses involved will negate the value of super-priority funding for many smaller companies, and whether it will routinely be possible to present the court, in the time available, with such a body of information as will allow it to make a commercially informed judgment on viability.

Rethinking charges on book debts Book debts are sums outstanding and owed to the troubled company. When the company enters a rescue procedure these book debts are often the only funds that are available for the purposes of financing continuing operations through the rescue period. The *Siebe Gorman* decision,[152] however, limited the possibility of such financing by holding that a creditor can take a fixed charge on present and future book debts provided that, under the terms of the charge, the creditor restricts both dealing with the debts and access to the proceeds of the debts. A fixed charge could thus cover future assets in a manner that, until *Siebe Gorman*, had been considered the exclusive domain of the floating charge.[153] According to *Siebe Gorman*, the creditor had to be able to prevent withdrawals from the account into which the proceeds of the book debts were paid but the cash flow implications of this position were not fully explored. In the wake of *Siebe Gorman*, an extensive case law has sought to delineate the conditions under which fixed charges can be held over book debts and their proceeds. Judges and commentators have struggled to make clear the basis for designating book debts charges as fixed or floating.[154] In practical terms this, moreover, is a distinction of some importance. If a bank is deemed to possess a floating charge over the book debts proceeds, it will rank behind preferential creditors; if the charge is deemed fixed, the charge holder will precede the preferential creditors in the queue for repayment.

152. *Siebe Gorman & Co. Ltd* v. *Barclays Bank Ltd* [1979] 2 Lloyd's Reports 142.

153. See R. M. Goode, 'Charges Over Book Debts: A Missed Opportunity' (1994) 110 LQR 592; A. Berg, 'Charges over Book Debts: A Reply' [1995] JBL 433; G. Moss, 'Fixed Charges on Book Debts: Puzzles and Perils' (1995) 8 *Insolvency Intelligence* 25; A. Zacoroli, 'Fixed Charges on Book Debts' (1997) 10 *Insolvency Intelligence* 41.

154. For discussion see, for example, Milman and Durrant, *Corporate Insolvency*, pp. 127–31; E. Ferran, *Company Law and Corporate Finance* (Oxford University Press, Oxford, 1999) pp. 518–33; M. Armstrong, ' "Return to First Principles" in New Zealand: Charges Over Book Debts are Fixed – But the Future's Not!' [2000] Ins. Law. 102; R. Gregory and P. Walton, 'Book Debt Charges: Following *Yorkshire Woolcombers* – Are We Sheep Gone Astray?' [2000] Ins. Law. 157; Gregory and Walton, 'Book Debt Charges: The Saga Goes On' (1999) 115 LQR 14; D. Capper and L. McHugh, 'Whither the Floating Charge?' [1999] Ins. Law. 162. The Cork Report urged statutory reversal of *Siebe:* paras. 1585–6.

In commercial terms, the significance of *Siebe Gorman* was that it reconciled the creditor's need to control the proceeds of the book debts (essential for the charge to be regarded as fixed) with the company's need to use the proceeds of the book debts to fund its business. Cases such as *Re Brightlife Ltd*[155] indicated, however, that where the charge restricted dealings with the debts but the company was free to deal with the debt proceeds, the charge would be classified as floating.

Over the years the courts have tended to differentiate between two frequently occurring situations. In the first of these, the chargee is a bank and the charge provides that the book debt proceeds must be paid into the company's account with the bank and not dealt with otherwise than in compliance with the bank's instructions. In such circumstances the charge has been treated as fixed. This will be the case (following *Siebe Gorman*) even if the bank does little to constrain dealings. Where, in contrast, the chargee is not a bank, the courts have tended to demand that, for a charge to be deemed fixed, the chargee's power of control should actually be exercised.[156]

A more recent trend in English cases has, however, moved away from *Siebe Gorman*.[157] The decision in *Re Atlantic Computer Systems plc*[158] concerned a clause dealing with the assignment of leases. This provided for the assignee to have the benefit of all rentals and moneys under certain subleases but no provision was made concerning the application of the individual rent payments made under these subleases. The Court of Appeal ruled that there might have been an intention for Atlantic Computer Systems to be free to use the rent instalments until the assignee intervened, but this did not mean that the charge was floating, rather than fixed. Nicholls LJ distinguished, however, between a charge on existing income-producing property (such as a lease) and a charge on present and future property (for example, a typical charge on present and future book debts).[159] The decision has thus been criticised as an old-fashioned approach inconsistent with the modern view that what distinguishes fixed and floating charges is not the nature of the asset but the location of the power to manage and control its use.[160]

155. [1987] Ch 200.
156. See Knox J in *Re New Bullas Trading Ltd* [1993] BCC 251; *Re Brightlife Ltd* [1987] Ch 200; Milman and Durrant, *Corporate Insolvency*, p. 127.
157. On recent developments see Ferran, *Company Law and Corporate Finance*, pp. 524–9; D. Milman, 'Company Charges: Recent Developments' [2000] 7 *Palmer's In Company* 1; A. Walters, 'Round Up: Corporate Insolvency' (2000) 21 Co. Law. 262 at 262–5.
158. [1992] Ch 505, [1992] 2 WLR 367, [1990] BCC 859 . See p. 290 above.
159. Ferran, *Company Law and Corporate Finance*, p. 525.
160. Ibid., pp. 525–6. See also Bridge, 'Company Administrators', pp. 396–7; *Re Atlantic Medical Ltd* [1992] BCC 653; *Re CCG International Enterprises Ltd* [1993] BCC 580.

A later development took place with *Re New Bullas Trading Ltd*[161] which involved 3i plc and a charge that was expressed to be fixed as to present and future debts owing to the company. A series of commonly encountered provisions prevented dealings with debts and provided for sums owed to be paid into a bank account specified by the chargee. Drawings on the account were only to be made in accordance with the chargee's directions. The proceeds of debts were, however, to be treated as released from the charge once they were paid into the bank account and until any directions on drawing or demands for payment were issued by the chargee. On such release from the fixed charge, the proceeds were subject only to the residual floating charge created in the same debenture. In the event, 3i did not give any directions but the Court of Appeal held that the fixed charge on unpaid debts was nevertheless valid. (The claim of 3i thus prevailed over that of the preferential creditors.) Nourse LJ gave the judgment of the Court of Appeal and noted that in cases such as *Siebe Gorman*, book debts and their proceeds had been treated as indivisible and thus *both* had to be controlled in order for a charge to be regarded as fixed. He accepted, however, that the drafters of the charge in question had taken a different approach and treated the debt and its proceeds (or fruits) as divisible. Nourse LJ held that this separation was legally possible so that the debts themselves could be subjected to a fixed charge and the proceeds to a floating charge once they had been paid into a designated account.

Re New Bullas Trading is open to criticism on a number of counts,[162] notably that it builds on a tree and fruit analogy that does not hold; that this approach involves accepting that the debt itself is destroyed by payment, an event which the holder of the security has no control over. The judgment, therefore, can be said to be difficult to reconcile with the idea that a fixed charge gives rise to a proprietary interest over the charged property that can only be released with the creditor's consent.[163]

---

161. [1994] BCC 36; see Berg, 'Charges over Book Debts: A Reply'.
162. See Goode, 'Charges over Book Debts'; Moss, 'Fixed Charges on Book Debts'; Zacoroli, 'Fixed Charges on Book Debts'; M. G. Bridge, 'Fixed Charges and Freedom of Contract' (1994) 110 LQR 340; I. Narey and P. Rubenstein, 'Separation of Book Debts and their Proceeds' [1994] CLJ 225; J. Naccareto and P. Street, '*Re New Bullas Trading Ltd*: Fixed Charges over Book Debts – Two into One Won't Go' [1994] JIBFL 109; S. Griffin, 'The Effect of a Charge over Book Debts: The Indivisible and Divisible Nature of the Charge' [1995] 46 NILQ 163; B. Collier, 'Conversion of a Fixed Charge to a Floating Charge by Operation of Contract: Is It Possible?' (1995) 4 AJCL 14; M. Armstrong, '"Return to First Principles"'.
163. Ferran, *Company Law and Corporate Finance*, p. 528. The 'tree and fruit' analysis is encountered *inter alia* in *Atlantic Computer* [1990] BCC 859 where it was applied to finance leases and the income stream derived therefrom.

In policy terms, the *Re New Bullas Trading* approach allowed for some fixed security while permitting continuing access to the proceeds of book debts.[164] There is a problem, though, in so far as cases such as *Siebe Gorman* and *Re New Bullas Trading* have a cumulative effect in undermining the position of preference that Parliament has created for certain debts in the insolvency legislation.[165] *Re New Bullas Trading* has, however, been held to have taken the wrong approach. In *Re Brumark Investments Ltd*[166] the New Zealand Court of Appeal construed a charge as floating where it had been expressed as fixed over future book debts which had been paid into a designated account and floating as regards other book debts that had been collected but were not yet required to be paid into the designated account – a procedure that allowed the company freedom to collect debts and use the proceeds in the ordinary course of business. The Privy Council[167] dismissed the appeal and Lord Millet delivered a judgment that supported the Court of Appeal, saying:

> Whether conceptually there was one charge or two, the debenture was so drafted that the company was at liberty to turn the uncollected book debts to account by its own act. Taking the relevant assets to be the uncollected book debts, the company was left in control of the process by which the charged assets were extinguished and replaced by

164. See also Berg, 'Charges over Book Debts: A Reply', who supports the decision in *Re New Bullas Trading Ltd*; R. Gregorian (1994) 15 Co. Law. 181, who argues that *Bullas* 'clarifies the law and promotes workable commercial arrangements between borrowers and lenders'.
165. See ch. 13 below; Insolvency Act 1986 ss. 40, 175, 386, 387 and Sched. 6; see further Goode, 'Charges Over Book Debts'.
166. *Re Brumark Investments Ltd* [1999] NZCA 227, [2000] 1 BCLC 353. The New Zealand Court of Appeal seemed concerned about the schizophrenic type of security validated in *Bullas*. On the *Brumark* decisions (NZCA and Privy Council) see Armstrong, '"Return to First Principles"'; Gregory and Walton, 'Book Debt Charges: Following *Yorkshire Woolcombers*' (2000) IL&P 157, 'Book Debt Charges: The Saga Goes On'; J. Verrill, '*Brumark Investments* and Fixed Charges on Book Debts' (2001) 3 *Finance and Credit Law*, No. 2; Walters, 'Round Up: Corporate Insolvency', pp. 264–5; D. McLauchlan, 'Fixed Charges over Book Debts: *New Bullas* in New Zealand' (1999) 115 LQR 365; F. Oditah, 'Fixed Charges over Book Debts after *Brumark*' (2001) 14 *Insolvency Intelligence* 49; L. S. Sealy, 'Company Charges: *New Bullas* Overruled – But is This the End of the Story?' [2001] 76 CCH *Company Law Newsletter* 1; A. Berg, '*Brumark Investments Ltd* and the "Innominate Charge"' [2001] JBL 532 ('*Atlantic Computer* shows that there is a third "intermediate" or "innominate" category of charge…English law should now recognise that the creation of valid equitable security which has features equally incompatible with a fixed or a floating charge is not conceptually impossible': at p. 539); F. Coulson and S. Hill, '*Brumark*: The End of Banking as We Know It?' (2001) *Recovery* (September) 16. For further analysis of the status of *Atlantic Computer Systems* ([1990] BCC 859) post *Brumark* see Oditah, 'Fixed Charges', pp. 53–4; G. Stewart, '*Brumark*: The World Stops Spinning on its Axis?' (2001) *Recovery* (September) 6, 7; Sealy, 'Company Charges', p. 4; D. Milman, 'Company Charges: A Return to Harsh Reality' [2001] Ins. Law. 135. See also New Zealand Personal Property Securities Act 1999.
167. Privy Council Appeal No. 35 of 2000 [2001] UKPC 28. Also reported as *Agnew* v. *Commissioner of Inland Revenue* [2001] 3 WLR 454.

different assets which were not the subject of a fixed charge and were at the free disposal of the company. That is inconsistent with the nature of a fixed charge. Their Lordships consider that *New Bullas* was wrongly decided.[168]

Doctrinally, the law on charges over present and future book debts has been afflicted by instability. It is likely that *Brumark* will be followed in English courts in the future[169] but it still leaves a number of uncertainties: on such matters as the types of receivables that are covered by the decision; the treatment of funds in hand; administration expenses; and effects on guarantors.[170] The judgment does not rule out a lender's being able to take a fixed charge over book debts, it merely gives some indication of the criteria that the courts will look to in examining the adequacy of control as a factor in categorising charges as fixed or floating. If, however, attention is refocused on the rescue implications of such charges, consideration should be given to a number of potential ways forward. Fixed charges over book debts could be abolished, the charged property could be realised in certain circumstances or fixed charges could be subjected to crystallisation on entry into insolvency procedures.[171]

It would be possible to use legislation to reverse the effect of *Siebe Gorman* and do away with the fixed charge over present and future book debts.[172] The effect would be that all of the book debts due to a company at the start of an insolvency proceeding (or arising thereafter) would be available to finance continued trading. The overall benefits to a company are not, however, certain. The assets involved might be caught by a floating charge and abolition would change the balance of lending between fixed and floating charges as well as make book debts subject to the claims of preferential creditors. Potential lenders to the troubled company would be less inclined to make funds available if floating rather than fixed security was to be available and claims deferred to those of preferential creditors. Overdraft financing by banks might, accordingly, be reduced[173]

---

168. Ibid., paras. 49–50. On fixed charges over 'other debts and claims' see G. Moss, 'The Chairman's View: A Look at Three Recent Cases' (2002) 15 *Insolvency Intelligence* 3 at 4–5.

169. See Oditah, 'Fixed Charges', p. 52; Stewart, '*Brumark*', p. 7; R3, *Technical Bulletin No. 44*, August 2001, section 44.1; and the approach in *Kleinwort Benson* v. *Lincoln City Council and Others* [1992] 2 AC 349.

170. See Oditah, 'Fixed Charges', p. 52; R3, *Technical Bulletin No. 42*, June 2001, section 1.

171. See also CLRSG, *Modern Company Law for a Competitive Economy: Registration of Company Charges* (October 2000) pp. 24–6, which asks if registrable debts should be extended beyond the present formulation of 'book debts', i.e. extended as far as an all money obligation.

172. See IS 2000, p. 34; Armstrong, ' "Return to First Principles" ' [2000] Ins. Law. 102, 109.

173. Armstrong, ' "Return to First Principles" ', pp. 109–10. See also Response by the SPI to the Consultation Paper of September 1999 (SPI, London, 12 November 1999).

and an anticipated outcome of abolition would be an increase in the assignment or discounting of book debts and debt factoring. As noted in chapter 3, there is already a trend away from term loan and overdraft financing towards an increasing use of asset-based financing and discounting.[174] Abolishing fixed charges over book debts may add to pressures that produce highly fragmented systems of financing with many players operating with different procedures, objectives and interests. In terms of rescue, the fear is that such arrangements do not lend themselves to turnarounds because creditor co-ordination costs and difficulties are increased and more obstacles are placed in the way of a successful rescue.[175]

A further way to make book debts available for rescue financing is to allow a company in administration or a CVA to dispose of its book debts subject to a fixed charge. The insolvency legislation provides for such a course of action. Section 15 of the Insolvency Act 1986 allows an administrator of a company to dispose of property subject to either a fixed or a floating charge, or goods subject to a hire purchase agreement. Such dispositions may be carried out as if the property were not subject to the security (or as if the rights of the owner under the hire purchase agreement were vested in the company) but court authorisation is required for fixed charges and the court must be satisfied that the disposal will promote one or more of the purposes of administration.[176] These provisions are mirrored in the Insolvency Act 2000 to deal with company dispositions during a CVA moratorium,[177] save that dispositions of property subject to fixed or floating charges need to be made with the security holder's consent or with court authorisation. Where property subject to a floating charge is disposed of under the above provisions, the holder of the security has the same priority with regard to the proceeds as he would have had in respect of the property itself. In the case of fixed charges the proceeds shall first be applied to discharging the sums secured or payable under the hire purchase agreement. In terms of rescue, section 15 of the Insolvency Act 1986 and Schedule 1, paragraph 20 of the Insolvency Act 2000 are useful in allowing an administrator or the company to effect turnaround and related realisations when a security holder or property owner refuses to co-operate.

---

174. Armstrong, '"Return to First Principles"'; Bank of England [1999] 31 *Quarterly Report on Small Business Statistics*, January 2000, pp. 24–5.
175. See IS 1999. Lack of 'creditor consensus' may thus be an increasing problem: see Armstrong, '"Return to First Principles"', p. 110; SPI Response to IS 1999, para. 4.1.3. Armstrong argues, however, that he has seen 'no empirical evidence to prove that increasing fragmentation of the small companies finance market frustrates rescue': p. 111.
176. Set out in the Insolvency Act 1986 s. 8(3).
177. See Insolvency Act 2000 Sched. 1, para. 20; see also ch. 10 below.

Can the courts use their discretion under these provisions to allow book debts secured by fixed charges to be used for funding rescues? A first problem here stems from the obligation to use the proceeds of disposition to meet the fixed charge holder's claim or that of the hire purchase owner. This will mean that funds will be available to fund rescues and continued trading only where there is a surplus. There are further difficulties. The provisions of the 1986 and 2000 Insolvency Acts still require it to be stated whether book debts are subject to fixed or floating charges, since this affects priorities regarding the proceeds of disposal. The courts, as has been noted, also face a number of difficult issues in deciding what proportion of fixed charge book debts shall be disposed of (and who should judge this); whether unsecured creditors need to be protected; and how the relevant book debts are to be identified. Such difficulties mean that this route is likely to assist in turnaround only exceptionally.

In 2000 the Insolvency Service recommended that, as an initial step to address the issue of funding company rescues, the law be changed to 'ensure that the extent of a fixed charge over a company's book debts be determined at the date of the company's entry into either a CVA moratorium or administration'.[178] Under this proposal the fixed charge on book debts would crystallise at the point of entry into an insolvency procedure. Book debts arising after the insolvency procedure commenced would fall outside its scope. They would, accordingly, be subject to any floating charge in existence but the new book debts would be available to finance continued trading. Additional finance would thus be made available for financing company rescues, argued the IS.[179]

This idea of crystallisation was rejected by the DTI in 1995 on the grounds that if a company proposing a CVA was genuinely viable it should be able to persuade the charge holder that 'it would not in the long term be disadvantaged by allowing the company to use charged book debts during the moratorium. If a company is viable the charge holder will probably have as much if not more to gain by supporting a rescue proposition.'[180] Such an argument is not, however, wholly convincing since a bank with such a fixed charge will have to decide whether to allow book debts to be used for rescue purposes at the start of a CVA and will be asked to give up part of its security at a time before it knows whether a viable rescue

---

178. IS 2000, p. 35.   179. Ibid., p. 34.
180. DTI/IS, *Revised Proposals for a New Company Voluntary Arrangement Procedure* (April 1995) ('DTI 1995'), p. 11.

can be delivered. A prudent banker, in these circumstances, would be liable to hold on to the security and seek to exercise control over corporate activities.

In response to this proposal it can be countered, first, that, as with abolition of the fixed charge over book debts, there might be problems in encouraging lenders to supply funds during moratoria when fixed security cannot be granted over book debts. There would, of course, be more funds coming into the company than would be the case in the absence of crystallisation but floating charges would take a proportion of these funds and any loans raised on the strength of the post-insolvency procedure book debts would be likely to flow from increased factoring or other asset-based financing methods rather than through term loans and overdrafts. The same worries as were voiced in relation to the abolition of fixed security over book debts would arise, notably concerning the difficulties of gaining the requisite creditor consensus for rescue in a context of diverse and fragmented financing. The main differences between abolition and crystallisation would be that abolition leaves more value with the floating charge but crystallisation recognises the value that lenders place on fixed charges over book debts and preserves lending on this basis. It cannot be assumed, however, that lenders would be strongly attracted to fixed charged lending on book debts if crystallisation might occur at the instigation of the directors and without any requirement of insolvency or near insolvency. Since entry into a CVA moratorium[181] might flow from actions of the directors and would not require the company to be near insolvency, the lenders might feel vulnerable in the face of the company's directors' power to restrict their security.

Equity conversions

A radical reform proposal put forward by Aghion, Hart and Moore[182] operates on the Jacksonian basis that the main goal of an insolvency procedure is to maximise the total value of the proceeds (measured in money terms) received by existing claimants and to preserve absolute priority. Aghion, Hart and Moore aim, additionally, to offer a regime that is quick, cheap and leaves minimal discretion in the hands of the judiciary and experts. The main evils that the proponents of equity conversion seek to counter are, first, the danger that senior creditors will vote for liquidation when

---

181. On the Insolvency Act 2000 CVA moratorium, see ch. 10 below.
182. P. Aghion, O. Hart and J. Moore, 'A Proposal for Bankruptcy Reform in the UK' (1993) 9 IL&P 103, summarised in DTI 1993, Appendix E.

this serves their interests but is not in the general interest of affected parties and, second, the tendency of the administrator when exercising discretion to be involved in inefficient and time-consuming bargaining in an attempt both to secure agreement on taking a firm forward and to decide how to distribute the resulting cash or securities.

The proposal is that when a firm is placed in administration a stay is put on creditors' claims and an individual is appointed to supervise the procedure. This person will convert the firm into an all equity firm and allocate rights to this equity among the former claim holders in exchange for their former claims. Senior creditors are given equity, junior creditors and former shareholders are given options to buy equity; the individual will solicit cash and non-cash bids for all or part of the 'new' firm. Non-cash bids may include proposals to reorganise the firm as a going concern and to take on new debts. These two tasks will be completed within a specified time, say within three months, and then junior creditors and former shareholders will decide whether to exercise their options. Following this stage, the new shareholders will vote on which bid to select and the firm will exit from insolvency.

Junior creditors would thus be required to buy out senior creditors before they receive anything. Claim disputes in such a process could be set aside and dealt with (together with late claims) once the firm has emerged from bankruptcy or been liquidated. Where a secured creditor's security does not fully cover the debt, he or she will be given an appropriate mix of shares and options. Floating charge holders will be granted shares according to their security and this favourable treatment of secured creditors might be expected to encourage financial institutions to lend to companies. Aghion, Hart and Moore's scheme was revised after consultation and would no longer involve an automatic equity for debt swap.[183] The revised procedure would constitute an option within receivership or administration or even replace administration.[184]

The regime's proponents point to a number of its supposed strengths.[185] First, conversion to equity gives the bank (assumed to be the main creditor holding a floating charge) a stake not merely in the recovery of its debt but in a growth in equity value beyond that point. This reduces the bank's incentive to enforce its debt prematurely when it is probable that waiting

183. See P. Aghion, O. Hart and J. Moore, 'Insolvency Reform in the UK: A Revised Proposal' (1995) 11 IL&P 67. (The proposal is described in Aghion, Hart and Moore, 'Proposal for Bankruptcy Reform'.)

184. Ibid., p. 69.

185. See Aghion, Hart and Moore, 'Insolvency Reform in the UK'.

would increase returns or rescue prospects. The bank also has an incentive to sell the company for as much as possible, rather than for merely enough to satisfy its security. Second, the banks may end up holding equity more often than at present and this may have a desirable effect on their propensity to appraise and monitor corporate debtor performance. Third, the system overcomes the problems that administrators face in attempting to negotiate resolutions of problems when different creditor groups have divergent interests. Fourth, the regime avoids the voting distortions that present administration arrangements may produce when junior creditors are placed in a position where they can, without justification, block plans and extract more money than they are allowed under priority. Finally, the system reduces the need for a moratorium (with its dangers of bad managers doing more damage to the company's financial state) because it allows the companies with good prospects to be saved within either administration or receivership.

A number of objections to the scheme and a number of potential difficulties can, however, be identified.[186] In the first instance, some confusion surrounds the issue of entitlement to instigate the equity conversion, with critics noting that a single unsecured creditor might be able to trigger the process irrespective of the amount owed and questioning whether a small unsecured creditor would have the right to displace an administrative receiver or an administrator appointed by the court.[187]

It can also be objected that if the procedure is not made compulsory it will add little to present procedures. In many schemes of arrangement, formal and informal, there is an element of debt/equity conversion and shareholders or junior creditors can always 'buy out' senior creditors: for example, by managerial buyouts of the business.[188] The position of the unsecured creditor in the scheme also gives ground for concern. Such creditors will only retain the right to claim outstanding debts if they exercise options to buy shares in the company by a specified date. All the equity in the scheme is, after all, given to the holder of the floating charge and unsecured creditors have to purchase their equity. This has been called a 'fundamental injustice' as it requires a group of creditors who have lost money to put up further funds to keep their debt alive.[189] Junior creditors

---

186. For criticism see Brown, *Corporate Rescue*, pp. 680–4.
187. See A. Campbell, 'The Equity for Debt Proposal: The Way Forward' (1996) 12 IL&P 14 at 15.
188. Brown, *Corporate Rescue*, p. 680, who concedes that Aghion, Hart and Moore acknowledge this point in 'Insolvency Reform in the UK', at p. 70.
189. J. Francis, Technical Secretary of the Society of Practitioners of Insolvency, 'Insolvency Law Reform: The Aghion, Hart and Moore Proposals' (1995) (Winter Edition) *Insolvency Practitioner*, p. 10, quoted in A. Campbell, 'Equity for Debt Proposal', p. 15.

may also be placed in a difficult position because there is, as yet, no flourishing market for distressed debt in the UK. The junior creditors, accordingly, may find it difficult to sell their options and, if these lapse, the effect will be to leave the senior creditors with all the equity.[190] The conversion proposal can indeed be seen as allowing floating charge holders to exploit their superior resourcing, information and bargaining positions in a manner that worsens the predicament of unsecured creditors. This is liable to be the case since the very factors that lead to the granting of unsecured loans will produce poor positioning to effect purchases of equity options, notably: informal modes of business operation; lack of familiarity with legal structuring in commercial relations; modest levels of staffing operations; and modes of business operation involving large numbers of small, fast-moving transactions and players. Of all creditors, the unsecured creditors are least likely to be able to put their hands on cash at short notice in order to purchase equity shares. As a result of their poor positioning, unsecured creditors will tend to be worse off within an equity conversion scheme than under many alternative arrangements. As is to be expected with proposals based on economic efficiency-seeking, there is a neglect of distributional justice issues and an in-built bias in favour of giving more to those who already have. Those who already have tend, after all, to be the parties who are best placed to make use of the opportunities on the table.

The deadlines involved in the conversion proposal only exacerbate the position of the unsecured creditor. Tight time limits are involved and options have to be exercised before the IP's plan is placed before the shareholders' meeting. As has been commented: 'At this stage it is unlikely that such creditors would have sufficient information to make an informed decision about the survival prospects of the company and exercising options could amount to throwing good money after bad.'[191] From the point of view of the strongest players – the banks with the floating charges – the position is, in contrast, rosy. The conversion process allows the bank to commence formal proceedings, trigger the conversion procedure and force the unsecured creditor to buy them out or else give up all their claims.[192]

As for the hope that an equity conversion scheme will keep transaction costs, and particularly legal costs, low, this may not be achievable in practice. There is the potential for much litigation and the need for a good deal of court supervision within the scheme in relation to issues of asset

190. Brown, *Corporate Rescue*, p. 680.
191. A. Campbell, 'Equity for Debt Proposal', p. 15.
192. Francis, 'Insolvency Law Reform', p. 4.

valuation, protections against abuse, control of the process and bias; the acceptability of the decisions of the IP; whether 'urgency procedures' can be used to meet deadlines; and the discretion exercised by the IPs. Administrators, in particular, may be placed in a difficult position if they are seeking bids for the company and, at the same time, assisting junior creditors to dispose of their options. As one commentator has cautioned: 'Widespread adoption of this procedure will generate new forms of potential duties and liabilities as administrators.'[193] The difficulty, in short, is that without legal oversight and controls, the very considerable discretions exercisable by IPs are open to abuse and liable to prompt many disputes in court. If, moreover, a high level of court supervision is involved, the scheme loses one of its heralded virtues. On the question of asset valuation, there are particular difficulties. The scheme's proponents suggest that disputes can be avoided by incorporating (in relation to fixed charges at least) 'forced sale' valuations by professional firms. Here there is a huge potential for fee paying, expense, litigation and delay. It is by no means the case, moreover, that a company's assets and liabilities can be ascertained quickly and easily.[194] Such calculations may be lengthy, fraught and highly contentious. Nor can such uncertainties be dealt with easily by Aghion, Hart and Moore's suggestion that disputes can be set aside and dealt with once the company has come out of insolvency. The existence of a body of contested claims will constitute, apart from anything else, a cloud of uncertainty that will hang over unsecured creditors' decisions on whether to exercise options and, as has been pointed out, such creditors may 'invest money to keep claims alive only to discover later that their equity holding is worth far less than they had calculated because of the existence of deferred claims'.[195] In sum, the equity conversion scheme has as its major probable effect the improvement of the position of banks at the expense of unsecured creditors. Nor is the deterioration of the unsecured creditors' position unconnected with the public interest in general. Commercial life depends to a large extent on the efficient giving of unsecured credit. In so far as unsecured creditors face large risks due to uncertain processes they will tend to resort to quasi-security devices and withdrawals of credit (demanding payment on the spot). Such a tendency will hinder rather than lubricate the wheels of commerce.

193. Brown, *Corporate Rescue*, p. 680.
194. A. Campbell, 'Equity for Debt Proposal', p. 16; Francis, 'Insolvency Law Reform', p. 9.
195. A. Campbell, 'Equity for Debt Proposal', p. 17.

Expertise

The earlier discussion on expertise raised the issue of whether IPs are sufficiently trained in rescue and orientated towards corporate or business turnaround. As noted above, many of the IS's consultees considered that IPs took sufficient steps to assist and promote rescue and recovery.[196] It is arguable, nevertheless, that higher levels of specialist knowledge may be introduced into rescues where the managers of the firm are given an input to rescue that is appropriate to their demonstrated level of competence. The suggestions made above on this front may accordingly increase expertise as well as efficiency.

The expertise of directors may contribute more tellingly to rescue, however, if it leads to earlier use of administration where this is appropriate. A number of respondents to the DTI argued that business people ought to be required to possess some sort of elementary qualification before they are allowed to act as company directors. Such qualifications would indicate that the individual has a basic understanding of company law and finance as well as the legal obligations going with directorship.[197] (They might also certify that the person possessed a basic knowledge of insolvency procedures and obligations.) The IS noted that a number of business people opposed a requirement to hold qualifications on the ground that this could operate as a brake on enterprise.[198] The directors consulted, however, said that they would be willing to undertake some sort of instruction provided that it was not expensive or time consuming and, overall, there was moderate support for the idea.[199] Mandatory basic training for directors could, furthermore, be advocated on the grounds that if legislation is passed in order to spell out directors' duties[200] and to create new insolvency regimes, this will only have limited effect if steps are not taken to bring those duties and regimes to the attention of directors. Some firms and directors will voluntarily acquaint themselves with the legal matters but these more responsible firms and directors are less likely to breach legal obligations or to meet financial troubles than more maverick operators. It is the latter who are disproportionately in need of training and higher standards. As for placing a brake on enterprise, it can be responded that ill-informed and irresponsible

---

196. See IS 2000, pp. 55–6.
197. See also V. Finch, 'Company Directors: Who Cares About Skill And Care?' (1992) 55 MLR 179 at 210.
198. IS 2000, para. 58.   199. Ibid.
200. See CLRSG, *Modern Company Law for a Competitive Economy: Developing the Framework* (March 2000); *Final Report*, 2001.

directorial behaviour may itself hinder enterprise. A world in which traders act defensively because of fears about their solvency or financial responsibilities is not a dynamic, responsive, low-transaction-cost world. It might be conceded that directors of firms with a level of turnover below a certain level should be exempted from the qualification requirement – this concession may be justifiable in order to encourage new business – but above that level the qualification could be mandatory. Those who object to the expense and difficulty of testing thousands of directors may be reminded, first, that each year huge numbers of would-be drivers of vehicles are tested in theory as well as in practice, and, second, that the actions of ill-informed directors may wreck businesses and lives, and, third, that a minimum competence may be a reasonable *quid pro quo* for the privilege of limited liability.[201]

Knowledge of directorial obligations and of insolvency procedures does not in itself ensure that directors will be inclined to start to seek help at an earlier stage of corporate decline than occurs now. What is needed, according to some commentators, is a cultural change in attitudes to insolvency. This change can be encouraged on a number of fronts: first, the notion that seeking help evidences managerial failure can be countered by public rejection of the condemnatory approach to insolvency. The speeches of Peter Mandelson when Trade Secretary exemplify such a rejection.[202] Second, as indicated already, directors, where possible, can be involved in rescue operations (under supervision arrangements) rather than excluded on the basis that they are inevitably culpable incompetents. Third, investors and large creditors can move to assure directors that taking early steps to secure help involves, in itself, no greater blot on the *curriculum vitae* than a decision to hire management consultants. Finally, such changes might be reinforced by tougher attitudes to those who indulge in wrongful and reckless trading, with greater use of the CDDA 1986 and stronger penalties imposed on errant directors.[203] Such measures may go some way towards

201. See ch. 15 below.
202. See the extract in M. Hunter, 'The Nature and Functions of a Rescue Culture' [1999] JBL 491 at 519; *The Times*, 14 October 1998; White Paper, *Our Competitive Future: Building the Knowledge Driven Economy* (Cm 4176, December 1998), 'Fear of Failure', paras. 212–14, which Hunter argues evidences the endorsement of this approach by Peter Mandelson's successor, Stephen Byers. See also *White Paper on Enterprise, Skill and Innovation* (2001), ch. 5, paras. 5.9–5.15: 'An entrepreneurial economy needs to support responsible risk taking. Insolvency law must be updated so that it strikes the right balance. It must deal proportionately with financial failure, whilst assuring creditors that it is handled efficiently and effectively' (para. 5.10).
203. See IS 2000, para. 59. See also A. Hicks, *Disqualification of Directors: No Hiding Place for the Unfit?* ACCA Research Report No. 59 (London, 1998). See ch. 15 below.

encouraging the view that failure to seek help is a more serious matter than being at the helm of a company that encounters difficulties.

Accountability and fairness

When looking to improve accountability and fairness in administration two central issues arise: should receivership be abolished and all creditors be directed through a single procedural gateway? Should the administration process take on board interests beyond those of creditors?

The abolition of receivership can be argued for on the ground that it operates in a manner that is unfair to creditors other than the appointing debenture holder and that it furthers the interests of the appointors at a potential cost to other creditors, employees, shareholders and the public. Abolition would give the court control over the debenture holder's enforcement of his or her security and it would demand that a supervising individual should act in the interests of all creditors or all affected parties.[204]

In 1999 the IS raised for consultation the idea of the 'single gateway', suggesting that imposing a single gateway through which all insolvent firms must pass would address concerns that the current regime:[205]

- is too complex. Hence management may not be aware of the range of options available to companies when they become insolvent;
- results in inefficient outcomes. Creditors exercising their private rights against insolvent companies may not result in the most efficient outcome in many cases.

The regime would act as a form of compulsory administration in which the IP would recommend to the court and creditors whether the company should be liquidated or preserved as a going concern. The idea of a unified insolvency procedure was not new: Germany had recently instituted such a system. The IS suggested that such a process might entail a period of observation by an IP, a moratorium for this period and a report to the court and creditors by the IP making recommendations (for reconstruction or liquidation) to be subject to a creditor note and court approval.[206]

---

204. See Phillips, 'Administration Procedure', p. 30. See also Milman and Mond, *Security and Corporate Rescue*, pp. 48–9, who argue that receivership should only be initiated by a court order: see ch. 8 above. See also the White Paper 2001 – *Productivity and Enterprise*, which proposes to restrict administrative receivership in favour of a streamlined system of administration. See ch. 8 above, pp. 269–71.
205. IS 1999, p.18.
206. As noted already the 2001 White Paper proposals to restrict administrative receivership have effects akin to single gateway proposals. The 2001 White Paper (para. 2.13) suggests that

A year later the IS put forward the single gateway for trading companies as a 'possible procedural innovation'[207] though no express recommendation was made as to its introduction. This procedure would incorporate the concept of the short-term or temporary administration as discussed earlier[208] and would operate as follows. Where the company had ceased trading the single gateway would be bypassed and liquidation entered into immediately.[209] Where a petition to wind up the company was made to court the court would make a temporary administration order. The administrator would be appointed from a panel of local IPs and would be given twenty-eight days to report to the court which could then order a winding up or an administration depending on the report's findings. A creditor secured by a floating charge would be able to enforce his or her security only by applying to court for an administration order, and section 8(3) of the Insolvency Act 1986 would be broadened to provide that the administrator should consider ways in which the interests both of the secured creditor and of the company could be served.[210] Any transition from administration to liquidation would be made smoother by allowing for the administrator to become the liquidator on the court ordering the company to be wound up.[211]

The single gateway proposal was responded to by IPs with what has been described as 'a mixture of hurt and outrage at the suggestion that they had failed to rescue numerous businesses through receivership'.[212] For their part, the banks argued that the single gateway would undermine the value of their security and lead to a reluctance to lend.[213] Responses to both stances can readily be made. To the practitioners' hurt and outrage it can be said that if they are acting with a proper regard for rescue and for wider interests in insolvency they should have little to fear in submitting

administrators be given twenty-eight days, not (as at present) three months, from appointment in which to state their proposals to creditors for consideration at a meeting.
207. IS 2000, p. 22.   208. See DTI 1993, ch. 6; and pp. 300–1 above.
209. Where the directors and shareholders of a trading company (solvent or not) decide that they are to liquidate the company then voluntary liquidation would proceed as at present (IS 2000, p. 22).
210. The 2001 White Paper proposes a similar regime, with floating charge holders applying for administration orders and administrators owing a duty of care to all creditors: paras. 2.8, 2.12.
211. A proposal echoed in the White Paper 2001 at para. 2.16.
212. Phillips, 'Administration Procedure', p. 30, who comments that this reaction 'completely missed the real point'. See the discussion of receivership at pp. 261–72 above. On 'idealised' notions of receivers within the Cork Report see G. McCormack, 'Receiverships and the Rescue Culture' [2000] 2 CFILR 229.
213. Phillips, 'Administration Procedure', p. 30.

to the increased court oversight that goes with the single gateway. As for the value of the bank's security, the key point, as indicated in the last chapter, is that the single gateway does not change priorities. It merely provides that interests other than those of the floating charge holders shall enter into consideration when this is possible without prejudice to the priorities regime. Any increases in transactional costs flowing from obligations of even-handedness and which have to be borne by banks can, of course, be passed on to consumers through marginal increases in interest rates. It is arguable that this is supportable since bank loans secured by floating charges can be said at present to be marginally too cheap where non-appointor interests are unfairly not considered and where financial risks are passed onto unsecured creditors.

Cork's concern regarding a single gateway can be seen in the Committee's fear that imposing a duty on a receiver to have regard for interests beyond those of the appointor would encourage legal challenges, cause delay and expense, and fail to advantage any party.[214] A point made in the preceding chapter can be repeated, however: non-floating charge holders, such as unsecured creditors, are ill-placed and poorly equipped to challenge IPs acting as receivers or administrators and fears of excessive litigation may, accordingly, be easily exaggerated. Where, moreover, IPs are able to serve, say, unsecured creditors' interests, without doing violence to priority, it is fair and in the public interest that they be obliged to do so: and it is also right that the courts should be able to enforce that obligation.

Conclusions: administration as practical rescue

It has been seen that much can be done to improve the performance of administration on the efficiency, expertise and accountability/fairness fronts. It may also be necessary, however, to take a broader look at the process of administration and reconsider how it is conceived and used. We have seen in the above discussions of receivership that a number of confusions and inconsistencies infuse current insolvency law. On the one hand, receivership is set up in terms of private interests. On the other, administration is seen by the Insolvency Act 1986 (section 8(3)) in a number of ways and oriented to: the survival of the company (or at least part of the business); arrangements between the company and creditors; or advantageous

214. Cork Report, para. 451.

winding up. (Cork's list of concerns in administration included employment and the public interest but these do not feature in section 8(3).) In
administration considerable value is placed on judicial oversight to ensure
fair treatment, but in receivership the courts take a back seat. Administration is avowedly a rescue device but it operates too late in corporate decline
to be effective as such; it fails to create incentives for directors to trigger rescue early; and it does not give creditors the access to decision-making that
would lead them to support rescue through administration. The sticks of
wrongful trading and disqualification are not matched by carrots that are
liable to induce directors to regard rescue without fear. There is, moreover, no consistent approach to the notion of a rescue procedure. Administration, for instance, gives shareholders no voice in decision-making, yet
a truly pre-insolvency rescue procedure would not deny the procedural
rights of shareholders on the grounds that in insolvency the shareholders'
interests are taken over by the creditors.

How can such tensions be resolved in a scheme of insolvency law based
on explicit values? First, the law can operate with a consistent view of
the purposes of insolvency procedures. The special treatment given to the
banks through receivership should be abandoned along the lines advocated in the 2001 White Paper on *Productivity and Enterprise* so that in all
rescue-oriented procedures consideration is given to all affected parties
whatever their position in the regime of priorities but without prejudice
to that listing of priorities. Receivership should be modelled on administration or even replaced by a single gateway system based on administration. Second, a consistent view can be taken of the *procedural* rights of
parties affected by the insolvency. These should not be dictated entirely
by formalities associated with pre-insolvency contracts but should take on
board the extent that a party stands in practice to be affected by the insolvency. Third, the law should clearly distinguish between pre-insolvency
(rescue) procedures and insolvency procedures. In the case of the former
the live (though often troubled) interests of shareholders should be recognised and their voices heard accordingly, whether or not the insolvency
process recognises the substantive rights of shareholders in a full insolvency. To distinguish between process rights and substantive rights in this
manner is the only way to ensure a fair consideration of interests at a period of corporate life when shareholder and creditor interests are in a state
of confusion.

Finally, a revised approach could be taken to the notion of fairness itself. At first glance it seems fair to grant to various parties equal

opportunities of access to decision-making. As our discussion of the equity conversion proposals showed, however, an opportunity of access is hardly fair if other parties are better placed to make use of that access. The effect of a fair race to access here may simply be to advantage the well-positioned and powerful parties further. If, when processes are designed, account is taken of the capacity of different parties to make use of those processes, a fairer set of insolvency rules (particularly for unsecured creditors) may result.

10

Company arrangements

This chapter looks at the statutory arrangements that companies may voluntarily enter into to deal with troubles or adapt to changes in market conditions. The two main procedures for effecting voluntary arrangements either within or outside administration or liquidation are schemes of arrangement under section 425 of the Companies Act 1985 and Company Voluntary Arrangements (CVAs) as provided for in the Insolvency Acts of 1986 and 2000.

Before looking at these two methods, it should be emphasised that informal arrangements made contractually can, as noted in chapter 7, provide very useful ways of attempting rescues before there is need to resort to the formalities of section 425 or CVA provisions. Informal steps, moreover, may be taken confidentially and, in the international context, may provide a useful way of negotiating between different insolvency systems.[1] Such contractual steps, however, possess a number of weaknesses. They are only binding on contracting parties and cannot tie dissenting parties to an agreement. They offer no form of moratorium to shield the company from its creditors and, even if approved by meetings of creditors and members, offer no protection from the enforcement of claims. Informal procedures may also lend themselves to domination by large secured creditors in a way unmatched by CVAs and section 425 processes.

Schemes of arrangement under the Companies Act 1985 sections 425–7

The roots of the scheme of arrangement lie in Victorian legislation[2] but, as set out in the Companies Act 1985, the process allows a 'compromise

---

1. See ch. 7 above; D. Brown, *Corporate Rescue: Insolvency Law in Practice* (J. Wiley & Sons, Chichester, 1996) p. 647.
2. Joint Stock Companies Act 1870.

or arrangement' to be agreed between a company and 'its creditors, or any class of them'.[3] An arrangement here may include a reorganisation of share capital by the consolidation of shares of different classes or by the division of shares into different classes.[4] Such schemes are commonly used to effect compromises and moratoria with creditors and, in recent years, schemes with policyholder creditors of insurance companies have been common.[5] They are also used in takeover and merger transactions and in reorganisation of rights allocated to classes of shares or debt, often where the articles or instruments constituting the capital are inadequate.[6]

The relevant procedure for a scheme involves an initial approach by the company to the court or else the summoning (with court approval) of meetings of the company's members and creditors. On such approval being obtained, the scheme must be approved by the court, which will consider issues of procedural fairness, hear objections from dissenters and decide whether the scheme is 'fair and reasonable'.[7] The court will, *inter alia*, consider whether each common interest group (for which there must be a separate meeting) is fairly constituted and whether the class's decision to approve the scheme was one that could reasonably have been made.[8]

One advantageous feature of the scheme of arrangement is that, if the arrangement is approved, it may modify the rights of shareholders and creditors and may do so without their consent. It is binding on all affected parties, not just those who approved it and not just those who were notified of the procedure (as with a CVA under the Insolvency Act 1986 sections 1–7).[9] Schemes, moreover, may be tailored to corporate needs. They

---

3. See generally A. Wilkinson, A. Cohen and R. Sutherland, 'Creditors' Schemes of Arrangement and Company Voluntary Arrangements' in H. Rajak (ed.), *Insolvency Law: Theory and Practice* (Sweet & Maxwell, London, 1993); D. Milman, 'Schemes of Arrangement: Their Continuing Role' [2001] Ins. Law. 145.

4. Companies Act 1985 s. 425(6)(b).

5. See CLRSG, *Modern Company Law for a Competitive Economy: Completing the Structure* (November 2000) ('CLRSG, *Completing the Structure*') p. 206.

6. Ibid.

7. *Re Anglo-Continental Supply Co. Ltd* [1922] 2 Ch 723, 726; *Re Dorman Long* [1934] 1 Ch 635; *Re NFU Development Trust Ltd* [1972] 1 WLR 1548; *Re RAC Motoring Services Ltd* [2000] 1 BCLC 307. See Wilkinson *et al.*, 'Creditors' Schemes of Arrangement', p. 330.

8. The court must be satisfied that the scheme does not operate unfairly between groups and will ask whether an intelligent and honest member of the class could reasonably have approved the proposal: see *RAC Motoring Services Ltd* [2000] 1 BCLC 307; D. Milman, 'Schemes of Arrangement' [2001] 6 *Palmer's In Company* 1.

9. A majority in number representing three-quarters in value of the creditors, or class of creditors, or members, or class of members, is binding on all creditors, or the class of creditors, or the members, or class of members, where the arrangement is sanctioned by the court: Companies Act 1985 s. 425(2). The court has complete discretion, when approving a scheme, to make consequential directions. This may be useful where the proposal put to the court differs from the proposal considered by the shareholders: *Re Allied Domecq plc* [2000] BCC 582; Milman, 'Schemes of Arrangement'.

are very flexible and there are no statutory prescribed contents for such schemes.[10] They can be used in conjunction with liquidation (in order to reach a particular compromise with creditors) or as an alternative to liquidation. Securities may be removed or rights to enforce securities may be curtailed and creditors' payment rights can be modified if the majority of secured creditors agree. (The court's powers under the Companies Act 1985 section 427 are more extensive here than in relation to administration orders.)

A second advantage, of relevance to rescue scenarios, is that schemes may be formulated and approved without any requirement that there be an impending insolvency. Early attention to corporate difficulties and timely responses to problems may, accordingly, be instituted. (This is a considerable advantage over administration.) A third favourable factor is that schemes of arrangement are in essence agreements between companies and their creditors and, accordingly, there is no need to involve an insolvency practitioner in formulating or in implementing the scheme. This allows the existing directors to stay in control of the company and the process does not deter them from taking remedial action by holding out the real prospect of a ceding of control to an outside IP. Schemes, moreover, can be applied to companies not registered in the UK, and, if the company has assets in the UK, the scheme can prevent enforcement against these. This overcomes jurisdictional problems. A final attraction of the scheme of arrangement is that it can be used to reorganise corporate groups: debt can be exchanged for equity and schemes can provide for the transfer of shares or assets between companies or even the amalgamation of a number of companies.[11]

In spite of such advantageous characteristics, schemes of arrangement have been used on relatively few occasions. This infrequency of resort is understandable once the disadvantages of the scheme of arrangement are considered. A major constraint on use has been that such schemes have been so rigorously protective of minority interests that, in practice, schemes have not been approved unless they have happened to satisfy the interests of all parties affected by them. This protective stance is seen in

10. Schemes must, however, be within the corporate powers of the company – *Re Ocean Steam Navigation Co. Ltd* [1939] Ch 41 – and must comply with the Companies Act requirements on reductions of capital or issues of redeemable shares: *Re St James Court Estate Ltd* [1944] Ch 6 and Companies Act 1985 ss. 135–41.
11. Note, however, that requirements may be imposed by regulations implementing the Third and Sixth Company Law Directives of the EC: the Companies (Mergers and Divisions) Regulation 1987 (SI 1987 No. 1991); EEC Council Directive 78/855, OJ 1978/295/36 and EEC Council Directive 82/891, OJ 1982/378/47.

the complexity of the approval arrangements. It is necessary to ensure that separate meetings are held for each different class of member or creditor affected by the proposed scheme. It is often difficult, however, to know what constitutes a class for these purposes, and the court will not offer guidance on such matters at the application stage.[12] Different types of shareholding clearly produce different classes, and preferential, secured and unsecured creditors will also be separately grouped. Other interest groups within these classes may also, however, have to be organised into different classes, and if such classes are not established properly from the start, the whole scheme will be nullified.[13]

There have, however, been recent signs of a less protective stance by the judiciary – a change of approach that has prompted some concern. When the Company Law Review Steering Group (CLRSG) looked at these issues it considered that, in an important case, the Court of Appeal had not given sufficient protection to minority creditors and members. The decision in *Re Hawk Insurance Co. Ltd*[14] was seen as worrying in so far as a scheme of arrangement under section 425 was approved where a single meeting of all the creditors had been held, notwithstanding that the creditors appeared to have had different rights. The courts have taken varying approaches to class definition[15] and the CLRSG looked favourably on legislating to define classes so as to restore the pre-*Hawk Insurance* position and state that the only persons entitled to attend and vote at a section 425 meeting would be 'persons whose rights are not so dissimilar as to make it impossible for

12. The CLRSG favoured the idea that the court should have discretion to decide class issues at the application stage: see CLRSG, *Modern Company Law for a Competitive Economy: Final Report* (July 2001) ('CLRSG, *Final Report*, 2001') para. 13.8.

13. A petition for approval of a scheme will be nullified: Practice Note [1934] WN 142.

14. [2001] EWCA Civ 241. Chadwick LJ: '…those whose rights are sufficiently similar to the rights of others that they can properly consult together should be required to do so, lest by ordering separate meetings the court gives a veto to a minority group. The safeguard against majority oppression … is that the court is not bound by the decision of the meeting'; see further R3, 'Legal Update' (2001) *Recovery* (September) 8. See also CLRSG, *Completing the Structure*, p. 215; *Report of the Review Committee on Insolvency Law and Practice* (Cmnd 8558, 1982) ('Cork Report') noted the difficulties of class definition (paras. 405–18), and CVA procedures avoid separations of classes in favour of remedial procedures for those who consider they have been unfairly prejudiced: see Insolvency Act 1986 s. 6.

15. On approaches to the definition of a class see Wilkinson *et al.*, 'Creditors' Schemes of Arrangement', pp. 326–7 and *Re BTR plc* [1999] 2 BCLC 675: 'those persons whose rights are not so dissimilar as to make it impossible for them to consult together with a view to acting in their common interest'. On which see *Sovereign Life Assurance Co. v. Dodd* [1892] 1 QB 573 (Bowen LJ) quoted in Wilkinson *et al.*, 'Creditors' Schemes of Arrangement', p. 327; *Re Osiris Insurance Ltd* [1999] 1 BCLC 182 (Neuberger J indicated that a single class might contain members whose interests were not exactly the same); a narrow interpretation of the notion of a class was adopted by Arden J at first instance in *Re Hawk Insurance Co. Ltd* [2001] BCC 57: if the interests of the parties were sufficiently dissimilar they constituted a separate class where approval had to be obtained.

them to consult together with a view to acting in their common interest'.[16] The CLRSG also suggested that the courts should be able to sanction a scheme even if classes had been wrongly constituted or, in appropriate circumstances, where separate meetings had not been held.[17]

On top of complications relating to definitions of classes, there are elaborate provisions that are designed to ensure that all members and creditors will be notified of the meetings and fully informed of the issues. A very extensive explanatory circular must be sent out with notices of meetings, and this circular will be both scrutinised in its terms and subjected to a power of approval by the court.[18] The court is thus involved in the procedure in at least two stages, first, on convening the necessary meetings of creditors and members and, second, on the petition to sanction the scheme as approved by the appropriate majorities of the meetings. On a petition for approval, moreover, a substantial review of information has to be provided to the court on such matters as the capital, business and financial history of the company, the terms of the scheme and the effects of the scheme on each relevant class of creditor or contributory. Dealings with the court on these matters involve substantial formality, routine and complexity as well as numerous attendances at court or chambers. Variations in schemes are also overseen by the court. When a scheme is approved by the court it must be filed at the Companies Registry and it cannot then be varied without court approval. In such circumstances the court will demand that further class meetings are held in order to approve the variation.

A further disadvantage of the scheme of arrangement is that, as noted, it involves no moratorium and thus offers a company little protection from the creditor who has the power to appoint a receiver. In the period between the initial formulation of a scheme and its becoming effective by court order, each individual creditor is able to exercise all the rights and remedies that he or she possesses against the company debtor. Cork estimated that, because of the complex procedure involved, this period of high vulnerability was unlikely to be less than eight weeks.[19] In this period the troubled company cannot prevent winding up or the random seizure of assets by individual creditors, and this will make it extremely difficult to launch even

---

16. CLRSG, *Final Report*, 2001, para. 13.8; see also *Re BTR plc* [1999] 2 BCLC 675.
17. CLRSG, *Final Report*, 2001, paras. 13.7, 13.8.
18. On information see Companies Act 1985 s. 426(2), s. 4 and Sched. 15B. The statement must state all relevant facts: *Re Dorman Long* [1934] 1 Ch 635; *Re Jessel Trust Ltd* [1985] BCLC 119.
19. Cork Report, para. 406 (discussing the Companies Act 1948 s. 206 scheme, the statutory predecessor of s. 425 of the Companies Act 1985).

the simplest scheme.[20] Schemes may, accordingly, have to be coupled with administration orders if any protection is to be secured. In 2000 the Insolvency Service recommended that it should liaise with the CLRSG to give full consideration to proposals for a moratorium in schemes of arrangement, one to resemble the CVA moratorium then proposed (and later implemented). The IS echoed Cork in dubbing the moratorium a 'valuable augmentation', and the case for such a period of protection is difficult to resist.[21]

It should, finally, be noted that the prominent role of the company's existing management in a scheme of arrangement may bring some advantages (for example, the mentioned lack of disincentives to respond to troubles) but there may be concurrent disadvantages. Schemes of arrangement depend substantially on the management of the company to take new initiatives, often defensively. These qualities may often be lacking in companies, particularly troubled companies. As Cork noted:

> It is, however, often the case that, where a company has become insolvent, the management has lost interest, or lost its grip, and there is a vacuum. All too often a scheme of arrangement with creditors would be of advantage to all concerned, but there is no one with the authority within the company, the means of information, and the energy to push the scheme through.[22]

In recent years the scheme of arrangement has revived in popularity and the 2000 CLRSG Consultation Paper, *Completing the Structure*, suggested that there would be 'strong support' for the retention of some procedure to enable those who promote reorganisation proposals to be able to impose these on a minority. The CLRSG noted the difficulties attending section 425–7 schemes (notably the problem that promoters of schemes have in identifying classes of creditors and members; the requirements for majority in number as well as 75 per cent in value approvals, and the length and inflexibility of processes).

20. Ibid., para. 408.
21. Insolvency Service, *A Review of Company Rescue and Business Reconstruction Mechanisms*, Report by the Review Group (DTI, 2000) ('IS 2000') para. 43. On the possibility of adding a moratorium to s. 425 schemes of arrangements, the CLRSG (*Final Report*, 2001, para. 13.11) recommended further DTI consideration. The Financial Services and Markets Act 2000 (s. 360) introduces the prospect of an administration order procedure for insurance companies and this might detract from use of schemes of arrangement. If, however, an interim moratorium was introduced into the s. 425 scheme of arrangement this would offer a vehicle for companies in difficulty but not technically insolvent companies, which at present cannot take advantage of administration or CVA mechanisms: see Milman, 'Schemes of Arrangement: Their Continuing Role', p. 146.
22. Cork Report, para. 417.

The CLRSG's Final Report of 2001 favoured, as noted, a definition of 'class' based on the approach taken in *Re BTR plc*.[23] It also advocated dropping the requirement that approvals at meetings be given by a majority in number as well as 75 per cent in value of creditors or members or classes.[24] Regarding the latter point, the CLRSG had argued that in many modern listed companies shareholders consisted to such a great extent of nominees that the decision of the true owners 'bears little or no relation to whether or not a majority in number is attained'.[25] No other meetings of members of a company, the Committee pointed out, required a majority other than by reference to value or voting powers.

Looking more broadly at reforms to section 425 procedures, there is a strong case for contending that the procedures for schemes of arrangement should be modelled along the lines of those relating to CVAs so that the class meeting regime as presently set up should be replaced with a statutory framework of meetings in combination with remedial powers to challenge the process by parties who are able to demonstrate that they have suffered prejudice – as per the Insolvency Act 1986 section 6 provisions on CVAs. Improvements in the transparency of the CVA process (as discussed below) should be applied to schemes of arrangement as should the CVA model of moratorium. Adopting this revised procedure for schemes of arrangement would offer a cheaper and quicker route to approval than mechanisms involving the court in routine approvals and decision-making on the procedural requirements of individual corporate circumstances. Cork, indeed, doubted whether 'painstaking perusal of documents by court officials with little or no experience of commerce or finance provides any real protection for creditors or contributories'.[26] There would be efficiency gains without material losses in fairness or accountability. As for the requirement of a numerical as well as a 75 per cent by value majority, the argument in favour of the existing rule is that this serves to limit the ability of creditors with large claims to impose their wills on their smaller creditor brethren. A further consideration is that if the schemes of arrangement process is streamlined so as to involve lower levels of court scrutiny and, if it continues to differ from the CVA by its non-reliance on the independent IP, there is a case for retaining small creditor protections in excess of those applicable to CVA procedures. Small

---

23. [1999] 2 BCLC 675: 'those persons whose rights are not so dissimilar as to make it impossible for them to consult together with a view to acting in their common interest'. See CLRSG, *Final Report*, 2001, para. 13.8.
24. CLRSG, *Final Report*, 2001, para. 13.10.   25. CLRSG, *Completing the Structure*, p. 216.
26. Cork Report, para. 419.

creditors, after all, might rightly complain about their exposed positions if very large creditors were able to agree arrangements with managers under conditions of low scrutiny and little independent oversight and small creditors could only rely on *ex post facto* challenges in court: challenges that might well have to be mounted by parties who are ill-resourced, ill-informed and generally very poorly placed to protect their positions.

Is there a case for retaining the scheme of arrangement process when resort might be made to other procedures such as CVAs and administrations? This is a matter to be returned to once the CVA device has been discussed.

Company voluntary arrangements

The CVA, like administration, owes its origins to the Cork Committee. Cork considered that the law it reviewed was deficient in failing to provide that a company, like an individual, could enter into a binding arrangement with its creditors by a simple procedure that would allow it to organise its debts.[27] Under the then law the company would have to obtain the separate consent of every creditor or else use the slow and cumbersome scheme of arrangement process.[28] The Insolvency Act 1986 sections 1–7 set out a simpler scheme based on the Cork recommendations, and these provisions were hailed as the arrival of a new 'rescue culture' in English insolvency procedures.[29] The Insolvency Act 1986 provides that the directors of a company can take the initiative in setting up a voluntary arrangement, though the first steps can be taken by the liquidator or the administrator if the company is being wound up or is in administration. It is not necessary for the company to be 'insolvent' or 'unable to pay its debts' for the procedure to be used. The directors may nominate an IP to act in relation to the CVA and may make a proposal for consideration by a meeting of the company's members and creditors. It is common for the directors to produce the proposal with the assistance of a licensed IP. The person nominated to act in a CVA as a trustee or supervisor must, within twenty-eight days[30] of notice of the proposal for a CVA, report to the court, stating whether, in

---

27. Cork Report, paras. 400–3.
28. See Companies Act 1985 ss. 425–7 (formerly Companies Act 1948 ss. 206–8), a scheme of compromise or arrangement; Companies Act 1985 s. 582 (formerly Companies Act 1948 s. 287), a scheme of liquidation and reconstruction; or Companies Act 1985 s. 601 (formerly Companies Act 1948 s. 306), a 'binding arrangement'.
29. M. Phillips, *The Administration Procedure and Creditors' Voluntary Arrangements* (Centre for Commercial Law Studies, QMW, London, 1996) p. 7.
30. Or longer if the court allows: Insolvency Act 1986 s. 2(2).

his opinion, meetings of the company and creditors should be summoned to consider the proposal.[31] The proposal needs to be approved by 75 per cent of creditors voting in person or by proxy by reference to the value of their claims. It also requires the approval of 50 per cent in value of the members/shareholders present at a shareholders' meeting. If approved[32] the scheme becomes operative and binding upon the company and all of its creditors who had notice of the meeting.[33] The scheme even binds those creditors who did not approve the proposal. The scheme is administered by a supervisor, usually the person who was the nominee,[34] who must be a qualified IP, and a CVA operates under the aegis of the court but without the need for court involvement[35] unless there is a disagreement requiring judicial resolution.

What a CVA does not do within the terms of section 4 of the Insolvency Act 1986 is affect, without agreement, the rights of secured creditors of the company to enforce their securities: meetings shall not approve any proposals or modifications that interfere with such enforcement rights except with the concurrence of the creditor concerned.[36] Similarly, company or creditors' meetings cannot approve proposals or modifications providing for the paying of preferential debts other than in priority to non-preferential debts or other than equally with other preferential debts.[37]

Nor did the Insolvency Act 1986 provide for a general moratorium and a period of protection during which the company can draw up and consider an arrangement.[38] A moratorium could only be achieved under the Act by combining a proposal for a CVA with an application to the court for the

---

31. Where the nominee is not the liquidator or administrator he must also state in his report whether, in his opinion, the proposed CVA has 'a reasonable prospect of being approved and implemented': Insolvency Act 2000 Sched. 2, para. 3.

32. Where there is a conflict between a creditors' meeting decision to approve a proposal and a shareholders' meeting decision, the creditors' meeting decision prevails, subject to a shareholders' right to challenge by application to the court: Insolvency Act 2000 Sched. 2, para. 5.

33. Unknown creditors (who would have been entitled to claim) are also bound if they come to light after the CVA is completed: Insolvency Act 2000 Sched. 2, paras. 6 and 7. On whether parties excluded from voting at a creditors' meeting are bound by a CVA (a question answered in the negative) see *Re TBL Realisations plc* (20 March 2001), *CCH Company Law Newsletter*, 2 May 2001, pp. 7–8.

34. Insolvency Act 1986 s. 7(2).

35. See the Insolvency Act 2000 Sched. 2, para. 3 for amendments to the circumstances in which the court may replace a nominee (i.e. for failure to submit a report; death or where impracticable or inappropriate for nominee to continue to act).

36. Insolvency Act 1986 s. 4(3).

37. The Insolvency Act 1986 Part I contains provisions obliging preferential creditors to accept a decision made by a majority of them even if passed in a separate class meeting. This contrasts with the Companies Act 1985 s. 425.

38. This contrasts with the 'interim order' available in the case of insolvent individuals under the Insolvency Act 1986 ss. 252–4.

appointment of an administrator.[39] This would constitute a complex and expensive procedure. The introduction of a CVA moratorium, as will be seen below, was the major change effected by the Insolvency Act 2000.

The CVA as efficient and effective rescue mechanism

If a CVA is to lead to rescue rather than liquidation it needs to achieve a number of results.[40] First, the business needs to generate cash profits that are sufficient to pay off past debts and deal with ongoing liabilities. Second, the credit control procedures of the company must be effective enough to avoid such an accumulation of bad debts as is likely to prejudice the recovery. Third, there will need to be a corporate strategy, implementable through the CVA proposal, that will lead to financial survival by taking all necessary steps, such as disposals of non-core activities or assets where appropriate. In order to achieve these results, a further requirement is likely to be directorial commitment and motivation. Enterprising directors will often possess incentives to leave a troubled company for greener corporate pastures, especially if they have no equity interest or do not require the business to succeed in order to protect their income. A CVA, accordingly, may need to create incentives for good directors to see the rescue through.

A number of difficulties will face the proponents of a CVA. Suppliers will often be reluctant to continue normal trading with the company and such suppliers, as well as main creditors, will have to be persuaded to support the CVA. Banks with fixed charges over book debts (i.e. debts owed to the company by other parties) will often have to be persuaded to allow the proceeds of those debts to be used to finance ongoing trading. This is because a troubled firm's book debts very often provide most of the potential income from which ongoing trading can be financed. The omnipresent danger is that a floating charge holder may appoint an administrative receiver, and those putting forward CVA proposals may often be suspected by creditors of using the CVA as a device that will allow the management to set up a phoenix operation in order to effect a transfer of the business and its assets and leave creditors empty handed. A further suspicion formerly may have been that, since a CVA did not involve a report on the directors' conduct, the arrangement was being used to avoid an investigation.[41]

---

39. Insolvency Act 1986 s. 8(3)(b).
40. See, for example, J. Alexander, 'CVAs: The New Legislation' (1999) *Insolvency Bulletin* 5.
41. See now Insolvency Act 2000 Sched. 2 para. 10: nominee required to report suspected offences to the Secretary of State. (See also Sched. 2, paras. 8 and 12 regarding false declarations by directors.)

Similarly, CVAs will rule out charges of wrongful trading on a subsequent liquidation[42] and directors' motives for seeking a CVA may be called into question for this reason.

The uptake of CVAs has been disappointingly low since 1986. In recent years the number of CVAs has approximated to the number of administrations. In 1999 there were 475 CVAs (and 440 administrator appointments) compared to 14,280 liquidations (compulsory and voluntary). In a series of reports[43] the DTI has reviewed the reasons why CVAs have not proved popular and the IS has played a central role in developing the reform proposals that were implemented with the Insolvency Act 2000.

Many of the reasons for the non-use of CVAs overlap with the reasons for the low resort to administration orders that were considered in the last chapter. Cost has been a material factor. Research has suggested that for very small companies the CVA may be too expensive a procedure to exploit.[44] In one survey only 8 per cent of companies undergoing CVA processes had turnover of less than £100,000 in the last financial year.[45] The DTI's 1993 Consultative Document included in its list of 'barriers to the use of CVA provisions': the secured creditor's right to appoint a receiver; the directors' lack of knowledge and IP's lack of experience of the provisions; fear by directors of provisions connected with the Insolvency Act 1986 and supervised by IPs; and rescues being attempted too late. Some of these barriers could nevertheless be reduced in effect, said the DTI. The lack of knowledge of directors could be countered by awareness campaigns and education, and directors' fears of insolvency processes might be responded to by placing rescue provisions in companies' statutes rather than in insolvency legislation, or by relabelling IPs as 'rescue consultants'. The lateness of rescue efforts could be remedied by improving directors' use of financial information and by raising the consciousness of auditors and non-insolvency advisors to make them more aware of, and more likely to recommend, rescue processes.[46]

Other barriers to use were, however, particularly severe in relation to CVAs. A major problem was lack of finance to fund corporate operations

---

42. Insolvency Act 1986 s. 214. See ch. 15 below.

43. DTI/IS, *CVAs and Administration Orders: A Consultative Document* (October 1993) ('DTI 1993'); DTI/IS, *Revised Proposals for a New CVA Procedure* (April 1995) ('DTI 1995'); Insolvency Service, *A Review of Company Rescue and Business Reconstruction Mechanisms*, Interim Report (DTI, September 1999) ('IS 1999'); Insolvency Service, *A Review of Company Rescue and Business Reconstruction Mechanisms, Report by the Review Group* (DTI, 2000) ('IS 2000').

44. See D. Milman and F. Chittenden, *Corporate Rescue: CVAs and the Challenge of Small Companies*, ACCA Research Report 44 (ACCA, London, 1995).

45. Ibid.   46. DTI 1993, p. 20.

during CVAs. Banks tended to act cautiously in consideration of their own shareholders' interests and in fear of 'throwing good money after bad'.[47] A number of tax considerations could also make CVAs an unattractive option, with preferential claims having to be paid in full and Crown creditors having to consider the revenue implications of agreeing to the proposed terms of a CVA. Similarly, the possibility of a continued right of distress (without need for court leave) during a CVA was reported by the DTI to be a cause of some concern.[48]

Foremost amongst the difficulties special to the CVAs under the Insolvency Act 1986 was, however, the absence of a moratorium. Without such protection it was difficult to prevent individual creditors from instituting enforcement actions against the company during the first stages of a CVA when negotiations were taking place. The DTI suggested that an immediate moratorium would be useful in allowing discussions to take place between the company, major creditors and secured lenders. It would also allow the company to carry on trading without facing such threats as landlord distraints or winding-up petitions or repossessions of goods under hire purchase or leasing contracts.[49] The arguments ranged against the moratorium, however, were that it is a device open to abuse by directors of companies that have no chance of turnaround and that it tends simply to prolong agonies, dissipate more assets and make realisations less efficient.

In 1993 the DTI concluded that on balance there would be advantages in introducing a moratorium to take effect on the filing in court by the directors of an intention to set up a CVA together with a consent to act by the nominee, but only if the moratorium was additional to the existing CVA procedure and involved an appropriate level of supervision.[50] It was proposed that the moratorium should be advertised, should last twenty-eight days and should bind all creditors. Any extension of a moratorium would require approval from a meeting of all creditors and should not bring the total duration beyond three months (save exceptionally to six months with court leave).

The 1993 proposals went to consultation and the DTI reported two years later that a 'broad consensus' had favoured a short moratorium for

---

47. Ibid., p. 15. On distributing moneys held by CVA supervisors once the company goes into liquidation see *Re Maple Environmental Services Ltd* [2000] BCC 93; *Re Brelec Installation Ltd, The Times*, 18 April 2000 (noted by S. Frieze at (2000) 13 *Insolvency Intelligence* 69–71).

48. DTI 1993, p. 23.

49. DTI 1993, p. 11. On landlords' right to peaceable re-entry see pp. 290–1 above.

50. So that companies which would be adversely affected by answering a stay on creditors' rights could take the more private and informal actions already available and that the existing CVA procedure would remain in place as an exit route for administration (DTI 1993, p. 12).

rescue purposes. The banks and others had opposed the suspension of their rights to appoint a receiver, but the DTI suggested that such a suspension was required in appropriate circumstances for the sake of rescue.[51] A proposed new CVA procedure was presented and aimed 'to make company rescue simpler, cheaper and more accessible, particularly for the smaller company'.[52] The key elements of the rescue procedure were the twenty-eight-day-moratorium, the continuation of management control of the company (but subject to supervision, a restriction on the disposal of assets and penalties for abuse of the rules on disposal) and the binding of the moratorium on all creditors, including secured creditors. Floating charge holders would be required to give five days' notice of their intention to appoint an administrative receiver, though this notice could be abridged with company consent or court leave.[53] During the moratorium a resolution might be passed or order made for winding up the company and assets subject to fixed or crystallised floating charges could not be disposed of without either the consent of the charge holder or the court's approval. The CVA would bind not merely all creditors but also all shareholders.

Reform

In February 2000 the Insolvency Bill was introduced into Parliament. It received Royal Assent on 30 November 2000.[54] Consistently with the DTI's proposals, the Insolvency Act 2000 allowed the directors of an 'eligible' company to obtain a moratorium when proposing a CVA under Part I of the Insolvency Act 1986 (Insolvency Act 2000 s. 1). A company is eligible under the Insolvency Act 2000, Schedule 1, para. 3 if, in the year before filing for a moratorium or the prior financial year, it has satisfied two or more of the requirements for constituting a small company under section 247(3) of the Companies Act 1985. This means that moratoria will only be available to companies with at least two of the following requirements: a turnover of not over £2.8 million per annum; less than fifty employees; and a balance sheet total which does not exceed £104 million.[55] These are

---

51. DTI 1995, p. 2.   52. Ibid.

53. During the five working days notice period the company must not dispose of assets other than in the ordinary course of business unless the court grants leave (DTI 1995, p. 4).

54. For comment see A. Smith and M. Neill, 'The Insolvency Act 2000' (2001) 17 IL&P 84.

55. Certain companies are not eligible for moratoria under Sched. 1, para. 2. These include, *inter alia*, insurance companies, certain banks, companies which are parties to market contracts and any company whose property is subject to a market charge or collateral security charge: see further Insolvency Act 2000 Sched. A1, paras. 2–4.

very small companies indeed: the current definition of small and medium-sized enterprises (SMEs) covers small companies with up to 200 employees and medium-sized companies with up to 500 employees. It can be argued that if moratoria are useful to small companies they should be of benefit to all companies.[56] In 1995 the DTI stated that the CVA procedure's time limits of five days to assess the CVA's viability and twenty-eight days to call a meeting of creditors had been designed with small companies in mind, but there was 'no reason why larger companies should be prohibited from filing for a moratorium'.[57] The Insolvency Act 2000 leaves open the possibility of extending the moratorium to larger companies by providing that the Secretary of State may promulgate regulations to modify the terms of eligibility for a moratorium.[58] One reason why eligibility might be extended arises from the vulnerability of the current rules to abuse. As the Law Society pointed out in its comments on the Insolvency Bill 2000,[59] a company might have an incentive to arrange its affairs so that it meets the requirements for being a small company in order to gain the protection of a moratorium for a CVA.

A company may not file for a moratorium if an administration order is in force; it is being wound up; an administrative receiver has been appointed; a CVA has effect; there is a provisional liquidator; a moratorium has been in force in the prior twelve months; or a CVA has ended prematurely and, in the twelve months before filing, a section 5(3)(a) order has been made.[60] Before a moratorium is obtained the directors will submit to the nominee the proposed term of the CVA and a statement of company affairs. The nominee will then indicate to the directors, in a statement, his opinion on whether the CVA has a reasonable prospect of approval and implementation; whether the company is likely to have sufficient funds to carry on its business; and whether meetings of the company and creditors should be summoned to consider the proposed CVA. Filing for a moratorium is carried out by the directors and involves submission to the court of a statement of proposals and of company affairs. The court also receives,

---

56. See Alexander, 'CVAs: The New Legislation', p. 8.
57. DTI 1995, p. 25.
58. In commenting on the Trade and Industry Committee Report on the draft Insolvency Bill, the Government said that 'the results of experience to date should be a significant factor in any decision to extend eligibility for a moratorium': see Trade and Industry Committee, Fourth Special Report, *Government Observations on the First and Second Reports from the Trade and Industry Committee* (session 1999–2000) HC 237.
59. Law Society Company Law Committee, *Comments on the Insolvency Bill*, March 2000, No. 396, p. 4.
60. Insolvency Act 2000 Sched. 1, para. 4.

inter alia, a nominee statement. The moratorium commences on filing the appropriate documents and lasts for twenty-eight days.[61]

The effects of the moratorium are to offer protection against petitions for winding up or administration orders, meetings of the company, winding-up resolutions, appointments of receivers and other steps 'to enforce any security over the company's property or to repossess goods in the company's possession under any hire purchase agreement except with the leave of the court'.[62] No other proceeding or execution or legal process or distress can be commenced, continued or levied against the company except by court leave nor can a landlord forfeit the lease of a company's premises by means of peaceable re-entry.[63]

Security granted during the moratorium is only enforceable if at the time of granting there were reasonable grounds for believing it would benefit the company.[64] The company is not allowed to obtain credit of over £250 during a moratorium unless the creditor has been informed of it.[65] Disposals of company property and payments of debts and liabilities existing prior to the moratorium are only permissible if there are reasonable grounds for believing that such actions will benefit the company or there was approval by a meeting of the company and its creditors (or the nominee in absence of such 'moratorium committees').[66] Property of the company subject to security or held in possession under hire purchase agreement can be disposed of with court leave or consent of the security holder/owner of the goods.[67] In the case of dispositions of property subject to a security which, as created, was a floating charge, the security holder's priority will not change regarding property representing the property disposed of.[68]

Where court leave is given as described, this is to be notified by the directors to the Registrar of Companies within fourteen days or liability to a fine results.[69] During the moratorium the nominee is obliged to monitor the company's affairs for the purposes of forming an opinion on whether the proposed CVA has a reasonable prospect of approval and implementation and whether the company is likely to have sufficient funds during the remainder of the moratorium to allow it to carry on its business.[70] The nominee must withdraw his or her consent to act if he or she forms the

---

61. Ibid., para. 8.   62. Ibid., para. 12(1)(g).

63. Ibid., para. 12(1)(h). On peaceable re-entry see P. McCartney, 'Insolvency Procedures and a Landlord's Right of Peaceable Re-entry' (2000) 13 *Insolvency Intelligence* 73 and ch. 9 above.

64. Insolvency Act 2000, Sched. 1, para. 14.   65. Ibid., para. 17.

66. Ibid., paras. 18, 19, 29 and 35.   67. Ibid., para. 20.   68. Ibid., para. 20(4).

69. Ibid., para. 20(9).   70. Ibid., para. 24(1).

opinion that such reasonable prospects of funds are no longer in prospect, if he or she becomes aware that the company was not at the date of filing eligible for a moratorium or if the directors fail to comply with their duty to supply the nominee with information needed to form an opinion on the above matters.[71] On withdrawal of nominee consent, the moratorium ends.

As for challenges to the nominees' actions, any creditor, director or member of the company or other person affected by a moratorium may apply to the court if dissatisfied with an act or omission or decision of the nominee during the moratorium.[72] The court is then empowered to confirm, reverse or modify any nominee decision, give him directions or make such other order as it thinks fit. The acts of directors within the moratorium can be challenged similarly.

The meeting of the company and creditors is to be called by the nominee when he or she thinks fit and these meetings shall decide whether to approve the proposed CVA with or without modifications.[73] Such modification shall not, however, affect the enforcement rights of secured creditors without consent or the priorities or *pari passu* payment of preferential debts.[74] A person entitled to vote at either meeting or the nominee has a right to challenge the CVA in court on the grounds that it unfairly prejudices the interests of the creditor member or contributory of the company; or that there has been a material irregularity in relation to or at either meeting.[75]

Once an approved CVA has taken effect, the person formerly known as the nominee becomes the supervisor of the CVA[76] and any of the company's creditors or other persons dissatisfied by any act, omission or decision of the supervisor may challenge this in court.[77]

What the 2000 Insolvency Act did not do was allow non-IPs or non-authorised persons to act as nominees and supervisors for CVAs[78] or allow the Secretary of State to require notice to be given before the appointment of an administrative receiver. Both of these potential provisions were opposed by the House of Commons Trade and Industry Committee which advocated that they be dropped from the Bill.[79] The Committee was not

---

71. Ibid., para. 25(2).   72. Ibid., para. 26.   73. Ibid., paras. 29–31.
74. Ibid., para. 35(4) and (5).   75. Ibid., para. 38.   76. Ibid., para. 39.
77. Ibid., para. 39(3).
78. The Insolvency Act 2000 s. 4(4) amends the Insolvency Act 1986 s. 389 and means that to act as a supervisor or nominee of a CVA the individual in question must be an IP or a person authorised to act as a supervisor etc. by a body recognised by the Secretary of State for that purpose.
79. Trade and Industry Committee, Second Report from the Trade and Industry Committee (Session 1999–2000) Draft Insolvency Bill, HC 112.

convinced that there was need for legislation to provide in advance 'a weapon to be used should the banks turn nasty in any future recession' and they thought it 'premature' to introduce a notice requirement in advance of the review of the 1997 Bankers' Code which was being undertaken.[80] The banks were particularly vocal in opposing the notice of receivership requirement and the Government dropped the clause from the Bill. The importance of this issue will recede, of course, if the Government implements its 2001 White Paper proposal to restrict the power to appoint a receiver to certain capital market transactions.[81] Reaction to the moratorium was favourable but modest. The Trade and Industry Committee acknowledged that there was 'broad consensus' on the moratorium but noted that this was 'not a panacea for companies in difficulty'.[82]

Achieving a successful rescue may also require that the directors are able to effect advantageous transactions with third parties. Here, however, the terms of the Insolvency Act 2000 create unhelpful uncertainties. Such third parties will be reluctant to deal with the directors if they are not certain that they will be protected from a subsequent failure of the moratorium or a non-approval of the voluntary arrangement. Schedule 1, paragraph 12(2) of the Insolvency Act 2000 suspends section 127 of the Insolvency Act 1986 (which prohibits property dispositions after the commencement of a winding up unless the court has otherwise authorised[83]). It does so where a petition for winding up has been presented before the beginning of the moratorium. The effect is that section 127 will not operate to render void any dispositions of property, transfers of shares or alterations in status of the members of the company during the moratorium. Such dispositions are then governed by the moratorium provisions. Uncertainties arise because there may not be a petition for winding up pending at the date of the start of the moratorium. The Law Society has argued that there should be an express provision confirming that 'the criteria for disposals, payments, charges and other permitted transactions during the moratorium regime fully supplant the criteria for escaping all the "normal" invalidating provisions of the Insolvency Act 1986 and third parties acting in good faith are protected in being party to such

---

80. Ibid., para. 27.
81. See DTI/Insolvency Service, *Productivity and Enterprise: Insolvency – A Second Chance* (Cm 5234, 2001) chapter 2. See also ch. 8 above.
82. Trade and Industry Committee, Second Report, Draft Insolvency Bill, paras. 11 and 12.
83. On the Insolvency Act 1986 s. 127 see L. S. Sealy, 'Company Liquidations: When Should Post-petition Banking Transactions be Avoided?' (2000) 57 CCH *Company Law Newsletter* 1; see further ch. 12 below.

transactions'.[84] If that is not the case, said the Society, there should be pro-visions allowing directors to seek court confirmation that any transactions are valid and proper. A danger is that if such worries are not countered, companies may be encouraged to petition for a winding up immediately before filing for a moratorium in order to protect transactions within the moratorium from being attacked as preferences or transactions at under-value under the Insolvency Act 1986 sections 239 and 238.

Efficiency

Have the Insolvency Act 2000 changes to CVAs produced a rescue regime that is likely to be efficient and effective? Recent figures produced by ICC, the on-line business data provider, suggest that in the majority of instances, CVAs may not prevent corporate failure.[85] ICC tracked the progress of nearly 3,000 troubled companies that survived by obtain-ing creditor backing for a management rescue plan. Of these companies, 63 per cent eventually failed and ICC concluded that although CVAs re-turn more than three times as much money to creditors as liquidation, in most cases the end product of a CVA was likely to be corporate failure.[86] ICC's managing director, moreover, suggested that the steps taken in the Insolvency Act 2000 were not likely to make the CVA more successful as a rescue device. Such figures, however, do not indicate that the business (rather than the company) has a very high failure rate. R3's Ninth Survey of Business Recovery, published in 2001, indicated that where CVAs are used there is a 74 per cent preservation rate.[87]

It remains to be seen whether the protection of a moratorium will im-prove the rescue potential of the CVA. General concerns have been voiced in relation to the role preferential creditors have played in CVA processes, the nominee's scrutiny role, rescue funding, corporate relations with land-lords or utility suppliers, and those who lease the tools of the trade to the company. It should be emphasised, moreover, that the new CVA morato-rium, as now set up, only applies to very small companies and here some

---

84. Law Society Company Law Committee, p. 6.
85. See *Financial Times*, 4 October 1999.
86. The SPI's Eighth Survey revealed that average returns to creditors in liquidations were 18 pence in the pound, in receivership the average return was 37 pence and in CVAs 41 pence. Overall preferential and secured creditors expected to recover 37 per cent of their debts and unsecured creditors 7 per cent. SPI, Eighth Survey, *Company Insolvency in the United Kingdom* (SPI, London, 1999).
87. The SPI Eighth Survey (covering 1997–8) indicated that where CVAs were used, 37 per cent of jobs were saved (receiverships saved 31 per cent, administrations 40 per cent and company voluntary liquidations 11 per cent). The SPI was renamed R3, the Association of Business Recovery Professionals, in January 2000.

particular problems may arise. Nominees, under the Insolvency Act 2000 arrangements, have to be prepared to state in writing at the outset that the CVA has a reasonable prospect of being approved and implemented and also that it is likely to have sufficient funds available during the moratorium to enable it to carry on business.[88] In order to place themselves in a position to make such a statement responsibly, nominees may have to engage in extensive consultations with proposed funders as well as major suppliers and other trading partners. Assurances from such parties will have to be sought and trading projections analysed. The overall effect, it has been suggested, may be that the amount of work involved, and the attendant expenses, will prevent the new CVA procedure from performing as a cost-effective device for smaller companies.[89] The new CVA, moreover, may be further reduced in its attractiveness because the moratorium does not protect the company during the period in which proposals are being developed and a nominee may fear that consulting with creditors before a moratorium comes into effect may trigger their taking precipitate action against the company.

Preferential creditors and CVAs

In the consultations that the IS held in its 1999 Review Group discussion paper on rescue and reconstruction mechanisms the 'most heartfelt' response on CVAs concerned 'the uncommercial attitude of the revenue departments (Inland Revenue and Customs and Excise) to proposals for CVAs'. Consultees urged that the revenue departments' insistence on 100 per cent payment and the time taken to consider proposals frustrated many CVA proposals that unsecured creditors would otherwise approve. Respondents consistently criticised the apparent unwillingness of these departments to deal with CVA proposals on their merits or to take a longer-term view of the prospects of a company's survival. The Review Group recommended that the Inland Revenue (IR) and Customs and Excise should work to develop a more commercial approach to CVAs so that proposals *were* judged on their merits and, where appropriate, less than 100 pence in the pound should be settled on if it was judged that a CVA would offer superior returns.[90]

In order to produce a more consistent and responsive approach to CVA proposals, the Review Group recommended that the two revenue

---

88. See Insolvency Act 2000 Sched. A1, para. 6; Sched. 2, para. 3.
89. See Smith and Neill, 'Insolvency Act 2000', p. 85. R3, the Association of Business Recovery Professionals, also made this argument: see R3, 'The Moratorium Provisions for the Company Voluntary Arrangement Procedure in the Insolvency Bill 2000' (2000) 16 IL&P 77.
90. IS 2000, p. 24.

departments should investigate integrating their work on CVAs, look at the staffing implications of a more responsive approach and consider the need to bring in private sector skills to bear on decisions relating to CVAs and their commercial viability. They should also, said the Review Group, explore with the Insolvency Service how to take a more proactive role in warning directors of the possible consequences of continuing to trade during insolvency and of the possible need for professional advice.

In accordance with these suggestions, the IR and the Customs and Excise set up a Voluntary Arrangements Service (VAS) in Worthing which has been up and running since 2 April 2001. It is managed by the IR on behalf of the Revenue and Customs departments.[91] The stated aims of the VAS are 'to help its customers, to work collaboratively with the private sector and other government departments and to make a full contribution to business rescue by supporting viable businesses through periods of temporary financial difficulty'.[92] To this end, the VAS publishes criteria by which it will judge the acceptability of proposals put to it by troubled companies.[93] Commentators will be sure to examine the work of the VAS closely in forthcoming years and to look for positive signs of rescue-friendly attitudes, notably instances of the revenue departments making concessions on their own debts for the sake of longer-term corporate rescue prospects.

A more radical approach, of course, would be to abolish the Crown's right to be paid as a preferential creditor. On whether this would produce more successful CVAs the Review Group reported a general acceptance that it would, since: 'the larger the dividend that can be proposed to unsecured creditors, and as importantly, the earlier it can be paid to them, the more likely they are to support proposals which would allow the survival of the company'.[94] Abolition of the Crown's preferential status is clearly a step that is consistent with a rescue philosophy and the Government has now proposed to move in this direction.[95]

The nominee's scrutiny role

An advantage of CVA procedure since the Insolvency Act 2000 is that protection from creditors can be achieved without the need to incur the trouble and expense of a court action. The IP who acts as nominee accordingly fulfils an important role in assessing prospects of success and filtering out non-viable proposals. This is a reason for insisting that the nominee be a

---

91. See D. Ellis, 'Inland Revenue and Business Rescue' (2001) *Recovery* (September) pp. 18–19.
92. Ibid, p. 18.
93. The criteria are at: www.inlandrevenue.gov.uk.
94. IS 2000, pp. 25–6. The Review Group added that it would be important that the benefits of abolition should accrue to unsecured creditors and not to the holders of floating charges.
95. White Paper, 2001 (*Productivity and Enterprise*), para. 2.19. See further ch. 13 below.

fully qualified IP, or a person authorised to act as a nominee or supervisor by a body recognised by the Secretary of State.[96] The role is, however, a difficult one since nominees rely heavily on information supplied to them by the directors and they will not have the power or time to conduct thorough investigations. One commentator described the predicament: 'If too much reliance is placed on the nominee as a filter it will inevitably lead to escalation in cost as nominees seek to protect their own position by "due diligence", or become conservative in recommending a CVA as viable; the result is that the proposed cheap and speedy procedure aimed at smaller companies will become prohibitively expensive and slow.'[97]

The Insolvency Act 2000 demands that when the nominee submits to the directors a statement[98] which indicates an opinion on, *inter alia*, whether the CVA has a reasonable prospect of approval and implementation, the nominee is 'entitled to rely on the information submitted to him' by the directors in their CVA proposal 'unless he has reason to doubt its accuracy'.[99] The Law Society cautioned that there was a 'clear danger' in the nominee simply relying on the information supplied by directors and the Society drew a contrast with procedures for an administration order. The latter procedure demands that the nominee satisfy himself on various matters and there is a provision for court scrutiny of the IP's report. With a CVA there is no court scrutiny of the nominee's statement and there is no requirement that he should have taken steps to check the accuracy of any information acted upon.[100] Concern has also been raised that for a nominee to be able to give the statement referred to above, he will need to be involved 'in the day to day management of the business and to have carried out a significant investigation'.[101] This could prove expensive. Concern was also expressed that the nominee will have significant responsibilities without authority in that he has no control over the assets which he would have if he were a provisional liquidator or other office holder, nor does he control the actions of the directors during the period of the moratorium.[102]

A further worry that was expressed by the Law Society perhaps evidenced a low opinion of the professional standards of IPs. The Society said: 'We are also concerned that companies will be encouraged to shop around amongst those authorised to act as nominees until they can

---

96. Insolvency Act 2000 s. 4.   **97.** Brown, *Corporate Rescue*, pp. 663–4.
98. Under Sched. 1, para. 6(2).   **99.** Insolvency Act 2000 Sched. 1, para. 6(3).
100. Law Society Company Law Committee, p. 5.
101. Alexander, 'CVAs: The New Legislation', pp. 8–9.   **102.** Ibid.

locate one prepared to provide an appropriate statement in order to secure a moratorium. This concern was shared by the Select Committee.'[103] The Society added that such loopholes created the potential for a voluntary arrangement to go badly wrong, bringing the whole process into disrepute amongst creditors.[104]

In defence of the Insolvency Act 2000 regime it could, however, be argued that nominee scrutiny, even if erring on the defensive side, is liable to be quicker and cheaper than resort to court and that the twenty-eight-day limit of the moratorium should restrict some of the dangers of abuse that are associated with the somewhat indefinite terms of the United States Chapter 11 moratorium.[105]

Rescue funding

A fundamental challenge for troubled companies is that of securing new funds in order to finance continuing activities while a CVA is being negotiated and in order to provide for the longer-term survival of corporate operations. The availability of longer-term financing will crucially affect the success or failure of the CVA since creditors are unlikely to agree to the company's proposals without the prospect of secure funding.[106] The SPI survey for 1997–8 suggested that in 43 per cent of cases the biggest barrier to turnaround was lack of appropriate finance[107] and R3's 1998–9 survey indicated that in one in five cases of companies with a turnover of over £5 million 'the main factor preventing a more positive outcome was the inability to secure funding'.[108]

In most cases it is the company's own bank that has to be persuaded that there is a viable future for the company and generally the IPs guiding the CVA will attempt to secure the bank's approval for proposals before other creditors are approached. Other sources of funds are also available. The DTI sponsors a Small Firms Loan Guarantee scheme which provides a guarantee for medium-term loans of two to seven years. Such funds cannot be used to pay existing debts but can provide new finance for eligible companies whose CVA is in place. The maximum amount available for an established business (one that has traded for two years or more) is £250,000[109]

---

103. Law Society Company Law Committee, pp. 4–5.

104. Ibid., p. 5.   **105.** See ch. 6 above.

106. DTI 1993, p. 5. On the importance of funding see IS 2000, pp. 33–5.

107. IS 1999, p. 12.

108. R3, Ninth Survey of Business Recovery in the UK. See also statement by R3, 'R3 Calls for Government to Commit to Action on Business Rescue' (2001: see r3.org.uk), that the 'most intractable problem in business rescue today is the provision of post-rescue finance'.

109. 2001 figures.

with a level of guarantee from the DTI to the lender of 85 per cent. Other financing options include new equity funding and the provision of funds by the firm's managers.

Short-term funding will generally be sought, as noted, through negotiation with the company's main lender (usually the bank); through negotiating limited credit periods with major suppliers; or by sale of assets. Negotiating supplier credit periods is, however, a fraught process for directors because such trading or credit may expose them to liabilities for fraudulent or wrongful trading[110] and it may involve further dissipation of the assets charged to creditors. Many such steps will in practice have to be carried out with the approval of secured lenders because the spending of money or selling of assets will reduce the security cover of such lenders.

Further options for enhancing funding during a moratorium might be offered by provision for super-priority or by changes to the rules on fixed securities on book debts. The issues surrounding such potential changes have been discussed in chapter 9 and will not be rehearsed here.

Landlords, lessors of tools and utilities suppliers

The rights of peaceable re-entry by landlords have been discussed in the last chapter and that debate will not be repeated. As for those who lease tools to the company and utilities suppliers, the Insolvency Act 2000 Schedule 1 provisions on the moratorium state that during the moratorium no steps may be taken 'to repossess goods in the company's possession under any hire purchase agreement except with the leave of the court. No other proceeding and no execution or other legal process may be commenced or continued and no distress may be levied against the company or its property except with the leave of the court.'[111]

This provision is based on sections 11(3)(c) (the administration order moratorium) and 10(4) of the Insolvency Act 1986 which, together with subsequent case law, make it clear that the moratorium on enforcement applies to goods supplied on hire purchase or similar agreements (which include conditional sale agreements, chattel leasing agreements and retention of title agreements).[112]

Utility supplies to troubled companies are protected at present by section 233 of the Insolvency Act 1986 which governs the situations in which an administration order is made, an administrative receiver or provisional

---

110. Insolvency Act 1986 s. 213 and s. 214; see further ch. 15 below.
111. Insolvency Act 2000 Sched. 1, para. 12(g), (h).
112. Hire purchase agreements and conditional sale agreements are defined in the Consumer Credit Act 1974 s. 189(1) (see Insolvency Act 1986 s. 436); and chattel leasing agreements and ROT agreements: are defined in the Insolvency Act 1986 s. 251.

liquidator is appointed, a CVA is approved by meetings of the company and of creditors, or the company goes into liquidation. In these circumstances where the office holder (administrator, administrative receiver and so on) requests that gas, electricity, water or telecommunications supplies be continued, the supplier may make it a condition of supply that the office holder personally guarantees payment of supplies, but that supplier shall not make it a condition of supply (or effectively make it a condition of supply) that any outstanding charges be paid. In the case of a CVA moratorium it would be appropriate to make such a provision effective at the time at which the CVA moratorium comes into force (when relevant documents are filed or lodged with the court).[113]

Expertise

The IP's expertise in and orientation to rescue has already been discussed[114] but consideration should be given to the CVA procedure and whether this is conducive to the making of informed and expert judgments on corporate rescues. Research into the operation of CVA procedures in the 1990s suggests that the expertise of IPs in operating CVA procedures may vary enormously. Flood and his colleagues found that knowledge about CVA processes was very highly concentrated within the body of IPs: 'three individuals' names arose time and time again'. These were the key players and other IPs tended to have very modest experience or knowledge concerning CVA procedures.[115] Other involved professionals moreover tended to have even less expertise. Levy Gee found in 1994 that bankers, accountants and solicitors in general had a 'surprisingly low' knowledge of CVAs with only 16 per cent of accountants claiming to have a good working knowledge.[116]

In the case of IPs there is no great financial incentive to develop CVA skills. One IP made the point to Flood *et al.* with the words: 'I get £25,000 over two years for a CVA whereas in receiverships you get £75,000 in six months.' Such factors favour wide variations in expertise. The few specialist IPs play a very highly expert role in CVAs whereas many practitioners supply a vastly less informed service.

---

113. Insolvency Act 2000 Sched. 1, paras. 7 and 8.
114. See ch. 5 above.
115. J. Flood, R. Abbey, E. Skordaki and P. Aber, *The Professional Restructuring of Corporate Rescue: Company Voluntary Arrangements and the London Approach*, ACCA Research Report 45 (ACCA, London, 1995) pp. 17–18. Note, however, that between 1990 and 1998 there was a tenfold increase in the use of CVAs, from around 50 to 500: see SPI Surveys for 1990 and 1998. This may encourage wider experience.
116. L. Gee, *How Effective are Voluntary Arrangements?* (Levy Gee, London, 1994).

If attention is focused, however, on the CVA process as a whole and its ability to deliver expert decisions, it should be remembered that this is not a procedure in which an IP lays down a judgment from on high. A CVA tends to involve an extended process of negotiation between the IP, the directors, the banks and other creditors. With this point in mind, a key issue is whether this is a negotiating process that is able to take on board the relevant information and produce sound decisions on rescue. One difficulty here may stem from the widespread ignorance of professional lawyers, bankers and accountants concerning CVAs. A second problem may centre on the need to generate trust within CVA procedures.[117] An important role of the IP is to develop such trust between different groups of creditors and the company directors. Without mutual confidence even the best-informed, most astute commercial judgments will come to nothing. Of central importance here is faith in the competence of the management team and its ability to turn fortunes around.[118] It follows that the expertise built into the CVA procedure will depend to a great extent on the skill not merely of the IP but also of the company's directors. Nor can the part to be played by the major creditors be ignored: these are the parties who have to be convinced that a CVA will succeed. The bankers have to possess the expertise in rescues that allows them to distinguish between good and less convincing CVA proposals.

Above all else then, the CVA demands a co-ordination of expertise. It is a procedure that might be thought to conduce to such co-ordination since the CVA provides a forum for discussion of the rescue scheme strengths and weaknesses. The quality of that discussion may, however, be suboptimal for a number of reasons. First, there may be conflict of interest between creditors of different classes who bear different levels of risk and who accordingly see proposed solutions in different lights. These conflicts may produce disagreements and conversations at cross-purposes. Second, the company's directors may not see solutions in the same light as other involved parties because they have different perspectives or interests. They may, for instance, be reluctant to accede to the IP's and creditors' wishes to install new directors because the directors' estimations of their own value to the company may be higher than those of the IPs and creditors. Third, such differences of interest may reduce levels of trust below optimal levels

---

117. The publicity generated by the Insolvency Service's Working Party Reports of 1999 and 2000 and the Insolvency Act 2000 will surely, however, lead to greater awareness of rescue mechanisms, including CVAs: see Alexander, 'CVAs: The New Legislation', p. 9.
118. See Flood *et al.*, *Professional Restructuring*, p. 19.

and this may affect information flows: when, for instance, directors conceal facts from the IP because they fear some adverse reaction such as replacement. Finally, the standard of participation in the negotiation may be low because the key players are not fully trained in CVA procedures or are not fully in touch with the company's state of affairs.

What can be done to improve expertise? If the CVA is seen as a broad-based negotiation it follows that it is not enough to improve the knowledge of IPs concerning CVAs. Other involved actors have to be brought up to speed also. Steps designed to improve performance here might involve training all company directors in basic insolvency procedures and the provision of similar training for bankers. Within the banking industry attention might also be given to the provision of a continuing expertise in insolvency at the appropriate organisational level. Over and above such sectoral training it may be appropriate to develop interdisciplinary skills so that accountants, bankers and lawyers can work on rescues together. As Flood *et al.* comment: 'It is worth reflecting that professional relationships across jurisdictional boundaries are crucial to the satisfactory resolution of something like the CVA.'[119]

Accountability and fairness

Information and transparency are vital prerequisites of accountability within CVAs. CVAs, as noted, only come into effect (under the Insolvency Act 1986 s. 5) when proposals have been approved by both the meeting of the company and the meeting of the creditors. Creditors who are considering the proposal put forward after discussions between the IP and the directors need to be given information on such matters as: the assets and valuations; projections of income on future contracts; cost savings and ongoing expenses; whether suppliers and customers will remain loyal; potential repossessions/forced sales; whether third party funds are available; the commitment of the directors; the positions of preferential creditors such as the IR and HM Customs and Excise;[120] and potential claims against the company.[121] The IP is obliged to take reasonable steps to be satisfied that assets and liabilities are not materially different from the position outlined in the proposal; that the proposal will be implemented as represented and that there is no 'already manifest yet unavoidable unfairness' in admitting, rejecting or valuing voting

---

119. Ibid., p. 23.   120. See ch. 13 below; White Paper, 2001, para. 2.19.
121. See R. Gregory, *Review of Company Rescue and Business Reconstruction Mechanisms: Rescue Culture or Avoidance Culture?* (CCH, Bicester, December 1999) p. 15.

claims.[122] Here much depends on the skill of the IP and his/her commitment to giving a full picture to the company and creditors. Guidelines on
best practice are made available to IPs by the Society of Practitioners in Insolvency.[123] There are, moreover, incentives to inform: as has been pointed
out, the IP's role in a CVA demands that central importance be given to the
creation of trust among affected parties.[124]

The process of holding the IP to account demands not merely that information be made available but that this can be used. For a creditor this
will mean that the creditors' meeting has to be attended or a proxy is
used. (Under the Insolvency Rules 1986 (Rule 1.17(1)) every creditor 'who
was given notice of the creditors meeting' is entitled to vote at the meeting.) There is no procedure, though, for advertising for creditors of whom
the company may not be aware at the time of summoning the meeting.
(The DTI had advocated a requirement to advertise the moratorium in
the *Gazette* and a newspaper in its 1995 paper.[125]) Under the Insolvency
Act 2000, however, advertising is called for when the moratorium comes
into force.[126] A CVA approved by a creditors' meeting, nevertheless, binds
all parties who are entitled to vote at the meeting (whether or not they
were present or represented) or who would have been so entitled had they
been given notice. Protection for unknown creditors is provided for in
Schedule A1, para. 38 of the Insolvency Act 2000, which gives parties who
have not been given notice of the creditors' meeting a power to apply to the
court to challenge a decision of the meeting on the grounds of unfair prejudice or material irregularity. They are given twenty-eight days from the
date of their awareness that the meeting has taken place to make such an
application to challenge. The court, if satisfied of the basis of such a challenge, can revoke or suspend the decision but can also direct the summoning of further meetings to consider revised CVA proposals. This provision
substitutes for the DTI's 1995 proposal that a further meeting of creditors
should be convened where the effect of unknown claims would be to reduce the payment to creditors by 10 per cent or more. It is arguable that an
advertising requirement would be fair to 'unknown' creditors likely to be

122. Ibid., pp. 15–16; *Greystoke* v. *Hamilton-Smith* [1997] BPIR 24, 28. It is a criminal offence for
a past or present officer of a company to make 'any false representation' or commit any other
fraud to obtain creditors' or members' approval: Insolvency Rules 1986 (SI 1986 No. 1925)
r. 1.30. An 'officer' here includes a shadow director (r. 130(2)). See also Insolvency Act 2000
Sched. A1, paras. 41 and 42; Sched. 2, paras. 8 and 12.
123. See SPI Statement of Insolvency Practice No. 3.
124. See Flood *et al.*, *Professional Restructuring*, pp. 5, 20–2.
125. DTI 1995, p. 22.   126. Insolvency Act 2000 Sched. 1, para. 10.

bound by the CVA; but it would enhance overall transparency and conduce to effective creditor communications.

Holding the directors to account may be as important in a CVA as the appropriate accountability of IPs. During a moratorium the directors will continue to manage the affairs of the company and secured creditors may fear that secured assets may be dissipated, with the possible result that if the CVA is not approved there will be little left over to enforce the security.[127] Some respondents to the DTI's 1993 proposals (notably IPs and lenders) expressed concern at the low level of monitoring involved in the CVA moratorium, but the 1995 revised proposals suggested that levels of supervision by the IP nominee would 'very much depend on the company's circumstances'.[128] The level of supervision should be settled before the nominee agrees to act, said the DTI, and it might include the nominee having full access to the company's records and premises. Variations in supervision levels were called for because the level of supervision appropriate for a company with a large number of retail outlets operating on a cash basis would differ from that called for in relation to an operation relying on one director serving two or three customers. What there should be, said the Department, was a statutory level of supervision comprising scrutiny of weekly management accounts by the nominee. Further control of directorial activities during the moratorium would be provided for by a series of provisions.[129] First, criminal sanctions and civil penalties would apply to directors who, for example, concealed, removed or destroyed assets and/or records; second, directors would only be able to dispose of assets (other than in the ordinary course of business) with the approval of the nominee and either the court or the creditors' committee; and third, there would be general provisions for creditors and shareholders to apply to the court for relief. The Insolvency Act 2000 duly makes provision for such criminal sanctions,[130] asset dispositions[131] and applications for relief.[132]

The philosophy underlying such control provisions was that directors who were left in control of the troubled company should be strongly aware of their obligations: 'the supervision and regulation of directors' activities and the existence of penalties for non-compliance are thought necessary to provide a very clear signal that abuse of the moratorium period will not be tolerated. It should also allay concerns that creditors may have about

127. Brown, *Corporate Rescue*, p. 666.   128. DTI 1995, p. 16.   129. See DTI 1995, p. 17.
130. See Insolvency Act 2000 Sched. 1, paras. 41–2.
131. Ibid., para. 18.   132. Ibid., para. 38.

management being left in charge of the company during the moratorium period.'[133]

The fairness of the approval process has been debated with regard to two main issues: whether the approval majority for creditors' meetings is set at the right level and whether shareholders should, through the company meeting, have a power to approve the CVA at all. The creditors' approval majority is set out in Rule 1.19 of the Insolvency Rules 1986 and demands that, to be effective, approvals must be given by a three-quarters majority in value of the creditors present in person or by proxy and voting on the resolution. This rule contrasts with the position for creditors of companies in administration, a simple majority by value of whom is required in order to agree restructuring proposals. The 75 per cent rule, said the DTI, was designed to encourage companies only to enter a moratorium if a successful rescue is likely and to provide an effective bar to unsound proposals being accepted.[134] The requirement was also said to recognise that the decision of the meeting would affect the return to all creditors. In 1999 the IS suggested that a way to promote more use of CVAs would be to change the voting provisions so as to reduce the threshold for acceptance by creditors.[135] Post-consultation, however, the IS doubted whether such a reform would be advisable. It was moved by the argument that lowering the threshold would not necessarily have any significant effect on acceptance levels; and that concerns would be aroused by binding creditors against their will by a simple majority.[136]

The argument that shareholders should not participate in the CVA approvals process through the company meeting can be represented thus: 'The present rules require there to be a meeting of shareholders. This gives them a veto over any CVA. Given that they have no economic interest in the insolvent company that is unjustifiable.'[137] This criticism of shareholder voting contrasts with the approach put forward by the DTI in 1995.[138] The Department argued that shareholders were not usually deprived of their shares when a CVA was proposed and that they should therefore have a right to receive information about the CVA and vote on it with or without modifications. The DTI considered, however, that the decisions of shareholders should not prevail over those of the creditors unless they could show to the court that they were being unfairly prejudiced. The reasoning here was that shareholders should not have any say in whether a CVA

133. DTI 1995, p. 17.   134. DTI 1995, p. 15.   135. IS 1999, p. 11.
136. IS 2000, p. 36.   137. Phillips, 'Administration Procedure', p. 24.
138. DTI 1995, p. 16.

was accepted if they did not have a demonstrable financial interest at the time. The proposal was thus akin to the situation in a liquidation: 'If the company is insolvent the shareholders are in no worse position than if the company were to go into insolvent liquidation rather than enter into a CVA. If, however, the company is saved their shares may begin to reflect real worth.'[139] The proposal to allow the shareholders to go to court on grounds of unfair prejudice was designed to allow shareholders' positions to be taken into account when there was an interest that was being unfairly affected.

The DTI view is preferable to the 'no economic interest' approach in so far as it is difficult to deny the actual and potential interest of a shareholder in the CVA. This is a procedure that does not necessarily commence with the company's insolvency: the directors can propose a CVA prior to insolvency (when shareholders still possess valid interests). What the Insolvency Act 2000 does is to provide that a decision to approve a CVA is effective if taken by both the creditors' and company meetings or the creditors' meeting on its own.[140] Where a CVA is approved it has effect as if made by the company at the creditors' meeting but where a decision of the creditors' meeting differs from one taken by the company meeting a member of the company can apply to the court which may either order the decision of the company rather than the creditors to have effect or make such order as the court thinks fit.[141] A person entitled to vote at either a creditors' or a company meeting has power to challenge a decision in court on the grounds of unfair prejudice or that there has been a material irregularity at either meeting.[142] If the court is satisfied on the 'unfair prejudice' or 'material irregularity' grounds, it is given powers of revocation, suspension or direction.[143] Provisions, accordingly, give primacy to the creditors' meeting but do allow creditors with interests that are liable to be prejudiced by a CVA to challenge the approval of the CVA or the process followed in such approval.

It might be questioned whether there is any purpose in providing for a members' meeting when the CVA can be approved by the creditors' meeting on its own.[144] Such a meeting does, however, provide shareholders with a forum and a route to information and discussion that would otherwise be lacking. Such a meeting, moreover, might, in some situations, alert

---

139. Ibid., p. 16.   140. Insolvency Act 2000 Sched. 1, para. 36(2).
141. Ibid., para. 36. See also Sched. 2, para. 5 regarding non-moratorium CVAs.
142. Insolvency Act 2000 Sched. 1, para. 38.   143. Ibid.
144. Phillips, 'Administration Procedure', p. 24.

shareholders to issues of potential prejudice of which they were unaware. It can be supported on that basis.

Whether CVAs are fair to secured creditors is a further issue that was much debated in the period leading up to the Insolvency Act 2000.[145] Under the Insolvency Act 1986, secured and preferential creditors were not to be prejudiced by an arrangement resulting from approval of a CVA proposal. If, however, a secured creditor allows a CVA to proceed and does not enforce a claim before proposals are put to creditors he or she might be disadvantaged since, once assets are in the hands of the CVA supervisor, they are, according to *Re Leisure Study Group Ltd*,[146] impressed with a trust in favour of scheme creditors.

The DTI considered the issue in its 1993 Consultative Document[147] and noted that a twenty-eight-day moratorium would only prevent a charge holder from appointing a receiver or administrative receiver for twenty-eight days unless a scheme were to be agreed.[148] It proposed that charge holders should have to give the company seven days' notice of their intention to appoint an administrative receiver during which time the directors would be able to file for a CVA. This was a proposal that amounted to a reversal of the position on administration petitions whereby the petitioner has to give five clear days' notice to a person who is entitled to appoint or who has appointed an administrative receiver.[149] The notice proposal was set out in the DTI's 1995 revised proposals as a five working days' requirement.[150] It was held out as effecting a fair balance between the nominees' need to have an opportunity to assess the prospects of rescue offered by CVA proposals and the concerns of the charge holders that their security would be diminished in the period of delay. As has been noted, however, the banks strongly opposed such a notice requirement[151] on the grounds that it would lead to defensive filings of CVA applications and undermine trust. No provision for such notice was contained in the Insolvency Act 2000 nor does the moratorium introduced by the 2000 Act

---

145. See Brown, *Corporate Rescue*, pp. 666–8.

146. [1994] 2 BCLC 65.   147. DTI 1993, pp. 17–18.

148. The White Paper of 2001 on *Productivity and Enterprise* proposed to limit to certain capital market transactions the power of the floating charge holder to appoint a receiver. If implemented this step would reduce potential interference with CVA procedures.

149. Insolvency Rules 1986 rr. 2.6, 2.7.   150. DTI 1995, pp. 11–13.

151. As did the House of Commons Trade and Industry Committee: see Fourth Special Report (HC 237, 1999–2000) p. 7, discussed in G. McCormack, 'Receiverships and the Rescue Culture' [2000] 2 CFILR 229, 241–3, who notes the dangers inherent in a notice requirement, particularly that banks stop cashing company cheques post-notice-giving and that directors react to notice by seeking an administration order rather than a CVA.

fail to provide protection for secured creditors. Assurances are offered by the Act's provisions on concealment by directors, on asset dispositions and on challenges for unfair prejudice or material irregularity at a creditors' or members' meeting.[152] On expiry of the moratorium a floating charge holder is again free to appoint a receiver.

Conclusions

CVA procedures have been enhanced by the moratorium introduced by the Insolvency Act 2000 but, in concluding this discussion, it is worth emphasising that legal provisions on CVAs can only go so far in effecting corporate rescues. The 2000 Act CVA does offer a reasonably accountable and fair mechanism for rescue but residual concerns must relate to the degree of co-ordination between directors and IP supervisors that any particular CVA will involve; the absence of provisions advertising proposed CVAs; whether a regime for super-priority funding is necessary for effective rescue; and whether training for directors is a prerequisite for effective rescue.

If seen in broader terms, the CVA procedure can be said to be based on a 'forum' approach to insolvency: one that operates on the basis that rescues can be negotiated into existence. This approach takes it that creditors will produce mutually acceptable solutions if all possibilities can be discussed openly and at low cost. This notion is open to criticism by those who see conflicts of interest as looming large in insolvency. From this perspective, it might be argued that the CVA is unlikely ever to offer the most popular or effective route to rescue because in most areas of corporate trouble the creditors tend to have such divergent interests and powers that rescue options are most likely to be arrived at by degrees of imposition rather than negotiation.

Drawing such a contrast suggests that a way to improve rescue prospects through CVAs may be to institute changes that will reduce the divergences of interest (or perceived divergences of interest) between different creditor groupings. How though can this be done consistently with allowing financing options to remain flexible? One route forward may be to revise the legal rules so that oppositions of interest are less starkly drawn. This can be done, for example, by obliging receivers to consider the

---

152. Insolvency Act 2000 Sched. 1, para. 38.

interests of unsecured creditors more fully,[153] or to offer more information to unsecured creditors or to opt for courses of action that favour unsecured creditors where this involves no cost to the charge holder. Another route would be to institute changes not through legal adjustments of interest but by measures designed to change the cultures, values and assumptions of involved parties: to encourage banks, for example, to identify their own long-term interests more closely with those of the body of unsecured creditors and employees.

Arguing from a further perspective, it might be contended that what really affects prospects of rescue is not so much the legal process involved or the arrays of interests encountered but the levels of business skill that are involved. Reforms reflecting this point of view could focus on steps designed to lift the skill levels of nominees and supervisors as well as those of directors. Improvements here might be secured through increased attention to training and the qualifications necessary for adopting any of the normal named roles. The measures might be constituted on a mandatory or a voluntary basis.

At this point we should return to a question posed earlier in relation to section 425 schemes of arrangement: is there a case for retaining these when resort can be made to CVAs or administration? The Company Law Review Steering Group suggested, as noted, that there would be strong support for a process allowing company managers to impose reorganisation proposals on a minority[154] and it is arguable that there are circumstances in which internally generated reforms may produce rescues more efficiently, expertly, accountably and fairly than procedures involving external practitioners. A streamlined version of the existing schemes of arrangement procedure may have a place in modern company law. Where the troubled company happens to be managed by directors who are able to initiate turnarounds and where these directors are able to see the need for such steps before prospects of rescue have become minimal, the scheme of arrangement has a valuable role. Again this raises the issues of directorial training and incentives within the insolvency process.

---

153. This, of course, would be the effect of the proposals in the DTI White Paper of 2001 on *Productivity and Enterprise* to restrict the floating charge holder's right to appoint a receiver (to certain capital market transactions) in favour of allowing such creditors streamlined access to an administration procedure in which the administrator will owe a duty of care to all creditors (see White Paper, 2001, ch. 2). See also the New Zealand Receivership Act 1993 s. 18 which requires receivers to exercise their powers with reasonable regard for the interests of unsecured creditors; McCormack, 'Receiverships and the Rescue Culture', p. 237; ch. 8 above.
154. CLRSG, *Completing the Structure*, p. 205.

Finally, it should be noted that schemes of arrangement and CVAs are both procedures that operate with distinct visions of the insolvency process in mind; ones that make numerous assumptions about the actors that should be involved, the procedural and substantive rights the parties should have and the ways in which prospects of rescue are best secured. The visions of insolvency seen within these processes may not be the same as the visions implied in other processes such as receiverships or administrations and it may be asked whether consistency between these visions (or even a single agreed vision) should be aimed for. This is an issue to be returned to in the next chapter.

Rescuing rescue

The last four chapters have looked at four formal rescue procedures as well as different approaches to informal rescue. If we ask whether English rescue procedures are appropriate or capable of improvement we should consider not merely the individual processes involved but the broad package of procedures on offer. If that package is assessed, this raises the issue of coherence and whether the different procedures hang together in sympathy or undercut each other. It may be argued that it is beneficial to provide companies with a number of different routes to rescue, but that contention will only hold if those routes are in harmony. If some modes of rescue undermine others, the effect of variety may not be benign choice but inefficiency and confusion.

An overall assessment of rescue procedures must also bear in mind that different procedures may be brought to bear on different stages of corporate troubles. Administration, for instance, demands that the company is, or is likely to be, unable to pay its debts. But the CVA procedure is not tied to insolvency or near insolvency. The importance of this point is that at different stages of corporate difficulty, the aspirations and objectives of parties may vary. At a very early stage of corporate trouble it will be natural for directors and other parties to focus on rescue and the machinery for achieving this. At the brink of insolvency, the law and the involved parties may be concerned with how the remaining assets can be most efficiently and effectively distributed to creditors. These differences of emphasis are also likely to be reflected in the extent to which different parties' rights stand to be adjusted so as to encourage rescue. When rescue is the chief end it will be appropriate to facilitate it by adjusting creditors' rights (for example, by prohibiting enforcement of these). When distribution is the main objective the emphasis will more properly be on the effective enforcement of creditors' rights.

A difficult situation arises when shareholder interests in a company are diminishing in a period just before insolvency. What is special about insolvency – and rescue more particularly – is that the nature of the game and even the list of players will vary as the company progresses through difficulties towards insolvency or turnaround. This can be seen in the position of a shareholder of a company. When a healthy company is operating, the directors may be perceived as working to further the shareholders' interests.[1] In an insolvency, the position has changed. The company cannot pay its debts and the directors are now operating not with the company/shareholders' assets but those of the creditors.[2] The interests of the creditors, at this stage, fall to be looked to as primary objects of directorial endeavour and procedural fairness to creditor interests becomes a first priority.

The difficulty for a designer of rescue procedures is that a procedure may operate across corporate life from the situation in which the company is essentially healthy but needs to reorganise or adjust operations, right through to the company's entry into insolvency. The procedure may thus have to protect rights that are shifting in relationship to each other and it will have to operate fairly when what is procedurally and substantively fair will change in accordance with the shifts in rights that occur as the company nears insolvency.

How then should a *system* of rescue procedures be designed? Do present rescue procedures match up to such a design? First, there should be clarity concerning the objectives in sight – the ends that are to be achieved efficiently and effectively. This means that a rescue system must be precise about the relative weights to be given to rescue and asset distribution.

---

1. On views of shareholders as the owners of the company or as the residual claimants of its assets see, for example, H. Butler, 'The Contractual Theory of the Corporation' (1989) 11 Geo. Mason UL Rev. 99; R. Sappideen, 'Ownership of the Large Corporation: Why Clothe the Emperor?' (1996–7) 7 King's College LJ 27. On different characterisations of the nature of a shareholder's interest see E. Ferran, *Company Law and Corporate Finance* (Oxford University Press, Oxford, 1999) pp. 131–3. On the status of groups other than shareholders as 'residual claimants' see Sappideen, 'Ownership'; G. Kelly and J. Parkinson, 'The Conceptual Foundations of the Company' [1998] 2 CfiLR 174. The Company Law Review Steering Group took the view that the basic duties of directors will still be to maximise shareholder wealth though this will be subject to a more 'inclusive' responsibility to have regard to other stakeholders: see *Modern Company Law for a Competitive Economy: Completing the Structure* (November 2000) ch. 3.
2. See *West Mercia Safetywear Ltd* v. *Dodd* [1988] 4 BCC 30, [1988] BCLC 250, per Dillon LJ. See also ch. 15 below.

Nor should it be forgotten that the same insolvency laws that serve rescues may also need to accommodate the purposes of healthy operating companies. It would not, for instance, make sense to create effective rescue procedures if the processes interfered unduly with, or imposed excessive costs on, healthy companies (for instance, because the rescue procedures can be abused for non-rescue reasons, as some fear may be the case with Chapter 11 in the USA). There is, accordingly, a balance to be set between rescue and operational concerns.

It may well be that at different stages of corporate life and decline, the optimal balances of different objectives will change. Rescue processes can cope with such difficulties but it is undesirable for different rescue procedures to target priorities divergently when operating at the same stage in corporate troubles. Here we see problems with the system of floating charges and the tension between administrative receivership and administration. The administration regime incorporates a moratorium and gives protection from creditors, and in doing so it effects a particular balance between ongoing corporate concerns (for example, to obtain financing when healthy), the interests of creditors and the wider interests to be served by rescue. The floating charge and administrative receivership system undermines administration (not to say schemes of arrangement and CVAs) and does so by setting out to achieve different ends (notably protection of the floating charge holder's interest) at the same time as schemes of arrangement and CVAs look to broader rescue interests.[3] It might be responded that insolvency law is offering here a choice of protections and procedural avenues to different parties but this misses the point. In reality, insolvency law is speaking with two voices and providing one procedure that is undermined by another. The route to a clearer design of insolvency/rescue regime is to decide on the appropriate balance of interests and to set up a procedure that pursues those interests consistently with that balancing. This argument favours the abolition of administrative receivership and a movement towards a 'single gateway' rescue regime.[4] It can also be questioned whether one procedure is suitable for all stages of corporate

3. It should of course be remembered that administrative receivership can itself block the appointment of an administrator: Insolvency Act 1986 s. 9(2), (3). The White Paper of July 2001 (DTI/Insolvency Service, *Productivity and Enterprise: Insolvency – A Second Chance* (Cm 5234, 2001)) proposes to ensure that collective procedures are used instead of administrative receivership, a development that builds on the Insolvency Service's Review Group's proposal to end the floating charge holder's right to veto the making of an administration order: see Insolvency Service, *A Review of Company Rescue and Business Reconstruction Mechanisms, Report by the Review Group* (DTI, 2000) ('IS 2000') para. 73.
4. The 'single gateway' proposal is discussed by the Insolvency Service in IS 2000, p. 22; see the discussion at pp. 269–72, 319–21 above.

decline and for all purposes relating to the troubled company. Administration, for instance, may commence at the point of near insolvency and run through to liquidation, and an examination of section 8(3) of the Insolvency Act 1986 reveals that administration is designed for such different purposes as the survival of the company[5] and realising the company's assets.[6]

A second prerequisite of clear rescue design is the identification of those values to be pursued in a rescue. Again these need to be targeted with consistency. This book, as indicated in chapter 2, argues that emphasis should be given to efficiency, expertise, fairness and accountability throughout the various stages of rescue. Efficiency, it has just been noted, demands clarity concerning objectives, and one recurring message of the last four chapters has been that efficiency in rescue may require that directors are able to resort to a rescue procedure *before* the chances of turnaround have become hopeless. Here the addition by the Insolvency Act 2000 of a moratorium to a new CVA procedure may be helpful, but questions can be asked about the continued requirement of section 8(1)(a) of the Insolvency Act 1986: that a court, if it is to make an administration order, must be satisfied that the company 'is or is likely to become unable to pay its debts'.

Turning to the issue of expertise, if we consider the allocations of managerial and oversight functions in English rescue procedures – and do so with a view to the trust impliedly being placed in different experts – we see quite different assumptions being made. Many informal rescue procedures, including the London Approach, rely on a process of negotiation between the companies, directors and the bank(s). If formal processes are examined, we see that schemes of arrangement place faith in the expertise of the directors, subject to court oversight, and there is no need to resort to an independent IP to formulate or implement the scheme. The directors remain in control and a great deal of faith is placed in their initiative and ability to take corrective steps to avert disaster. The CVA, in contrast, places control in the hands of an external expert. The company's directors, as noted, may propose a CVA but this must provide for a nominee to supervise the CVA's implementation and the nominee must be qualified to act as an IP in relation to the company.[7] This faith in the expertise of the independent IP may sometimes be well placed but, as was noted in chapter 10, some IPs have limited knowledge of CVA procedures and any

---

5. Insolvency Act 1986 s. 8(3)(a).   6. Ibid., s. 8(3)(d).

7. Note that with the new, small company CVA established by the Insolvency Act 2000, nominees do not specifically have to be IPs: see ch. 10 above.

expert judgment may have to survive an extended negotiation procedure, involving the IP, the directors, the banks and other creditors. This negotiation, moreover, may be conducted in a context of only limited trust. At the end of the day, then, expertise has to flow from a process of co-ordination with the IP at the helm.

In administration, the expertise of the IP is again central in both setting up the process and implementing it, but, given the role of the company's directors in instituting four-fifths of all administrations, the skill of those directors in seeing the need to institute an administration is also important. As noted, the company has to be near to, or actually, insolvent for an administration order to be granted and the window of rescue opportunity is, accordingly, very narrow. This gives more prominence to the galvanising role of the company directors. The law here trusts the directors' expertise too little to allow the debtor to stay in possession, but sets up a procedure whose rescue prospects depend crucially on the same directors.

In administrative receivership the expert running the procedure is the qualified IP who acts as the receiver and is appointed by the floating charge holder/debenture holder. As noted, this individual is independent to the extent that the appointor may issue no instructions, though the receiver may apply to court for directions.

To summarise, in looking for the expertise that will generate successful rescues, insolvency law operates with a scattergun approach rather than a considered analysis of informational position, training, disinterestedness, specialist knowledge of the market, ability to judge financing options or commitment to implementation for rescue purposes. The formal procedures relevant to rescue again speak with inconsistent voices: schemes of arrangements are marked by high trust in directors; CVAs look to independent experts and negotiated or group expertise; administrations look to independent experts that rely on expert directorial triggers; and receivership emphasises the highly distanced model of independent expert. To repeat, a system of insolvency law that is thought through should operate on assumptions concerning expertise that are consistent rather than vacillating. These assumptions, moreover, could be based on analyses of the kind of factors noted above, along with the host of others that together underpin the exercise of independent judgment.

A discussion of accountability within rescue procedures proceeds on similar lines. Schemes of arrangement involve no oversight of directors by IPs but control by meetings of creditors and members together with judicial oversight. CVAs also require that IPs structure directors' proposals and the latter also have to be approved by creditors and members. The skill of the IP is crucial to the flow of information and accountability to creditors and members in a CVA. An array of criminal sanctions and civil liabilities also serves to hold directors to account in cases of concealment, removal or distribution of assets and/or records. General court scrutiny is also available by provisions allowing creditors and shareholders to apply for relief. In administration considerable emphasis is placed on court involvement. Accountability to shareholders is, however, absent in so far as the members are not involved in approval of the administrator's proposals (which are approved by the creditors alone).[8]

The administrative receiver's accountability contrasts with the above descriptions. Cork opposed direct accountability[9] and the insolvency legislation follows Cork in this respect: administrative receivers' primary obligations are to act *bona fide* to realise the assets of the company in the interests of debenture holders and to exercise a limited duty of care.[10] There is, however, no duty to obey the company or to provide the company with details and information concerning the conduct of the company's affairs.

Looking at accountability in different insolvency procedures, we again see not only varying rules but divergent philosophies. This is most notably the case with administrative receivership where notions of accountability to creditors in general, or to members, employees or business partners, all give way to the idea that it is appropriate for the receiver to engage in a disinterested, almost mechanical, pursuit of the appointing floating charge holder's interest. Even in relation to the other procedures there are tensions. Schemes of arrangement build on the notion that directors can be left largely free from monitoring by IPs but CVAs and administrations imply that there is considerable value in specialist control over the directors' behaviour, proposals and informational roles. In administrations there is no need for shareholders' approval. This contrast with schemes of arrangement procedures may be defended by some on the grounds that administration necessarily occurs when the company is close to insolvency but it is perhaps jumping the gun to argue that shareholders should drop out of the approval process completely when insolvency is a likelihood, rather than a given.

---

8. Shareholders can, however, apply to the court under the Insolvency Act 1986 s. 27 if they have a complaint that the proposals will prejudice them.
9. *Report of the Review Committee on Insolvency Law and Practice* (Cmnd 8558, 1982) para. 444.
10. See *Medforth v. Blake* [1999] BCC 771, [1999] 3 All ER 97 and discussion in ch. 8 above.

Finally, the issue of fairness falls to be considered. Considerable emphasis is placed on fairness to minority interests in schemes of arrangement. Meetings of creditors and shareholders have to approve proposals and, as noted in chapter 10, it is the court's protective stance on this front that produces a complex process with elaborate provisions on notice. In relation to CVAs one means of ensuring fair treatment of creditors is through the approvals mechanism and the requirement of 75% in value approvals. As noted, though, this rule contrasts with the simple majority required in administration and CVAs have to be approved by shareholder meetings whereas administrations do not. As argued above, the exclusion of shareholders from votes on administrations may be difficult to justify, at least in the pre-insolvency situations that section 8(1)(a) of the Insolvency Act 1986 covers. It can also be contended that administrations do not fairly take on board those interests of parties beyond creditors, notably employees. The purpose of making an administration order under section 8(3)(a) of the Insolvency Act 1986 is 'the survival of the company and the whole or any part of its undertaking, as a going concern' but the employee stakeholders whose livelihoods are at stake are offered no formal input into the decision-making process governing administration.

Turning to administrative receivership, the abolition of this procedure can be justified principally on the grounds that it operates in a manner that is unfair to creditors other than the appointing debenture holder and that it furthers the interests of the appointor at potential cost not merely to other creditors but also to employees, shareholders and the public.

To summarise on fairness, we see that the law relating to the four insolvency procedures operates with divergent assumptions on the rights of parties involved in insolvency. As a result, the models of fairness implicit in the four processes are inconsistent. The law does have to confront the difficult problem of changing balances between the interests of certain classes. This is apparent in the position of the shareholder in, say, the administration procedure since the shareholder's interest can be said to be considerable pre-insolvency but diminishing as full insolvency looms. An organised approach to insolvency law would decide which parties have which rights at which stages of insolvency and set the rules accordingly and consistently across the four procedures. This is not what is found in the law, and the anomalous framework of administrative receivership makes this manifest.

To conclude on rescue procedures, the individual procedures possess strengths and weaknesses as outlined, but as an overall system they constitute a disjointed package. There are a number of potential explanations for this state of affairs. Many such explanations are historical and political. Long-established deference to security interest holders as major property owners has created a resistance to organised rescue strategies and sets of laws that might be seen as interfering with such property rights.[11] Cork's recommendations were cherry picked and post-Cork law reforms in this area have been piecemeal efforts that have failed to take on the broader strategic issues. That the law has, for whatever reasons, ended up dealing with rescue in the present way does not, however, make the law acceptable. Nor does the political commitment of powerful institutions to such processes as administrative receivership make these processes unobjectionable.

My argument has been that insolvency law can and should take on board the shifting nature of rights and relationships in troubled corporate affairs. Other things being equal, however, it should offer a range of insolvency processes that caters for the values of efficiency, expertise, accountability and fairness and does so on the basis of assumptions that are consistent across different procedures. At present formal rescue procedures speak with many voices but the effect of this may not be so much to offer choice to parties as to create confusion.

---

11. See A. Clarke, 'Security Interests as Property: Relocating Security Interests within the Property Framework' in J. W. Harris (ed.), *Property Problems from Genes to Pension Funds* (Kluwer, London, 1997).

Part IV

Gathering and distributing the assets

12

Gathering the assets: the role of liquidation

Liquidation is the end of the road for the troubled company. It involves its winding up and the gathering in of the assets for subsequent distribution to creditors. Liquidation nevertheless raises issues of efficiency, expertise, accountability and fairness as much as processes involving prospects of rescue. This chapter explores those issues as well as the conceptual underpinnings of liquidation. To set the scene it is necessary to set out the varieties of liquidation and the legal framework that supports the liquidation process.

The voluntary liquidation process

Liquidations are encountered in three main forms: voluntary, compulsory and public interest. A voluntary liquidation of a solvent company is termed 'a members' voluntary winding up' and where an insolvent company is involved this is then known as 'a creditors' voluntary winding up'.[1] This distinction flows from the Insolvency Act 1986 sections 89 and 90 which provide that if the directors have made a statutory declaration of solvency under section 89, a members' voluntary liquidation occurs, but that the liquidation is a creditors' voluntary liquidation in the absence of such a declaration.

Both types of voluntary liquidation are, however, triggered by the actions of the company's members. These members can initiate a liquidation by passing a special resolution in favour of a voluntary liquidation or by passing an extraordinary resolution declaring that the company 'cannot by reason of its liabilities continue its business and that

---

1. See D. Milman and C. Durrant, *Corporate Insolvency: Law and Practice* (3rd edn, Sweet & Maxwell, London, 1999) p. 77.

it is advisable to wind up'.[2] Both forms of resolution require three-quarters majority votes[3] and trigger voluntary liquidation at the date passed. Resolutions must be advertised in the *Gazette* within fourteen days of passing (on penalty of a fine where the officers of a company are in default[4]).

Creditor involvement in creditors' voluntary winding up is provided for in the rule that a company must call a creditors' meeting within fourteen days of the meeting at which the resolution for voluntary liquidation is to be proposed.[5] Such creditors, moreover, must be given at least seven days' warning and a notice of the meeting has to be placed in the *Gazette* and two local newspapers. This advertisement must give the name of the IP who is qualified to act as the company's voluntary liquidator and it must also indicate the place where a list of creditors can be found.

A main source of information to creditors is the Statement of Affairs that the Insolvency Act 1986 section 99 requires the company directors to lay before the creditors' meeting. The directors, moreover, must nominate one of their number to run the creditors' meeting.[6] The creditors at that meeting are able to nominate a liquidator. The members of the company may also nominate a liquidator at their meeting but if members and creditors choose divergently, the nominee of the creditors will be appointed.[7] Where the company is not content with a creditors' choice a challenge may be made in court within seven days.[8] As for the powers of the company's directors, these are limited by section 114 of the Insolvency Act 1986 which covers the period prior to the appointment of a

---

2. Insolvency Act 1986 s. 84(1)(c). Section 84(1)(a) also provides that when the period fixed (if any) for the duration of a company in the articles expires, the company in general meeting can pass a resolution requiring it to be wound up voluntarily (an ordinary resolution requires a simple majority).

3. Companies Act 1985 s. 378. A special resolution normally requires not less than twenty-one days' notice (unless waived under the Companies Act 1985 s. 378(3)), but an extraordinary resolution can be carried with more urgency.

4. Insolvency Act 1986 s. 85(2).

5. Ibid., s. 98; Insolvency Rules 1986 rr. 4.51 (as amended), 4.53, 4.62. See Milman and Durrant, *Corporate Insolvency*, pp. 78–9 and the decision of *Re Centrebind Ltd* [1967] 1 WLR 377. That case held that failure to comply with the specified meetings procedures did not invalidate proceedings but, now, Insolvency Act 1986 s. 166 prevents a liquidator, as a general rule, from exercising any section 156 powers (e.g. of property disposal) until the creditors' meeting required by section 98 has been held. Section 166(5) of the Insolvency Act 1986 gives the court powers to make directions where there has been a failure to comply with sections 98 and 99: on the exercise of these see R. Tateossian, 'The Scope of Section 166(5) Insolvency Act 1986: An Analysis' (2001) *Finance and Credit Law* 4.

6. Failure of the nominated director to attend the meeting will not necessarily invalidate proceedings. See *Re Salcombe Hotel Development Co. Ltd* [1991] BCLC 44.

7. Insolvency Act 1986 s. 100(2).   8. Ibid., s. 100 (3); Insolvency Rules 1986 r. 4.103.

liquidator and only allows directorial powers to be exercised with the sanction of the court or in order to secure compliance with section 98 provisions on the creditors' meeting or section 99 on the directors' statement of affairs.

The person chosen to act as a liquidator in a creditors' voluntary winding up must be a qualified IP.[9] IPs, moreover, often have a strong influence on choice of liquidator. As Milman and Durrant indicate:

> IPs commonly offer a service to their commercial clients of attending on their behalf at creditors' meetings of their insolvent debtors and reporting on the proceedings free of charge. Professionals in the field, usually representatives of the larger accountancy firms, are well known to each other, and commonly discussions take place before the meeting to find out which of them commands the most voting power, now measured by value of the debt under Rule 4.63(1). By arrangement, some of the professionals attend the creditors' meeting, and frequently one of them proposes the appointment of one of the others, either as liquidator, in place of the members' nominee, or, more commonly nowadays, as joint liquidator.[10]

Joint liquidators may be appointed by such a process and the court has power to appoint a further liquidator to join a sole liquidator.[11] On appointment any liquidator has fourteen days in which to advertise his appointment in the *Gazette* and to notify the Companies Register.

In a creditors' voluntary liquidation, creditors play a central control function. They are placed in a fiduciary position regarding the company and its assets and act in the main through the Liquidation Committee.[12] This body has a maximum membership of five creditors and five contributories. Creditors, moreover, have more power since they can veto all or any of the contributories (under section 101(3) of the Insolvency Act 1986). The quorum for such a committee is two members, and any member may be removed by the creditors at large. It has a right to information as the liquidator is advised to report all relevant matters to it. Members may require meetings to be called but generally meetings are at the discretion of the liquidator.

Creditors may apply to the court for directions;[13] they have powers to remove liquidators[14] or apply to the court for removal of a voluntary

---

9. Insolvency Rules 1986 r. 4.101.   10. Milman and Durrant, *Corporate Insolvency*, p. 80.
11. *Re Sunlight Incandescent Ltd* [1906] 2 Ch 728.
12. See Insolvency Act 1986 s. 101. On the duties, functions and procedural rules relating to Liquidation Committees see Statement of Insolvency Practice (SIP) 15 (E & W), (2001).
13. Insolvency Act 1986 s. 112.   14. Ibid., s. 171(2).

liquidator; and they may ask the court to have the company compulsorily wound up under the Insolvency Act 1986 section 116.[15]

As for court supervision of voluntary liquidations, this is light and it is not a day-to-day activity. The court may, nevertheless, become involved where there is a request to remove a liquidator or where a liquidator, contributory or creditor applies to it to determine a question arising in the winding up or to use the powers it might employ in a winding up by the court to enforce calls or other matters.[16]

When voluntary liquidation is entered into the general powers of the directors, as noted, cannot be exercised,[17] but a series of powers is given to the liquidator under section 165 and Schedule 4 of the Insolvency Act 1986. The liquidator, with the sanction of the Liquidation Committee,[18] may pay any class of creditors in full; make compromises or arrangements with creditors or alleged creditors; compromise calls, debts, potential debts, claims and any question relating to the assets or the winding up of the company. Security, moreover, may be taken in the course of discharging these claims.

The sanction of the Liquidation Committee is not required in relation to the exercise of a number of other powers, including: the bringing or defending of actions or legal proceedings on behalf of the company; carrying on the business of the company as is necessary for a beneficial winding up;[19] selling or transferring any of the company's property; executing deeds for the company and using its seal; proving in the insolvency of any contributory; dealing in bills of exchange; borrowing against the security of a company's assets; taking out letters of administration to the estate of a deceased contributory; appointing an agent to perform business; and doing all such other things as may be necessary for the winding up of a company's affairs and distribution of its assets.

These powers described are general and implied. A number of statutory powers sit alongside these, however. All types of liquidator may disclaim onerous property under the Insolvency Act 1986 sections 178–82. This may be done without court leave[20] and notwithstanding the liquidator

---

15. See *Re Lowestoft Traffic Services Co. Ltd* [1986] 2 BCC 98.

16. Insolvency Act 1986 s. 112.   17. Ibid., s. 103.

18. Obtainable in advance or by ratification.

19. The onus appears to be on an objector to establish that an action was not beneficial to the winding up: see *Hire Purchase Co.* v. *Richans* (1887) 20 QBD 387; Milman and Durrant, *Corporate Insolvency*, p. 82.

20. A notice of disclaimer has to be filed in court under Insolvency Rules 1986 r. 4.187.

taking possession of the property, attempting to sell it or exercising rights of ownership in it.[21] Onerous property here includes unprofitable contracts or other property that is not saleable or readily saleable or such that may create a liability to pay money or perform an onerous act.[22] The effect of disclaiming is to terminate the rights and liabilities of the company with regard to the property disclaimed, but rights and liabilities of other parties are not affected.[23] In exercising this power the liquidator's hand may be pressed by interested parties who may require the liquidator to decide whether there is an intention to disclaim, and the liquidator has twenty-eight days to give notice of disclaiming or then forfeit the right to disclaim. If, moreover, persons suffer a loss as a result of the liquidator's disclaiming, they can prove as creditors in the winding up.

As will be discussed further below, the statutory powers of liquidators allow them to set aside prior transactions at undervalue or transactions which amount to preferences. Liquidators, moreover, may obtain orders for the examination of company affairs in order to secure information[24] and may apply for an order that directors or former directors make a contribution to the assets.[25] If the liquidator wishes to obtain court guidance on questions relating to a winding up, an application can be made under section 112 of the Insolvency Act 1986 and the court may also be asked to appoint a special manager.[26] When a liquidator is appointed he or she is not personally bound by pre-liquidation contracts enforceable against the company, except where he or she has actually adopted them.[27] Such contracts, however, retain their force with regard to the company unless they are disclaimed by the liquidator. Contracts entered into by liquidators for

---

21. Insolvency Act 1986 s. 178(2).   22. Ibid., s. 178(3).

23. *Hindcastle Ltd* v. *Barbara Attenborough Associates* [1996] 2 WLR 262. See also *Re Park Air Services* (*Christopher Moran Holdings Ltd* v. *Bairstow and Ruddock*) [1999] BCC 135, [1999] EGCS 17 (House of Lords guidance on calculating compensation for landlord where liquidator disclaims lease); T. Withyman, 'Disclaimer: Practical Tips on the Consequences' (2000) *Insolvency Bulletin* 5; C. Swain, 'The Landlord's Claim: The *Park Air Services* Case' (1999) *Insolvency Bulletin* 6; A. Clarke, 'Overcompensation for Disclaimer?' [1998] 2 CfiLR 248. On disclaimers and waste management licences see *Official Receiver of Celtic Extraction and Bluestone Chemicals* v. *Environment Agency* [2000] BCC 487, [1999] 4 All ER 684 (waste management licences held by the Court of Appeal to be disclaimable); J. Armour, 'Who Pays When Polluters Go Bust?' (2000) 116 LQR 200; P. de Prez, 'The Power of Disclaimer and Environmental Licences' [2000] Ins. Law. 87; C. Abbot, 'Liquidator Escapes Liability by Disclaiming Waste Management Licence' [2000] 1 *Palmer's In Company* 1; A. Pickin, 'Getting Rid of Waste Management Licences' (1999) 13 *Insolvency Intelligence* 79; C.-A. Png, 'Conflicting Obligations in Insolvency Cases' (2001) 22 Co. Law. 281.

24. Insolvency Act 1986 s. 236.   25. Ibid., s. 214. See ch. 15 below.

26. Insolvency Act 1986 s. 177.   27. *Re S. Davies & Co. Ltd* [1945] Ch 402.

the purposes of effecting a winding up do not bind them personally since they act in this regard as agents of the company.[28]

As for the duties of the liquidator, the first of these is to realise the company's assets effectively and to apply the company's property 'in satisfaction of the company's liabilities *pari passu*'[29] so that there is a distribution 'among the members according to their rights and interests in the company'. There is a duty to contact known creditors and meet their claims as well as an obligation to consider all known debts before distributing assets.[30] Where dividends are to be paid, liquidators must give notice of their intention to declare a dividend[31] and must provide for debts relating to claims undetermined at that time and the claims of creditors who may not have had time to establish their proofs because of the distance of their place of residence.[32] When a dividend is declared, however, creditors who have not proved cannot disturb the dividends. Dividends must be paid by the liquidator when this is possible and proper accounts, minutes of meetings and records must be kept.[33] The liquidator is in a fiduciary position in relation to the company and must not derive personal profit from his role: this rules out employing him or herself to do legal work flowing from the winding up.[34]

Liquidators can be removed by the court or the creditors and may only resign by reasons of ill-health, retirement from insolvency practice, conflict of interests or changes in personal circumstances that make it impossible for them to continue to act. Where a resignation is to be effective, a creditors' meeting must be called and asked to accept this. In the absence of such an acceptance, the liquidator may apply to the court. A creditors' voluntary winding up terminates normally with the realisation of all available assets and their distribution to claimants in order of priority. After this is done, the liquidator must call final meetings of members and creditors[35] to which accounts of realisations and distributions must be submitted. These accounts must, in turn, be sent to the Companies Registry within a week of the meeting. The

---

28. But see *Plant (Engineers) Sales Ltd* v. *Davis* (1969) 113 Sol. Jo. 484 regarding contracts under seal.

29. Insolvency Act 1986 s. 107. For discussion of the *pari passu* principle see chs. 13 and 14 below.

30. See *Re Armstrong Whitworth Securities Ltd* [1947] Ch 673; *Argylls Ltd* v. *Coxeter* [1913] 29 TLR 355.

31. Insolvency Rules 1986 r. 4.180(2).   32. Insolvency Rules 1986 r. 4.182.

33. Insolvency Regulations 1994 (SI 1994 No. 2507).

34. See Milman and Durrant, *Corporate Insolvency*, p. 91; *Re Gertzenstein Ltd* [1997] 1 Ch 115; rule 4.149 of the Insolvency Rules 1986 allows the court to set aside dealings between the liquidator and his associates which involve company assets.

35. Insolvency Act 1986 s. 106.

Registrar will then record the liquidator's account and return under the Insolvency Act 1986 section 201 and the company is deemed dissolved three months from registration of a return.[36] After this date the company does not exist and can neither be sued nor initiate court proceedings.

Compulsory liquidation

Compulsory liquidation generally involves actions initiated against the company's wishes, in contrast to members' or creditors' voluntary windings up. Proceedings are commenced by a petition that may be presented by any creditor (including contingent or prospective creditors),[37] the company, the directors (with all directors joining the petition acting as a board following unanimous or majority resolution), a contributory or the clerk of a magistrates' court in enforcement of a fine.[38] Receivers and administrators are also able to present petitions: in the case of the former, to aid realisation of the assets and, in the case of the latter, under court authorisation.[39] In the case of creditors whose claims are disputed by the company, the court will exercise a discretion and will tend not to accede to the petition where the company disputes the claim on substantial grounds and in good faith.[40] The creditor whose claim is genuinely disputed is thus poorly placed to assert that the company has 'neglected to pay' the debt. Where, moreover, the debtor company has an enforceable cross claim against the petitioner – for a sum exceeding the claim – the court may dismiss or stay a winding-up petition.[41]

The primary grounds for a winding-up petition are that 'the company is unable to pay its debts'.[42] The Insolvency Act 1986 deems this inability

36. Ibid., s. 106.
37. Insolvency Act 1986 s. 124(1). Where a voluntary winding up has been commenced and the majority of creditors wish it to continue, a petitioning creditor has to show some good reason for there to be a compulsory winding up: see *Re Ziceram Ltd* [2000] BCC 1048.
38. Insolvency Act 1986 s. 124(1).
39. See Milman and Durrant, *Corporate Insolvency*, pp. 100–1.
40. *Re London and Paris Banking Corporation* (1875) LR 19 Eq 444; *Brinds Ltd* v. *Offshore Oil* [1986] 2 BCC 98. See generally Milman and Durrant, *Corporate Insolvency*, p. 99; A. Keay, 'Disputing Debts Relied on by Petitioning Creditors Seeking Winding Up Orders' (2000) 22 Co. Law. 40. Keay argues (p. 46): 'To qualify as a substantial dispute a dispute must be real and not fanciful, but it does not matter that the company bears malice towards the petitioner… But, where at least £750 is indisputably owed to the petitioner, after taking into account the disputed part of the debt, courts may decline to dismiss the petition.'
41. See *Re Bayoil SA* [1999] 1 WLR 147, though the court may decide to deal with a cross claim in the litigation: see *Re Richbell Information Systems Inc.* v. *Atlantic General Investments Trust Ltd* [1999] BCC 871.
42. Insolvency Act 1986 s. 122(1)(f). See further ch. 4 above.

to occur: (a) if a creditor who is owed over £750 has served the company with a written demand for payment (in prescribed form at the company's registered office) and the company has 'for three weeks neglected to pay the sum or to secure or compound for it to the reasonable satisfaction of the creditor';[43] or (b) if, in England and Wales, execution or other process issued on a judgment, decree or order of the court in favour of a creditor of the company is returned unsatisfied in whole or in part;[44] or (c) if it is proved to the satisfaction of the court that the company is unable to pay its debts as they fall due;[45] or (d) if it is proved that the value of the company's assets is less than the amount of its liability, taking into account its contingent and prospective liabilities.[46] Petitions based on the above grounds will also commonly refer to the grounds set out in the Insolvency Act 1986 section 122(1)(g) that 'the court is of the opinion that it is just and equitable that the company should be wound up'.[47]

Procedurally, a winding-up petition has to be served on the company and other parties as well as advertised according to the Insolvency Rules.[48] Service at the company's registered office is demanded and advertising must take place at least seven days after service and at least seven days before the hearing. The period between presentation of a winding-up petition and its hearing is a difficult one for the company and the petitioner. The company will often want to continue trading and petitioners may fear that the directors will dissipate assets and devalue their claims. In anticipation of these potential problems, the law provides that where a petitioner can show that there is a serious risk that the directors will dissipate the company's assets and prejudice their claim, the court can appoint a provisional or interim liquidator to oversee the assets until the petition is heard.[49] This person may be a private IP but usually the Official Receiver will be appointed. Protection for claimants is also offered by the rules on avoidance of transactions and the retrospectivity of the rule governing the start of a winding up. When a winding-up order is made, the winding up is deemed to commence at the time of presenting the petition.[50] Section 127

43. Insolvency Act 1986 s. 123(1)(a).   44. Ibid., s. 123(1)(b).   45. Ibid., s. 123(1)(e).
46. Ibid., s. 123(2).
47. See *Ebrahimi v. Westbourne Galleries Ltd* [1973] AC 360; *Re J. E. Cade & Son Ltd* [1991] BCC 360. Section 122(1) also provides that a company may be wound up if: the company has by special resolution resolved that it be wound up by the court; it, being a public company, has not been issued with a share capital requirement certificate within a year of registration; it is an 'old company'; it does not commence or operate business for a whole year; or the number of its members is reduced below two.
48. Insolvency Rules 1986 rr. 4.8–4.10.   49. Insolvency Act 1986 s. 135.
50. Ibid., s. 129(2).

of the Insolvency Act 1986 covers dispositions of company property after this time and provides that any such dispositions and transfers of shares or alterations in the status of the company's members shall be void unless the court otherwise orders.[51]

More general shielding of the company is offered by sections 126 and 128 of the Insolvency Act 1986, which provide that during winding up a company creditor or contributory may apply to the court for a stay of legal proceedings against the company and that, again during a winding up, any attachment, sequestration, distress or execution in force against a company is void.

As for the discretion of the court to grant a winding-up order, this will normally be exercised in favour of the petitioner if there is no opposition.[52] The court may, however, refuse an order under section 125 of the Insolvency Act 1986 if it is opposed by the majority of creditors. In deciding this issue, the court will look to the numbers of opposing creditors, to the value of the debts owed and to the quality of those creditors.[53] On this last point, the court will give less weight to the claims of creditors who are connected with the company (for example, as directors or shareholders[54]) or who are fully secured[55] (and so have a limited interest in the liquidation). The court, moreover, will resist the use of liquidation to serve the petitioners' ulterior motive rather than general creditor benefit.[56]

As soon as a winding-up order is made, the Official Receiver automatically assumes the role of the liquidator until another liquidator is appointed.[57] After this time no legal actions may be taken against the company without the leave of the court and, subject to any conditions imposed

---

51. See *Bank of Ireland v. Hollicourt (Contracts) Ltd* [2001] 2 WLR 290, [2001] 1 All ER 289, [2001] 1 BCLC 233 (CA). (Where a bank which is merely acting as an agent of a troubled company honours a cheque drawn on co-account unaware of a petition's presentation, the liquidator can recover from the payee only. The bank was not liable under section 127 to make restitution to the company of amounts paid to the company's creditors out of its account following presentation of a winding-up petition.) See also Lightman J in *Coutts & Co. v. Stock* [2000] BCC 247 (on the confused state of the law in this area); L. S. Sealy, 'Company Liquidations: When Should Post-petition Banking Transactions be Avoided?' (2000) 57 CCH *Company Law Newsletter* 1; G. Stewart, 'Section 127 in the Court of Appeal' (2001) *Recovery* (February) 9; C. Pugh, '*Hollicourt* to Reduce Banks' Exposure under Section 127' (2001) 17 IL&P 53; H. Mistry, '*Hollicourt*: Bringing the Authorities Out of Disarray' (2001) 22 Co. Law. 278.
52. Conversion to compulsory liquidation may be supported by the court, particularly where there is a deemed need for investigation into the directors' conduct.
53. See, for example, *Re Holiday Stamps Ltd, The Times*, 11 July 1985; *Re Flooks of Bristol (Builders) Ltd* [1982] Com LR 53.
54. *Re Vuma Ltd* [1960] 1 WLR 1283.   55. *Re Flooks of Bristol (Builders) Ltd* [1982] Com LR 53.
56. Milman and Durrant, *Corporate Insolvency*, pp. 107–8; *Re Greenwood* [1900] 2 QB 306; *Re A Company (No. 0013925 of 1991) ex parte Roussel* [1992] BCLC 562; *Re Leigh Estates Ltd* [1994] BCC 292.
57. Insolvency Act 1986 s. 136(2).

by the court, the winding-up order ends the powers of the directors, passes control of the company's assets to the Official Receiver and operates as notice discharging the employees (except where the business continues for the purposes of beneficial winding up, the liquidator indicates a wish that employment should continue and the employees agree to continuation[58]). A winding-up order does not, in itself, however, repudiate other types of contract and the company is not deprived of the legal title to its assets.[59]

The liquidator is an officer of the court and has powers (and is obliged) to take into his custody or control all the property of the company.[60] Under section 144 of the Insolvency Act 1986 this includes all the property to which the company appears entitled. He or she may call on officers and employees of the company to provide statements of affairs[61] and, as in a voluntary liquidation, there is a power to disclaim onerous property and contracts. There is, in addition, a discretion to call meetings of creditors and contributors, though these parties may compel the calling of a meeting if they have the support of one tenth in value of their body.[62]

Turning to controls over the liquidator in a compulsory winding up, he or she will be answerable to the Liquidation Committee of a company's creditors set up under section 141 of the Insolvency Act 1986. The liquidator may, with the sanction of the court or the Liquidation Committee, exercise any of the powers set out in Parts 1 and 2 of Schedule 4 of the Insolvency Act 1986 (payment of debts, compromise of claims etc., institution and defence of proceedings, carrying on of business of the company) and, as in a voluntary liquidation, the liquidator may carry out, without the need for court approval, the set of powers contained in Part 3 of Schedule 4. In compulsory liquidations, however, liquidators will be subject to control to a greater degree than in voluntary liquidations. They will, for example, require the sanction of the court or committee to initiate or defend legal proceedings in their name, in the name of the company or to carry on the business of the company.[63] Court review of liquidator activities is provided for by section 168(5) of the Insolvency Act 1986 which allows any person

58. See R. M. Goode, *Principles of Corporate Insolvency Law* (2nd edn, Sweet & Maxwell, London, 1997) p. 117; *Re Oriental Bank Corporation (Macdowell's Case)* (1886) 32 Ch D 36.

59. *Ayerst v. C and K Construction Ltd* [1976] AC 167.

60. On the implications of status as an officer of the court see, e.g., C. Villiers, 'Employees as Creditors: A Challenge for Justice in Insolvency Law' (1999) 20 Co. Law. 222.

61. Insolvency Act 1986 s. 131; Insolvency Rules 1986 rr. 4.32–4.38.

62. Insolvency Act 1986 s. 168.

63. Ratification is, however, possible for uncontentious actions: see r. 4.184(2).

aggrieved by a liquidator's act or decision to apply to the court, whereupon the court may confirm, reverse or modify the act/decision and make orders as it thinks fit.

The key function of the liquidator is to 'secure that the assets of the company are got in, realised and distributed to the company's creditors and, if there is a surplus, to the persons entitled to it'.[64] Failure to fulfil that function may result in penalties for the liquidator, which may involve misfeasance actions,[65] deprivations of costs[66] and actions for negligence.[67] Duties that must be discharged include keeping proper accounts and lodging with the Insolvency Service's account at the Bank of England any funds realised. The accounts of the liquidator will be audited by the Secretary of State and there is an obligation to file accounts and returns under section 170 of the Insolvency Act 1986. It is, moreover, the duty of the liquidator to keep minutes of meetings and administrative records, to act independently and to avoid conflicts of interest.

The end of a compulsory liquidation occurs when the liquidator has realised all the potential assets of the company and distributed all available funds. The liquidator will then report to the final meeting of creditors which may release him. If the liquidator is not so released he or she may apply to the Secretary of State.[68] The liquidator must report the outcome of the final meeting to the court and the Companies Registry and, when three months have elapsed, the company will automatically dissolve.[69]   *WINDING UP IN THE PUBLIC INTEREST.*

A further method of compulsory winding up is winding up in the public interest as provided for by section 124A of the Insolvency Act 1986.[70] This power to wind up is triggered by the Secretary of State following investigation by the DTI or other official inquiries. It is a power that bypasses the requirement that creditors must be owed in excess of £750 if

---

64. Insolvency Act 1986 s. 143(1).   65. Ibid., s. 212.

66. *Re Silver Valley Mines* (1882) 21 Ch D 381; Milman and Durrant, *Corporate Insolvency*, p. 113.

67. IRC v. *Hoogstraten* [1985] QB 1077.   68. Insolvency Rules 1986 r. 4.121.

69. An expedited process for dissolving a company is available in Insolvency Act 1986 s. 202 where the company's realisable assets will not cover the cost of the liquidation and where full investigation of the company's affairs is not required. Here the OR may apply to the Registrar of Companies for an early dissolution order, though twenty-eight days' notice of the intention to apply has to be given to the company's creditors and contributories and administrative receiver (if there is one).

70. Inserted in the Insolvency Act 1986 by the Companies Act 1989. See D. Milman, 'Winding Up in the Public Interest' [1999] 3 *Palmer's In Company* 1 at 1–2; A. Keay, 'Public Interest Petitions' (1999) 20 Co. Law. 296; C. Campbell, 'Protection by Elimination: Winding Up of Companies on Public Interest Grounds' (2001) 17 IL&P 129. Cork recognised the public interest value of winding up in these circumstances: – see *Report of the Review Committee on Insolvency Law and Practice* (Cmnd 8558, 1982) ('Cork Report') para. 1747.

they are to petition the court for a winding up and it is useful where, for instance, it comes to light that a company is defrauding large numbers of creditors of relatively small sums of money: as where 40,000 football World Cup tickets were sold by a company but no tickets were supplied.[71]

This is a power that the Secretary of State can employ when forming the view that it is expedient and in the public interest to wind up the company. It is operated in a modest number of instances (eighty-five in 2000–1)[72] and involves the making of a 'public interest petition' and the court being persuaded that it is just and equitable to wind up the company. No proof of insolvency is required. Petitions requesting that the court should order a winding up have to be advertised and the company at issue must be given seven days' notice of advertising in order to allow it to apply to the court to prevent this.

The reasons for presenting such petitions have included:[73] the absence, during the company's lifetime, of sufficient paid-up capital; serious Companies Act breaches; fraudulent conduct, misrepresentation or conspiracy; inadequate record keeping and misleading of the public; and lack of authorisation to conduct an investment or insurance business. A winding-up order does not, however, flow automatically from the presenting of a petition by the Secretary of State. The court will satisfy itself that an order is in the public interest and submissions from the Secretary of State will be considered and tested in the same manner as those of other parties.[74]

Once a public interest petition has been presented, the Secretary of State may apply for the appointment of a provisional liquidator and the court may think this to be an especially appropriate course where there is a need for speedy and urgent investigation of the company's affairs: as where a fraud on the public is alleged.[75] The Secretary of State may petition for a winding up of the company under section 124A of the Insolvency Act 1986 even if the company is registered outside Great Britain, even if the company is solvent and even if no illegality is alleged.[76] Where a registration is outside Great Britain the company's principal place of business

71. See Campbell, 'Protection by Elimination', p. 131.
72. Insolvency Service, Annual Report 2000–1.
73. See Keay, 'Public Interest Petitions', p. 297.
74. See *Re Walter L. Jacobs Ltd* [1989] 5 BCC 244, 251; *Re Secure & Provide plc* [1992] BCC 405; *Secretary of State for Trade and Industry* v. *Travel Time (UK) Ltd* [2000] BCC 792; Keay, 'Public Interest Petitions', p. 298.
75. See *Re A Company (No. 007070 of 1996)* [1997] BCLC 139.
76. *Re SHV Senator Hanseatische Verwaltungs Gesellschaft mBH* [1997] BCC 112, [1996] 2 BCLC 562.

must, however, be England or Wales[77] and there must be a sufficient connection with the jurisdiction of the English courts.[78]

Generally, winding-up petitions are heard in public (though hearing in chambers is possible[79]) and petitions have to be advertised in the *London Gazette* when presented.[80] A company may, nevertheless, ask the court to restrain publication if it is able to show that this may result in serious damage to its reputation and financial stability.[81] Where the Secretary of State obtains a winding-up order the DTI will usually be able to recover the costs from the company,[82] and the Court of Appeal has confirmed that costs may be recoverable from a controlling director where the costs of defending a petition were expended in the director's individual interest.[83]

The concept of liquidation

When the Cork Committee reviewed the state of insolvency procedures in 1982 it was concerned that liquidation, like other ways of dealing with insolvency, was based on a myth: that creditors would control processes. The principle underlying insolvency law, from at least Victorian times to the 1980s, was said to be that: 'Since the estate is being administered primarily for the benefit of the creditors, they are the persons best calculated to look after their own interests.'[84] In accordance with this notion, the Companies Act 1948 section 246 obliged the liquidator to have regard to any directions given by the creditors in general meeting or by the committee of inspection and, in exercising certain powers, the liquidator required express authority from the committee of inspection.

It was suggested to the (receptive) Cork Committee that the system of creditor control was illusory because of apathy and indifference on the part of the creditors. Three reasons were given for the weakness of creditor oversight: first, the general belief that most liquidators were efficient, reliable and experienced; second, the propensity of business creditors to

77. *Re Normandy Marketing Ltd* [1994] Ch 198, [1993] BCC 879.
78. See Keay, 'Public Interest Petitions', p. 300; *Re Titan International Inc.* [1998] 1 BCLC 102.
79. Insolvency Rules 1986 r. 7.6(1).   80. Ibid., r. 4.11(1).
81. *Re A Company (No. 007923 of 1994)* [1995] BCC 634, 639; *Re Golden Chemical Products Ltd* [1976] 1 Ch 300.
82. *Re Xyllyx plc (No. 2)* [1992] BCLC 378, 385.
83. *(Re Northwest Holdings plc) Secretary of State for Trade and Industry* v. *Backhouse* [2001] EWCA Civ 67. On FSA petitions to wind up on 'just and equitable' grounds, see FSMA 2000 s. 367.
84. Cork Report, para. 912.

allow for occasional bad debts in fixing prices and to write these off so as to reduce taxable profits, a propensity producing a lack of real interest in insolvency processes; and, third, an acceptance that in most cases of insolvency the general body of creditors was likely to receive only a small dividend. Such factors produced a situation, said Cork, in which creditors were reluctant to attend meetings or serve on committees and where there was an indifference towards the supervision of insolvency processes.

Cork made a number of recommendations that were designed to encourage ordinary creditors to play an active role in insolvency proceedings.[85] A broader solution was, however, to involve a rethinking of the insolvency procedures '[t]o move away from the concept of creditor control toward one based on creditor participation'. This shift, in turn, would be achieved by requiring liquidators (like receivers and administrators) to give more information to creditors generally and to reduce the duties placed upon creditors.

In terms of the benchmarks employed throughout this book, what Cork proposed was a change in emphasis so that liquidation could be seen less as a matter of accountability and control (by creditors) and more as an issue of expert (professional) management by the IP: though in combination with higher levels of transparency and more modest (but more realistic) levels of creditor supervision. Whether liquidation operates in a manner that is supportable by reference to the chapter 2 benchmarks is my next concern.

Efficiency

Central to liquidators acting efficiently is the effective protection of the entitlements of creditors in the gathering together of the insolvency estate. In such endeavours, liquidators are assisted by the Insolvency Act 1986 which seeks to avoid a number of transactions that might defeat creditors, notably actions involving: dispositions after presentation of the winding-up petition;[86] late executed floating charges;[87] transactions at undervalue;[88] preferences;[89] and transactions defrauding creditors.[90]

---

85. For example, Cork's proposals to increase the share in the distribution available for the general body of creditors by reducing preferential debt and conferring a stake in receiver realisation. See ch. 3 above and chs. 13 and 14 below.
86. Insolvency Act 1986 s. 127.   87. Ibid., s. 245.   88. Ibid., s. 238.   89. Ibid., s. 239.
90. Ibid., s. 423. Other provisions also seek to prevent transactional avoidance such as Insolvency Act 1986 s. 244 (extortionate credit transactions); Companies Act 1985 s. 395

Such provisions, if enforced, allow creditors' entitlements to be restored and, furthermore, in the case of wrongful trading, provide for compensatory payments to be paid by directors.[91] Efficient application of these laws may also deter the directors of troubled companies from taking actions that prejudice legitimate creditor interests.[92] Such efficient enforcement action by liquidators is only possible if there is access to the funding that is necessary to pursue cases against errant directors.[93] This section of the chapter accordingly focuses on the funding of liquidator actions but also considers whether liquidators are well placed to amass the information that is necessary for the effective deploying of legal challenges. Whether liquidation and the rules on the avoidance of transactions operate substantively fairly as between different creditors (or between creditors and others) is left to the next section, but overlaps are inevitable and fairness clearly demands efficient and effective enforcement.

The background to funding and its importance to liquidators is that liquidators will often view litigation from a position of reluctance to pursue some actions (for example, avoidable transactions) where there are economically powerful defending parties (for example, banks) or where lucrative professional relationships (with, say, banks) are liable to be soured. As Parry and Milman note: 'It should not be forgotten that the receivership and investigation work, which banks put the way of IPs, will be a far more lucrative source of income than transaction avoidance.'[94]

(non-registration of charges). See generally D. Milman and R. Parry, *A Study of the Operation of Transactional Avoidance Mechanisms in Corporate Insolvency Practice*, Insolvency Lawyers' Association Research Report (1997); R. Parry and D. Milman, 'Transaction Avoidance Provision in Corporate Insolvency: An Empirical Study' (1998) 14 IL&P 280.

91. See Insolvency Act 1986 s. 214; see further ch. 15 below.

92. See R. Parry, 'Funding Litigation in Insolvency' [1998] 2 CfiLR 121.

93. In *Re Leyland DAF Ltd* [2001] 1 BCLC 419 Rimer J held, at first instance (upheld Feb. 2002, CA) that certain expenses properly incurred by a liquidator in a winding up are payable out of assets comprised in a floating charge in priority to the claims of the chargee, a position that was the same whether the floating charge had crystallised before or after the commencement of the liquidation (see *contra Re M. C. Bacon (No. 2)* [1990] BCC 430; *Re Portbase Clothing Ltd* [1993] Ch 388, [1993] BCC 96). See, however, the discussion of *Re Floor Fourteen Ltd* ([2001] 3 All ER 499, [2001] 2 BCLC 392) below. On *Re Leyland DAF* see S. Foster, '*Leyland DAF*: The Importance for Banks and Receivers' (2001) 69 *CCH Company Law Newsletter* 1; T. Pope and M. Woollard, 'The Balance of Power in the Expenses Regime: Part 1 – *Leyland Daf*' (2001) 14 *Insolvency Intelligence* 9, 'Part 2 – *Lewis*' (2001) 14 *Insolvency Intelligence* 20; M. Steiner, 'Receivers v. Liquidators v. Preferential Creditors v. Unsecured Creditors: Practitioners Beware!' (2001) 17 IL&P 3. It has now, furthermore, been held that corporation tax accruing in a liquidation on the realisation of an asset is payable as an expense of the liquidation: see *Commissioners of Inland Revenue* v. *Kahn* [2001] BCC 373 (also reported as *Re Toshoku Finance (UK) plc* [2000] 3 All ER 938) (CA)), [2002] BCC 110 (HL); see Pope and Woollard, 'Balance of Power – Part 2', p. 21.

94. Parry and Milman, 'Transaction Avoidance', p. 282. On conflicts of interest between banks, receivers and liquidators see Foster, '*Leyland DAF*'.

Liquidators, moreover, have to protect the insolvency estate by enter-ing a game in which their own funding problems will routinely be ex-ploited by defenders as a tactic designed to kill the case.[95] As for those funding problems, a number will be faced by liquidators.[96] The diffi-cult reality a liquidator encounters is that actions will have to be taken when a company is insolvent and necessarily short of funds, a position not aided by the non-eligibility for legal aid of a company in administra-tion or liquidation.[97] The Cork Committee commented that the task fac-ing the liquidator was 'too difficult' and led to a paucity of challenges to illegitimate payments,[98] and to date a series of problems confronts the liquidator.

In some circumstances there may be sufficient liquid funds in the pool of realised assets to fund litigation. If the liquidator wishes to litigate to protect creditor interests, he or she will need the approval of the creditors' Liquidation Committee to bring an action in the company's name.[99] In the case of an unsuccessful action brought by the liquidators in their name personally, they may claim indemnification in respect of costs borne, but a significant issue here is the place in the order of priorities that such claims will occupy. Here the judges have not always ruled in a manner that assists the effective funding of liquidator actions. In *Re M. C. Bacon Ltd (No. 2)*[100] Millet J ruled that the costs of unsuccessful preference and wrongful trad-ing actions could not rank, for priority purposes, as taken for the pur-pose of preserving, realising or getting in the assets within Rule 4.218(1) of the Insolvency Rules 1986,[101] nor could they be regarded as expenses of the winding up for the purposes of section 115 of the Insolvency Act 1986. Millet J held that the causes of action involved could not be viewed as as-sets of the company and the actions were not brought by or on behalf of the company. This meant that such costs would rank below the claims of float-ing charge holders and would be payable only out of any assets remaining for distribution to unsecured creditors: a position offering considerable discouragement to liquidators.

95. Parry and Milman, 'Transaction Avoidance', p. 282. On the difficulties of office holders where the costs and expenses of insolvency proceedings exceed the assets in the estate see H. Anderson, 'Insolvent Insolvencies' (2001) 17 IL&P 87. For an instance in which a director was ordered to pay the costs of a successful winding-up petition in the public interest as he induced the company to defend the petition to serve his ulterior interests, see *Secretary of State for Trade and Industry v. Backhouse* [2001] EWCA Civ 67.
96. See Milman and Parry, *A Study*, ch. 2.   97. Legal Aid Act 1988 s. 2(10).
98. Cork Report, para. 1257.
99. In compulsory liquidation this will require the court's sanction.
100. [1990] 3 WLR 646.   101. See also *Re Yagerphone* [1935] Ch 392.

The *Katz* v. *McNally*[102] decision was only concerned with transaction avoidance, not wrongful trading (as in *Re M. C. Bacon (No. 2)*), but the Court of Appeal went some way in countering the reasoning of Millet J in *Re M. C. Bacon (No. 2)*. In *Katz* the court considered that Rule 12.2 made it clear that the expenses of an avoidance action constitute 'expenses of a winding up' and that section 115 of the Insolvency Act 1986 conferred priority on all expenses properly incurred by the liquidator in the course of his duties. Morritt LJ, moreover, held the view that reimbursement of the liquidator could be justified on equitable principles if the liquidator was acting as a trustee or at least in being in a fiduciary position.[103] The significance of *Katz* was clear: office holders were assured that litigation expenses could be met from the company's assets.

The judicially restrictive approach has, however, been reasserted post-*Katz*. In the case of *Re Floor Fourteen Ltd, Lewis* v. *Commissioners of Inland Revenue*[104] the Court of Appeal approved *Re M. C. Bacon (No. 2)*. The liquidator in *Re Floor Fourteen* sought to use the company's funds in his hands to pursue proceedings against the company's directors for wrongful trading and preferences. The preferential creditors successfully opposed the liquidator's application for court approval of this course of action and Peter Gibson LJ accepted that *Re R. S. & M. Engineering Co. Ltd, Mond* v. *Hammond Suddards*,[105] which expressly approved *Re M. C. Bacon (No. 2)*, was binding on the court. Gibson LJ stated that the contrary view in *Katz* was *obiter* and that no independent right to recoup litigation expenses out of the assets could be founded on section 175 of the Insolvency Act 1986.[106] The rights of action of a liquidator to recover preferences and for wrongful trading – and the fruits of such actions – were not property of the company and the costs were not necessary (even if properly incurred) so as to bring them within Rule 4.218(1)(m).[107] The court did not entirely close the door on the

102. [1997] BCC 784.   103. See Parry, 'Funding Litigation in Insolvency', p. 130.
104. [2001] 3 All ER 499, [2001] 2 BCLC 392. See A. Walters, 'Re Floor Fourteen Ltd in the Court of Appeal' (2001) 22 Co. Law. 215; Steiner, 'Receivers v. Liquidators'.
105. [2000] Ch 40, [1999] 3 WLR 697.
106. See 64 CCH Company Law Newsletter, 23 May 2000.
107. M. C. Bacon (No. 2) [1990] 3 WLR 646; Re Oasis Merchandising Services Ltd (1997) BCC 282, Ward v. Aitken [1997] BCC 282; but for a different approach see Re Exchange Travel Holdings Ltd (No. 3) [1997] 2 BCLC 579 where (in a case decided before Mond) the Bacon approach was not embraced warmly: see G. Stewart, 'Legal Update' (2001) Recovery (July) 8. In Scotland a different position obtains under rule 4.67 of the Insolvency (Scotland) Rules 1986, para. 1(a), which allows the payment of 'outlays...incurred by the liquidator in carrying out his functions in the liquidation': see the comment by R. Robinson (2001) Recovery (July) 34. For criticism of Re Floor Fourteen see Editorial, (2001) 17 IL&P 41 which argues that a restrictive view of 'assets of the company' serves neither commercial morality nor the creditor-protective

liquidator, however. It ruled that if the court had a discretion to permit the liquidator to recoup costs (a matter on which it was uncertain) an application might be made to the Companies Court. The Court of Appeal did not have sufficient information to reach a proper conclusion on this issue, and for this reason was not prepared to exercise any such discretion.

An appeal to the House of Lords is awaited in *Re Floor Fourteen Ltd* but if the law remains as set out in the Court of Appeal, liquidators will receive little assistance from the court in providing efficient protection for the estate for distribution, unless they can achieve funding from outside the liquid funds of the company. The effect of *Re Floor Fourteen*, in combination with *Leyland DAF*,[108] is that the expenses a liquidator incurs properly in a winding up can have priority over the claims of a floating charge holder to assets covered by the floating charge and over liquidation preferential creditors,[109] but any costs of unsuccessful litigation or of successful claims under sections 214 or 239 of the Insolvency Act 1986 will not have this priority.[110] As one commentator has observed: 'So long as a category of preferential creditors remains, then liquidators are likely to find themselves handicapped in bringing what could be perfectly justified proceedings which are likely to succeed.'[111]

One method of securing financing from beyond the company is to obtain funds from individual creditors so that their interests can be protected. Such creditors, however, may be slow to provide cash for a number of reasons.[112] First, they may be wary of the lengthy legal processes involved, the uncertainties of any positive result and the potential wrecking tactics of defendants. Small creditors may prefer to cut their losses and large creditors may be happier to absorb the loss rather than become involved in funding a deal whose outcome is uncertain. Second, creditors may be wary of the motives of the liquidator and may fear that actions are taken not so much to protect creditors as to increase professional fees or to enforce commercial morality. If creditors believe that public interest concerns are driving the liquidator's strategy, they may be highly unenthusiastic about subsidising protection of these. Third, creditors may fear that if they fund an action that fails, the court might make a costs order

---

aims of the statutory provisions and rule 4.218, a view echoed in Pope and Woollard, 'Balance of Power – Part 2', pp. 20–1.
108. *Re Leyland DAF* [2001] 1 BCLC 419, upheld Feb. 2002 (CA)   **109.** See ch. 13 below.
110. See Foster, '*Leyland DAF*', p. 2.   **111.** Steiner, 'Receivers v. Liquidators', p. 8.
112. See Editorial, (1998) 14 IL&P 3; Milman and Parry, *A Study*, pp. 18–20; D. Milman, 'Litigation: Funding and Procedural Difficulties' (1997) *Amicus Curiae* 27.

against them under the Supreme Court Act 1981 section 51.[113] Fourth, creditors who are asked to fund an action cannot be offered, in return, a higher proportion of the proceeds of an action than is to be distributed to other creditors: the *pari passu* principle will apply. (Here there is a contrast with the position in Australia where the court can order distributions of recoveries that reward funding creditors.[114])

The case of *Katz*[115] suggested that a party lending money to the liquidator might be granted a first charge over any recoveries in respect of the funding provided (but the priority of a lending creditor's original debt would be unaffected).[116] *Katz* may, however, be limited in scope to cases of voluntary liquidation since section 156 of the Insolvency Act 1986 requires court approval for expenses to be met in compulsory liquidation. Even in voluntary liquidation the court may decline to allow the costs of the action to be met in priority and questions may arise as to whether expenses have been 'properly incurred' (according to section 115 of the Insolvency Act 1986) where company assets are small.[117] As already noted, though, doubts have been cast on *Katz* by the Court of Appeal in *Re Floor Fourteen Ltd*[118] which adhered to the line of *M. C. Bacon (No. 2)* and held the view that litigation expenses of the liquidation were not expenses of the winding up. This goes some way to undermining the argument, based on *Katz*, that creditor loans to liquidators for litigation are possible subjects of first charges over recoveries.[119]

A further method of financing litigation might be for the liquidator to agree with an outside funder that the latter will be assigned the claim for an agreed sum or will finance the action in return for a share in the fruits of the litigation. The case of *Re Oasis Merchandising Services Ltd*[120] involved

---

113. See Milman, 'Litigation': D. Milman, 'Security for Costs: Principles and Pragmatism in Corporate Litigation' in B. Rider (ed.), *The Realm of Company Law* (Kluwer, London, 1998); *Eastglen Ltd* v. *Grafton* [1996] BCC 900: refusal of third party costs against a funding creditor where genuine interest and good faith shown.

114. See Corporations Law s. 464 cited in Milman, 'Litigation', p. 27; *Re Glenisla Investments Ltd* (1996) 18 ACSR 84; *Bell Group* v. *Westpac Banking Corp.* (1996) 22 ACSR 337.

115. *Katz* v. *McNally* [1997] BCC 784.

116. See Parry, 'Funding Litigation in Insolvency', p. 131.   117. Ibid.

118. *Re Floor Fourteen Ltd, Lewis* v. *Commissioners of Inland Revenue* [2001] 3 All ER 499, [2001] 2 BCLC 392.

119. Parry, 'Funding Litigation in Insolvency', p. 31 was confident that the Court of Appeal's approach in *Katz* would 'surely lead to *Bacon* being overturned by the Court of Appeal in the future'. Unfortunately the opportunity was forgone in *Re Floor Fourteen Ltd*.

120. [1997] BCC 282; [1997] 2 WLR 764. For discussion see A. Walters, 'Staying Proceedings on Grounds of Champerty' [2000] Ins. Law. 16; Walters, 'Enforcing Wrongful Trading: Substantive Problems and Practical Disincentives' in B. Rider (ed.), *The Corporate Dimension* (Jordans, Bristol, 1998) pp. 153–9; Walters, 'Anonymous Funders and Abuse of Process' (1998) 114 LQR 207; Walters, '*Re Oasis Merchandising Services Ltd* in the Court of Appeal' (1997) 18 Co.

such selling of the fruits of an action. In that Court of Appeal decision attention was paid to *Grovewood*,[121] which had considered that a sale of the fruits of an action was not 'sale' for the purposes of the Insolvency Act 1986, Schedule 4, para. 6 and so was not exempt from the rules on champerty.[122] *Oasis* was more favourably disposed than *Grovewood* to allow such sales and the Court of Appeal noted that there was much to be said for allowing liquidators to sell the fruits of actions, provided that the purchasers were not given the right to influence the liquidator's conduct of the proceedings.[123] More negative, however, was the *Oasis* attitude to the disposal of rights of action that are personal to the liquidator (as are many transactional avoidance rights). In that case, the Court of Appeal rejected an arrangement whereby the liquidator assigned the potential proceeds of an Insolvency Act 1986 section 214 wrongful trading action in return for litigation finance provided by a commercial body. The court, moreover, held that an assignment was not possible because the fruits of the wrongful trading action were not 'property' subject to the liquidator's power of sale under Schedule 4, para. 4 of the Insolvency Act 1986. An important distinction was drawn between assets that are the property of a company (including rights of action open to the company *prior* to winding up) and assets arising only after liquidation and recoverable only by the liquidator. The latter were not to be regarded as the 'company's property' under Schedule 4, para. 6. Particular court objection was also taken in *Oasis* to the reservation by the funder of certain powers of control over the litigation. The Court of Appeal noted that the wrongful trading provisions possessed a penal aspect[124] and was of the view that acts of such a nature should remain within the control of the office holder (an official acting under court direction).

Law. 214; Walters, 'A Modern Doctrine of Champerty?' (1996) 112 LQR 560; Walters, 'Foreshortening the Shadow: Maintenance, Champerty and the Funding of Litigation in Corporate Insolvency' (1996) 17 Co. Law. 165; K. Houston, 'Agreement to Share Fruits of Wrongful Trading Claim Void' (1997) 18 Co. Law. 297.

121. *Grovewood Holdings* v. *James Capel & Co.* [1995] BCC 760.

122. The rule on champerty prohibits the selling of a cause of action or its fruits to a party with no legitimate interest in the proceedings. As a general rule such sales are not champertous in insolvency if it is within the office holder's power (under Insolvency Act 1986, Sched. 4, para. 6) to sell or dispose of the assets of the company: see Parry, 'Funding Litigation in Insolvency', p. 123. See Walters, 'A Modern Doctrine of Champerty?'; P. Winterborne, 'The Second Hand Cause of Action Market' (2001) 14 *Insolvency Intelligence* 65 (who notes, at p. 66, the conflicting public policy considerations operating in assignment of causes of action cases, namely (1) that causes of action should not be traded and that persons without a legitimate interest in litigation should not become involved, and (2) that office holders should not be prevented from pursuing legitimate causes of action (and recovering valuable funds for creditors) due to lack of funding).

123. [1997] 2 WLR 764, 777H; *ANC Ltd* v. *Clark Goldring and Page Ltd* [2001] BPIR 568. See Milman and Parry, *A Study*, p. 21.

124. See discussion in ch. 15 below.

Objections to the restrictiveness of *Oasis* can, however, be taken.[125] It might be argued that allowing the funding of liquidator actions through the assignment of proceeds would do more potential good (in assisting creditor protection and deterring errant directorial behaviour) than it would cause harm in undermining the administration of justice (by giving a commercially uninvolved party an interest in the case or allowing 'trafficking' in cases[126]). The dangers involved in such funding arrangements can, moreover, be reduced by restrictions on the degree of control over the litigation process that can be conceded to a funder[127] – perhaps limiting this to such matters as choice of lawyer or a voice in settlement negotiations – for, as has been pointed out, commercial realities demand that funders be given some influence.[128]

A second objection is that the *Oasis* approach gives too little attention to the merits of a case when it deems a stay of proceedings to be the appropriate judicial response to the funding of liquidation litigation by the assignment of proceeds. Where the case is strong and there is good evidence of malpractice to the detriment of creditor interests, it is arguable that the courts should take this factor into account in deciding whether to allow an action to proceed.[129]

A further difficulty with *Oasis* is that a funding distinction is drawn between the Insolvency Act 1986 section 212 misfeasance actions (which the law treats as corporate property able to be assigned) and section 214 wrongful trading actions (which cannot). This produces perverse incentives to 'overload' misfeasance and bring actions under s. 212 or to test the limits of directors' duties at common law when claims may fall squarely within s. 214. One commentator has dubbed this 'absurd'.[130]

Conditional fee arrangements (CFAs) offer another potential means of funding liquidator actions.[131] Under such agreements, the liquidator will pay no lawyers' fees in an unsuccessful action but will be charged a 'success fee' or 'uplift' by the legal firm if the desired outcome is achieved.[132]

125. See generally Walters, 'Staying Proceedings', 'Enforcing Wrongful Trading'.
126. Walters, 'Staying Proceedings', p. 20; Milman and Parry, *A Study*, p. 40.
127. See the judgment of Peter Gibson LJ at [1997] 2 WLR 764 at 777; *Giles* v. *Thompson* [1994] 1 AC 142 (some funder interference acceptable).
128. Walters, 'Staying Proceedings', p. 22.
129. Ibid., p. 23. See *Abraham* v. *Thompson* [1997] 4 All ER 362; *Stocznia Gdanska SA* v. *Latvian Shipping Co. (No. 2)* [1999] 3 All ER 822 (proceedings only to be stayed if, on the particular facts, the likelihood of abuse is sufficient to deny access to justice).
130. Walters, 'Enforcing Wrongful Trading', p. 158.
131. Permitted by the Conditional Fee Agreement Order, 1995 (SI 1995 No. 1674), Conditional Fee Agreement Regulations, 1995 (SI 1995 No. 1675).
132. Note that conditional fees are not like contingency fees employed in the USA. The US style agreements often provide for a client to pay the lawyer a percentage of the damages

Proceedings by liquidators relating to companies being wound up are 'specified proceedings' to which conditional fee arrangements can be applied.[133] Lawyers' costs are usually the largest element of the sums that liquidators require in order to pursue those assets that a debtor may have hidden away. The liquidator's ability to retain lawyers on a conditional fee basis is designed to facilitate actions since the risk of legal fees is transferred to the liquidator's own lawyer and the risk of having to pay the other side's costs in an unsuccessful case can be covered by insurance.

The introduction of conditional fee arrangements has been found, however, not to have made a huge impact in the insolvency sector.[134] This may be because informal arrangements of a similar nature are already being used by solicitors and liquidators and because restrictions have limited the enthusiasm of practitioners. It has, for instance, been suggested that solicitors have not warmed to the upper limit of 25 per cent that is imposed on their demanded recoveries.[135] A further difficulty has arisen because conditional fees do not adequately deal with adverse costs, which, under the Insolvency Lawyers' Association Model Conditional Fee Agreement, have to be borne by the liquidator or the estate as client. Insurance for adverse costs is possible, as noted, and recent years have seen a growth in the availability of legal costs insurance. The London market in such insurance has been said to have been boosted by the Government's decision to widen the use of no-win no-fee agreements: solicitors' firms that take on such conditional fee work will very often insist that their clients take out insurance to cover opponents' costs in the event of a lost case. (In 1999, indeed, the *Financial Times* reported that the largest legal costs insurance policy ever placed in the London market – a £15.6 million policy – had been bought by the liquidators of the Australian-based Bell Group.[136]) Liquidators, nevertheless, may see such insurance as not entirely problem free. In order to obtain cover, a counsel's opinion will often be required and this may be costly. Liquidators have to find the premiums out of the available company funds and premiums have risen sharply in recent years. The Law Society operates the most widely used conditional fee insurance scheme

---

if the client wins. An English lawyer is still restricted from agreeing with a client to be paid a percentage of the recoveries from an action. See further LCD Consultation Paper, *Access to Justice with Conditional Fees*, March 1998.

133. Conditional Fee Agreements Order, 1995 (SI 1995 No. 1674).

134. Milman and Parry, *A Study*, p. 21. See also BDO Stoy Hayward Survey (reported in (1999) 12 *Insolvency Intelligence* 48) which concluded, *inter alia*, that there was a lack of overall assessment by firms surveyed of the impact of CFAs on their practice.

135. Milman and Parry, *A Study*.   136. *Financial Times*, 2 December 1999.

but raised one set of premiums by around 90 per cent in 1997 alone. The conditions that insurers impose on such cover (for example, demanding the use of lawyers on the insurance company's panel) may also restrict the liquidator's enthusiasm for such arrangements.[137] There is, moreover, evidence that solicitors' firms will tend to demand a very strong case indeed before proceeding on a conditional fee basis. This is reflected in evidence from the personal injury sector which reveals a success rate for solicitors of 98 per cent.[138]

The above analysis suggests that efficient liquidator action to protect the interests of creditors is likely to be impeded by funding difficulties. Milman and Parry,[139] in their Insolvency Lawyers' Association funded research of 1997, found that in cases where there appeared to practitioners to be a cause for action under sections 238, 239, 245 and 423 of the Insolvency Act 1986, between 33 per cent and 50 per cent of the office holders said that they instituted proceedings 'rarely'.[140] The reason in around 60 per cent of cases was lack of funding, and the next most cited reason – lack of evidence – figured in around 30 per cent of cases.[141]

What can be done to ease such funding difficulties? A first step would be to amend the law as stated in the Insolvency Act 1986 so as to allow liquidators to assign shares in the fruits of an action, provided that they do not cede control of such claims.[142] As Milman and Parry conclude: 'A much wider range of parties [should be allowed] to undertake transactional avoidance litigation. Commercial organisations, which are increasingly prominent in the area of litigation finance, should be permitted to purchase and prosecute actions to avoid dubious transactions and the courts should be prepared to reconsider their traditional hostility to such "trafficking".'[143]

---

137. See BDO Stoy Hayward Survey (1999), revealing that 75 per cent of those questioned considered that such restrictive clauses in insurance agreements were a deterrent to taking out cover.

138. Ibid.   139. Milman and Parry, *A Study*.

140. The percentages of office holders responding 'rarely' varied from section to section as follows: Insolvency Act 1986 section 238 – 38.6 per cent; section 239 – 33.7 per cent; section 245 – 50.5 per cent; section 423 – 49.4 per cent: Milman and Parry, *A Study*, pp. 25–6.

141. Ibid., p. 30.

142. Milman and Parry, *A Study*, p. 39. Winterborne suggests that the claims that office holders can bring (under sections 339, 340, 214, 238 or 239 of the Insolvency Act 1986) cannot be assigned because this would be to delegate a statutory power. Where, in contrast, a claim is one that the company could have brought, the cause, as noted, is an asset that can be sold by the office holder for the benefit of creditors with the terms of Schedule 4, para. 6: Winterborne, 'Second Hand Cause of Action Market', p. 67. See also *ANC Ltd* v. *Clark Goldring and Page Ltd* [2001] BPIR 568.

143. Milman and Parry, *A Study*, pp. 39–40. See also Winterborne, 'Second Hand Cause of Action Market'.

State funding of 'public interest' litigation to prevent avoidance has also been put forward as a response to funding difficulties,[144] and the Harmer Report[145] on insolvency law reform in Australia recommended this for the corporate insolvency area. This funding might be organised around a levy on directors or companies and reimbursement of the fund could be provided for in the case of successful liquidator actions.[146] This is not, however, a problem-free area and processes would have to be established so as to avoid the taking of speculative cases or cases that lack real merit and are pursued for tactical reasons.

A further way of funding avoidance litigation would be to make use of the profits of the Insolvency Services Account (ISA) (which imposes a levy on liquidation funds paid into and out of the account). The profits of the ISA are presently used to investigate the past conduct of parties (including directors) for the purposes *inter alia* of bringing prosecutions or disqualification proceedings. It has been argued[147] that the deterrent effects of disqualification are undramatic and that:

> The funds in the ISA could be better employed in subsidising…the costs of investigating and bringing financial claims against directors, shadow directors and recipients of the benefits of voidable transactions. Financial claims against them…would be a far more effective deterrent and public protection and, what is more, would bring more tangible benefits to the creditors.[148]

A further move in the direction of Australian law might also be desirable. In that country the court has the power to approve an arrangement in which a creditor who has indemnified the liquidator against the costs of proceedings can be allocated a higher share of the proceeds recovered: one that reflects the degree of risk assumed by the creditor.[149] In the UK the court might be given the power to approve such arrangements between liquidators and funders as seem appropriate and fair to all affected creditors.

Funding is not the only difficulty that liquidators face in attempting to combat transaction avoidance. The substantive rules of insolvency law

144. Milman and Parry, *A Study*.
145. Australian Law Reform Commission, *General Insolvency Inquiry*, Report No. 45 (Canberra, 1988) 26.
146. Ibid. See also Editorial, (1998) 14 IL&P 185–6.   147. Editorial, (1998) 14 IL&P 185–6.
148. Ibid., p. 186.   149. See *Re Glenisla Investments Ltd* (1996) 18 ACSR 84.

can also be criticised as giving secured creditors, normally banks, excessive levels of protection.[150] The law on the avoidance of preferences, for instance, is set out in section 239 of the Insolvency Act 1986 and is designed to protect *pari passu* distribution by stopping an insolvent company from favouring one creditor at the expense of others. Section 239 modified the law, in a manner prompted by Cork,[151] so as to allow a liquidator to succeed in a challenge by establishing that one contributing influence behind the transaction was the desire to prefer.[152] In the case of *M. C. Bacon Ltd*,[153] however, Millet J held that a defence exists if it can be shown that the directors entered a transaction not in order to prefer but with a view to securing financing in order to keep the business going. This focus on subjective motivation increases the liquidator's problems of proof, though in the case of beneficiaries to the transaction who are connected persons there is onus reversal so that such a person has to show that the transaction is not influenced by a desire by the company to prefer.[154] An objective or 'effects' test in the law of preferences would eradicate the problems brought to the fore by *Re M. C. Bacon Ltd* and would correspond to the approach taken in other jurisdictions such as Australia and the USA.[155] An alternative step of assistance to liquidators would be the institution of a statutory presumption of preference where there is a grant of security so that the court should set this aside unless the debenture holder is able to give good reason for sustaining it. Liquidators would also benefit by abolition of the requirement (in sections 238, 239 and 245 of the Insolvency Act 1986) that the liquidator should show that the company was unable to pay its debts within the meaning of section 123 of the Insolvency Act 1986. The incompleteness of company financial records and problems of valuation may make proof of insolvency at the relevant time very difficult for the liquidator, who would be assisted by abolition of this requirement in favour of establishing that the company subsequently became insolvent within the specified time period.[156] Milman and Parry have argued that in dealing with transactions at undervalue the law should recognise (contra Millet J in *Re M. C. Bacon Ltd*) that creating a security does devalue a company's assets so that in looking to section 238 of the Insolvency Act 1986 (transactions at undervalue) a devaluation effected in this way is only

---

150. Milman and Parry, *A Study*, p. 36.   151. Cork Report, paras. 1241–88.
152. See Insolvency Act 1986 s. 239(5).   153. [1990] BCLC 324.
154. *Re Exchange Travel Holdings* [1996] 2 BCLC 524; discussed by R. Parry [1997] Ins. Law. 11–13.
155. See Milman and Parry, *A Study*, p. 36.   156. Ibid., p. 38.

acceptable if the recipient of the transaction can show that a corresponding economic benefit has accrued to the company.[157]

There may also be a case for a more general change in the burden of proof so as to assist liquidators. In Australia a trustee in bankruptcy may give notice to the recipient of a suspectedly void transfer and demand a return to the estate. Where the recipient then wishes to contest that notice he or she will bear the burden of proving that no preference was given.[158] Finally, a hardening of the law's position on the recipient of a benefit from an insolvency company might contribute to liquidator effectiveness in protecting the estate.

Turning now to information, there is little utility in providing for a properly funded liquidation system if liquidators are ill-informed concerning the extent and whereabouts of the insolvent company's assets or concerning relevant directors' dealings. The liquidator's powers, as already outlined, do, however, contain extensive powers to gather information, and section 235 of the Insolvency Act 1986 provides that officers, employers, administrators or administrative receivers of the company (past and present) have a duty to provide the liquidator with such information as may reasonably be required.[159] The liquidator may also ask the court to exercise its powers under section 236 of the Insolvency Act 1986 to call before it for examination any officer of the company, any person known or suspected of having in their possession any property of the company or any person supposed to be indebted to the company; or any person whom the court thinks capable of giving information concerning the business dealings, property etc. of the company. Account books, papers or records may also be demanded by the court and powers of seizure and arrest are provided for in section 236(5).

The court has a broad discretion to conduct examinations in order to further a winding up and the liquidator will have some influence on the exercise of that discretion. The view of an office holder that an

---

157. Ibid., p. 36. See also A. Clarke, 'Security Interests as Property: Relocating Security Interests within the Property Framework' in Harris, *Property Problems*, pp. 119–20.

158. See Bankruptcy Act 1966 s. 139ZQ introduced in 1991; A. Keay, *Avoidance Provisions in Insolvency Law* (LBC Information Services, Sydney, 1997) pp. 298–308; Milman and Parry, *A Study*, p. 38.

159. Note also that company officers are required to be proactive, and not merely reactive, under Insolvency Act 1986 ss. 206–11: see *Re McCredie, The Times*, 5 October 1999, per Henry LJ. (The Insolvency Act 1986 s. 208(1), for example, makes it a criminal offence to fail 'fully and truly to discover to the liquidator all the company's property' and to fail to deliver up company property under the director's custody and control. The same applies to books and papers.)

examination is required is normally given 'a good deal of weight'[160] but the power to examine is not designed to offer liquidators special advantages in ordinary litigation and should not be operated oppressively.[161] Its purpose has been described as allowing the office holder 'to get sufficient information to reconstitute the state of knowledge a company should possess'.[162] The House of Lords has held that an order could properly be made to extend to all documents and information which office holders reasonably require to carry out their functions.[163]

Liquidators are placed in a strong informational position by the Insolvency Act 1986 but, of course, their ability to deploy this information to good effect depends greatly upon their expertise: a matter to which we now turn.

Expertise

A liquidator must be a qualified IP[164] and the general characteristics of IPs have been discussed in chapter 5 above. The issue of particular concern here is whether the winding up process as presently set up is consistent with the exercise of an appropriate level of expertise.

In asking this question it is not necessary to assess the potential of the liquidator as an agent of possible rescue. His or her role is more focused than that of, say, an administrator and centres on gathering in the assets and distributing them. It is in the gathering process that there is a particularly strong role for expertise. At this stage of operations the liquidator has both to defend the body of corporate assets and seek to increase it. The former task is evident in liquidator dealings with those who claim that property in the possession of a company does not form part of the

---

160. *Joint Liquidators of Sasea Finance Ltd* v. *KPMG* [1998] BCC 216, 220. See further C. Campbell, 'Investigations by Insolvency Practitioners – Powers and Restraint: Part I' (2000) 16 IL&P 182.
161. *Re Embassy Art Products Ltd* [1987] 3 BCC 292.
162. Browne-Wilkinson VC in *Re Cloverbay Ltd* [1991] Ch 90, 102; [1990] BCC 415, 419–20.
163. *Bristol and Commonwealth Holdings plc (Joint Administrators)* v. *Spicer and Oppenheim (Re British and Commonwealth Holdings plc No. 2)* [1993] AC 426. On the potential impact of the Human Rights Act 1998 here, see W. Trower, 'Bringing Human Rights Home to the Insolvency Practitioner' (2000) 13 *Insolvency Intelligence* 52. See also Insolvency Act 2000 s. 11, which amends Insolvency Act 1986 s. 219 which had allowed answers obtained under powers of compulsion, derived from the Companies Act 1985, to be used as evidence against that person. In *Saunders* v. *UK* [1997] BCC 872 the ECHR decided that for the prosecution to use answers given pursuant to a power of compulsion in subsequent criminal proceedings infringed Mr Saunders' rights under Article 6 of the European Convention on Human Rights. The Insolvency Act 2000 therefore amends section 219 to make it compatible with the Convention.
164. Insolvency Act 1986 s. 388.

estate: because, for instance, it is asserted that the owner has retained title. Socio-legal studies of practice reveal, in this area, a high level of IP expertise and dominance.[165] Claimant suppliers to companies are often out
of their depth and IPs tend to be in possession of the goods, to know the
supply needs and to be both legally competent and familiar with the legal
game being played. They are sophisticated repeat players who will use devices such as delay and bluff to protect the assets of the estate.[166] Liquidators, moreover, have an incentive to deploy their expertise to the full: their
fees have to be paid out of the assets that are realised and the less that is
removed from the company by, say, successful uses of the retention of title
device the more remains for fee-paying purposes. Questions may arise as
to the fairness of such arrangements but lack of liquidator expertise is not
the primary issue.

The challenge to the expertise of the liquidator is perhaps more severe
when he or she attempts not to retain assets but to secure these, for example, by using the avoidance powers given to liquidators to challenge transactions that prejudice creditors. What is clear from the empirical research,
however, is that the self-policing of insolvency professionals can operate
in a manner that upholds ethical or professional standards, as where IPs
use their powers in order to remove from office at the creditors' meeting a
liquidator of whose conduct they did not approve.[167]

Running counter to such expert upholding of standards, however, is
the tendency of IPs to use their professional expertise at creditors' meetings not to further transparency in liquidation processes but to engage in
self-serving activities of a collective or individual nature. Wheeler argues
that the creditors' meeting is often used by IPs as a public forum to pa-
rade their standards of practice; to compete for the work involved in the
liquidation (by 'stealing' the liquidation from the provisional liquidator
through use of rhetoric to gain creditor support); and to sideline creditors
and exclude trade creditors from a process amounting to an 'exclusionary
discourse'.[168] Such an account, of course, emphasises the danger of evaluating insolvency processes by using a benchmark of expertise without reference to objectives: liquidation may be a process that lends itself to certain
misdirections of expertise.

165. See S. Wheeler, 'Capital Fractionalised: The Role of Insolvency Practitioners in Asset
Distribution' in M. Cain and C. B. Harrington (eds.), *Lawyers in a Post Modern World: Translation
and Transgression* (Open University Press, Buckingham, 1994).
166. Ibid., p. 90. See also ch. 3 above and ch. 14 below.
167. S. Wheeler, 'Empty Rhetoric and Empty Promises: The Creditors' Meeting' (1994) 21
Journal of Law and Society 350, 360.
168. Ibid., pp. 367–9.

Accountability

In both voluntary and compulsory liquidations the liquidator is obliged to convene a meeting of creditors to consider his removal from office if he is requested to do so by more than 25 per cent in value of the creditors, and if he fails to do so the creditors may apply to the court to order such a meeting.[169] At such a meeting a simple majority of those present and voting may remove the liquidator.

Such may be the formal position but on the ground the accountability of a liquidator – particularly to the creditors' meeting – may operate quite differently. Legal accountability may be described as 'empty rhetoric'.[170] As was seen in the last section, IP expertise and repeat playing may produce dominance over the creditors' meeting rather than accountability so that such meetings are seen by IPs and liquidators not so much as holdings to account as opportunities for pursuing or defending business.

Does the Human Rights Act 1998 (HRA) introduce the prospect of greater legal accountability for liquidators?[171] The HRA applies to the decision-making procedures of all public bodies and it is unlawful under section 6 for a public authority to act in a way that is incompatible with a Convention right. A liquidator is liable to be considered as a public authority under section 6(3) as he or she undertakes a public function, for the benefit of society as a whole. (An administrator of a company is also likely to be seen as a 'public authority'.[172])

The European Court of Human Rights (ECHR) has held that Article 6 is satisfied where there is a proper right of appeal to a court and the determining of rights is properly reviewable by the court after a fair hearing.[173] In the case of liquidator activities relating to a company being wound up by the court, the Insolvency Act 1986 provides for court control in sections 167(3) and 168(5). The courts, however, have indicated that they will

---

169. Insolvency Rules 1986 r. 4.114-CVL and 4.115.

170. Wheeler, 'Empty Rhetoric and Empty Promises'.

171. See M. Simmons and T. Smith, 'The Human Rights Act 1998: The Practical Impact on Insolvency' (2000) 16 IL&P 167; J. Lowry and L. Watson, *Company Law* (Butterworths, London, 2001) pp. 410–13; W. Trower, 'Human Rights: Article 6 – The Reality and the Myth' [2001] Ins. Law. 48; Trower, 'Bringing Human Rights Home'; D. Kapper, 'Insolvency and the Human Rights Act 1998: Early Northern Ireland Perspectives' [2001] Ins. Law. 119.

172. The position is less clear in relation to administrative receivers, supervisors of voluntary arrangements and office holders when not undertaking 'public functions': see Simmons and Smith, 'Human Rights Act 1998', p. 170.

173. See I. F. Fletcher, 'Juggling with Norms: The Conflict between Collective and Individual Rights under Insolvency Law' in R. Cranston (ed.), *Making Commercial Law* (Clarendon Press, Oxford, 1997) pp. 411–14.

only interfere with a liquidator's decision on grounds of reasonableness,[174] and it has been questioned whether this meets Article 6 requirements.[175] Suggested areas where liquidators may face HRA attack have included: preventing trading by presenting a winding-up petition;[176] exercising investigative powers;[177] and using confidential statements.[178] The potential impact of the HRA should not, however, be exaggerated since the concept of 'justifiable interference' will shield the decisions of many office holders as will the usual array of informational, evidential and resource restraints that limit challenges through court action.

If Wheeler's portrait of the creditors' meeting rings true and there is less to creditor scrutiny than meets the eye, what is to be done? Here it could be argued that the answer is not to increase levels of judicial oversight: that would do little for the less well-informed and less well-positioned creditors and might do much to increase costs and delays. The appropriate response may be for the IP profession to police its professional standards more rigorously so that greater attention is paid to informing creditors and listening to them rather than holding them at a distance by conducting an arcane 'players' dialogue'.

Fairness

Avoidance of transactions

Fairness in liquidation demands that the general body of creditors be protected from dispositions of the company's assets in the period leading up to liquidation which confer improper advantages on certain creditors or other parties. It demands that the collective nature of the insolvency process be protected. The law on the avoidance of transactions, accordingly, seeks to protect collectivity and the principle of *pari passu* distribution and to deal with the unjust enrichment of a particular party at the expense of the general body of creditors.[179] This section of the chapter

---

174. See *Re Edennote Ltd, Tottenham Hotspur plc* v. *Ryman* [1996] BCC 718; *Leon* v. *York-O-Matic Ltd* [1966] 1 WLR 1450; *Mitchell* v. *Buckingham International plc* [1998] 2 BCLC 369.

175. See Simmons and Smith, 'Human Rights Act 1998', p. 170.

176. Insolvency Act 1986 s. 127.

177. Ibid., ss. 235–6; see *Re Esal Commodities Ltd* [1988] PCC 443 at 457–8.

178. Insolvency Act 1986 s. 236. See Simmons and Smith, 'Human Rights Act 1998', p. 170.

179. See generally D. Prentice, 'Some Observations on the Law Relating to Preferences', in R. Cranston (ed.), *Making Commercial Law* (Clarendon Press, Oxford, 1997); A. Keay, 'Preferences in Liquidation Law: A Time for Change' [1998] 2 CfiLR 198; Keay, 'The Recovery of Voidable Preferences: Aspects of Restoration' [2000] 1 CFILR 1; Keay, 'The Avoidance of Pre-Liquidation Transactions: Anglo-Australian Comparison' [1998] JBL 515; M. Hemsworth, 'Voidable Preference: Desire and Effect' (2000) 16 IL&P 54; J. Verrill, 'Attacking Antecedent Transactions' [1993] 12 JIBL 485; Milman and Durrant, *Corporate Insolvency*, ch. 11.

discusses the major avoidance provisions that are found in the Insolvency Act 1986, namely: preferences (sections 239–41); transactions at undervalue and transactions defrauding creditors (sections 238, 240–1, 423); and avoidance of floating charges (section 245).

Preferences

A preference occurs when a creditor – to the detriment of other creditors – receives more from a company before it goes into liquidation than he or she would have obtained in a formal distribution in liquidation. The broad aim of preference law is to ensure the fair treatment of creditors in a liquidation, but it can also be claimed that preference laws increase the assets available for distribution to creditors by protecting the collective nature of the liquidation process.[180] Preference laws may thus be thought to discourage the piecemeal dismembering of the estate in the lead up to liquidation and thus to maximise its value. As Prentice points out, however,[181] preference law claws back transactions only where there is a desire to prefer and this means that the law will only deter such dismembering if the parties involved are aware of the impending insolvency of the company.[182]

Under the terms of the Insolvency Act 1986 sections 239–41, a liquidator can successfully challenge a transaction as a preference by showing that: the transaction was entered into within six months of insolvency,[183] or within two years if the defendant is a person 'connected with a company';[184] the recipient is a creditor, surety or guarantor of any of the company's debts; the company does anything which places the recipient in a position that, in the event of the liquidation, will be better than the position he would have been in had the thing not been done; the company was influenced in deciding to enter into the impugned transaction by a desire to make a preference; and at the time of, or as a result of, the preference the company was unable to pay its debts and was insolvent within the meaning of the Insolvency Act 1986 section 123.

---

180. On the advantages of collectivity see the discussion in ch. 2 above, pp. 28–9; T. H. Jackson, *The Logic and Limits of Bankruptcy Law* (Harvard University Press, Cambridge, Mass., 1986) pp. 16–17.

181. 'Some observations', p. 443.

182. Directors may, however, fear that if they grant a preference they may be vulnerable to a disqualification order under the Company Directors' Disqualification Act 1986 Sched. 1, Part 2, para. 8 which makes preferences relevant in assessing unfitness to take part in the management of the company: see ch. 15 below.

183. Insolvency is defined in the Insolvency Act 1986 s. 240(3) as the date of the commencement of the winding up (at the time of presentation of the petition for winding up per s. 129(2) or the passing of the resolution for winding up in a voluntary winding up per s. 86). Administrators can also challenge preferences: s. 239 (1) and (2).

184. Insolvency Act 1986 s. 240(1)(a).

A controversial aspect of the law here is its subjective basis, as seen in the need for the liquidator to show that the company was 'influenced' by a 'desire' to prefer. On this point, Cork examined the case for objectivity but concluded that proof of intention to prefer should be retained in the law and that 'genuine pressure by a creditor should continue to afford a defence'.[185] The law, said Cork, should be reluctant to allow the recovery of payments made to discharge lawful debts due and Cork considered that recovery was only justifiable if the payment was 'really improper'. As critics have suggested, however,[186] this misses the point since it may well be thought to be improper to subvert *pari passu* by preferring one creditor to another in the lead up to insolvency. What is clear is that the liquidator's task in protecting both the estate and the principle of equal distribution is made harder by the need to show the influence of a desire to prefer. On how dominant the section 235(5) desire to prefer must be, the case of *Re M. C. Bacon Ltd*[187] casts some light. Millet J, in an influential judgment, stated that it was not necessary to adduce direct evidence of the desire – which could be inferred from the circumstances of the case – but the desire must have influenced the decision or the transaction being attacked by the liquidator. It was not necessary to show that the desire was the only or the decisive factor behind the preference: it might only be one of the influencing factors. In the case of preferences to persons connected with the company, there is some assistance for the liquidator in section 239(6) of the Insolvency Act 1986 which creates a (rebuttable) presumption of a section 239(5) desire to prefer.[188]

The use of a subjective test here has been dubbed 'unrealistic and unreasonable'.[189] It is always difficult for a court to ascertain subjective motive[190] and especially problematic in the case of a corporate body with no easily identifiable mind.[191] The courts have proved reluctant to make inferences concerning the mind of the debtor company[192] and in many cases

---

185. Cork Report, para. 1256.
186. Prentice, 'Some Observations'; Keay, 'Preferences in Liquidation Law'.
187. [1990] BCLC 324.
188. See e.g. *Weisgard* v. *Pilkington* [1995] BCC 1108 where directors failed to rebut the presumption of a desire to prefer. In *Re 38 Buildings Ltd* [1999] BCC 260 the family beneficiaries of a trust executed by a troubled family company were held not to be preferred connected persons since the trustees of the fund were collectively to be treated as creditors for the purposes of s. 239.
189. Keay, 'Preferences in Liquidation Law'.
190. As recognised by the Cork Report at para. 1253.
191. See Keay, 'Preferences in Liquidation Law', pp. 206–7; and more generally J. Coffee, ' "No Soul to Damn: No Body to Kick": An Unscandalized Inquiry into the Problem of Corporate Punishment' (1981) 79 Mich. L Rev. 386.
192. *Re Beacon Leisure Ltd* [1991] BCC 213; *Re Fairway Magazines Ltd* [1992] BCC 924.

troubled companies make payments to creditors not in order to execute a preference but in order to ease creditor pressure or to ensure continuity of business activity.[193] If, accordingly, the creditor is not a 'connected' person, the liquidator faces an uphill task in establishing the desire to prefer as well as the company's insolvency.[194]

A further difficulty for the liquidator is that a payment to a creditor may be made when a company is acting in a disorganised fashion. In this confusion it may be especially difficult to show the influence of a desire to prefer and it can be argued that fairness – through protection of *pari passu* distribution – is as deserving of protection from transfers that are unthinking as from those that are designed to prefer.[195] The argument for a subjective approach is weak if couched simply in terms of Cork's desire to see companies pay 'lawful debts properly due'.[196] Cork also argued that the diligent creditor 'might in principle be allowed to retain the fruits of his diligence'[197] but this contention has limited force in the period leading to a liquidation: if accepted it gives the green light to a creditors' race to collect. It encourages precipitous actions and it undermines the collective approach to liquidation with all its advantages of efficiency and fairness.

Cork also favoured adherence to the established legal rule that transfers made under pressure from creditors could be defended as there was no free intention to prefer in such circumstances.[198] Again, however, the position is difficult to sustain as it undermines collectivity by rewarding those who indulge in a race to collect. The position invites creditors to apply pressure (again precipitately) and it favours more powerful creditors who are given an incentive to collude with companies to give the appearance of pressure.[199]

What, though, of the argument that an objective 'effects-based' approach to preferences is undesirable as it would make creditors nervous

---

193. Keay, 'Preferences in Liquidation Law', p. 207.

194. See Offer, 'Influential Desire and Dominant Intention' (1990) 3 *Insolvency Intelligence* 42.

195. On the centrality of protecting *pari passu* in preference law, see the Privy Council in *Lewis v. Hyde* [1997] BCC 976, 979. On *pari passu* see ch. 13 below.

196. Cork Report, para. 1256(a).   197. Ibid., para. 1256(b).

198. Ibid., para. 1256. See *Alderson v. Temple* (1768) 6 Burr. 2235; 97 ER 165; *Scott v. Thomas* (1834) 6 C&P 661; *Re Liebert* (1873) 8 Ch App 283; *Smith v. Pilgrim* (1876) 2 Ch D 127; *Re FLE Holdings* [1967] 1 WLR 140 (where it was indicated by the court that if the company mistakenly believed it had to pay because of the pressure its intention was not to grant a preference but to save itself).

199. Keay, 'Preferences in Liquidation Law', pp. 211–12. I. F. Fletcher, 'Voidable Transactions in Bankruptcy Law: British Law Perspectives' in J. Ziegel (ed.), *Current Developments in International and Comparative Corporate Insolvency Law* (Clarendon Press, Oxford, 1994) pp. 307, 309.

of having any dealings with the troubled company; that it would chill commercial activity in a generally undesirable way? In response it can be said that financing for companies is not likely to be less forthcoming (or less continuing) under an effects rule than under a subjective rule that positively encourages them to demand repayment of their loan at the first sniff of trouble. Should the contrary prove to be the case, a 'creditor's defence' rule could be introduced to protect transactions that are made in good faith as part of the ordinary course of business (a defence seen in some jurisdictions[200] that adopt effects-based preference rules). This kind of rule should, however, not be endorsed without good cause since it makes the liquidator's task of protecting *pari passu* distribution more difficult and, again, favours the powerful creditor.

To conclude on preferences, it cannot be claimed that the current law with its subjective test operates in a manner that comes near to maximising creditor fairness. The present subjective approach and its weak protection of *pari passu* has the effect of adding further to the unfair burden that unsecured creditors bear: they, after all, are the parties that depend on strong application of the *pari passu* principle.[201] An objective approach has been seen to lead to more frequent and more successful liquidator actions to set aside unfair preferences and, overall, would increase fairness.[202]

Transactions at undervalue and transactions defrauding creditors
Under section 238(4) of the Insolvency Act 1986 a transaction at undervalue is entered into by a company if, at a relevant time,[203] it makes a gift to a person or enters into a transaction on terms giving the company no consideration or enters a transaction for a consideration whose value in money or money's worth is significantly lower than the value of the consideration provided by the company.[204]

---

200. See New Zealand Companies Act 1955 s. 266(2); *Countrywide Banking Corporation Ltd* v. *Dean* [1998] BCC 105 (PC) (payment not in course of business but part of disposition of business).
201. See further chs. 13 and 14 below.   **202.** Keay, 'Preferences in Liquidation Law', p. 215.
203. Within two years (connected person) or six months (unconnected person) of insolvency: the rule on the relevant time is the same as for a preference and is contained in the Insolvency Act 1986 s. 240.
204. Dealings with different parties may be treated collectively in assessing the transaction as a whole and the consideration given: *Phillips* v. *Brewin Dolphin Bell Lawrie Ltd* [2001] 1 WLR 143. See K. Dawson, 'Transaction Avoidance: *Phillips* v. *Brewin Dolphin* Considered' (2001) 72 *CCH Company Law Newsletter* 1; G. Stewart, 'Legal Update'; R. Parry, 'Case Commentary' [2001] Ins. Law. 58; B. Hackett, 'What Constitutes a Transaction at an Undervalue?' (2001) 17 IL&P 139; D. Milman, Editorial, 'Swelling the Assets' [2001] Ins. Law. 85; R. Mokal, 'Consideration, Characterisation, Evaluation: Transactions at Undervalue after *Phillips* v. *Brewin Dolphin*' [2001] JCLS 359. In *Brewin Dolphin* the goodwill of a stockbroking business was obtained in return for the cost of redundancy payments to employees, valued at a fraction of the value of

The company must have been unable to pay its debts at the time or become unable to do so because of the transaction. Excluded from coverage, however, are transactions entered into by the company in good faith for business purposes where there were reasonable grounds for believing the transaction would benefit the company.[205]

In contrast with the law on preferences, the liquidator's power to challenge transactions at undervalue does not depend on establishing any particular intention or motive on the part of the company, but the 'in good faith and for the purpose of carrying on its business' defence[206] favours parties seeking to sustain a transaction. If, however, the liquidator succeeds in a section 238 challenge, the court must make such an order as it thinks fit for restoring the position to what it would have been had the company not entered the transaction.[207] This will have the effect of placing the recovered assets back in the pool and making them available for the benefit of creditors generally.

As a device for ensuring the fair treatment of creditors in liquidation, this action is limited by the 'in good faith and for the purpose of carrying on its business' defence. Liquidators, for instance, might find it difficult to challenge golden handshakes; or *ex gratia* payments to retiring directors, dividend payments or grants of security for existing unsecured loans.[208] In the case of the latter, in particular, there is again considerable opportunity for powerful creditors such as banks to benefit, to the eventual cost of the body of smaller unsecured trade creditors.[209]

A further problem in relation to section 238 of the Insolvency Act 1986 is that this section only applies where the company is insolvent at the time or becomes insolvent as a result of the transaction. Section 320 of the Companies Act 1985 requires general meeting approval for transactions with directors or persons connected with them during times when the company is trading. This section, however, offers little protection where directors control the general meeting. The CLRSG argued that if a transfer of assets to a phoenix company[210] had taken place, an effective remedy for a liquidator, one compensating creditors, was to enforce remedies under

the business. The House of Lords concluded that there had been a transaction at undervalue and in doing so looked beyond the artificial division of the agreement that the participants made.

205. Insolvency Act 1986 s. 238(5)(a); *Re Inns of Court Hotel Co.* (1868) LR 6 Eq 82.

206. Insolvency Act 1986 s. 238(5)(a).   207. Insolvency Act 1986 s. 238(3).

208. See J. H. Farrar and B. M. Hannigan, *Farrar's Company Law* (4th edn, Butterworths, London, 1998) p. 730. Administrators can also use s. 238–s.238(1).

209. See *Re M.-C. Bacon Ltd* [1990] BCC 78.

210. The term 'phoenix' company was used to describe the practice of putting a company into voluntary liquidation (or receivership) at a time when it owed large sums to its unsecured

section 320.[211] The CLRSG accordingly recommended that section 320 should be amended to state that where, at the time of a section 320(1)(a) transaction, the company is insolvent (or becomes insolvent because of the transaction and goes into insolvent liquidation within twelve months of the approval) and the second party to the transaction is a connected person or a director, the resolution will not be valid for section 320 purposes if it would not have been passed without the votes of the director (and/or connected persons) unless the transaction in question was supported by an independent valuation. Such a revised rule would offer the same Companies Act 1985 section 322 remedies as would obtain in the absence of approval, including the right of the company to set the transaction aside and to sue the director to account for his profits or to indemnify the company against its losses.

Transactions at undervalue are also dealt with under the heading of 'Transactions defrauding creditors' in section 423 of the Insolvency Act 1986.[212] This remedy has its roots in the bankruptcy laws of the sixteenth century and operates with the same definition of a transaction at undervalue as is used in section 238. Section 423 actions, however, differ from those under section 238 in so far as they incorporate no time limits for the transactions challenged.[213] Liquidators do not have to show that the company was insolvent at the time of the transaction but they do have to establish that the company had entered into the deal with an intention to put the assets beyond the reach of, or otherwise prejudice, a person[214] who is making or who may make a claim against the company.[215] A further

creditors; the liquidator (or receiver) would frequently be appointed by a controlling shareholder (who may have also taken a floating charge over the company's undertaking); and the liquidator (or receiver) would sell the entire business at a knock-down price to a new company incorporated by the former controllers of the defunct company. Consequently what was essentially the same business would be carried out by the same people under the same or a similar name in disregard of the claims of the creditors of the first company – the second, new company rising 'phoenix-like' from the ashes of the old. Section 216 of the Insolvency Act 1986 is aimed at countering the 'phoenix' syndrome: see further ch. 15 below.

211. CLRSG, *Modern Company Law for a Competitive Economy: Final Report* (July 2001) pp. 327–30. The CLRSG recommended amending the Insolvency Act 1986 s. 216 so that the court would not ordinarily grant leave under section 216 if there was a material transfer of assets (within twelve months prior to liquidation) to a new company in which a director of the first company was also interested, unless there was compliance with the (amended) section 320.

212. See S. Elwes, 'Transactions Defrauding Creditors' (2001) 17 IL&P 10.

213. The Insolvency Act 1986 s. 423 arguably cannot be used to extend the time zone for contesting preferences: see *Re Lloyd's Furniture Palace Ltd, Evans v. Lloyd's Furniture Palace Ltd* [1925] Ch 853.

214. This may be a single creditor, and it has been said to be immaterial that creditors as a whole are not prejudiced: see *National Westminster Bank plc v. Jones, The Times*, 7 July 2000.

215. See *Arbuthnot Leasing International Ltd v. Havelet Leasing (No. 2)* [1991] 1 All ER 591. The requirement of prejudice in s. 423(3)(b) will not be satisfied where a party transfers an asset

difference between sections 238 and 423 of the Insolvency Act 1986 powers is that, in the case of the former, the court shall make an order to restore the position prior to the transaction, but under section 423 the court is empowered to make a similar order or to protect the interests of persons who are victims of the transaction: a power that will allow the court to order property to be handed over or reimbursement to be made to a particular prejudiced party.

Avoidance of floating charges

A liquidator may seek to increase the fund available for unsecured creditors by challenging the practice of lenders obtaining new floating charges during a company's troubled times in order to better their position in an anticipated insolvency distribution. The liquidator can resort to section 245 of the Insolvency Act 1986 which is designed to invalidate floating charges that are executed close to insolvency and which secure post-indebtedness without providing new assets or benefits to the company. Section 245 provides for challenge where the charge has been made with a connected person within two years ending with the onset of insolvency; or with any other person within twelve months of that date. A charge will not be invalidated under this section to the extent that the assets have been increased by the sum of the value of fresh money, goods or services supplied to the company at the same time as[216] or after the charge; any discharges or reductions of any debt of the company (again at the same time or after the creation of the charge); and such interest as is payable on the above consideration. Such fresh sums must have been passed to the company and it is not enough if those are forwarded by the lender to the company's bank to reduce an overdraft that the third party has guaranteed. This is because the money paid to the bank has not become freely available to the company and so is not paid to it within the meaning of section 245.[217]

This is an area of statute law that has proved difficult for liquidators to put to good effect. Section 245 covers floating, but not fixed charges, and

that is so encumbered that it lacks value or if, prior to the transaction, the company has no asset of value: see *Pinewood Joinery* v. *Starelm Properties Ltd* [1994] 2 BCLC 412. The intention to place assets out of reach of creditors does not have to be the *sole* purpose of the debtor: see *Chohan* v. *Saggar & Another* [1992] BCC 306, 321; *Spa Leasing Ltd* v. *Lovett & Others* [1995] BCC 502; Elwes, 'Transactions Defrauding Creditors'.

216. On the 'same time as' see *Re Shoe Lace Ltd (sub nom. Power* v. *Sharpe Investments Ltd)* [1994] 1 BCLC 111 where Sir Christopher Slade stated (at p. 123) that, in order to come within the terms of s. 245(2)(a), moneys paid before the execution of the debenture would have to be paid at a 'minimal' interval so that payment and execution could be regarded as 'contemporaneous'.

217. See *Re Fairways Magazines Ltd* [1993] 1 BCLC 643; *Farrar's Company Law*, pp. 734–5.

it does not have purchase where the company has paid off the debenture holder secured by the floating charge.[218] If the floating charge is in favour of an unconnected person, the liquidator will have to prove that the company was then unable to pay its debts per section 123 of the Insolvency Act 1986 or was, as a result of the transaction, unable to pay its debts as they fell due.[219] The effect of the loan under which the floating charge was created has to be taken into account and the liquidator may have a complex and difficult case to make out: section 245(4) places the onus on the liquidator as challenger of the charge to show that the company was insolvent. Overall, then, section 245 is designed to increase fairness in the insolvency process but its effect is limited by the noted difficulties experienced by the liquidator.

Fairness to group creditors

In asking whether liquidation processes operate fairly, it is necessary to take some time to consider the special position of creditors of groups of companies. What constitutes a group is not formally defined in English law[220] but it is a concept understood commercially as a family of related companies or businesses in which one company (the parent or holding company) maintains effective control over the others through shareholding and managerial controls.[221] Issues of fairness arise if it is asked whether

218. The effect of a successful challenge is to invalidate the floating charge but the debt is not extinguished.

219. See the definition in *Re Patrick and Lyon Ltd* [1933] Ch 786. Additional tests of inability to pay debts (e.g. the balance sheet test) also operate here: see ch. 4 above.

220. But parent and subsidiary undertakings are dealt with in the Companies Act 1985 s. 736 (dealing with legal control) and Companies Act 1985 s. 258 (the broader economically based parent company/subsidiary undertaking definition which forms the basis of the consolidated accounts requirements under the EU Seventh Directive. See also the Companies Act 1985 s. 227 for requirements for consolidated group accounts). On the definition of the corporate group for accounting purposes see E. Ferran, *Company Law and Corporate Finance* (Oxford University Press, Oxford, 1999) pp. 27–30; C. Napier and C. Noke, 'Premium and Pre-Acquisition Profits; the Legal and Accounting Professions and Business Combinations' (1991) 54 MLR 810.

221. On groups generally see K. Hopt (ed.), *Groups of Companies in European Laws* (de Gruyter, Berlin, 1982); T. Hadden, *The Control of Corporate Groups* (IALS, London, 1983); Hadden, 'The Regulation of Corporate Groups in Australia' (1992) UNSW LJ 61; Lord Wedderburn, 'Multinationals and the Antiquities of Company Law' (1984) 47 MLR 87; C. Schmitthoff and F. Wooldridge (eds.), *Groups of Companies* (Sweet & Maxwell, London, 1991); J. McCahery, S. Piccoitto and C. Scott (eds.), *Corporate Control and Accountability* (Oxford University Press, Oxford, 1993) chs. 16–20; M. Gillooly (ed.), *The Law Relating to Corporate Groups* (Butterworths, Sydney, 1993); R. Grantham, 'Liability of Parent Companies for the Actions of the Directors of their Subsidiaries' (1997) 18 Co. Law. 138; S. Wheeler and G. Wilson, *Directors' Liabilities in the Context of Corporate Groups* (Insolvency Lawyers' Association, Oxfordshire, 1998); J. H. Farrar, 'Legal Issues Involving Corporate Groups' (1998) 16 *Corporate and Securities Law Journal* 184; D. Milman, 'Groups of Companies: The Path towards Discrete Regulation' in D. Milman (ed.), *Regulating Enterprise* (Hart, Oxford, 1999); R. Austin, 'Corporate Groups' in R. Grantham

the law imposes risks on creditors (of parent companies or subsidiaries) that are inequitable. This question is the first concern here. A second issue – whether any unfairnesses the law imposes in the group context are justifiable as economically efficient – is one which will be returned to. Unfairness in this discussion will be treated as being involved where risks are imposed on parties who are significantly less well placed than others to evaluate risks; to adjust their terms of business to reflect such evaluations; or to bear the consequences of economic harms that result from such risk bearing.[222]

Here we are dealing with no small issue. The corporate group has developed during the last century to become an almost uniform form of business and one that routinely crosses national and regulatory boundaries.[223] Most businesses of any size or substance now conduct their operations through subsidiaries that are owned by a parent company. The essential problem, however, is that there is a disjuncture between the law's vision of the limited liability company and the reality of commercial life. The law does not hold parent companies liable for subsidiaries because it treats companies as juristic persons with separate corporate personality.[224] The reality is that groups operate as economically and managerially cohesive operations, often with high levels of unity. They move resources around and operate as organically whole institutions.

For managers and shareholders of the parent company there are a number of reasons for operating via the group mechanism.[225] It has been suggested that a primary reason is to distribute risks in a manner that serves the group as a whole.[226] The group device, however, also provides a degree of managerial autonomy for buying, selling or operating certain business activities; it allows geographically dispersed businesses to be managed separately; it caters for compliance with local laws (where,

and C. Rickett (eds.), *Corporate Personality in the Twentieth Century* (Hart, Oxford, 1998); J. Dine, *The Governance of Corporate Groups* (Cambridge University Press, Cambridge, 2000).

222. See the discussion of non-adjusting creditors at pp. 428–37, 484 below.

223. On the development of the group see J. Wilson, *British Business History 1720–1994* (Manchester University Press, Manchester, 1995); T. Hadden, 'Inside Corporate Groups' (1984) 12 *International Journal of Sociology of Law* 271.

224. *Salomon* v. *A. Salomon & Co. Ltd* [1897] AC 22. See also the reaffirmation of the separation of parent and subsidiary obligations in *Adams* v. *Cape Industries* [1990] 2 WLR 657 (CA). If a subsidiary acts as an agent for the parent company the latter will incur liability on ordinary agency principles: see *Canada Rice Mills Ltd* v. *R* [1939] 3 All ER 991; Ferran, *Company Law and Corporate Finance*, p. 35. On a parent company liability through guarantees or in tort see Ferran, *Company Law and Corporate Finance*, pp. 35–7.

225. See, for example, Austin, 'Corporate Groups'; T. Eisenberg, 'Corporate Groups' in Gillooly, *Law Relating to Corporate Groups*; CLRSG, *Modern Company Law for a Competitive Economy: Completing the Structure* (DTI, November 2000) ch. 10.

226. See CLRSG, *Completing the Structure*, p. 177.

for example, a country demands a home-based corporate presence); it can allow tax advantages to be achieved; it may usefully limit the influence of anti-trust laws or a regulator (by removing parent companies from the regulator's domain); it allows legal liabilities of various kinds to be shifted and limited in ways that protect the parent company; it provides a means of keeping labour costs down;[227] and it allows for investments, profits and losses to be distributed in ways that maximise benefits to the group.[228]

In spite of the prevalence of the group, insolvency law very largely fails to take on board the interdependency of many companies. The law is still focused almost exclusively on the individual company; there is no legally developed doctrine of group enterprise or notion of 'group interest'; there are no clear rules on the liability of the parent company for the firms within its group; and there is virtually no legal control over the complexity of the group's structure.[229] The creditors of companies within a group can only assert claims against their particular debtor company, not the group. The potential for unfair treatment stems from the ability of a parent company's directors to manipulate the rules governing limited liability companies to the group's or parent company's advantage. A typical large group may involve more than a hundred subsidiaries or subsidiaries of subsidiaries and some of the latter may be placed as far as five removes from the main board of directors.[230] These extended organisations are tied together by arrangements of ownership, contract, management and economic interdependence yet the companies involved are regarded by the law as so many independent units.

This difference between commercial reality and legal framework can result in unfair allocations of risk to creditors for a number of reasons. The creditors of a subsidiary face at least the following difficulties.[231] They may face enormous costs in calculating the risks they are bearing, because the

---

227. See H. Collins, 'Ascription of Legal Responsibility to Groups and Complex Patterns of Economic Integration' (1990) 53 MLR 731.

228. See T. Hadden, 'Insolvency and the Group: Problems of Integrated Financing' in R. M. Goode (ed.), *Group Trading and the Lending Banker* (Chartered Institute of Bankers, London, 1988).

229. See T. Hadden, 'Regulating Corporate Groups: International Perspectives' in McCahery *et al.*, *Corporate Control*.

230. Collins, 'Ascription of Legal Responsibility', p. 733; Hadden, *Control of Corporate Groups*, p. 9.

231. See J. Landers, 'A Unified Approach to Parent, Subsidiary and Affiliate Questions in Bankruptcy' (1975) 42 U Chic. L Rev. 589 (see reply by R. Posner, 'The Rights of Creditors of Affiliated Corporations' (1976) 43 U Chic. L Rev. 499; and reply by Landers, 'Another Word on Parents, Subsidiaries and Affiliates in Bankruptcy' (1976) 43 U Chic. L Rev. 527).

parent company enjoys freedom to move resources and risks around the group in a manner that favours the group rather than the subsidiary.[232] Corporate decisions will be made with a view to maximising overall returns rather than ensuring the health of any subsidiary and it may be extremely difficult to assess the financial or risk position of a subsidiary at any one time. Creditors of subsidiaries within a group may be misled about the ownership of assets that are available to pay their debts; transactions within groups may not be conducted at arm's length; assets may be transferred, or loans given, at non-market rates; and guarantees and dividends may be given without reference to the interests of the companies affected.[233] A firm may be made excessively dependent on others for funds, business or both, and one firm may be used clandestinely within the group as a dumping ground for losses, liabilities and risks. A further problem for a subsidiary creditor is that amidst the above complexities it may be difficult to find out such basic matters as which companies are members of the group and which inter-company dependencies are intra-group.[234] Nor can creditors of subsidiaries take comfort in the rules governing directors' duties. The tradition of the law dictates that directors owe duties to their own company, not to the subsidiaries that their decisions may affect.[235] The directors of a parent company, moreover, may use cross-holdings to entrench themselves in control of the group, yet they may have very small commitments of capital themselves.

The above considerations may make creditors of a subsidiary nervous.[236] Other consequences of the law may move them towards indignation. The Cork Report noted a scenario in which a wholly owned subsidiary is mismanaged and abused for the benefit of a parent company but in which loans from the parent company are employed. When the subsidiary goes into liquidation its creditors find that the parent company submits a proof in respect of its loan and a substantial proportion of the

232. 'Firms enjoy considerable freedom both in law and practice to determine the limits of their boundaries': see Collins, 'Ascription of Legal Responsibility', pp. 736–8, on 'the capital boundary problem'.

233. See Cork Report, para. 1926. On the 'implied statutory duty' (under the Insolvency Act 1986 s. 238) of a lending bank to consider, in seeking the security of a corporate guarantee, the interests of the surety's creditors, see D. Spahos, 'Lenders, Borrowing Groups of Companies and Corporate Guarantees: An Insolvency Perspective' [2001] JCLS 333.

234. See Milman, 'Groups of Companies', pp. 222–3.

235. *Lindgreen v. L & P Estates Ltd* [1968] 1 Ch 572; *Charterbridge Corp. Ltd v. Lloyds Bank* [1970] 1 Ch 62.

236. If a subsidiary becomes insolvent the parent and other subsidiaries may still prosper 'to the joy of the shareholders without any liability for the debts of the insolvent subsidiary': see *Re Southard* [1979] 1 WLR 1198 (CA), per Templeman LJ.

funds realised by the liquidator go to the parent company and (where the loan is secured) do so before the unsecured creditors of the subsidiary are repaid.[237]

Cork saw such a legal position as 'undoubtedly defective'[238] and one commentator has noted widespread criticism of the process by which 'the liberal creation of undercapitalised subsidiaries [creates] a second level of limited liability protection for businesses wishing to insulate themselves from enterprise liabilities'.[239] Realigning the law so as to deal with the problems posed by groups has, however, not proved easy. The difficulties can be outlined by considering the main proposals that have been canvassed to date. These can be grouped into three broad responses: subordinating debts owed to companies within the group to the claims of non-group creditors; consolidating group debts; and tightening directors' obligations and liabilities.

Subordination was a route advocated in limited form by Cork.[240] Several parties who gave evidence to the Cork Committee argued that all debts owed by a company in liquidation to other companies in the same group should be deferred to the claims of external creditors. Cork, however, drew a distinction between debts arising from ordinary trading activities between group companies and debts 'which in substance represent long term working capital and which arise from finance provided by the parent company'.[241] In making this distinction, Cork drew on the US courts' equitable jurisdiction to subordinate, as preserved by statute,[242] under which the courts looked at the conduct of parties and tended to look for fraud, mismanagement, wrongful conduct or under-capitalisation

---

237. The rules on transactional avoidance may come into play: see Insolvency Act 1986 ss. 239 and 245; *Re Shoe Lace Ltd (sub nom. Power* v. *Sharp Investments)* [1994] 1 BCLC 111; Milman, 'Groups of Companies', p. 225. Proof of debt between group members was allowed in *Re Polly Peck International plc (No. 3)* [1996] 1 BCLC 428. On instances where the parent company may not deny liability see Milman, 'Groups of Companies', pp. 226–8.

238. Cork Report, para. 1934; the words 'seriously inadequate' are used of the law at para. 1950. See also paras. 1924 and 1928 for reflections of views that the position was 'offensive to ordinary canons of commercial morality' and that it was 'absurd and unreal to allow the commercial realities to be disregarded'.

239. See Milman, 'Groups of Companies' p. 225, and for judicial concern see Staughton LJ in *Atlas Maritime Co.* v. *Avalon Maritime Ltd (No. 1)* [1991] 4 All ER 769 at 779. On the capacity of groups to avoid the legal regulation of business transfers and TUPE (on TUPE see ch. 16 below) see *Michael Peters Ltd* v. *Farnfield & Michael Peters Group plc* [1995] IRLR 190; S. Hardy, 'Some TUPE Implications for Insolvency Lawyers' [2001] Ins. Law. 147 at 149.

240. Cork Report, paras. 1958–65.

241. Ibid., para. 1960.

242. 11 USC s. 510(C) 1978, giving statutory recognition to the 'Deep Rock' doctrine (the name being taken from a subsidiary company featuring in *Taylor* v. *Standard Gas and Electric Co.* (1939) 306 US 307) where the claims (as a creditor) of a controller of a company can be subordinated to the claims of the other creditors: see Landers, 'Unified Approach', pp. 597–606.

where finance was by the controlling shareholder.[243] Cork suggested that it would not be equitable to subordinate in the case of ordinary trading debts but it would be fair to do so in the case of liabilities, secured or unsecured, which are owed to connected persons or companies and which represent all or part of the long-term capital of the company.[244]

One problem with Cork's approach (which has not been implemented) is that the distinction upon which it builds constitutes an invitation to lengthy and expensive litigation.[245] A further issue, however, relates to the broad exemption of ordinary trading debts. In a group there are, as noted, real dangers that transactions at other than market value will be entered into for manipulative reasons (for example, to shift risks onto a subsidiary whose creditors are ill-placed to respond to such a risk shift). There seems no reason why such transactions should escape subordination because they are encountered in an ordinary trading context. If the objective is fairness to creditors of subsidiaries, debts to group companies relating to such transactions should be subordinated.

A second major response to unfair risk shifting is to consolidate (to lift the veil on the group[246]) to deal with the commercial realities and to order pooling of assets of related companies in liquidation so as to improve the dividend prospects for creditors. There are a number of ways to implement such an approach. In Germany the legislation of 1965 (*Konzernrecht*) dealt with the issue in a formalistic way by seeking to lay down the parameters of

---

243. See Milman, 'Groups of Companies', p. 230; R. Schulte, 'Corporate Groups and the Equitable Subordination of Claims on Insolvency' (1997) 18 Co. Law. 2; *Taylor* v. *Standard Gas and Electric Co.*
244. Cork recommended that where such liabilities were secured by fixed or floating charges that security should be invalid as against the liquidator, administrator or any creditor to the company until all claims to which it had been deferred were met: Cork Report, para. 1963.
245. See Milman, 'Groups of Companies', p. 229. Cork's rejection of subordination for 'ordinary trading activity' claims was not argued out: the Committee merely reported hostility in the United States Congressional hearings and the fact that it was 'not persuaded' on its own account.
246. On the English courts' approach to lifting the veil in the group context see *Adams* v. *Cape Industries* [1990] 2 WLR 657; discussed by S. Griffin in (1991) 12 Co. Law. 16. See also *Farrar's Company Law*, pp. 73–4. The European Court of Justice shows more inclination to treat a group of companies as a single economic entity: see *Istituto Chemioterapico Italiano SpA* v. *EC Commission*, Case 6, 7/73 [1974] ECR 223; *SAR Schotte GmbH* v. *Parfums Rothschild SARL*, 218/86 [1992] BCLC 235. In the USA the flexible concept of equitable subordination has been adopted and piercing the veil of incorporation is also resorted to. On piercing the veil in the United States context, see Landers, 'Unified Approach', who would pierce the veil whenever the parent company has failed to endow the subsidiary with sufficient resources to make it economically viable or failed to observe the legal formalities for creating a separate corporation. See also P. Blumberg, *The Law of Corporate Groups: Procedural Problems in the Law of Parent and Subsidiary Companies* (Little, Brown, Boston, Mass., 1983) ch. 1.

formal legal relations between the companies in a group.[247] The drawback of such a strategy is that it produces a somewhat rigid legal framework that may unduly restrict enterprise, prove poor at adapting to change and yet not remove the need for judicial intervention. An alternative method relies more explicitly on the use of judicial discretion. In New Zealand, legislation passed in 1980 empowered the courts to order one company in a group to *contribute* towards the assets of a fellow group company in the event of the latter's insolvency.[248] Such orders are to be granted when the court considers this just and equitable, and attention will be paid to the role of the parent company, especially its part in the subsidiary's collapse.[249] In the case of collapses of the group as a whole, the New Zealand law grants judges an analogous discretion to *pool* the assets and liabilities of the group.[250] Here the New Zealand courts must have regard to the extent to which the related company took part in the management of any of the other companies; the conduct of any of the companies towards the creditors of any of the other companies; the extent to which the businesses have been combined; the extent to which the causes of the liquidation of any of the companies are attributable to the actions of any of the other companies; and such other matters as the court thinks fit.[251] A similar approach has been adopted in Ireland,[252] and was also advocated by the Harmer Committee in Australia.[253] In the USA the court may order consolidation

247. See Milman, 'Groups of Companies', p. 231; J. Rinze, 'Konzernrecht: Law on Groups of Companies in Germany' (1993) 14 Co. Law. 143; K. Hopt, 'Legal Elements and Policy Decisions in Regulating Groups of Companies' in Schmitthoff and Wooldridge, *Groups of Companies*; D. Sugarman and G. Teubner (eds.), *Regulating Corporate Groups in Europe* (Nomos, Baden-Baden, 1990). In the European Draft Ninth Directive (Commission Document III/1639/84-EN) an approach modelled on the German group regime was promoted but this measure received a hostile reception and has not been implemented. On the possibility of future European initiatives regarding regulation of corporate groups see K. Hopt, 'Legal Issues and Questions of Policy in the Comparative Regulation of Groups' [1996] *I Gruppi di Societas* 45.

248. Companies Amendment Act 1980 (New Zealand); see now Companies Act 1993 s. 271(1)(a); see further Austin, 'Corporate Groups', pp. 84–6.

249. See *Rea* v. *Barker* (1988) 4 NZCLC 6, 312; *Rea* v. *Chix* (1986) 3 NZCLC 98, 852; *Bullen* v. *Tourcorp Developments Ltd* (1988) 4 NZCLC 64, 661.

250. See Companies Act 1993 s. 271(1)(b); *Re Dalhoff and King Holdings Ltd* [1991] 2 NZLR 296; *Re Pacific Syndicates (NZ) Ltd* (1989) 4 NZCLC 64, 757; Milman, 'Groups of Companies', p. 230; Austin, 'Corporate Groups', pp. 83–6. There is some evidence that Australian courts may be sympathetic to such pooling if it is 'for the benefit of creditors generally': see Austin, 'Corporate Groups', p. 84 and *Dean-Willcocks* v. *Soluble Solution Hydroponics Pty Ltd* [1997] 13 ACLC 833, 839.

251. Companies Act 1993 (New Zealand) s. 272(1).

252. Companies Act (Ireland) 1990 s. 140 (contributions) and s. 141 (pooling). In France statutory provisions address the parent–subsidiary relationship on a number of points but also rely on judicial discretion: see Milman, 'Groups of Companies', p. 231.

253. Australian Law Reform Commission, *General Insolvency Inquiry*, Report No. 45 (Canberra, 1988) para. 857: discussed in Austin, 'Corporate Groups', p. 86.

(known as 'substantive consolidation'[254]) under the auspices of its general equitable powers and will do so where the companies' affairs are inextricably linked or the creditors can be shown to have dealt with the debtor companies as a single economic unit. In such consolidations the group assets and liabilities are dealt with as a single unit as part of a pooling arrangement.[255]

A further route to consolidation, parent company contributions and an acknowledgement of commercial realities lies through treating the parent company as a shadow director of the insolvent subsidiary.[256] In English law, liability for wrongful trading under section 214 of the Insolvency Act 1986 also applies to shadow directors, who are defined (in section 251) as persons 'in accordance with whose directions or instructions the directors of the company are accustomed to act...'.[257] The concept of a shadow director can encompass a parent company and this paves the way for liability for wrongful trading and contributing to the insolvent company's assets by order of the court (under section 214(1)). Such use of the shadow direction concept does not make parent companies generally liable for the debts of subsidiaries but it may cover situations of wrongful trading and it looks to the realities of economic control rather than the formalities of ownership.[258]

The courts have dealt with the matter of parent companies as shadow directors. In *Hydrodan*[259] it was made clear that the issue was whether the directors of a subsidiary exercise their own independent discretion and judgment and that, to prove shadow directorship, it had to be shown that the board of the subsidiary did not exercise this discretion and judgment but acted in accordance with the directions of the parent company.

---

254. As opposed to procedural consolidation where the bankruptcy proceedings of different entities are consolidated for procedural purposes only, having no effect on creditors' substantive rights. On US 'substantive consolidation' see further A. Borrowdale, 'Commentary on Austin' in Grantham and Rickett (eds.), *Corporate Personality*, pp. 91–2.

255. For an account of the informal pooling arrangements in the BCCI group liquidations see C. Grierson, 'Issues in Concurrent Insolvency Jurisdiction: English Perspectives' in Ziegel (ed.), *Current Developments*. On US consolidation see further C. Frost, 'Operational Form, Misappropriation Risk and the Substantive Consolidation of Corporate Groups' (1993) 44 Hastings LJ 449; C. Grierson, 'Shareholder Liability, Consolidation and Pooling' in E. Leonard and C. Besant (eds.), *Current Issues in Cross-Border Insolvency and Reorganisations* (Graham and Trotman, London, 1994); Landers, 'Unified Approach'; Borrowdale, 'Commentary on Austin'.

256. On shadow directors see ch. 15 below.

257. The concept is borrowed from the Companies Act 1985 s. 741.

258. See Collins, 'Ascription of Legal Responsibility', p. 741, who argues that the concept opens the possibility of offering a powerful response to the 'capital boundary problem'.

259. *Re Hydrodan (Corby) Ltd* [1994] BCC 161.

A broadening of approach can be discerned in *Deverell*[260] where, in the Court of Appeal, Morritt LJ suggested *inter alia* that the fact that the board of directors may be characterised as subservient clearly indicated the existence of a shadow directorship.[261] *Deverell* thus opens the door to the liability of a parent company to a subservient subsidiary's creditors, but there are limitations to this remedy. As noted, it only applies where wrongful trading is established and, second, it looks to instances in which the parent board dominates the subsidiary board as a matter of governance. Whether it will cover instances where the companies are commercially linked but are formally and managerially independent is far less certain.[262]

It is noteworthy that Cork declined to recommend that a holding company be liable for an insolvent subsidiary company's debts.[263] Some of the Committee favoured the radical view (that the parent company should always be liable) and other members of the Committee favoured the New Zealand discretionary approach. Cork, however, drew back from making a recommendation because of anticipated effects on entrepreneurship, difficulties of apportioning liability, potential impacts on long-term existing creditors and other ramifications outside insolvency: notably that the directors of a parent company would have to have regard for not only the interests of that company but also the interests of other group companies. Such matters were so important, said Cork, that a wide review covering company and insolvency law issues was needed.[264] The response to the point concerning widening directors' duties, of course, may be that the directors of parent companies now possess such extensive powers to influence subsidiaries by methods of such extremely low transparency that such a broadening of directors' obligations could be healthy.

A further method of making holding company assets available to creditors in subsidiaries is the proposal discussed by the CLRSG in 2000.[265] In the mooted 'elective regime' the parent company would guarantee the liabilities of the subsidiary and would satisfy certain publicity requirements, and the subsidiary, in return, would be exempted from Companies Act requirements relating to annual accounts and audit. By 2001, however, the CLRSG had been convinced by consultees that there was no solid case for

---

260. *Secretary of State for Trade and Industry* v. *Deverell* [2000] 2 WLR 907, [2000] BCC 1057.
261. [2000] 2 WLR 907 at 919–20.
262. See Collins, 'Ascription of Legal Responsibility', p. 742. See also J. Payne, 'Casting Light into the Shadows: *Secretary of State for Trade and Industry* v. *Deverell*' (2001) 22 Co. Law. 90; D. Milman, 'A Fresh Light on Shadow Directors' [2000] Ins. Law. 171.
263. See the discussion in Ferran, *Company Law and Corporate Finance*, pp. 39–40.
264. Cork Report, paras. 1951–2.   265. See CLRSG, *Completing the Structure*, ch. 10.

'the elective regime'.[266] Concerns were expressed to the CLRSG about the details and the regime's low potential to reduce burdens on groups significantly. The most telling objection, however, was that there would be an unacceptable loss of publicly available information at the individual company level. The proposal was not recommended and it seems rightly so since it would have distanced the creditor of a subsidiary from information needed to assess risks.[267]

A third canvassed response[268] to the difficulties faced by group creditors is to develop the concept of duties of dominant shareholders. Thus it has been suggested that a dominant shareholder (the parent company) should owe fiduciary duties (of loyalty and fairness) to its subsidiary and other subordinated companies and that the dominant parent should have the burden of proving that transactions with the dominated company are fair, unless those transactions have been authorised by 'disinterested' shareholders.[269]

All the above suggestions are designed to reduce the unfairnesses that stem from the facility with which the directors of a parent company can shift risks to the creditors of a subsidiary. The broad objections to this 'family' of proposals are that they would interfere unwarrantably with directors' managerial freedoms, would violate the separate entity principle, would stifle enterprise and would create uncertainty – that it is better to tolerate present unfairnesses than to escalate overall costs very substantially in pursuit of fairness.[270] This seems, however, no answer to the case for subordinating parent company debts to other debts. That case is based on the unfairness of allowing companies who control subsidiaries to prove for debts alongside other creditors of the subsidiary. The strategic and informational advantages enjoyed by the parent company are adequate compensation for subordination. As far as consolidation is concerned, the least legally uncertain proposal is the radical one – that a parent company should automatically be responsible for the liabilities of a subsidiary.

266. CLRSG, *Final Report*, 2001, pp. 179–80.

267. Assessment of risk may still be necessary despite a guarantee of liabilities since there are residual risks of the parent company. For creditors of subsidiaries analysing parent company risks may be complex and time-consuming.

268. One posited as building on US *Principles of Corporate Governance*, American Law Institute, Draft No. 5 (1986).

269. See A. Tunc, 'The Fiduciary Duties of a Dominant Shareholder' in Schmitthoff and Wooldridge, *Groups of Companies*. See also M. Lower, 'Good Faith and the Partly Owned Subsidiary' [2000] JBL 232.

270. See, for example, the Law Council of Australia objections discussed by Austin, 'Corporate Groups', p. 86 and by J. O'Donovan, 'Group Therapies for Group Insolvencies' in Gillooly, *Law Relating to Corporate Groups*.

It might be argued, however, that practical uncertainties would raise capital costs unduly. Objectors would contend that a welcome effect of limited liability is that the suppliers of credit know the risks they face, they know that these risks are limited and so are induced to lend on reasonable rates. Shareholders and creditors benefit by the certainties generated.[271] If parent groups are liable for subsidiaries, it could be said, such benefits of limited liability are undermined because it is difficult to assess risks across groups.

This argument can, however, be overstated. The shareholders of the parent company will still be shielded from personal liability by the limited liability that they enjoy.[272] It is true that inefficiencies are caused by the uncertainties that flow from the complexities of risk assessments within groups. These do have to be paid for, but non-liability of the parent company for its subsidiaries creates perhaps greater overall uncertainties through incentives to produce poor information flows to lenders to the group.[273] Those lenders will charge rates that reflect uncertainties. Directors of parent companies that are not liable for subsidiaries will perhaps not be too worried: they will consider the balance between the higher capital costs they face across the group (due to the nervousness of lenders to group subsidiaries) and their ability to offload risks onto the creditors of subsidiaries, notably trade creditors. The banks lending to the parent company may not be very concerned either because they will have confidence that insolvency risks are being shifted away from the parent company to the subsidiary and its creditors. Such powerful decision-makers are likely, accordingly, to favour a regime that is highly uncertain and high cost, provided that other parties (the unsecured creditors of subsidiaries) are bearing those costs. Those other parties, however, would be unlikely to welcome such a system.

The advantage of making the parent company liable is that its managers may be induced to take risks responsibly and the parties bearing the risks will be those that are best informed and best able to control the flow of finances. Where the parent is not liable its managers will be prone to engage in excessive risk taking because they can shift risks to subsidiaries.[274] Indeed, without the parent liability, the managers of a subsidiary may

271. See Posner, 'Rights of Creditors', pp. 501–3.
272. See Ferran, *Company Law and Corporate Finance*, p. 32.
273. See Landers, 'Another Word on Parents', p. 539: 'the present system effectively rewards owners who can hide from public view'.
274. See P. Blumberg, *The Multinational Challenge to Corporation Law: The Search for a New Corporate Personality* (Oxford University Press, New York, 1993) p. 134.

also take excessive risks because they may be confident of relocation to another company within the group that has benefited from the excessive risk bearing of the first subsidiary.[275] The creditors and the directors of the parent company will be more efficient risk bearers than the creditors of subsidiaries because the former have far better levels of information. Posner objects to the parent company liability approach on the grounds that lenders to the parent company will have to investigate the creditworthiness of the group's subsidiaries[276] but (given their access to group information) it is easier for them to do this than for the subsidiary's trade creditors to review the whole group's financial risks. General levels of uncertainty, moreover, are likely to be lower where the parent company is liable because the broad incentives favour openness and transparency rather than manipulation and secrecy. Apart from anything else, parent company liability would reduce the tendency to construct massively complex group corporate structures for non-productive reasons (for example, to avoid regulatory obligations or to create 'dump' subsidiaries).[277] The answer to Posner, in short, is not that a parent company is losing its limited liability advantages but that it is retaining these and losing its facility to shift risks unfairly – losing the subsidy to entrepreneurship that is now being paid for by the creditors of insolvent subsidiary companies.

The case for parent company liability accordingly seems strong but, as has been seen above,[278] such a radical reform is politically unlikely. A discretionary regime is politically more likely to be introduced but it is more vulnerable to attacks for uncertainty. Lenders to companies within the group are liable to charge rates that reflect the difficulties of assessing when and whether the courts will impose liability on the parent company. One proposed solution to this problem is to exempt the parent company from such potential liability where subsidiaries are specified: 'provided that those subsidiaries are financially managed in a manner which segregates their assets and liabilities from the assets and liabilities of the rest of the group and that the segregation is documented in a manner that would permit a liquidator to trace the assets affected by it'.[279] It is difficult, however, to see how such preservation of the separate entity could be managed within the commercial interrelationships and complexities of a group's

275. F. H. Easterbrook and D. Fischel, *The Economic Structure of Corporate Law* (Harvard University Press, Cambridge, Mass., 1991) pp. 56–7.
276. Posner, 'Rights of Creditors', p. 517.
277. See further Hadden, 'Regulating Corporate Groups'.
278. See Milman, 'Groups of Companies', p. 231, and pp. 414–15 above.
279. See Austin, 'Corporate Groups', p. 87.

structure and how, if attempted, it could be achieved without such restrictiveness as would negate the advantages of group membership.

The discretionary route, it seems, has to face up to the likelihood that it will involve time-consuming and expensive litigation in circumstances where finances are highly constrained. As commentators have observed, this may explain the poor success rate of such mechanisms and even steps to reverse the onus of proof (so that parent companies are presumed liable for subsidiaries' debts unless they show that they have operated at arm's length) will not avoid considerable costs.[280] If the creditors of group subsidiaries are to be protected, yet costs kept to a reasonable level, it may be necessary to be bold and to opt for a regime of consolidation.

Conclusions: concepts of liquidation

The above account outlines a number of respects in which the process of liquidation is open to criticism and improvement on the efficiency, expertise, accountability and fairness fronts. Questions also arise as to the value of a single gateway approach to insolvency, a matter discussed in chapter 9 and not for repetition here. A further issue concerns the conceptual underpinnings of liquidation. These should be examined to see if there is value in approaching liquidation in terms that differ from the model implicit in current English insolvency law. Cork espoused a shift from a 'creditor control' to a 'creditor participation' model of insolvency proceedings but there are other directions from which to approach liquidation. One such direction involves seeing liquidation as other than a process that centres precisely on a set of formal legal rules. This is perhaps against the inclination of lawyers who devote much attention to extensive sets of statutory provisions, but it is already clear from the above account that liquidation can be portrayed in a number of non-rule-centric ways: as an institutional contest involving such different parties as expert insolvency practitioners, banks, directors, shareholders, unsecured trade creditors, the courts and the DTI – participants with very different aims, interests, incentives, levels of information, expertise and access to the insolvency process. Liquidation, moreover, can be seen as a reflection of long-established conventions of deference to powerful institutions. On this view, an observer might explain much of the liquidation process in terms of the exalted positions that English insolvency law has

---

280. Milman, 'Groups of Companies', p. 231.

long given to powerful secured creditors.[281] Linked to this vision are notions that modern English liquidation is driven in shape and operation by those who possess information and skill. It is on this view the preserve of the repeat players, as exemplified by the manner in which IPs dominate creditors' meetings.

Different portraits of liquidation can also be placed in opposition to each other. On the one hand, it can be seen as a process in which professions act in a detached way so as to ensure that creditors are dealt with fairly and the public interest is served by monitoring the behaviour of directors *ex post facto*. On the other, liquidation can be seen in strictly private interest terms with IPs, creditors, directors and others all pursuing their own interests in a highly focused manner.

Alternative visions of liquidation can also be generated by moving one's disciplinary viewpoint away from law. Economists would be liable to espouse a private interest approach but sociologists and anthropologists, for instance, would emphasise the social and cultural contexts within which liquidation takes place and the extent to which liquidation is driven by group-based ideas, understandings and traditions. Psychologists might be expected to place more emphasis on the attitude of the individual and might focus on the approaches that individual IPs tend to adopt because of their background and training.

What, though, do these different ways of seeing liquidation tell us about issues of design, reform and evaluation? A key message is that achieving better performance on the efficiency, expertise, accountability and fairness fronts will not come simply through changes in the legal rules. The world is not that rule-centred and other approaches have to be embraced.[282] Training, for example, is a strategy with considerable potential. The liquidation process may be improved through refinements in the training of IPs (in, for example, consultative techniques) or in directorial training (to cover ongoing company contexts and insolvency or near insolvency situations and rescue processes, as well as information-gathering techniques[283]). Institutional roles, moreover, might be reconceived so that, for instance, the part played by the courts in scrutinising processes is reformulated. One way in which this could be done is to replace resort to court with other processes, such as the use of administrative

---

281. See ch. 3 above and ch. 14 below.

282. On the extent to which behaviour is rule-governed see, for example, Mary Douglas' discussion of 'grid' and 'group' relations in M. Douglas, *In the Active Voice* (Routledge, London, 1982).

283. See V. Finch, 'Company Directors: Who Cares About Skill and Care?' (1992) 55 MLR 179.

powers.[284] Liquidators, on this model, could be empowered to adopt a designated administrative power to 'call in' property that has been transferred out of the estate in a suspect manner. Such a regime could make resort to court[285] a secondary matter rather than a primary process in relating to the relevant set of issues.[286]

Finally, a fresh look might be taken at the overall objectives of the liquidation process – a review that bears in mind the balance between ends such as efficiency and fairness. Consistency between this area of insolvency law and others is a matter to be borne in mind here. It would be muddled thinking to give efficiency primacy of place in relation to one insolvency process but (without reason) to give greater emphasis to, say, fairness or accountability in another. There may, of course, be reasons for differences of emphasis but consistency and clarity demand that we should be clear about these. One such reason may be that liquidation, unlike other insolvency processes, can be seen in non-rescue terms and as relating to a narrower set of interests than, say, administration. To conclude, there is, as noted, much to be done to refine insolvency law as it affects liquidation but insolvency law and processes must be seen in the round and we should be aware of the improvements that can be gained by looking beyond the narrowly legal and towards adjustments in cultures, traditions, incentives, expectations, institutions, training and roles.

284. On mediation and alternative dispute resolution see M. Humphries, E. Pavlopoulos and P. Winterborne, 'Insolvency, Mediation and ADR' (1999) *Insolvency Bulletin* 7.
285. See Insolvency Act 1986 s. 208 (misconduct in the course of winding up), s. 234 (getting in the company's property), s. 235 (duty to co-operate with the office holder), s. 236 (inquiry into company's dealings, etc.).
286. It should be remembered, as noted above (pp. 397–8), that human rights issues may arise. Under the Human Rights Act 1998 and Article 6 of the Convention there is a right to an independent and impartial tribunal. If an office holder determines the rights of a person, there may be a lack of independence where the office holder is an administrative receiver: see generally Simmons and Smith, 'Human Rights Act 1998'; Trower, 'Human Rights'; Lowry and Watson, *Company Law*, pp. 410–13.

13

The *pari passu* principle: when everyone is equal?

A fundamental rule of corporate insolvency law is said to be enshrined in the *pari passu* principle.[1] This holds that in a winding up creditors shall share rateably in those assets of the insolvent company that are available for residual distribution. 'Rateably' here means in common proportions according to the extent of their pre-insolvency claims: as opposed, for instance, to ranking in order of the time at which the claim was established.[2]

This, and the following chapter, consider whether the *pari passu* principle operates in an efficient and fair manner and whether there is a case for approaching post-insolvency distribution in a different way. Issues of accountability and expertise will not be addressed since *pari passu* is a substantive rule governing the distribution of goods and little is to be gained by asking whether a principle is, in itself, accountable or expert. Whether insolvency principles are administered accountably and expertly are matters dealt with in other chapters.

As noted previously in chapter 12, creditors are free, prior to winding up, to pursue whatever enforcement measures are open to them: for example, repossession of goods or judgment execution. Indeed, the race goes to the swiftest. Liquidation puts an end to the race as the liquidator is responsible for the orderly realisation of assets for the benefit of all unsecured

---

1. See D. Milman, 'Priority Rights on Corporate Insolvency' in A. Clarke (ed.), *Current Issues in Insolvency Law* (Stevens & Sons, London, 1992) p. 51. *Report of the Review Committee on Insolvency Law and Practice* (Cmnd 8558, 1982) ('Cork Report') para. 1220. The *pari passu* principle is now contained in the Insolvency Act 1986 s. 107 (voluntary winding up) and the Insolvency Rules 1986 r. 4.181(1) (compulsory winding up). For an argument that *pari passu* should not be treated as a fundamental rule see R. Mokal, 'Priority as Pathology: The *Pari Passu* Myth' [2001] CLJ 581.
2. See ch. 14 below.

creditors and for distributing the net proceeds *pari passu*. The *pari passu* principle, however, can only apply to unencumbered assets of the insolvent company that are available for distribution. If a company holds property as a bailee or trustee, that property is not part of the common pool for distribution. Similarly, goods possessed by the company under a contract of sale that reserves title to the seller until completion of payment do not form part of the pool. Where, moreover, the company has given security rights over property this constitutes an asset available for distribution only to the extent that its value exceeds the sum of the secured indebtedness.[3]

Corporate insolvency law is faced here with two important challenges: how to stipulate which assets will be available for distribution and whether exceptions should be made to the *pari passu* rule in distributing those available assets. This chapter focuses on the latter issue and chapter 14 considers the construction of the insolvent company's estate for distribution.

At this point, the discussion of insolvency law rationales that was contained in chapter 2 should be recalled. Different visions of corporate insolvency law will produce different approaches to the distribution and construction of the insolvency estate. If corporate insolvency law is seen as centrally concerned to maximise the assets available for distribution to creditors,[4] creditors' rights in a liquidation will be treated as governed by prior non-insolvency entitlements. What has been bargained for in advance will dictate priorities in a subsequent liquidation. If, on the other hand, insolvency law is seen as having a redistributional role – one that allows prior private bargains to be adjusted in the public interest or in pursuit of democratically established policies – creditors' rights in a liquidation will be influenced by a range of factors other than rights established outside insolvency.[5]

3. See R. M. Goode, *Principles of Corporate Insolvency Law* (2nd edn, Sweet & Maxwell, London, 1997) p. 48. On the limits to *pari passu* see F. Oditah, 'Assets and the Treatment of Claims in Insolvency' (1992) 108 LQR 459 at 468–76; Mokal, 'Priority as Pathology', pp. 585–90; pp. 424–49, 452–83, 485–87 below.

4. See T. H. Jackson, *The Logic and Limits of Bankruptcy Law* (Harvard University Press, Cambridge, Mass., 1986); D. G. Baird and T. Jackson, 'Corporate Reorganisations and the Treatment of Diverse Ownership Interests: A Comment on Adequate Protection of Secured Creditors in Bankruptcy' (1984) 51 U Chic. L Rev. 97; D. G. Baird 'Loss Distribution, Forum Shopping and Bankruptcy: A Reply to Warren' (1987) 54 U Chic. L Rev. 815. Arguably the *pari passu* principle, *stricto sensu*, with collectivity mimics the notional 'creditors' bargain' posited by Jackson. See also the discussion in S. S. Cantlie, 'Preferred Priority in Bankruptcy' in J. Ziegel (ed.), *Current Developments in International and Comparative Corporate Insolvency Law* (Clarendon Press, Oxford, 1994).

5. See, for example, E. Warren, 'Bankruptcy Policy' (1987) 54 U Chic. L Rev. 775; Warren, 'Bankruptcy Policymaking in an Imperfect World' (1993) 92 Mich. L Rev. 336.

As indicated in chapter 2, the approach taken in this book rejects the narrow 'creditor wealth maximising' vision of corporate insolvency law and sees insolvency law as properly concerned with redistributional and public interest aspects as well as with respect for private bargains and property. This implies, first, that exceptions to *pari passu* may be entertained on their public interest merits and, second, that in constructing the estate of the insolvent company that is available for distribution, it may be legitimate to restrict the extent to which private bargaining will be allowed to circumvent the principles of collectivity and *pari passu* distribution.

Before considering whether certain exceptions to *pari passu* can be justified on efficiency or on fairness grounds, the rationale for *pari passu* should be noted. In terms of efficiency, the case for *pari passu* is that within a mandatory, collective regime it conduces to an orderly means of dealing with unsecured creditor claims. Legal costs and delays are said to be kept low by a simple *pari passu* rule because, in the absence of any legislative direction to differentiate between unsecured creditor claims, it avoids the need for courts to make difficult choices, as would be involved were they to adopt other possible principles: for example, distribution according to need or inability to sustain losses.[6] In terms of the economic efficiency of the 'creditors' bargain' and 'creditor wealth maximisation' theories, compulsory, collective proceedings are held out as reducing strategic costs and increasing the aggregate pool of assets.[7] The collectivity of dealings with unsecured creditors as a class is enhanced by the *pari passu* principle and is efficient in so far as it avoids the costs of dealing with claims on their individual merits.[8]

Fairness in the procedural and substantive senses may also be said to be assured by the *pari passu* principle in so far as it prevents an intra-class race to enforce claims that is destined to be won by the strongest and swiftest and it also involves equality of treatment between unsecured creditors.[9]

---

6. See Milman, 'Priority Rights', p. 59.

7. See T. H. Jackson, *Logic and Limits of Bankruptcy Law*, ch. 1; see also ch. 2 above.

8. Mokal argues ('Priority as Pathology', p. 593) that it is collectivity not *pari passu* that avoids value-destroying races to collect; that *pari passu* is not necessary for efficiency. Value, however, is lost by processes additional to the race to collect, notably in incurring high costs to deal with claims individually. *Pari passu* reduces such costs within the class of unsecured creditors and accordingly may be justified on efficiency (as well as fairness) grounds. There is, in short, more to securing efficiency than stopping the race to collect and having creditors form an orderly queue. The claims of parties in the queue have to be dealt with efficiently. It can be conceded, however, that the claims of unsecured creditors could be dealt with collectively and at low cost without reference to *pari passu*, for example by paying debts according to date of loan. On the acceptability of alternatives to *pari passu* see ch. 14 below.

9. On justice in insolvency see J. Finnis, *Natural Law and Natural Rights* (Clarendon Press, Oxford, 1980) p. 190; see also ch. 14 below.

This will be the case at least where the principle is not undermined by exceptions.

Exceptions to *pari passu*

Liquidation expenses and post-liquidation creditors

Liquidation expenses rank ahead of all other claims on the estate and are paid in full before even preferential debts.[10] In order to effect the most beneficial winding up of a company the liquidator may have to sustain a period of continued trading for a given time. This may benefit all creditors. During this period, funds may be required in order to keep employees in post and to achieve continuity in the supply of materials. If creditors were asked to supply funds during this post-liquidation period they would be unlikely to oblige if the debts involved were to enjoy no priority over those of pre-liquidation creditors.[11] Such super-priority can, however, be achieved by treating the liquidator's transactions with such creditors as expenses of the liquidation so that post-liquidation creditors do not have to prove for a dividend in competition with other creditors.[12] Expenses of the liquidation (including post-liquidation creditors' claims) are thus paid first, followed by the claims of preferential creditors,[13] and only the remaining pool of assets[14] becomes available for distribution to the general body of unsecured creditors. While it is clear that new transactions by the liquidator constitute post-liquidation claims, difficulties may arise in relation to obligations under existing contracts or leases. The relevant test

10. Secured creditors will be entitled to be paid out of the proceeds of their security ahead of all other claims, but if the security is by way of a floating charge, liquidation expenses and debts that are preferential debts must be paid first. See Insolvency Act 1986 ss. 115, 107; Insolvency Rules 1986 r. 4.180(1). See Insolvency Act 1986 ss. 115, 156, 175(2)(a) regarding liquidators' costs and expenses. See further Insolvency Lawyers' Association/AAG, 'The Liquidation Expenses Principle' [2000] Ins. Law. 126; G. Moss and N. Segal, 'Insolvency Proceedings: Contract and Financing – The Expenses Doctrine in Liquidation, Administration and Receiverships' [1997] 1 CfiLR 1. For further discussion of liquidators and expenses see ch. 12 above.

11. See Goode, *Principles of Corporate Insolvency Law*, p. 154.

12. Rule 12.2 of the Insolvency Rules 1986 lists items to be regarded as expenses of the winding up and rule 4.218 gives the order of priority for payment of expenses of the winding up – subject, however, to the courts' powers under the Insolvency Act 1986 s. 156. On paying corporation tax (on interest receivable after the start of a winding up) as a necessary disbursement and an expense of the winding up see *Commissioners of Inland Revenue v. Kahn (Re Toshoku Finance (UK) plc)* [2001] BCC 273 (CA), (affirmed [2002] BCC 110 (HL); D. Milman, 'Post Liquidation Tax as a Winding Up Expense' [2000] Ins. Law. 169. See also *Re Leyland DAF Ltd* [2001] 1 BCLC 419: assets covered by a crystallised floating charge are available to be used to recoup properly incurred liquidation expenses (affirmed Feb. 2002 (CA)).

13. See Insolvency Act 1986 s. 175(2)(a) and (b).

14. Which will have been depleted, of course, by payment to any floating charge holders.

is whether the liquidator had adopted the transaction and taken it over for the purposes of the winding up.[15]

Before the Insolvency Act 1986, this treatment of post-liquidation debts placed utility companies in a strong position relative to other trade suppliers. The large providers of gas, electricity, water and telecommunications services could use their dominant market positions to compel the payment of debts on accounts incurred before the commencement of a winding up. They would do this by threatening to cut off a supply unless arrears were paid in full or payment was personally guaranteed by the liquidator or receiver.[16] Where the supply was essential to preserve the company's assets, payment was difficult to avoid and the effect was to pay the utility debt in priority even to the statutory preferential creditors.[17] Following strong criticism of this process in the Cork Report,[18] section 233 (as amended) of the Insolvency Act 1986 prohibited resort to this practice. The supplier may now require the office holder to undertake personal responsibility for payment of any new supply but may not make the availability of a new supply conditional on receiving payment or security for the old supply.

Preferential debts

The Cork Committee noted that *pari passu* distribution of uncharged assets was in practice seldom, if ever, attained because, in the overwhelming majority of cases, the existence of preferential debts frustrated such distribution.[19] Preferential debts are unsecured debts which, by force of statute, fall to be paid in a winding up in priority to all other unsecured debts (and to claims for principal and interest secured by a floating charge[20]) but

---

15. See *ABC Coupler and Engineering Co. Ltd (No. 3)* (1970) 1 All ER 656; *Re Downer Enterprises Ltd* [1974] 2 All ER 1074; *Re Oak Pits Colliery Co.* (1882) 21 Ch D 322; *Re National Arms and Ammunition Co.* (1885) 28 Ch D 474.

16. In receivership private suppliers of strategic raw materials may also enjoy powerful bargaining positions: see *Leyland DAF Ltd* v. *Automotive Products plc* [1993] BCC 389.

17. The legality of this practice was upheld in *Wellworth Cash & Carry (North Shields Ltd)* v. *North Eastern Electricity Board* [1986] 2 BCC 99, 265.

18. Cork Report, ch. 33, esp. para. 1462.

19. Ibid., p. 317. Preferential debts were introduced in the Preferential Payments in Bankruptcy Act 1897.

20. Preferential creditors rank in priority not only above unsecured creditors, but also above debenture holders with assets covered by floating, not fixed, charges: see Insolvency Act 1986 s. 175(2)(b). See also Insolvency Act 1986 s. 251 which defines 'floating charge' so as to include a charge, which, though originally floating, has since become fixed. Thus, any charge which was originally a floating charge but has become a fixed charge (e.g. by crystallisation or by a notice of conversion) before the 'relevant date' defined by s. 387 will be subordinated to the preferential debts under s. 175(2)(b), thus depriving such decisions as *Re Woodroffes Ltd* [1986]

which abate rateably as amongst themselves. Preferential debts are listed in Schedule 6 of the Insolvency Act 1986[21] and include rates and certain taxes;[22] wages or salaries of employees; accrued holiday remuneration of employees[23] and earnings-related social security contributions. Assessed taxes such as income tax and corporation tax were not given preferential status in Schedule 6 of the Insolvency Act 1986 since the government yielded to Cork's arguments that there was no case for priority in such instances.[24] Taxes collected by the taxpayer for the Crown (for example, PAYE and National Insurance contributions) were, however, listed as preferential, being treated in effect as moneys which the taxpayer has collected and held in an arrangement analogous to a trust for further delivery to the Crown. Such a stark distinction between the treatment of 'assessed' and 'collected' taxes has, however, been eroded since 1986 because subsequent additions to the Schedule 6 list of taxes have reasserted the principle of Crown preference on the introduction of new forms of assessed taxation such as insurance premium tax, beer excise duty, lottery duty, air passenger duty and levies on coal and steel production.[25] There is, moreover, no restriction on the sums for which the Crown can assert its preference, provided that the debts at issue have become due within the stipulated

Ch 366, *Re Brightlife Ltd* [1987] Ch 200 and *Re Griffin Hotel Co. Ltd* [1941] Ch 129 of force. Conversely, where a charge was originally a fixed charge and is converted to or replaced by a floating charge, the preferential debts have no priority: *Re New Bullas Trading Ltd* [1994] BCC 36 (cf. *Re Brumark Investments Ltd (Agnew v. Commissioner of Inland Revenue)* [2001] 3 WLR 454, [2001] UKPC 28).

21. See also Insolvency Act 1986 ss. 386, 387; Insolvency Act 1986 s. 175 (winding up), s. 40 (receivership: see *Re H & K Medway Ltd* [1997] BCC 853).

22. The decision in *Re Toshoku (UK) plc* [2001] BCC 273 (CA [2002] BCC 110 CHL), as noted above, makes it clear that corporation tax liabilities arising after the start of a winding up are properly to be treated as expenses of the winding up and are therefore to be paid in advance of preferential debts: see Milman, 'Post Liquidation Tax'.

23. See Category 5 of the sixth Schedule.

24. See Cork Report, paras. 1409–50, where the Committee accepted that the Crown was an involuntary creditor in relation to such taxes but stressed that abolition of the Crown preference would not lead to significant net losses and 'the ancient prerogative of the Crown to priority … cannot be supported by principle or expediency' (para. 1417). Different considerations were said, however, to apply to taxes such as PAYE or national insurance, VAT and car tax since the Crown's claim in such cases was for money collected by the debtor from other parties and the debtor could properly be viewed as a tax collector rather than a tax payer. Unless such debts were given priority the moneys collected would swell the insolvent's estate to the benefit of private creditors rather than the state.

25. See, for example, Finance Act 1994 Sched. 7, para. 7(2) (insurance premium tax); Finance Act 1991 Sched. 2, para. 21A (beer duty); Finance Act 1993 s. 36(1) (lottery duty); Insolvency (ECSC Levy Debts) Regulations 1987 (SI 1987 No. 2093) (levies on coal and steel production). See also I. F. Fletcher, 'The Counter Reformation by Stealth: Crown Preference for Unpaid Taxes' [1995] JBL 604–6. These additions can be seen to run counter to the basic philosophy of the Cork Committee.

reference period.[26] The Crown recovers some £60–90 million of preferential debt in insolvencies each year.[27]

Can preferential debts be justified in economic efficiency terms?[28] A general argument relating to unsecured creditors asserts that if parties constitute involuntary, non-adjusting creditors, their debtors will not bear the full costs of defaulting and so will not take optimal care to avoid default. The debtor will thus take excessive risks with, say, the credit offered by the Crown tax authorities and by employees and there will be an inefficient allocation of resources in society. The Crown, it can be claimed, is in no position to choose whether to offer credit to a company and, similarly, employees who are paid in arrears have little option but to provide credit to their employing company for the period between wage payments.[29]

As for the ability to adjust credit terms, this is crucially important. If the Crown and employees could adjust the terms on which they provide credit so as to take account of default risks, the inefficiencies noted would not arise (the risk-related component of the credit arrangement would induce the appropriate level of credit provision and care taken). Here, however, it may be proper to draw a distinction between the Crown and a company's employees. The Crown is able to position its tax levels in a manner that anticipates default rates. It will spread default risks across taxpayers when taking this action. In doing so it does not adjust the cost of credit to take on board the default risk relating to the particular company at issue. The risk, as noted, is spread across taxpayers. This produces inefficiency in so far as subsidies are effected from non-defaulting to defaulting taxpayers. Companies who are at low risk of insolvency are paying too much tax because they are sharing the burdens occasioned by companies that do default on their debts.

---

26. See Fletcher, 'Counter Reformation by Stealth'. The reference period is usually six months (e.g. VAT) or twelve months (e.g. PAYE payments, social security contributions, Customs and Excise payments). Employees' claims for arrears of wages or salary, however, are subject to a four-month period of reference (para. 9(b) of Sched. 6) and are subject to a maximum limit fixed by the Secretary of State: £800 according to the Insolvency Proceedings (Monetary Limits) Order 1986 (SI 1986 No. 1996) Art. 4.

27. See Insolvency Service, A *Review of Company Rescue and Business Reconstruction Mechanisms*, Interim Report (DTI, September 1999) ('IS 1999') para. 8(b). On Government proposals to abolish the Crown's preferential status see pp. 431–5 below and the DTI/Insolvency Service White Paper, *Productivity and Enterprise: Insolvency – A Second Chance* (Cm 5234, 2001) ('White Paper, 2001') para. 2.19.

28. See generally Cantlie, 'Preferred Priority in Bankruptcy'; V. Finch, 'Is *Pari Passu* Passé?' [2000] Ins. Law. 194, 206.

29. See Cantlie, 'Preferred Priority in Bankruptcy', pp. 422–3.

Employees, in contrast, are ill-positioned to adjust their credit rates to take account of default risks.[30] When they negotiate employment contracts with a firm there will be little discussion of insolvency risks, the employee is liable to lack the information or expertise necessary to calculate the extent of such risks and, even if employees could make the appropriate calculations, they might well be unable to negotiate wages that incorporate a risk element because they face severe competition in the market for jobs and because others in that market may be unable or disinclined to hold out for such risk elements in their wages. Arguments about the general inefficiencies of unsecured credit do not, however, explain why the Crown or employees should be more sympathetically treated than other ordinary (e.g., trade) creditors. The latter, as was noted in chapter 3, may also be poorly placed to adjust their terms to cope with default risks.

All unsecured creditors might be covered by general protections in the shape of 10 per cent funds and, as argued in chapter 3, this would to some extent limit these inefficiencies in credit supply that stem from non-adjustment of rates. In deciding whether, over and above this, it is desirable in efficiency terms to give the Crown and employees protection beyond that enjoyed by trade creditors, it is necessary to consider the possible basis for favouring some non-adjusting creditors rather than others.

A key factor here concerns the costs of risk bearing. Where given levels of risk are allocated in a manner that gives rise to inefficiency because the decision-maker relieved of risk is liable to behave with sub-optimal care, it is relevant to consider variations in the costs of bearing undue risks. It may, in turn, be desirable to give most protection to those who will incur the greatest costs in bearing the risks at issue.[31]

The ability to spread risks increases a party's capacity to withstand the consequences of default.[32] Thus, the Crown is generally able to spread risks across taxpayers and is accordingly well equipped to sustain losses from defaults, or even to pass those losses on to other taxpayers who are likely to be able to cope with marginal increases in tax rates without suffering catastrophic consequences.[33] Trade creditors will have a certain

---

30. See generally B. Gleig, 'Unpaid Wages in Bankruptcy' (1987) 21 UBC L Rev. 61–83. On employees, see C. Villiers, 'Employees as Creditors: A Challenge for Justice in Insolvency Law' (1999) 20 Co. Law. 222; ch. 16 below.
31. See Cantlie, 'Preferred Priority in Bankruptcy', p. 430.
32. Ibid., pp. 433–44.
33. On the extent of moneys owed to the Crown – the Inland Revenue estimated that it was owed between £100m and £150m of preferential debt as at October 1995 and HM Customs and Excise wrote off £198m of preferential debt in 1995 – see A. Keay and P. Walton, 'Preferential Debts: An Empirical Study' [1999] Ins. Law. 112 at 113.

capacity to spread risks but small suppliers may be very hard hit by defaults. The costs of default in their cases may be high, with employees losing jobs or even businesses folding. Employees, as noted, are seldom able to spread default risks and so will suffer considerable hardship: for example, where lack of moneys owed prevents them from generating or gaining further employment. Not only are employees poor self-insurers against debtor default (their lack of diversification prevents effective self-insuring) but they will be unlikely to find insurance markets in which they can contract to spread risks.[34] What makes shifting risks to employees especially undesirable is that the costs of such a risk shift are liable to be higher than when insolvency risks are placed elsewhere. On this reasoning, tort creditors do not merit especially high levels of protection in insolvency because they are less likely than employees to be highly vulnerable to instances of default and, accordingly, they will not usually be extremely high-cost risk bearers. They will routinely have other sources of income, funds and products and risks will be spread by such diversification.

It has been proposed that other creditors (including secured creditors) should be deferred to tort claimants in insolvency[35] but a further consideration here is the special effect that deferment to tort creditors may have on major lenders. Banks, for instance, might be deterred from advancing funds on the basis of secured loans where they face risks of giving way to potentially huge tort claims. As argued in chapter 3,[36] other ways of protecting involuntary tort creditors – such as compulsory tort liability insurance for companies – might prove more consistent with efficient corporate financing.

The issue of vulnerability to risks may also militate against placing prepaying consumer creditors in a better position than ordinary unsecured creditors. Ogus and Rowley have contended[37] that there are material reasons for giving consumer pre-payers special protection – reasons based on economic efficiency. Their argument, in brief, is that few problems arise in the general provision of credit when there is voluntary choosing of investments, full information and equal bargaining power. In so far as such conditions are lacking in a trading relationship there may be a case for

---

34. Cantlie 'Preferred Priority in Bankruptcy', p. 437.
35. For discussion see D. Leebron, 'Limited Liability, Tort Victims and Creditors' (1991) 91 Colum L Rev. 1565, at 1643–50; H. Hansman and R. Krackman, 'Towards Unlimited Shareholder Liability for Corporate Torts' (1991) 100 Yale LJ 1879; V. Finch, 'Security, Insolvency and Risk: Who Pays the Price?' (1999) 62 MLR 633 at 657.
36. See pp. 95–7 above.
37. A. Ogus and C. Rowley, *Prepayments and Insolvency* (OFT Occasional Paper, 1984).

protecting the ill-placed party and, in so far as one group of creditors is liable to be more poorly placed than another, a relatively superior level of protection is appropriate. Consumer pre-payers, Ogus and Rowley state, may be eligible for such superior protection because they tend to be 'distanced from the company in a way that the trade creditor typically is not and may well regard the cost of negotiating over the risk of insolvency as excessive in relation to the amount at stake'.[38]

Consumer pre-payers may also be geographically dispersed (for example, in mail order contracting) which weakens their position, and they will rarely have easy access to such information on the trader as will allow them to assess insolvency risks. (The Office of Fair Trading has reported that it 'does not regard it as feasible' that consumers be expected to check on the financial standing of traders.[39]) Finally, many consumer creditors may fail to see themselves as creditors of the company at all, especially where they are led by the trading company to believe that the period of prepayment is short.

Whether consumer creditors are placed in positions materially worse than those occupied by small trade creditors is, however, open to argument. For its part, the Cork Committee decided against special treatment for consumers, saying of consumer and trade creditors: 'There is no essential difference. Each gives credit and if the credit is misplaced, each should bear the loss rateably.'[40] What is more strongly arguable is that consumer creditors tend to be lower-cost risk bearers than employees because their risks are more widely spread (across products). This argument suggests that if preferential treatment should be given, employees, not consumer creditors, should be favoured.[41]

A second factor that may influence the case for protecting an unsecured creditor is his or her ability to prevent default and the taking of inefficiently low levels of care. If a party is able to intervene and forestall disaster we may, on fairness grounds, be less inclined to protect them from default risks by giving them priority than we would in the case of someone who has no power to intervene.[42] On this front, the Crown is poorly placed since it can often do little to stop a company from running up ever larger tax

38. Ibid., p. 12.   39. Ibid., para. 5.11.   40. Cork Report, para. 1052.
41. In the survey reported by Keay and Walton, 'Preferential Debts: An Empirical Study', 60 per cent of IP respondents said that they would not introduce a new preference category for prepayment consumer creditors.
42. See A. Keay and P. Walton, 'The Preferential Debts Regime in Liquidation Law: In the Public Interest?' [1999] CfiLR 84 at 96; *Report of the Study Committee on Bankruptcy and Insolvency Legislation*, Canada (1970), para. 3.2.076–7; M. Shanker, 'The Worthier Creditors (and a Cheer for the King)' (1975–6) 1 Canadian Bus. LJ 341.

debts. Trade creditors in a regular supply relationship with a debtor may occasionally be able to impose conditions on supply and may adjust terms or decline to supply further items. Small suppliers to a large number of customers are, however, unlikely to be in this position and, in the case of all trade creditors, market conditions and competitive pressures may rule out the institution of preventative measures. Employees may decline to supply further labour if worried about their employer's solvency but, in a market where alternative employment is unavailable, this may be difficult. If the employee occupies a managerial position in the employing company there may, however, be opportunities to influence decision-making so as to limit default dangers, but such opportunities and influence may be very limited in many cases. Tort creditors, in contrast, will rarely, if ever, be able to take steps to influence default rates, or levels of care, and consumer creditors will occupy a similar position. The above points indicate that in terms of ability to prevent default there is no particularly strong case for sustaining exceptions to the *pari passu* principle.

An economic efficiency consideration should, however, also be considered. It might be argued that giving preferential treatment to the tax authorities leads to inefficiencies in so far as it creates an excessive incentive for those authorities to initiate liquidation proceedings; that this kills off enterprises that might survive and contribute to the economy. This issue has been officially considered in recent years. A review was announced in the 1998 White Paper, *Our Competitive Future*,[43] which stated that the Government would review the costs and benefits of any changes to the Crown's preferential status. In February 1999 the Trade and Industry Secretary, Stephen Byers, set up an Insolvency Service Review Group to consider insolvency law reforms and, by the autumn of that year, the Review Group had issued a consultation document that was taken by the financial press to place the tax authorities' preferential status in serious question.[44] The consultation document stated that the tax authorities were responsible for initiating 2,223 insolvency proceedings in the year to 31 March 1998 (17.6 per cent of total initiated proceedings) but that the Revenue and Customs supported between 70 and 80 per cent of rescue plans put to them.[45] The tax authorities denied to the Review Group that they drove

---

43. DTI, *Our Competitive Future: Building the Knowledge Driven Economy* (Cm 4176, 1998) esp. paras. 2.12–2.13.
44. See J. Kelly, 'Byers Questions Crown's Status as First Creditor', *Financial Times*, 20 September 1999; Keay and Walton, 'Preferential Debts: An Empirical Study'.
45. Figures from HM Customs and Excise suggest that that body instituted 4,374 winding-up petitions in 1998/9 and that 2,485 orders were made.

potentially sound businesses into insolvency and the Review Group stated that these authorities' attitude to voluntary arrangements was 'likely to be positive'.[46] This assessment was supported by the Society of Practitioners of Insolvency's 1999 Survey, *Company Insolvency in the United Kingdom*.[47] The results of this survey of 1,000 licensed insolvency practitioners threw cold water on the assumption that it is the creditors who are best placed to recover their money in a liquidation or receivership who stand in the way of innovative attempts to keep companies afloat.[48] The tax authorities resisted rescues *via* insolvency procedures in only 3 per cent of cases. The same was true of banks and other secured creditors, but unsecured creditors resisted in almost 10 per cent of cases. These figures, accordingly, suggested that there was little case for ending the Crown's preferential status simply because it creates an incentive to bring companies inefficiently to precipitate ends.[49]

When the Review Group issued its follow-up report in 2000[50] the case for reform had strengthened. Consultees had responded strongly in describing the 'uncommercial' attitude of the revenue departments (Inland Revenue and Customs and Excise) to proposals for CVAs.[51] The insistence of these departments on payment in full had been seen to frustrate many proposals that unsecured creditors would have otherwise approved. 'Consistent criticism' centred on the unwillingness of the Revenue and the Excise to deal with proposals on their merits or take a longer term view of the prospects of corporate survival.[52] There was concern that the Revenue and the Excise could bring down potential CVAs by rejecting them too late to allow more acceptable proposals to be developed. As for the need for

---

46. IS 1999, para. 8(c).

47. SPI, Eighth Survey, *Company Insolvency in the United Kingdom* (SPI, London, 1999).

48. The SPI Eighth Survey revealed that in 2 per cent of cases suppliers or customers recover all their money in insolvency procedures but in 24 per cent of cases banks do so and in 30 per cent of cases the tax authorities do so. Preferential and secured creditors were expected to recover 37 per cent of debts but unsecured creditors would recover on average only 7 per cent. The survey by Keay and Walton, 'Preferential Debts: An Empirical Study', found, however, that 78 per cent of IP respondents said that Crown preference diminished the possibility of rescue and 62 per cent of respondents thought that the Crown had a general policy of voting against rescue. Half of respondent IPs thought that the Crown would become more amenable to rescue packages if preferential status was abolished. Over 60 per cent of respondents favoured abolishing the Crown's preferential status but 95 per cent would not end the priority enjoyed by employees.

49. For a contrary view see ICAEW memorandum TECH 13/99, *A Review of Company Rescue and Business Reconstruction Mechanisms* (1999), which argues that removing the Crown's preferential status would encourage more company rescues.

50. Insolvency Service, *A Review of Company Rescue and Business Reconstruction Mechanisms, Report by the Review Group* (DTI, 2000) ('IS 2000').

51. On CVAs (company voluntary arrangements) see ch. 10 above.

52. IS 2000, p. 24.

legislative reform of Crown preference, there was 'considerable support' for abolition of the preferential status. There was little merit seen in the argument that preferential status was an appropriate compensation for the Crown's position as an involuntary creditor: 'A consistent observation was that the Government, which recovers between £60m to £90m a year by way of preferential debts from insolvencies, was in a far better position to absorb the effect of such bad debts than the average trade creditor of an insolvent company.'[53]

The Review Group made a number of recommendations to change the administration of claims to Crown preference. First, it suggested that the Inland Revenue and Customs and Excise should use their existing discretionary powers to develop 'a more commercial approach' to CVAs so that CVA proposals could be dealt with on their merits and that there would be clear scope to accept less than 100p in the pound if it was judged that a CVA would offer superior returns. Second, it recommended that the Revenue departments should notify the CVA nominee of the Crown's intentions in good time for the creditors' meeting. Third, the Customs and Excise was recommended to establish a central unit to deal with CVAs and to consider bringing private sector expertise into the unit. The unit would be given clear terms of reference 'to ensure that decisions to give up, in whole or in part, the Crown's preferential claim in a particular CVA were commercially justified'.[54] This was seen as an approach that would advantage unsecured creditors, improve the Crown's ability to pursue commercial debt arrangement and benefit the economy. Fourth, the Review Group argued that the Revenue departments, together with the Insolvency Service, should explore ways in which they could be more productive in warning directors of their financial troubles and pointing out such matters as the consequences of continuing to trade and the need for professional advice. The matter of legal abolition of Crown preference was said to be 'ultimately a political choice' though the Review Group noted a 'general acceptance' that abolition or waiver of the Crown's right to be paid as a preferential creditor in a CVA would encourage more CVAs to be proposed and accepted. The larger (and earlier) the dividend payment that was proposed to unsecured creditors the more likely they were to support proposals that would allow the company to survive. The Group concluded by stressing the importance of 'directing the benefits of any adjustments in Crown Preference towards unsecured creditors rather than floating charge holders'.[55]

---

53. Ibid., p. 25.   54. Ibid., p. 25.   55. Ibid., p. 26.

The thrust of these arguments has subsequently been endorsed in the Government's 2001 White Paper proposals to abolish Crown preferences in all insolvencies and to direct benefits to unsecured creditors by adopting a 'mechanism that ringfences a proportion of the funds generated by the floating charge'.[56] As for the Review Group's suggestions on administering the Crown's preferential claims, the Inland Revenue and Customs and Excise set up the Voluntary Arrangements Service in April 2001 to ensure that rescue proposals were given support.[57]

Do considerations of fairness suggest that certain non-adjusting creditors should be preferred to others in insolvency? Here we come to the issue that for Cork was central:

> Since the existence of any preferential debts militates against the principle of *pari passu* distribution and operates to the detriment of ordinary unsecured creditors, we have adopted the approach that no debt should be accorded priority unless this can be justified by reference to principles of fairness and equity which would be likely to command general public acceptance.[58]

In the case of the Crown it might be argued that it is an involuntary creditor that cannot choose its debtors or tailor its credit terms and that it is wrong to burden creditors with risks that they are in no position to recognise, calculate, adjust terms to, or protect themselves against.[59] This contention, as noted, found little resonance with consultees of the Insolvency Service Review Groups 1999–2000. Many unsecured creditors cannot adjust and the rationale offers no justification for giving priority to one category of unsecured creditors over another. Fairness considerations point in the direction of general protections for unsecured creditors – as offered by the 10 per cent rule – but not towards more particular safeguards.

The Insolvency Service Review Group noted the 'historical' argument that Crown debts are due to the public purse and the benefits to society in collecting taxes outweigh the benefits to, or claims of, individual creditors (except, to an extent, employees).[60] Cork, however, 'unhesitatingly'

---

56. See White Paper, 2001 (on *Productivity and Enterprise*), para. 2.19.
57. See DTI, *Opportunity for All in a World of Change – A White Paper on Enterprise, Skill and Innovation* (DTI, February 2001) ch. 5, paras. 5.14–5.15. On the Voluntary Arrangements Service (VAS) see further ch. 10 above. A User Forum is also to be set up to consider matters of policy: see [2001] *Simon's Tax Intelligence* 165; see ch. 10 above.
58. Cork Report, para. 1398.
59. Cantlie, 'Preferred Priority in Bankruptcy', p. 419. See IS 1999, p. 15.
60. IS 1999, p. 15.

rejected the view that debts owed to the community[61] or the Crown should be given priority over debts owed to private creditors, and such rejection seems both well founded and consistent with the sentiments of Review Group consultees[62] as well as the Government which, as noted above, stated in 2001 that it would abolish Crown preferential status in all insolvencies.[63] The Crown, when offering unsecured credit, is at least as capable of adjusting to, or protecting against, risks of default as private creditors such as trade suppliers, litigants with judgments for costs[64] or victims of breaches of contract or of tortious actions.[65] It might seem clear from surveys that the system of preferential debts causes considerable discontent in the ranks of unsecured creditors[66] but it might be warned that the position of unsecured creditors would not necessarily be improved if the Crown's preferential status was removed: 'In cases where a company had assets which were subject to a floating charge such removal would in the first place benefit the floating charge-holder. Only if there were sufficient funds to repay the charge-holder in full would unsecured creditors benefit at all.'[67]

To warn that an unfairness will not be fully remedied is, however, no reason for denying that a partial remedy has value. In any event the Government, as already indicated, has now stated that: 'we would ensure that the benefit of abolition of preferential status goes to unsecured creditors. We will achieve this through a mechanism that ring fences a proportion of the funds generated by the floating charge.'[68]

Does fairness demand priority for employee creditors?[69] Most employees are likely to be poorly placed to assess the financial standing of their employers, or to insist on employment terms that protect them against

---

61. Cork Report, para. 1410.   62. See IS 2000, p. 25, para. 90.

63. See White Paper, 2001 (on *Productivity and Enterprise*), para. 2.19.

64. On arguments regarding the treatment of 'inchoate security creditors' (i.e. those who have taken the initiative to enforce rights by litigation) see D. Prentice, 'The Effect of Insolvency on Pre-liquidation Transactions' in B. Pettet (ed.), *Company Law in Change* (Stevens & Sons, London, 1987) and pp. 447–9 below. For staunch support (by the Court of Appeal) of the *pari passu* principle as regards judgment creditors see *Re Buckingham International plc* [1998] BCC 943.

65. Cork Report, para. 1414.

66. The survey reported by Keay and Walton, 'Preferential Debts: An Empirical Study', reveals that 68 per cent of respondent IPs thought that there was unsecured creditor discontent.

67. IS 1999, para. 8(f).   68. White Paper, 2001, para. 2.19.

69. See Cantlie, 'Preferred Priority in Bankruptcy'; Keay and Walton, 'Preferential Debts Regime in Liquidation Law'; Gleig, 'Unpaid Wages in Bankruptcy'; C. Symes, 'The Protection of Wages When Insolvency Strikes' (1997) 5 *Insolvency Law Journal* 196; D. Zalman, 'The Unpaid Employee as Creditor' (1980) 6 Dalhousie LJ 148; Villiers, 'Employees as Creditors'.

insolvency risks. Cork, however, rejected the case for employee creditor priority on the grounds that it would give 'an excessive degree of indemnity to higher paid employees, including directors and senior management, at the expense of ordinary creditors who in many cases may be more deserving of sympathy'.[70] Employees are protected by the Employment Protection Acts,[71] said Cork, and there was no need for overlapping insolvency law protections. At present the Employment Rights Act 1996 (ERA) offers employees of an insolvent company more extensive protection than the Insolvency Act 1986. The 1986 Act gives preferential priority to unpaid wages to a maximum of £800 and accrued holiday pay owed. The ERA provides for payment by the Secretary of State for up to eight weeks of pay arrears during the statutory minimum period,[72] up to six weeks' holiday pay and a basic award for unfair dismissal.[73] The Secretary of State makes such payments out of the National Insurance Fund and stands in the shoes of the employee in attempting to recover such funds from the liquidator. Less than a quarter of the money paid out of the ERA scheme can be claimed by the Crown as preferential.[74] Current law, accordingly, gives employees limited priority in relation to unpaid wages and the ERA gives further protection. The effect of limited priority in such a regime is to allow the National Insurance Fund to recover a proportion of sums paid out to employees. To abolish employees' preferential status under the 1986 Act would consequently impose a loss not on employees but on the National Insurance Fund. It would, in doing so, make available considerable sums for other unsecured creditors. This may be no bad thing in efficiency terms since the Crown is likely to be a lower cost risk bearer than the other unsecured creditors referred to, but it may be objected that it is unfair for taxpayers to foot part of the bill for an insolvency when they have enjoyed no direct involvement with the company.[75] What the body of taxpayers has enjoyed, it could be riposted, is the prospect of gaining

---

70. Cork Report, para. 1430.

71. See now the Employment Rights Act 1996 (ERA 1996). On employees more generally see ch. 16 below.

72. I.e. up to eight weeks at up to £240 per week: ERA 1996 s. 186(1)(a); SI 1999 No. 3375.

73. ERA 1996 ss. 182, 186, 167.

74. See Keay and Walton, 'Preferential Debts Regime in Liquidation Law', p. 100, who note that on 31 March 1996 £762 million was owed by insolvent employers to the Fund, of which only £177 million (23 per cent) ranked as preferential.

75. The Cork Report, para. 1433, favoured replacing insolvency law priority with statutory employment protection. If Crown preferential rights are surrendered (White Paper, 2001, para. 2.19) and the resulting fund is ringfenced, then calls for abolition of employees' preferential status may have more force: see, for example, D. Milman, 'Insolvency Reform' [2001] Ins. Law. 153; Mokal, 'Priority as Pathology', pp. 616–20.

tax revenue from the potentially successful company. Having been happy to accept tax from a viable company and, in this sense, having shared in profits, such taxpayers, it could be said, are in no position to complain if they stand to bear some of the costs of failure. The Cork Committee,[76] for its part, favoured the Canadian approach in which the State's subrogated rights are not preferential. Cork noted Canadian thinking – that leaving a greater body of funds for unsecured creditors would be useful in encouraging them to play a more active part in the administration of the insolvent company's estate – but the Committee stressed that the case for meeting employees' debts was rooted in social policy considerations.[77]

In such discussions the further question arises as to the appropriateness of treating all employees who are owed wages in like terms. It is possible to distinguish some employee groups from others on the issue of fairness. Directors, for instance, might be thought to be less worthy of protection from the risks of unpaid wages than other employee creditors on the grounds that they can be taken to be better informed about risks, are better able to monitor the activities of the company, share *ex officio* some responsibility for the company's insolvency and are better able to gain compensation for insolvency risks than other employees and creditors.[78] This reasoning might be thought to justify excluding company directors from the group of those creditors able to benefit from a 10 per cent fund; giving no priority to such directors' claims to unpaid wages; and rendering directors ineligible for benefits from the National Insurance Fund in relation to unpaid wages. Directors' claims would, on such reasoning, be subordinated/deferred to those of other creditors. Such steps might, however, be considered to be too draconian and to exaggerate the extent to which company directors are able to self-inform concerning their company's insolvency risks, to influence financial risk-taking or to exit from excessively risky situations.[79]

---

76. Ibid., para. 1434.

77. Ibid., para. 1435. Australia has abolished the Crown's preferential status (Corporations Law as amended 1992). Canada has also done away with the notion of preferred status for Crown debts but the Crown does have broader access to secured status in bankruptcy: see Cantlie, 'Preferred Priority in Bankruptcy'.

78. See generally K. Van Wezel Stone, 'Policing Employment Contracts Within the Nexus-of-Contracts Firm' (1993) 43 U Toronto LJ 353.

79. On Cork's approach to discouraging irresponsibility to creditors on the part of directors see Cork Report, ch. 43; and ch. 15 below. See also White Paper, *A Revised Framework for Insolvency Law* (Cmnd 9175, 1984) which emphasised that all directors should ensure they have full awareness of their company's financial position; D. Milman, 'Insolvency Act 1986' (1987) 8 Co. Law. 61.

Set-off

A well-established principle of insolvency law is that where there are mutual debts existing between a creditor and a company in liquidation, the smaller debt is to be set against the larger debt and only the balance is to be paid to the creditor out of the insolvency estate.[80] Thus, if company A has supplied materials to now insolvent company B and is owed £10,000 for these but company A also owes company B £6,000 for equipment supplied by company B to company A, the principle of set-off means that £6,000 of the £10,000 debt is extinguished. There is no defence or counterclaim to an action involved here. Company B does not have to go to court to establish a counterclaim, it merely uses the debt to pay off part of the debt to company A. The effect of this, as will be returned to below, is that where company A has provided the £10,000 credit without security, it is placed in a better position than insolvent company B's other unsecured creditors with regard to the £6,000 debt which is effectively paid back to company A before other unsecured debts are looked to.

Insolvency set-off applies within the terms of Rule 4.90 of the Insolvency Rules 1986 which applies where, before liquidation,[81] there have been 'mutual credit, mutual debts or other mutual dealings between the company and any creditor of the company proving or claiming to prove for a debt in liquidation'. If there have been such mutual dealings then 'account shall be taken ... and the sums due from one party shall be set-off against the sums due from the other'.[82] Mutuality is essential: sums due from the company to another party will not be included in the set-off.[83] Mutuality demands that the two parties each have a debt owed by and to the other but the claims involved need not be

---

80. See Finch, 'Is *Pari Passu* Passé?', pp. 197–8. See generally Cork Report, ch. 30; Goode, *Principles of Corporate Insolvency Law*, ch. 8; P. Wood, *English and International Set-Off* (Sweet & Maxwell, London, 1989); R. Derham, *Set-Off* (2nd edn, Oxford University Press, Oxford, 1996); D. Milman and C. Durrant, *Corporate Insolvency: Law and Practice* (3rd edn, Sweet & Maxwell, London, 1999) pp. 182–7; S. McCraken, *The Banker's Remedy of Set Off* (2nd edn, Butterworths, London, 1998); D. Capper, 'Contracting Out of Insolvency Set-off: Irish Possibilities' [2000] Ins. Law. 248; C. Lynch, 'Insolvency Set-Off: A Review of Current Issues' (1994) 10 IL&P 161. On varieties of set-off see P. Ridgway, 'Corporation Tax in Insolvency: Part 3 – Equitable Set-Off and Crown Debts' (2000) 13 *Insolvency Intelligence* 9.
81. On the arising of a right of set-off see *Rother Iron Works* v. *Canterbury Precision Engineers Ltd* [1974] QB 1 but compare *Business Computers Ltd* v. *Anglo-African Leasing Ltd* [1977] 1 WLR 578. See Milman and Durrant, *Corporate Insolvency*, pp. 182–3.
82. Insolvency Rules 1986 r. 4.90(2).
83. Ibid., r. 4.90(3). See *Smith (Administrator of Coslett (Contractors) Ltd)* v. *Bridgend CBC (Re Coslett (Contractors) Ltd (in administration))* [2001] BCC 740 (HL): conversion of a company's property was not a mutual dealing between the Council and the company (Lord Hoffmann at p. 748).

connected or of the same type. They may be in contract, tort, restitution, statutory or other legal origin. Both claims, however, must be monetary in nature.[84] If one debt is proprietary in nature then no set-off is allowed.

The set-off rule applies to all companies in liquidation, be this compulsory or voluntary, where the English courts have jurisdiction to wind up. It does not apply to companies in administration, those subject to the appointment of an administrative receiver or companies in voluntary arrangements with creditors. The credits and debits involved must have taken place before the company 'goes into liquidation': that is, before the time of the winding-up order or the passing of the resolution to wind up the company.[85]

When a debtor company goes into insolvency the statutory rules set out in Rule 4.90 of the Insolvency Rules 1986 are mandatory[86] and displace all other forms of set-off not exercised prior to the winding up.[87] The courts have, however, had to come to grips with various attempts to exclude the mandatory application of insolvency set-off. Thus, in *Rolls Razor* v. *Cox*[88] the court held that a washing-machine salesman was entitled to set-off £106 of sale proceeds against the £406 of retained commission that the now insolvent company owed him. The set-off that was involved, said the court, could not be excluded by the contractual agreement between the parties which had purported to rule it out.[89]

---

84. On the requirements of mutuality see *Morris* v. *Agrichemicals Ltd (Morris* v. *Rayners Enterprises Inc.)* (BCCI No. 8) [1997] BCC 965 at 973–4 ('*Morris* v. *Agrichemicals*').

85. Note that this is not the same definition of the 'commencement of winding up' that is used elsewhere in the Insolvency Act 1986, which refers, for other purposes, to the time the petition was presented or the resolution is passed.

86. On the mandatory nature of statutory set-off see *National Westminster Bank Ltd* v. *Halesowen Presswork and Assemblies Ltd* [1972] AC 785; *Morris* v. *Agrichemicals*.

87. See Goode, *Principles of Corporate Insolvency Law*, pp. 174–7, where the five types of set-off are listed as: (1) independent set-off; (2) transaction set-off; (3) current account set-off; (4) contractual set-off; and (5) insolvency set-off.

88. [1967] 1 QB 552.

89. For criticism of this decision see Goode, *Principles of Corporate Insolvency Law*, p. 192. See also *National Westminster Bank Ltd* v. *Halesowen Presswork and Assemblies Ltd* [1972] AC 785 where the House of Lords held that a person for whom a right exists cannot waive that right so as to exclude the statutory rules of set-off: see discussion at pp. 440–2. In *British Eagle International Airlines Ltd* v. *Compagnie Nationale Air France* [1975] 1 WLR 758, [1975] 2 All ER 390 ('*British Eagle*') debts were cleared through a clearing house with seventy-six IATA member airlines. The court held that the liquidator of British Eagle had a legitimate claim for the net sum owed by Air France to British Eagle (after sums owed by the latter to the former had been set-off under the statutory rules). To allow pre-insolvency clearing arrangements to continue post-liquidation would offend the *pari passu* principle as sums due from Air France to British Eagle would, on clearing, be used to satisfy the debts of clearing house member creditors to the 'detriment' of non-members. For criticism of the *British Eagle* decision see, *inter alia*, Oditah, 'Assets', p. 466; R. Mokal, 'Priority as Pathology', pp. 598–601.

A recent case reviewing the issue of set-off was *Morris* v. *Agrichemicals*.[90] In that instance the bank, BCCI, had loaned money to A but had taken a deposit from B, a majority shareholder in the borrower company. The issue for the court was whether the bank was required to apply the rules of insolvency set-off and use the deposits from B to reduce the debts owed to the bank by the borrower company. The House of Lords held that the depositors could not insist on set-off because there was no mutuality: the borrowers owed the bank the sums of the loans but the bank owed the depositors the amount of the deposits. This was the case because the borrower and depositor were legally separate entities, though they were not separate economically. The decision in *Morris* thus contrasted with that of *MS Fashions*[91] where the facts were generally similar but with a key difference: here the depositors had not only pledged their deposits for the loans but they had guaranteed the obligation of the borrower and had thus established mutuality of claims for the purposes of mandatory set-off.[92]

Why should insolvency set-off be mandatory? Should contracting out of insolvency set-off be resisted on efficiency or fairness grounds? As one commentator has asked: 'What is so special about insolvency set-off which makes contracting out of it totally impossible whereas contracting out of the *pari passu* rule is to be possible provided the contracting out operates to the detriment rather than the benefit of the creditor which is a contracting party?'[93]

---

90. [1997] 3 WLR 909; [1997] BCC 968 *(Re BCCI (No. 8))*. The House of Lords in *Morris* also considered whether a bank can take an effective charge over its own customer's credit balance (answering in the affirmative) or whether this amounted to a contractual set-off and not a true security at all: see further R. Calnan, 'Fashioning the Law to Suit the Practicalities of Life' (1998) 114 LQR 174; R. M. Goode, 'Charge-Backs and Legal Fictions' (1998) 114 LQR 178; G. McCormack, 'Charge-Backs and Commercial Certainty in the House of Lords *(Re BCCI (No. 8))*' [1998] CfiLR 111; R. Mokal, 'Resolving the *MS Fashions* "Paradox"' [1999] CfiLR 106; J. de Lacy, 'The Legality of Charge-Back Security Interests' [1998] 5 *Palmer's In Company*; M. Evans, 'Decision of the Court of Appeal in *Morris* v. *Agrichemicals Ltd*: A Flawed Asset' (1996) 17 Co. Law. 102; G. McCormack, 'Security Interests in Deposit Accounts: The Anglo-American Perspective' [2002] Ins. Law. 7.
91. *MS Fashions* v. *Bank of Credit and Commerce International SA (No. 2)* [1993] BCC 70; Mokal, 'Resolving the *MS Fashions* "Paradox"'.
92. As the depositors owed an obligation to the bank under the guarantee and the bank owed the depositors an obligation in respect of the deposit.
93. See E. Ferran, 'Subordinated Debt Agreements' (1993) *CCH Company Law Newsletter* (28 June 1993) 8, 9; Ferran, *Company Law and Corporate Finance* (Oxford University Press, Oxford, 1999) pp. 552–4; D. Capper, 'Contracting Out of Insolvency Set-off'. On contracting out of *pari passu* to the detriment of the contracting creditor see *Re Maxwell Communications Corp. (No. 2)* [1994] 1 BCLC 1, [1993] BCC 369, [1994] 1 All ER 737 ('*Maxwell Communications*') and discussion below.

The Cork Committee noted the efficiency benefits of allowing contract-ing out.[94] When the law allowed contracting out of set-off[95] a company in financial difficulties, attempting to reorganise its affairs, found it useful to open a new account with the bankers to whom it was indebted. This account would be maintained in credit and the bank would agree that in a subsequent liquidation it would not set-off any credit balance on the account against existing indebtedness. This meant that the funds in the new account would be handed over intact to the liquidator and the bank would not become preferred to other creditors through the funds in the new account. For its part, the company would be able to run the business on a cash basis for the general benefit of all creditors. After contracting out was legally prevented such a company might open a new account with a new bank but not, if properly advised, its former bank. Cork deemed this to be an 'unnecessary and undesirable complication'.[96] The Committee urged that contracting out should be allowed. There was no sound reason of policy for the prohibition and there were good commercial reasons for ending it.

In *Maxwell Communications Corporation (No. 2)*[97] Vinelott J urged, in con-trast, that the mandatory nature of insolvency set-off could be justified in efficiency terms because this was a procedure from which the company and the body of creditors could benefit. The creditor could settle at least part of his debt without having to prove for it and the troubled company would be relieved of the need to engage in potentially expensive proceed-ings in order to recover the debt due to it. Complications such as determi-nation of whether a dividend was owing in the liquidation to a creditor who had waived set-off in circumstances where proceedings against him were still afoot could also be avoided with a mandatory rule. In the *Hale-sowen* case,[98] also, Lord Simon stressed that set-off was part of the proce-dure whereby insolvent estates are administered in a proper and orderly way. It was not a private right which those who benefited from it were free to waive; it was a matter in which the commercial community generally had an interest and accordingly this was a right that could not be con-tracted out of. A central issue, then, may be whether allowing parties to contract out of set-off would benefit creditors generally by removing the

---

94. See Cork Report, paras. 1341–62.
95. That is, until the decision in *National Westminster Bank Ltd v. Halesowen Pressworks and Assemblies Ltd* [1972] AC 785.
96. Cork Report, para. 1341.
97. [1993] BCC 369, [1994] 1 BCLC 1, [1994] 1 All ER 737.   98. [1972] AC 785.

preferred status of the contractor (in relation to the debt owed from the insolvent company) or would prejudice creditors generally by increasing transaction costs.[99]

Will mandatory set-off, however, lead to disadvantages for companies in some circumstances? In certain scenarios, it can be contended, mandatory set-off can introduce difficulties for a troubled company because it makes it harder for the company to refinance its operations by arranging additional credit facilities. This will happen where existing creditors will not agree to the refinancing deal if it involves a new creditor being given preference through set-off.[100] Implementation of the Cork recommendation to allow contracting out of set-off would give greater financing flexibility in such scenarios.

Is mandatory set-off fair? In *Forster* v. *Wilson*[101] the aim of insolvency set-off was said to be to do 'substantial justice' between the parties.[102] This implies that if creditor A owes troubled company B £1,500, yet A is owed £2,000 by B, it is just that the £1,500 debt is allowed to be set-off. The effect is to repay to A £1,500 of his debt as a matter of preference over other creditors of B (who, when deciding to lend, may have seen the debt in the company (B's) account as an asset). Allowing set-off worsens the position of other creditors who are not engaged in a mutual debt relationship with the company. The effect of set-off is to remove from the insolvency estate the asset that is the debt due from the creditor to the company.[103] An alternative would be for A to pay the £1,500 debt to B and then prove for the £2,000 in Company B's insolvency, taking a percentage dividend on the sum owed alongside other unsecured creditors. To an independent observer this alternative arrangement might seem fairer than set-off because set-off 'rewards', with priority, those solvent creditors who happen also to have borrowed from an insolvent company.[104]

---

99. But note that in *Halesowen* an agreement which would have increased the remaining creditors' insolvency estate was struck down. Contracting out is allowed in Scotland and the United States: on Scotland see Insolvency Act 1986 s. 440(2)(b); Capper, 'Contracting Out of Insolvency Set-off', p. 252.

100. Mandatory set-off is likely, of course, to make creditors more willing to lend to the troubled company. If those creditors also owe debts to the company they will be able to set-off their own debts against debts owed to them by the company.

101. (1843) 12 M&W 191 at 203–4. See Oditah, 'Assets', p. 467.

102. The 'substantial justice' purpose attributed to Parke B in *Forster* v. *Wilson* has been quoted with approval several times: see, for example, *Stein* v. *Blake* [1996] 1 AC 243 at 251E; *Gye* v. *McIntyre* [1991] 171 CLRT 609 at 618.

103. Of course, the principal limiting requirement is that of mutuality. Insolvency set-off is usually said to guard against injustice to the solvent party, i.e., against the solvent party's having to pay in full knowing it will in turn merely get a few pence in the pound.

104. See discussion in Carruthers and Halliday, *Rescuing Business*, pp. 181–6.

Subordination

It is clear from the above that the *pari passu* principle is not one that can be bypassed to one's advantage by simple contractual agreements with no proprietary effect.[105] It is also clear that statutory exceptions to *pari passu* are encountered: the Insolvency Rules make set-off mandatory and, again, there is no contracting out of set-off within current corporate insolvency law. On the matter of contractual subordination,[106] however, it is possible to make an effective agreement that one's own debt will rank behind the other unsecured debts of a company. The ground-breaking decision here was *Re Maxwell Communications Corporation plc (No. 2)*.[107] The question before the court was whether the holders of convertible subordinated bonds might effectively contract not to be repaid until after the general unsecured creditors had been satisfied in full. Vinelott J did not see why bondholders, who had entered into an investment arrangement fully aware of the subordination of their claims, should be elevated to the level of the rest of the creditors at the time of insolvency. The bondholders had freely contracted with relevant knowledge and the court saw no reason to re-open the contractual bargain. Contracting out of the *pari passu* principle was thus allowed on the basis that a creditor would be permitted to waive a debt in full (or in part) and that this might be agreed in advance of, or after, a liquidation. After all, noted Vinelott J, a creditor could waive a right to prove in liquidation and could agree to postpone his debt after winding up had commenced. Other creditors, indeed, might have given credit on the understanding that another creditor's subordination

---

105. See *British Eagle* [1975] 2 All ER 390; and see *MMI* v. *LSE* [2001] 4 All ER 223 and NeubergerJ's ten propositions, concerning 'deprivation provisions' and the *British Eagle* principle; see G. Stewart, 'The British Eagle has Landed' (2001) *Recovery* (December) 7–8; ch. 14 below, p. 451. On whether direct payment clauses in construction contracts offend the *pari passu* principle see D. Capper, 'Direct Payment Clauses and the *Pari Passu* Principle' [1998] CfiLR 54; A. Emden, *Emden's Construction Law* (Butterworths, London, 1997) Issue 39, section 111, paras. 3167–206; G. McCormack, '*Pari Passu* Distribution and Construction Contracts' (1993) 8 IL&P 169; McCormack, *Proprietary Claims and Insolvency* (Sweet & Maxwell, London, 1997) pp. 17–25; R. Davis, *Construction Insolvency* (Chancery, London, 1991) ch. 6. **106.** On contractual subordination see generally B. Johnston, 'Contractual Debt Subordination and Legislative Reform' [1991] JBL 225; F. Oditah, *Legal Aspects of Receivables Financing* (Sweet & Maxwell, London, 1991); R. Nolan 'Less Equal than Others: *Maxwell* and Subordinated Unsecured Obligations' [1995] JBL 484; McCormack, *Proprietary Claims and Insolvency Law*, pp. 145–6; Ferran, *Company Law and Corporate Finance*, pp. 549–61; E. Ferran, 'Recent Developments in Unsecured Debt Subordination' in B. Rider (ed.), *The Realm of Company Law* (Kluwer, London, 1998); S. Rajani, 'Enforceability of Subordination of Debt in a Liquidation' (2000) 15 IL&P 58 (dealing with the implications of the Contracts (Rights of Third Parties) Act 1999). On trust subordination and contingent-debt subordination see Ferran, *Company Law and Corporate Finance*, pp. 561–4; K. Thomas and C. Ryan, 'Section 459, Public Policy and Freedom of Contract' (2001) 22 Co. Law. 199 at 200–1. **107.** [1994] 1 All ER 737.

agreement would be effective. Vinelott J also noted that contractual subordination was effective in other leading common law and civil law jurisdictions[108] and he considered that, given that such agreements were recognised as effective, to strike them down would be a triumph of form over
substance.

What may be difficult to deny is the value of subordinated borrowing
as a form of corporate finance. Subordination may be useful in a number of circumstances,[109] notably: to allow shareholders or directors to inject funds into a company where existing creditors will not allow further
unsubordinated borrowings; to allow parent companies to enhance the
credit of a subsidiary that is issuing securities (so that an appropriate rating for the securities will be obtained); to allow companies to appeal to investors who seek high incomes in return for higher risk bearing; and to
allow a bank to issue funds for treatment as capital for capital adequacy
purposes.

Why, however, allow contracting out of *pari passu* on subordination but
not on set-off or more generally? The key consideration is fairness. On this
matter the courts have consistently taken the view that an agreement that
purports to improve the position of a creditor who would normally be subject to the *pari passu* rule will not, for reasons of public policy, be effective when the debtor company is in liquidation.[110] Subordination, as mentioned above, however, has been seen, notably by Vinelott J in the *Maxwell
Communications* case, as worsening only the position of the contracting
party and, accordingly, as a manoeuvre involving no unfairness to other
creditors.[111] This would be the case if such contracts could not be terminated or adjusted in the periods leading up to insolvency.

It is possible, however, to think of circumstances in which, under current conditions, unfairness could be occasioned by use of a subordination
agreement. If bank A agrees to advance funds to company B in difficult
times and agrees to subordinate its debt to those of creditors C, D and E,
creditors C, D and E may be inclined to increase their lending to company B in the knowledge that A's advance is subordinated to their own

---

108. For example, Australia and New Zealand: see Ferran, 'Recent Developments', pp. 206–9
for a discussion of provisions and case law.
109. See Ferran, 'Recent Developments', p. 201.
110. See *British Eagle* [1975] 2 All ER 390.
111. For Commonwealth judgments consistent with the line of Vinelott J in *Maxwell* see *Horne
v. Chester & Fein Property Development Pty Ltd and Others* (1986–7) 11 ACSR 485; *Ex parte de Villiers,
Re Carbon Developments (Pty) Ltd (in liquidation)* [1993] 1 SA 493.

claims.[112] If, at a later date, A renegotiates the terms of its loan to B and ends the subordination, lenders C, D and E may have been led to make loans available in unfair conditions. If, in the alternative, the debtor company seeks to make payments to the allegedly subordinated creditor, the unsubordinated unsecured creditors are poorly positioned to protect their own interests as they are not parties to the subordination agreement and the doctrine of privity of contract will rule out enforcement against the company.[113] Nor do arguments that contractual subordinations constitute waivers of statutory rights give the unsubordinated creditors any rights of enforcement or allow them to prevent variations in the terms of the subordination agreement.[114] The potential to subordinate at will creates uncertainties in the lending regime, it makes the task of liquidation more complex and this, in itself, will increase costs. Where lenders C, D and E gain the relevant information on subordination (or non-subordination) by A, they are liable to increase their interest rates to reflect any uncertainties in the system. Moving beyond a simple subordination agreement – in which a creditor agrees to rank behind all other creditors of a particular debtor – that creditor may wish to agree to rank behind some, but not all, of the other creditors.[115] A group of creditors, indeed, may seek to agree a ranking order amongst themselves, so that, for example, A, B and C agree to rank behind all other general creditors but to rank between themselves, A first, B second and C last. The central issue here is whether the *British Eagle* ruling is offended by such arrangements and parties are seeking to opt out of *pari passu* to their own advantage. Where a creditor agrees to subordinate to some, but not all, other creditors it is arguable that the *pari passu* principle is not breached because the subordinator gains no advantage over parties who are not involved in the subordination agreement. Where, as in the example of A, B and C above, a ranking order is agreed, third party creditor

---

112. On reliance on subordination by third party creditors see Nolan, 'Less Equal than Others', p. 495 who argues that there is little that third party creditors can do to protect themselves against variations in subordination terms. The advent of liquidation should, however, prevent variations after the start of the winding up: see Ferran, 'Recent Developments', p. 214.

113. See Nolan, 'Less Equal than Others', p. 495; *Dunlop Pneumatic Tyre Co. Ltd* v. *Selfridge & Co. Ltd* [1915] AC 847 at 853.

114. See Nolan, 'Less Equal than Others', pp. 496–7 who also reviews arguments that unsubordinated creditors might be able to secure damages from a liquidator who distributes in breach of valid contracts of subordination and arguments that restitution could be sought from subordinated creditors who have received funds contrary to the terms of the subordination agreement: see *Ministry of Health* v. *Simpson* [1951] AC 251.

115. See Ferran, *Company Law and Corporate Finance*, pp. 554–6.

interests are not prejudiced but A will gain a priority advantage over B and C. This is a consensual agreement, however, that has been treated in Commonwealth case law as not infringing the public policy of the *pari passu* rule.[116]

Deferred claims

Claims may be deferred by statute, that is placed in priority *below* the claims of other creditors.[117] Thus section 215(4) of the Insolvency Act 1986 provides that 'where a court makes a declaration under [sections 213 or 214 of the Insolvency Act 1986] in relation to a person who is a creditor of the company, it may direct the whole or any part of any debt owed by the company to that person and any interest thereon shall rank in priority after all other debts owed by the company and after interest on those debts'. Similarly the Insolvency Act 1986 defers sums due to members of the company by way of dividends, profits or otherwise. Such claims are ranked below those of all other creditors.[118] It is clear, however, from the case of *Soden*[119] that the relevant section (section 74(2)(f)) subordinates to the rights of unsecured creditors only sums due to a member 'in his character as member'. This covers sums due under the section 14 (Companies Act 1985) statutory contract which draws a contract out of the terms of the company's memorandum and articles and other obligations imposed by the Companies Act. Sums due to a member independently of that section 14 membership contract are excluded as, for example, are sums due as court awards in an action for misrepresentation, as in the *Soden* decision itself. Such sums owed would not be deferred but would rank *pari passu* with unsecured creditors. The broader importance of the *Soden* decision is the approach it lays down concerning the ranking of claims of members whose financial relationship with their company goes beyond simply share ownership. Issues of set-off are also affected since *Soden* holds that

---

116. See Horne v. *Chester & Fein Property Development Pty Ltd and Others* (1986–7) 11 ACSR 485, discussed in Ferran, *Company Law and Corporate Finance*, p. 555. See also *US Trust Corporation* v. *Australia and New Zealand Banking Group* (1995) 17 ACSR 697.

117. See Finch, 'Is *Pari Passu* Passé?', p. 199. See generally Goode, *Principles of Corporate Insolvency Law*, pp. 160–1. Goode notes the development in the USA of the doctrine of equitable subordination but suggests that in England the terms of the Insolvency Act 1986 give the courts the powers they need. On the doctrine of equitable subordination and inter-company loans see ch. 12 above. See also Justice, *Insolvency Law: An Agenda for Reform* (Justice, London, 1994) p. 25. For a discussion of an adjustable priority rule involving the deferral of secured claims to the unsecured claims of non-adjusting parties see ch. 14 below at pp. 459–60.

118. Insolvency Act 1986 s. 74(2)(f).

119. *Soden* v. *British & Commonwealth Holdings plc (in administration)* [1997] BCC 952.

sums arising out of the statutory membership contract will provide no set-off from, say, non-fully-paid-up shares, but other independent claims outside the statutory contract may be set-off against the obligation of contribution.

Conclusions: rethinking exceptions to *pari passu*

The following chapter considers whether *pari passu* is so frequently bypassed and flawed in shape and application that it is necessary to look to alternative approaches in order to achieve more satisfactory modes of distribution. Here, however, it is necessary to consider whether the current exceptions to *pari passu* are in need of reform. Thus far it has been indicated that there may be a case for abolishing Crown preferences and for revising the rules on set-off.

Are there, however, other classes of unsecured creditor that are in need of greater or lesser protection than at present? In the case of one group put forward for greater priority – that of consumer creditors – we have seen difficulties with the argument for favourable treatment. The problem with this proposal is that it is difficult to distinguish 'consumer' from 'trade' creditors since there will be similarity between many of the contractual and practical arrangements entered into by such parties. Many trade creditors, moreover, may not have been repeat players in their dealings with the insolvent company yet many consumer creditors may have sustained a continuing relationship. We have seen that, compared with employees, the case for protecting the consumer creditor may be weak since the consumer is likely to enjoy a greater freedom to contract or decline to contract with the company; is more able to exit from the relationship in favour of forming a connection with another company; is more likely to spread risks by relying on more than one company to supply its required consumer goods; and is accordingly a lower-cost risk bearer than the typical employee.

A further proposal is designed to protect those creditors who have acted in a manner that benefits their fellow creditors. Prentice has argued that where creditor A takes action through the courts to enforce a debt but that action is overtaken by a winding-up order,[120] the court should have a discretion to award creditor A the costs of the litigation but not the benefit of any judgment.[121] Awarding such costs to such creditors would give priority

---

120. Thereby staying the enforcement of all actions: see further ch. 12 above.
121. See D. Prentice, 'Effect of Insolvency on Pre-liquidation Transactions'.

to those costs and would compensate creditor A for the expenses of an action that is likely to benefit other creditors by signalling to them that the debtor company's viability may be at issue. The court discretion, the argument runs, could be used to keep the floodgates closed on precipitate actions to enforce debts and would discourage enforcement races. The award of such court costs would also prevent debtor companies from prevaricating when asked to settle accounts while using the threat of a voluntary winding up to discourage creditors from pressing their claims: the threat would be empty if the creditor would be liable to recover costs. This might, in turn, prevent unnecessary liquidations. Finally, the principle of *pari passu* would be respected by limiting the effective priority being given to the costs of the action only.

A difficulty with the proposal is that, as we have seen in chapter 3, signalling is a flawed process. When creditor A seeks to enforce a debt against company B in court, this may be the product of A's lack of information and panicky state of mind rather than any process of rational evaluation of B's viability. There may, moreover, be reasons for A's seeking to enforce a debt at a particular time that are entirely unrelated to B's viability: the state of A's own financial affairs (or internal corporate politics) may be the driving factor behind the legal action. It could be responded that the envisaged judicial discretion regarding costs might be employed in a manner that rewards only actions offering good signalling to other creditors but this is to presuppose unrealistic levels of information in the hands of the judiciary. The extent of a discretion to award costs, rather than a right to costs, might be said also to undermine any incentives that creditors might have to bring actions and send signals to creditors. The state of the present law does allow creditors other than creditor A to nullify the benefits of any judgment obtained by A: the other creditors can simply await A's judgment and then present a winding-up petition. It could be argued, however, that creditor A did have the option of presenting a winding-up petition him- or herself and that accordingly he/she has no basis for complaint. This argument holds except that the courts will not allow a creditor to use a winding-up procedure to collect small debts.[122] Overall, the case for the proposed discretion to award litigation costs to A seems not to be made out. It is based on assumptions about signalling that are difficult to sustain and it would create, at least to a degree, an incentive to litigate that is liable to render the

---

122. I.e. under £750: see Insolvency Act 1986 s. 123(1)(a), though creditors may combine their debts to qualify: *Re Leyton & Walthamstow Cycle Co.* [1901] WN 275; see ch. 12 above.

overall costs of winding up a company higher than would otherwise be the case.

To conclude, it should be emphasised that, in considering exceptions to *pari passu*, it is the *relative* cases for preferring the different types of creditor that are at issue. In the above discussion the group for whom the strongest case for a protected status can be sustained is that of company employees and the criteria relevant to an assessment of that case included: ability to gain and use information concerning default risks; ability to adjust terms to take on board such risks; capacity to exit from excessively risk-laden arrangements; vulnerability to risks; and status as a low- or high-cost bearer of risks. Employees are, however, protected in employment protection legislation and if White Paper proposals to abolish the Crown's preferential status are implemented, the rationale for current employee preferential status may be undermined.

14

Bypassing *pari passu*

The main potential bases for supporting *pari passu* as a principle of corporate insolvency law are that it provides an efficient and fair ground rule for allocating the insolvency estate. As was seen in the last chapter, however, exceptions to *pari passu* produce a principle that is unduly complex and uncertain. This chapter considers the extent to which *pari passu* can be bypassed and a central issue will be whether bypassing is so easily and frequently practised that the value of *pari passu* is undermined. Here, therefore, we return to the second of the two key problems that corporate insolvency law faces in this area: how a company's insolvent estate is to be constructed.

As a preliminary point it should be emphasised that the law does not readily countenance contracting out of collective arrangements for dealing with the insolvency estate. It was noted in chapter 13 that parties may be allowed by the courts to enter into contracts in a manner that worsens their status in the distribution of an insolvent company's estate.[1] What the courts will not do is allow creditors to 'contract with [their] debtor [to] enjoy some advantage in a bankruptcy or winding up which is denied to other creditors'.[2] The House of Lords made it clear in the *British Eagle* case[3] that this would be contrary to public policy whether or not the contractual provision was expressed to take effect only on

1. Cf. *National Westminster Bank Ltd* v. *Halesowen Presswork and Assemblies Ltd* [1972] AC 785 where an agreement (altering a creditor's priority position) was struck down despite the fact that it would have increased insolvency value to the remaining creditors.
2. Vinelott J in *Re Maxwell Communications Corporation plc (No. 2)* [1994] 1 All ER 737 at 750.
3. *British Eagle International Airlines Ltd* v. *Compagnie Nationale Air France* [1975] 1 WLR 758, [1975] 2 All ER 390 ('*British Eagle*'). See also *Re Rafidain Bank* [1992] BCLC 301; D. Milman and C. Durrant, *Corporate Insolvency: Law and Practice* (3rd edn, Sweet & Maxwell, London, 1999) ch. 8; D. Capper, 'Direct Payment Clauses and the *Pari Passu* Principle' [1998] CfiLR 54.

insolvency.[4] Effect would not be given to a contractual arrangement that attempted to avoid collectivity by purporting to allow certain creditors to opt out of *pari passu* distribution of the residual estate to their advantage.[5] British Eagle[6] was a member of an International Air Transport Association (IATA) clearing house scheme in which moneys due from airlines to each other would be netted out each month. When British Eagle went into liquidation it owed money to a number of airlines but it had a claim against Air France which the liquidator sought to recover. Air France argued that British Eagle's liquidator was bound by the contractual regime of the clearing house scheme and could only collect the sum due after netting out the claims of those creditors who were creditors of British Eagle. The liquidator successfully contended that such a process would breach the *pari passu* principle because it would remove from British Eagle's estate the sum due from Air France – a sum that, otherwise, would be available to the body of British Eagle's general creditors.[7] In accepting this contention, a bare majority of the House of Lords accepted crucially that British Eagle's claim against Air France was a direct one, with IATA acting simply as a collecting agent, rather than a mere element in British Eagle's net balance with the principal IATA.[8]

Creditors may not be able to contract out of the *pari passu* principle to their advantage but they can take a series of other steps that will bypass *pari passu*. In taking these steps they are taking advantage of the fact that

---

4. See also *Carreras Rothmans Ltd* v. *Freeman Mathews Treasure Ltd* [1985] 1 Ch 207 at 226; M. Simmons, 'Avoiding the *Pari Passu* Rule' (1996) 9 *Insolvency Intelligence* 9.

5. Contracts that prevent property from entering the estate – i.e. contracts with proprietary effect such as retention of title clauses – will be recognised, as will be seen. For decisions focusing on the intent, rather than the effect, of a contract see *Ex parte Mackay* (1873) LR 8 Ch App 643; F. Oditah, 'Assets and the Treatment of Claims in Insolvency' (1992) 108 LQR 459 at 466. It may be the case that if the insolvent estate is deprived of property as a result of an arrangement that was not designed to escape insolvency rules, the courts may allow that deprivation as an exception to the *British Eagle* principle: see Neuberger J in *MMI* v. *LSE* [2001] 4 All ER 223; G. Stewart, 'The British Eagle Has Landed' (2001) *Recovery* (December) 7–8. (A company was liquidated and the London Stock Exchange (LSE), in accordance with the LSE articles, deprived the company of its shares on the Exchange. Neuberger J noted that there was no coherent set of rules to enable one to assess where a 'deprivation' provision fell foul of the *British Eagle* principle but he extracted ten propositions derived from case law. On the facts of the case before him Neuberger J concluded that the deprivation provision fell within an exception to the general *British Eagle* principle and the liquidator could not sustain his claim.)

6. See [1975] 2 All ER 390.

7. See R. M. Goode, *Principles of Corporate Insolvency Law* (2nd edn, Sweet & Maxwell, London, 1997) pp. 180–2.

8. The absence of mutuality precluded set-off of third party claims. If the House of Lords had treated IATA as a principal then set-off would have been applicable: see Goode, *Principles of Corporate Insolvency Law*. For a criticism of *British Eagle* see Oditah, 'Assets', p. 466; R. Mokal, 'Priority as Pathology: The *Pari Passu* Myth' [2001] CLJ 581 at 598–601.

it is only the assets in which the company has a beneficial interest that are available to creditors. Property held, for instance, on trust by the company will not enter the estate and where the company has granted security over property the asset enters the estate only to the extent of the equity of redemption (the difference between the value of the asset and the sum of the secured indebtedness).[9] Here, as Goode notes, the distinction between property rights and personal rights is vitally important for insolvency purposes: the holder of a property right can enforce it ahead of the general body of creditors, whereas the holder of a personal right can only prove for a dividend in competition with other creditors.[10]

As will be seen below, there may be a strong case for the law allowing holders of property rights to enforce these ahead of creditors' rights in the insolvency estate. As we will also see, however, the ability to make assets available to a company while avoiding entry of those assets into the corporate estate leads to a deterioration in the position of the ordinary unsecured creditor. 'Every new property right, every added security interest, every proprietary restitutionary remedy, every equity has eroded his or her stake in the insolvency process.'[11]

It is time to consider in detail the devices that can be used to avoid entry into the residual estate and thereby to bypass *pari passu* distribution.

Security

If creditors take security over loans they will *take* and *keep* property rights for themselves by way of such security. The property subject to the secured claim thus belongs to the secured claimant to the value of the claim and accordingly it does not enter the insolvency estate and become available for distribution.[12] Such arrangements may involve fixed or floating charges. As was noted in chapter 3, the institution of security can be supported on broad efficiency grounds, though elements of inefficiency are involved in so far as risks may be loaded excessively upon unsecured creditors. The earlier discussion of attendant issues will not be rehearsed here but the

---

9. See Goode, *Principles of Corporate Insolvency Law*, pp. 48–9.
10. R. M. Goode, *Commercial Law in the Next Millennium* (Sweet & Maxwell, London, 1998) p. 62.
11. Goode, *Principles of Corporate Insolvency Law*, p. 50.
12. Statute may, however, make certain debts (e.g. preferential ones) payable from the estate in priority to rights to property that is not part of the estate (e.g. that forming the subject of a floating charge). On floating charges see also ch. 3 above.

further question of whether security taking involves unfairness should be addressed at this point.[13]

To give priority to secured creditors and to allow the bypassing of *pari passu* can be argued to lead to no unfairness to unsecured creditors. This contention rests on three main arguments: that the security has been freely bargained or contracted for; that it does not deprive the company of value; and that relevant parties are given due notice of security arrangements and so cannot, with justice, complain.[14]

The essence of the 'bargain' justification is as follows.[15] When a debtor company grants a security interest to a creditor this will increase the risks faced by the other creditors because it reduces their expected value in an insolvency. Other creditors will, however, be aware of this risk and will adjust loan rates accordingly or seek their own security or quasi-security. Voluntary contracting parties, accordingly, are treated fairly because they are free to contract at the rates and on the terms they consider appropriate.

The first objection to the 'bargain' argument is that those who enter into arrangements for credit in the commercial world do not always do so from equal negotiating positions.[16] Inequalities, indeed, can be quite striking. Small trade creditors, for reasons discussed in chapter 3, may often be in no position to gain the information that would make them equal bargainers with those seeking security. They may lack the resources, expertise and time to evaluate risks accurately and the nature of their products and business arrangements may not allow for the appropriate adjustments of business terms.

Competitive conditions in the market may also undermine the small trade creditor's ability to renegotiate interest rates when new securities are offered. (Contractual terms reflecting such conditions may also rule out such rate adjustments.) If equality of bargaining power was evenly spread

---

13. This discussion draws on V. Finch, 'Security, Insolvency and Risk: Who Pays the Price?' (1999) 62 MLR 633 at 660–7.

14. See J. Hudson, 'The Case Against Secured Lending' (1995) 15 *International Review of Law and Economics* 47 at 55; R. M. Goode, 'Is the Law Too Favourable to Secured Creditors?' (1983–4) 8 Canadian Bus. LJ 53.

15. See T. H. Jackson and A. T. Kronman, 'Secured Financing and Priorities Among Creditors' (1979) 88 Yale LJ 1143 at 1147–8; F. Buckley, 'The Bankruptcy Priority Puzzle' (1986) 72 Va. L Rev. 1393; *Salomon v. A. Salomon & Co. Ltd* [1897] AC 22 at 52: 'Every creditor is entitled to get and to hold the best security the law allows him to take', per Lord Macnaghten.

16. See B. G. Carruthers and T. C. Halliday, *Rescuing Business: The Making of Corporate Bankruptcy Law in England and the United States* (Clarendon Press, Oxford, 1998) p. 171; L. LoPucki, 'The Unsecured Creditor's Bargain' (1994) 80 Va. L Rev. 1887 at 1896–8; M. G. Bridge, 'The *Quistclose* Trust in a World of Secured Transactions' (1992) 12 OJLS 333 at 341; Justice, *Insolvency Law: An Agenda for Reform* (Justice, London, 1994) p. 6 on dissatisfaction with the imbalance of power between the large, secured creditors and the trade and other unsecured creditors.

between different types of creditor, one would expect a random distribution of security-taking across all types of creditor but, in fact, the vast majority of security arrangements involve banks, finance houses or building societies, not firms in commercial business.[17] Small trade creditors suffer not only from information asymmetries in relation to banks but also from a lack of economies of scale. Banks, who repeat play (with regard to small as well as large loans), operate with large volumes of lending and offer longer terms of credit than trade creditors, tend to make extensive use of security, to have specialist advisers and to have lower set-up and monitoring costs.[18] This all increases their bargaining power in relation to other creditors.

A second objection to the 'bargain' rationale is that a number of creditors are truly involuntary. They cannot take account of security arrangements because they did not choose to become creditors at all.[19] In this position, particularly, are tort victims. When parties agree security arrangements, they expropriate value that otherwise would rest, at least partly, with the body of involuntary creditors.

There are few reasons, furthermore, for treating freedom of contract as sacrosanct. The law has a long history of laying down the kinds of security that can be agreed to (all of which stipulations curtail the contractual freedoms of parties) and Parliament has clearly recognised that the right of a creditor to take security needs to be constrained if a fair balance is to be drawn between the interests of all creditors.[20]

A final concern is that the 'bargain' argument might have impetus where all affected parties are included in the bargaining process but it has little persuasive power when a bargain between a creditor and debtor imposes costs on others: 'freedom of contract arguments have force only with respect to arrangements that do not create direct externalities…[W]hen the contract directly impinges on the rights of third parties, there is no prima facie presumption of freedom of contract.'[21] Arrangements

---

17. See Hudson, 'Case Against Secured Lending', p. 55
18. Ibid., p. 56.
19. See LoPucki, 'Unsecured Creditor's Bargain', pp. 1896–7.
20. See *Report of the Review Committee on Insolvency Law and Practice* (Cmnd 8558, 1982) ('Cork Report') pp. 335–6. Freedom of contract is ignored, for example, when avoiding pre-insolvency transactions: Insolvency Act 1986 ss. 238–41, 245; preferential creditors are given priority even though they have not 'bargained' for it: Insolvency Act 1986 ss. 40, 175, 386, 387; Insolvency Act 1986 Scheds. 6 and 13.
21. L. Bebchuk and J. Fried, 'The Uneasy Case for the Priority of Secured Claims in Bankruptcy' (1996) 105 Yale LJ 857 at 933; cf. A. Schwartz, 'Taking the Analysis of Security Seriously' (1994) 80 Va. L Rev. 2073 at 2082.

that allow debtors to increase the insolvency share of one party, and which come at the expense of other parties, involve externalities. Priority seeking is, after all, central to security taking.[22]

The 'value' argument offers a response to the last point. It asserts that when a creditor takes security for new value[23] this does not prejudice third party unsecured creditors because the secured creditor is not withdrawing from the company more than he or she paid in.[24] A particular difficulty, however, is that after-acquired property clauses may draw assets into the original security arrangement.[25] As each new asset is acquired by the debtor, more and more security builds up without the injection of fresh value by the original secured creditor. That creditor enjoys the windfall benefit of diminishing risks of default and the existing interest rate proves increasingly advantageous to them. New assets do not enter the pool for the potential benefit of unsecured creditors but create such windfalls. The floating charge has thus long been criticised as a device that unfairly allows a charge upon all future property[26] and Cork suggested that: 'The matter for wonder is that such a device should ever have been invented by a Court of Equity.'[27]

The argument from 'notice' urges that security is justified when other creditors are duly apprised of the situation.[28] These creditors, it is contended, can be in no position to complain about secured loans when they have been supplied with adequate information. This justification, however, fails to give due consideration to the position of involuntary creditors or to those voluntary creditors who cannot reasonably be expected to adjust their terms to the granting of security. Particular problems, moreover, arise with the floating charge. As Cork noted, the requirement that such

---

22. See Cork Report, ch. 35. Indeed, some US commentators describe the grant of security as the issue of insolvency rights: see A. Schwartz, 'Security Interests and Bankruptcy Priorities: A Review of Current Theories' (1981) 10 *Journal of Legal Studies* 1; Buckley, 'Bankruptcy Priority Puzzle', who argues (at p. 1406) that unsecured creditors should not demand insolvency distribution rights for which they have not paid. See also Bridge, '*Quistclose* Trust', pp. 340–1.

23. I.e. contemporaneous or subsequent value: see further Goode, 'Is the Law Too Favourable to Secured Creditors?', pp. 60–3.

24. See ibid. This assumes the terms of the loan are not unreasonable and thus require adjustment or setting aside.

25. See *Holroyd* v. *Marshall* (1862) 10 HL Cas 191; I. Davis, 'The Trade Creditor and the Quest for Security' in H. Rajak (ed.), *Insolvency Law: Theory and Practice* (Sweet & Maxwell, London, 1993); M. G. Bridge, 'Form, Substance and Innovation in Personal Property Security Law' [1992] JBL 1.

26. See Buckley J in *Re London Pressed Hinge Co. Ltd* [1905] 1 Ch 576 at 583; Cork Report, para. 107.

27. See Cork Report, para. 107.

28. See Goode, 'Is the Law Too Favourable to Secured Creditors?', p. 63.

charges be registered does little to assuage the feelings of grievance generated by such charges since the register gives very inadequate information
to the trade creditor.[29] Where floating charges secure bank overdrafts[30]
the amount outstanding on the latter may fluctuate daily. It is, accordingly, impossible to tell from the register how much the floating charges
secure. Even the latest company balance sheet offers little further assistance on this front since it is usually out of date by some months and
will be unlikely to disclose contingent liabilities such as guarantees of
the overdrafts of associated companies, which may also be secured by
the floating charge. English law, moreover, offers little protection to
unsecured creditors where they are misled by the late filing of a security
interest.[31] The twenty-one-day time limit as a condition of validity has,
indeed, been dubbed 'inappropriate', since the proper sanction for failure
to make a timely filing is subordination to a subsequent interest before
the filing and (in the case of eve of insolvency filing) voidability as a
preference.[32]

Registration and notice requirements in English law are further weakened by their non-applicability to retention of title under a conditional
sale or hire purchase agreement. Where unsecured creditors are not informed about such quasi-security devices they are unaware of the additional risks they face and the force of the notice argument is again spent.[33]

Notice, moreover, is a procedural protection and may not protect unsecured creditors against substantive unfairness. One area in which there
is potential scope for substantive unfairness concerns the actions of receivers. A receiver appointed by secured creditors has a duty to take
proper care to secure the best price reasonably obtainable when selling

---

29. Cork Report, para. 109. For proposals on a new notice-filing system for registrable
charges see CLRSG, *Modern Company Law for a Competitive Economy: Final Report* (July 2001)
('CLRSG, *Final Report*') ch. 12. Registrable charges would include floating charges, all charges
on goods and complex, but not simple, retentions of title. Where specific types of property
(e.g. land) are dealt with by specialist registers there would be dual registration with
Companies House to allow single searches of creditworthiness to be undertaken. See further
D. Milman, 'Company Law Review: Company Charges' [2001] Ins. Law. 180.
30. Most companies grant floating charges to their bankers to secure 'all sums due or to
become due' on their current overdrafts.
31. See Companies Act 1985 s. 404 regarding the court's power to grant an extension of time.
An order which will be made without prejudice to the rights of third parties acquired
between the date of creation of the charge and the date of its registration. Ordinary
unsecured creditors are not, however, protected by this wording.
32. Goode, 'Is the Law Too Favourable to Secured Creditors?', p. 64. On preferences see
Insolvency Act 1986 s. 239 and ch. 12 above.
33. See text at pp. 110–16 above on ROT clauses. On accounting recommendations see ICAEW
Statement, *Guidance for Auditors on the Implications of Goods Sold Subject to Reservation of Title*
(1977); A. Belcher and W. Beglan, 'Jumping the Queue' [1997] JBL 1, 16–17.

the charged assets.[34] In *Medforth* v. *Blake*[35] the Court of Appeal made it clear that a receiver managing a mortgaged business possessed duties going beyond mere duties to act in good faith. Those duties might depend on the facts and circumstances of the case but, subject to the primary duty to try to meet the secured debt, there was an obligation owed to those with interests in the equity of redemption to manage the business with due diligence if managing the business had been undertaken. Secured creditors, nevertheless, owe no duty to refrain from appointing receivers where this would unnecessarily harm the company. They may act wholly selfishly.[36] A mortgagee, for example, may choose to appoint a receiver when a market is at rock bottom even though a delay would, at no cost, benefit other creditors.[37] Even post-*Medforth*[38] the receiver's primary duty is to the debenture holder. The receiver is not obliged to carry on the business in order to benefit parties other than the appointing debenture holder and satisfaction of the primary duty may be achieved by breaking up a company even though a greater return to the pool of creditors would be achieved by selling the company as a going concern.[39]

English law on security exacerbates the position of the unsecured creditor again in the framework of rescues. Most company rescue operations, if they are to succeed, demand that the companies' assets and undertakings be retained largely intact so that the businesses[40] can be managed as going concerns. A major rescue procedure, however, can be arrested by the appointment of an administrative receiver by a debenture holder whose floating charge (alone or combined with 'one or more other securities') covers substantially all of the relevant company's

---

34. See *Downsview Nominees Ltd* v. *First City Corporation Ltd* [1993] AC 295. See further A. Berg, 'Duties of a Mortgagee and a Receiver' [1993] JBL 213; H. Rajak, 'Can a Receiver be Negligent?' in B. Rider (ed.), *The Corporate Dimension* (Jordans, Bristol, 1998); A. Hogan, 'Receivers Revisited' (1996) 17 Co. Law. 226; R. M. Goode, 'Proprietary Rights and Unsecured Creditors' in B. Rider (ed.), *The Realm of Company Law* (Kluwer, London, 1998) pp. 192–3. The receiver owes no separate duty to unsecured creditors: *Lathia* v. *Dronsfield Bros. Ltd* [1987] BCLC 321. See further ch. 8 above.

35. [1999] 3 All ER 97. See the discussion in ch. 8 above.

36. *Shamji* v. *Johnson Matthey Bankers Ltd* [1991] BCLC 36.

37. See Goode, 'Proprietary Rights and Unsecured Creditors', p. 192.

38. [1999] 3 All ER 97.

39. But see *AIB Finance Ltd* v. *Alsop and Another* [1998] BCC 780, concerning a mortgagee appointed under a charge which contained a power to carry on business. See also *Hadjipanayi* v. *Yeldon et al.* [2001] BPIR 487 at 494–5.

40. A company's business (or part of it) can be hived off or sold by receivers or supervisors of voluntary arrangements; part of the company's business can be sold by administrators, but a complete hive-down of the company's viable businesses is seemingly not possible (*Re Rowbotham Baxter Ltd* [1990] BCC 113; Insolvency Act 1986 s. 8(3)(a)).

assets.[41] An administrator[42] can only come onto the scene if the debenture holder consents.[43] This framework gives secured creditors a number of powers and, in exercising these, they may look utterly to their own interests. The unsecured creditors' concerns may not come into play at all.[44] It might, of course, be argued that unsecured creditors will often be aware of the law's kindness to secured creditors and will adjust their terms accordingly. Leaving aside the problems of adjustment already noted, unsecured creditors will have particular difficulties in assessing risks when those assessments demand that predictions be made about the actions that may be taken by secured creditors in exercise of broad discretionary powers. For unsecured creditors, uncertainties (and the costs of reducing these) are thus increased and the burdens of risk bearing are added to. There are, moreover, enhanced incentives for unsecured creditors to take refuge in self-help mechanisms such as quasi-security devices: incentives which, if followed, are liable (as noted above) both to undermine the efficiencies that priority does bring and to worsen the position of their weakest unsecured brethren.

To summarise: the bargain, value and notice arguments are used in asserting the fairness of bypassing *pari passu* by excluding secured property from the insolvency estate. There are, however, material problems concerning the inequalities, competitive conditions and third party effects of secured credit bargains, not to say their relevance to involuntary creditors. The value argument is undermined by such provisions as relate to after-acquired property and the notice contention is unconvincing in relation to involuntary creditors or to those who cannot adjust, suffer from

41. Insolvency Act 1986 s. 29(2). In the case of composite security the appointment must be made under the floating charge element: *Meadrealm Ltd v. Transcontinental Golf Construction Ltd* (1991, unreported); see Marks (1993) 6 *Insolvency Intelligence* 41.

42. Administration, a procedure designed primarily for corporate rescue found in the Insolvency Act 1986 Part 11, owed much to the Cork Report's commitment to a rescue philosophy: see Cork Report, ch. 9.

43. Insolvency Act 1986 s. 9(2). Any person having the right to appoint an administrative receiver must be notified to allow exercise of his *de facto* power of veto of appointing an administrative receiver. On reform of the power of veto see chs. 8 and 9 above.

44. See Goode, 'Proprietary Rights and Unsecured Creditors', pp. 193–4: the ability of the debenture holder to block the making of an administration order 'drives at the very foundation of the rescue culture. Without an administration order there is no moratorium, for a CVA does not attract a moratorium.' On proposals to restrict the floating charge holder's right to appoint an administrative receiver to the enforcement of market charges within the context of the separate insolvency regime for capital markets introduced by the Companies Act 1989 Part VII, see DTI/IS White Paper, *Productivity and Enterprise: Insolvency – A Second Chance* (Cm 5234, 2001) ('White Paper, 2001') paras. 2.5 and 2.18; see also ch. 8 above. (On CVA regimes see ch. 10 above.)

poor information or are affected by a quasi-security device. The ability of secured creditors, in many circumstances, to act purely selfishly and the narrowness of receivers' duties are both factors that undermine assertions that security is fair.

If abolishing security would be inadvisable on efficiency grounds, what could be done to make the balance between secured and unsecured creditors fairer? Looking, first, to the problems of unequal bargaining, a simple redress would be to reduce the effect of this by providing that 10 per cent of the net realisations of assets subject to charges be made available for distribution among ordinary, unsecured creditors. As noted in chapter 3, the 10 per cent fund was proposed by Cork[45] with reference to floating charges and was advocated on fairness grounds, as a response to the 'real injustice'[46] that floating charges were capable of producing. It was not unfair, said Cork, to insist on a concession from floating charge holders for the benefit of the general body of creditors.[47] Cork did not bring assets subject to fixed charges within the remit of the 10 per cent fund (indeed the Report was silent on the subject). Fixed charges, however, may draw within their scope after-acquired assets of the originally specified class. Where the sum of assets covered by the fixed charge grows in value there is a transfer of insolvency wealth from non-adjusting unsecured creditors and an issue of fairness arises. Adjustment in relation to such charges is potentially easier than with floating charges because a view of the registration documents will reveal a specification of assets that offers unsecured creditors some guidance as to the types of asset movement which may affect their potential insolvency claims.

In relation to fixed charges, unsecured creditors' problems of adjustment are likely to be less severe than with floating charges for another reason: relevant asset movements are liable to be fewer in the case of fixed charges because the debtor has to obtain the fixed charge holder's permission for asset substitution.[48] With floating charges, of course, the debtor is free to deal with the charged assets on their own account and without reference to the chargee. These points suggest that the need for a 10 per cent fund is perhaps less pressing in relation to fixed charges. The

---

45. See Cork Report, paras. 1523–49; and see now the White Paper, 2001, para. 2.19, which proposes to 'ringfence' a proportion of funds generated by the floating charge for the benefit of unsecured creditors.

46. Cork Report, para. 1527.

47. For other advocates of a 10 per cent fund see Goode, 'Is the Law Too Favourable to Secured Creditors?', p. 67; D. Milman, 'The Ten Per Cent Fund' [1999] Ins. Law. 47.

48. Where debtors anticipate the need for routine asset substitution they are very likely to agree to the grant of a floating charge.

10 per cent fund is no complete answer but it does have the merit of reducing the possibility that unsecured creditors will be faced with empty coffers.

Inequalities in enforcement might also be addressed. It has been noted above that secured creditors are free, on corporate insolvency, to enforce their security interests in a manner that prejudices the interests of other creditors. Harms such as the removal of assets vital to the running of the company's business or making untimely realisations may be as severe in receiverships as in liquidations.[49] Cork argued that there should be a twelve-month freeze on enforcement of a security on the appointment of a receiver or administrator[50] and there may be a similar case for such a freeze when the debtor goes into liquidation.

The duties of care of the secured creditor's agent, the receiver, might, moreover, be reformulated so as to oblige the enforcers of security to act in the interests of the general body of creditors at least where this would involve no material loss to themselves. The proposals in the DTI's White Paper – to reduce the role of administrative receivership in favour of a streamlined administration in which the administrator will owe a duty of care to all creditors – would have this welcome effect.[51] In England, the pre-*Medforth*[52] freedom of the debenture holder and the receiver to act purely selfishly was criticised[53] but the more extensive duty of care that is encountered post-*Medforth* still has its limitations. It cannot be said with certainty, for instance, that the receiver has to take such actions as will benefit creditors generally provided that the appointing debenture holder's interests are not prejudiced. *Medforth* may in coming years be treated as demanding no more than that the receiver manage the business with due diligence where it is decided to continue operating the business. We cannot be confident that any obligation to continue the business in the general interest of creditors will be read into *Medforth*.[54]

49. See Goode, 'Is the Law Too Favourable to Secured Creditors?', pp. 70–1. In winding up, security rights may be asserted so as to inhibit the liquidator's ability to deal with the company's trading stock for the purpose of beneficial winding up of the business.
50. Cork Report, paras. 1506–7: the secured creditor would, however, have a right to apply to court where delay in enforcement would prejudice him. The American Bankruptcy Reform Act 1978 ss. 361–4 imposes a stay and gives a trustee broad rights to use, sell and lease charged assets, rights covering both bankruptcy and rehabilitation proceedings.
51. See White Paper, 2001, para. 2.12.
52. *Medforth v. Blake* [1999] 3 All ER 97. See ch. 8 above.
53. See *Palk v. Mortgage Services Funding plc* [1993] Ch 330 (Sir Donald Nicholls VC); Goode, 'Proprietary Rights and Unsecured Creditors', pp. 192–3.
54. See the Australian Corporate Law Reform Act 1992 s. 232(4) – receivers to exercise the degree of care and diligence that a reasonable person in a like position in a corporation would

There is similarly a case for supporting the 2001 White Paper approach[55] and restricting the ability of the debenture holder to throw a spanner in the process leading to the making of an administration order by appointing an administrative receiver. This ability may not only produce inefficiencies (in so far as rescue may demand that the company be retained as a going concern by the administrator) but it may also produce unfairness to unsecured creditors whose interests will suffer disproportionately as the company's operations are impeded.

A more radical approach to balancing creditor interests is to repackage the floating charge, as discussed above, and place it within a new, statutory regime to cover all security and quasi-security interests along North American lines, in which conflicts between secured and third parties are resolved with reference to considerations of fairness and practicality rather than the particular form of the transaction.[56] This may provide an opportunity to reduce potential injustices to small, unsecured creditors and might, for instance, offer protection to buyers of goods in the ordinary course of business whether or not there is knowledge of the prior security interest.[57] The notion that such creditors have constructive knowledge of prior security is thus abandoned.[58] Such a repackaging of the floating charge[59] would not only allow a wholesale review of a

exercise in the corporation's circumstances; Canadian Bankruptcy and Insolvency Act 1992 s. 247 – receivers to deal with the assets in a commercially reasonable manner; New Zealand Receivership Act 1993 s. 18 – an obligation *inter alia* to exercise powers with reasonable regard to the interests of unsecured creditors, guarantors and others claiming an interest in property through the debtor.

55. See White Paper, 2001, paras. 2.5 and 2.18 on the proposal to restrict the right to appoint an administrative receiver to holders of floating charges granted in connection with transactions in certain capital markets.

56. Including, for example, ROTs and conditional sales. On Article 9 of the Uniform Commercial Code (UCC) see generally Bridge, 'Form, Substance and Innovation'; R. M. Goode, 'The Exodus of the Floating Charge' in D. Feldman and F. Meisel (eds.), *Corporate and Commercial Law: Modern Developments* (Lloyd's of London Press, London, 1996). See also G. McCormack, 'Personal Property Security Law Reform in England and Canada' [2002] JBL 113. McCormack urges caution before England goes down the Article 9 route: 'Theoretical perfection may safely be sacrificed at the altar of practical utility' (p. 142).

57. I.e. granting such purchasers priority over the 'floating charge' holder (on the grounds that trade and turnover are the lifeblood of commerce): see Article 9:307(1) UCC and Bridge, 'Form, Substance and Innovation', p. 14.

58. See Bridge, 'Form, Substance and Innovation', p. 13.

59. On the case for abolishing the floating charge see *Report of the Committee on Consumer Credit* (Cmnd 4596, 1971) ('Crowther Report'), para. 5.5.6. The Diamond Report, *A Review of Security Interests in Property* (DTI, HMSO, 1989), suggests that a new register of security interests is all that is needed (paras. 11.6.2, 16.8) though Diamond recommends that negative pledge clauses should be registered (para. 16.10). In 2000 the Company Law Review Steering Group published a consultation document on the subject of registering company charges (*Modern Company Law for a Competitive Economy: Registration of Company Charges* (URN 00/1213) (October 2000)). It invited views, *inter alia*, on the merits of going over to the North American approach

confused mass of law but would provide an opportunity to state that the interests of unsecured creditors should not give way to those of secured creditors where this would be unfair in the substantive or the procedural senses.[60]

Changes might also be made so as to reinforce the 'value' justification for security, which holds that security is fair when it does not dilute the interests of others. One such reform would be to outlaw secured lending on existing corporate assets (while allowing it on new assets). As noted in chapter 3, however, such a severe restriction on the raising of finance might lead many companies into difficulty. A less draconian step would be to echo Article 9,[61] again, and provide that priority would be given to 'purchase money security interests' (PMSIs)[62] as against earlier creditors with perfected securities.[63] The PMSI is a security interest that favours a creditor who advances sums to fund the acquisition of a particular asset when those sums are in fact so used. Such an interest prevails over all others in a priority conflict.[64] Recognising PMSIs would mean that where a financier provides new assets to the company, the assets would not be drawn into the scope of the floating charge covering after-acquired property. This would reduce the unfairness involved in the floating charge holder gaining the windfall benefit of security in after-acquired assets and doing so at the expense of the later creditor. The PMSI holder can also point to

of a 'notice filing' system under which priority is determined by the date of filing. The CLRSG *Final Report* of 2001 (ch. 12) advocated the introduction of a notice-filing system. See also ch. 3 above.

60. Policy decisions would have to be made concerning the position of preferential creditors (who now rank before floating, and after fixed, charge holders in priority). On Diamond's position see Diamond Report, p. 85.

61. See Bridge, 'Form, Substance and Innovation', p. 14; Jackson and Kronman, 'Secured Financing', p. 1171; Diamond Report, paras. 11.7.5–11.7.7.

62. On English judicial efforts in this direction see *Abbey National Building Society* v. *Cann* [1991] 1 AC 56; *Re Connolly Bros. Ltd (No. 2)* [1912] 2 Ch 25. See further J. Jeremie, 'Gone in an Instant: The Death of "*Scintilla Temporis*" and the Growth of Purchase Money Security Interests in Real Property Law' [1994] JBL 363; J. de Lacy, 'The Purchase Money Security Interest: A Company Charge Conundrum' [1991] LMCLQ 531; de Lacy, 'Retention of Title, Company Charges and the *Scintilla Temporis* Doctrine' [1994] Conv. 242; H. Bennett and C. Davis, 'Fixtures, Purchase Money Security Interests and Dispositions of Interests in Land' (1994) 110 LQR 448; A. Schwartz, 'A Theory of Loan Priorities' (1989) 18 *Journal of Legal Studies* 209. (Note also the proposals of the DTI/IS, *Company Voluntary Arrangements and Administration Orders: A Consultative Document* (October 1993) and the Insolvency Service's *Reviews of Company Rescue and Business Reconstruction Mechanisms* (1999) and (2000) for statutory super-priority for providers of *capital* during a rescue/reconstruction procedure giving these lenders priority over all existing *lenders*.) See further ch. 9 above.

63. I.e. those who had registered their interests or given possession of the asset to the debtor.

64. For a definition of the PMSI see Article 9:107 UCC. On procedural requirements to obtain 'perfection' see Article 9:312(3). On the operation of simple ROT clauses as PMSIs see Diamond Report, pp. 88–9.

the new value added to the company and the lack of any attendant prejudice to other creditors' security interests. This is because purchase money loans contemplate payments that correspond to the new asset's depreciation and so repossession normally satisfies the PMSI creditor. The cushion of free assets that protects earlier lenders against default is accordingly unaffected.[65]

A further way to reinforce the value justification for security is to strengthen preference rules. These rules are designed to prevent insolvent companies from preferring one creditor to another within a specific period leading to a winding up.[66] At present, these rules are subjectively phrased in looking to whether the company desired to confer a preference in giving a security. A strengthening of the law would involve a move in the direction of the Australian and US regimes and the adoption of an objective approach.[67] The issue would then be whether the *effect* of granting the security was to improve the position of one creditor at the expense of others, and the company's desires would drop out of account.[68]

Turning to the issue of notice, unfairness can be reduced by improving information flows to unsecured creditors. As noted, proposals have been made that secured creditors might have to go beyond mere registration and take reasonable steps to inform unsecured creditors of their intentions if they are to place the latter in a subordinate position.[69] Again, however, it should be emphasised that such requirements may increase costs and the supply of information and notice is only of value to certain unsecured

---

65. See Davis, 'Trade Creditor and the Quest for Security', pp. 57–8.

66. See Goode, 'Proprietary Rights and Unsecured Creditors'. On preferences generally see D. Prentice, 'Some Observations on the Law Relating to Preferences' in R. Cranston (ed.), *Making Commercial Law* (Clarendon Press, Oxford, 1997); D. Milman and R. Parry, *A Study of the Operation of Transactional Avoidance Mechanisms in Corporate Insolvency Practice*, ILA Research Report (1997); A. Keay, 'Preferences in Liquidation Law: A Time for Change' [1998] 2 CfiLR 198; I. F. Fletcher, 'Voidable Transactions in Bankruptcy Law: British Law Perspectives' in J. Ziegel (ed.), *Current Developments in International and Comparative Corporate Insolvency Law* (Clarendon Press, Oxford, 1994). See also ch. 12 above.

67. On these regimes see Keay, 'Preferences in Liquidation Law'; M. Shanker, 'The American Bankruptcy Preference Law: Perceptions of the Past, the Transition to the Present, and Ideas for the Future' in Ziegel, *Current Developments*.

68. See Keay, 'Preferences in Liquidation Law'; Goode, 'Proprietary Rights and Unsecured Creditors', p. 187: defences such as good faith or change of position would still, however, be relevant. An objective approach to preferences is likely to facilitate the prevention of unfair grantings of security on past rather than new value; cf. *Re M. C. Bacon Ltd* [1990] BCC 78. See ch. 12 above.

69. See LoPucki, 'Unsecured Creditor's Bargain', p. 1948; S. Block-Lieb, 'The Unsecured Creditor's Bargain: A Reply' (1994) 80 Va. L Rev. 1989. Article 9 filing of a security agreement will not, in itself, ensure that detailed information flows to other creditors since a filing notice may give bare outlines only: it is the right to call for particulars of the security agreement that yields valuable information. See Bridge, 'Form, Substance and Innovation', p. 15; Diamond Report, p. 94.

creditors. It is of little assistance to involuntary creditors or to those who are unable to adjust for the variety of reasons already discussed.[70]

To sum up, then, it can be said that bypassing *pari passu* by excluding secured property from the insolvent company's estate is difficult to justify in fairness terms with reference to arguments based on bargaining and freedom of contract, supply of value and sufficiency of notice: at least this is so given the present state of English law. Inequalities of bargaining positions, information asymmetries, impositions of externalities and enforcement biases undermine the free bargaining rationale. After-acquired property clauses and weak preference rules detract from claims to the supply of new value, and inadequacies of registration processes and inabilities to adjust place question marks against assertions that notice is adequate.

Steps can be taken to reduce unfairness on most of the above fronts and in some cases the same reforms would also improve overall efficiency. A fixed fraction rule would, for instance, limit unfairness to non-adjusting unsecured creditors and reduce inefficient value transfers. Compulsory tort liability insurance could reduce the unfairness involved in subsidies from involuntary non-adjusting, unsecured tort creditors.

Retention of title and quasi-security

In chapter 3 it was noted that many companies raise finance and arrange the use of assets by using sale arrangements in a manner that substitutes for security. 'Quasi-security' devices such as retentions of title, hire purchase and leasing agreements, factoring and sale and lease-back contracts are used in order to supply credit but avoid the scope of *pari passu* by keeping the assets at issue out of the corporate insolvency estate. The efficiency considerations attending the use of such devices were considered in chapter 3[71] and concerns noted on a number of fronts: that quasi-security devices may produce inefficient transfers of insolvency wealth away from unsecured creditors; that quasi-security undermines the efficiencies associated with security because it increases the uncertainties associated with lending; that poor information on the use of quasi-security devices and legal unknowns produce unnecessary uncertainties; and that quasi-security devices do not, in reality, deliver real protection for creditors who resort to them.

---

70. See pp. 95–7, 427–31 above.   71. See pp. 110–16 above.

Before questions of fairness are addressed it is as well to make clear the nature of the legal limitations that affect quasi-security devices. Rather than deal with all varieties of quasi-security, one example of the genre – the retention of title (ROT) clause – will be focused on here. To commence, the terms upon which title to goods can be retained by a creditor should be outlined.[72]

A simple ROT clause will involve a provision in a contract of sale that stipulates that property in the goods being sold will not pass from seller to buyer until the purchase price has been paid in full.[73] Such a clause will not require registration as a security interest in order to be effective.[74] In more complex arrangements, sellers may attempt to reserve title not merely in the original goods (for example, raw materials) but also in the proceeds of sale of such goods or in products manufactured from such goods or in the proceeds of sale of such products.[75] In the *Romalpa* case[76] the Court of Appeal held that when a seller S supplies goods to buyer B under a ROT clause and authorises B to sell the goods on condition that B accounts for the proceeds of sale, S may, on B's insolvency, rely on the fiduciary relationship established[77] and have an equitable right to trace those proceeds and prevent them from falling into the insolvent estate

---

72. See generally S. Wheeler, *Reservation of Title Clauses* (Oxford University Press, Oxford, 1991); Wheeler, *Reservation of Title Clauses: Impact and Implications* (Clarendon Press, Oxford, 1992); G. McCormack, *Reservation of Title* (2nd edn, Sweet & Maxwell, London, 1995); I. Davies, *Effective Retention of Title* (Fourmat, London, 1991); G. Moffat, *Trusts Law: Text and Materials* (3rd edn, Butterworths, London, 1999) ch. 15, paras. 600–11. On the importance and enforcement of ROT clauses see S. Wheeler, 'Capital Fractionalised: The Role of Insolvency Practitioners in Asset Distribution' in M. Cain and C. B. Harrington (eds.), *Lawyers in a Post Modern World: Translation and Transgression* (Open University Press, Buckingham, 1994). On the interaction of unjust enrichment, restitutionary techniques and retention of title see G. McMeel, 'Retention of Title: The Interface of Contract, Unjust Enrichment and Insolvency' in F. Rose (ed.), *Restitution and Insolvency* (Lloyd's of London Press, London, 2000).
73. See Sale of Goods Act 1979 s. 19(1) (the statutory basis for ROT clauses). If a seller attempts to reserve merely equitable, as opposed to legal, title to the goods this will be treated as a charge void for non-registration: see *Re Bond Worth Ltd* [1979] 3 All ER 919. On the EC Late Payment Directive and Member States' obligations to recognise contractually agreed-upon ROT clauses see G. McCormack, 'Retention of Title and the EC Late Payment Directive' [2001] 1 JCLS 501.
74. See *Aluminium Industrie Vaassen BV* v. *Romalpa Aluminium Ltd* [1976] 1 WLR 676; *Armour* v. *Thyssen Edelstahlwerke AG* [1990] 3 WLR 810, [1991] 2 AC 339; Companies Act 1985 s. 395(2).
75. The danger with a complex ROT clause is that it will be found by the courts to create a registrable charge and will be void if not registered under the Companies Act 1985 ss. 395, 396(1)(c): see, for example, *E . Pfeiffer WW GmbH* v. *Arbuthnot Factors Ltd* [1988] WLR 150, [1987] BCLC 522; *Carroll Group Distributors Ltd* v. *Bourke Ltd* [1990] ILRM 285; *Compaq Computers Ltd* v. *Abercorn Group Ltd* [1992] BCC 484.
76. *Aluminium Industrie Vaassen BV* v. *Romalpa Aluminium Ltd* [1976] 1 WLR 676.
77. For criticisms of this point see J. Ulph, 'Equitable Proprietary Rights in Insolvency: The Ebbing Tide?' [1996] JBL 482 at 498; R. Bradgate, 'Reservation of Title Ten Years On' (1987) Conv. 434 at 440; J. de Lacy, '*Romalpa* Theory and Practice under Retention of Title in the Sale of Goods' (1995) 24 *Anglo-American Law Review* 327 at 337.

of B. The goods must be kept distinct and the relationship between the parties must be fiduciary rather than merely that of debtor to creditor.[78] By such use of a ROT clause, S is given a right *in rem* in the proceeds and does not have to compete with the creditors for a share in B's insolvency estate.[79]

In the *Romalpa* instance the aluminium foil had not been processed or mixed with other goods. When, however, materials are supplied subject to a ROT clause and there is such a processing or mixing, an issue is whether the seller can rely on the ROT clause to trace into the product that results from processing or mixing. In the *Borden*[80] decision the Court of Appeal held that if S sells goods to a manufacturer knowing that the goods will be subject to the manufacturing process before being sold, there is no fiduciary relationship between S and B and S cannot rely on a simple ROT clause to ensure tracing: a right over the finished product will have to be provided for by express contractual stipulation. *Borden* thus leaves open difficult issues concerning the point at which the seller's goods lose their identity and become a new product.[81] Where the sold goods have been mixed with other goods but are identifiable readily and can be separated easily then the seller can retain them.[82] Case law post-*Borden* suggests that when attempts are made to draft ROT clauses so as to retain title in new products or proceeds thereof, the courts will construe these as intending to vest legal ownership of the manufactured product in the hands of the buyer subject only to a registrable charge in favour of the seller.[83] It may, however, be possible for the seller and buyer to agree which of them is to become the owner of any manufactured product: this was the suggestion of Goff and Oliver LJJ in *Clough Mill Ltd* v. *Martin*.[84]

---

78. See G. Lightman and G. Moss, *The Law of Receivers of Companies* (2nd edn, Sweet and Maxwell, London, 1994) p. 196.

79. If a buyer has become insolvent then the seller can achieve 'debt recovery' via his ability to assert a right *in rem*. If, on the other hand, the proprietary remedy available to the seller is confined to operating by way of a security charge, then, as noted above, ROT sellers invariably lose out upon the buyer's insolvency due to their failure to register the security charge as per Companies Act 1985 s. 395.

80. *Borden (UK) Ltd* v. *Scottish Timber Products Ltd* [1981] Ch 25. See also *Re Bond Worth Ltd* [1980] Ch 228; *Re Peachdart* [1984] Ch 131.

81. For discussion see J. de Lacy, 'Processed Goods and Retention of Title Clauses' [1997] 10 *Palmer's In Company*; de Lacy, 'Corporate Insolvency and Retention of Title Clauses: Developments in Australia' [2001] Ins. Law. 64 (analysing the decision of *Associated Alloys Pty Ltd* v. *ACN* (2000) 171 ALR 568); Ulph, 'Equitable Proprietary Rights in Insolvency'; A. Hicks, 'When Goods Sold Become a New Species' [1993] JBL 485; P. Birks, 'Mixing and Tracing' (1992) 45(2) *Current Legal Problems* 69.

82. *Hendy Lennox (Industrial Engines) Ltd* v. *Grahame Puttick Ltd* [1984] 1 WLR 485.

83. *Re Peachdart* [1984] Ch 131.

84. [1985] 1 WLR 111, 115, 124. See further de Lacy, 'Corporate Insolvency and Retention of Title Clauses', pp. 70–5.

From a creditor's point of view, a particularly useful version of the ROT clause is the 'all-monies' provision which retains title in the seller's hands until all debts owed to the seller on any grounds are fully paid. (It has been suggested that about half of all ROT clauses are of the 'all-monies' kind.[85]) In an insolvency a benefit of such a clause is that it is not necessary to identify which items in a stock of supplied goods have been paid for: with an 'all-monies' clause all of the stock remains the seller's property. It is arguable that such reference to obligations unconnected with the immediate sale should be viewed as involving a charge, but in the *Armour*[86] case the House of Lords did not regard such a clause as creating a right of security and unanimously held that all-monies clauses are 'legitimate retention of title'.[87]

The value of an all-monies clause is particularly high when the value of the goods sold is rising. If, for example, paintings are supplied by A to a gallery B under an all-monies arrangement, retained ownership of these will operate in effect as security for the debt the purchaser owes in relation to the purchase price for the paintings but also for other debts (for example, relating to furnishings supplied by A to B under other contracts). Keeping an asset of escalating value out of the insolvency estate has the effect of advancing in priority a series of formerly unsecured debts beyond the immediate transaction. It places that asset out of the reach of floating charge holders[88] and ordinary unsecured creditors.[89]

Do ROT clauses offer a means of bypassing *pari passu* that creates unfairness? A first key consideration here is that, as noted, ROT clauses do not have to be registered.[90] Unsecured creditors may, accordingly, be unfairly misled concerning the insolvency risks they are running when they supply goods on credit to a company.[91] Trade suppliers, for instance, may see an array of assets in their debtor's possession but these assets may belong to other parties and there is no register that can be resorted to so as to reveal

---

85. See A. Hicks, 'Retention of Title: Latest Developments' [1992] JBL 398 at 400; J. Spencer, 'The Commercial Realities of Reservation of Title Clauses' [1989] JBL 220 at 227: in Spencer's survey 59 per cent of materials suppliers (of various sizes) said that they used ROT clauses.
86. *Armour* v. *Thyssen Edelstahlwerke AG* [1990] 3 All ER 481, [1990] 3 WLR 810.
87. See Hicks, 'Retention of Title', p. 403 and also the discussion therein on part-payment.
88. But see judge's comments re the hypocrisy of banks complaining of ROTs when they have the floating charge: *Re Clough Mill Ltd* [1985] 1 WLR 111.
89. The Cork Report, para. 1645, recommended that ROTs should be restricted to the price outstanding on the goods involved in the transaction and that securing the payment of moneys beyond this should be achieved by the creditor using a fixed or floating charge.
90. The CLRSG recommended in 2001 that a notice-filing system be introduced for company charges. Complex retention of title clauses would be registrable but not simple ROTs: see CLRSG, *Final Report*, para. 12.60.
91. See Cork Report, paras. 1631–65.

this information. The existence, never mind the nature and extent, of the ROT clauses will remain invisible.[92] Not only is the *pari passu* principle by-passed but so are the disclosure protections attending the use of security devices.

Matters are made yet worse for the unsecured creditors referred to because corporate accounts will routinely treat goods supplied under ROT arrangements as purchases by the debtor company. Goods which are not the property of the company concerned thus commonly appear as assets in the balance sheet and it is rare for auditors' notes on accounts to mention retentions of title.[93] As has been commented about ROTs: 'they remain invisible until they become important'.[94]

When the Cork Committee took evidence on ROTs a 'cry for certainty' was made by 'consultee after consultee'.[95] The complaint was that claims involving ROTs were often confused and that without clarity the prospect of expensive litigation overshadowed commercial life. Cork's response was to accept that such complexities could not be avoided and could be negotiated around.[96] It could be contended, however, that all unnecessary legal uncertainties compound the informational unfairness that ROTs can occasion.

A second basis for seeing ROTs as conducing to unfairness is that such devices are not equally available to all creditors. The costs of using ROTs may be relatively low for many suppliers because standardised contracts can be employed but, as noted in chapter 3, the suppliers of certain goods, such as fuels, paint, food and fodder, are unable to use ROTs at all because such materials disappear on consumption and leave the creditor with an unsecured claim.[97] The effect is to load insolvency risks unduly onto the shoulders of those suppliers who happen to deal in goods that are consumed in the short term. A similar point can be made in relation to those suppliers who are repeat players and those who are engaged in a series of 'one-off' transactions. The latter may find it far more difficult to impose ROT clauses on their debtors.

A third cause of unfairness may arise from the use of ROTs to secure debts beyond the immediate transaction. As already noted, this is a

92. See Belcher and Beglan, 'Jumping the Queue', pp. 16–17.
93. C. Williams, 'Retention of Title: Some Recent Developments' (1991) 12 Co. Law. 54.
94. Belcher and Beglan, 'Jumping the Queue', p. 17.
95. Cork Report, para. 1627.   96. Ibid., paras. 1628–9.
97. Contrast the situation and approach taken regarding processed goods in the Antipodes: see *Re Weddel (NZ) Ltd* [1996] 5 NZBLC 104; *Associated Alloys Pty Ltd* v. *ACN* (2000) 171 ALR 568; de Lacy, 'Processed Goods and Retention of Title Clauses' and 'Corporate Insolvency and Retention of Title Clauses'.

particularly acute problem where the asset involved is of escalating value. That growth in value, combined with an all-monies (or all-liabilities) clause, will not be a windfall that becomes available to the body of unsecured creditors but will serve to prioritise certain unsecured debts (those owed to the asset supplier) and will ultimately[98] leave other unsecured creditors looking at a smaller insolvency estate than they anticipated.

Such unfairnesses as are noted may be compounded by inequalities of bargaining power. Powerful creditors will be able to impose ROT clauses on debtors but those with less market power (or subject to more competitive circumstances) may be unable to retain title.[99] The ROT is accordingly a device that may prove unfair in so far as it shifts insolvency risks to those who are the newest and weakest players in the market.

There is an argument, however, that use of ROT clauses can be conducive to fairness. The Cork Committee did not advocate the outlawing of ROT clauses in insolvency, noting that this would usually benefit floating charge holders, not unsecured creditors, and stating:

> suppliers have opted for reservation of title clauses precisely because they seek to avoid the unfairness which results when they supply goods on credit, a floating charge crystallises and a receiver then takes the goods and realises them for the benefit of the debenture-holder leaving the supplier with nothing. It seems to us that suppliers are entitled, in such circumstances, to take steps to protect themselves and that it would be wrong to deny them the protection they seek.[100]

Cork was disposed not to curtail contractual freedoms more than necessary[101] but was faced with its respondents' 'wide unanimity' of view that ROTs should be subjected to disclosure. The Committee recommended that a disclosure requirement along the lines of Article 9 of the US Uniform Commercial Code should be adapted to English needs so that there should be disclosure of names of suppliers imposing ROTs; descriptions of the types or classes of goods covered by the ROT; and the maximum

---

98. Of course the floating charge holder is the first to 'suffer'.

99. See *Leyland DAF Ltd* v. *Automotive Products plc* [1993] BCC 389 which demonstrates the potential for a ROT clause to *contribute* to a supplier's bargaining power, i.e. where continued supplies are vital to a receiver's attempts to keep a company running (noted in Belcher and Beglan, 'Jumping the Queue', pp. 18–19).

100. See Cork Report, paras. 1633–4; G. Elias, *Explaining Constructive Trusts* (Clarendon Press, Oxford, 1990) p. 135: 'It is only fair that suppliers of goods to businessmen should be able to stipulate for ROTs in respect of the goods which they supply. It would be unprincipled to give the power to take property rights by way of security to the lending institutions and nobody else.'

101. Cork Report, para. 1637.

amount that at any one time could be secured by the ROT.[102] Consumer goods, as covered by the Sale of Goods Act 1979 (covering goods ordinarily bought for private use or consumption), would, on Cork recommendations, not be covered by a disclosure requirement. Cork did not take a view on how far tracing should be allowed to extend but, as noted, did consider that a duly registered ROT should be limited to the price outstanding on the goods immediately contracted for and should not take the all-monies or all-liabilities form.

Were the Cork recommendations to be implemented they would go some way to meet criticisms based on the unavailability of information concerning ROTs and the unfairness of extending ROTs beyond the immediate transaction.[103] Action on these lines has yet to be taken, however, in spite of the added weight of the reports of the Diamond and Crowther Committees[104] which both advocated a new register of 'security interests' that would have included retentions of title to secure the payment of money.[105] In France and Italy, like the USA, ROTs require registration to be effective but the EC Draft Directive would not require registration.

Trusts

Parties involved in commercial relations with a company may, for reasons discussed above, find it difficult to take security or retain title so as to protect themselves against a potential insolvency. The consumer, for example, who pays in advance for goods may be ill-placed to resort to such measures. Another kind of refuge may, however, be available by reference to equitable doctrines which separate property held on trust from property forming part of the insolvent company's estate.[106] As the Cork Committee

---

102. Ibid., para. 1638.

103. On ROT registration generally see S. Wheeler, 'The Insolvency Act 1986 and ROTs' [1987] JBL 180.

104. Diamond Report, para. 9.3.2.

105. The Company Law Review Steering Group's 2000 Consultation Document (*Registration of Company Charges*) puts forward proposals for defining those retention of title clauses that are deemed registrable but, as noted, the CLRSG's *Final Report* (ch. 12) would treat complex, but not simple, ROTs as registrable in its proposed notice-filing system. See also de Lacy, 'Corporate Insolvency and Retention of Title Clauses', p. 75, who queries whether any fundamental reform in this area will result 'given the rather dismissive tone' of the (Company Law Review's *Registration of Company Charges*) Consultation Paper.

106. On trusts and insolvency see generally Moffat, *Trusts Law*, ch. 15; A. Belcher, *Corporate Rescue* (Sweet & Maxwell, London, 1993) ch. 9; H. Anderson, 'The Treatment of Trust Assets in English Insolvency Law' in E. McKendrick (ed.), *Commercial Aspects of Trusts and Fiduciary Obligations* (Clarendon Press, Oxford, 1992); Cork Report, ch. 22; A. Oakley, 'Proprietary Claims and their Priority in Insolvency' [1995] CLJ 377.

stressed, property held by an insolvent company on trust for others has never passed to the liquidator representing the general body of the company's creditors because the liquidator takes on the 'free assets' of the insolvent company.[107] Proprietary interests in favour of third parties prevail against the general body of creditors unless, of course, they are invalidated under any particular statutory provisions (e.g., those relating to the avoidance of floating charges or non-registration of charges). If a lender is placed in the position of a beneficiary of a trust imposed on the company, that lender has a claim *in rem* against the money at issue in priority to all others claiming against the company's assets.[108] As with retention of title it is thus possible to avoid *pari passu* distribution by keeping property out of the body of assets available for settling the company's debts.

This section of the chapter outlines the conditions under which the law will recognise trusts in the corporate insolvency context. It then considers efficiency issues arising from the use of trusts and finally looks to questions of fairness. (Questions of accountability and expertise were dealt with in chapter 12 when assessing liquidation processes in which the principle of *pari passu* distribution is applied to the residual estate.)

The recognition of trusts

For a trust relationship to be recognised the courts must find there to exist both an equitable proprietary interest in the property in question and a fiduciary relationship.[109] Circumstances satisfying these conditions may involve three distinct types of trust: express, resulting and constructive.[110] For an express trust to be established there are 'three certainties' to be shown to be present:[111] of intention, subject matter and objects. On the first point, intention will not necessarily involve writing (unless land is involved[112]) and the key issue is whether in substance a sufficient

---

107. See Cork Report, para. 1042.

108. See Milman and Durrant, *Corporate Insolvency*, p. 161.

109. See Oakley, 'Proprietary Claims', pp. 381–3; *Agip (Africa) v. Jackson* [1989] 3 WLR 1367 at 1386; *Re Diplock* [1948] Ch 465.

110. See S. Worthington, *Proprietary Interests in Commercial Transactions* (Clarendon Press, Oxford, 1996) pp. 44–5, who argues that some judges and commentators describe a single express trust while others require two trusts: a primary express trust linked with a secondary trust which operates if the primary trust fails, the secondary trust being variously described as an express trust, a resulting trust or even a constructive trust.

111. See Milman and Durrant, *Corporate Insolvency*, p. 166.

112. See *Re Kayford Ltd* [1975] 1 All ER 604 at 607. As Milman and Durrant (*Corporate Insolvency*, p. 166) note: 'a trust can arise even though the transaction is not framed in terms of a trust; the crucial factor, as always, is the substantive operation of the arrangement'. See, for example, *Re English & American Insurance Co.* [1994] 1 BCLC 649 and *Re Fleet Disposal Services Ltd* [1995] 1 BCLC 345 but compare *Swiss Bank Corp. v. Lloyds Bank Ltd* [1981] 2 WLR 893. The lack of certainty of intention was critical in *Re Multi Guarantee Co. Ltd* [1987] BCLC 257.

intention has been manifested.[113] As for subject matter, it must be possible to identify the property that is covered by the trust: a special difficulty where money is involved and where trust claims are liable to succeed only if the money at issue is retained in a separate bank account.[114]
Certainty of objects requires clarity concerning the purposes of the trust
relationship. If, for instance, there is an intended trust relationship but
it is unclear when funds are to be distributed in a particular way, the
trust will fail and money held by a company will, on an insolvency, enter the insolvency estate. This was the position in *Re Challoner Club Ltd
(in liquidation)*[115] where members of a company (an incorporated club) do-
nated funds to the troubled company which attempted to create a trust
over those funds. The trust terms were too uncertain to identify when
the money was to return to the members and consequently the trust
failed.

Resulting trusts are based on the presumed intentions of the settlor and
are generally held to arise where a party purchases property in the name of
another[116] or transfers property into the name of another.[117] Constructive
trusts[118] are trusts imposed independently of the intentions of the parties
and can be seen as devices used by the courts in pursuit of justice. Recent
cases suggest that claims to constructive trusts are difficult to establish
and in practical insolvency contexts the constructive trust is of limited
importance.[119]

In relation to corporate insolvency trusts are of particular importance
in two contexts which are worthy of more detailed attention. These are
where funds are advanced for particular purposes and where consumers
make payments for goods or services in advance.

---

113. See *Re Kayford Ltd* [1975] 1 All ER 604.
114. See also *Re London Wine Shippers Ltd* [1986] PCC 121; *Re Ellis, Son & Vidler Ltd* [1994] BCC 532;
Export Credits Guarantee Dept. v. *Turner* 1981 SLT 286. See further Ulph, 'Equitable Proprietary
Rights in Insolvency', pp. 489–93.
115. *The Times*, 4 November 1997.
116. See Oakley, 'Proprietary Claims,' p. 386; *Dyer* v. *Dyer* (1788) 2 Cox Eq 92.
117. *Vandervell* v. *Inland Revenue Commissioners* [1967] 2 AC 291. See also the discussion of
'presumed' and 'automatic' trusts by Megarry J in *Vandervell*.
118. See *Re Goldthorpe Exchange Ltd* [1995] 1 AC 74 (PC).
119. Regarding remedial constructive trusts see *Re Polly Peck International (No. 4)*, *The Times*, 18
May 1998, per Mummery LJ: 'The insolvency road was blocked off to the remedial
constructive trusts, at least when judge-driven in a vehicle of discretion…to a trust lawyer
and, even more so to an insolvency lawyer, the prospect of a court imposing such a trust was
inconceivable.' See further G. Stewart, 'No Remedial Trust in Insolvency' (1998) (August)
Insolvency Practitioner 8; Worthington, *Proprietary Interests*, p. 50. See generally C. Rickett,
'Of Constructive Trusts and Insolvency' in F. Rose (ed.), *Restitution and Insolvency* (Lloyd's
of London Press, London, 2000); D. Wright, 'The Remedial Constructive Trust and
Insolvency' in Rose, *Restitution and Insolvency*.

Advances for particular purposes

During the nineteenth century the suppliers of funds for speculative enterprises commonly protected their investments by advancing moneys not to companies directly but to trustees.[120] The latter would then release funds as required and if the company involved became insolvent any funds left in the hands of the trustees would be recoverable by the investors.[121] Such a procedure offered protection but it did involve the inconvenience of using intermediaries.

Whether funds advanced directly to the company for a specific purpose might be held on trust was the issue considered by the House of Lords in *Barclays Bank Ltd* v. *Quistclose Investments Ltd*.[122] In that case Rolls Razor Ltd was in difficulties but declared a dividend on its shares and Quistclose loaned the company £209,719 solely for the purpose of paying the dividend. The sum was paid into a separate account with Barclays Bank, with whom Rolls Razor were currently overdrawn. Barclays were aware of the payment by Quistclose. Rolls Razor then went into liquidation before the dividend was paid and Barclays claimed to be entitled to set off the money from Quistclose against the overdraft. The House of Lords decided unanimously, however, that the money had been received by the company on trust to pay the dividend and that, the primary trust having failed, that money was held on a secondary trust for Quistclose. Since Barclays had been given notice of the trust disposition, its own claim failed.

The *Quistclose* type of arrangement is now commonly used and its effect is to give the lender protection in relation to sums not yet expended on the specific purpose.[123] Such an arrangement differs from a secured loan in that it does not have to be registered and there is no public notice given of the transaction.

Consumer prepayments

When consumers make payments in advance to companies for goods or services – for example, by sending money to mail order firms – they run considerable risks. If the company becomes insolvent before the goods or services are supplied, the consumers have no remedies except as unsecured

---

120. See Milman and Durrant, *Corporate Insolvency*, p. 161.
121. *National Bolivian Navigation Co.* v. *Wilson* (1880) 5 App Cas 176.
122. [1970] AC 567, [1968] 3 All ER 651.
123. For recognition of a purpose trust in the context of payments made to administrators to facilitate the discharge of liabilities owed to third parties by the company in administration see *Re Niagara Mechanical Services International Ltd (in administration)* [2001] BCC 393, described (2000) *Recovery* (August 7), [2001] 80 *CCH Company Law Newsletter* 6.

creditors, a position in which they are unlikely to receive even a substantial portion of their money back. The Cork Report[124] noted that a good deal of public and media concern attended this state of the law and in 1984 an Office of Fair Trading (OFT) survey suggested that there were at least 15 million prepayments per year, that 2 per cent of these involved a loss of money and that total losses exceeded £18 million.[125]

Such difficulties have been responded to in a variety of ways. A number of trade associations have established voluntary compensation schemes[126] and certain statutes deal with prepayments in particular sectors. The Estate Agents Act 1979 section 13 thus requires a client's money to be held in trust in a separate bank account.[127] General legislation also plays a part here in so far as the Sale of Goods (Amendment) Act 1995 provides that pre-paying buyers of part of a bulk will obtain undivided proprietary rights in the bulk.[128] This amending legislation went some way in helping with problems of identifying the subject of the trust (though the bulk of goods may itself present difficulties of identification) but such legislative responses have not solved all the problems and uncertainties left by judicial decisions in this area.

A key such decision is that of *Re Kayford*.[129] This case concerned a company (K) that ran a mail order business. K had loaned its main supplier considerable sums of money but the supplier entered financial difficulties. This, in turn, threatened K's solvency. K was advised by an accountant to open a separate 'Customers' Trust Deposit Account', to pay into it any money received from customers of goods which had not yet been delivered and to withdraw money only on delivery of the goods. K accepted the device but, in the first instance, paid money into a dormant deposit account in the company's name, only at a later stage altering the name of the account. After K had entered involuntary liquidation Megarry J found sufficient evidence of an intention to create a trust. This was contained in the discussions of K's managing director, the accountant and the bank manager. Megarry J found that the three certainties of a trust were established and commented:

124. Cork Report, paras. 1048–9.
125. OFT, *The Protection of Consumer Prepayments: A Discussion Paper* (1984) ('OFT'). See also Moffat, *Trusts Law*, ch. 15.
126. Moffat, *Trusts Law*, p. 587, notes those of the Newspaper Proprietors Association and the Mail Order Protection Scheme.
127. See OFT, paras. 3.1–3.13; G. Howells and S. Weatherill, *Consumer Protection Law* (Dartmouth, Aldershot, 1995).
128. See Ulph, 'Equitable Proprietary Rights in Insolvency'.
129. [1975] 1 All ER 604, [1975] 1 WLR 279.

No doubt the general rule is that if you send money to a company for goods which are not delivered you are merely a creditor of the company unless a trust has been created. The sender may create a trust by using appropriate words when he sends the money…or the company may do it by taking suitable steps on or before receiving the money. If either is done the obligations in respect of the money are transformed from contract to property, from debt to trust.[130]

Megarry J suggested, further, that it was entirely 'proper and honourable' for a company to use such a trust account as soon as there were doubts about the firm's ability to fulfil its obligations. He, indeed, welcomed the taking of such steps.

Effectiveness and efficiency

Do trust devices offer an effective and efficient way for parties to protect themselves when advancing funds or making prepayments? A first problem is the restrictiveness and uncertainty of much of the law relating to trusts. As already noted, the impact of remedial constructive trusts on commercial life is liable to be very modest.[131] In relation to express trusts and resulting trusts, as encountered in *Quistclose*, there are issues of uncertainty.[132] As commentators have pointed out,[133] the precise nature of the equitable right to see that the loan is applied 'for the primary designated purpose' is unclear and it is not always apparent when the primary purpose is fulfilled, the 'trust' spent and the equitable right extinguished. Moffat also notes: 'Similar uncertainty surrounds the status of the particular class of creditors for whose benefit the primary trust in *Quistclose* was created, i.e. the shareholders post-declaration of a dividend. Are they beneficiaries under a private express trust with associated rights of enforcement? If not, are we presented with an example of a "purpose trust" infringing the beneficiary principle?'[134]

Questions also arise as to the characterisation of the assets to be placed in trust. This area of uncertainty is encountered in the *Carreras Rothmans*[135] case. Rothmans owed an advertising agency money for services

---

130. [1975] 1 WLR 279 at 282.
131. See also *Re Goldthorpe Exchange Ltd* [1995] 1 AC 74 and *Re Wait* [1927] 1 Ch 606 for judicial expressions of caution in regard to importing trust concepts into the commercial law area; see Ulph, 'Equitable Proprietary Rights in Insolvency', pp. 486–7.
132. See Moffat, *Trusts Law*, pp. 595–8.
133. Ibid.; J. Heydon, W. Gummow and R. Austin, *Cases and Materials on Equity and Trusts* (4th edn, Butterworths, Sydney, 1993) p. 476.
134. Moffat, *Trusts Law*, p. 595.
135. *Carreras Rothmans Ltd* v. *Freeman Mathews Treasure Ltd* [1985] 1 Ch 207, [1984] 3 WLR 1016.

and renegotiated an agreement so that the sums involved were paid by the agency into a special account for the purpose of paying these expenses. The agency went into liquidation and Rothmans contested their claim to the funds with the liquidator. The case was decided on *Quistclose* lines and the funds were said never to have belonged to the agency and to be re-payable to Rothmans. Such an approach is, however, questionable since the agency had effectively made an existing asset (the Rothmans' debt) available exclusively to one class of creditor, and this should probably now be seen as a preference or contrary to the principle established in *British Eagle*.[136]

Quistclose, it should also be noted, involved an attempted corporate res-cue, and the extent to which *Quistclose* principles are liable to be extended by the courts to cover more routine advances of corporate finance is a fur-ther area of uncertainty.[137] The courts may well act consistently with the advice of commentators and be less inclined to recognise trusts where res-cues are not involved and where the language used does not evidence the intention to establish a trust in rigorous terms.[138] Here, again, the philo-sophical underpinnings of *Quistclose* are unclear and further cases raise the questions whether the *Quistclose* trust is to be seen as an express trust or a constructive trust and whether it is to be viewed in pure trusts law terms or remedially.[139]

Such uncertainties reduce the present value of the *Quistclose* type of trust as an effective and efficient means of protecting investors but there is no necessary reason why the courts or the legislature could not bring new clarity into this area of the law. If it is asked whether such trusts hold out the promise of effective and efficient protection in routine cases of lending, other considerations have to be taken into account. First, a cred-itor may demand that a debtor company should place the funds at issue into a special account to be used for a specific purpose but the company may resist such a request for a number of reasons. Administrative costs will be incurred by the company and these may be seen as excessive and unnecessary. Other creditors may insist on similar separate accounts and there may be fears of a deluge of such requests that, overall, would impose tight and inconvenient restraints on the uses to which money can be put.

---

136. On preferences see Insolvency Act 1986 ss. 239, 240 and ch. 12 above; *British Eagle International Airlines Ltd* v. *Compagnie Nationale Air France* [1975] 1 WLR 758, [1975] 2 All ER 390 and ch. 13 above.

137. See Belcher and Beglan, 'Jumping the Queue', p. 7.

138. See Bridge, '*Quistclose* Trust'.

139. See Belcher and Beglan, 'Jumping the Queue', p. 8; C. Rickett, 'Different Views on the Scope of the *Quistclose* Analysis: English and Antipodean Insights' (1991) 107 LQR 608.

The company, moreover, may consider that it is not possible to designate specific purposes for its borrowings without giving up the flexibility of financing that it needs to compete in the marketplace. In the face of such company resistance to the use of a *Quistclose* trust, the small supplier of funds or the infrequent/one-off supplier may be ill-positioned to insist on the arrangement and may be ill-equipped to calculate the advantages, disadvantages and ways of arranging such a trust.

Turning to consumer prepayments and the *Kayford* type of trust, this also possesses limitations.[140] In the first instance it requires that the consumer, on forwarding money, should use appropriate words to manifest the intention to establish a trust, or the company supplying the goods must itself take actions demonstrating such an intention.[141] Most consumers will not be aware of the possibilities offered by *Kayford* trusts and are unlikely to use the required forms of words when making purchases. They may not occupy bargaining positions that allow them to insist on such arrangements and the trading companies themselves will have weak incentives to establish *Kayford* trusts. A second difficulty arises from the need to identify the funds at issue. The law provides rules to trace assets in mixed accounts but these rules are complex and do not allow involved parties to predict legal effects clearly. Legal uncertainties also infect the process of establishing a *Kayford* type of trust. Thus, the courts may refuse to recognise such trusts where they are deemed to infringe the *pari passu* principle of residual insolvency distribution and when such infringements will be declared is a matter of some uncertainty.[142]

Focusing on allocative efficiency prompts the question whether it is desirable to offer consumer pre-payers the protections of *Kayford* trusts and to place them ahead of other unsecured creditors in whose body they would take their place in the absence of a trust. In the last chapter it was argued that consumer creditors were less worthy of special protection than employee creditors. Practical considerations, moreover, may also undermine the efficiency case for creditor protections through trusts. Even if the case for creditor protection was accepted it could be argued that trusts do not provide the best route to such protection. The OFT recognised in 1984 that administrative costs for firms might be high if separate

---

140. See W. Goodhart and G. Jones, 'The Infiltration of Equitable Doctrine into English Commercial Law' (1980) 43 MLR 489; Moffat, *Trusts Law*, pp. 590–1; A. Ogus and C. Rowley, *Prepayments and Insolvency* (OFT Occasional Paper, 1984).
141. See Ogus and Rowley, *Prepayments and Insolvency*, p. 6.
142. See Cork Report, para. 1068; *British Eagle International Airlines Ltd* v. *Compagnie Nationale Air France* [1975] 2 All ER 390.

accounts and trusts were routinely employed.[143] These costs would have a disproportionate effect on small new companies. Public policing of such practices might prove expensive since firms would possess incentives to transfer funds from special to general accounts before contracts were fulfilled. Prepayments also provide, in many cases, an 'essential part of the trader's working capital'.[144] Ogus and Rowley suggest that in general terms there is no efficiency presumption that such financing is better provided by commercial rather than customer creditors (though they qualify this comment by stating that if poorly informed consumers falsely maintain uneconomic market operations there may be efficiency losses on society). A danger that can be pointed to with more confidence, however, is that if superior protections were given to consumer creditors that effect would be to increase the incentives of other parties to take security and to leave fewer assets available for unsecured creditors. A further danger is that funds to replace those currently provided by prepayment might be hard to come by. Ogus and Rowley caution: 'Given capital market imperfections, it is by no means clear that alternative finance would be available, save at loaded rates of interest, even where the trader was essentially solvent, especially in the case of new enterprise.'[145] The risk is that gains for consumers would be achieved at the price of significant increases in legal and administrative costs.

Other means of consumer protection have been suggested.[146] In rejecting preferred status for consumer creditors and compulsory trust accounts, the Cork Committee relied on more general measures to discourage irresponsible corporate behaviour or limit its effects. These came in the form of tighter disqualification rules for errant directors and the introduction of the wrongful trading concept together with the proposed 10 per cent fund which would be available for consumer as well as other unsecured creditors. Ogus and Rowley pointed out that a number of protective arrangements had already been introduced (most following negotiations with the OFT) so as to protect consumers in relation to certain types of transaction. Thus, certain statutes such as the Estate Agents Act 1979 demand that clients' money must be held in trust in a separate

---

143. Ogus and Rowley, *Prepayments and Insolvency*, paras. 6.9–6.24.
144. Cork Report, para. 1050.
145. Ogus and Rowley, *Prepayments and Insolvency*, p. 28; cf. P. Richardson, 'Consumer Protection and the Trust' [1985] JBL 456.
146. See the Customer Prepayment (Protection) Bill 1982 which was introduced into Parliament as a Private Member's Bill but failed to progress beyond first reading; C. M. Schmitthoff, 'A Consumers' Prepayment (Protection) Bill?' [1984] JBL 105.

account.[147] Some trade associations, moreover, had voluntarily established compensation schemes to reimburse disappointed consumers: these were encountered, for instance, in the newspaper, periodical, travel agency, vehicle building and glazing installation sectors. As for further responses to the predicament of consumer pre-payers, these commentators backed Cork on wrongful trading controls as a way forward, and viewed as promising the institution of steps to educate traders on the causes of collapse (where possible involving the banks and expert creditors); the wider dissemination of corporate accounting information; 'the linking of bank guarantees to the obtaining of secured creditor status – thereby inducing self-interested monitoring of trading company performance'; and the encouraging of voluntary trust funds and insurance bonds. There was, they added, no clearly established public interest case for the compulsory introduction of any of the above solutions.

Before leaving the question of efficiency and effectiveness in relation to trusts, the special case for 'rescue fund trusts' should be considered. The argument for regularising arrangements whereby finances are supplied to a troubled company for the purposes of assisting in its survival is that it may be in the economic interest of the community to encourage the supply of funds (by consumers, bankers or traders) in circumstances that facilitate rescues and increase corporate survival rates.[148] This type of arrangement could operate on a regularised *Quistclose* basis when a purchaser of goods offers prepayment expressly on the basis that this funding is to assist in a rescue and is given for a specific purpose to be held on trust. Recognition of the trust would thus keep the fund of the insolvency estate and encourage rescue funding by traders as well as banks.

The possible problem with the trust-based regime as described is that it may be open to the same criticisms as were made of the statutory super-priority (SSP) as proposed by the DTI/Insolvency Service in 1993, dropped in 1995 after consultation[149] and mooted again in 1999.[150] SSP would give providers of funding during a moratorium a statutory super-priority over all existing creditors. (Such lenders would be *at the head* of the queue for the insolvency estate, not placed *outside* the queue as would be the case in

---

147. Section 13.
148. See R. Austin, 'Commerce and Equity: Fiduciary Duty and Constructive Trust' (1986) 6 OJLS 444 at 455.
149. DTI Consultative Documents: *Company Voluntary Arrangements and Administration Orders* (1993), *Revised Proposals for a New Company Voluntary Arrangement Procedure* (1995).
150. See Insolvency Service, *A Review of Company Rescue and Business Reconstruction Mechanisms* (1999).

a trust-based system.) The proposal was dropped in 1995 on the grounds that it might militate against the proper consideration of the viability of the business by a lender: it would lead to inefficiently large incentives to lend and to unjustifiable financing.[151] In such a scenario the supposed danger is that the highly protected investor encourages the company to continue trading beyond the point where this is justified and this results in greater damage to existing creditors than would otherwise be the case.

Such reasoning, however, is open to question. In a *Quistclose* type of arrangement where the lender to the troubled company places funds on trust and is well informed, there is no excessive incentive to invest because the investor is not free riding on the security of other parties but is able to calculate the relevant investment risks and to agree a price or interest rate accordingly. The use of a separate trust account, in this regard, keeps the affairs of the new finance supplier separate from those of the creditors of the company. (It is, of course, the requirements of specific purpose and separate accounting that, as noted, restrict the potential role of the *Quistclose* trust as a general form of flexible corporate financing.) Inefficiencies might arise where such new trust-based finance suppliers are ill-informed (a position likely where consumer prepayments are involved) or where the company's creditors have no information on the trust-based funding. (The latter issue can be responded to with a disclosure requirement.) From the point of view of a company's existing creditors there is a balance to be considered in assessing the desirability of encouraging 'rescue fund trusts'. On the one hand, there are dangers that their positions will be worsened by ill-informed funders allowing the company to descend into greater troubles than would otherwise be the case; on the other hand, it is to their advantage if prospects of corporate decline can be reduced by encouraging injections of rescue funds. This emphasises that any problems in this area stem from deficiencies in information supplies and use rather than from resort to *Quistclose*-type trusts.

Fairness

Do trusts of the *Quistclose* type operate consistently with the fair treatment of corporate creditors? It can be argued that in *Quistclose* no creditors were misled into making further loans by the existence of a separate dividend account and the bank was aware of the agreement between the parties. This will not always be the case, however.[152] *Quistclose*-type arrangements

---

151. DTI, *Revised Proposals*, para. 2.2.   152. Moffat, *Trusts Law*, p. 594.

are not subject to the registration and disclosure requirements associated with security and one effect, indeed purpose, of a *Quistclose*-type transaction 'may be to create an impression of commercial solidity so as to enable the borrower to continue trading and avoid insolvency, with the consequence that fresh liabilities to creditors will probably be incurred'.[153] Actual and potential creditors of a company may, thus, be deceived in so far as they are led to see the potential insolvency estate as larger than it really is: the property held on an undisclosed trust will lie at the heart of the 'deception'. Similarly with a *Kayford* trust, the firm's general creditors may observe a high level of economic activity and stocking but may not realise that a proportion of this is funded out of consumer prepayments and the involved moneys and assets will at no time enter the insolvency estate. When, moreover, an existing asset (a debt in *Carreras Rothmans*) is placed in trust for a particular creditor or class of creditor, there is, as has been noted above, a transaction approaching a preference or a breach of *British Eagle* principles.[154] In *Kayford* the company chose unilaterally to protect a particular set of (new) customers by means of a new trust arrangement. Megarry J decided that this did not constitute a fraudulent preference because the case involved 'the question not of preferring creditors but of preventing those who pay money from becoming creditors, by making them the beneficiaries under a trust'.[155] As Goodhart and Jones have argued,[156] however, it is difficult to accept that the customers in *Kayford* were never creditors since that would demand acceptance that the money received from the customers was subject to a trust the moment it was received. The facts were, however, that the customers forwarded money without any binding undertaking from Kayford to pay it into a trust account. It would clearly be a preference for a company to take money from general funds and pay this into a trust account for the benefit of certain creditors but it is difficult to see how the arrangement adopted in *Kayford* differed materially from such a process.[157] In summary, then, it is arguable that a *Kayford* arrangement is likely to infringe *British Eagle* principles and to involve unfairness for that reason.[158]

Are trust arrangements equally available to all suppliers of corporate funds? Here the problem in relation to the *Kayford* trust is that it is the voluntary action of the receiving company that establishes the trust and,

---

153. Ibid.   154. See pp. 475–6 above.   155. [1975] 1 WLR 279 at 281.
156. Goodhart and Jones, 'Infiltration of Equitable Doctrine', p. 496.
157. Ibid., p. 497.
158. See the comments of Templeman LJ in *Borden (UK) Ltd* v. *Scottish Timber Products Ltd* [1979] 3 WLR 672.

accordingly, that company may act in a selective or discriminatory manner beyond the control of any particular fund supplier. With a *Quistclose* trust instituted by the fund provider disparities of information collection and handling will create a bias in favour of better resourced funders and repeat players will be advantaged as compared to one-off providers. Overall, as with many other modes of bypassing *pari passu*, the effect of such trust mechanisms will be to disadvantage the poorly resourced, ill-informed, one-off trade creditor who will at the end of the day constitute an unsecured creditor surveying a shrunken insolvency estate.

Such a situation could be avoided, as already noted, by instituting statutory reforms to oblige suppliers to hold consumer prepayments in separate accounts and on trust.[159] Leaving aside efficiency issues and the problem of removing working capital from the company, can a case be made out for such a course of action on grounds of fairness? Treating consumer creditors preferentially (as compared to unsecured trade creditors) might be argued for on the basis of their special vulnerability.[160] Consumer creditors, it could be said, tend to be less wealthy than other creditors; are less likely and able to spread risks through diversification or self-insurance; and are not fully voluntary creditors because they are poorly informed concerning insolvency risks, are ill-placed to negotiate terms with traders and, indeed, may not see themselves as credit suppliers.

The Cork Committee was unmoved by these arguments, though it did not respond to them in detail and merely urged that consumer creditors extend credit like traders and said that between the two groups, there is 'no essential difference'. The problem for the proponents of consumer protection lies in any contention that consumers are in a worse position than all unsecured trade creditors. The small unsecured trade creditor who is not in a continuing relationship with a debtor company may (as indicated in chapter 13) be very poorly positioned to evaluate risks, may not consider himself as a credit supplier and, arguably, may be more vulnerable than the average consumer in cases of default. The consumer may be deprived, on default, of a luxury consumer item; the small trade creditor may lose out on the payment that allows his business to continue. The consumer may suffer a personal loss; the small trader's loss may affect a host of employees very significantly. Any rationale for preferential treatment based on a vulnerability assessment might have to include numbers

---

159. See n. 146 above and Cork Report, para. 1053, for rejection of this proposal.
160. See Ogus and Rowley, *Prepayments and Insolvency*, paras. 5.39, 5.11.

of unsecured trade creditors as well as consumers. Given these consider-ations the case in fairness for special treatment of consumers as a general class seems not to be made out.

To conclude on the use of trust devices, there may be a case for en-couraging the use of trust-based protections for parties who supply funds in rescue scenarios. Any potential prejudice to the general body of cor-porate creditors may then be compensated for by attendant increases in the company's prospects of survival. In relation to non-rescue situa-tions the case for trust devices seems highly questionable on efficiency and fairness grounds. Widespread use of trust arrangements is likely to lead to inflexible regimes of financing that are not efficient and consis-tent with dynamism in the marketplace. Unfairness is also likely to re-sult because of informational and resourcing disparities, with the end result of worsening the positions of unsecured creditors. Legal uncer-tainties further compound these problems. The way forward on trust may, as Goodhart and Jones suggest,[161] be to treat fund suppliers as *de facto* creditors and to seek to ameliorate the position of unsecured creditors more generally rather than to create yet another protected group.

Alternatives to *pari passu*

In moving to consider possible alternatives to *pari passu* it is useful to focus again on what a regime for distributing an estate post-insolvency should achieve. The contention in this book is that insolvency laws and processes should be designed to produce acceptable combinations of efficiency, ex-pertise, fairness and accountability characteristics.[162] This implies that the devices and processes that make up the regime for distribution should offer players in the marketplace a range of low-cost modes of protection against insolvency risks but that they should also avoid allocating risks in ways that produce unfairness or inefficiency and should satisfy principles of accountability and transparency in seeking to ensure that both fairness and efficiency concerns are satisfied.

The means for delivering the above desiderata may, accordingly, be to offer a range of devices (for example, security, retentions of title, trusts) but to set those devices up so that they are legally certain as well as

---

161. Goodhart and Jones, 'Infiltration of Equitable Doctrine', p. 512.
162. See ch. 2 above.

identifiable and employable at minimal cost. The protections offered
by insolvency law should also be designed to protect vulnerable parties
who would bear insolvency risks inefficiently or unfairly if left unpro-
tected.

How are the vulnerable to be identified?[163] It can be repeated, first, that
parties will *not* be vulnerable if they can (at reasonable cost) secure preferential positions in distributions or if they can (again at reasonable cost)
adjust terms and loan rates to reflect risks borne. The Crown, as noted, is
able to position its tax levels in a manner that anticipates default rates.
Employees, in contrast, exemplify parties who are ill-positioned to adjust
their credit rates to take account of default risks.[164] Some traders may be
unable to adjust rates because the time scales they work to are too short,
the costs of information collection are too high or relevant data may be unavailable. Accepted commercial procedures within a trade may, moreover,
make accurate risk assessment non-feasible.

Another sign of vulnerability – one also noted in chapter 13 – is a low capacity to absorb losses. The ability to spread risks increases a party's capacity to withstand the consequences of default.[165] The Crown, again, is well
placed and can spread default risks across taxpayers who, in turn, are likely
to be able to cope with marginal increases in tax rates without suffering
catastrophic consequences. Resilient traders tend to be those whose businesses are not totally dependent on the viability of one particular debtor[166]
and who are involved in the supply of goods or services to a large number
of customers. If one of their customers becomes insolvent they are less exposed to disaster than those trade creditors who deal with only one main
customer. Most trade creditors are relatively protected in this respect, as
are many tort victims. Employees, on the other hand, are seldom able to
spread default risks and so are highly vulnerable.[167] Tort creditors and consumer creditors, as has been seen, will tend to be lower-cost risk bearers
than employees since they will usually have other sources of income, funds
and products, and risks will be spread by such diversification.

Bearing in mind such issues of fairness to the vulnerable and efficiency,
it is almost time to consider particular alternatives to *pari passu* but before

---

163. This section builds on V. Finch, 'Is *Pari Passu* Passé?' [2000] Ins. Law. 194 at 206–10.
164. See generally B. Gleig, 'Unpaid Wages in Bankruptcy' (1987) 21 UBC L Rev. 61–83. But see
p. 449 above.
165. S. S. Cantlie, 'Preferred Priority in Bankruptcy' in Ziegel, *Current Developments in
International and Comparative Corporate Insolvency Law*, pp. 433–44.
166. Ibid.   167. Ibid.

doing so we should map out the limitations of the role that *pari passu* plays in the insolvency process.

The first such limitation is in the breadth of that role. It can be argued that by the time the *pari passu* principle comes into play many of the difficult insolvency law questions have been posed and answered.[168] There is force in this point. The role of *pari passu* is defined by the shape of exceptions and bypassing arrangements that insolvency law allows. As has been indicated, those exceptions and bypassing devices raise, in themselves, numerous issues of efficiency and fairness (not to mention expertise and accountability). To allow the use of such devices is not merely to reduce the role of *pari passu*, it introduces principles and priorities to override *pari passu*. When teachers say 'The sweets will be distributed equally to all children in the class' we see a single, clear principle of fairness. When they say 'All red-haired children's appetites will, however, be satisfied first and then equal distribution will take place', the fairness of *Animal Farm* comes to mind.

Limitations of scope do not in themselves, however, constitute reasons for abandoning *pari passu*. Questions arise as to the acceptability of the overriding principles that qualify *pari passu* but it could still be argued that *pari passu* is the most appropriate method of redistributing residual assets and that other principles would, even in relation to the residual assets, produce significantly different (perhaps less acceptable) results for residual claimants.

If, however, the role of *pari passu* is seen in terms of ensuring that unsecured creditors are dealt with in an efficient and fair way, it should be noted that there are approaches to this issue that go beyond asking how the residual assets should be distributed and that these can be seen as further limitations on the importance of *pari passu*. Five such approaches can be noted. These look to protect unsecured creditors through:

- rethinking how the estate is constructed (for example, by considering priorities and deferrals[169]);
- procedural protections (for example, improving transparency and disclosure through insolvency regimes);

---

168. For a sustained argument that *pari passu* has limited practical impact and should not be viewed as a fundamental rule underpinning insolvency law see Mokal, 'Priority as Pathology', esp. pp. 587–8.

169. A class of creditor that might be dealt with specifically by statute is the company director: see ch. 13 above, pp. 437.

- substantive protections (for example, augmenting the residual estate with a 10 per cent fund rule[170] or directors' contribution through personal liability);
- reducing insolvency risks (for example, through training of directors, corporate governance improvements, educating traders in reasons for corporate collapse, encouraging banks and secured creditors to monitor);
- spreading insolvency risks: either across groups of companies;[171] or through compensation schemes;[172] or through insurance mechanisms.[173]

If these alternatives are borne in mind it can be concluded that the role of *pari passu* is modest, given that issues concerning *pari passu* are linked to, and surrounded by, a host of not inconsiderable questions. This does not, however, mean that *pari passu* is of insignificant importance.

A second limitation of *pari passu*'s role is that it is not wholly clear. The principle can be said to be weak because it operates in a confused manner due to the multiplicity of potential exceptions and bypassing arrangements encountered in law and practice. The above discussion suggests that there is scope for clarifying the rules governing exceptions and bypasses. Such clarification might be expected to reduce the costs incurred by parties seeking to protect themselves from insolvency risks but distributional consequences may flow: ordinary creditors who are still ill-placed to secure protections may be faced with a yet smaller residual estate as other parties take greater advantage of newly facilitated protections.

A number of questions are raised. A first issue is whether particular exceptions and bypasses are justifiable in themselves. This chapter and the last have explored a number of issues that arise on that front. A further matter, however, is whether, as a collectivity, the array of exceptions and bypasses involves too great a degree of confusion and too large a mass of uncertainty to offer efficiency and fairness. Viewed collectively, the question is whether a simpler, more rational and legally certain array of devices

---

170. See Cork Report, paras. 1538–41 and for discussion see Milman, 'Ten Per Cent Fund'; Carruthers and Halliday, *Rescuing Business*, chs. 4 and 7.

171. On insolvency issues raised by corporate groups see ch. 12 above, pp. 406–18.

172. As in the travel industry via ABTA.

173. On insurance limitations and availability see S. Shavell, 'On Liability and Insurance' (1982) 13 *Bell Journal of Economics* 120; S. Harrington, 'Prices and Profits in the Liability Insurance Market' in R. Litan and C. Winston (eds.), *Liability: Perspectives and Policy* (Brookings Institution, Washington D.C., 1988); V. Finch, 'Personal Accountability and Corporate Control: The Role of Directors' and Officers' Liability Insurance' (1994) 57 MLR 880 at 887–92.

might be devised. If it is accepted that well-resourced, well-informed creditors will take any steps they think rational to protect themselves against the risks of insolvency, the challenge is to allow them to do this at lowest cost consistent with the fair treatment of other unsecured creditors: to achieve an acceptable balance of efficiency-serving and distributionally fair ends. At present, it could be argued, the worst of two worlds is achieved: the well-resourced expend too much money and time on protection and the poorly-resourced are left with too small a fund to draw from. Such reasoning suggests that a statutory clarification of the law relating to exceptions and bypasses would have much to offer provided that this reduced legal uncertainties and the costs of achieving protections while, at the same time, it provided adequate protections (in the shape of, for example, 10 per cent funds) for those who cannot reasonably be expected to negotiate themselves into protected positions.

The final question for consideration in this chapter is whether the residual ordinary creditors who are left with a collectively 'fair' fund should be allocated shares in it *pari passu* or by other principles of distribution. To return to the children in our Orwellian classroom, distribution to the pupils might be governed by a principle of evenness but alternatives could be argued for. Larger shares could, for instance, be given to well-behaved children; to those who lodge confectionary claims first; to those who shout loudest; to those who need sugar most; to those who fared badly in prior distributions; or to those who would create most trouble if not favoured.

Let us now turn to consider the main alternatives to *pari passu* distribution of the residual estate.

Debts ranked chronologically

A first alternative to *pari passu* is to provide that debts be repaid from the residual estate with reference to the date of accrual on a first-come-first-served basis. Those with debts established at the earliest dates would, accordingly, be paid first. Such a regime might involve recording and disclosure mechanisms that would allow each creditor to assess the position before entrenching funds.

Such a regime would not, in itself, address the problems of exceptions and bypassing noted above and there might be efficiency costs. As a company entered troubled economic waters it would become progressively more difficult to raise funds since prospective creditors would know that, arriving 'late', they would rank low in the distributional order. The effect would be an increasing resort to security, quasi-security and trust devices and transaction costs would accordingly rise. The newly strong incentive to avoid the estate would, in turn, create increased uncertainty for other prospective unsecured creditors because assessing their lending risks would demand ever more complex and time-consuming analyses of the estate-avoiding measures that have been used in relation to the company. This would involve not only inefficiency but unfairness to the most poorly placed unsecured creditors since the latter would be in no position to evaluate their loan risks.

Debts ranked ethically

It would be possible to pay unsecured creditors according to their, or society's, needs, so that repayments would be organised on an ethical basis: say, in order to maximise the sum of human happiness.[174]

Such a utilitarian approach would be vulnerable to the standard criticisms of utilitarianism: how is happiness to be calculated and measured? Whose happiness counts? Does happiness achieved by unethical, even monstrous, means count?[175] Even if the tenets of utilitarianism were accepted, however, applying such an approach to insolvency would be difficult. There would be high levels of creditor uncertainty since predicting positions in the repayment queue would be nearly impossible (how does one unsecured creditor assess the likely advent of another unsecured creditor who is more worthy or needing of payment?). This would produce huge inefficiencies unless simpler, more predictable, more collectivist distributional rules were employed.[176]

Ethical approaches to repayment, however, raise general issues of collectivity. If the individual position or worth of a creditor is taken into account in distributing the residual estate then that individual position – whether it is assessed according to utilitarian principles or corrective

---

174. On ethics and insolvency generally see J. Kilpi, *The Ethics of Bankruptcy* (Routledge, London, 1998). For a utilitarian strategy see P. Shuchman, 'An Attempt at a "Philosophy of Bankruptcy"' (1973) 21 UCLA L Rev. 403.

175. On the limits of utilitarianism see e.g. A. Sen and B. Williams (eds.), *Utilitarianism and Beyond* (Cambridge University Press, Cambridge, 1982). On utilitarianism, legal and ethical efficiency issues see R. Posner, 'Utilitarianism, Economics and Legal Theory' (1979) 8 *Journal of Legal Studies* 103; R. M. Dworkin, 'Is Wealth a Value?' (1980) 9 *Journal of Legal Studies* 191; Dworkin, *A Matter of Principle* (Clarendon Press, Oxford, 1986) ch. 13; V. Finch, 'The Measures of Insolvency Law' (1997) 17 OJLS 227 at 239–40; ch. 2 above.

176. On rule utilitarianism and artificial virtues see D. Hume, *A Treatise of Human Nature*, L. Selby-Bigge and P. Nidditch (eds.) (Oxford University Press, Oxford, 1978); Shuchman, 'Philosophy of Bankruptcy', pp. 460–5.

justice[177] or other ethical principles – will be difficult to assess in advance and inefficiencies and unfairnesses would be caused by the inability of creditors to assess present and future risks. This is not to say that certain *classes* of creditor (for example, consumers, employees or other non-adjusting groups) might not merit special protections on ethical grounds. Reference to such classes in principles of estate distribution would be possible without the uncertainties involved in individual assessments and we see this approach already in the statutory treatment of preferential creditors. Questions arise, however, concerning the definition of such classes; the relative claims of different classes; the wide divergence of claims to deserve protection within the class membership; and the need to translate such ethical approaches into democratically endorsed policy form.

Debts ranked on size

It might be argued that small creditors should be paid at a higher rate of return than those ordinary unsecured creditors who have loaned larger sums to troubled firms. (David Milman has suggested a £750 threshold below which such special treatment should be applicable.[178]) The basis for doing so would be that small creditors are more vulnerable and deserve high levels of protection.

The problem with such a proposal is that it is difficult to correlate the size of the loan with the vulnerability of the creditor. Small lenders, for instance, may be better and more energetic risk spreaders than medium or large lenders: their businesses may involve large numbers of small loans rather than fewer loans of greater size. Small lenders may be able to adjust their loan rates quite effectively because the market may offer a range of deals and attendant risks. Small creditors may be more risk resilient and lower-cost risk bearers than some larger creditors: where, for example, the former's financial eggs are not all in one basket, they can absorb an insolvency loss fairly easily and there are not substantial ripple effects flowing from the loss. Nor can it be assumed that small creditors are necessarily less well informed, expert or strongly positioned to negotiate than larger creditors. This may depend on the particular market or organisational

---

177. See Ogus and Rowley, *Prepayments and Insolvency*, p. 15; R. Epstein, 'A Theory of Strict Liability' (1973) 2 *Journal of Legal Studies* 151; Schwartz, 'Security Interests and Bankruptcy Priorities'. See also Kilpi, *Ethics of Bankruptcy*.
178. See D. Milman, 'Priority Rights on Corporate Insolvency' in A. Clarke (ed.), *Current Issues in Insolvency Law* (Stevens & Sons, London, 1991) p. 78.

set-up involved, the relevant regulatory regime or even the state of the economy.

Debts paid on policy grounds

If policy grounds underpin the placing of some creditors ahead of the residual estate this is not so much an alternative way of residual estate distribution as an alternative construction of the estate as a whole. A genuine alternative to *pari passu* in relation to the residual estate would involve paying different ordinary creditors at different rates. One mooted candidate for special treatment is the consumer creditor. It has been argued that this class of unsecured creditor might be entitled to a higher rate of return as compared to trade creditors because the latter 'should be more aware of the risks involved in extending credit to the company' and because 'bad debt insurance is increasingly available to trade creditors'.[179] Consumer creditors, moreover, are said to suffer disproportionately on the debtor's insolvency.[180]

It might be countered that the mooted special treatment would make life more difficult for IPs, would increase transaction costs and should be opposed on that basis. Such efficiency costs might be worth paying, however, if more than compensated for by attendant improvements in fairness. On these points, however, reference can be made to the last chapter's discussion of preference for consumer creditors and, to recap, it could be said that many trade creditors are far more harshly affected by corporate insolvencies than the average consumer creditor: their livelihood may depend on payment, and some trade creditors may be less able to evaluate risks, adjust terms or insure against bad debts than some consumers. On such questions of creditor vulnerability much turns, again, on such matters as the type of transaction involved, the pattern of risk spreading, the mode of payment, the market traditions, the levels of competition in the sector, the quality of information on suppliers that is available and the rate of turnover of business in the sector. If one is really concerned with fairness, it could be said, attention should be paid not to consumers as a class but to protections for individual creditors who are ill-positioned to evaluate risks or sustain economic shocks. Here, though, proponents of change are in a difficult position. It is difficult to make a general class claim, and to take on board individual circumstances introduces the uncertainties and inefficiencies noted above in relation to ethical approaches.

179. Ibid.   180. Ibid., p. 78.

Conclusions

Any discussion of *pari passu* has to bear in mind the link between issues of residual estate distribution and issues of estate construction as a whole. The import of the above discussion is that if fairness and efficiency are sought in the distribution of the residual estate, the case for a collective approach is a strong one. To take on board individual positions, vulnerabilities or ethical merits produces too great an accumulation of uncertainties and transaction costs to provide either fair or efficient processes.

It has also been argued above, however, that concerns for the fair and efficient treatment of creditors may be served by looking beyond questions of residue distribution. A blinkered focus on *pari passu* should, accordingly, be avoided. Not only is it relevant to look to questions of estate construction more generally but attention should be paid to protections for 'vulnerable' risk bearers in the form of procedural requirements (of information provision and disclosure); to substantive protections of a general nature (such as a 10 per cent fund for ordinary unsecured creditors); to ways of reducing overall risks of insolvency (for example, by improvements in managerial standards and training); and to modes of lowering risks to the vulnerable by spreading insolvency risks. This spreading can be achieved, for instance, by extending risks across corporate groups; by establishing compensation regimes and by relying on (or instituting and requiring) insurance provision.

Pari passu plays a role in insolvency proceedings but this role is limited by the context described above. Improvements in the legal regime are possible, however. Exceptions and bypasses could be clarified and steps could be designed to limit the extent to which poorly placed creditors bear undue risks because of their inability to adjust terms in the light of assessable risks. One general development would be the infusion of greater transparency and more readily available information into insolvency processes (for example, by disclosure rules on ROT clauses). There seems no strong case for major new allocations of preferential status,[181] however, and this points to a broad strategy of improving the general position of the unsecured ordinary creditor by steps such as the 10 per cent fund.

---

181. A minor new allocation might be claimants seeking restitution of unjust enrichments: see V. Finch and S. Worthington, 'The *Pari Passu* Principle and Ranking Restitutionary Claims' in Rose, *Restitution and Insolvency*.

As for the contention that *pari passu* is not the best way to distribute the residual estate, those alternatives to *pari passu* that are based on assessments of the individual position or merit of the creditor would be objectionable, as noted, on grounds of uncertainty, inefficiency and unfairness. Those based on new approaches to the definition of classes face problems of heterogeneity in class membership and in demonstrating why classes selected for new special rates of repayment have claims that are generally stronger than competing classes.

Part V

The impact of corporate insolvency

15

Directors in troubled times

The rules and processes that make up insolvency law operate as a set of incentives and constraints that influence how company directors behave at times of both good and bad corporate fortune. This chapter considers how those incentives and constraints operate and examines the assumptions and philosophies that underpin the role of the company director in insolvency law. The analysis offered here continues the approach set out in chapter 2 and asks whether current insolvency law deals with directors in a manner that renders directors appropriately accountable, makes the best use of directorial expertise, conduces to efficient outcomes and is consistent with the fair treatment of directors and parties affected by directorial behaviour. For the purposes of clarity of exposition, the issue of accountability will be considered first, since this involves a mapping out of the broad array of influences and constraints that insolvency law applies to directors – a mapping exercise that should provide a useful background to the discussions of expertise, efficiency and fairness that follow.

Accountability

Directorial accountability can operate through a variety of devices – which will be considered below – but the purposes to be served by such devices may also vary. Insolvency law, for instance, might set out to punish an errant director; to protect creditors at risk from directorial actions; to compensate parties who have suffered losses at the hands of directors; and insolvency law and company law may also seek to achieve a number of other ends such as raising standards of business conduct and entrepreneurship.

A search for the purposes underlying current corporate insolvency law controls over directors can begin with the Cork Report.[1] Cork emphasised that the function of insolvency law was not merely to distribute the insolvency estate to creditors. Other objectives were to encourage debt recovery (and persuade debtors to pay or propose settlements of debts) and, through investigations and disciplinary actions, to meet 'the demands of commercial morality'.[2] Central here, then, was the notion that insolvency law and investigative processes would uncover assets concealed from creditors, ascertain the validity of creditors' claims, and expose the circumstances surrounding the debtor's failure. Anything less, said Cork, would be unacceptable in a trading community and would lead to 'a lowering of business standards and an erosion of confidence in our insolvency law'.[3] This was a matter not merely of punishing the errant, said Cork, but of exposing affairs to creditors and encouraging public scrutiny.[4] Society had an interest in insolvency processes and attention, accordingly, needed to be paid to whether or not fault or blame attached to the conduct of the insolvent party; whether punishment was merited; whether the party should be restricted so as to prevent repetition of errant conduct; and whether responsibility for the insolvency was attributable to someone other than the director.[5] Cork, thus, emphasised the need for insolvency law to promote the 'highest standards of business probity and competence' and noted, in particular, the disquiet that was widespread in the commercial and practitioner communities concerning the lenient manner in which the law dealt with the directors of insolvent companies, which was often compared unfavourably with the law's stricter approach to the individual bankrupt.[6] Cork accepted that a fresh approach was justified, not least to deal with the dishonesty and malpractices of 'fly by night' operators and the losses imposed on ordinary unsophisticated creditors. That fresh approach was to be implemented through Cork's proposals *inter alia* for a new concept of wrongful trading liability and broader powers for court disqualification of delinquent directors (with automatic exposure to personal liability for certain debts). These were proposals

---

1. *Report of the Review Committee on Insolvency Law and Practice* (Cmnd 8558, 1982) ('Cork Report').
2. Cork Report, para. 235; see B. G. Carruthers and T. C. Halliday, *Rescuing Business: The Making of Corporate Bankruptcy Law in England and the United States* (Clarendon Press, Oxford, 1998) pp. 266–83.
3. Cork Report, para. 238.   4. Ibid., para. 239.   5. Ibid., para. 1735.
6. See further W. R. Cornish and G. de N. Clark, *Law and Society in England 1750–1950* (Sweet & Maxwell, London, 1989) ch. 3, part 2. On proposed reforms to bankruptcy law and attitudes to bankrupts see Insolvency Service, *Bankruptcy: A Fresh Start* (2000); DTI/IS White Paper, *Productivity and Enterprise: Insolvency – A Second Chance* (Cm 5234, July 2001).

infused with rationales ranging from punishment to restitution; prevention to retribution.[7] It should not be forgotten, however, that Cork saw proposals that were designed to impose stricter controls on directors as merely one aspect of a package of reforms that, amongst other things, aimed to facilitate rescues and to limit the losses that might result from directorial deficiencies or other misfortunes.

The statutory legacy of Cork will be dealt with below but it is worth noting first that recent years have seen a shift in emphasis away from Cork's concerns both to redress the law's lenient treatment of directors and to do something about 'phoenix company' problems.[8] The Blair Government has been marked by a stress on the virtues of entrepreneurship and risk taking as necessary components of wealth creation. The White Paper on Enterprise, Skill and Innovation of 2001[9] encapsulated this approach with its aims to 'help create an ambitious business culture' and proposals including 'significantly relaxing insolvency rules so that honest businesses and individuals who go bankrupt have a better chance of starting again quicker while cracking down on the fraudulent and irresponsible'. Peter Mandelson, when Trade Secretary, paved the way for such an 'entrepreneurial' approach and, in 1998, he made a series of speeches on encouraging entrepreneurial risk taking.[10]

As for cracking down on 'rogue' directors, Companies House, in 1997, created a new website listing directors subject to disqualification orders.[11] In 1998 a 'hotline'[12] was set up to allow the public to report rogue

7. See Carruthers and Halliday, *Rescuing Business*, pp. 274–7.

8. The 'phoenix' syndrome occurs when the activities of a failed company are continued by those responsible, using the vehicle of a new company, or where a director engages in serial corporate failure, leaving creditors stranded with those failures, and moves on to a new company while concealing past failures from the public: see Company Law Review Steering Group, *Modern Company Law for a Competitive Economy: Final Report* (2001) paras. 15.55–15.77. Data from CCN, the credit investigation agency, suggests that there are more than 300,000 directors with more than one failed company behind them and, of these, 4,000 have ten or more failures behind them: see N. Cohen, 'Dangerous Directors', *Financial Times*, 16 December 1996.

9. DTI, *Opportunity for All in a World of Change – A White Paper on Enterprise, Skill and Innovation* (DTI, February 2001).

10. See ch. 6 above; DTI White Paper, *Our Competitive Future: Building the Knowledge Driven Economy* (December 1998) paras. 2.12–2.14; Insolvency Service, *A Review of Company Rescue and Business Reconstruction Mechanisms*, Interim Report (1999); *A Review of Company Rescue and Business Reconstruction Mechanisms, Report by the Review Group* (2000). On the European Commission's approach to insolvency as part of its strategy for promoting entrepreneurship and 'desirable risk taking' see European Commission, *Communication from the Commission to the Council and the European Parliament: Progress Report on the Risk Capital Action Plan*, COM (2000) 658 final (18 October 2000) p. 14.

11. See http://www.companieshouse.gov.uk. On disqualification of directors see pp. 521–37, 548–9 below.

12. The number is: 0845 601 3546.

directors to the Insolvency Service (IS) and the IS took over 2,300 calls from January 1998 to April 2001. A further significant step was taken in 2000 when the Minister for Competition and Consumer Affairs, Dr Kim Howells, announced the setting up by the IS of a specialist team to investigate directors who asset-strip companies which then become insolvent. The Forensic Insolvency Recovery Service (FIRS) was established as a team of private sector and IS partners comprising lawyers, insolvency practitioners and enquiry agents. The team was given powers to take legal actions to recover assets.[13] Dr Howells urged in April 2001 that there should be 'no hiding place' for unscrupulous directors.

The 2001 White Paper on Enterprise, Skill and Innovation emphasised the importance of distinguishing between honest and culpable failures. This line was particularly salient in the White Paper's treatment of personal bankruptcies, where it was promised that honest failures would not be punished or stigmatised, while those which were fraudulent or culpable would be dealt with more severely. In the case of companies, the White Paper promised legislation to promote a rescue culture and to speed up the disqualification of unfit company directors. It was, nevertheless, clear from press releases that the distinction between honest and culpable failures was one that the government applied as much to the corporate as to the individual sphere of insolvency.[14]

What then are the mechanisms that insolvency law establishes for holding directors to account? If the rules on disqualification are left out of account – for consideration later under the heading of expertise – accountability mechanisms can, perhaps, best be set out by discussing, first, the array of rules that provide for liability and, second, the associated issues of

---

13. See D. Milman, 'Controlling Managerial Abuse: Current State of Play' [2000] Ins. Law. 193; DTI Press Notice P/2000/510. In the year to 31 March 2001 there were 1,548 disqualifications: Insolvency Service Annual Report 2000–1, p. 17; see further pp. 502, 532–7, 548–9 below.

14. See, for example, 'DTI to Back "Honest Failure"', *Observer*, 15 July 2001. The courts have also played a role regarding 'culpable' corporate failures and have, *inter alia*, extended the notion of a 'shadow director' for the purposes of Company Directors' Disqualification Act 1986 s. 22(5)). In *Secretary of State for Trade and Industry* v. *Deverell* [2000] 2 WLR 907 the Court of Appeal widened the category of persons who may be 'shadow directors' to look to the reality of action within the company, emphasise public protection and include those whose frequent non-professional advice is acted upon. Board subservience was not a precondition of being a shadow director: see J. Payne, 'Casting Light into the Shadows: *Secretary of State for Trade and Industry* v. *Deverell*' (2001) 22 Co. Law. 90–1; see further p. 435 below. On stricter judicial approaches to disqualification see *Secretary of State for Trade and Industry* v. *Gray* [1995] 1 BCLC 276; R. Gilby and R. Pugh, 'Caveat Director!' (1995) 11 IL&P 21; see further pp. 524–6 below. See also Editorial, 'Enterprise Culture v. Stakeholder Protection' (2001) IL&P 121–3, referring to the UK's 'comprehensive and sophisticated set of sanctions' at p. 121.

enforcement. A starting point is the set of common law duties that a director owes to a company.

Common law duties

In general a director cannot be made liable in insolvency for the obligations of his or her company.[15] It has long been established, however, that a director owes a fiduciary duty to act *bona fide* in the best interests of the company[16] and, in an insolvency, this duty may come into play. A liquidator, for instance, may mount a claim against the director personally where the director's negligent conduct has diminished the insolvency estate.[17]

A second set of issues surrounds the set of duties that directors owe to company creditors. Here a review of case law reveals that the courts have taken divergent views on the nature of the duty owed by directors to creditors. Is it to be seen as an aspect of the traditional fiduciary duty of directors to act *bona fide* in the interests of the company,[18] or is it an independent, positive duty owed directly to creditors and founded either on ordinary principles of directors' duty of care or on tortious principles?[19]

In favour of the idea that duties to creditors flow from the traditional fiduciary duty to act in the best interests of the company, there are a number of English court decisions that build on a series of Commonwealth cases. Notable among the latter is *Walker* v. *Wimborne*[20] in which the Australian High Court spoke of 'directors of a company in discharging their duty to the company [having to] take account of the interest of its shareholders and its creditors' (Mason J). Similarly, in *Nicholson* v.

---

15. *Salomon* v. *A. Salomon & Co. Ltd* [1897] AC 22.

16. See *Re Smith and Fawcett Ltd* [1942] Ch 304. On the degree of care owed see Romer J in *Re City Equitable Fire Insurance Co.* [1925] Ch 407; *Dorchester Finance Co. Ltd* v. *Stebbing* [1989] BCLC 498; V. Finch, 'Company Directors: Who Cares About Skill and Care?' (1992) 55 MLR 179.

17. See *Re D'Jan of London Ltd* [1993] BCC 646, discussed in S. Griffin, *Personal Liability and Disqualification of Company Directors* (Hart, Oxford, 1999) pp. 27–9.

18. See *Re Smith and Fawcett Ltd* [1942] Ch 304.

19. This account draws on V. Finch, 'Creditors' Interests and Directors' Obligations' in S. Sheikh and W. Rees (eds.), *Corporate Governance and Corporate Control* (Cavendish, London, 1995) and Finch, 'Directors' Duties: Insolvency and the Unsecured Creditor' in A. Clarke (ed.), *Current Issues in Insolvency Law* (Stevens, London, 1991). On directors' duties to creditors see also R. Grantham, 'The Judicial Extension of Directors' Duties to Creditors' [1991] JBL 1; D. Prentice, 'Creditors' Interest and Directors' Duties' (1990) 10 OJLS 265; L. S. Sealy, 'Directors' "Wider" Responsibilities: Problems, Conceptual, Practical and Procedural' (1987) 13 Monash LR 164; J. S. Ziegel, 'Creditors as Corporate Stakeholders' (1993) 43 U Toronto LJ 511; C. Riley, 'Directors' Duties and the Interests of Creditors' (1989) 10 Co. Law. 87.

20. [1976] 50 ALJR 446 at 449. Noted: R. Baxt (1976) 50 ALJ 591.

Permakraft[21] Cooke J, sitting in the New Zealand Court of Appeal, concluded *obiter* that directors' duties to the company 'may require them to consider *inter alia* the interests of creditors'.[22] During the 1980s the English courts echoed this approach. In *Lonrho* v. *Shell Petroleum*[23] Diplock LJ indicated that the 'best interests of the company' might not be exclusively those of shareholders 'but may include those of creditors'. Buckley LJ in *Re Horsley and Weight Ltd*[24] referred to the 'loose' terminology of 'directors owing an indirect duty to creditors not to permit any unlawful reduction of capital to occur' and stated that it was more accurate to say that directors 'owe a duty to the company in this respect'. In both the Court of Appeal and the House of Lords decisions in *Brady* v. *Brady*[25] it was indicated (by Nourse LJ and Lord Oliver) that directors needed to consider creditors' interests if they were to act in the interests of the company.

Contrasting with this approach are dicta suggesting that there is a direct and specific duty that is owed to creditors. Thus, in *Winkworth* v. *Edward Baron Developments Co. Ltd*[26] Lord Templeman stated: 'A duty is owed by the directors of the company and to the creditors of the company to ensure that the affairs of the company are properly administered and that its property is not dissipated or exploited for the benefit of directors themselves to the prejudice of creditors.'[27] His Lordship's distinction between the company and the creditors here implied the notion of a specific duty to the latter.[28] The most recent indications are, however, that the courts may be unwilling to recognise a duty owed directly to creditors.[29] In the *Yukong* case[30] Toulson J considered *West Mercia*[31] and stated that where a director acted in breach of his duty to the company by causing assets of the company to be transferred in disregard of the interests of its creditor or creditors, he was answerable through the scheme Parliament had provided in the Insolvency Act 1986 section 212, but 'he does not owe a direct fiduciary

---

21. [1985] 1 NZLR 242.
22. Ibid., at 249. Noted: [1985] JBL 413. See also *Kinsela* v. *Russell Kinsela Pty Ltd* (1986) 4 ACLC 215, noted Baxt (1986) 14 ABLR 320.
23. [1980] 1 WLR 627 at 634.   24. [1982] 3 All ER 1045 at 1055–6.
25. [1989] 3 BCC 535 (CA), [1988] 2 All ER 617 (HL). See Riley, 'Directors' Duties and the Interests of Creditors'.
26. [1987] 1 All ER 114.   27. Ibid., at 118.
28. See also *Hooker Investments Pty Ltd* v. *Email Ltd* (1986) 10 ACLR 443.
29. See further pp. 508–10, 519 below. See also Prentice, 'Creditors' Interest', p. 275; L. S. Sealy, 'Personal Liability of Directors and Officers for Debts of Insolvent Corporations: A Jurisdictional Perspective (England)' in J. Ziegel (ed.), *Current Developments in International and Comparative Corporate Insolvency Law* (Clarendon Press, Oxford, 1994) p. 486.
30. *Yukong Lines Ltd of Korea* v. *Rendsburg Investments Corporation and Others* [1998] BCC 870; see also T. Ogowewo, 'A Perfect Case for the Application of Section 423 of the Insolvency Act 1986: *Yukong Line of Korea* v. *Rendsburg Investments Corp. of Liberia (No. 2)*' [1999] Ins. Law. 106.
31. *West Mercia Safety Wear Ltd* v. *Dodd* [1988] 4 BCC 30.

duty towards an individual creditor nor is an individual creditor entitled to sue for breach of the fiduciary duty owed by the director to the company'.[32] It remains to be seen if *Yukong* is the last word. If a direct duty to creditors *were* to be resuscitated by the courts then the question as to the nature of that duty would arise. Is the duty, for example, to be seen as an extension of the directors' traditional duty of care or is it to be seen as one grounded in tortious principles?[33]

To view duties to creditors as part of the traditional duty to act *bona fide* in the company's interests is not without problems: are creditors' interests to be considered independently or merely in so far as they are relevant to the company's interests?[34] Are creditors' interests to be part of a package of claims (i.e. including those of shareholders and employees), in which case how will directors proceed if these constituent company interests conflict?[35] Is, moreover, directorial consideration of creditors' interests to be assessed subjectively or objectively? Subjectivity may be consistent with principle[36] but would pose problems of accountability[37] and an objective approach could draw the judges into assessment of directors' business decisions.[38] The judges have yet to resolve these questions, but judicial opinion does currently favour treating the duty as part of the interests of the company.[39]

The beneficiaries of the duty

Judges have tended to speak of creditors as a homogeneous group but have failed to state clearly whether directors owe a duty to creditors generally, to

32. *Yukong Lines Ltd of Korea* v. *Rendsburg Investments Corp. of Liberia (No. 2)* [1998] BCC 870 at 884.
33. See further Finch, 'Creditors' Interests and Directors' Obligations'.
34. See P. Finn (ed.), *Equity and Commercial Relationships* (Law Book Co., Sydney, 1987) ch. 5 ('Directors' Duties and the Company's Interests') where Hayden argues that conduct which injures a creditor may also injure the company in that it may force a receiver's appointment, damaging the reputation and life of an otherwise successful company.
35. See V. Finch, 'Directors' Duties Towards Creditors' (1989) 10 Co. Law. 23.
36. See *Re Smith and Fawcett* [1942] Ch 304: the duty is to act *bona fide* in what the director considers, not what the court considers, is in the company's interests (per Lord Greene). See also *Regentcrest plc (in liquidation)* v. *Cohen* [2001] BCC 494, where Jonathan Parker J, in dismissing a claim brought by liquidators against a director for breach of his fiduciary duty to act *bona fide* in the best interest of the company, stated the duty was to be judged on a subjective basis: if (the director) 'honestly believed that he was acting in the best interests of the company' he was not in breach.
37. How could creditors ever be secure in the knowledge that consideration of their interests was ever more than lip service? See Sealy, 'Directors' "Wider" Responsibilities'.
38. See *Carlen* v. *Drury* (1812) 1 Ves & B 154. But see dicta of Temple LJ in *Re Horsley and Weight Ltd* [1982] 3 All ER 1045: 'the directors ought to have known the facts', at 1056; Cooke J in *Nicholson* v. *Permakraft* [1985] 1 NZLR 242 at 250 also favoured an objective approach.
39. See, for example, the Federal Court of Australia in *Re New World Alliance Pty Ltd*, Fed. No. 332/94, 26 May 1994. See also *Kuwait Asia Bank EC* v. *National Mutual Life Nominees Ltd* [1991] 1 AC 187; *Yukong Line of Korea* v. *Rendsburg Investments Corporation and others* [1998] BCC 870.

individual creditors, or to a class of creditors. Attempts have been made to distinguish the interests of existing creditors from those of future creditors but, even in this endeavour, inconsistent approaches are to be encountered. Thus, in *Nicholson* v. *Permakraft*[40] Cooke J indicated that future creditors might normally be expected to 'take the company as it is' and guard their own interests, whereas in *Winkworth* v. *Edward Baron*[41] Lord Templeman urged that 'duties were owed to creditors present and future to keep its property inviolate and available for the payment of debts'.

As for existing creditors, these may possess highly conflicting interests: the unsecured trade creditor is in a quite different position from the bank with a floating charge over the company's property.[42] The courts have yet to offer clear guidance to the director who has to choose between such competing interests[43] and an undifferentiated approach may reduce the force of such a duty quite considerably: 'Where duties are owed to persons with potentially opposed interests, the duty bifurcates and fragments so that it amounts ultimately to no more than a vague obligation to be fair ... If the law does this it abandons all effective control over the decision maker.'[44] Distinguishing between classes of creditor seems necessary, if nothing else, for the purposes of rendering duties potentially effective. If unsecured creditors are to be protected, the judges would have to construe the duty as owed to them either individually or as a specific class and the latter approach would seem more consistent with the notion of bankruptcy as a collective procedure concerned with *pari passu* distribution according to pre-bankruptcy entitlements.[45]

A further issue the courts have yet to resolve concerns the exclusivity of the attention that directors should give to creditor interests when those

40. [1985] 1 NZLR 242.

41. [1987] 1 All ER 114; see also *Kinsela* v. *Russell Kinsela Pty Ltd* (1986) 4 ACLC 215 at 221 (future creditors); *Jeffree* v. *National Companies & Securities Commission* (1989) 7 ACLC 556 at 561 (contingent creditors).

42. See Riley, 'Directors' Duties and the Interests of Creditors'.

43. For example, directors may have to choose between using remaining assets to pay off preferential creditors or continuing trading in the hope of benefiting unsecured creditors. (Of course, choosing to trade on for the benefit of unsecured creditors rather than immediately paying preferential debts is not necessarily improper: see *Re CU Fittings Ltd* [1989] 5 BCC 210 (a disqualification case, noted in V. Finch, 'Disqualification of Directors: A Plea for Competence' (1990) 53 MLR 385).)

44. Sealy, 'Directors' "Wider" Responsibilities', p. 175.

45. To give unsecured creditors a class action would guide directors rather than leaving them to attempt to be fair 'to all creditors' and would not seem prejudicial to secured creditors who would be able to realise their security or appoint a receiver to act on their behalf: see further Finch, 'Directors' Duties: Insolvency and the Unsecured Creditor', p. 105. See also T. H. Jackson, *The Logic and Limits of Bankruptcy Law* (Harvard University Press, Cambridge, Mass., 1986); Jackson, 'Bankruptcy, Non-bankruptcy Entitlements and the Creditors' Bargain' (1982) 91 Yale LJ 857.

interests fall to be considered.[46] Some authorities come close to making creditor interests an exclusive focus. Thus, in *Brady* v. *Brady*,[47] Nourse LJ, in the Court of Appeal, indicated that after the advent of insolvency (or doubtful insolvency) the interests of the company 'are in reality the interests of existing creditors alone'.[48] This implies that the directors have a duty to pursue the advantage of creditors, an approach consistent with the comments of Street CJ in *Kinsela*[49] to the effect that in an insolvent company it is the creditors' and not the shareholders' assets that are under the management of the directors.[50]

A contrasting approach allows directors to act post-insolvency in the interests of the company as a whole, provided that actions do not prejudice creditors. Thus, in *Re Welfab Engineers Ltd*,[51] Hoffmann J considered the position where a company was insolvent but had not been placed in the hands of a receiver. He stated that although the directors were not, at such a stage, entitled to act in a manner leaving the creditors in a worse position than on a liquidation, they had not failed in their duty to the company when they had borne in mind the effect on employees of different courses of action.[52]

A way to resolve such tensions is to read dicta in *Brady* and *Kinsela* as being concerned with the reorientation of focus from shareholder to creditor interests that occurs around the point of insolvency rather than being concerned to address the issue of exclusivity of interest. The judges could endorse *Welfab* and stress that creditor interests fall to be considered on insolvency (or doubtful insolvency) but that such interests do not have to be the exclusive concerns of directors. Just as directors are entitled to look beyond shareholder interests before insolvency[53] they should be given a degree of flexibility in relation to the interests of the creditors, who, on insolvency, have stepped into the shoes of the shareholders.[54]

---

46. See generally R. Grantham, 'Directors' Duties and Insolvent Companies' (1991) 65 MLR 576.

47. [1989] 3 BCC 535.

48. Ibid., p. 552. This appears unaffected by the House of Lords' decision in *Brady* and indeed is impliedly accepted by Lord Oliver: see [1988] 2 All ER 617 at 632.

49. (1986) 4 ACLC 215.   **50.** Ibid., at p. 730.   **51.** [1990] BCC 600.

52. See Grantham, 'Directors' Duties and Insolvent Companies', p. 578: 'the importance of *Welfab* lies in Hoffmann J's affirmation that, while they should not be exploited, so long as creditors leave the company in the directors' hands, the company will not be run primarily for their benefit'.

53. See Sealy 'Directors' "Wider" Responsibilities'; Companies Act 1985 s. 309.

54. See the discussion of the Company Law Review Steering Group proposals at pp. 508–10 below.

When does the duty arise?

Even if it is accepted that the duty to creditors flows from the traditional duty to act in the company's interests, the courts have been tentative in stating when creditors' interests fall to be considered by directors as part of those company interests. Three positions on the issue can be distinguished:

(a) When a company becomes insolvent the interests of creditors are company interests.
(b) Creditors' interests transform into company interests as the company approaches insolvency or when insolvency is threatened.
(c) The interests of the company include those of creditors and directors should bear in mind creditors' interests at all times.

The judges have hovered, sometimes uneasily, between these three positions. In support of position (a) is the *West Mercia*[55] decision of the Court of Appeal in which a director effected a fraudulent preference and was found to be guilty of a breach of duty (the director had, for his own purposes, made a transfer between accounts in disregard of the interests of the general creditors of the insolvent company). *West Mercia* indicated that where a company is insolvent, a director's duty to act in the best interests of the company includes a duty to protect the interests of the company's creditors. Dillon LJ noted with approval Street CJ's statement in the Australian case of *Kinsela* v. *Russell Kinsela Property Ltd*:[56]

> In a solvent company the proprietary interests of the shareholders entitle them as a general body to be regarded as the company when questions of the duty of directors arise … But where a company is insolvent the interests of creditors intrude. They become prospectively entitled, through the mechanism of liquidation, to displace the power of the shareholders and directors to deal with the company's assets.

Whether insolvency is a precondition of creditor interests being subsumed within company interests is, however, a matter not beyond doubt. A number of cases extend the principle to incipient insolvency or even threatened insolvency. Thus the Court of Appeal in *Re Horsley & Weight Ltd*[57] stated that insolvency, or near insolvency, was a precondition, and a similar stance appeared to be taken by the New Zealand Court of Appeal in *Nicholson* v. *Permakraft*.[58] In *Nicholson* the company was solvent at the relevant time

55. [1988] 4 BCC 30.   56. (1986) 4 ACLC 215 at 401.   57. [1982] 3 All ER 1045.
58. [1985] 1 NZLR 242. See also *Grove* v. *Flavel* (1986) 4 ACLC 654 where the court rejected the argument that there was a general duty owed by directors to protect creditors' interests irrespective of the company's financial position.

but Cooke J considered situations in which directors should consider creditors' interests. These included circumstances of insolvency or near insolvency or doubtful insolvency or if the 'contemplated payment or other course of action could jeopardise its solvency'. Such reasoning may accord to some extent with position (b) and the idea that creditor interests fall to be considered in so far as insolvency looms. This is echoed in, for example, Nourse LJ's dicta in *Brady v Brady*[59] where His Lordship considered the meaning of 'given in good faith in the interest of the company' in section 153 of the Companies Act 1985[60] and stated that where the company is insolvent or even doubtfully solvent, the interests of the company are in reality the interests of the existing creditors alone.

Certain cases go further and adopt a stance close to position (c) by suggesting that insolvency *per se* is no precondition to consideration of creditors' interests. In the High Court of Australia in *Walker v. Wimborne*[61] Mason J indicated that creditors' interests should be considered even before insolvency because 'those interests may be prejudiced by the movement of funds between companies in the event that the companies become insolvent'. Thus, creditors' interests could always be relevant given the theoretical possibility of future insolvency.[62] *Nicholson v. Permakraft*[63] is not far short of this position in referring to circumstances in which a contemplated payment or other course of action might jeopardise solvency. There are dicta, moreover, in two House of Lords decisions in which duties to creditors are mooted and the issue of insolvency is not even referred to.[64]

The courts have thus adopted a variety of positions on directors' duties to creditors[65] and, although *West Mercia*[66] sought to clarify the common law in pointing to an intrusion of creditors' interests on insolvency or

---

59. See [1989] 3 BCC 535 at 552.
60. Nourse LJ assumed that the words in the Companies Act 1985 s. 153(1)(b) had the same meaning in that context as when considering directors' fiduciary duties.
61. (1976) 137 CLR 1; (1978) 3 ACLR 529. See also *Facia Footwear Ltd (in administration) v. Hinchliffe* [1998] 1 BCLC 218; *Galladin Pty Ltd v. Aimnorth Pty Ltd* (1993) 11 ACSR 23; *Wright v. Frisnia* (1983) 1 ACLC 716.
62. See Barrett (1977) 40 MLR 229.   63. [1985] 1 NZLR 242.
64. In *Lonrho v. Shell Petroleum* [1980] 1 WLR 627, Lord Diplock, when speaking of the best interests of the company not necessarily being those of shareholders alone but possibly including those of creditors, made no mention of solvency or insolvency. Neither did Lord Templeman in *Winkworth v. Edward Baron Developments Co. Ltd.* [1986] 1 WLR 1512, when he was speaking of the duty apparently directly owed to creditors.
65. Per Giles JA in *Linton v. Telnet Pty Ltd* (1999) 30 ACSR 465 at 473: there is significant difficulty in deciding when directors should have regard to creditors' interests and it depends on the particular facts.
66. [1988] 4 BCC 30.

prospective insolvency, a good deal of further clarification is required. *West Mercia* did not explain in a satisfactory manner how to identify the point at which a prospective insolvency becomes real enough to call for the reorientation of directors' attitudes towards creditors. *West Mercia*, moreover, did not address the issue of whether the directors' state of appreciation of the company's solvency was to be judged objectively or subjectively.

On the 'prospect of insolvency' issue, the Cork Committee[67] acknowledged that although insolvency arises at the moment when debts have not been met as they fall due, 'the moment is often difficult to pinpoint precisely'. The English courts, nevertheless, would not be without guidance in seeking to devise a test. Cooke J in *Nicholson* suggested that, although balance sheet solvency and the ability to pay capital dividends were important in assessing any actions taken, nevertheless:

> as a matter of business ethics it is proper for directors to consider also whether what they will do will prejudice the company's practical ability to discharge promptly debts owed to current and likely continuing trade creditors…because if the company's financial position is precarious the futures of such suppliers may be so linked with those of the company as to bring them within the reasonable scope of the directors' duty.[68]

An alternative approach to definition might be derived from the statutory criteria of the Insolvency Act 1986: for example, the definition of inability to pay debts found in section 123(2) which, *inter alia*, adopts the liabilities test and the strict balance sheet approach of total assets exceeding total liabilities, 'taking into account contingent and prospective liabilities'. Section 123(1)(e), on the other hand, provides a cash flow test by which a company is deemed unable to pay its debts 'if it is proved to the satisfaction of the court that the company is unable to pay its debts as they fall due'.[69]

As for the test to be applied regarding the director's state of appreciation of the company's solvency, different approaches, again, might be taken. Templeman LJ took an objective approach in *Horsley & Weight* in stating that if expenditure threatens the existence of the company 'the directors ought to have known the facts'.[70] In contrast, it can be argued that the subjective approach is appropriate in all cases involving the general fiduciary duty of directors to act in good faith in the interest of the

---

67. Cork Report, para. 205.   68. [1985] 1 NZLR 242, 249.
69. See ch. 4 above; R. M. Goode, *Principles of Corporate Insolvency Law* (2nd edn, Sweet & Maxwell, London, 1997) ch. 4.
70. [1982] 3 All ER 1045 at 1056.

company. Thus Jonathan Parker J has recently stated that this duty is what the director can, and does, honestly believe to be in the company's best interest.[71]

One reason for moving to greater objectivity, however, is the argument that creditors' interests warrant greater protection than can be offered by a subjective test. After all, it can be contended, if creditors' interests only enter the scene when solvency is at issue and if creditors are disadvantaged *vis-à-vis* shareholders in so far as they are likely to have less information as to the company's solvency, then a director's appreciation of whether a transaction will prejudice the creditors further should be measured against an objective benchmark. Such reasoning favours the approach adopted in the wrongful trading provisions of the Insolvency Act 1986 section 214.[72] According to this approach directors should be expected to exhibit the same degree of appreciation of their company's viability as would reasonably be expected of a diligent person exercising their functions in the company. A standard of performance is demanded, accordingly, which is consistent with the idea of a minimum level of competence.[73] Directors, on this view, would be bound to give good faith consideration to creditors' interests from the moment they know *or ought to have concluded* that the company's solvency is at the very least doubtful.

To summarise, then, the judges have failed to state clearly when the duty arises or what state of mind or knowledge renders the director potentially liable. Directors seeking guidance on the former issue have to rely on a confusion of dicta and statutory tests. Judges may inevitably have to exercise discretion in assessing the point of doubtful solvency in particular contexts but more coherent structuring of that discretion is necessary if directors and creditors are to know where they stand.

An Institute of Directors survey of members was published in 1999[74] and revealed that there was widespread uncertainty in UK boardrooms over directors' obligations to consider the interests of different groups

---

71. *Regentcrest plc (in liquidation)* v. *Cohen* [2001] BCC 494.

72. See Insolvency Act 1986 s. 214(4)(a). On section 214, however, and problems of inconsistency of judicial approach, see pp. 512–15 below.

73. For discussion of the influence of the 'statutory lead' of Insolvency Act 1986 s. 214 on the general duty of skill and care, see Finch, 'Company Directors', pp. 202–4; D. Arsalidou, 'The Impact of Section 214(4) of the Insolvency Act 1986 on Directors' Duties' (2000) 21 Co. Law. 19; Law Commission and Scottish Law Commission, *Company Directors: Regulating Conflicts of Interest and Formulating a Statement of Duties* (Law Commission Report No. 261, Scottish Law Commission Report No. 173, 1999) paras. 15.3–15.5 and 15.9–15.10; CLRSG, *Modern Company Law for a Competitive Economy: Developing the Framework* (March 2000) ch. 3; *Modern Company Law for a Competitive Economy: Completing the Structure* (November 2000) ch. 13.

74. News Digest, (1999) 20 Co. Law. 302.

of stakeholders when considering corporate actions. Three-quarters of respondents thought that directors' duties were difficult to understand; over half thought that they had to account to creditors and employees;[75] a quarter thought the same of customers and suppliers, and 87 per cent believed that the law needed to be clarified if directors were to understand their obligations.

The Company Law Review Steering Group has now considered the case for a statutory statement of directors' duties to creditors in a situation where the company is insolvent or threatened by insolvency.[76] The CLRSG's consultations led it close to the view that such a statement was needed.[77] There were difficulties of legal formulation, said the CLRSG, but these could be overcome, and to fail to make such a statutory statement would risk misleading directors by omitting an important part of the overall picture. The central issue was when the normal rule[78] – that a company is run in the interest of its members, or shareholders – should be modified by (or give way to) an obligation to have regard to the interests of creditors. On the latter issue – of displacement of the duty so as to favour creditors – the CLRSG advocated including in the statutory restatement of the law a duty modelled on that of the Insolvency Act section 214 to take every step to minimise losses to creditors that a person exercising due care and skill would take.[79] This duty would come into play at a time when a director knows (or would know but for a failure of his to exercise due skill and care) that 'there is no reasonable prospect of the company's avoiding going into insolvent liquidation'.[80]

As for the director's obligations at an earlier stage of corporate decline, the CLRSG noted the argument that directors should have to take a balanced view of risks to creditors at these stages. The rule as encountered in Australia and the *West Mercia* case[81] might, the CLRSG said, be 'regarded as of considerable merit' and, in the CLRSG formulation, would take effect 'at a time when a director of a company knows and would know, but for a

---

75. On employees see ch. 16 below.
76. See CLRSG, *Modern Company Law for a Competitive Economy: Final Report* (July 2001) pp. 42–5.
77. The initial draft statement had not advocated such a statement of a special duty to creditors: see CLRSG, *Developing the Framework*, paras. 3.72–3.73.
78. See CLRSG, *Final Report*, 2001, Schedule 2: General Principles, para. 2.
79. 'Due care and skill' here is defined by the General Principles, para. 4, as that which would be exercised by a reasonably diligent person with both (a) the knowledge, skill and experience which may reasonably be expected of a director in his position; and (b) any additional knowledge, skill and experience which he has.
80. See CLRSG, *Final Report*, 2001, p. 348, General Principles, para. 9.
81. See *West Mercia Safetywear Ltd* v. *Dodd* [1988] BCLC 250; CLRSG, *Final Report*, 2001, p. 44.

failure of his to exercise due care and skill, that it is more likely than not that the company will at some point be unable to pay its debts as they fall due'. The director would be obliged, in exercising his powers, to take such steps 'as he believes will achieve a reasonable balance between – (i) reducing the risk that a company will be unable to pay its debts as they fall due; and (ii) promoting the success of the company for the benefit of its members as a whole'. The CLRSG draft states[82] that what is reasonable must be decided in good faith, giving more or less weight to the need to reduce risk as the risk is more or less severe. In deciding what is to promote the success of the company for the benefit of its members as a whole the director must take account, in good faith, of all the material factors that it is practicable in the circumstances for him to identify (which includes the need to achieve outcomes that are fair between members).

Such a statutory duty brings with it dangers that directors will act excessively cautiously, fail to take reasonable risks and flee from companies at the first signs of trouble. The CLRSG was aware of these issues.[83] The heralded answer, however, was provided by the subjective statement of the duty (in the phrase 'as he believes will achieve a reasonable balance'). The duty, it should be emphasised, would arise not only when the director knows that it is more probable than not that the company will be unable to pay its debts, but also when the director would know this but for a failure of his to exercise due care and skill. The CLRSG, nevertheless, concludes: 'Directors could thus safely be advised that it is only the greater than even probability of such failure which they need to take account of.'[84]

Some members of the CLRSG favoured the formulation set out in the CLRSG Final Report[85] but others took the view that the draft 'gives inadequate guidance to directors and depends on their being able to discern an intermediate stage on the path to insolvency which is not identifiable in reality'.[86] There was, at the end of the day, no agreed view in the CLRSG and the Group ended by recommending that the DTI should consult on the matter.

It follows from what has been said earlier that the present author would favour the CLRSG formulation of the 'intermediate' duty as to the arising of the obligation and would accept the subjectivity built into the formulation of the content of the director's obligation in so far as it

---

82. CLRSG, *Final Report*, 2001, p. 347.   **83.** Ibid., p. 44.   **84.** Ibid., p. 45.
85. Ibid., p. 347, para. 8.
86. Ibid., p. 45. See further p. 35, on the possible consequences of not adopting the draft formulation.

balances consideration of creditors' interests with a reasonable degree of protection for directors.

Another issue arises where a company is the tortfeasor and it is generally not possible to recover from a director on the basis of the latter's liability. He or she is protected by the company's separate personality.[87] If the director authorises the commission of a tortious act he or she may be personally liable on some authorities,[88] but the House of Lords has taken a restrictive line in the *Williams* case.[89] In that decision their Lordships indicated that the key issue was whether the defendant director, or anybody on his behalf, could say directly or indirectly that the defendant was to assume personal responsibility towards the affected parties. In *Williams* the director of a one-man company was sued personally for a negligent misstatement but there was no personal liability, said the House of Lords, because the individual involved had held himself out at all times as the managing director of a limited liability company and never assumed to involve himself in personal liability. There was no evidence of the director having personally vouched for the negligent statements at issue and so no duty of care arose. The policy indication given out by the House of Lords in *Williams* was that, in protecting the advantages of limited liability for small entrepreneurs, the courts would be reluctant to attribute personal liability in tort to directors.[90] In contract a similar line is to be expected. A company director will not generally be personally liable on company contracts[91] unless he or she gives the impression that personal liability is being assumed.[92]

Statutory liabilities

Turning to statutory provisions creating personal liability, directors may be liable to compensate creditors where they have been party to fraudulent

87. See D. Milman and C. Durrant, *Corporate Insolvency: Law and Practice* (3rd edn, Sweet & Maxwell, London, 1999) p. 225.
88. *Evans (C) and Sons Ltd v. Spritebrand Ltd and Sullivan* [1985] 1 WLR 317; *Mancetter Developments Ltd v. Garmanson Ltd et al.* [1986] 2 WLR 871; *Fairline Shipping Corporation v. Adamson* [1974] 2 All ER 967; *Thomas Saunders Partnership v. Harvey* (1990) 9 Trad LR 78.
89. *Williams v. Natural Life Health Foods* [1998] 1 WLR 830. See comments by R. Grantham and C. Rickett (1999) 62 MLR 133; R. Mullender (1999) 20 Co. Law. 121; G. Shapira (1999) 20 Co. Law. 130.
90. Milman and Durrant, *Corporate Insolvency*, p. 226. See also V. Finch and J. Freedman, 'Limited Liability Partnerships: Pick and Mix or Mix Up?' [2002] JBL (forthcoming, September).
91. *Henry Brown & Sons v. Smith* [1964] 2 Lloyd's Rep 476.
92. *The Swan (Bridges & Salmon v. Swan, The (Owner))*, [1968] 1 Lloyd's Rep 5; *Rolfe Lubell & Co. v. Keith* [1979] 1 All ER 860; cf. *Bondina Ltd v. Rollaway Shower Blinds Ltd* [1986] 1 WLR 517. See Milman and Durrant, *Corporate Insolvency*, p. 221.

trading by the company. Section 213 of the Insolvency Act 1986 provides:

(1) If in the course of the winding up of the company it appears that any business of the company has been carried on with intent to defraud creditors of the company, or creditors of any other person, or for any fraudulent purpose, the following has effect.

(2) The court, on the application of the liquidator, may declare that any persons who were knowingly parties to the carrying on of the business in the manner above mentioned, are liable to make such contributions (if any) to the company assets as the court thinks proper.

This section has a long history and, indeed, was introduced particularly to protect unsecured creditors from the abuse of 'filling up' floating charges.[93] Now, however, it is recognised[94] that the aim of fraudulent trading provisions – to discourage directors from carrying on business at the expense of creditors – is severely restricted by the requirement of dishonest intent[95] and the courts' insistence on strict standards of pleading and proof.[96] Such an approach may be understandable for criminal liability under section 458 of the Companies Act 1985, but its imposition on the civil liability provided for in section 213 of the 1986 Act has led to the latter section's virtual obsolescence. This obsolescence is now even more apparent with the advent of section 214, the 'wrongful trading'[97] provision.

As for the criminal offence of fraudulent trading under section 458 of the Companies Act 1985, the CLRSG concluded that this constituted 'a

---

93. A process whereby directors lent money secured by floating charges to their asset-less companies, bought stock on credit which became subject to the floating charges, then appointed receivers who sold off the stock to satisfy the directors' charges, leaving the creditors 'whistling'. Now, however, the company would have to be kept afloat for two years to avoid the operation of the Insolvency Act 1986 s. 245: see ch. 12 above.

94. See Cork Report, p. 398.

95. In the subjective sense: 'actual dishonesty...real moral blame' per Maugham J in *Re Patrick and Lyon Ltd* [1933] Ch 786 at 790. Maugham J noted that the provision was 'by no means easy to construe'. For High Court guidance on what a liquidator must prove in order to establish a case of fraudulent trading see *Morphites* v. *Bernasconi* [2001] 2 BCLC 1 (mere preferring of one creditor over another is not enough but it need not be shown that any individual creditors were misled into providing credit by the defendant's fraudulent actions: it is the intention that is critical). See also *Re William Leach Brothers Ltd* [1932] 2 Ch 71; *Re L. Todd (Swanscombe) Ltd* [1990] BCC 127; *R* v. *Miles* (1992) Crim. L Rev. 657.

96. Ian Fletcher has noted the degree of uncertainty 'whether civil or criminal proceedings for fraudulent trading will prove to be successful in any given case': *The Law of Insolvency* (2nd edn, Sweet & Maxwell, London, 1996) p. 660.

97. Section 214, according to the marginal note, is concerned with 'wrongful trading', but it is notable that the word 'trading' is not used in the text of the Act: see further L. S. Sealy and D. Milman, *Annotated Guide to the Insolvency Legislation* (5th edn, CCH, Bicester, 1999) pp. 245–6.

valuable weapon in countering crime'.[98] There were, however, problems of under-deterrence and the CLRSG proposed that the penalty for the offence should be raised to a level comparable with that for deception under the Theft Act.

Section 214 of the Insolvency Act 1986 is the section which owes its birthright to the Cork Committee,[99] and, as stated previously, was the White Paper's great hope for the unsecured creditor.[100] In terms of increasing directors' duties to unsecured creditors section 214 provides that where a company is in liquidation a liquidator can apply to the court to have a person who is or has been a director declared personally liable to make such contribution to the company's assets as the court thinks proper. The liquidator must establish that at some time before the commencement of the winding up of the company that person knew or ought to have concluded that there was no reasonable prospect that the company would avoid going into insolvent liquidation and that the respondent was either a director or a shadow director[101] of the company at that time.

A defence is, however, available if the respondent director shows that, having reached the state of knowledge referred to, he took *every step* with a view to minimising potential loss to the company's creditors that he ought to have taken (section 214(3)). Here there is a movement away from the subjective test of skill and care applied to directors in the common law cases such as *Re City Equitable Fire Insurance Co.*[102] Under section 214 a director is judged not only by the knowledge, skill and experience that he actually has (section 214(4)(b)) but also by the 'general knowledge, skill and experience that may reasonably be expected of a person carrying out the same functions' (section 214(4)(a)). A director can, therefore, under this limb be judged by standards of the 'reasonable director' even though he may be well below those standards himself.[103]

98. See CLRSG, *Final Report*, 2001, para. 15.7. The CLRSG recommended that the offence should be extended to companies incorporated overseas and trading in the UK and to individuals and partnerships.

99. Cork Report, ch. 44.

100. Academics and practitioners also saw section 214 as a potentially valuable tool: see Prentice, 'Creditors' Interest'; F. Oditah, 'Wrongful Trading' [1990] LMCLQ 205.

101. That is, a person in accordance with whose instructions the directors of the company are accustomed to act. On shadow directors see Insolvency Act 1986 s. 251; Company Directors' Disqualification Act 1986 s. 22(5); Companies Act 1985 s. 741(2); p. 535 below.

102. [1925] Ch 407.

103. This sets a minimum standard and, in deciding whether this minimum has been obtained, regard can be had to the particular company and its business: see *Re Produce*

The wrongful trading section has, however, proved to be a great disappointment in so far as its impact has been low.[104] Between 1989 and 1993 there were 92,500 corporate insolvencies in England and Wales but only four wrongful trading actions reached court.[105] Problems in the funding of such actions have clearly not helped to develop wrongful trading as a strong force for directorial accountability and these have been discussed above.[106] Judicial approaches to section 214 have, however, not added to the efficacy of the provision. This is an area where there has been an unhelpful confusion about the role and purpose of the law. Cork had envisaged that civil liability for wrongful trading would effect a balance between encouraging the growth of enterprises and discouraging 'downright irresponsibility'.[107] This balancing, as involved in section 214, has allowed different judges to adopt different approaches to wrongful trading and a degree of uncertainty has resulted. In *Re Produce Marketing Consortium Ltd*[108] Knox J treated the section 214 jurisdiction as 'primarily

Marketing Consortium [1989] 5 BCC 569 per Knox J at 594. For a further discussion of this case, see Prentice, 'Creditors' Interest'; L. S. Sealy [1989] CLJ 375. See also Park J in *Re Continental Assurance Co. of London plc* [2001] BPIR 733 for a judicial analysis of the nature of individual directors' potential liabilities, quantum and issues of several liability versus joint and several liability under section 214; see futher A. Walters, 'Wrongful Trading: Two Recent Cases' [2001] Ins. Law. 211.

104. See, for example, A. Walters, 'Enforcing Wrongful Trading: Substantive Problems and Practical Disincentives' in B. Rider (ed.), *The Corporate Dimension: An Exploration of Developing Areas of Company and Commercial Law* (Jordans, Bristol, 1998); Griffin, *Personal Liability*, p. 6; C. Cook, 'Wrongful Trading: Is it a Real Threat to Directors or a Paper Tiger?' [1999] Ins. Law. 99; P. Godfrey and S. Nield, 'The Wrongful Trading Provisions: All Bark and No Bite?' (1995) 11 IL&P 139; D. Milman, 'Wrongful Trading Actions: Smoke without Fire?' [1995] 8 *Palmer's In Company* 1; A. Hicks, 'Wrongful Trading: Has it been a Failure?' (1993) 8 IL&P 134; Hicks, *Disqualification of Directors: No Hiding Place for the Unfit?*, ACCA Research Report No. 59 (London, 1998) pp. 125, 134; A. Campbell, 'Wrongful Trading and Company Rescue' [1994] 25 CLJ 69; Arsalidou, 'Impact of Section 214(4)'; S. Shulte, 'Enforcing Wrongful Trading as a Standard of Conduct for Directors and a Remedy for Creditors: The Special Case for Corporate Insolvency' (1999) 20 Co. Law. 80.

105. See Godfrey and Nield, 'Wrongful Trading Provisions', p. 140. There have subsequently been only a small number of reported cases: see *Re Hydrodan (Corby) Ltd* [1994] BCC 161; *Re Sherborne Associates Ltd* [1995] BCC 40; *Re Brian D. Pierson (Contractors) Ltd* [1999] BCC 26. Other cases, such as *Re Farmizer (Products) Ltd* [1995] BCC 926 (appeal from this decision dismissed in [1997] BCC 655), have dealt with procedural issues relating to a section 214 claim, while others have focused on other matters relating to a section 214 claim: see *Burgoine* v. *London Borough of Waltham Forest* [1997] BCC 347. *Re Oasis Merchandising Services Ltd* [1995] BCC 911 dealt indirectly with section 214 but its focus was on champerty and funding arrangements: see A. Keay, 'The Duty of Directors to Take Account of Creditors' Interests: Has it Any Role to Play?', paper presented to SPTL Company Law Section, SPTL Annual Conference, September 2000. Since 1986 there have been, on average, around 18,000 insolvent liquidations per annum and Griffin has commented: 'it is surely a hallmark of the provision's ineffectiveness that more actions have not been taken', *Personal Liability*, p. 97.

106. See ch. 12 above, pp. 383–92.　　**107.** Cork Report, para. 1805.

108. [1989] 5 BCC 569.

compensatory rather than penal'.[109] It is clear, however, from other cases such as *Re Sherborne Associates Ltd*[110] that the wrongful trading provisions are being seen by some judges not so much as a civil remedy to raise standards among directors and to compensate creditors, but as a way to punish directors whose actions are seen as immoral. Such a punitive conception may also sit more comfortably with a 'pro-enterprise'/'pro-rescue' stance rather than a 'pro-creditor' position.[111] In *Sherborne* the actions were dismissed and the judge was sympathetic to the honest, hard-working, well-respected businessmen who acted as directors in times of difficulty.[112] Even on a finding of liability under section 214, the court may, in deciding the appropriate amount of a director's compensation, exercise its discretion under section 214(1) and may take account of the degree of culpability exhibited by the director.[113] The court can, therefore, note whether the director's conduct resulted from a failure to appreciate rather than from a deliberate course of wrongdoing; whether or not there were heeded or unheeded warnings from the auditors;[114] and whether there was any misappropriation of assets by the directors for their own benefit.[115] In *Re Purpoint Ltd*,[116] however, Vinelott J did not look kindly on directors who failed to monitor their company's financial affairs and in *Re DKG Contractors Ltd*[117] there was a similar approach to directors who failed to implement the basics of company law. Thus, in exercising their discretions to order directorial contributions, the courts may, as noted, vary their responses according

109. Ibid., at 597. On the public law function of section 214 in prescribing standards of directorial behaviour see Robert Walker J in *Re Oasis Merchandising Services Ltd* [1995] BCC 911 at 918.

110. [1995] BCC 40. See Godfrey and Nield, 'Wrongful Trading Provisions'.

111. Terms used by Walters, 'Enforcing Wrongful Trading', p. 149. It can similarly be argued that there is a tension between compensatory and standard-raising rationales: see Shulte, 'Enforcing Wrongful Trading'.

112. Note, however, that the principal director had died by the time of the hearing and consequently the court may have been anxious not to judge with hindsight someone who was unable to defend himself: see I. F. Fletcher, 'Wrongful Trading: "Reasonable Prospect" of Insolvency' (1995) 8 *Insolvency Intelligence* 14. The dangers of acting on hindsight (noted in *Re Sherborne* itself), and of assuming that what has happened was always bound to happen and was apparent, were noted in *Re Brian D. Pierson (Contractors) Ltd* [1999] BCC 26 when Hazel Williamson QC, in the Chancery Division, declined to be 'wise with hindsight' and gave respect to the directors' judgment as to the company's prospects. Nevertheless, on the facts, she was satisfied that the directors ought to have concluded that there was no reasonable prospect of avoiding insolvent liquidation and they were liable under section 214. In *Re Continental Assurance Co. of London plc* [2001] BPIR 733, however, a sympathetic view of directors appears to have been taken again when Park J rejected a wrongful trading action, noting that the directors had not acted unreasonably in difficult circumstances when they sought expert advice and, reasonably, traded on.

113. See M. Simmons, 'Wrongful Trading' (2001) 14 *Insolvency Intelligence* 12.

114. *Re Brian D. Pierson (Contractors) Ltd* [1999] BCC 26.

115. *Re Produce Marketing Consortium Ltd (No. 2)* [1989] BCLC 520, [1989] 5 BCC 569.

116. [1991] BCLC 491.   **117.** [1990] BCC 903.

to their espousal of different approaches to section 214, be these compensatory (as in *Re Produce Marketing*[118]) or inclined to advert to issues of culpability (as discernible, for example, in such cases as *Re Sherborne, Re Purpoint* and *Re DKG Contractors*[119]). The bite of the wrongful trading provisions is, therefore, diminished not merely by the legal uncertainties that liquidators face on seeing widely varying judicial rulings, but also by the propensity of the judiciary to look to culpability (rather than pure compensation) as a factor of relevance in deciding both whether to declare a liability to contribute and subsequent issues of quantum.

Personal liability for directors also arises in relation to sections 216 and 217 of the Insolvency Act 1986, the provisions designed to deal with the 'phoenix syndrome'. These sections prohibit a director of a company that has entered insolvent liquidation from being involved, for the next five years, in the management of a company using the same name as the insolvent company or a name so similar as to suggest association with it. The rule also applies to any director who has left a company within twelve months of liquidation. Breach of the rule involves criminal penalties but an individual may seek the court's leave to act as the director of a similarly named company and there is evidence that the courts will be well disposed to grant such leave where the applicant was not to blame for the failure of the initial company.[120] Section 217 provides that a director who breaches section 216 has unlimited liability for the debts of the 'successor' company after he became director.

Further areas of directorial liability relate to transactions at undervalue and preferences and transactions defrauding creditors under sections 238, 239 and 423 of the Insolvency Act 1986. These provisions and their enforcement have, however, been discussed in chapter 12 and will not be dealt with here.

The above discussion sets out the main rules governing the potential liability of directors in cases of corporate insolvency. Matters of enforcement

---

118. [1989] 5 BCC 569.

119. [1995] BCC 40; [1991] BCLC 491; [1990] BCC 903. See also *Re Continental Assurance Co. of London plc* [2001] BPIR 733 where Park J seemed much influenced by the directors' 'wholly responsible and conscientious attitudes'.

120. See *Penrose* v. *Official Receiver* [1996] 1 BCLC 389; *Re Lightning Electrical Contractors Ltd* [1996] 2 BCLC 302. See further the discussion on the 'phoenix' problem by the CLRSG, *Final Report*, 2001, paras. 15.55–15.77. The Review Group, *inter alia*, distinguishes between 'good phoenix' situations (i.e. where 'honest individuals may, through misfortune or naïve good faith, find that they can no longer trade out of their difficulties... and the only way to continue an otherwise viable business... may be for them to do so in a new vehicle using the assets and trading style of the original company') and 'bad phoenix situations' (i.e. those 'who seek to abuse the system or deliberately evade their responsibilities'). On the rarity of use of section 216 see further para. 15.61.

need, however, to be considered if the real accountability of directors is to be assessed. In relation to the common law duties that directors owe to creditors there are considerable enforcement difficulties. The judges have tended to see directors' duties to creditors in exhortatory terms and so have failed to grasp the enforcement nettle. If creditors' interests derive from general duties owed to the company then breaches should properly be dealt with by the company as contemplated in *Nicholson*[121] and *Walker v. Wimborne*.[122] The problem, however, is that enforcement of the duty is likely to be difficult before the company goes into administration, receivership or liquidation since creditors cannot rely on the existing board or the shareholders to complain about the ill-treatment of creditors' interests. On liquidation, the possibility arises of a misfeasance action under section 212 of the Insolvency Act 1986, which allows proceedings where a director has been guilty of 'any misfeasance or breach of any fiduciary or other duty in relation to the company'.[123] Duties to creditors may thus arise at the stage of doubtful solvency but creditors *per se* are given a right of action only on winding up.

Such enforcement may, of course, offer little assistance to unsecured creditors since funds will go to company assets and will come within the scope of any floating charge.[124] As for secured creditors, the receiver, as the company's agent,[125] might assist their cause by bringing an action against the directors for breach of duty, and case law indicates that shareholders cannot extinguish the duty to creditors by ratifying directorial breaches of it.[126]

Are creditors, however, in a good position to enforce duties against directors? As has been argued elsewhere,[127] effective enforcement demands an ability to acquire and use information; expertise or understanding of the relevant activity; a commitment to act; and an ability to bring pressure or sanctions to bear on the party to be controlled.

---

121. [1985] 1 NZLR 242.
122. [1976] 50 ALJR 446, (1976) 137 CLR 1, (1978) 3 ACLR 529.
123. The Insolvency Act 1986 extended the ambit of misfeasance to 'include breach of any duty including the duty of care': per Hoffmann LJ in *Re D'Jan of London Ltd* [1994] 1 BCLC 561 at 562. On misfeasance see further F. Oditah, 'Misfeasance Proceedings against Company Directors' [1992] LMCLQ 207; *Re Brian D. Pierson (Contractors) Ltd* [1999] BCC 26; *Re Westlowe Storage & Distribution Ltd* [2000] BCC 851; *Re Continental Assurance Co. of London plc* [2001] BPIR 733.
124. See *Re Anglo-Austrian Printing and Publishing Co.* [1895] Ch 152 (damages received from directors for misfeasance are available to the charge holder).
125. See *Gomba Holdings UK Ltd and Others v. Homan and Bird* [1986] 1 WLR 1301; Insolvency Act 1986 s. 44(1)(a).
126. See *Kinsela* (1986) 4 ACLC 215; *Re Horsley & Weight* [1982] 3 All ER 1045; *Nicholson v. Permakraft* [1985] 1 NZLR 242.
127. Finch, 'Company Directors'.

On the first issue, creditors may have not inconsiderable access to information. The disclosure rules operating throughout company legislation generally reflect the principle that these operate for creditors' as well as shareholders' benefit. Creditors, like shareholders, can obtain information on the financial state of the company at the Company Registry in the form of copies of certain classes of resolution, annual accounts and directors' and auditors' reports. Copies of these documents have, moreover, to be sent to 'all debenture holders'. When a company enters or nears insolvency, further sources of information arise. Receivers appointed by debenture holders must be furnished with a statement of affairs from the company's officers and must report in turn to all creditors and creditors' meetings.[128] Where voluntary arrangements are made in order to conclude an agreement with creditors, the directors' proposal and statement of the company's affairs will become available to creditors,[129] and when administrators or liquidators act they will provide creditors' meetings with a body of information. Data concerning directorial behaviour may also flow from the creation of contractual rights to information.[130] The terms of debentures may provide for the supply of information and financial data and detailed figures, for example, may be requested on a periodic basis by financial creditors.

The value of information deriving from insolvency-related regimes may, however, be questioned. Creditors may well gain much information only at a very late stage in corporate troubles and this tardiness will often rule out actions designed to forestall directorial failures or negligence. As with shareholders, however, informal sources of information may assist creditors and major financial creditors will often use their influence to obtain a steady flow of information from senior managers. Major creditors may also obtain representation on the company's board and subsequently will gain access to new sources of information. Trade creditors will be less likely to use such sources but if a continuing trading relationship has been formed, they may acquire information informally.

Can more be done to inform creditors? One potential response to the 'phoenix syndrome' has been put forward by the Federation of Small Businesses (FSB) which has argued[131] that the DTI should designate certain

128. Insolvency Act 1986 ss. 47(1), 48(1) and (2).
129. Insolvency Act 1986 s. 2(2) and (3); Insolvency Act 2000 Sched. A1, para. 30; Insolvency Rules 1986 rr. 1.3(1) and (2); Insolvency Rules 1986 rr. 1.5(1) and (2), 1.12(3); Insolvency Act 1986 s. 3(2) and (3).
130. See J. Day and P. Taylor, 'The Role of Debt Contracts in UK Corporate Governance' (1998) *Journal of Management and Governance* 171; C. Smith and J. Warner, 'On Financial Contracting: An Analysis of Bond Covenants' (1979) 7 *Journal of Financial Economics* 117.
131. See Cohen, 'Dangerous Directors'.

individuals as 'provisional directors' where they have been at the helm of several failed companies. Such directors would then be required to disclose their track records so that trade creditors, for instance, would be aware of these. Monthly financial returns for the companies of such directors might also be demanded so that creditor monitoring of financial health could be facilitated. The FSB argument here is that such steps offer smaller creditors lower-cost information sources and help them to assess risks. There seems an arguable case for such requirements also on grounds of fairness to unsecured creditors.

Even when creditors possess information, however, they may have problems in using it. Creditor expertise, indeed, may vary considerably. Financial creditors might be expected to be expert in assessing risks and managerial performance, but trade creditors may possess expertise in a particular business sector only and may be less able to evaluate directorial performance beyond those areas.

Will creditors be committed to enforcing directorial duties? They may be where they foresee any threat to their prospects of repayment but, in general, creditors are not disposed to review the actions of managers. Factors that might, nevertheless, affect the propensity to enforce might be the size of the investment, the nature of any security, the type of business and the levels of directorial discretion that are usual in the sector. For small trade creditors such factors may well not come into play unless the debtor is a major purchaser of the creditor's product. Such creditors will tend to look for supply elsewhere rather than to continue a relationship in the hope of recovering from directors on the basis of a breach of duty.

What incentive, indeed, is there for creditors to seek to recover from directors? Secured creditors will focus on realising their security by appointing a receiver. Only if such realisation fails to meet the sum outstanding will such creditors have anything to gain from the contributions of directors. In the case of creditors secured with floating charges, incentives may similarly operate only to cover shortfalls (directorial contributions will form part of the company's assets). Ordinary unsecured trade creditors will possess questionable incentives to pursue errant directors since they will be paid after floating charge holders.

After a liquidation has been initiated by qualifying creditors, actions may be brought by creditors against directors under a number of heads: for example, misfeasance actions for breaches of fiduciary or other duties in relation to the company.[132] Such duties, however, are, as noted already, owed to the company and contributions obtained from directors as a

132. See further Finch, 'Company Directors', p. 193.

result will go to the company assets for the benefit of all creditors. Individual creditors may be discouraged from bringing such actions, moreover, because the liquidator may proceed similarly on behalf of all creditors and will have investigative powers that individual creditors do not possess.[133] As for liquidators' actions, we have seen in chapter 12 that creditors may have to indemnify costs where it is anticipated that there may be insufficient assets to support litigation, especially since the Court of Appeal decision in *Re Floor Fourteen*[134] adhered to the *M. C. Bacon (No. 2)*[135] approach that litigation expenses of the liquidation were not expenses of the winding up.[136]

The common law duty offers little to the unsecured creditor since it is owed to the general body of creditors rather than unsecured creditors individually or as a class. A duty owed directly to individual creditors seems, as already noted, to have been discredited after *Yukong*[137] and would conflict with insolvency's collectivist principles, might lead to a multiplicity of suits, and could lead individual creditors to place improper pressure on directors to settle their particular claim.[138] As has been argued elsewhere, the alternative may be to place directors under a duty to unsecured creditors as a class.[139] Such a class action could exceptionally allow unsecured creditors collectively to seek injunctions where necessary to prevent directors from acting in a manner jeopardising the company's solvency or to ensure the consideration of unsecured creditors' interests in circumstances of marginal solvency.[140]

The position of creditors generally might be strengthened by another reform: one to allow creditors to take action in the company's name in enforcement of directorial duties. The CLRSG has recommended that shareholders' derivative actions for breaches of directors' duties should be put on a statutory footing[141] but are there good reasons for a creditors'

---

133. Insolvency Act 1986 ss. 131–4, 235. 134. [2001] 3 All ER 499, [2001] 2 BCLC 392.
135. [1991] Ch 127.
136. See ch. 12 above; M. Steiner, 'Receivers v. Liquidators v. Preferential Creditors v. Unsecured Creditors: Practitioners Beware!' (2001) 17 IL&P 3.
137. *Yukong Lines Ltd of Korea* v. *Rendsburg Investments Corp. of Liberia (No. 2)* [1998] BCC 870, [1998] 1 WLR 294; see pp. 500–1 above.
138. See further Finch, 'Directors' Duties: Insolvency and the Unsecured Creditor' and 'Creditors' Interests and Directors' Obligations'; D. Prentice, 'Directors, Creditors and Shareholders' in E. McKendrick (ed.), *Commercial Aspects of Trusts and Fiduciary Obligations* (Clarendon Press, Oxford, 1992) pp. 74–5.
139. See Finch, 'Directors' Duties: Insolvency and the Unsecured Creditor'.
140. For their part, directors might have few grounds to fear that unsecured creditors would interfere in the workings of the company. Such creditors would have to demonstrate to a court reasonable cause to anticipate that insolvency would result from the action in question and this would be an onerous burden to discharge.
141. See CLRSG, *Final Report*, 2001, p. 165. On the case for a new statutory derivative action for shareholders see Finch, 'Company Directors:', pp. 204–6. See generally I. Ramsay, 'Corporate

counterpart? Could creditors be included in the potential class of applicants for a derivative action (as well as directors and officers and creditors of related companies)?[142] One reason advanced for the inclusion of creditors has been that, in some circumstances, creditors might be in receipt of better relevant information than is available to 'other outsiders'.[143] The opportunity of using creditors as monitors of corporate management seems, however, a less convincing argument than the need to protect creditor interests. If, as was indicated in *Horsley, Nicholson* and *Brady*, creditor interests become company interests not merely post-insolvency but also when insolvency threatens, and if the CLRSG's views regarding directorial consideration of creditors' interests come to fruition,[144] then it *may* be appropriate to allow creditors to act before the liquidator comes onto the scene (so as to protect their interests) by injuncting any directorial actions that are likely to prejudice solvency severely.[145]

Enforcement of the statutory controls over such matters as fraudulent or wrongful trading, transactions at undervalue and preferences depends on action, not by a creditor, but by an office holder of the company. As was made clear in chapter 12, however, liquidators face severe funding problems in resorting to law in order to enforce directors' duties. Such practical difficulties combine with problems of legal uncertainty, particularly in the case of wrongful trading, to produce an accountability regime of seemingly low impact.[146]

Governance, Shareholder Litigation and the Prospects for a Statutory Derivative Action' (1992) 15 UNSW LJ 149 at 165–6; Law Commission, Report No. 246, *Shareholder Remedies* (Cm 3769, 1997); Consultation Paper No. 142, *Shareholder Remedies* (1996) (for comment see D. Sugarman (1997) 18 Co. Law. 226 and 274; J. Lowry (1997) 18 Co. Law. 247; C. Riley (1997) 18 Co. Law. 260; L. Moran (1997) 18 Co. Law. 264); DTI, *Shareholder Remedies: A Consultation Document*, URN 98/994 (November 1998); CLRSG, *Developing the Framework*, 2000, paras. 4.65 and 4.115.

142. See Australian Companies and Securities Law Review Committee, *Enforcement of the Duties of Directors and Officers of a Company by Means of a Statutory Derivative Action* (Report No. 12, 1990) ('CSLRC'). See also *Report of House of Representatives Standing Committee on Legal and Constitutional Affairs, Corporate Practices and the Rights of Shareholders* (1991).

143. CSLRC, p. 50.

144. See CLRSG, *Final Report*, 2001, pp. 42–5. The need to consider creditors would arise when, in the exercise of due care and skill, directors realise that it is more likely than not that the company will be unable to pay its debts: see pp. 508–10 above.

145. Section 1234 of the Australian Corporations Law of 1991 enabled the courts to grant injunctive relief to 'any person' affected by contraventions of the Corporations Law. The CLRSG, *Final Report*, 2001, p. 312 and CLRSG, *Developing the Framework*, 2000, para. 13.71 suggest codification of civil remedies for breach of directors' duties but the question of rights of enforcement of the duty of consideration of creditors' interests is seemingly left open.

146. Lack of visible enforcement of the wrongful trading provisions may give an excessively negative view of their impact, however, since insolvency practitioners may use the threat of proceedings to concentrate directors' minds, extract sums from directors in order to settle claims and force quick settlements: see Walters, 'Enforcing Wrongful Trading', p. 159;

Expertise

Does insolvency law encourage directorial behaviour that is expert, honest and free from incompetence? Here focus will rest on the rules on disqualification before note is made of alternative means of influencing directorial expertise. In so doing it is necessary to consider both the rationales that the judges espouse in disqualifying directors and whether the rules are enforced in a manner that actually encourages expert, honest and competent company direction.

The director of an insolvent company may be found unfit to run a limited liability company and disqualified by the courts under section 6 of the Company Directors' Disqualification Act 1986 (CDDA).[147] The Secretary of State[148] or Official Receiver[149] may apply to the court for such a disqualification and, on a finding of unfitness, the court must disqualify the director from being concerned in the management of a company for a minimum of two years.[150] It is the use of mandatory disqualification that sets section 6 apart from the other provisions of the CDDA which involve judicial discretion to disqualify and may be used, for example, where there is misconduct in relation to the company (involving, perhaps, conviction of an indictable offence in relation to the company,[151] persistently breaching companies legislation on documents and returns,[152] or participation in frauds or fraudulent trading[153]); where there is a finding of unfitness following the Secretary of State's application on an inspector's report or departmental investigation;[154] or where there is a wrongful trading,[155]

C. Williams and A. McGee, 'A Company Director's Liability for Wrongful Trading', ACCA Research Report No. 30 (London, 1992) p. 16.

147. See CDDA 1986 s. 6(2) for definition of 'insolvent'. For the background to section 6 and to the importance of disqualification in insolvency law's investigative role, see Cork Report, paras. 235–40, 1813–18. See also I. F. Fletcher, 'Genesis of Modern Insolvency Law: An Odyssey of Law Reform' [1989] JBL 365. See generally Griffin, *Personal Liability*; L. S. Sealy, *Disqualification and Personal Liability of Directors: A Guide to the Changes made by the Insolvency Legislation of 1985 and 1986* (5th edn, CCH New Law, Kingston upon Thames, 2000).

148. Per CDDA 1986 s. 7(3) it is the duty of liquidators, official receivers, administrators or administrative receivers to report cases of suspected 'unfitness' to the Secretary of State.

149. At the Secretary of State's discretion, CDDA 1986 s. 7(1).

150. CDDA 1986 s. 6(1)(4). Mandatory disqualification for a minimum period reflected the Cork Committee's concern for the tightening up of the previous discretionary jurisdiction of Companies Act 1985 s. 300.

151. CDDA 1986 s. 2.   152. Ibid., ss. 3 and 5.

153. Ibid., s. 4; Companies Act 1985 s. 458; Insolvency Act 1986 s. 10.

154. CDDA 1986 s. 8.

155. Ibid., s. 10. On allowing the company to trade when insolvent even where this does not amount to wrongful trading, see C. Bradley, 'Enterprise and Entrepreneurship' (2001) 1 *Journal of Corporate Law Studies* 53 at 66; *Secretary of State for Trade and Industry v. Imo Synthetic Technology Ltd* [1993] BCC 549; *Re Bath Glass* [1988] 4 BCC 130.

company direction by an undischarged bankrupt[156] or failure to pay under a County Court administration order.[157]

In applying the disqualification provisions different judicial philosophies or rationales can be discerned.[158] What might be called a 'rights' approach sees directing a company incorporated with limited liability as a valuable asset or right worthy of protection in the exercise of commercial ventures. This model reflects the 'business enterprise' perspective on company law, which sees the director as a taker of business risks, subject to a company law that respects and enables his or her freedom to manage rather than make managerial decisions liable to judicial second guessing.[159] An alternative standpoint sees incorporation with limited liability as a privilege, a facility to be used in the public interest. This view could be said to reflect the social responsibility perspective on company law which looks not merely at the interests of investors, managers, directors and creditors but to the 'legitimate needs, too, of the public interest, of the consumer, of the employee'.[160]

The respective logics of the rights and privileges approaches may be represented as two packages each comprising a distinct set of tenets. The rights approach implies, in its pure form, the following: that interference with the right to direct a limited liability company is only merited where culpability is present; that culpability is relevant in assessing the period of disqualification on, *inter alia*, retributive principles; that the process of disqualification is accordingly best seen as a penal one; that withdrawal of the right to direct not only deprives the person concerned of an asset but involves stigma; that the onus is on the 'prosecution' to justify disqualification; and that unfitness should be proved beyond reasonable doubt in satisfaction of the criminal burden of proof. Furthermore, the *mens rea* required should be intention, recklessness or, at least, gross negligence.

---

156. CCDA 1986 s. 11.

157. Ibid., s. 12. The CDDA is thus aimed at catching a plethora of directorial wrongdoing: for example, paying some creditors but not others (see *Re Carecraft Construction Co. Ltd* [1993] 4 All ER 499, 511; *Re New Generation Engineers* [1993] BCLC 435; *Official Receiver* v. *Barnes (Re Structural Concrete Ltd)* [2001] BCC 478 (regarding non-payment of Crown debts)) and paying the director's own debts (see *Secretary of State* v. *Imo Synthetic Technology Ltd* [1993] BCC 549).

158. This discussion builds on V. Finch, 'Disqualifying Directors: Issues of Rights, Privileges and Employment' (1993) ILJ 35. See also Finch, 'A Plea for Competence'.

159. See, for example, L. S. Sealy, *Company Law and Commercial Reality* (Sweet & Maxwell, London, 1984) p. 46.

160. K. W. Wedderburn, *Company Law Reform* (Fabian Society, London, 1965) p. 10; Wedderburn, 'The Social Responsibility of Companies' (1985) 15 Mel. ULR 4.

In contrast, the privilege approach is consistent with the notion that disqualification is most appropriately justified by the need to protect the public rather than to punish the director.[161] Thus the process of disqualification is seen as non-penal. Withdrawal of the privilege of direction, moreover, is not on this view stigmatic and the period of withdrawal is seen as assessable on protective principles. Nor are employment prospects held to be dashed on a disqualification since business may be carried out by other methods (for example, in partnership or as a sole trader) rather than by the exercise of the privilege of incorporating a limited liability company. Culpability is, therefore, not required in order to justify disqualification: 'mere' incompetence will suffice. Accordingly, the proceedings not being penal, unfitness may be proved on a balance of probabilities according to the usual civil standard.

Were the judiciary to follow the logic of either of the above approaches in a consistent manner, decisions on section 6 CDDA would possess a coherence they now lack. As things stand, some decisions can be placed firmly within the rights approach, some reflect the privilege viewpoint and some have a foot in both camps.

The rights approach is marked, as noted, by an emphasis on culpability and an eye to retributive notions of justice.[162] Thus judges have distinguished between the fitness of directors of the same company on the basis of their culpability. In *Re Cladrose*[163] a director lacking accounting qualifications escaped disqualification following a complete failure to produce audited accounts and to file annual returns. His colleague, a qualified accountant, was, however, disqualified because of his 'unwarrantable' conduct in his failing *vis-à-vis* the accounts and returns. The latter's qualifications, it was stressed, rendered his omissions 'far more blameworthy' than those of his co-director.[164]

---

161. See *Re Lo-Line Electric Motors Ltd* [1988] 4 BCC 415; *Re Westmid Packaging Services Ltd, Secretary of State for Trade and Industry v. Griffiths* [1998] 2 All ER 124, [1998] BCC 836; *R v. Evans* [2000] BCC 901; *Re Westminster Property Management Ltd, Official Receiver v. Stern* [2001] BCC 121. On disqualification undertakings under the Insolvency Act 2000 being seen as protective rather than punitive see *Re Blackspur Group plc* (23 May 2001, unreported); see pp. 536, 549 below. On treating disqualification in ordinary civil terms rather than as a quasi-criminal process, see A. Walters, 'Directors' Disqualification' (2000) 21 Co. Law. 90 at 91.

162. See *R v. Young* [1990] BCC 549 where the court declared that a disqualification order was 'unquestionably a punishment' and ruled that it was inappropriate to link such an order with a conditional discharge. On the retributive tradition see, for example, R. Nozick, *Philosophical Explanations* (Clarendon Press, Oxford, 1981). For arguments favouring conceptualisation of the possible purposes of the disqualification regime in terms of retribution and protection see C. Riley, [2000] CFILR 372 at 373–4.

163. [1990] BCC 11.   164. See further Finch, 'A Plea for Competence'.

Not only does the rights approach stress culpability, it, as indicated, treats interfering with company direction as stigmatic and involving a serious interference with substantive, rather than merely procedural, rights. Thus in *Re ECM (Europe) Electronics*[165] Mervyn Davies J found no 'blameworthiness' sufficient to justify 'stigmatizing' the director and in *Re Crestjoy Products Ltd*[166] Harman J stressed the 'substantial interference with the freedom of the individual' involved in section 6 disqualifications. This emphasis has been echoed in other decisions. Thus in *R v. Holmes*[167] Tucker J said of the disqualification of a director: 'It deprived him of a businessman's best asset, that is recognition in the eyes of the public that he is fit to act as a director of a limited company.'[168]

The mandatory nature of disqualification involved under section 6 of the 1986 Act has encouraged such a rights view on the part of some judges. Thus Harman J argued in *Re Crestjoy Products Ltd*[169] that the statutory predecessor of section 6, section 300 of the Companies Act 1985, had given the judges a discretion on whether to disqualify following a finding of unfitness, a discretion exercisable in the public interest. He contrasted this with the position under section 6 CDDA which implied the appropriateness of a more penal approach: 'disqualification under the former disqualification provision was not penal . . . [I]t seems to me, however, that when I am faced with a mandatory two year disqualification if facts are proved, the matter becomes more nearly penal.'[170] When Hoffmann J decided *Re Swift* in 1992[171] he felt able to comment in unequivocal terms: 'these being penal proceedings Mr Ettings must, I think, be given the benefit of the doubt'[172] while in 1995, in *Secretary of State v. Gray*,[173] Hoffmann LJ (now in the Court of Appeal) was again clearly influenced by the mandatory nature of section 6, indicating that the purpose of making the section mandatory was to ensure that everyone whose conduct fell below the appropriate standard was disqualified for at least two years whether 'the individual court thought this was in the public interest or not'.[174]

---

165. [1991] BCC 268.   **166.** [1990] BCC 23 at 26.   **167.** [1991] BCC 394.
168. Ibid., p. 396. See also *Re ECM (Europe) Electronics Ltd* [1991] BCC 268 at 275.
169. [1990] BCC 23. See also Mummery J in *Re Cedac* [1990] BCC 555 at 558–9. But cf. Court of Appeal in *Re Cedac* [1991] BCC 148.
170. [1990] BCC 23 at 26. See also *Re Cedac Ltd* [1990] BCC 555; *Secretary of State for Trade and Industry v. Langridge* [1991] Ch 402 at 412: 'While a disqualification order is not of itself penal, it is clearly restrictive of the liberty of the person against whom it is made, and its contravention can have penal consequences', per Balcombe LJ.
171. *Re Swift 736 Ltd* [1992] BCC 93.   **172.** Ibid., p. 95.   **173.** [1995] 1 BCLC 276.
174. See also *Re Living Images Ltd* [1996] 1 BCLC 348 where Laddie J spoke of 'moral turpitude' and the need for 'cogent evidence'.

That the judges adopt a penal approach is further evidenced by instances in which factors bearing on culpability rather than public protection are deemed relevant in assessing the appropriate period of disqualification. In *Re Sevenoaks Stationers*[175] Dillon LJ accepted as a mitigating factor the director's personal monetary losses and lack of personal gain.[176] In *Re Churchill Hotel (Plymouth) Ltd*[177] Peter Gibson J decided not to disqualify, noting *inter alia* that the director had apologised for his defaults and 'expressed regret' for the failure of the companies.[178] Similarly in *Re Swift*[179] Hoffmann J noted that the director had 'already suffered considerable misfortune' and had gained nothing financially out of his failure of duty as a director. Consequently he was disqualified for just a year longer than the minimum period. All of these matters relate more readily to culpability and questions of retribution than to issues of public protection.[180] In *Re Chartmore*[181] Harman J imposed the minimum disqualification period on a director who had *inter alia* failed to keep proper accounts, traded on the back of creditors and exhibited a 'total lack of attention to proper duties'. The basis of this leniency was that the director was 'still only about 30', and, in his Lordship's words, was 'really very young' and 'pretty young' respectively when the two relevant companies went down.[182] This indicated, said Harman J, 'conduct at the bottom end of the scale of blameworthiness'. Either Harman J possessed a highly optimistic view of maturation as a public protection, or, as formerly in *Crestjoy*,[183] he was assessing conduct on punitive principles.

175. [1990] BCC 765, [1991] Ch 164. Note that in *Re Sevenoaks* three levels of unfitness to be a director were related to different lengths of the disqualification period.
176. [1990] BCC 765 at 780. See also *Re Pamstock* [1994] 1 BCLC 716; cf. *Re Firedart* [1994] 2 BCLC 340 where Arden J refused to accept, as a matter of mitigation, the fact that the director had personally guaranteed the company's overdraft and had provided security over his own property to the bank.
177. [1988] BCC 112.   178. Ibid., p. 122.   179. [1992] BCC 93 at 97.
180. For a case in which culpability and protection are linked, see *Re Barings plc, Secretary of State for Trade and Industry v. Baker* [1998] BCC 583 at 590, in which Sir Richard Scott VC urged that evidence of a director's 'general conduct in discharge of the office of director goes to the question of the extent to which the public needs protection'.
181. [1990] BCLC 673.
182. In *Re Melcast (Wolverhampton) Ltd* [1991] BCLC 288 the age of the director was again considered to be a mitigating factor in imposing a more lenient disqualification period. The director was aged sixty-eight and his conduct was deemed by Harman J to warrant a ten-year disqualification period. The director was nevertheless disqualified for seven years because the judge considered that by the age of seventy-five it was unlikely that the director would ever again be concerned in the management of a company. In *Re Moorgate Metals Ltd* [1995] 1 BCLC 503 at 520, in contrast, Warner J considered that the age of the director (seventy) should not be considered as a mitigating factor.
183. [1990] BCC 23.

Some cases take an approach that is penal but they are not based principally on retributive notions of punishment: rather they call for denunciation[184] of certain conduct. Thus in Re D. J. Matthews (Joinery Design) Ltd[185] the errant director's counsel argued that his client had evidenced unfitness in directing two previous companies but had 'learned his lessons', was now managing a third company successfully and that, accordingly, the public no longer needed protection from the director's acting irresponsibly. Peter Gibson J was, however, less inclined to gloss over the past culpability, saying: 'Just as there is joy in heaven over a sinner that repenteth, so this court ought to be glad that a director, who has been grossly in dereliction of his duties, now wishes to follow the path of righteousness. But I must take into account the misconduct that has occurred in the past.'[186]

Turning to the privilege approach, the purpose of disqualification for unfitness has been said to be the protection of the public 'against those who use limited liability to abuse the privileges of limited liability and to… "rip off" the public'.[187] This offers a view of limited liability as a privilege accorded upon terms and susceptible to withdrawal for the public good rather than because of any need for retribution or denunciation.[188] The approach is consistent with the notion that disqualification may protect the public in three ways: by keeping unfit directors 'off the road'; by deterring unfit directors from repeating their misconduct; and by encouraging other directors to act properly so as to raise standards of corporate governance.[189] A director may on such a view be disqualified for 'mere' incompetence. Thus in Re Bath Glass[190] Peter Gibson J indicated that for a finding of unfitness: 'the court must be satisfied that the director has been guilty of serious failure…whether deliberately or through incompetence to perform those duties of a director which are attendant on

184. On denunciatory principles see Denning LJ, Report of the Royal Commission on Capital Punishment (Cmd 8932, 1953) p. 18.
185. [1988] 4 BCC 513.
186. Ibid., p. 518. See also Re Samuel Sherman plc [1991] BCC 699 at 712 concerning, unusually, a public company, and CDDA 1986 s. 8; Re Blackspur Group plc (No. 2) [1998] 1 WLR 422, [1998] BCC 11: disqualification intended to have a real deterrent effect on others.
187. Harman J in Re Douglas Construction Services Ltd [1988] BCLC 397 at 402. See also Re Cladrose Ltd [1990] BCC 11 at 18; Secretary of State for Trade and Industry v. Gray [1995] Ch 241; Re Westmid Packing Services Ltd, Secretary of State for Trade and Industry v. Griffiths [1998] 2 All ER 124, [1998] BCC 836 (CA); R v. Evans [2000] BCC 901; Re Westminster Property Management Ltd, Official Receiver v. Stern [2001] BCC 121.
188. Re Rolus Properties [1988] 4 BCC 446 at 449 (Harman J).
189. See Walters, 'Directors' Disqualification', 91. On the raising of standards rationale see Re Swift 736 Ltd [1993] BCC 312 at 315 (CA); Secretary of State for Trade and Industry v. McTighe [1997] BCC 224.
190. [1988] 4 BCC 130 at 133.

the privilege of trading through companies with limited liability'. Consistent with such a concern for both deliberate shortcomings and incompetence has been a judicial movement away from language focusing on turpitude to that of public protection; from asking whether the director has manifested a 'want of commercial morality',[191] towards examining if regard has been paid to 'proper standards'[192] of 'probity and competence'.[193]

The privilege approach thus justifies actions against two very different kinds of errant director, 'the person who is simply exploiting limited liability in a cynical way with a disregard for proper responsibility' or alternatively the director who is exploiting it 'because he is so stupid and ignorant that he is quite incapable of appreciating what has happened and thereby causes large losses by in a sense incompetence'.[194] In both of these cases it has been indicated that there is a need to 'protect the public' from further abuse of the privilege of limited liability.[195]

The privilege approach does not imply that disqualification is a penal process – rather it is a public policy decision that pays heed to the *procedural* rights of directors. Thus, in *Re Lo-Line*[196] disqualification was portrayed in

191. For examples of the language of turpitude see *Re Dawson Print Group Ltd* [1988] 4 BCC 322 ('breach of standards of commercial morality'); *Re CU Fittings Ltd* [1989] 5 BCC 210 ('commercial impropriety' needed); *Re Cedac Ltd* [1990] BCC 555 (Mummery J: 'a lack of commercial probity' or 'commercially culpable manner'); *Re Park House Properties Ltd* [1997] 2 BCLC 530 (Neuberger J: 'attributable to ignorance born of a culpable failure to make enquiries or, where enquiries were made, of culpable failure to consider or appreciate the results of those enquiries').

192. See Harman J in *Re Keypack Homecare Ltd (No. 2)* [1990] BCC 117; Peter Gibson J in *Re Churchill Hotel (Plymouth) Ltd* [1988] BCC 112 at 117.

193. *Re Landhurst Leasing* [1999] 1 BCLC 286 at 344. The standard may vary according to the nature and size of the company and the role which the defendant played in its affairs: *Re Continental Assurance Co. of London plc (sub nom. Secretary of State for Trade and Industry v. Burrows)* [1996] BCC 888, [1997] BCLC 48; *Re Barings plc* [1998] BCC 583 at 586; *Re Barings plc (No. 5)* [1999] 1 BCLC 433; *Re Kaytech International plc* [1999] BCC 390; *Official Receiver v. Vass* [1999] BCC 516.

194. Harman J in *Re Douglas Construction Services Ltd* [1988] BCLC 397 at 402. In *Baker v. Secretary of State for Trade and Industry* [2001] BCC 273 the Court of Appeal upheld the trial judge's disqualification order covering a director who had failed to heed clear warning signals, 'hoped for the best' and showed 'incompetence to a high degree'.

195. *Re Douglas Construction Services Ltd*, at 402. In *Re Westminster Property Management Ltd*, *Official Receiver v. Stern* [2001] 1 All ER 633, [2001] BCC 121, the Court of Appeal held that the imposition of disqualification (whose primary purpose was deemed not penal but to protect the public against those whose past record as a director has shown them to be a danger to creditors and others) was compatible with, as a justified derogation from, Article 43 (freedom of establishment) and Article 49 (freedom to provide services) of the European Community Treaty. Note also that the CLRSG has canvassed the idea that the Secretary of State might be provided with a power to apply to the court for an interim order preventing a director from acting as such. This power would be employable before proceedings for disqualification were heard and is designed to cope with the phoenix syndrome and the time lag for proceedings against directors: see *Final Report*, 2001, p. 332.

196. *Re Lo-Line Electric Motors Ltd* [1988] 4 BCC 415.

the following terms:

> The primary purpose... is not to punish the individual but to protect
> the public against the future conduct of companies by persons whose
> past records as directors of insolvent companies have shown them to be
> a danger to creditors and others. Therefore, the power is not
> fundamentally penal. But... disqualification does involve a substantial
> interference with the freedom of the individual. It follows that the
> rights of the individual must be fully protected.[197]

From the privilege perspective, it matters little whether disqualification
affects a director's personal employment prospects adversely: the public interest is the dominant consideration. The courts, nevertheless, have
tended, when applying the privilege approach, to stress that loss of the
facility of limited liability does not end all employment prospects. In *Re
Southbourne Sheet Metal Co. Ltd*[198] Harman J stated that the disqualification
jurisdiction was 'of a somewhat hybrid character'. It was not a prosecution
neither was it an ordinary civil proceeding:

> it is not a penal proceeding. It is not intended to punish the director. It
> is a proceeding where the DTI or the Official Receiver... is proceeding
> with a view to protecting the public by removing from a man the
> privilege of trading under the cover of limited liability. It does not stop
> a man's freedom to trade, either as a sole trader or in a partnership,
> upon... 'his own bottom', where he is liable down to his last collar
> stud.[199]

The errant director might well take a more serious view of disqualification
and its effects, particularly when, in the aftermath, he or she seeks credit
under the cloud of such an order. Harman J has, nevertheless, repeatedly
stressed that it is always open to any disqualified person to carry on trading
in business, on their own account or as a partner.[200]

The *strength* of the procedural protections offered to a director may also
depend on the courts' conception of the disqualification process as non-
penal or penal. Thus a notice requirement is more likely to be seen as
directory rather than mandatory when a court stresses public protection
rather than private interest.[201] Balcombe LJ in *Re Tasbian Ltd (No. 3)*[202] put

---

197. Ibid., p. 419.   198. [1991] BCC 732.   199. Ibid., p. 734.
200. See also *Re Chartmore Ltd* [1990] BCLC 673 at 675; *Re Probe Data Systems Ltd (No. 3)* [1991]
BCC 428 at 434 (see Court of Appeal at [1992] BCC 110). For an example of plans to continue
trading accepting personal liability after disqualification, see *Re D. J. Matthews (Joinery Design)
Ltd* [1988] 4 BCC 513 at 518.
201. Contrast the majority and minority judgments in *Re Cedac Ltd* [1990] BCC 555, [1991] BCC
148 (Court of Appeal), concerning application of CDDA 1986 s. 16(1).
202. [1992] BCC 358.

the unanimous Court of Appeal view in stating that it would not be right to preclude trial of a disqualification issue 'merely' because the Official Receiver had supported an *ex parte* application with inaccurate facts. His Lordship stressed: 'this is public interest litigation'.[203]

Is there a discernible judicial trend favouring either the rights or the privilege approach? It seems not. Decisions offer examples, as noted, of both approaches, with, for example, *ECM Europe*[204] and *Southbourne*[205] offering quite different perspectives. Individual judges have also been seen to adopt elements of both the rights and privilege standpoints. Thus Harman J has been noted under the rights heading in *Crestjoy*[206] and *Chartmore*[207] and as paying heed to privilege-based factors in *Southbourne*.[208] Even within individual judgments the language associated with the two approaches intermixes. Thus Dillon LJ's judgment in *Re Sevenoaks*[209] stresses both the public protection rationale of disqualification and the absence of personal gain on the director's part. A similar confusion is encountered in *Re Keypack*[210] and in *Griffiths*[211] where disqualification was based on ostensibly protective principles but where the period of disqualification for the 'offence' was approached by assessments of culpability.[212]

203. Ibid., p. 366. For those concerned with employment issues more generally, an attractive feature of the privilege approach, with its focus on the public interest, may be its attention to the wider employment implications of disqualification. Under the former section 300 of the Companies Act 1985 the judicial discretion to disqualify or not on a finding of unfitness was, on numerous occasions, exercised so as to avoid undue consequences for clients or employees of the director's other companies. Thus in *Re Majestic Sound Recording Studios Ltd* [1988] 4 BCC 519 and in *Re Lo-Line Electric Motors Ltd* [1988] 4 BCC 45 (see also *Re Artic Engineering Ltd (No. 2)* [1986] BCLC 253) directors were allowed to continue in office but subject in each case to supervisory arrangements. The mandatory nature of disqualification under CDDA 1986 s. 6 might be expected to rule out such courses of action and demand that concessions be made only at the stage of establishing unfitness. That some flexibility of judicial approach remains possible has, however, been made clear in *Re Chartmore Ltd* [1990] BCLC 673, in which Harman J granted leave to waive disqualification in respect of a particular company for a one-year trial period subject to conditions. It may be the case, therefore, that by resort to CDDA 1986 ss. 1(1) and 17 – the bases for the waiver in *Chartmore* – continued attention can be given to the employment effects of disqualification. On leave to act under CDDA 1986 s. 17 see further Griffin, *Personal Liability*, pp. 189–93; *Secretary of State for Trade and Industry v. Baker* [1999] 1 All ER 1017; *Secretary of State for Trade and Industry v. Rosenfeld* [1999] BCC 413; *Re TLL Realisations Ltd, Secretary of State for Trade and Industry v. Collins* [2000] BCC 998.
204. *Re ECM (Europe) Electronics* [1991] BCC 268, [1992] BCLC 814.
205. *Re Southbourne Sheet Metal Co. Ltd* [1991] BCC 732.
206. *Re Crestjoy Products Ltd* [1990] BCC 23, [1990] BCLC 677.
207. *Re Chartmore Ltd* [1990] BCLC 673.   208. [1991] BCC 732.
209. *Re Sevenoaks Stationers (Retail) Ltd* [1990] BCC 765, [1991] Ch 164.
210. *Re Keypack Homecare Ltd* [1987] BCLC 409; *(No. 2)* [1990] BCC 117.
211. *Secretary of State for Trade and Industry v. Griffiths, Re Westmid Packaging Services Ltd (No. 3)* [1998] BCC 836, the Court of Appeal stating that while protection of the public is the primary purpose of disqualification, in truth the exercise engaged in when making a disqualification order is little different from any sentencing exercise.
212. See also *Re Manlon Trading Ltd, Official Receiver v. Haroon Abdul Aziz* [1995] 1 All ER 988, per Evans-Lombe J: 'The legislature must have envisaged that it was in the public interest that a businessman whose past conduct had justified disqualification should, after an appropriate

Both policy considerations and conceptual coherence favour adopting a single approach to disqualification: one based on the notion of privilege/public protection rather than rights/penality. A contrast may here be drawn between disqualification and fraudulent trading,[213] which may appropriately be deemed penal. Looking to wrongful trading, we have seen above that this contains a strong compensatory dimension.[214] In parallel with such an approach, there seems no good case for adopting an exclusively penal viewpoint in relation to unfitness where the director's behaviour does not fall foul of explicitly criminal provisions.[215]

It has been argued that a combined approach may be necessary since 'disqualification periods are, and can often only be, decided on the basis of a penal principle not a solely protective one'.[216] It has also been suggested that public opinion demands a punitive response to 'dishonest and fraudulent directors'.[217] If, however, a privilege approach is adopted this does not mean that a director's misconduct or moral turpitude is irrelevant. Rather (as indicated in *Lo-Line*[218]) it means that disqualification may, where appropriate, be used to protect the public against the potential misbehaviour of a person who has manifested an undesirable attitude to the privilege of limited liability. The 'dishonest and fraudulent director' is thus likely to be dealt with sufficiently severely to assuage public opinion. Central to the privilege approach is, however, a rejection of using disqualification per section 6 merely for the purposes of punishment in the retributive sense.

What, then, of the denunciatory approach which proposes disqualification as a means of stamping certain behaviour as unacceptable? The privilege viewpoint, with its lack of concern to punish, again suggests that denunciation is not an appropriate end for the disqualification process. If a director has acted fraudulently or committed other criminal offences or has engaged in wrongful trading then he or she can be dealt with by provisions other than section 6.[219] If past conduct indicates untrustworthiness

period in which the public was to be protected and during which it must be presumed he became aware of the consequences of his past failings, have restored to him the right to manage businesses with the protection of limited liability', at 1003.

213. Insolvency Act 1986 s. 213. See *Re Produce Marketing Consortium Ltd (No. 2)* [1989] 5 BCC 569 at 594.

214. See *Re Produce Marketing Consortium Ltd*, at p. 597. But see discussion at pp. 513–14 above.

215. For example, CDDA 1986 ss. 2, 4, 5. See also CDDA 1986 s. 10 re disqualification for fraudulent trading and wrongful trading. See *R v. Holmes* [1991] BCC 394 regarding the 'difficulty' in reconciling a compensation order, per Insolvency Act 1986 s. 213, and a disqualification order.

216. S. Wheeler (1990) IL&P 174 at 175.

217. See Newbegin, 'Disqualifying Directors', *The Lawyer*, 24 September 1991.

218. [1988] 4 BCC 415 at 419.

219. See, for example, Insolvency Act 1986 ss. 213, 214; Companies Act 1985 s. 458.

or other characteristics that raise doubts about future conduct then the privilege approach justifies disqualification on the grounds of public protection. Where a director is not a person from whom the public needs protection now or in the future, then he or she should not be disqualified under section 6. In relation to past behaviour, advocates of the privilege approach may thus argue that denunciation, like retribution, may be needed in relation to certain illegal directorial acts but that such needs are catered for outside the disqualification process; that introducing denunciatory and retributive principles into disqualification involves unnecessary and inappropriate confusion.

A privilege standpoint emphasises that incompetence may provide a basis for disqualification.[220] (Incompetence, after all, is, when combined with mismanagement, the major cause of corporate insolvency.[221]) Being non-penal, the burden of proof should, according to such a view, be on balance of probabilities, as indicated in *Re Southbourne*.[222] A privilege approach does not, however, imply that a director's interests are to be ignored. The errant director does not, on such a view, have a substantive right to retain the facility of limited liability but does possess procedural rights. These exist in the CDDA[223] and offer some protection against potential prejudice in spite of the courts' increased inclination, on adopting a privilege approach, to treat them as directory rather than mandatory.[224]

A case such as *Re Chartmore*[225] suggests that the courts are capable of giving section 6 a degree of flexibility. Recent cases do not, however, show that a consistent or coherent approach to section 6 disqualifications has been arrived at. The privilege rationale offers a route to such coherence. More importantly it emphasises that, in removing the facility of limited liability, public protection is paramount.[226]

So much for the rationales underpinning the use of disqualification. The second issue for consideration is whether the disqualification

---

220. *Re Bath Glass Ltd* [1988] 4 BCC 130, at 133.

221. See ch. 4 above; J. Argenti, *Corporate Collapse: The Causes and Symptoms* (McGraw-Hill, London, 1976); J. R. Lingard, *Corporate Rescues and Insolvencies* (2nd edn, Butterworths, London, 1989); C. Campbell and B. Underdown, *Corporate Insolvency in Practice: An Analytical Approach* (Chapman, London, 1991) ch. 2.

222. *Re Southbourne Sheet Metal Co. Ltd* [1991] BCC 732 at 734.

223. See CDDA 1986 ss. 7 and 16; see also S. Wheeler [1991] IL&P 141.

224. See, for example, *Re Cedac Ltd* [1991] BCC 148 (CA), re CDDA 1986 s. 16(1). See *Re Probe Data Systems Ltd (No. 3)* [1992] BCC 110 and *Re Tasbian Ltd (No. 3)* [1992] BCC 358: Court of Appeal judgments re CDDA 1986 s. 7(2) applications.

225. [1990] BCLC 673.

226. Whether the judges are prepared to accept this approach is, of course, an issue: see 'The Fourth Annual Leonard Sainer Lecture – The Rt Hon. Lord Hoffmann', (1997) 18 Co. Law. 194. See further p. 533 below.

rules actually make a difference to expertise, honesty and competence on the ground. On this point a number of commentators have argued that the impact of the rules has been small.[227] Two National Audit Office (NAO) Reports (of 1993 and 1999)[228] respectively criticised the efficiency of the Insolvency Service's administration of the CDDA and cautioned that disqualification was perceived as having only a marginal effect on improving the behaviour of directors generally.[229] A later survey also revealed that insolvency practitioners were sceptical concerning the effectiveness of disqualification which was 'not influential ... not well placed and ... difficult to enforce'.[230] One explanation for the low incidence of disqualification orders may be that the officials who are involved in implementation are no more consistent about the aims and objectives of disqualification than the judiciary. Wheeler, for instance, argues that the disqualification process involves a 'unique mix of public regulation, public interest and private funding'.[231] She stresses that lack of resources and inefficiencies in the enforcing agency are not sufficient explanations of low numbers of disqualifications and that much can be explained by the inconsistencies of approach that are found amongst IPs and between IPs and the enforcing agency. Her portrait is of an implementation breakdown born out of philosophical differences. In selecting cases for disqualification, she argues, many actions fail to proceed because a large number of conduct reports contain 'moral frames and end goals which do not accord with the goals and resulting construction of the public interest used by the Disqualification Unit'.[232]

---

227. See, for example, A. Hicks, 'Director Disqualification: Can It Deliver?' [2001] JBL 433; Hicks, *Disqualification of Directors*; A. Walters, 'Directors' Disqualification after the Insolvency Act 2000: The New Regime' [2001] Ins. Law. 86; Walters, 'Directors' Duties: The Impact of the Directors' Disqualification Act 1986' (2000) 21 Co. Law. 110.

228. NAO, *Company Director Disqualification* (October 1993, HC 907), *Company Director Disqualification: A Follow Up Report* (May 1999, HC 424). See S. Wheeler, 'Directors' Disqualification: Insolvency Practitioners and the Decision-making Process' (1995) 15 *Legal Studies* 283.

229. The 1993 NAO Report stated that 18,165 reported cases of alleged unfit conduct had resulted in at most 1,712 disqualification orders: Wheeler, 'Directors' Disqualification', p. 285; the Insolvency Service's Annual Report 2000–1 stated that in 2000–1 its Disqualification Unit received 5,551 reports identifying elements of unfit conduct by directors: 3,328 from IPs and 2,223 from the Official Receiver (1999–2000, 3,311 and 2,285). In 2000–1 1,456 disqualification proceedings were issued, marginally down on 1999–2000. The number of disqualification orders obtained in 2000–1 was 1,548. Of these, 887 involved two to five years' disqualification; 614 involved six to ten years and 47 involved eleven years. Disqualifications were most numerous in the textile, clothing and manufacturing sectors; and the construction and demolition sectors (at 13 per cent of total in each case).

230. See Hicks, 'Can It Deliver?', p. 437.

231. Wheeler, 'Directors' Disqualification', p. 286.   **232.** Ibid., p. 304.

In the 1996 Sainer lecture[233] Lord Hoffmann argued that disqualification had done little to raise standards of skill and care and that disqualification for incompetence was extremely rare, with the courts tending to emphasise conduct which breaches standards of accepted commercial morality. 'It is said that incompetent directors ought to be put off the road for a while like incompetent drivers, simply for the protection of the public. But the courts have never completely accepted this philosophy.'[234]

Sympathy with a 'rights' approach to direction may thus make judges reluctant to disqualify in a manner that produces a dramatic impact on standards. Lord Hoffmann noted that the courts were often mindful of the serious impact of disqualification on an individual. More practical factors, however, reduce the protective effect of disqualification for unfitness.[235] The law requires no prior qualification for becoming a company director,[236] limited liability companies can be incorporated at minimal cost and it is not easy to fix an *ex post facto* standard of competence for disqualification.[237] The disqualification process, moreover, only comes into play in cases where the incompetence (or 'unfitness') at issue is followed by insolvency (which may be a matter of happenstance). Routine investigations and the making of unfit conduct reports by administrative receivers, administrators or liquidators only follow entry into formal insolvency proceedings.[238] The conduct of directors of companies that are merely struck off the register and dissolved is not investigated.[239] Many incompetent directors may escape disqualification due to good fortune or the skill of other parties. Another factor is the period of time needed to collect evidence for a formal hearing: this may be so considerable as to lead to a number of disqualifications being dropped because they are out

233. Note, 'Hoffmann Plays Down Law's Contribution to the Efficiency of Corporate Management' (1997) 18 Co. Law. 56; Lord Hoffmann, 'Sainer Lecture'.

234. Note (1997) 18 Co. Law. 56. For an argument that there is a 'growing judicial intolerance of honest or uninformed incompetence' see E. Ferran, *Company Law and Corporate Finance* (Oxford University Press, Oxford, 1999) p. 234.

235. See Hicks, 'Can It Deliver?', pp. 439–40 and *Disqualification of Directors*, pp. 68–9.

236. Lord Hoffmann made the point that it was difficult to find an *ex post facto* standard of competence for disqualification because the law does not require any qualification to become a director: Lord Hoffmann, 'Sainer Lecture' at 197.

237. Schedule 1 of the CDDA 1986 gives a definition of improper conduct but offers the well-intentioned director little guidance on standards of best practice to creditors.

238. On investigative powers of office holders see C. Campbell, 'Investigations by Insolvency Practitioners – Powers and Restraints: Part I' (2000) 16. IL&P 182.

239. See Hicks, 'Can It Deliver?', pp. 443–5. On 1996–7 figures, 80 per cent of companies removed from the register were struck off without any investigation or reporting at all.

of time.[240] Periods of disqualification, furthermore, tend to be short (on average five years[241]) and the enforcement of orders is difficult. In the case of self-employed directors, these individuals may avoid the impact of disqualification by setting up in their own name. It is, indeed, arguable that disqualification is a sanction that is most effective when applied to professional, employed executives but one that in practice is used more widely in relation to the self-employed individual with regard to whom it has less impact.[242] Yet further considerations reducing the protective impact of the disqualification regime are that the deterrent effect of disqualifications may be low because directors have little awareness of disqualification or its associated penalties; the chances of disqualification, post-insolvency, are small; and disqualification does not remove ill-gotten gains.

Finally, the realities of funding have to be taken into account. The primary investigator of directorial conduct is usually the liquidator but if a company has few assets, the creditors are unlikely to press for a winding up and no investigation or report on the directors' conduct will be carried out.[243] There is, moreover, an undesirable incentive effect here: the more drastically directors remove residual assets from a company the less likely it is that a formal insolvency procedure will be instigated and the directors' conduct investigated.

In the last decade there have, nevertheless, been improvements in the disqualification system. After the NAO Report of 1993 and its criticism of the Insolvency Service's enforcement endeavours there has been a considerable increase in the volume of disqualification proceedings.[244] Over 1,500 disqualification orders are now being made annually by the courts.[245] In 1998, as noted above, the IS set up a disqualification hotline[246]

240. See CDDA 1986 s. 7: the application for disqualification must be made within two years from the date the company 'became insolvent', but the court may, exceptionally, give leave to make a later application (s. 7(2)); *Re Probe Data Systems Ltd (No. 3)* [1992] BCC 110 at 111: Scott LJ's factors to be taken into account when considering whether to grant leave.

241. See NAO Report (1999); Hicks, 'Can It Deliver?', p. 440.

242. See Hicks, 'Can It Deliver?', p. 446.

243. Administrative receivers are, however, required to report on the conduct of directors. In compulsory liquidations the Official Receiver has a duty to investigate the causes of failure and conduct of directors but a voluntary liquidator has fewer obligations and powers of investigation: the IP involved will only report on the conduct of directors on the basis of information coming to light in the investigation of assets. See further Hicks, 'Can It Deliver?', p. 444. See also CLRSG, *Final Report*, 2001, para. 15.25: the Review Group suggests extending to administrators the (liquidator's) duty of reporting of offences.

244. See Walters, 'New Regime'.

245. The Insolvency Service's Annual Report for the year to 31 March 2001 indicated that there were 1,548 disqualification orders during those twelve months.

246. See p. 497 above; in 2000–1 449 calls were made, resulting in 232 substantive complaints and 47 cases being referred to the DTI legal service, 28 to Official Receivers and 13 to other agencies. Nine convictions arose from hotline complaints: IS Annual Report 2000–1, p. 20.

to enable members of the public to report possible contraventions of prohibitions on direction and, in 2000, the Government announced the setting up by the IS of a specialist team to investigate directors who asset-strip companies. This Forensic Insolvency Recovery Service (FIRS) was given the power to take legal action to recover money from fraudulent and negligent directors of failed companies.

The Court of Appeal has also played a role in extending the scope of disqualification. Section 22 of the CDDA extends liability for disqualification on the grounds of unfitness to shadow directors, defined by section 22(5) of the CDDA as persons 'in accordance with whose directions or instructions the directors of a company are accustomed to act (but that person is not deemed a shadow director by reason only that the directors act on directions given by him in a professional capacity)'.[247] In *Secretary of State for Trade and Industry* v. *Deverell*[248] the concept of the shadow director in CDDA section 22 was at issue and the court widened the category of persons who may be regarded as such directors and so may be covered *inter alia* by the rules on directors' liability and disqualification. Morritt LJ was concerned 'to identify those with real influence in the corporate affairs of the company'. He stated that the intention of Parliament was to protect the public and that 'all that is required is that what is said by the shadow to the board is not by way of professional advice but is usually followed over a wide enough area and for long enough'. Subservience by the board was not required and the influence of the shadow director need not extend to the whole field of the company's activities. Whether a communication amounted to 'directions or instructions', moreover, was to be objectively assessed.[249]

In *Re Kaytech*[250] the court took a similarly practical approach for determining whether a person is a *de facto* director and amenable to the directors' liability and disqualification rules: all relevant internal and external factors were to be taken into account, to be determined as a question of fact and not by applying one single test.[251]

247. See G. Morse, 'Shadow Directors and De Facto Directors in the Context of Proceedings for Disqualification on the Grounds of Unfitness and Wrongful Trading' in Rider (ed.), *The Corporate Dimension*; S. Griffin, 'The Characteristics and Identification of a *De Facto* Director' [2000] 1 CFILR 126; G. Bhattacharyya, 'Shadow Directors and Wrongful Trading Revisited' (1995) 15 Co. Law. 313; L. Jones, 'Distinguishing Shadow Directors' (1994) Sol. Jo. 440.
248. [2000] 2 WLR 907.
249. See Payne, 'Casting Light'; D. Milman, 'A Fresh Light on Shadow Directors' [2000] Ins. Law. 171. For an earlier restrictive view see *Re PFTZM Ltd* [1995] BCC 280.
250. [1999] 2 BCLC 351; compare with *Re Hydrodan (Corby) Ltd* [1994] BCC 161: see N. Campbell, '*Re Hydrodan (Corby) Ltd*' [1994] JBL 609.
251. See Payne, 'Casting Light'.

The Insolvency Act 2000 introduced a new fast-track procedure for processing disqualifications. Section 6 of that Act inserts a new section 1A into the CDDA to establish a process for achieving disqualification without the involvement of the court.[252] In this process the Secretary of State is empowered to accept consensual undertakings from directors that are equivalent in effect to disqualification orders.[253] The parties can, accordingly, negotiate and agree on a period of disqualification in a form of plea bargain. The aim of the new procedure is to reduce enforcement costs; make regulation more responsive (by reducing the period during which proceedings are pending and directors are still empowered to act); save court resources and reduce the uncertainties involved in lengthy disqualification processes.[254]

It remains to be seen how the new process works but there may be some way to go. A thousand disqualifications a year has been said to 'make little impact on the legions of the unfit'.[255] There are around 3 million directors with millions more who could buy a company off the shelf and so current levels of disqualification may have a small impact and a small deterrent effect. There are, moreover, risks in a plea-bargaining approach, notably that periods of disqualification will be reduced overall and that the deterrent and control effects of disqualification will be weakened. From the directors' point of view, there are dangers that the new regime creates incentives to accept disqualification early in negotiations (to avoid escalating costs[256]) and that they will be economically distanced from a just hearing of their case.[257]

252. See Insolvency Act 2000 (Commencement No. 1 and Transitional Provisions) Order 2001 (SI 2001 No. 766) (C27).

253. Formerly the Secretary of State would have been restricted in accepting compromises by the ruling in *Re Blackspur Group plc, Secretary of State for Trade and Industry v. Davies* [1998] 1 WLR 422: see Walters, 'New Regime', p. 88. Before the 2000 Act parties might, however, have negotiated a disqualification for a specified period and asked the court to approve this without a full hearing: see *Re Carecraft Construction Co. Ltd* [1994] 1 WLR 172; Practice Direction [1996] 1 All ER 445; Special Briefing, 'Practice Note' [1996] 9 *Insolvency Intelligence* 22; *Official Receiver v. Cooper* [1999] BCC 115; *Re SIG Security Services Ltd, Official Receiver v. Bond* [1998] BCC 978.

254. Commenting on the new powers, Kim Howells, Consumer Affairs Minister, said: 'Ensuring that the business community and consumers are protected from the activities of rogue directors at the earliest opportunity is vital. The new power to disqualify administratively will save time in the courts.' See Comment, ' "Fast Track" Disqualification is Under Way' (2001) 22 Co. Law. 213 at 214. On the tension between the public interest in 'quickie' disqualifications and the public interest in the promotion of good corporate governance see A. Walters, 'Bare Undertakings in Directors' Disqualification Proceedings: The Insolvency Act 2000, *Blackspur* and Beyond' (2001) 22 Co. Law. 290.

255. Comment (1999) 20 Co. Law. 97. *The Times*, 4 June 1998, described disqualification as a 'limp lettuce leaf'. As indicated above, 1,548 disqualification orders were obtained in 2001.

256. See Walters, 'New Regime', p. 93; Practice Direction: Directors' Disqualification Proceedings [1996] 1 All ER 445, para. 28.1.

257. See further pp. 548–9 below.

If disqualification were to be relied upon significantly to boost the expertise of directors, then steps would have to be taken to overcome its inherent weaknesses. Enforcement costs and periods could be reduced further by establishing a specialist tribunal;[258] sanctions could be made more severe and also more flexible; more rigorous policing could be directed at those who breach disqualification orders;[259] more information could be given to directors and the public on disqualifications[260] and a greater emphasis placed on protecting the public.[261] More radically, there could be a rethinking of the conditions under which directorial conduct is the subject of reporting so that the current dependency on formal insolvency processes is reduced and investigations can be instigated following such events as complaints or examples of errant behaviour that do not lead to insolvency.[262]

It should not be forgotten that other approaches to improving directorial expertise can be considered. The criminal law has a role to play in limiting the worst forms of directorial misbehaviour and directors may be held to account by such mechanisms as fraudulent trading,[263] which, as noted, the CLRSG considered a valuable weapon in countering crime.[264] Laws providing for the personal liability of directors (for example, for wrongful trading) might also be said to encourage directorial expertise and standards. The use of criminal laws, however, demands that high standards of proof be satisfied and it has been pointed out that the criminal offences established in the Companies Acts are hugely under-enforced.[265] As for compensatory liabilities, it has been noted above that factors such as funding difficulties for liquidators very significantly reduce regulatory effects. Hicks has, nevertheless, argued that evidential problems in the current law might be overcome and that 'New, strict liability offences and civil penalties which preclude the misuse of corporate property to the

---

258. As advocated by Hicks, 'Can It Deliver?', p. 446.

259. As noted, the CLRSG recommended in 2001 that the duty on a voluntary liquidator to report offences (introduced in the Insolvency Act 2000) should be extended to administrators: see CLRSG, *Final Report*, 2001, para. 15.25.

260. This might involve the issue of guidance to directors on their duties and responsibilities together with the expected standards of behaviour: see Hicks, 'Can It Deliver?', pp. 449–51. The Law Commission recommended in 1999 that the Companies House form signed by persons becoming directors should contain a statutory statement of their duties: the form would be signed to acknowledge its having been read; See Law Commission, *Regulating Conflicts of Interest*.

261. See Hicks, 'Can It Deliver?'; Finch, 'Disqualifying Directors'.

262. On DTI investigations under the Companies Act 1985 Part XIV, see J. Boyle, J. Birds, E. Ferran and C. Villiers, *Boyle and Birds' Company Law* (4th edn, Jordans, Bristol, 2000), pp. 589–99.

263. Companies Act 1985 s. 458.   264. CLRSG, *Final Report*, 2001, para. 15.7.

265. See Hicks, 'Can It Deliver?', p. 454.

detriment of creditors could be highly effective, being easier to prove than the broad and uncertain test of unfitness.'[266]

A statement of statutory duties to creditors that was understood by directors might raise standards by increasing directors' awareness of their obligations in times of trouble. What is clear is the extent of work that has to be done. A 2001 survey of directors of companies with an average of over 700 employees and £167 million annual turnover revealed that they were 'fundamentally ignorant' about their duties and liabilities on insolvency.[267] Two-thirds of finance, legal and managing directors were unaware that their personal liability might be higher if they had above-average expertise and experience. The same proportion did not know that their company could continue to trade if it was insolvent provided that it had a reasonable prospect of avoiding liquidation.

The issue of information for directors has been considered by the Law Commission and the Scottish Law Commission[268] as well as by the CLRSG.[269] The CLRSG wanted 'greater clarity on what is expected of directors' and to make the law more accessible as well as to bring the law into line with modern business practice: 'clear, accessible and authoritative guidance for directors on which they may safely rely, on the basis that it will bind the courts and thus be consistently applied'.[270] As noted already, however, no detailed blueprints can be set down and the courts must still be relied upon to give flesh to the rules.[271] It may, moreover, be the case that it will be the brightest, best and most competent directors that make themselves aware of their duties, rather than the less able and less competent. The effect may be to polish the standards of directors who already perform well rather than to raise the standards of those who cause

---

266. See Hicks, *Disqualification of Directors*, p. v, who suggests that disqualifying courts might be empowered to make compensation orders and that the IS might provide resources for pursuing wrongful trading and other compensation claims.

267. Survey by Taylor, Joynson and Garrett, *Legal Director* magazine, reported in *Financial Times*, 1 November 2001.

268. Law Commission and Scottish Law Commission, *Regulating Conflicts of Interests*.

269. CLRSG, *Final Report*, 2001, pp. 42–5. See also CLRSG, *Developing the Framework*, paras. 3.12–3.85; CLRSG, *Completing the Structure*, ch. 3.

270. CLRSG, *Final Report*, 2001, para. 3.9.

271. On questioning whether the judges are equipped to review directors' actions near insolvency, or to assess business risks, see T. Telfer, 'Risk and Insolvent Trading' in R. Grantham and C. Rickett (eds.), *Corporate Personality in the Twentieth Century* (Hart, Oxford, 1998) pp. 138–9; G. Varollo and J. Fukelstein, 'Fiduciary Obligations of Directors of the Financially Troubled Company' (1982) 48 *Business Lawyer* 239; D. Wishart, *Company Law in Context* (Oxford University Press, Auckland, 1994).

greatest losses to creditors. It can be pointed out, moreover, that knowledge of one's duties is not the same as knowing how to turn around a company's fortunes in times of trouble. It is only one of many expectations that we may have of directors in troubled times.[272] More rigorous standards, of course, might prompt directors to behave more responsibly but it can be argued that such steps have to be combined with new training initiatives to have real effects.

Other proposals on raising directorial expertise relate to company direction in general, rather than to performance in the specific context of insolvency, and space does not allow a full review here.[273] Steps such as professionalisation and training[274] and the monitoring and regulation of directorial behaviour may, however, encourage higher standards of performance across the spectrum of corporate fortunes.[275] The market, indeed, may supply incentives that may raise directors' standards. Thus banks may consider the training and track records of directors when assessing loan risks and may require personal guarantees in the case of less impressive directors. A straw poll at a recent INSOL conference, moreover, revealed that a 'sizeable majority' of delegates favoured a compulsory competence test that directors would sit (along 'driving test' lines) before being allowed to act as directors.[276] Informational solutions are also being increasingly advocated. It has been suggested that the Government could prepare directors' 'information packs' to advise new directors on

---

272. See L. Hitchens, 'Directorships: How Many Is Too Many?' (2000) CFILR 359.

273. See Finch, 'Company Directors'.

274. Ibid. The Institute of Directors (IOD) introduced the concept of a 'chartered director' in 1999. To achieve this status directors must have experience as a director, must pass an examination and must subscribe to the IOD's Code of Professional Conduct: see further R. Esen, 'Chartered Directors' Qualification: Professionalism on UK Boards' (2000) 21 Co. Law. 289; IOD website, http://www.iod.co.uk/profdev/howto.cd.html. The IOD has also developed a Diploma in Company Direction and promoted a range of measures designed to improve directorial competence. Degrees in company direction are now available at various academic institutions. It is, however, questionable whether this burgeoning demand is raising the standards of the most able and competent rather than the performance of those individuals most likely to underperform: see Finch, 'Company Directors'. On the issuing of guidance for directors and the need to deal with functions as well as duties, see Hitchens, 'Directorships', pp. 367–8. The CLRSG rejected the notion that company directors should be required to have formal qualifications or age limits: see CLRSG, *Final Report*, 2001, para. 3.49. The CLRSG's preferred route lay through developing the rules on disclosure: para. 6.18.

275. The Combined Code recommends that on first appointment to be a director of a listed company directors should be given training on their role, but directors of listed companies are only a small minority of directors: see Hitchens, 'Directorships', p. 366; C. Riley, 'The Company Director's Duty of Care and Skill: The Case for an Onerous but Subjective Standard' (1999) 62 MLR 697.

276. See Editorial, (2001) 17 IL&P 121.

their functions and obligations[277] and, in practice, bodies such as R3 are taking information solutions forward with business 'survival guides' for directors.[278]

Such approaches can, however, offer no guarantees that directorial expertise will save companies in a given situation: enterprise necessarily involves risks. What *insolvency* procedures should not do is discourage directors from seeking help or prevent directors from applying their skills in times of corporate troubles: for instance, by creating excessive incentives to depart from troubled companies or by excluding directors too fully from, or at too early a stage in, rescue or insolvency processes.

Efficiency

Do insolvency laws and processes induce directors to behave in ways that efficiently balance the protection of creditor interests with needs to pursue rescue options and encourage enterprise?[279] It has been pointed out above that certain insolvency processes (e.g. administration) can be criticised as offering directors too weak a set of incentives to apply their expertise to rescue or creditor protection objectives in times of trouble. That discussion will not be repeated, nor is there the space here to discuss how the law generally conduces to directorial skill and care.[280] What can be done is to focus on the position of the director during corporate troubles and the efficiency of controls and incentives operating at such times. As a preliminary issue, then, the efficiency implications of imposing incentives and disincentives on directors, rather than corporations, should be noted. A first reason for targeting directors is that the total costs of sanctioning directors may be lower than the costs involved in controlling corporations so as to achieve the same reductions in wrongdoing.[281] Personal liability, moreover, is less liable to impose costs on a firm that will either increase the likelihood of insolvency or worsen the position of creditors in an insolvency. Making directors liable may also provide an efficient way to raise

---

277. Ibid. The suggestion is to fund such packs by a modest levy on companies each time a notice of appointment or change of directors is filed with the Registrar of Companies.

278. See R3 (formerly SPI), *Ostrich's Guide to Business Survival* (R3, London, 2001).

279. This, it will be seen, is not a Jacksonian test of whether the law conduces to maximising the pool of assets available to all the company's creditors. On the reasons for rejecting this test see ch. 2 above.

280. On which see Finch, 'Company Directors'; Riley, 'Company Director's Duty of Care and Skill'.

281. See R. H. Kraakman, 'Corporate Liability Strategies and the Cost of Legal Controls' (1984) 93 Yale LJ 857; V. Finch, 'Personal Accountability and Corporate Control: The Role of Directors' and Officers' Liability Insurance' (1994) 57 MLR 880 at 881–7.

standards of management as it assists investigators by providing them with levers with which to bargain with managers for information concerning other corporate failings.

A further efficiency-related advantage of holding directors liable is that this may leave risk evaluation and risk spreading to those individuals who are the best acquirers of information concerning corporate risks, levels of capitalisation, internal control systems and insurance. It thus permits managers to select the optimal strategies for dealing with risks.[282] Finally, of course, personal liability improves the prospects of compensation by bringing the pocket of the wrongdoer within range of the victim, and where that pocket is deep, it may produce compensation for wrongdoing that is unavailable from the insolvent company.

A number of further points can be gleaned by examining a particular rule in more detail. Here it is worth looking at the wrongful trading provision and asking whether insolvency processes leave directors prone to undesirable diversion from the efficient and balanced pursuit of rescue or creditor protection objectives and whether the costs of ensuring that directors pursue such ends, rather than personal interests, are excessive.[283]

A central issue here, as has been pointed out,[284] is one of agency costs.[285] These costs relate to three main areas of potential directorial inefficiency. First, the managers of a troubled firm may expend assets in a desperate gamble to trade out of trouble and save their jobs. They will, in doing so, take inefficiently large risks because the risk bearers are in the first instance the shareholders (to be followed increasingly by the creditors as the firm declines).[286] A second danger is that managers will act in ways that prejudice the interests of creditors who were granted loans at early stages of corporate life: by, for example, taking out later secured loans that involve draconian terms and are not justified by the chances of potential recovery. Third, directors may, in times of trouble, act in a manner biased towards

---

282. See Kraakman, 'Corporate Liability Strategies', p. 874.

283. The wrongful trading section, Insolvency Act 1986 s. 214, it should be noted, does not attack the incompetence or mismanagement that may have brought a company to the verge of insolvency. It covers the taking of proper steps to protect creditors beyond the point when the company's failure seems inevitable.

284. See R. Mokal, 'An Agency Cost Analysis of the Wrongful Trading Provisions: Redistribution, Perverse Incentives and the Creditors' Bargain' [2000] 59 CLJ 335.

285. The costs a principal incurs in ensuring that an agent acts in his, rather than the agent's, own interests: see generally M. C. Jensen and W. H. Meckling, 'Theory of the Firm: Managerial Behaviour, Agency Costs and Ownership Structure' (1976) 3 *Journal of Financial Economics* 305.

286. On the 'perverse' incentive for an insolvent company to continue to trade see Telfer, 'Risk and Insolvent Trading'; D. Prentice, 'Creditors' Interest'. On excessive risk aversion see p. 544 below.

their shareholders and they may be able to do so because their information is superior to that possessed by creditors.

It has been argued that shareholders and creditors would be likely to agree to an open-ended section 214 type of directorial duty as a way of dealing with such problems.[287] They are likely to do so, the argument runs, because the efficient mode of applying the right incentives is for creditors to be allowed to decide on the efficient balance between, on the one hand, spending on control or monitoring activity, and, on the other, adjusting loan terms to take on board the risks of adverse actions by directors. Shareholders are likely to be content both that the company will pay the loan rates that are set in this manner and for directors to look to creditor interests as insolvency looms, because such a creditor-centred regime is cheaper overall than one in which shareholders and creditors seek, *ex ante*, to anticipate and agree all the steps that managers should take in troubled times.[288] The company, after all, will pay interest rates that are reduced in reflection of the creditor orientation that comes with insolvency.

It may, however, be the case that in certain circumstances there are ways of reducing agency costs that are more efficient than a section 214 type of duty. In assessing these alternatives, it has to be borne in mind that, as noted, section 214 may be formulated and enforced in a manner that renders it a control device of low impact, low control effect, low deterrence and poor compensation.[289] Under-deterrence may, indeed, occur because the wrongful actions of directors may produce losses to creditors that vastly exceed any sums liable to be forfeited by directors.[290] The pessimistic view of personal liability rules generally is that they tend to be difficult to enforce because of organisational secrecy, the numbers of responsible parties involved and the evidential problems that are associated with attempts to isolate culprits and prove cases. In many cases, relevant knowledge (e.g. about the nature of the corporate decline) may, rightly or wrongly, be scattered across the management or firm and not held by one individual.[291] Personal liability rules,

---

287. See Mokal, 'An Agency Cost Analysis', p. 349; cf. B. Cheffins, *Company Law: Theory, Structure and Operation* (Clarendon Press, Oxford, 1997) pp. 541–2.

288. Mokal, 'An Agency Cost Analysis'.

289. 'Section 214 has in reality failed to fulfil its objectives of achieving an efficient means by which the wrongful trading activities of directors can be successfully penalised': Griffin, *Personal Liability*, p. 96.

290. See S. Shavell, 'Liability for Harm Versus Regulation of Safety' (1984) 13 *Journal of Legal Studies* 357; S. Polinsky and S. Shavell, 'Should Employees be Subject to Fines and Imprisonment Given the Existence of Corporate Liability?' (1993) 13 *International Review of Law and Economics* 239.

291. See generally C. D. Stone, 'The Place of Enterprise Liability in the Control of Corporate Conduct' (1980) 90 Yale LJ 1.

moreover, may discourage the conscientious from acting as directors while failing to provide effective deterrence for, or remedies against, cavalier directors.[292]

As for the argument that personal liability rules will encourage intra-company monitoring of potential wrongdoing, the effects of such rules on non-executive directors may be undesirable.[293] Executive directors tend to dominate corporate boards and possess considerable advantages over outsiders *vis-à-vis* their time, resources, quality of information and access to board policy-making procedures.[294] The outsider faces severe obstacles in monitoring board activity and the prospect of being held personally liable for failing in such monitoring functions may prove an excessive deterrent to non-executive direction, notably when the economic benefits of non-executive direction are seen to be dwarfed by potential liabilities for damages. Companies may, in spite of such relevant factors, persuade non-executive directors to serve on their boards but the prospect of personal liability may result in such directors demanding high-risk premiums; perhaps excessive investment by the company in monitoring for offences; and the avoidance of conduct that is potentially profitable but gives rise to legal uncertainties.[295] Alternatively, companies, when selecting outside directors, may seek to avoid such problems by choosing directors who are either non-risk averse or uncritical of risk taking. An incentive to select on such a basis would run counter to notions of outside directors constituting checks on corporate folly.

The imposition of personal liability can have further cost and efficiency implications. Thus, the costs of compensating managerial risk bearers may be greater than the costs of deterrence by means of enterprise liability since directors bear risks of an undiversified kind. Unlike shareholders who can spread risks across a portfolio, the directors' eggs are in the one corporate basket.[296] It is preferable, say the Chicago school,[297] to punish

---

292. See J. Freedman, 'Limited Liability: Large Company Theory and Small Firms' (2000) 63 MLR 317, who notes (at p. 344) that if the 'device' of making directors personally liable is to be relied upon, 'it may be important for a clear and reasonably consistent body of case law to be built up in order to provide guidance and for principles drawn from this case law to be communicated to business owners prior to incorporation. Such reliance, however, presupposes a highly rational system of deterrence in which directors show a high level of understanding of detailed legal information.'

293. See Finch, 'Personal Accountability and Corporate Control', pp. 885–6.

294. See Finch, 'Company Directors', pp. 197–200; V. Brudney, 'The Independent Director: Heavenly City or Potemkin Village?' (1982) 95 Harvard LR 597.

295. See Kraakman, 'Corporate Liability Strategies', p. 892.

296. Ibid., pp. 865, 887; D. Mayers and C. Smith, 'On the Corporate Demand for Insurance' (1982) 55 *Journal of Business* 281 at 283.

297. See R. Posner, *Economic Analysis of Law* (5th edn, Aspen Law and Business, New York, 1998).

the corporation. This will create incentives for internal corrective action[298] and the firm is better positioned than the state to deter misconduct by its employees and to do so efficiently.[299]

Another danger of personal liability is that those who *are* prepared to operate as company directors will become excessively risk averse, so much so that they are unwilling to take commercially justifiable risks for fear of triggering personal liability. Either such risks may be left untaken (an inefficient result[300]) or those properly responsible may evade their responsibilities. Risk avoidance can be achieved most readily by delegating legally awkward tasks to subordinates,[301] closing companies down too early[302] or by shifting risks to outside consultants.[303] Inefficiencies may result in so far as managers shy away from decisions, fail to trade or assume responsibilities, desist from establishing effective lines of control and delegate decisions to parties less well positioned to decide relevant issues. Even where the right levels of risks are taken by directors, it may be the case that statutory regulation causes directors to spend an inordinate amount of time on compliance issues and that this may impose ongoing costs on the company that outweigh the value of any protections that ensue. In 1962 the Jenkins Report raised this issue, asking whether further statutory regulation would 'to any significant extent hamper or impede the company in the efficient conduct of its legitimate business'.[304]

---

298. Incentives perhaps dependent on the firm itself facing high levels of punishment and probability of detection: see Stone, 'Place of Enterprise Liability', p. 30.

299. Where, however, the firm itself is unlikely to suffer sanctions, it may even endorse directorial wrongdoing: see J. Coffee, ' "No Soul to Damn: No Body to Kick": An Unscandalized Inquiry into the Problem of Corporate Punishment' (1981) 79 Mich. LR 386 at 408.

300. See R. Rosh, 'New York's Response to the "D & O" Insurance Crisis' (1989) 54 Brooklyn LR 1305 at 1317. On economic theory behind risk aversion see, *inter alia*, Jensen and Meckling, 'Theory of the Firm'; Stone, 'Place of Enterprise Liability', pp. 34–5; Telfer, 'Risk and Insolvent Trading', pp. 135–7.

301. Kraakman, 'Corporate Liability Strategies', p. 860.

302. See T. Cooke and A. Hicks, 'Wrongful Trading: Predicting Insolvency' [1993] JBL 338.

303. R. Daniels and S. Hutton, 'The Capricious Cushion: The Implications of the Directors' and Officers' Insurance Liability Crisis in Canadian Corporate Governance' (1993) Canadian Bus. LJ 182 at 187; R. H. Kraakman, 'Gatekeepers: The Anatomy of a Third Party Enforcement Strategy' (1986) *Journal of Law, Economics and Organization* 53 at 55–7. Relying on advice will not always protect a director from, for example, disqualification: see *Re Bradcrown Ltd*, 2 November 2000 (CCH *Company Law Newsletter*, 8 January 2001).

304. *Report of the Company Law Committee* (Cmnd 1749, 1962) p. 3; Telfer, 'Risk and Insolvent Trading', p. 134; D. Wishart, 'Models and Theories of Directors' Duties to Creditors' (1991) 14 NZULR 323; J. Mannolini, 'Creditors' Interests in the Corporate Contract' (1996) 6 *Australian Journal of Corporate Law* 1; M. Byrne, 'An Economic Analysis of Directors' Duties in Favour of Creditors' (1994) 4 *Australian Journal of Corporate Law* 275; M. Moffat, 'Directors' Dilemma: An Economic Evaluation of Directors' Liability for Environmental Damages and Unpaid Wages' (1996) 54 U Toronto Fac. LR 293 at 306.

Nor may directors find reassurance in judicial responses. Heavy reliance on personal liability places a good deal of faith in the courts as arbiters of the business decisions of directors. As has been seen above, however, the judges have left the wrongful trading law in an uncertain state that (if enforced) would be likely to chill efficient directorial risk taking. This uncertainty might make directors 'likely to shy away from taking the sort of bold resolute decisions that are required to maximise profits'.[305]

It may be the case, however, that the disciplines of the labour market will reinforce the wrongful trading and other insolvency provisions, so as to give directors incentives to behave properly during times of decline. The optimistic argument here is that a director's value in the market will be influenced by his reputation for behaving reasonably: 'He has an incentive to signal to the market that he is capable of effectively doing all that any reasonably competent manager would do to abate the damage done to the company's creditors.'[306] In response to such optimism, however, it can be said that even if a director was governed by the labour market this would not necessarily demand that an efficient balancing of creditor and shareholder interests was ensured by the director. Such a market might look to issues of basic competence, but a 'balanced' approach to different interests would only be valued by a market that itself reflected such interests. A labour market dominated by shareholder concerns would reward directors who favoured members' rather than creditors' interests.

As for the power of the labour market, this, like the market for corporate control, may encounter severe informational problems in assessing directorial behaviour, especially during periods of corporate difficulty when affairs move fast, data may not be collected efficiently, there is confusion and blame-shifting as 'tracks are covered'. For all these reasons it is difficult to see the labour markets as making up for the deficiencies of personal liability rules in encouraging efficient company direction.

---

305. Cheffins, *Company Law*, p. 541. See also Cooke and Hicks, 'Wrongful Trading'; Grantham, 'Judicial Extension'. On the 'liability chill' see R. Daniels, 'Must Boards Go Overboard?: An Economic Analysis of the Effects of Burgeoning Statutory Liability on the Role of Directors in Corporate Governance' in J. Ziegel (ed.), *Current Developments in International and Comparative Corporate Insolvency Law* (Clarendon Press, Oxford, 1994); F. H. Easterbrook and D. Fischel, *The Economic Structure of Corporate Law* (Harvard University Press, Cambridge, Mass., 1991); Telfer, 'Risk and Insolvent Trading'.
306. Mokal, 'An Agency Cost Analysis', pp. 351–2; R. Daniels, 'Must Boards Go Overboard?' (1994–5) 24 Canadian Bus. LJ 229 at 241.

Does insolvency law place creditors in a position in which they can police directors' behaviour in times of trouble?[307] It is certainly the case that creditors possess significant power that is capable of being exercised at such times. Secured creditors can apply real pressure merely by threatening to exercise their legal rights upon default or even prospective default of debenture terms. Such creditor stances would impinge on directors' reputations and prompt reappraisals of company plans and top management. Unsecured trade creditors are unlikely to exert the same broad influence as financial creditors but, where a company fails to pay its debts, trade creditors may apply pressure by threatening to disclose this fact to other suppliers, the market and the public. As the company moves from financial difficulty to financial crisis, creditor power increases further. The company's prospects of survival almost wholly depend on creditor cooperation. Financial creditors may be able and inclined to demand broad changes as conditions of assistance.

Threats cease and legal steps are initiated when rescue is deemed inappropriate.[308] At this stage, secured creditors may replace the directors with a receiver, and qualifying creditors may initiate a liquidation. At this time actions potentially covering negligence may be brought against directors personally. Such actions, as we have seen, may be brought under a number of heads. First, like a shareholder, any creditor may bring a misfeasance action against past or present company officers for a breach of fiduciary or other duty in relation to the company.[309] This action, however, demands a certain altruism on the petitioning creditor's behalf. Such duties are owed to the company: thus any contributions or compensation received from negligent directors will go to the company's assets and, as such, will be available to all creditors generally. These actions are, in addition, made less attractive because a misfeasance action can also be brought by the liquidator as the representative of the general creditors. Thus, liquidators, on behalf of creditors, can collect and evaluate the evidence for taking action against former directors, aided by investigative powers unavailable to individual creditors.[310] Action by liquidators, however, is not always to be assumed even if the evidence of directiorial negligence exists. Wheeler has noted the pragmatism of liquidators:

---

307. On the creditors' position to monitor directors and their role in controlling general directorial competence see Finch, 'Company Directors', pp. 189–95.
308. On corporate rescues see Lingard, *Corporate Rescues and Insolvencies*; 'Britain Needs a "Rescue Culture" Now', Cork Gully Discussion Paper No. 1 (London, June 1991).
309. Insolvency Act 1986 s. 212(1), (3).
310. See Insolvency Act 1986 ss. 131–4. See also ch. 12 above.

An important concern is with the location and realisation of saleable assets, from which their fees will be paid…A fruitless but well-intentioned search for assets is unlikely to be a cost-effective use of time. An action of misfeasance, for example, becomes a reality only after a balancing exercise of factors such as cost, time involved, and the financial situation of the directors from which the recovery is sought.[311]

Will such creditor-driven actions lead directors to behave responsibly? The danger is that funding and enforcement difficulties in relation to such actions as wrongful trading and misfeasance may lead to under-deterrence. Under-deterrence may also occur because errant directors' pockets may not be sufficiently deep to induce creditors to incur the expenses of enforcing their rights.[312] Some lenders can resort to third party security to make up for such deficiency. They may accordingly seek charges from shareholder-managers of closely held firms to cover personal property, even homes.[313] Such actions may, however, only be feasible for powerful banks that are dealing with smaller companies in circumstances where third parties hold considerable assets.

In concluding, then, it can be said that the present law falls short in conducing to efficient company direction in times of corporate trouble. A number of key difficulties can be identified. Funding problems render the enforcement of actions such as wrongful trading suits a blunted and inefficient tool. Similarly, when liquidators or creditors face high costs in gaining relevant information about company affairs, inefficiency results. Such high costs may result from an excessive reliance on the use of outside professionals in insolvency processes and sets of incentives (or uncertainties) that lead directors to depart too early from the company scene. Legal uncertainties, as seen in the wrongful trading law, create inefficiencies by both chilling desirable risk taking by directors and by reducing the ability of shareholders and creditors to assess and manage risks at lowest cost. If it is asked whether the current statutory scheme would have been arrived at by allowing participants to negotiate,[314] one thing is clear. Participants in such a discussion would have wanted a regime in which directors, creditors and shareholders could assess and allocate risks in as clear a fashion as possible. That is the precondition for maximising returns. From an efficiency perspective what matters is certainty, what is undesirable is the

---

311. S. Wheeler, 'Disqualification of Directors: A Broader View' in H. Rajak (ed.), *Insolvency Law: Theory and Practice* (Sweet & Maxwell, London, 1993) p. 193.
312. See A. Hicks, 'Advising on Wrongful Trading: Part 1' (1993) 14 Co. Law. 16.
313. See Mokal, 'An Agency Cost Analysis', p. 359.
314. See Telfer, 'Risk and Insolvent Trading', pp. 146–7; Cheffins, *Company Law*, pp. 540–4.

chill wind of unknown risks.[315] From this point of view the current formulation of the law on directors' duties fails to deliver.

Finally, the broad limitations of individual liability rules have to be returned to. Efficient deterrence of sub-optimal behaviour requires not merely that legal rules are efficiently applied but that sanctions are efficient; that there is a correspondence between the assets that a director puts at risk, and the potential losses that directorial actions may place on creditors or shareholders. This condition is rarely satisfied and, accordingly, responses such as improved directorial training, intra-company controls and accountability regimes have to be looked to.

Fairness

Directors might complain that, in a number of respects, they are treated unfairly by the laws and processes discussed above. Disqualification under the CDDA may have very serious implications for individuals but, as has been seen above, the courts have failed to offer clear guidance on the position of the director. Some judges have applied a 'rights' approach to company direction. Others have seen direction of a company incorporated with limited liability as a privilege. If the judiciary were to follow the logic of either of the above approaches in a consistent manner, directors might not be placed to complain that the law was incoherent, inconsistent and unfair. A single consistent judicial trend, however, is yet to emerge and decisions, as noted, often contain elements of both 'rights' and 'privileges' approaches.[316]

Before the Insolvency Act 2000, company directors might have complained that the disqualification process was so slow as to constitute an unfair regime. The Insolvency Service's 2000 Report on Company Rescue and Business Reconstruction Mechanisms[317] noted that:

> There were strong arguments made that for many honest directors of failed companies, the length of time which it currently takes the Secretary of State...to bring on disqualification proceedings (or to reach a decision that proceedings will not be brought) acts as a considerable inhibition on any attempts they may wish to make to go back into business.[318]

---

315. See generally P. Halpern, M. Trebilcock and M. Turnbull, 'An Economic Analysis of Limited Liability in Corporation Law' (1980) 30 U Toronto LJ 117.

316. See pp. 529–30 above and, for example, *Secretary of State for Trade and Industry* v. *Griffiths, Re Westmid Packaging Services Ltd (No. 3)* [1998] BCC 836; *Re Keypack Homecare Ltd (No. 2)* [1990] BCC 117.

317. Report by the Review Group (DTI, 2000).   318. Ibid., para. 104.

The Review Group recommended that steps be taken to speed up the disqualification process and the Insolvency Act 2000 section 6 offered a response by developing the 'fast-track' procedure. As already noted, this procedure empowers the Secretary of State to accept consensual undertakings equivalent to disqualification orders without a full court hearing.[319] Another potential complaint of unfairness, however, emerges with this process. The Institute of Directors, among others, has complained that a plea-bargaining culture may develop in which directors will be placed under undue economic pressure to accept disqualification rather than have their day in court.[320] One commentator has argued that the new procedure 'will do little to dissuade the rogue with deep pockets. The real danger is that directors with limited resources and no desire for litigation against the Secretary of State will be persuaded to agree a disqualification undertaking with little or no professional advice.'[321]

Moving away from disqualification to the other personal liabilities of directors, the latter may again complain of unfairness on the grounds that uncertainty infuses a host of liability provisions. In relation to wrongful trading, for instance, it has been suggested that the key finding – whether the director knew, or ought to have concluded, that there was 'no reasonable prospect' of avoiding insolvent liquidation – poses a question that is 'inherently elusive'.[322] A director can 'only speculate whether injecting more capital, cajoling other directors to take corrective action, tightening up accounting procedures, pursuing plans to achieve a turnaround, consulting an insolvency practitioner, or putting the company into liquidation will be sufficient'.[323] Nor, indeed, has this been a short-lived and recent complaint. In the early 1980s Bishop argued that

---

319. The Secretary of State may, however, require a statement of grounds for the undertaking in terms of those set out in *Carecraft*: see *Re Blackspur Group plc*, 23 May 2001.

320. See Walters, 'New Regime', pp. 92–3. See also M. Simmons and T. Smith, 'The Human Rights Act 1998: The Practical Impact on Insolvency' (2000) 16 IL&P 167, for suggestions (at p. 172) that it is a breach of Article 6 for the individual to face 'such proceedings without proper legal representation' and that if directors are unable to 'contest the proceedings effectively due to financial considerations' this too could amount to a breach of Article 6.

321. R. Tateossian, 'The Future of Directors' Disqualification' (2000) *Insolvency Bulletin* 6 at 7. An Editorial in the *Financial Times* (16 November 1999) suggested that prior to the Insolvency Act 2000 directors were faced with a Hobson's choice: 'either accept the ban, and be barred from business for at least two years; or run the risk of a long, extremely expensive court battle to try to clear your name'. Sir Richard Scott, the Vice Chancellor, argued to the Chancery Bar Association in 1999 that a solution might be to allocate costs under the 'just and reasonable' test of criminal cases, rather than the 'loser pays all' civil litigation formula: see (2000) 21 Co. Law. 90.

322. D. Prentice, 'Corporate Personality, Limited Liability and the Protection of Creditors' in R. Grantham and C. Rickett (eds.), *Corporate Personality in the Twentieth Century* (Hart, Oxford, 1998) p. 119.

323. Cheffins, *Company Law*, pp. 542–3, quoted by Telfer, 'Risk and Insolvent Trading', pp. 139–40.

'in many situations the law today is in such a state of flux and insufficiently clear that an honest and conscientious executive may very well find himself threatened with...if not actually subjected to liability for conduct which at the time he, not unreasonably, regarded as ethical and prudent'.[324]

Such complaints of unfairness and demands for legal certainty are given added weight when it is remembered that, in times of corporate trouble, directors will very often be compelled to make decisions within short deadlines and under extreme pressure. It is similarly the case with regard to the common law duties of care, skill and diligence: it is difficult to discern a coherent statement of the law from the cases or to offer, on the basis of those cases, a set of helpful guidelines for directors.[325] A director has a duty to consider creditors' interests at some stage in a company's decline but whether this duty begins to operate when the company is insolvent, of 'doubtful solvency' or at some point earlier is a matter of guesswork.[326] The director's difficulties are only added to by further uncertainties in determining when a company is insolvent and which approach to accounting data should be used in making this calculation.[327] English directors are not protected by a 'business judgment rule' as encountered in the USA and some commentators have questioned whether judges are qualified to strike the right balance in judging the performance of directors.[328] If there are any doubts about the ability of the judges to produce commercially operable, consistent and legally acceptable rules on directors' duties, it may be unwise to leave in their hands a set of common and statutory laws that constitute invitations to ad hocery.

For its part, as we noted above, the CLRSG has accepted the case for making a legislative restatement of directors' duties, and has done so in order to give the law greater clarity and accessibility; to attune the law to current business practice; and to reflect modern business needs and wider expectations of responsible business behaviour.[329] Such objectives are to

---

324. J. Bishop, *The Law of Corporate Officers and Directors' Indemnification and Insurance* (1981) paras. 36–7.

325. See Finch, 'Directors' Duties: Insolvency and the Unsecured Creditor'; A. Hicks, 'Directors' Liability for Management Errors' (1994) 110 LQR 390. Note that the CLRSG now proposes a legislative restatement of the principles for directors' general duties including those of care, skill and diligence: see *Developing the Framework* (March 2000) paras. 3.39–3.40; *Completing the Structure* (November 2000) ch. 3. The CLRSG's draft statutory statement seeks to align the standard of care with the objective/subjective test based on section 214(4) of the Insolvency Act 1986. See further CLRSG, *Final Report*, 2001, paras. 3.7–3.11.

326. See Finch, 'Creditors' Interests and Directors' Obligations'. See pp. 504–6 above.

327. See Riley, 'Directors' Duties and the Interests of Creditors', p. 542; ch. 4 above.

328. See Cheffins, *Company Law*, p. 543.   329. See CLRSG, *Final Report*, 2001, pp. 40–1.

be welcomed but the 2001 Final Report is disappointing in so far as the CLRSG, as discussed above, came to no agreed view on whether a duty to have regard to creditor interests should operate before the section 214 point (of knowing that there is 'no reasonable prospect' of avoiding insolvent liquidation), namely when the director knows 'that it is more likely than not that the company will at some point be unable to pay its debts as they fall due'.[330] The CLRSG also adheres to the section 214 formulation of the wrongful trading provision and, accordingly, offers little response to the criticisms (referred to above) that this gives the judges too much leeway to continue to make decisions on a case-by-case basis in an area in which there has been little consistency of judicial approach.

Conclusions

The current regime of insolvency laws and processes fails to deal with company directors in a convincing manner. The sections above have identified deficiencies on the accountability, expertise, efficiency and fairness fronts. In many ways the root cause of insolvency law's failure is one that has been alluded to already. Present insolvency law is not underpinned by a conception of the company director, or the company director's insolvency role, that is explicable in relation to a sustained set of values or principles. Instead, we see an institutional inconsistency in which company directors are sometimes seen as competent and trustworthy individuals with private rights to direct limited liability companies that are worthy of strong protection. On other occasions directors are seen as fortunate individuals who exercise the privilege of directing limited liability companies and who should not be too surprised if, in the public interest, they lose that right in order to protect the public or to raise standards of direction as a matter of policy.

Present governmental policy, we have seen, is to promote enterprise and competitiveness, represent a modern view of the balancing of interests between participants and be as simple and accessible as possible.[331] To this end statutory statements of directors' duties and insolvency rules can be developed but a look at the history of directors' common law duties or section 214 of the Insolvency Act 1986 (and its restatement) tells us that there is no easy way to indicate in a statute precisely when a particular

---

330. The drafting suggested for consideration by CLRSG is found in its *Final Report*, 2001, at p. 347 para. 8.
331. CLRSG, *Final Report*, 2001, p. vii.

director should start to treat creditors rather than shareholders as risk bearers whose interests are to be taken into account. Similarly, there is no precise blueprint available to state what a duty of skill and care demands in a given context. The judges have to be relied upon to put flesh on such rules. What can be avoided are unexplained divergences of philosophy. Directors cannot rightfully complain if the judges produce laws that are complex; they can complain if the laws are philosophically confused.

16

Employees in distress

The insolvency of a company may prove traumatic for employees,[1] especially those who have invested years of effort and skill in the enterprise. A range of outcomes for employees may be triggered by insolvency, and the law, in some respects, seeks to minimise the negative consequences of insolvency for employees. Insolvency law, however, has other interests to look to, notably those of creditors and possibly those of shareholders and the state. Issues of fairness come to the fore as do considerations of rescue and the design of rules that allow efficient transfers of enterprises.

This chapter begins by outlining how the law treats employees in an insolvency. It then moves to a now familiar set of issues by asking four questions. Do insolvency laws relating to employees lead to efficient rescue processes and corporate operations? Do these laws make best use of employee expertise? Are employees given an appropriate voice within the schemes of accountability that operate in insolvency? Does the law allocate rights to employees that are fair? A further, more general issue is then

---

1. In law a company director is an office holder but he or she may also be an employee. This is a matter of fact in the individual case and turns on the director's relationship with a company. The Employment Appeal Tribunal in *Eaton v. Robert Eaton Ltd* [1988] IRLR 83 gave guidance on the factors to be considered: (a) Did the director have a descriptive title (for example, managing director)? (b) Was there an express contract of employment, minute or memorandum agreeing to employment as an employee per Companies Act 1985 s. 318? (c) Was remuneration by salary or directors' fees? (d) Was remuneration fixed in advance or paid on an ad hoc basis? (e) Was remuneration by entitlement or in effect gratuitous? (f) Did the director merely act in a directorial capacity or was he or she under the control of the board in respect of the management of his or her work? Other factors are whether the director paid Schedule E (PAYE) income tax and Class 1 National Insurance contributions. See generally SPI, *Treatment of Directors' Claims as 'Employees' on Insolvency* (SPI Technical Release 6, 1999); *McQuisten v. Secretary of State for Employment*, EAT 1298/95, 11 June 1996; *Buchan v. Secretary of State for Employment, Ivey v. Secretary of State for Employment* [1997] IRLR 80; *Secretary of State for Trade and Industry v. Bottrill* [1999] IRLR 326, [1999] BCC 177; *Brooks v. Secretary of State for Trade and Industry* [1999] BCC 232. See also M. Jefferson, 'Directors, Controlling Shareholders, Employees and Rights on Insolvency' (1998) 19 Co. Law. 307.

discussed: whether insolvency law's conception of the employee evidences a coherent and appropriate philosophy.

Protections under the law

When a company becomes insolvent, employees of the company may constitute creditors for such matters as unpaid wages, sick pay and holiday pay. They may also be contractually entitled to pay in lieu of notice under their contracts of employment and may be able to make other contractual claims.[2] At common law, employees are merely unsecured creditors but the Insolvency Act 1986[3] gives preferential status to some limited employee claims. These are claims regarding wages and holiday pay entitlement accruing in the four months prior to proceedings,[4] subject to an overall limit of £800. They rank ahead of other unsecured creditors' claims and also ahead of those of secured creditors with floating charges (but not fixed charges). Claims beyond this £800 limit are dealt with on an ordinary unsecured basis and in many insolvencies even the preferential claims of employees will be reduced or defeated by the prior claims of creditors with fixed security. When, moreover, the expenses of the liquidation and the secured creditors have been paid, the employees share their priority rateably with other preferential creditors which include the Inland Revenue.[5]

A second, and often more productive, source of protection flows from employment law and the social security system.[6] Employees of a company which has entered insolvency proceedings are entitled to claim against the state National Insurance Fund (NIF) on the terms set out in the Employment Rights Act 1996 ss. 166–70 and ss. 182–90. These provisions enable employees to claim in respect of unpaid arrears of wages (for up to eight

2. On employee claims generally see D. Pollard, *Corporate Insolvency: Employment and Pension Rights* (2nd edn, Butterworths, London, 2000); C. Villiers, 'Employees as Creditors: A Challenge for Justice in Insolvency Law' (1999) 20 Co. Law. 222; S. Cantlie, 'Preferred Priority in Bankruptcy' in J. Ziegel (ed.), *Current Developments in International and Comparative Corporate Insolvency Law* (Clarendon Press, Oxford, 1994) ch. 17; P. L. Davies, 'Employee Claims in Insolvency: Corporate Rescue and Preferential Claims' (1994) 23 ILJ 141; L. Clarke and H. Rajak, '*Mann* v. *Secretary of State for Employment*' (2000) 63 MLR 895; R. Morgan, 'Insolvency and the Rights of Employees' [1989] *Legal Action* 21.
3. Insolvency Act 1986 s. 175 and Sched. 6.
4. More precisely, four months to the 'relevant date', as defined in the Insolvency Act 1986 s. 387 (the date varies according to the particular insolvency procedure involved).
5. On proposals to abolish Crown preference see DTI/Insolvency Service, White Paper, *Productivity and Enterprise: Insolvency – A Second Chance* (Cm 5234, 2001) para. 2.19. On preferential creditors generally see ch. 13 above.
6. See, for example, Clarke and Rajak, '*Mann* v. *Secretary of State*'; H. Collins, K. Ewing and A. McColgan, *Labour Law Text and Materials* (Hart, Oxford, 2001) ch. 10.

weeks at up to £240 per week),[7] notice pay, holiday pay, the basic award for unfair dismissal compensation, any statutory redundancy pay and any award made by an industrial tribunal for failure to consult with representatives of the workforce. The effect is that if the Secretary of State/NIF makes any payments to employees the NIF is then subrogated, by statute, to the rights of the employees against the insolvent employer (including their rights as preferential creditors).[8]

From the employee's point of view, the advantages of the NIF route are that NIF entitlements are guaranteed as opposed to preferred.[9] Employees are thus certain to be paid such entitlements in full (up to the statutory limit) even if the insolvent employer has no funds. They are also spared the delays involved in allowing insolvency processes to run their full course in meeting their preferential claims and they avoid the danger that the claims of fixed charge security creditors will exhaust the insolvency estate before the preferential claims come to be dealt with.[10]

Employees are also protected by a series of laws that conduce to the continuation of their paid employment. When the employer company becomes insolvent prospects of payment diminish. If the company remains the employer during rescue attempts, the employees' claims for wages are protected by the priority rules already noted. Where, however, the administrative receiver becomes their employer, wage and other payment claims are part of the expenses of the receivership. The receiver will be indemnified by the secured creditor and the effect is to give retained workers 'super-priority' for their wages. Under the Insolvency Act 1986 section 44,[11] administrative receivers are personally liable for 'qualifying liabilities'[12] on contracts of employment which they adopt, but no adoption can take place within fourteen days of the receiver's appointment.

---

7. Employment Rights Act 1996 s. 186(1)(a); SI 1999 No. 3375.

8. The law here implements EC Directive 80/987/EEC on the approximation of the laws relating to the protection of employees in the event of the insolvency of their employer. For an example of such a claim see *McMeechan* v. *Secretary of State for Employment* [1997] ICR 549 (CA). On the European aspects (and when a company is in insolvency) see *Mann* v. *Secretary of State for Employment* [1999] IRLR 566 (discussed by Clarke and Rajak (2000) 63 MLR 895); Collins *et al.*, *Labour Law*, pp. 1031–3; *Regeling* v. *Bestur van de Bedrijfsvereniging voor de Metaalnijverheid* [1999] IRLR 379 (ECJ); *Everson and Barrass* v. *Secretary of State for Trade and Industry and Bell Lines Ltd (in liquidation)* [2000] IRLR 202 (ECJ).

9. Claimants on the NIF do, however, have to establish their redundancy claims before a tribunal: see Morgan, 'Insolvency'.

10. See Morgan, 'Insolvency'; Clarke and Rajak, '*Mann v. Secretary of State*', p. 89, who also note the danger that increasingly wide drafting of fixed charges is tending to reduce the value of statutory preferential status; see further ch. 9 above.

11. As amended by the Insolvency Act 1994.

12. See Insolvency Act 1986 s. 44(1)(b), 44(2A).

This provision gives fourteen days of grace in which an administrative receiver can decide whether and how to effect a rescue. Adopting employee contracts preserves employment and makes the administrative receiver the guarantor of the wages but, from the employee's perspective, the personal liability and super-priority mentioned above only apply to wages and entitlements under occupational pension schemes, not to such items as claims for dismissal.[13]

The Insolvency Act 1986 also attaches some liability for contracts of employment to administrators.[14] Again, a fourteen-day period of grace applies, but, if adopted after this time, the Act binds administrators by a first priority regarding claims on the assets of the company for certain 'qualifying liability'[15] sums including termination payments and continuing wages due to employees. By adopting the contract, therefore, administrators risk their expenses since adoption gives employees 'super-priority' over all other creditors: a contrast with receivers who attract personal liability for contractual liabilities (including back wages).[16]

Another set of laws covers the situation in which there is a sale of the company or part of the business: a sale that might be made as part of a rescue operation or the realisation of assets by the liquidator, administrator or receiver. Employees in such scenarios may be faced with new owners who wish to vary terms of employment, close down some units or downsize by dismissing a portion of the workforce. General employment laws cover workforce reductions and variations of contract and will not be discussed here.[17] Mention should be made, however, of the Transfer of Undertakings (Protection of Employment) (TUPE) Regulations 1981 which implemented the European Acquired Rights Directive 77/187.[18]

13. For discussion see ch. 8 above, pp. 243–5.
14. Insolvency Act 1986 s. 19(4), (5) and (6). See *In re FJL Realisations Ltd (IRC v. Lawrence)* [2001] ICR 424, [2001] BCC 663 regarding the status of PAYE and National Insurance contributions deducted from employees' salaries in adopted employee contracts.
15. Insolvency Act 1986 s. 19(6). See pp. 286–8 above
16. See Villiers, 'Employees as Creditors'; *Powdrill v. Watson* [1995] 2 All ER 65.
17. See generally N. Selwyn, *Law of Employment* (11th edn, Butterworths, London, 2000); Collins *et al.*, *Labour Law.*
18. On TUPE see, for example, R. Eldridge, 'TUPE Operates to Damage Rescue Culture' (2001) *Recovery* (September) 21; S. Hardy, 'Some TUPE Implications for Insolvency Lawyers' [2001] Ins. Law. 147; S. Frisby, 'TUPE or not TUPE? Employee Protection, Corporate Rescue and "One Unholy Mess"' [2000] 3 CFILR 249; J. Armour and S. Deakin, 'Insolvency, Employment Protection and Corporate Restructuring: The Effects of TUPE' (ESRC Centre for Business Research, Cambridge, Working Paper No. 204, June 2001); J. McMullen, *Business Transfers and Employee Rights* (2nd edn, Butterworths, London, 1992); H. Collins, 'Transfer of Undertakings and Insolvency' (1989) 18 ILJ 144; P. L. Davies, 'Acquired Rights, Creditors' Rights, Freedom of Contract and Industrial Democracy' (1989) 9 *Yearbook of European Law* 21; B. Hepple, 'The Transfer of Undertakings (Protection of Employment) Regulations' (1982) 11 ILJ 29.

This Directive was designed to preserve the contractual rights of employees on a transfer of their employing business.[19] The TUPE Regulations were introduced by a 'reluctant' government[20] and affected transfers in insolvency and non-insolvency situations.

Under the common law, a business transfer terminates all employment contracts[21] and employees of insolvent companies that are involved in a transfer are able to rely only on their preferential claims or their access to the NIF. Before TUPE, therefore, the purchaser of a going concern sale of an insolvent business would not be liable for the acquired rights of its employees. Following TUPE, matters were different. Under Regulation 5 of TUPE, a transfer of an undertaking passes contracts of employment over to the transferee and previously employed persons become employees of the transferee under the same terms and conditions as are set out in their initial contracts. Unsatisfied liabilities of the transferor also pass to the transferee. For the purposes of this section, employees are persons 'employed immediately before the transfer'.[22]

Under Regulation 8(1) of TUPE, employees dismissed because of the transfer, or a reason connected with it, are deemed to have been unfairly dismissed and are accordingly entitled to compensation for unfair dismissal. This rule does not apply, however, if the reason or principal reason for dismissal is an 'economic, technical or organisational' (ETO) reason entailing changes in the workforce of the transferor or transferee 'before or after the relevant transfer'.[23]

The insolvency implications of TUPE have depended a great deal on the courts. One central issue has been whether the purchaser of an insolvent business could avoid inheriting employee liabilities if the IP acting as agent of the transferor company effected dismissals prior to the transfer. Matters here turn on the construction of the phrase 'employed immediately before the transfer' in Regulation 5(3). An opportunity to avoid

---

19. On the definition of a 'transfer', the construction of 'identity', the effect of amending Directive 98/50/EC and contracting out, see Case C-172/99, *Oy Liikenne Ab* v. *Pekka Liskjarvi and Pentti Juntunen* [2001] IRLR 171 (ECJ) and P. Davies, 'Transfers: The UK Will Have to Make Up its Own Mind' (2001) 30 ILJ 231. See also V. Shrubsall, 'Competitive Tendering, Out-sourcing and the Acquired Rights Directive' (1998) 61 MLR 85.

20. See David Waddington MP, Under-Secretary of State for Employment, HC Deb. vol. 14, col. 680.

21. Frisby, 'TUPE or not TUPE?', p. 250; *Nokes* v. *Doncaster Amalgamated Collieries* [1940] AC 1014.

22. TUPE Regulation 5(3): where the transfer is effected by a series of transactions this rule includes persons employed immediately before any of those transactions.

23. TUPE Regulation 8(2).

employee-related obligations was provided by the *Spence* case[24] where the
Court of Appeal held that an employee dismissed three hours in advance of
a transfer was not employed 'immediately before' that event. The House of
Lords, however, took a different view in *Litster*[25] where there was an hour's
gap between dismissal and transfer. Their Lordships focused on the purpose of the Acquired Rights Directive – which they said was to ensure the
protection of acquired rights of employees – and accordingly read Regulation 5(3) in the light of Regulation 8(1). The effect was to add to the words
'employed immediately before the transfer' the phrase 'or would have
been so employed if he had not been unfairly dismissed in circumstances
described in Regulation 8(1)'.[26] Unfair dismissal according to Regulation 8(1) includes instances where the transfer, or a reason connected
with it, is a principal reason for dismissal.[27] This meant that the strategy of
dismissing employees in the lead up to a transfer was undermined.[28] The
real issue had become the reason for dismissal rather than the exact time at
which it was effected. Employees were thus more strongly protected than
under *Spence* though it was up to them to establish that the reason for dismissal was connected with the transfer.[29] They could, moreover, claim unfair dismissal compensation from the purchaser even if dismissed prior
to the sale.[30] Cases subsequent to *Litster* such as *Re Maxwell Fleet Facilities
Management Ltd* (No. 2)[31] have also indicated that where a hive-down[32] takes
place in an effort to avoid the transfer of employment liabilities, the courts

24. *Secretary of State for Employment* v. *Spence* [1986] ICR 651. But see *Bork International A/S* v.
Foreningen 101/87 [1988] ECR 3057, [1990] 3 CMLR 701 (ECJ rules that if a worker is dismissed
before transfer at the behest of the transferee, and in breach of Article 4(1), the worker is
regarded as being employed at the time of transfer).
25. *Litster* v. *Forth Dry Docks and Engineering Co. Ltd* [1990] 1 AC 546.
26. See Frisby, 'TUPE or not TUPE?', p. 256; Lord Oliver in *Litster* [1990] 1 AC 546 at 563A–B.
27. On conflicting authorities regarding the connection between a dismissal and the transfer
see Eldridge, 'TUPE Operates to Damage Rescue Culture'; *Harrison Bowden Ltd* v. *Bowden*
[1994] ICR 186; *Kerry Foods Ltd* v. *Creber* [2000] IRLR 10; *Collins* v. *John Ansell & Partners* [2000] ELR
555; *Honeycombe 78 Ltd* v. *Cummins and Others* (unreported, EAT 100/99).
28. Regulation 8 would also apply to dismissals post-transfer (with no fixed time limit) if
they were connected to the transfer. Regulation 12, moreover, states that any provision of any
agreement that purports to exclude or limit the effect of a regulation should be void: see
Credit Suisse First Boston (Europe) Ltd v. *Litster* [1999] ICR 794 (CA); *Wilson* v. *St Helens Borough
Council, British Fuels Ltd* v. *Baxendale* [1999] 2 AC 52, [1998] ICR 1141 (HL).
29. *Willis* v. *McLaughlin and Harvey plc* [1996] NI 427.
30. The court will not make an order for specific performance so that a purchaser is
compelled to continue employment (except when other statutory rights of reinstatement or
re-engagement apply). See *Wilson* v. *St Helens Borough Council, British Fuels Ltd* v. *Baxendale* [1999]
2 AC 52 (HL).
31. [2000] 2 All ER 860.
32. A hive-down involves the transfer of viable parts of a business to a subsidiary of the
insolvent company incorporated for that purpose (usually bearing a similar name to the
troubled company). A buyer is then sought for the subsidiary. The supposed advantage lies in
providing a 'clean commercial package': see Davies, 'Acquired Rights', pp. 32–3.

will treat the device unsympathetically and apply the *Litster* approach. The courts will thus ensure that where dismissals are made prior to the eventual transfer of the hive-down vehicle, the employment liabilities will pass through to the ultimate transferee.

A further complication flows from Regulation 8(2) of TUPE which offers the employer a defence. The dismissal will not be unfair if, as already noted, there was an 'economic, technical or organisational reason' for it (the ETO defence).[33] The courts have held that improving the price of a sale will not constitute such a reason and tend to look for a justification connected with the prospects of operating the business as a going concern.[34] The courts have developed case law on Regulations 5 and 8[35] but, from the IP's point of view, a concern is that this is bedevilled by uncertainties on a number of points: for instance, regarding the ETO defence and the connection between a dismissal and the transfer.[36] Such a practitioner would, in an ideal world, be able to calculate the reliability of any TUPE-avoiding measures and his or her exposure to potential employee claims. On present evidence that practitioner is faced with a legal state of affairs that is uncertain and far from ideal.[37]

Efficiency

In assessing whether the law's treatment of employees leads to efficiency in insolvency processes, it is necessary to keep the efficiency question separate from the issue of fairness or distributional justice. Central fairness questions (to be returned to below) are whether employees' acquired employment rights should be recognised and, if so, whether creditors, the state or other parties should bear the associated costs. Key efficiency questions are whether the law conduces to low-cost rescues

---

33. See, for example, Eldridge, 'TUPE Operates to Damage Rescue Culture', p. 20.

34. Collins *et al.*, *Labour Law*, p. 1038; *Whitehouse* v. *Charles A. Blatchford & Sons Ltd* [2000] ICR 542 (CA); *Wheeler* v. *Patel and J. Goulding Group of Companies* [1987] ICR 631 (EAT); *Gateway Hotels Ltd* v. *Stewart* [1988] IRLR 281 (EAT); McMullen, *Business Transfers*, p. 20 and the approach of the ECJ: see *Abels* v. *Bedrijfsvereniging voor de Metall-Industrie en de Electrotechnische Industrie* (Case C-135/83) [1987] 2 CMLR 406, but compare more recent approaches in the ECJ in *Jules Dethier Equipment SA* v. *Dassy* (Case C-319/94) [1998] ICR 541.

35. See, for example, Frisby, 'TUPE or not TUPE?'; Collins *et al.*, *Labour Law*.

36. Frisby, 'TUPE or not TUPE?', p. 259, for instance, asserts: 'Both insolvency practitioners and transferees will never be entirely certain whether "financial constraints" dismissals will be adjudged to be unconnected to a transfer.'

37. See, for example, M. Sargeant, 'Business Transfers and Corporate Insolvencies: The Effect of TUPE' (1998) 14 IL&P 8; Eldridge, 'TUPE Operates to Damage Rescue Culture', p. 20. In 2001 the Government announced that it planned to reform TUPE in order to promote greater flexibility in the rules on transfers; see pp. 561, 563–4 below.

or realisations (and distributions) of the insolvent company's assets and whether the law creates inefficient distortions in the allocation of resources. In answering these questions it is necessary to bear in mind the broad array of employees' protections outlined above, though this discussion will focus centrally on the TUPE regulations.

A first point to make is that employee protections may in some circumstances conduce to the efficient negotiation of insolvency solutions. As indicated, the system of employee 'super-priority', the rules on contract adoption, the set of employment protections and, in particular, the TUPE regulations, will sometimes operate to encourage key employees to stay with a troubled company and to help it out of its troubles. This may prove more efficient than a position in which employees rush for the door and companies that might have been turned around and rescued are liquidated. As commentators have argued: 'The first step to assist a corporate rescue is to induce the retained workforce to continue to work. Employees will be reluctant to help, however, unless they receive a better assurance that they will receive their wages than a promise from an insolvent company.'[38]

Protections for employees, especially those giving some feeling of security, may also help to shore up morale. It has been noted that office holders tend to fear that employees who feel that a business is doomed have a propensity to withdraw co-operation and 'are apt to develop mysterious illnesses' or simply not to apply very much effort once they know that they are certain to be made redundant.[39] Similarly, some protective rules, notably those on employee consultation, may encourage the successful pursuit of solutions. As Armour and Deakin have commented: 'On the positive side, TUPE provides a basis on which a designated representative of the employee – either the recognised trade union or unions in the enterprise concerned, or the default representatives provided for by statute – has the power to enter into negotiations with the employer over the terms on which the restructuring may take place.'[40]

Contrary to this optimistic view, however, are ranged a number of objections. Uncertainties in the law will tend to raise transaction costs,

---

38. Collins *et al.*, *Labour Law*, p. 1034.
39. Armour and Deakin, 'Insolvency, Employment Protection and Corporate Restructuring', p. 37.
40. Ibid., p. 46. See also the arguments for employees' participation in M. Armstrong and A. Cerfontaine, 'The Rhetoric of Inclusion? Corporate Governance in Insolvency Law' [2000] Ins. Law. 38.

produce solutions inefficiently and render rescues more difficult. Against the contention that the law leads to low-cost bargaining, it can be said that employee representatives under the present law find it difficult to offer clear undertakings to employees and purchasers of businesses because uncertainty surrounds the basis upon which employment rights subject to TUPE can be waived and whether an employee representative has the power to compromise the claims of some employees in order to help others.[41]

Article 4A(2)(b) of the amended Acquired Rights Directive 98/50 (yet to be implemented in the UK) takes a step towards permitting this kind of bargaining in insolvency proceedings under the supervision of a 'competent public authority'.[42] A Member State may, under the Directive, provide that transferees, transferors and employee representatives may (in so far as current law or practice permits) agree alterations 'to terms and conditions of employment designed to safeguard employment opportunities by ensuring the survival of the undertaking, business or part of the undertaking or business'. In its September 2001 Consultation Document on reform, the DTI argued that the underlying aim of this provision was to promote the sale of insolvent businesses as going concerns, an objective in line with the rescue culture it wished to promote.[43] The Government, therefore, proposed to take up this option and provide accordingly. Legislation on this point will offer a chance to clarify the legal position on such agreements.[44]

Present TUPE case law, as indicated above, is also uncertain on a number of other points so that it is difficult for a transferor or a transferee to judge whether redundancies made pre- or post-transfer in order to reduce a wage bill will produce costs to transferees following the application

---

41. See Armour and Deakin, 'Insolvency, Employment Protection and Corporate Restructuring', pp. 46–7 and *Wilson* v. *St Helens Borough Council, British Fuels Ltd* v. *Baxendale* [1999] 2 AC 52. For a discussion of the difficulties attending this course of action see P. L. Davies, 'Amendments to the Acquired Rights Directive' (1998) 27 ILJ 365.

42. In the UK the 'competent public authority' would be an IP and the 'insolvency proceedings' covered would be administration, company and individual voluntary arrangements and creditors' voluntary windings up but not administrative receiverships or any other kind of receiverships or members' voluntary windings up: DTI, *TUPE: Government Proposals for Reform: Public Consultation Document* (DTI, 2001, URN 01/1133) para. 27.

43. DTI, *TUPE*, 2001. On the amended Directive (Directive 78/50/EC) and the Government's consultation see further M. Sargeant, 'Proposed Transfer Regulations and Insolvency' [2002] JBL 108.

44. Matters requiring clarification could include the meaning of 'ensuring the survival of the enterprise', the assessment of appropriate representatives of employees and the problem of tight timescales: see further Sargeant, 'Proposed Transfer Regulations', pp. 110–11.

of Regulations 5 and 8 by tribunals.[45] Researchers, tellingly, have found that involved practitioners hold the widespread belief that the law is so uncertain as to make reliable predictions of costs impossible.[46]

A second issue is whether (leaving uncertainties aside) shifting acquired rights costs onto the purchasers of insolvent companies obstructs rescues and thereby involves inefficiency. Here much depends on the particular circumstances.[47] In cases where there is no prospect of rescue, acquired rights have no effect. In instances where there is a clear case for a going concern sale, acquired rights are likely not to affect the rescue although purchasers will discount the price paid in reflection of their expected liabilities to employees (a solution principally raising issues of fairness rather than efficiency). In some cases, however, the transfer of acquired rights will mean that an office holder will raise more through a break-up sale than by selling as a going concern to a buyer who will make an offer that is acquired rights discounted. Armour and Deakin thus quote as 'largely representative' the following comment from a party experienced in the conduct of administrations and administrative receiverships: 'The Acquired Rights Directive I think is bad news for employees because it makes businesses harder to sell and therefore jobs harder to rescue...[A]t the margin I'm sure there are cases where the businesses didn't sell because of the burdens that the purchaser would have had to take on.'[48]

In these marginal cases the overall effect may be inefficient when the state National Insurance Fund pays out for redundancies in circumstances where continuing employment for some of the workforce would have lowered net costs.[49] Whether the process of protecting acquired rights actually impedes rescue rather than merely reduces sale price may, again, depend on a number of considerations, such as the number of employees involved, the length of their service and the quality and timing of information possessed by the potential purchaser.[50]

---

45. See G. Morris, 'Transferring Liability for Employee Claims' [2000] JBL 188; Frisby, 'TUPE or not TUPE?', p. 265.

46. Frisby, 'TUPE or not TUPE?', pp. 265–6 where an interviewee is quoted as calling TUPE 'one unholy mess'; Sargeant, 'Business Transfers and Corporate Insolvencies'; Armour and Deakin, 'Insolvency, Employment Protection and Corporate Restructuring', p. 38.

47. See Armour and Deakin, 'Insolvency, Employment Protection and Corporate Restructuring', pp. 25–39.

48. Ibid., p. 31. The European Court of Justice considered this issue in the case of *Abels* v. *Bedrijfsvereniging voor de Metaal-Industrie en de Electrotechnische Industrie*, Case 135/83 [1987] 2 CMLR 406.

49. Frisby, 'TUPE or not TUPE?', p. 264.   **50.** Ibid., p. 265.

An efficient regime of protecting acquired rights would be one that reduced uncertainties and did not 'chill' efficient rescues (that is, rescues where overall value is greater with a going concern than with a break-up sale). The amended Acquired Rights Directive seeks to further rescues[51] by allowing Member States to exempt the need to transfer rights (under Articles 3 and 4) from any transfer where the transferor is the subject of bankruptcy proceedings 'or any analogous insolvency proceedings which have been instituted with a view to the liquidation of the assets of the transferor', provided the proceedings are under the supervision of a competent public authority (such as an IP). The DTI suggests in its Consultation Document that the procedures covered by this would include compulsory winding up, bankruptcy and possibly creditors' voluntary winding up.[52] Additionally, as noted above, where Articles 3 and 4 *do* apply, then employers' and employees' representatives can agree changes in terms and conditions so as to ensure rescue. Where the debts arise before transfer[53] and the Member State offers protections at least equivalent to those set out in Council Directive 80/987/EEC relating to protection of employees in the event of the insolvency of their employer,[54] the transferor's pre-existing debts towards employees will, furthermore, not pass to the transferee. In such a regime, acquired rights costs would fall on the NIF rather than the transferee – or rather the creditors of the transferor, if it is assumed that they tend to suffer when transferees make reduced offers in anticipation of having to meet acquired rights costs. This state funding might save jobs and prove efficient in cases where the balance between the returns from, on the one hand, break-up sales and, on the other, ongoing basis disposals, turns on who bears the acquired rights costs.

The DTI consultation of 2001 argued in favour of this course of action on the basis that benefits 'are expected to outweigh the relatively modest

---

51. See the *Abels* decision (Case 135/83, ECR 469) in which the ECJ was concerned that transfers of acquired rights might inhibit rescues and distinguished between those insolvencies whose purpose was liquidation and those whose aim was rescue of the enterprise. The 1977 Directive, said the court, covered rescue-orientated proceedings but not those whose purpose was liquidation. The *Abels* distinction is reflected in the amending Directive 98/50. As has been pointed out, though, this leaves difficult issues of identifying the purposes of different proceedings at different times: see M. Sargeant, 'More Flexibility for Insolvent Transfers: The Amended Acquired Rights Directive' (1999) 15 IL&P 6; Sargeant, 'An Amended Acquired Rights Directive' [1998] JBL 577. See also Hardy, 'Some TUPE Implications' and the 'continued trading' test of Case C-319/94, *Jules Dethier Equipment SA v. Dassy* [1998] ICR 541.
52. DTI, *TUPE*, 2001, para. 26.
53. So that dismissals are effected by the transfer: see Directive 98/50 Article 4A(2)(a).
54. Directive 98/50 of 29 June 1998: DTI, *TUPE*, 2001, para. 27. See Sargeant, 'More Flexibility for Insolvent Transfers' and 'Proposed Transfer Regulations', pp. 109–10.

additional "deadweight" costs' in insolvency payments from the NIF.[55] The Government, therefore, proposed that where appropriate insolvency proceedings had opened, any outstanding debts to employees would either be met by the NIF (if within the categories and statutory upper limits on amounts guaranteed under the Employment Rights Act 1996) or pass to the transferee, as at present (if not within those categories or limits).

There may be dangers, however. Employees might receive redundancy payments (up to the statutory ceiling) but would not be able to recover unfair dismissal compensation from the NIF. Such a system could also induce IPs to engage routinely in pre-transfer dismissals.[56] On this last point, however, something may turn on the information possessed by the IP. If the quality of information is high, it might be hoped that the IP would assess the need to dismiss or retain on the (acceptable) basis of the employee's value to the ongoing business. On grounds of certainty there may be a case for this version of state-funded acquired rights rather than one in which proof of an 'objective' case for dismissal is a precondition of the NIF's paying for acquired rights costs rather than the transferee.[57] A more pessimistic view of the IPs' motivation might, however, suggest a tendency to take advantage of 'tactical' dismissals: which might involve, for example, the shedding of senior staff and replacing them with more junior personnel possessing fewer acquired rights. This vision does point to the need to restrict access to the NIF by distinguishing between justifiable and unjustifiable dismissals.[58]

Expertise

The law would contribute to the best use of employee expertise at times of trouble if it induced loyalty on the part of those employees whose expertise is necessary to ensure an efficient sale or rescue. As the law stands, however, the employees of a troubled company are confronted by all of

55. DTI, *TUPE*, 2001, para. 30. (Some costs would be offset by savings in benefit payments to employees who lost their jobs on liquidation.)

56. A concern expressed by Frisby, 'TUPE or not TUPE?', p. 268. Cost to the state would, however, be limited in the DTI's proposed regime as the NIF would only pay up to statutory limits.

57. Frisby, 'TUPE or not TUPE?', p. 269, suggests that uncertainties involved in distinguishing 'objective', or justifiable, dismissals from others can be reduced by introducing a rebuttable presumption that a dismissal is not justifiable.

58. For example, by holding a dismissal to be economically justifiable when the employee is surplus to the ongoing requirements of the business.

the uncertainties described above and they will tend to be far less well equipped than transferors, IPs or transferees to assess their levels of job security or the financial risks they would run if they decided to stay with the company. From the narrow perspective of employee expertise, therefore, the case for measures to increase certainty can be made with special force. Here, again, therefore, there may be an argument for the state to bear acquired rights costs. Such a set up would, as noted, allow IPs and other involved parties to assess whether there is a case for dismissal on legitimate economic grounds. There is liable to be far greater consistency between that process of reasoning and the employee's deliberations on his or her value to the firm than between the latter deliberations and an employee's assessment of the security that he or she is likely to derive from the statutory and case law on acquired rights.

Accountability

Are employees given an appropriate voice in insolvency procedures? Insolvency law, together with employment law, protects that voice in a number of respects.[59] First, the law on unfair dismissal requires a 'reasonable' employer to engage in consultation with an individual employee prior to dismissal and, where the employee is represented by an independent union recognised by the employer, that reasonable employer will also give as much warning as possible to the union and consult the union as to the best way to achieve the desired result with minimum hardship to employees.[60] The law on unfair dismissal thus can collectivise worker participation in decisions about economic dismissals, but this depends on there being a relevant union and an employee may not enjoy such rights if the tribunal is satisfied that the outcome would not have differed had consultation been conducted.[61] A second protection derives from the Trade Union and Labour Relations (Consolidation) Act 1992 ss. 188–98 which provide that if an employer proposes to dismiss twenty or more workers at one establishment for economic reasons, he or she must consult in good time with representatives of the workforce[62] with a view to agreeing ways of avoiding or

59. See Collins et al., Labour Law, pp. 1056–67.
60. Williams v. Compair Maxam [1982] ICR 156 (EAT).
61. Where an employer fails to act in a reasonable manner procedurally and this does not affect the outcome, the unfairly dismissed employee will often, at the discretion of the tribunal, receive no compensation in excess of the redundancy payment (Polkey v. A. E. Dayton Services Ltd [1988] ICR 142 (HL)). This development 'subverts the procedural protections in almost every case of redundancy': Collins et al., Labour Law, p. 1059.
62. Who may be the recognised trade union or (in the absence of one) elected representatives.

reducing dismissals or mitigating the consequences of dismissal. Failure to comply with this requirement may result in a tribunal making a protective award[63] to the dismissed employee.

A third source of employee process rights covering the sale of a business is TUPE. The TUPE Regulations 1981, as amended, oblige the transferor and transferee to consult and consider representations from a recognised trade union or (in the absence of a union) other workforce representatives. Failure to observe this requirement may mean that the employer has to pay 'just and equitable'[64] compensation to 'affected employees' of up to thirteen weeks pay over and above existing contractual entitlements.[65]

Finally, note should be taken of collective agreements made between trade unions and employees. Such agreements in the UK do not generally envisage that the trade unions will be empowered to prevent economic dismissals or have a right to be consulted so as to agree the need for dismissal. Where, however, the terms of collective agreements are incorporated into contracts of employment, enforceable rights may arise.[66]

Overall, the effect of these provisions is to give employees only the most modest voice in insolvency.[67] As has been stated: 'The notion that the workforce should routinely participate in managerial decisions that might affect their livelihoods seems like a distant peak of the horizon of British industrial relations ... The culture of British management seems to be one of preferring to keep strategic decisions confidential and to regard business reorganisations as part of the managerial prerogative.'[68]

Employee rights, then, hardly impinge on the governance of insolvency processes[69] but they may have some effects. The TUPE obligations of consultation are backed up by potentially punitive provisions and this creates an incentive for managers to collectivise negotiations in troubled

---

63. Consisting of wages for the period during which proper consultation should have taken place.

64. Having regard to the seriousness of the employer's failure to comply with the consultation duty.

65. TUPE 1981, Regulation 11(11). These provisions do not cover sales of shares or takeovers, their principal importance concerning situations where the transferee introduces variations in terms: Collins *et al.*, *Labour Law*, p. 1062. In the case of takeover bids there is a (sanction free) duty merely to provide information under the City Code on Takeover and Mergers, Rule 24.1: see S. Deakin and G. Slinger, 'Hostile Takeovers, Corporate Law and the Theory of the Firm' (1997) 24 *Journal of Law and Society* 124.

66. See *Anderson* v. *Pringle of Scotland Ltd* [1998] IRLR 64.

67. See B. Cheffins, *Company Law: Theory, Structure and Operation* (Clarendon Press, Oxford, 1997) p. 574; Armstrong and Cerfontaine, 'Rhetoric of Inclusion?', p. 40.

68. Collins *et al.*, *Labour Law*, p. 1066.

69. See Armour and Deakin, 'Insolvency, Employment Protection and Corporate Restructuring', p. 17.

times. This may lower the cost of planning and implementing new strategies,[70] which may bring a number of further advantages.[71] It may facilitate planning reorganisations. It may increase employee loyalty, by offering reassurance, and help avoid the destructive effects of industrial action. A further gain from listening to the worker voice may be that expertise and knowledge within the workforce may be tapped, so that more efficient or fairer ways of realising reorganisational objectives may be arrived at. The co-operation of the workforce may also result in financial assistance: where, for example, employees make wage concessions in an effort to make a turnaround work. Finally, there may be social gains from consultation. If employees are given advance notice of reorganisations, they may find new jobs, retrain, retire or take other steps that will lower the overall impact of an insolvency on society.

Such advantages suggest that (assuming transaction costs can be kept modest) there is a case in efficiency terms for strengthening the voice of employees within insolvency processes and reorganisation procedures. With reference to fairness also it can be argued that it is socially just to increase the voice of those parties who have committed their efforts and working lives to the enterprise.[72] It is, indeed, to issues of fairness that we should now turn.

Fairness

Is insolvency law's application of employee rights fair? In answering this question we may ask whether the acquired rights of employees should be recognised and, if they are to be recognised, who should bear the cost of compensating the employees of insolvent companies. (In this discussion we might note that the issues are similar whether the transfer is made via a liquidator, a receiver or an administrator.)[73] On the recognition issue, responses may vary according to different ways of conceptualising the employee. One vision of the employee sees him or her as merely another unsecured creditor. As was seen in chapter 13, however, there is a case, even within such a vision, for giving employees rights that are superior or preferential to those of other unsecured creditors. It would be unfair, for

---

70. Collectivising negotiations may lower costs in so far as employers can deal with the unions or worker representatives rather than engage in protracted individual negotiations, but, as noted, TUPE rights cannot be negotiated away by the union and so there is a limit to the role of collective agreements: ibid., pp. 22–3.

71. See Collins *et al.*, *Labour Law*, p. 1057.   72. See Villiers, 'Employees as Creditors'.

73. See Davies, 'Acquired Rights'.

instance, not to recognise that employees are especially high-cost risk bearers who tend to enjoy modest levels of information and have very limited abilities to adjust rates or negotiate terms so as to reflect risks.[74] Such protections as are offered by the Insolvency Act 1986 section 175's preferential treatment for employees' accrued wages and the 'super-priority' given to employees' wage and payment claims from a receiver, are, for the time being, on this view, justified.[75]

Another approach, however, might treat the employee not as some species of unsecured creditor but as a stakeholder, who has an entitlement to rights and protections that derives from his or her contribution to the assets of the company.[76] That contribution, it could be argued, is different in kind from that of an individual who supplies finance or goods to the company. Labour and working commitment, on this view, are factors that create superior moral claims based on desert and contribution as well as need.[77] A similar argument can be made in implied contractual terms. Employees, it could be said, are engaged with the company on the basis of implicit expectations of careers, continuing prospects and pensions and these expectations should be recognised by insolvency law.[78]

A comparative perspective on these issues can be achieved by looking across the Channel. In France a series of reforms followed the election of Mitterand's socialist government in 1981. These promulgated a strong participatory model of the employee.[79] This model fully recognises the employee as a 'participant' in the company, in good times as well as bad. Indeed, the more a company experiences difficulties, the more the employee representative institutions have a voice and powers of action. Employees enjoy rights not only to be informed and consulted but to influence decision-making. The judges, moreover, have endorsed this

---

74. See pp. 428–31 above.

75. Note, however, that if the White Paper 2001 proposal (para. 2.19) to abolish the Crown's preferential status is implemented, the rationale for employee preferential status may be undermined: see ch. 13 above.

76. See Collins *et al.*, *Labour Law*, p. 1029; Armstrong and Cerfontaine, 'Rhetoric of Inclusion?'; G. Bastin and P. Townsend, 'Should We Make the Redundancy Scheme Redundant?' (1996) 17 Co. Law. 252.

77. See Villiers, 'Employees as Creditors', p. 229; D. R. Korobkin, 'Rehabilitating Values: A Jurisprudence of Bankruptcy' (1991) 91 Colum. L Rev. 717; Korobkin, 'Contractarianism and the Normative Foundations of Bankruptcy Law' (1993) 71 Texas L Rev. 541; M. Walzer, *Spheres of Justice* (Basil Blackwell, Oxford, 1995); J. Finnis, *Natural Law and Natural Rights* (Clarendon Press, Oxford, 1980); P. Shuchman, 'An Attempt at a "Philosophy of Bankruptcy"' (1973) 21 UCLA L Rev. 403; A. Gewirth, *The Community of Rights* (University of Chicago Press, Chicago, 1996).

78. I am grateful to Hugh Collins for suggesting this point.

79. See Armstrong and Cerfontaine, 'Rhetoric of Inclusion?'.

vision so that employee representatives in France constitute an organ comparable to the board of directors or the general meeting.[80] In 1985 the legislature made employees' interests part of the 'interests of the company', and employee representative institutions are entitled to intervene very extensively as participants in insolvency procedures.[81]

Employee participation is firmly entrenched in France but it has not proved a panacea for troubled companies since insolvency tends to be a small company problem and to occur where employee representation is non-existent.[82] It may be the case that further steps are required to assist SMEs but proponents of the French system urge the strong ethical basis of the participatory model, as 'social justice has an imperative quite independent of efficiency rationales'.[83]

If it is accepted that employees have acquired rights that should be recognised in an insolvency, who should pay? When such acquired rights are passed onto transferees who discount the prices that they pay for troubled firms, the costs of acquired rights are, as noted, liable in practice to be borne by the secured creditors of the insolvent company.[84] These creditors are the parties who stand to take the lion's share of the residual estate and they will be the first to suffer from a strict transfer of acquired rights. If, on the other hand, rights do not transfer, the state and taxpayer (through the NIF) will compensate those employees who lose their jobs (though payments are subject, in practice, to limitations). In discussing efficiency we saw that (if low levels of 'tactical' dismissals can be assumed) there may be a case for state funding of acquired rights protections on the grounds that this will reduce uncertainty. Is such a solution fair to the taxpayer though?

A risk-based analysis might raise difficult questions here. It is arguable that the state is an involuntary creditor who may find it easy to spread risks but who is very ill-placed to monitor and influence risk taking and who will not reap the benefits of risk taking. It could be argued that it would be unfair to burden taxpayers for these reasons and that it would be more equitable to burden creditors with employee-related costs. Creditors, especially the banks, are, after all, not only efficient risk spreaders but they are parties who advance loans voluntarily, can adjust their terms to

---

80. Ibid., p. 42.

81. Law 85–98 January 1985, Article 10. An administrator, for instance, must inform and consult with employees on the evaluation of a company's position and proposals as well as on the resultant report. Valid recovery plans must have been consulted on with employee institutions: Armstrong and Cerfontaine, 'Rhetoric of Inclusion?', p. 44.

82. Ibid., p. 44.   83. Ibid.

84. And by unsecured creditors if assets are sufficient to satisfy secured creditors' claims and leave a fund.

perceived risks, are well informed and stand to benefit (at least through interest mechanisms and sales of ancillary bank services) from the profits made by the enterprise. There are, however, some reasons why the state can be said to enjoy the benefits of risk taking and should be prepared on grounds of fairness to fund acquired rights. Entrepreneurial risk taking will be encouraged by such funding and this will conduce to wealth creation which in turn will benefit the state in many ways.[85] It would allow rescues and redistributions to occur in a lower friction manner than would be possible under a regime demanding that creditors should bear such costs. This may prove fair to taxpayers in so far as there is a return to the state for its efforts: the lower friction regime of enterprise would be likely to produce, overall, greater wealth for the state.

On both efficiency and fairness fronts, it seems there is a case for state funding of acquired rights in two situations.[86] First, if the anticipated incidence of abuse through 'tactical' dismissals is reasonably small – and outweighed by gains in net wealth creation – it would be sensible to fund *all* insolvency-related dismissals from state sources. If, however, the likelihood of such abuse is high, it will be necessary to distinguish, at lowest cost, between objectively necessary dismissals (which would be state funded) and unjustifiable or 'tactical' dismissals (which would not be paid for by the NIF). Guidance on these choices can best be derived from research into the severity of risks that state funding might be abused and into the potential of new laws and processes (such as reversals of proof)[87] to reduce the uncertainties and transaction costs that flow from efforts to separate economically necessary from unjustifiable dismissals.

Conclusions

Employees are in some ways the lost souls of insolvency law. Their working contributions are the lifeblood of companies, yet the law does remarkably little to involve them in insolvency procedures. This is because the law has failed to develop on the basis of a coherent and appropriate conception of the employee. On the one hand, insolvency law sometimes

---

85. Amongst other things there would, as noted above, be savings on NIF benefit payments where rescues are effected.
86. On the (attractive) case for socialising employee claims, see Davies, 'Acquired Rights', p. 53.
87. See Frisby's suggestion (noted above) of lowering costs by applying a rebuttable presumption that a dismissal is not objectively necessary where dismissal and re-engagement occurs pre- and post-transfer: Frisby, 'TUPE or not TUPE?', p. 269.

sees the employee as a creditor who merits a certain amount of protection. On the other, he or she is occasionally treated in a manner consistent with the rhetoric of stakeholding. Policies on employees, moreover, are driven, in relation to some issues, by considerations of economic efficiency yet on others they are shaped by reference to ethical and social justice arguments. The way to resolve such difficulties is, first, to develop a solid informational and research base so that the implications of dealing with employees in different ways can be calculated rather than guessed at. Some of the works referred to in this chapter offer evidence that the foundations of such research are now being laid. There is now, for instance, some empirical data (albeit small scale) on matters such as the transfer effects of TUPE. Much more work needs to be done, however, before reliable judgments can be made on issues such as the role of employee loyalty within rescues; the quality of information that tends to be available to potential parties to rescue; or the role played by employee representatives in designing and achieving turnarounds. Second, there needs to be greater clarity not merely about the objectives of insolvency law as a whole, but about the conception, nature and extent of employees' rights in the corporation. Finally, and building on these developments, there needs to be a greater openness (even political honesty) regarding the trade-offs of risks, values and interests that are involved in insolvency law.[88] This means that tensions between the interests of shareholders, creditors, employees, the state and other stakeholders have to be confronted rather than hidden away.

---

88. See, for example, Armstrong and Cerfontaine, 'Rhetoric of Inclusion?', p. 45 and the authors' attack on DTI approaches as 'tinkering'.

Conclusion

In some ways corporate insolvency law has come a long way since the Cork Report.[1] Numerous statutes, court decisions and administrative reforms have sought to develop the law so as to remedy deficiencies and secure newly appreciated needs. On the political front, recent years have seen the UK Government showing a renewed desire to attune insolvency laws to the needs of enterprise while, at the same time, avoiding abuses and injustices. In other ways, however, corporate insolvency law can be seen, to date, as an area marked by missed opportunities and modest achievements. It has, first, failed to develop as an organised, consistent and purposeful body of rules and processes. This has been a legal sector in which Cork's prescriptions were cherry-picked and where, subsequently, particular issues have been dealt with piecemeal by both legislators and judges. Corporate insolvency law has, secondly, been developed without close co-ordination with relevant legal sectors and processes. It has not been linked sufficiently closely with company law – in spite of its relevance to the ongoing needs of healthy companies – nor has it been tied in with an analysis of the arrangements for providing finances for companies that are found in the UK. As was made clear in chapter 3, corporate insolvency law is faced with a pattern of corporate funding that is dictated very largely by the legal frameworks that govern the provision of credit, notably those relating to security and quasi-security. To design insolvency law without looking at those arrangements is to cut the cloth without measuring the wearer.

A third difficulty has been that this has been an area of law that has developed without a consistent guiding philosophy. As has been stressed in chapter 11, different procedures have been developed on the basis of

---

1. *Report of the Review Committee on Insolvency Law and Practice* (Cmnd 8558, 1982).

inconsistent assumptions not only about the values and objectives that are properly to be pursued, but also about the potential and roles of the different actors that are involved in insolvency processes. Directors and employees are central figures in corporate insolvency law and processes, but the law is based on notions of directorial roles and employee rights that are multiple, inconsistent and competing. This leads to a host of confusions, uncertainties, inefficiencies, unfairnesses and misplaced accountabilities. The broad end product has been a system of corporate insolvency law that offers not so much a choice of processes that pull together harmoniously as an ill-organised array of procedures that, in many respects, undermine each other. We see this not least in the way that receivership has been allowed to ride roughshod over other corporate insolvency mechanisms such as administration and company voluntary arrangements.

Putting such a consistent guiding philosophy into effect is, however, no simple matter. To return to a point already made, insolvency law meshes with other legal domains, notably company law and employment law. Consistency of philosophy means not only that insolvency law has to be characterised by purpose and direction but that company and employment laws need to be both internally coherent and consistent with insolvency law. The chapter 15 and 16 discussions of directors and employees give an indication of the dangers and challenges being confronted here. To give a simple example, it is of little value designing insolvency laws that are rescue friendly if laws on employment protection offer strong disincentives to the corporate transfers that are necessary to keep businesses alive.

The returns from philosophical consistency are, moreover, important. At various points throughout this book it has been argued that legal uncertainties produce high costs, inefficiencies and unfairnesses. It might be responded, though, that laws can never be certain, that judges have to apply rules to differing circumstances, and that judges need to adjust criteria, standards and rules to cope with changes in such matters as business practices and ways of setting up commercial relationships. There is, however, an important distinction to be drawn between the unavoidable uncertainties that flow from the factors just noted and the unnecessary uncertainties that arise because inconsistent philosophies are vying with each other in driving legal developments. If, for example, punitive approaches to company direction are sustained in competition with public protection philosophies (or if rescue-oriented and creditor protection responses are set against each other) a great deal of uncertainty will unnecessarily arise if there is no set of overarching principles that indicates which of the competing approaches will prevail in which circumstances, or what balance between the approaches is appropriate.

It is philosophical consistency – within and across the areas of insolvency, company and employment law – that offers such guiding principles. This, it should be emphasised, does not mean that a single substantive blueprint has to be laid down: in a changing world such blueprints rapidly pass their sell-by dates. What is required is an approach that confronts competitions between values and objectives and explains how these can be understood and argued out. It is the ability to explain – and so to understand and predict – that reduces uncertainties.

This book has set out to respond to these questions of philosophical deficiency. It has done so, first, by making out the case for an 'explicit values' approach to the design and evaluation of corporate insolvency processes. This is an approach that is applicable to all corporate insolvency procedures and encourages the development of mechanisms that are consistent in so far as they link to a common philosophy and to a limited number of identifiable values. Second, this book has set out to examine not merely the formal rules of corporate insolvency law but also the procedures, actors and institutions that give substance to the law as an aspect of corporate life and decline. It is, after all, not achieving a great deal if formal laws are harmonious but confusions and inconsistencies of approach pervade the processes and institutional structures that are needed to implement these laws. Attending to procedures, actors and institutions means that difficult questions have to be tackled concerning not merely the substantive and procedural rights of individuals, groups and firms but also the capacities and incentives of these parties to deliver the appropriate levels of managerial skill and commitment to rescue or winding-up processes. The return from coming to grips with these issues is that corporate insolvency law can be assessed and redesigned with an eye to operational matters and not merely to the formal rules.

A third way of responding to the current problems that are encountered in the law has been to examine whether the assumptions that underpin existing laws, procedures and institutions need to be challenged so that new ways of conceiving rules, processes and actors are necessary if an explicit values approach is best to be served.

The chapters above have presented arguments in favour of a number of changes that seem likely to lead to gains in efficiency, expertise, accountability or fairness without unduly negative side-effects. On the financing of corporate organisations, current arrangements involve significant dangers that transfers of insolvency wealth will be effected from unsecured to secured creditors and to parties who are well equipped to make use of quasi-security devices. Such transfers, where they occur, may prejudice healthy companies' needs as well as the interests, in insolvencies, of certain creditor classes (notably the unsecured trade creditors). Procedures could and should be adopted to allow unsecured creditors to inform themselves more easily about the risks they are running when they provide credit. This is not a complete answer for all unsecured creditors but it is a step that will help reduce inefficiencies and unfairness in the case of certain parties.

Wealth transfers away from creditors who cannot adjust their terms to cope with risks could be responded to by introducing a fixed-fraction rule, as proposed by Cork and alluded to in the 2001 White Paper,[2] whereby a given percentage of secured creditors' claims is to be treated as unsecured. Compulsory insurance against certain categories of tort liability could also provide a way of reducing the inefficient subsidies that are provided by a particular group of involuntary non-adjusting unsecured creditors.

As for the system of financing corporate operations overall, a problem currently stems from the confusion of devices that are available. This creates uncertainty and increases transaction cost unnecessarily. Similarly, the system of priorities is rendered uncertain and confused by the capacity of 'creditors' to employ quasi-security devices such as retention of title clauses. Steps can be taken to reduce such confusions and, in turn, to lower general transaction costs. Thus, for example, a more rigorous approach to the registration of retentions of title would increase transparency and reduce the costs of borrowing by lowering the levels of financial uncertainty that creditors face when providing funds.

The processes and grounds for ending corporate lives are also matters of concern. If certain parties, such as floating charge holders, possess incentives to end such lives at times when this may not be in the general interest of all those parties who are affected by the insolvency, this may be inefficient as well as unfair. There is a case, as the Government now seems to recognise, for abolishing the right of a floating charge holder to appoint a receiver in a way that overrides rescue procedures.

Turning to the major actors in corporate insolvency processes – the IPs – it has been argued above that there is no strong case for reforms to

2. DTI/Insolvency Service, *Productivity and Enterprise: Insolvency – A Second Chance* (Cm 5234, 2001) para. 2.19.

replace IPs with court officials or civil servants. There may be good grounds, however, for tightening the mechanisms used to regulate IPs, for rethinking the breadth of the duties that IPs owe in insolvency procedures and for subjecting IP regulation to more rigorously independent oversight.

Current governmental endorsements of a rescue orientation in corporate insolvency procedures are to be welcomed but the discussion of rescue in chapters 6 to 11 revealed considerable scope for improvements in present arrangements. First, there is a need for harmonisation so that different rescue procedures do not undermine each other. This, again, points to the case for curtailing the rights of floating charge holders to appoint receivers and for moving towards a 'single gateway' approach to rescue procedures. Efficiency in rescues may also be served by giving directors greater incentives and capacities to resort to rescue procedures before the company's chances for turnaround have evaporated. Thought should be given, for instance, to ending the requirement, in the Insolvency Act 1986 section 8(1)(a), that a court must be satisfied that a company is, or is likely to become, unable to pay its debts before it can make an administration order. Consistent assumptions ought also to be made across rescue procedures concerning the roles of different actors such as directors or IPs. Such assumptions, moreover, should be based not on traditions of deference or unexplored notions of culpability but on a considered analysis of factors such as informational position; training; incentives; specialist knowledge of the relevant market; ability to assess financial options; and commitment to rescue.

Accountability within rescue procedures should, again, be ensured in reflection of a philosophy that is consistent across procedures. To this end, the narrowness of the administrative receiver's accountability – and its focus on the interests of the appointing debenture holder – should be addressed. There may also be a case for reconsidering whether shareholders should be excluded from the approval process in administrations when insolvency is merely likely. Such an exclusion may not be fairness-enhancing and it may, similarly, be argued that fairness demands that the interests of employee stakeholders should be reflected in greater access to, or recognition in, the decision-making processes governing administration. Considerations of fairness also reinforce the case for abolishing administrative receivership or, if it is to be retained, imposing obligations on the receiver to take on board interests beyond those of the appointing debenture holder.

As far as the substantive principles governing post-insolvency contributions are concerned, it is collectivity and the *pari passu* principle that has long occupied centre stage as regards residual assets. *Pari passu* has, however, been subjected to a variety of exceptions and bypassing arrangements. Of those exceptions, it has been argued above that the case for abolishing Crown preferences and for revising the rules on set-off is one not to be dismissed. It is difficult to support proposals for giving consumer creditors increased priority – largely because it is so difficult to distinguish 'consumer' from 'trade' creditor vulnerability – but employees can, for the moment, be identified as the creditor group most deserving of special treatment because of their status as non-adjusting, high-cost risk bearers.[3] On replacing the *pari passu* principle with another approach to distribution of the residual assets, it has been argued that alternatives that involve assessing the individual position or merits of the creditor would give rise to much uncertainty and would involve both inefficiencies and unfairnesses. New approaches to the definition of creditor classes face severe difficulties in dealing with heterogeneities within the memberships of such redefined classes and there would be problems in showing why such newly favoured classes would have claims that are stronger than those of competing classes.

It has been emphasised in chapter 14 that *pari passu* only comes into operation once the relevant, residual, insolvency estate has been constructed. Values such as efficiency and fairness have, accordingly, to be pursued in constructing the estate more generally and in establishing protections for 'vulnerable' risk bearers in the form of procedural requirements (of information provision and disclosure); substantive protections (such as a 10 per cent fund for unsecured creditors); ways of reducing overall risks of insolvency (for example, by improving directorial standards and training); and ways of spreading insolvency risks and, thereby, lowering risks borne by vulnerable parties.

The position of employees needs to be clarified not merely for the sake of employed persons but so that parties buying and selling companies can do so without excessive costs. A way forward, in the corporate transfer area, may lie through greater state funding of employees' acquired rights costs in corporate transfers post-insolvency. The law should move towards a conception of the employee that recognises his or her participatory rights and contributions to the company. The relationship between

---

3. This special treatment may not be merited if the 2001 White Paper proposal to abolish Crown preferential status is enacted.

this conception of the employee and the dictates of economic efficiency should be set out clearly in the law and such a relationship sustained in a consistent manner by the judiciary. As an underpinning to such developments in the law, more research should be undertaken (and state funded) on such matters as the potential role of the employee in rescues. Only against a reliable background of research can legislators, policy-makers, judges or others make informed judgments on implications for employees, other creditors or the variety of affected parties when they are shaping corporate insolvency processes or deciding issues.

As a final conclusion, a return should be made to the nature of the corporate insolvency law philosophy that is being argued for here. The 'explicit values' approach, it should be emphasised, is one that seeks to embrace both the public and private dimensions of corporate insolvency law. It is always difficult to reconcile public interests with those of private contractors, especially where private contractors vary sharply in their economic power, information levels, expertise and so on. A way to effect a 'least-worst' reconciliation, and to argue out the merits of this, is, however, to identify the values that are sought to be furthered within corporate insolvency processes. This, in the first instance, helps us to identify the ways in which different rules, processes and institutional arrangements affect various parties in divergent ways. Greater transparency is thus given to decisions about trade-offs. We can be clearer, for instance, on how much a new statutory requirement might affect small trade creditors compared to large secured bank lenders. Such an approach also helps us to identify more easily the contradictory effects and assumptions that are associated with different processes and arrangements.

If corporate insolvency law is to move forward as a coherent, consistent and purposeful set of rules and processes, it is necessary to rethink a number of its elements in the light of such transparency. Some of those elements have been identified here and one route towards greater clarity of design and evaluation has, I hope, been mapped out in this book.

Bibliography

The publisher has used its best endeavours to ensure that the URLs for external websites referred to in this book are correct and active at the time of going to press. However, the publisher has no responsibility for the websites and can make no guarantee that a site will remain live or that the content is or will remain appropriate.

Abbot, C., 'Liquidator Escapes Liability by Disclaiming Waste Management Licence' [2000] 1 *Palmer's In Company* 1

Adler, B., 'Financial and Political Theories of American Corporate Bankruptcy' (1993) 45 Stanford L Rev. 311

  'A World Without Debt' (1994) 72 Wash. ULQ 811

Aghion, P., O. Hart and J. Moore, 'A Proposal for Bankruptcy Reform in the UK', Discussion Paper No. 167 (LSE Financial Markets Group, 1993)

  'Insolvency Reform in the UK: A Revised Proposal', Special Paper No. 65 (LSE Financial Markets Group, January 1995) and in (1995) 11 IL&P 67

Agnello, R., 'Administration Expenses' (2000) *Recovery* (March) 24

Alexander, J., 'CVAs: The New Legislation' (1999) *Insolvency Bulletin* 5

Altman, E. I., 'Financial Ratios, Discriminant Analysis and the Prediction of Corporate Failure' (1968) 23 *Journal of Finance* 589

  Corporate Bankruptcy in America (D. C. Heath, London, 1971)

Anderson, H., 'Insolvency Practitioners: Professional Independence and Conflict of Interest' in A. Clarke (ed.), *Current Issues in Insolvency Law* (Stevens, London, 1991)

  'The Treatment of Trust Assets in English Insolvency Law' in E. McKendrick (ed.), *Commercial Aspects of Trusts and Fiduciary Obligations* (Clarendon Press, Oxford, 1992)

  'Receivers Compared with Administrators' (1996) 12 IL&P 54

  'Insolvent Insolvencies' (2001) 17 IL&P 87

Anderson, J., 'Receivers' Duties to Mortgagors. Court of Appeal Makes a Pig's Ear of It' (1999) 37 CCH *Company Law Newsletter* 6

Argenti, J., *Corporate Collapse: The Causes and Symptoms* (McGraw-Hill, London, 1976)

Armour, J., 'Share Capital and Creditor Protection: Efficient Rules for a Modern Company Law' (2000) 63 MLR 355

  'Who Pays When Polluters Go Bust?' (2000) 116 LQR 200

Armour, J. and S. Deakin, 'Norms in Private Insolvency Procedures: The "London Approach" to the Resolution of Financial Distress', ESRC Centre for Business

Research, Cambridge, Working Paper Series No. 173, September 2000, reprinted in [2001] 1 JCLS 21

'Insolvency, Employment Protection and Corporate Restructuring: The Effects of TUPE', ESRC Centre for Business Research, Cambridge, Working Paper Series No. 204, June 2001

Armour, J. and S. Frisby, 'Rethinking Receivership' (2001) 21 OJLS 73

Armstrong, M., '"Return to First Principles" in New Zealand: Charges Over Book Debts are Fixed – But the Future's Not!' [2000] Ins. Law. 102

Armstrong, M. and A. Cerfontaine, 'The Rhetoric of Inclusion? Corporate Governance in Insolvency Law' [2000] Ins. Law. 38

Arora, A., 'The Human Rights Act 1998: Some Implications for Commercial Law and Practice' (2001) 3 *Finance and Credit Law* 1

Arsalidou, D., 'The Impact of Section 214(4) of the Insolvency Act 1986 on Directors' Duties' (2000) Co. Law. 19

Austin, R., 'Commerce and Equity: Fiduciary Duty and Constructive Trust' (1986) 6 OJLS 444

'Corporate Groups' in R. Grantham and C. Rickett (eds.), *Corporate Personality in the Twentieth Century* (Hart, Oxford, 1998)

Australian Law Reform Commission, *General Insolvency Inquiry*, Report No. 45 (Canberra, 1988)

Ayer, J., 'Goodbye to Chapter 11: The End of Business Bankruptcy as We Know It' (Mimeo, Institute of Advanced Legal Studies, 2001)

Bacon, A. and R. Cowper, 'The Moratorium Emasculated: Another Blow for Corporate Recovery?' (1997) 10 *Insolvency Intelligence* 73

Baggott, R. and L. Harrison, 'The Politics of Self-Regulation' (1986) 14 *Policy and Politics* 143

Baird, D. G., 'The Uneasy Case for Corporate Reorganisations' (1986) 15 *Journal of Legal Studies* 127

'Loss Distribution, Forum Shopping and Bankruptcy: A Reply to Warren' (1987) 54 U Chic. L Rev. 815

Baird, D. G. and T. Jackson, 'Corporate Reorganisations and the Treatment of Diverse Ownership Interests: A Comment on Adequate Protection of Secured Creditors in Bankruptcy' (1984) 51 U Chic. L Rev. 97

Cases, Problems and Materials on Security Interests in Personal Property (Foundation Press, Mineola, N.Y., 1987)

Baister, S., 'Late Interest on Debts' (1999) *Insolvency Bulletin* 5

Baldwin, R., 'Health and Safety at Work: Consensus and Self-Regulation' in R. Baldwin and C. McCrudden (eds.), *Regulation and Public Law* (Weidenfeld & Nicolson, London, 1987)

'The Next Steps: Ministerial Responsibility and Government by Agency' (1988) 51 MLR 622

Rules and Government (Oxford University Press, Oxford, 1995)

Baldwin, R. and M. Cave, *Understanding Regulation* (Oxford University Press, Oxford, 1999)

Baldwin, R. and C. McCrudden (eds.), *Regulation and Public Law* (Weidenfeld & Nicolson, London, 1987)

Balz, M., 'Market Conformity of Insolvency Proceedings: Policy Issues of the German Insolvency Law' (1997) 23 *Brooklyn Journal of International Law* 167

Bank of England, Occasional Paper, 'Company Reorganisation: A Comparison of Practice in the US and the UK' (Bank of England, 1983)

Finance for Small Firms, Fifth Report (Bank of England, 1998)

[1999] 31 *Quarterly Report on Small Business Statistics*

Finance for Small Firms, Sixth Report (Bank of England, 1999)

Finance for Small Firms, Eighth Report (Bank of England, March 2001)

Bardach, E. and R. A. Kagan, *Going by the Book: The Problem of Regulatory Unreasonableness* (Temple University Press, Philadelphia, 1982)

Barnes, R., 'The Efficiency Justification for Secured Transactions: Foxes with Soxes and Other Fanciful Stuff' (1993) 42 Kans. L Rev. 13

Bastin, G. and P. Townsend, 'Should We Make the Redundancy Scheme Redundant?' (1996) 17 Co. Law. 252

Bates, J., *The Financing of Small Businesses* (3rd edn, Sweet & Maxwell, London, 1982)

Bayfield, D., 'Receiver Can Use Vulnerability of Customer' (2000) 13 *Insolvency Intelligence* 38

BDO Stoy Hayward Survey, reported in (1999) 12 *Insolvency Intelligence* 48

Bebchuk, L. and J. Fried, 'The Uneasy Case for the Priority of Secured Claims in Bankruptcy' (1996) 105 Yale LJ 857

Beetham, D., *The Legitimation of Power* (Macmillan, London, 1991)

Belcher, A., 'The Economic Implications of Attempting to Rescue Companies' in H. Rajak (ed.), *Insolvency Law: Theory and Practice* (Sweet & Maxwell, London, 1993)

Corporate Rescue (Sweet & Maxwell, London, 1997)

Belcher, A. and W. Beglan, 'Jumping the Queue' [1997] JBL 1

Bennett, H. and C. Davis, 'Fixtures, Purchase Money Security Interests and Dispositions of Interests in Land' (1994) 110 LQR 448

Bentley, L., 'Mortgagee's Duties on Sale: No Place for Tort?' (1990) 54 *Conveyancer and Property Lawyer* 431

Berg, A., 'Duties of a Mortgagee and a Receiver' [1993] JBL 213

'Charges over Book Debts: A Reply' [1995] JBL 433

'*Brumark Investments Ltd* and the "Innominate Charge"' [2001] JBL 532

Bhandari, J. S. and L. A. Weiss (eds.), *Corporate Bankruptcy: Economic and Legal Perspectives* (Cambridge University Press, Cambridge, 1996)

Bhattacharyya, G., 'Shadow Directors and Wrongful Trading Revisited' (1995) 15 Co. Law. 313

Bird, C., 'The London Approach' (1996) 12 IL&P 87

Birks, P., 'Mixing and Tracing' (1992) 45(2) *Current Legal Problems* 69

Black, F., 'Bank Funds in an Efficient Market' (1975) *Journal of Financial Economics* 323

Black, J., 'Constitutionalising Self-Regulation' (1996) 59 MLR 24

Rules and Regulators (Clarendon Press, Oxford, 1997)

Blackstone, W., *Commentaries on the Laws of England* (8th edn, Clarendon Press, Oxford, printed for W. Strahan, T. Cadell and D. Prince, 1778 (facsimile of 1st edn, 1765–9))

Block-Lieb, S., 'The Unsecured Creditor's Bargain: A Reply' (1994) 80 Va. L Rev. 1989

Blumberg, P., *The Law of Corporate Groups: Procedural Problems in the Law of Parent and Subsidiary Companies* (Little, Brown, Boston, Mass., 1983)

The Multinational Challenge to Corporation Law: The Search for a New Corporate Personality (Oxford University Press, New York, 1993)

Borrowdale, A., 'Commentary on Austin' in R. Grantham and C. Rickett (eds.), *Corporate Personality in the Twentieth Century* (Hart, Oxford, 1998)

Boshkoff, D. and R. McKinney, 'The Future of Chapter 11' (1995) 8 *Insolvency Intelligence* 6

Bowers, W., 'Whither What Hits the Fan? Murphy's Law, Bankruptcy Theory and the Elementary Economics of Loss Distribution' (1991) 26 Ga. L Rev. 27
'Rehabilitation, Redistribution or Dissipation: The Evidence of Choosing Among Bankruptcy Hypotheses' (1994) 72 Wash. ULQ 955
Boyle, J., J. Birds, E. Ferran and C. Villiers, *Boyle and Birds' Company Law* (4th edn, Jordans, Bristol, 2000)
Bradgate, R., 'Reservation of Title Ten Years On' (1987) Conv. 434
Bradley, C., 'Corporate Control: Markets and Rules' (1990) 53 MLR 170
'Enterprise and Entrepreneurship' (2001) 1 *Journal of Corporate Law Studies* 53
Bradley, M. and M. Rosenzweig, 'The Untenable Case for Chapter 11' (1992) 101 Yale LJ 1043
Bratton, W. W., 'The "Nexus of Contracts Corporation": A Critical Appraisal' (1989) 74 Cornell L Rev. 408
Breyer, S., *Regulation and Its Reform* (Harvard University Press, Cambridge, Mass., 1982)
Bridge, M. G., 'Company Administrators and Secured Creditors' (1991) 107 LQR 394
'Form, Substance and Innovation in Personal Property Security Law' [1992] JBL 1
'The *Quistclose* Trust in a World of Secured Transactions' (1992) 12 OJLS 333
'Fixed Charges and Freedom of Contract' (1994) 110 LQR 340
Brierley, P., 'The Bank of England and the London Approach' (1999) *Recovery* (June) 12
'Britain Needs a "Rescue Culture" Now', Cork Gully Discussion Paper (London, 1991)
British Bankers' Association, *Description of the London Approach* (Mimeo, 1996)
Banks and Business Working Together (London, 1997)
Voluntary Code of Practice (1997)
British Chamber of Commerce, *Small Firm Survey No. 24: Finance* (July 1997)
Broude, R., 'How the Rescue Culture Came to the United States and the Myths that Surround Chapter 11' (2001) 16 IL&P 194
Brown, D., *Corporate Rescue: Insolvency Law in Practice* (John Wiley & Sons, Chichester, 1996)
Brudney, V., 'The Independent Director: Heavenly City or Potemkin Village?' (1982) 95 Harv. L Rev. 597
Buckley, F., 'The Bankruptcy Priority Puzzle' (1986) 72 Va. L Rev. 1393
Bulman, S. and L. Fitzsimons, 'To Run or Not to Run…(the Borrower's Business)' [1999] Ins. Law. 306.
Butler, H., 'The Contractual Theory of the Corporation' (1989) 11 Geo. Mason UL Rev. 99
Byrne, J. and L. Doyle, 'Can a Landlord Forfeit a Lease by Peaceable Re-entry?' [1999] Ins. Law. 167
Byrne, M., 'An Economic Analysis of Directors' Duties in Favour of Creditors' (1994) 4 *Australian Journal of Corporate Law* 275
Cabinet Office, *The Citizens' Charter: Five Years On* (London, 1996)
Calabresi, G. and A. Melamed, 'Property Rules, Liability Rules and Inalienability: One View of the Cathedral' (1972) 85 Harv. L Rev. 1089
Calnan, R., 'Fashioning the Law to Suit the Practicalities of Life' (1998) 114 LQR 174
Campbell, A., 'Wrongful Trading and Company Rescue' [1994] 25 CLJ 69
'The Equity for Debt Proposal: The Way Forward' (1996) 12 IL&P 14
Campbell, C., 'Investigations by Insolvency Practitioners – Powers and Restraints: Part I' (2000) 16 IL&P 182
'Protection by Elimination: Winding Up of Companies on Public Interest Grounds' (2001) 17 IL&P 129

Campbell, C. and B. Underdown, *Corporate Insolvency in Practice: An Analytical Approach* (Chapman, London, 1991)

Campbell, N., '*Re Hydrodan (Corby) Ltd*' [1994] JBL 609

Cane, P. (ed.), *Atiyah's Accidents, Compensation and the Law* (5th edn, Weidenfeld & Nicolson, London, 1993)

Cantlie, S. S., 'Preferred Priority in Bankruptcy' in J. Ziegel (ed.), *Current Developments in International and Comparative Corporate Insolvency Law* (Clarendon Press, Oxford, 1994)

Capper, D., 'Direct Payment Clauses and the *Pari Passu* Principle' [1998] CfiLR 54
'Contracting Out of Insolvency Set-off: Irish Possibilities' [2000] Ins. Law. 248

Capper, D. and L. McHugh, 'Whither the Floating Charge?' [1999] Ins. Law. 162

Carlson, D. G., 'Philosophy in Bankruptcy (Book Review)' (1987) 85 Mich. L Rev. 1341

Carruthers, B. G. and T. C. Halliday, *Rescuing Business: The Making of Corporate Bankruptcy Law in England and the United States* (Clarendon Press, Oxford, 1998)

CBI, *Cutting Through the Red Tape: The Impact of Employment Legislation* (November 2000)

Cheffins, B., *Company Law: Theory, Structure and Operation* (Clarendon Press, Oxford, 1997)

Chesterman, M., *Small Businesses* (2nd edn, Sweet & Maxwell, London, 1982)

Chuah, J., 'EC Regulation on Insolvency Proceedings' (2000) *Finance and Credit Law* 6 (November/December)

City University Business School, *The Role of Leasing in the Financing of Small and Medium Sized Companies* (London, 1997)

Clarke, A., 'Corporate Rescues and Reorganisations in English Law after the Insolvency Act 1986' (Mimeo, University College, London, 1993)
'Security Interests as Property: Relocating Security Interests within the Property Framework' in J. W. Harris (ed.), *Property Problems from Genes to Pension Funds* (Kluwer, London, 1997)
'Overcompensation for Disclaimer?' [1998] 2 CfiLR 248

Clarke, F., G. Dean and K. Oliver, *Corporate Collapse: Regulatory, Accounting and Ethical Failure* (Cambridge University Press, Cambridge, 1997)

Clarke, L. and H. Rajak, '*Mann v. Secretary of State for Employment*' (2000) 63 MLR 895

CLRSG, *Modern Company Law for a Competitive Economy: Developing the Framework* (March 2000)
Consultation Document, *Modern Company Law for a Competitive Economy: Registration of Company Charges* (October 2000)
Modern Company Law for a Competitive Economy: Completing the Structure (November 2000)
Modern Company Law for a Competitive Economy: Final Report (July 2001)

Coffee, J., '"No Soul to Damn: No Body to Kick": An Unscandalized Inquiry into the Problem of Corporate Punishment' (1981) 79 Mich. L Rev. 386

Cohen, J., 'History of Imprisonment for Debt and its Relation to the Development of Discharge in Bankruptcy' (1982) 3 *Journal of Legal History* 153

Collier, B., 'Conversion of a Fixed Charge to a Floating Charge by Operation of Contract: Is It Possible?' (1995) 4 AJCL 14

Collins, H., 'Transfer of Undertakings and Insolvency' (1989) 18 ILJ 144
'Ascription of Legal Responsibility to Groups and Complex Patterns of Economic Integration' (1990) 53 MLR 731

Collins, H., K. Ewing and A. McColgan, *Labour Law Text and Materials* (Hart, Oxford, 2001)

Companies and Securities Law Review Committee, *Enforcement of the Duties of Directors and Officers of a Company by Means of a Statutory Derivative Action* (Report No. 12, 1990)

Connell, R., 'Chapter 11: The UK Dimension' (1990) 6 IL&P 90

Cook, C., 'Wrongful Trading: Is it a Real Threat to Directors or a Paper Tiger?' [1999] Ins. Law. 99

Cook, G. and K. Pond, 'Swedish Corporate Rescue' (2001) *Recovery* (September) 27

Cooke, T. and A. Hicks, 'Wrongful Trading: Predicting Insolvency' [1993] JBL 338

Cork Advisory Committee, Cmnd 6602 (1976). Interim report to the Minister, published in July 1980 as *Bankruptcy: Interim Report of the Insolvency Law Review Committee* (Cmnd 7968, 1980)

Cork, K., *Cork on Cork: Sir Kenneth Cork Takes Stock* (Macmillan, London, 1988)

Cornish, W. R. and G. de N. Clark, *Law and Society in England 1750–1950* (Sweet & Maxwell, London, 1989)

Cosh, A. and A. Hughes, *Enterprise Britain: Growth, Innovation and Public Policy in the Small and Medium Enterprise Sector* (ESRC Centre for Business Research, Cambridge, 1998)
British Enterprise in Transition (ESRC Centre for Business Research, Cambridge, 2000)

Coulson, F. and S. Hill, '*Brumark*: The End of Banking as We Know It?' (2001) *Recovery* (September) 16

Countryman, V., 'The Concept of a Voidable Preference in Bankruptcy' (1985) 38 Vand. L Rev. 713

Cousins, J., A. Mitchell, P. Sikka, C. Cooper and P. Arnold, *Insolvency Abuse: Regulating the Insolvency Service* (Association for Accounting and Business Affairs, 2000)

Craig, P. P., 'The Monopolies and Mergers Commission, Competition and Administrative Rationality' in R. Baldwin and C. McCrudden (eds.), *Regulation and Public Law* (Weidenfeld & Nicolson, London, 1987)
Public Law and Democracy in the United Kingdom and the United States of America (Clarendon Press, Oxford, 1990)

Cranston, R., *Principles of Banking Law* (Oxford University Press, Oxford, 1997)

Crompton, *Practice Common-placed: Or, the Rules and Cases of the Practice in the Courts of King's Bench and Common Pleas*, LXVII (3rd edn, 1786)

Cruickshank, D., *Competition in UK Banking: A Report to the Chancellor of the Exchequer* (HMSO, London, 2000)

CSO Annual Abstract of Statistics (DTI, 1996–7)

Cuming, R., 'Canadian Bankruptcy Law: A Secured Creditor's Haven' in J. Ziegel (ed.), *Current Developments in International and Comparative Corporate Insolvency Law* (Clarendon Press, Oxford, 1994)
'The Internationalization of Secured Financing Law: The Spreading Influence of the Concepts UCC, Article 9 and its Progeny' in R. Cranston (ed.), *Making Commercial Law: Essays in Honour of Roy Goode* (Clarendon Press, Oxford, 1997)

Dahan, F., 'The European Convention on Insolvency Proceedings and the Administrative Receiver: A Missed Opportunity?' (1996) 17 Co. Law. 181

Dal Pont, G. and L. Griggs, 'A Principled Justification for Business Rescue Laws: A Comparative Perspective, Part II' (1996) 5 *International Insolvency Review* 47

Daley, C. and C. Dalton, 'Bankruptcy and Corporate Governance: The Impact of Board Composition and Structure' (1994) 37 *Academy of Management Journal* 1603

Daniels, N. (ed.), *Reading Rawls: Critical Studies on Rawls' 'A Theory of Justice'* (Blackwell, Oxford, 1975)

Daniels, R., 'Must Boards Go Overboard?: An Economic Analysis of the Effects of Burgeoning Statutory Liability on the Role of Directors in Corporate Governance' in J. Ziegel (ed.), *Current Developments in International and Comparative Corporate Insolvency Law* (Clarendon Press, Oxford, 1994)

'Must Boards Go Overboard?' (1994–5) 24 Canadian Bus. LJ 229, 241

Daniels, R. and S. Hutton, 'The Capricious Cushion: The Implications of the Directors' and Officers' Insurance Liability Crisis in Canadian Corporate Governance' (1993) Canadian Bus. LJ 182

Davies, I., *Effective Retention of Title* (Fourmat, London, 1991)

'The Trade Creditor and the Quest for Security' in H. Rajak (ed.), *Insolvency Law: Theory and Practice* (Sweet & Maxwell, London, 1993)

Davies, P. L. 'Acquired Rights, Creditors' Rights, Freedom of Contract and Industrial Democracy' (1989) 9 *Yearbook of European Law* 21

'Employee Claims in Insolvency: Corporate Rescue and Preferential Claims' (1994) 23 ILJ 141

'Amendments to the Acquired Rights Directive' (1998) 27 ILJ 365

'Legal Capital in Private Companies in Great Britain' (1998) 8 *Die Aktien Gesellschaft* 346

'Transfers: The UK will have to Make Up its Own Mind' (2001) 30 ILJ 231

Davies, P. L. (ed.) (with contributions from D. D. Prentice), *Gower's Principles of Modern Company Law* (6th edn, Sweet & Maxwell, London, 1997)

Davis, R., *Construction Insolvency* (Chancery, London, 1991)

Dawson, I., 'The Administrator, Morality and the Court' [1996] JBL 437

Dawson, K., 'Transaction Avoidance: *Phillips* v. *Brewin Dolphin* Considered' (2001) 72 CCH *Company Law Newsletter* 1

Day, J. and P. Taylor, 'The Role of Debt Contracts in UK Corporate Governance' (1998) *Journal of Management and Governance* 171

'Financial Distress in Small Firms: The Role Played by Debt Covenants and Other Monitoring Devices' [2001] Ins. Law. 97

de Lacy, J., 'The Purchase Money Security Interest: A Company Charge Conundrum' [1991] LMCLQ 531

'Retention of Title, Company Charges and the *Scintilla Temporis* Doctrine' [1994] Conv. 242

'*Romalpa* Theory and Practice under Retention of Title in the Sale of Goods' (1995) 24 *Anglo-American Law Review* 327

'Processed Goods and Retention of Title Clauses' [1997] 10 *Palmer's In Company*

'The Legality of Charge-Back Security Interests' [1998] 5 *Palmer's In Company*

'Corporate Insolvency and Retention of Title Clauses: Developments in Australia' [2001] Ins. Law. 64

de Prez, P., 'The Power of Disclaimer and Environmental Licences' [2000] Ins. Law. 87

Deakin, S. and A. Hughes, 'Economics and Company Law Reform: A Fruitful Analysis?' (1999) 20 Co. Law. 212

'Economic Efficiency and the Proceduralisation of Company Law' [1999] CfiLR 169

Deakin, S. and G. Slinger, 'Hostile Takeovers, Corporate Law and the Theory of the Firm' (1997) 24 *Journal of Law and Society* 124

Delaney, K., *Strategic Bankruptcy: How Corporations and Creditors Use Chapter 11 to their Advantage* (University of California Press, Berkeley, 1989)

Deregulation Unit, Cabinet Office, *Checking the Cost of Regulation: A Guide to Compliance Costs Assessment* (1996)

Regulation in the Balance: A Guide to Regulatory Appraisal Incorporating Risk Assessment (1998)

Derham, R., *Set-Off* (2nd edn, Oxford University Press, Oxford, 1996)

Devlin, P., *The Enforcement of Morals* (Oxford University Press, London, 1965)

Diamond, A. L., *A Review of Security Interests in Property* (Diamond Report) (DTI, HMSO, London, 1989)

Dine, J., *The Governance of Corporate Groups* (Cambridge University Press, Cambridge, 2000)

Douglas, M., *In the Active Voice* (Routledge, London, 1982)

Doyle, L., 'The Residual Status of Directors in Receivership' (1996) 17 Co. Law. 131

    'The Receiver's Duties on a Sale of Charged Assets' (1997) 10 *Insolvency Intelligence* 9

Draper, M., 'Taking a Leaf out of Chapter 11?' (1991) 17 *Law Society Gazette* 28

Drewry, G., 'Forward from FMI: The Next Steps' (1988) PL 505

    'Next Steps: The Pace Falters' (1990) PL 322

Drukwczyk, J., 'Secured Debt, Bankruptcy and the Creditors' Bargain Model' (1991) 11 *International Review of Law and Economics* 201

DTI, *Burdens on Business* (1985)

    Counting the Cost to Business (1990)

    Cutting Red Tape for Business (1991)

    Checking the Cost to Business (1992)

    Cutting Red Tape (1994)

    Thinking about Regulation (1994)

    Encouraging Debt/Equity Swaps (1996)

    Consultation Paper, *Improving the Payment Culture* (July 1997)

    Shareholder Remedies: A Consultative Document (URN 98/994) (November 1998)

    Opportunity for All in a World of Change – A White Paper on Enterprise, Skill and Innovation (February 2001)

    TUPE: Government Proposals for Reform: Public Consultation Document (URN 01/1133) (2001)

DTI/Insolvency Service, *Company Voluntary Arrangements and Administration Orders: A Consultative Document* (October 1993)

    Revised Proposals for a New Company Voluntary Arrangement Procedure (April 1995)

    A Review of Company Rescue and Business Reconstruction Mechanisms: Report by the Review Group (2000)

    Productivity and Enterprise: Insolvency – A Second Chance (Cm 5234, July 2001)

Dunscombe, J., 'Bankruptcy: A Study in Comparative Legislation' (1893) 2 *Columbia University Studies in Political Science* 17

Dworkin, R. M., *Taking Rights Seriously* (Duckworths, London, 1977)

    'Is Wealth a Value?' (1980) 17 *Journal of Legal Studies* 191

    A Matter of Principle (Clarendon Press, Oxford, 1986)

Dyson, K. and S. Wilks, 'The Character and Economic Content of Industrial Crisis' in Dyson and Wilks (eds.), *Industrial Crisis: A Comparative Study of the State and Industry* (Blackwell, Oxford, 1985)

Easterbrook, F. H. and D. R. Fischel, 'Voting in Corporate Law' (1983) 26 *Journal of Law and Economics* 395

    'The Corporate Contract' (1989) 89 Colum. L Rev. 1416

    The Economic Structure of Corporate Law (Harvard University Press, Cambridge, Mass., 1991)

Eisenberg, T., 'Corporate Groups' in M. Gillooly (ed.), *The Law Relating to Corporate Groups* (Butterworths, Sydney, 1993)

Eldridge, R., 'TUPE Operates to Damage Rescue Culture' (2001) *Recovery* (September) 21

Elias, G., *Explaining Constructive Trusts* (Clarendon Press, Oxford, 1990)

Ellis, D., 'Inland Revenue and Business Rescue' (2001) *Recovery* (September) 18

Elwes, S., 'Transactions Defrauding Creditors' (2001) 17 IL&P 10

Emden, A., *Emden's Construction Law* (Butterworths, London, 1997) Issue 39

Epstein, R., 'A Theory of Strict Liability' (1973) 2 *Journal of Legal Studies* 151

Esen, R., 'Chartered Directors' Qualification: Professionalism on UK Boards' (2000) 21 Co. Law. 289

Evans, M., 'Decision of the Court of Appeal in *Morris* v. *Agrichemicals Ltd*: A Flawed Asset' (1996) 17 Co. Law. 102

Everett, D., *The Nature of Fixed and Floating Charges as Security Devices* (Monash University, Victoria, 1988)

Fairburn J. and J. Kay (eds.), *Introduction to Mergers and Merger Policy* (Oxford University Press, Oxford, 1989)

Fama, E. F., 'Agency Problems and the Theory of the Firm' (1980) 88(1) *Journal of Political Economy* 288

Farrar, J. H., 'Company Insolvency and the Cork Recommendations' (1983) 4 Co. Law. 20
'Legal Issues Involving Corporate Groups' (1998) 16 *Corporate and Securities Law Journal* 184

Farrar, J. H. and B. M. Hannigan, with contributions by N. E. Furey and P. Wylie, *Farrar's Company Law* (4th edn, Butterworths, London, 1998)

Federation of Small Businesses Report, *Barriers to Survival and Growth in UK Small Firms* (2000)

Fennell, S., 'Court-appointed Receiverships: A Missed Opportunity?' (1998) 14 IL&P 208

Fenning and Hart, 'Measuring Chapter 11: The Real World of 500 Cases' (1996) 4 *American Bankruptcy Institute Law Review* 119

Ferguson, R. B., 'Self-Regulation at Lloyds' (1983) 46 MLR 56

Ferguson, R. B. and A. C. Page, 'The Development of Investor Protection in Britain' (1984) 12 *International Journal of Sociology of Law* 287

Ferran, E., 'The Duties of an Administrative Receiver to Unsecured Creditors' (1988) 9 Co. Law. 58
'Floating Charges: The Nature of the Security' [1988] CLJ 213
'Subordinated Debt Agreements' (1993) *CCH Company Law Newsletter*
'Recent Developments in Unsecured Debt Subordination' in B. Rider (ed.), *The Realm of Company Law* (Kluwer, London, 1998)
Company Law and Corporate Finance (Oxford University Press, Oxford, 1999)

Ferris, J., 'Report of Mr Justice Ferris' Working Party on *The Remuneration of Office Holders and Certain Related Matters*' (London, 1998)
'Insolvency Remuneration: – Translating Adjectives into Action' [1999] Ins. Law. 48

Finch, V., 'Directors' Duties Towards Creditors' (1989) 10 Co. Law. 23
'Disqualification of Directors: A Plea for Competence' (1990) 53 MLR 385
'Directors' Duties: Insolvency and the Unsecured Creditor' in A. Clarke (ed.), *Current Issues in Insolvency Law* (Stevens, London, 1991)
'Board Performance and Cadbury on Corporate Governance' [1992] JBL 581
'Company Directors: Who Cares About Skill and Care?' (1992) 55 MLR 179
'Disqualifying Directors: Issues of Rights, Privileges and Employment' (1993) ILJ 35
'Corporate Governance and Cadbury: Self-Regulation and Alternatives' [1994] JBL 51
'Personal Accountability and Corporate Control: The Role of Directors' and Officers' Liability Insurance' (1994) 57 MLR 880
'Creditors' Interests and Directors' Obligations' in S. Sheikh and W. Rees (eds.), *Corporate Governance and Corporate Control* (Cavendish, London, 1995)

'The Measures of Insolvency Law' (1997) 17 OJLS 227

'Insolvency Practitioners: Regulation and Reform' [1998] JBL 334

'Controlling the Insolvency Professionals' [1999] Ins. Law. 228

'Security, Insolvency and Risk: Who Pays the Price?' (1999) 62 MLR 633

'Is *Pari Passu* Passé?' [2000] Ins. Law. 194

Finch, V. and S. Worthington, 'The *Pari Passu* Principle and Ranking Restitutionary Claims' in F. Rose (ed.), *Restitution and Insolvency* (Lloyd's of London Press, London, 2000)

Finn, D., 'Conflict of Interest' (1999) *Insolvency Bulletin* 13

Finn, P. (ed.), *Equity and Commercial Relationships* (Law Book Co., Sydney, 1987)

Finnis, J., *Natural Law and Natural Rights* (Clarendon Press, Oxford, 1980)

Fish, S., *Doing What Comes Naturally: Change, Rhetoric and the Practice of Theory in Literary and Legal Studies* (Clarendon Press, Oxford, 1989)

Flaschen, E. and T. DeSieno, 'The Development of Insolvency Law as Part of the Transition from a Centrally Planned to a Market Economy' (1992) 26 *International Lawyer* 667

Flessner, A., 'Philosophies of Business Bankruptcy Law: An International Overview' in J. S. Ziegel (ed.), *Current Developments in International and Comparative Corporate Insolvency Law* (Clarendon Press, Oxford, 1994)

Fletcher, I. F., 'Genesis of Modern Insolvency Law: An Odyssey of Law Reform' [1989] JBL 365

'Voidable Transactions in Bankruptcy Law: British Law Perspectives' in J. Ziegel (ed.), *Current Developments in International and Comparative Corporate Insolvency Law* (Clarendon Press, Oxford, 1994)

'Adoption of Contracts of Employment by Receivers and Administrators: The *Paramount* Case' [1995] JBL 596

'The Counter Reformation by Stealth: Crown Preference for Unpaid Taxes' [1995] JBL 604

'Wrongful Trading: "Reasonable Prospect" of Insolvency' (1995) 8 *Insolvency Intelligence* 14

The Law of Insolvency (2nd edn, Sweet & Maxwell, London, 1996)

'The European Union Convention on Bankruptcy Proceedings: An Overview and Comment with US Interests in Mind' (1997) 23 BJIL 25

'Juggling with Norms: The Conflict between Collective and Individual Rights under Insolvency Law' in R. Cranston (ed.), *Making Commercial Law* (Clarendon Press, Oxford, 1997)

'Administration as Liquidation' [1998] JBL 75

Insolvency Law in Private International Law (Clarendon Press, Oxford, 1999)

'A New Age of International Insolvency: The Countdown Has Begun – Parts I and II' (2000) *Insolvency Intelligence* 1

Flood, J., R. Abbey, E. Skordaki and P. Aber, *The Professional Restructuring of Corporate Rescue: Company Voluntary Arrangements and the London Approach*, ACCA Research Report 45 (ACCA, London, 1995)

Flood, J. and E. Skordaki, *Insolvency Practitioners and Big Corporate Insolvencies*, ACCA Research Report 43 (ACCA, London, 1995)

Floyd, R., 'Corporate Recovery: The London Approach' (1995) 11 IL&P 82

Foster, C., *Financial Statement Analysis* (2nd edn, Prentice-Hall, Englewood Cliffs, N.J., 1986)

Foster, S., '*Leyland DAF*: The Importance for Banks and Receivers' (2001) 69 *CCH Company Law Newsletter* 1

Francis, J., 'Insolvency Law Reform: The Aghion, Hart and Moore Proposals' (1995) (Winter edn) *Insolvency Practitioner*

Franks, J. and C. Mayer, 'Capital Markets and Corporate Control: A Study of France, Germany and the UK' (1990) 10 *Economic Policy* 191

Franks, J. and O. Sussman, 'The Cycle of Corporate Distress, Rescue and Dissolution: A Study of Small and Medium Size UK Companies', IFA Working Paper 306 (2000)

Franks, J. and W. Torous, 'Lessons from a Comparison of US and UK Insolvency Codes' in J. S. Bhandari and L. A. Weiss (eds.), *Corporate Bankruptcy: Economic and Legal Perspectives* (Cambridge University Press, Cambridge, 1996)

Freedman, J., 'Accountants and Corporate Governance: Filling a Legal Vacuum?' (1993) *Political Quarterly* 285

'Limited Liability: Large Company Theory and Small Firms' (2000) 63 MLR 317

Freedman, J. and M. Godwin, 'Incorporating the Micro Business: Perceptions and Misperceptions' in A. Hughes and D. Storey (eds.), *Finance and the Small Firm* (Routledge, London, 1994)

Frieze, S., 'Exit from Administration' (2001) 14 *Insolvency Intelligence* 41

Frisby, S., 'Making a Silk Purse out of a Pig's Ear: *Medforth* v. *Blake and Others*' (2000) 63 MLR 413

'TUPE or not TUPE? Employee Protection, Corporate Rescue and "One Unholy Mess"' [2000] 3 CFILR 249

Frost, C., 'Operational Form, Misappropriation Risk and the Substantive Consolidation of Corporate Groups' (1993) 44 Hastings LJ 449

Frug, G. E., 'The Ideology of Bureaucracy in American Law' (1984) 97 Harv. L Rev. 1277

Gaffney, M., 'Small Firms Really Can Be Helped' (1983) *Management Accounting* (February)

Galen, M. with C. Yang, 'A New Page for Chapter 11?' *Business Week*, January 25, 1993

Galligan, D. J., *Discretionary Powers: A Legal Study of Official Discretion* (Clarendon Press, Oxford, 1986)

Ganguly, P. and G. Bannock (eds.), *UK Small Business Statistics and International Comparisons* (published on behalf of the Small Business Research Trust, Harper & Row, London, 1985)

Gee, L., *How Effective are Voluntary Arrangements?* (Levy Gee, London, 1994)

Gewirth, A., *The Community of Rights* (University of Chicago Press, Chicago, 1996)

Gilby, R. and R. Pugh, 'Caveat Director!' (1995) 11 IL&P 21

Gillooly, M. (ed.), *The Law Relating to Corporate Groups* (Butterworths, Sydney, 1993)

Gilson, S., 'Management Turnover and Financial Distress' (1989) 25 *Journal of Financial Economics* 241

'Bankruptcy, Boards, Banks and Blockholders' (1990) 27 *Journal of Financial Economics* 355

'Managing Default: Some Evidence on How Firms Choose between Workouts and Chapter 11' in J. S. Bhandari and L. A. Weiss (eds.), *Corporate Bankruptcy: Economic and Legal Perspectives* (Cambridge University Press, Cambridge, 1996)

Gilson, S. C., K. John and L. H. P. Lang, 'Troubled Debt Restructurings: An Empirical Study of Private Reorganisation of Firms in Default' (1990) 27 *Journal of Financial Economics* 323

Gilson, S. and M. Vetsuypens, 'Creditor Control in Financially Distressed Firms: Empirical Evidence' (1994) 72 Wash. ULQ 1005

Gleig, B., 'Unpaid Wages in Bankruptcy' (1987) 21 UBC L Rev. 61

Godfrey, P. and S. Nield, 'The Wrongful Trading Provisions: All Bark and No Bite?' (1995) 11 IL&P 139

Goetz, C. J. and R. E. Scott, 'Liquidated Damages, Penalties and the Just Compensation Principle: Some Notes on an Enforcement Model and a Theory of Efficient Breach' (1977) 77(4) Colum. L Rev. 554

'Principles of Relational Contracts' (1981) 67 Va. L Rev. 1089

Goode, R. M., 'Is the Law Too Favourable to Secured Creditors?' (1983–4) 8 Canadian Bus. LJ 53

Legal Problems of Credit and Security (2nd edn, Sweet & Maxwell, London, 1988)

'Surety and On-Demand Performance Bonds' [1988] JBL 87

'Charges Over Book Debts: A Missed Opportunity' (1994) 110 LQR 592

Commercial Law (2nd edn, Penguin Books, London, 1995)

'The Exodus of the Floating Charge' in D. Feldman and F. Meisel (eds.), *Corporate and Commercial Law: Modern Developments* (Lloyd's of London Press, London, 1996)

Principles of Corporate Insolvency Law (2nd edn, Sweet & Maxwell, London, 1997)

'Charge-Backs and Legal Fictions' (1998) 114 LQR 178

Commercial Law in the Next Millennium (Sweet & Maxwell, London, 1998)

'Proprietary Rights and Unsecured Creditors' in B. Rider (ed.), *The Realm of Company Law* (Kluwer, London, 1998)

Goode, R. M. and L. Gower, 'Is Article 9 of the Uniform Commercial Code Exportable? An English Reaction' in J. Ziegel and W. Foster (eds.), *Aspects of Comparative Commercial Law* (Oceana, Montreal, 1969)

Goodhart, W. and G. Jones, 'The Infiltration of Equitable Doctrine into English Commercial Law' (1980) 43 MLR 489

Gough, W., 'The Floating Charge: Traditional Themes and New Directions' in P. Finn (ed.), *Equity and Commercial Relationships* (Law Book Co., Sydney, 1987)

Company Charges (2nd edn, Butterworths, London, 1991)

Gower, L. C. B., *Review of Investor Protection* (Cmnd 9125, 1984)

Graham, C., 'Self-Regulation' in G. Richardson and H. Genn (eds.), *Administrative Law and Government Action* (Clarendon Press, Oxford, 1994)

Grantham, R., 'Directors' Duties and Insolvent Companies' (1991) 65 MLR 576

'The Judicial Extension of Directors' Duties to Creditors' [1991] JBL 1

'Liability of Parent Companies for the Actions of the Directors of their Subsidiaries' (1997) 18 Co. Law. 138

'Refloating a Floating Charge' [1997] CfiLR 53

Green, R. and E. Talmor, 'Asset Substitution and the Agency Costs of Debt Financing' (1986) 10 *Journal of Banking Law* 391

Green Paper, *Bankruptcy: A Consultative Document* (Cmnd 7967, 1980)

Gregory, A., University of Exeter Study of Domestic Takeovers in 1984–92 (1997)

Gregory, R., 'Receiver's Duty of Care Considered' (1992) *CCH Company Law Newsletter* 9

'Insolvency Law Reform' (14 December 1993) *CCH Company Law Newsletter*

Review of Company Rescue and Business Reconstruction Mechanisms: Rescue Culture or Avoidance Culture? (CCH, Bicester, December 1999)

Gregory, R. and P. Walton, 'Book Debt Charges: The Saga Goes On' (1999) 115 LQR 14

'Book Debt Charges: Following *Yorkshire Woolcombers* – Are We Sheep Gone Astray?' [2000] Ins. Law. 157

Grier, I. and R. E. Floyd, *Voluntary Liquidation and Receivership* (3rd edn, Longman, London, 1991)

Grierson, C., 'Issues in Concurrent Insolvency Jurisdiction: English Perspectives' in J. S. Ziegel (ed.), *Current Developments in International and Comparative Corporate Insolvency Law* (Clarendon Press, Oxford, 1994)

'Shareholder Liability, Consolidation and Pooling' in E. Leonard and C. Besant (eds.), *Current Issues in Cross-Border Insolvency and Reorganisations* (Graham and Trotman, London, 1994)

Griffin, S., 'The Effect of a Charge over Book Debts: The Indivisible and Divisible Nature of the Charge' [1995] 46 NILQ 163

Personal Liability and Disqualification of Company Directors (Hart, Oxford, 1999)

'The Characteristics and Identification of a *De Facto* Director' [2000] 1 CFILR 126

Gross, K., 'Taking Community Interests into Account in Bankruptcy: An Essay' (1994) 72 Wash. ULQ 1031

Guide to the Professional Conduct of Solicitors (8th edn, Law Society, 1999)

Hackett, B., 'What Constitutes a Transaction at an Undervalue?' (2001) 17 IL&P 139

Hadden, T., *The Control of Corporate Groups* (IALS, London, 1983)

'Inside Corporate Groups' (1984) 12 *International Journal of Sociology of Law* 271

'Insolvency and the Group – Problems of Integrated Financing' in R. M. Goode (ed.), *Group Trading and the Lending Banker* (Chartered Institute of Bankers, London, 1988)

'The Regulation of Corporate Groups in Australia' (1992) UNSW LJ 61

'Regulating Corporate Groups: International Perspectives' in J. McCahery, S. Piccoitto and C. Scott (eds.), *Corporate Control and Accountability* (Oxford University Press, Oxford, 1993)

Hain, P., *Regulating for the Common Good* (GMB Communications, London, 1994)

Halpern, P., M. Trebilcock and M. Turnbull, 'An Economic Analysis of Limited Liability in Corporation Law' (1980) 30 U Toronto LJ 128

Hamilton, R., B. Halcroft, K. Pond and Z. Liew, 'Back from the Dead: Survival Potential in Administrative Receiverships' (1997) 13 IL&P 78

Hansman, H. and R. Krackman, 'Towards Unlimited Shareholder Liability for Corporate Torts' (1991) 100 Yale LJ 1879

Hanson, R., 'Landlords' Right to Effect Peaceable Re-entry Against Tenants in Administration' (1999) *Insolvency Bulletin* 7

Hardy, S., 'Some TUPE Implications for Insolvency Lawyers' [2001] Ins. Law. 147

Hare, D. and D. Milman, 'Corporate Insolvency: The Cork Committee Proposals I' (1983) 127 Sol. Jo. 230

Harlow, C. and R. Rawlings, *Law and Administration* (2nd edn, Butterworths, London, 1997)

Harmer, R., 'Comparison of Trends in National Law: The Pacific Rim' (1997) 1 *Brooklyn Journal of International Law* 139

Harrington, S., 'Prices and Profits in the Liability Insurance Market' in R. Litan and C. Winston (eds.), *Liability: Perspectives and Policy* (Brookings Institution, Washington D.C., 1988)

Harris, J. W. (ed.), *Property Problems from Genes to Pension Funds* (Kluwer, London, 1997)

Harris, S. and C. Mooney, 'A Property Based Theory of Security Interests: Taking Debtors' Choices Seriously' (1994) 80 Va. L Rev. 2021

Hart, H. L. A., *Law, Liberty and Morality* (Oxford University Press, Oxford, 1963)

Haugen, R. and L. Senbet, 'Bankruptcy and Agency Costs' (1988) 23 *Journal of Financial and Quantitative Analysis* 27

Heidt, K. R., 'The Automatic Stay in Environmental Bankruptcies' (1993) 67 *American Bankruptcy Law Journal* 69

Hemsworth, M., 'Voidable Preference: Desire and Effect' (2000) 16 IL&P 54

Hepple, B., 'The Transfer of Undertakings (Protection of Employment) Regulations' (1982) 11 ILJ 29

Heydon, J., W. Gummow and R. Austin, *Cases and Materials on Equity and Trusts* (4th edn, Butterworths, Sydney, 1993)

Hicks, A., 'Retention of Title: Latest Developments' [1992] JBL 398

'Advising on Wrongful Trading: Part 1' (1993) 14 Co. Law. 16

'When Goods Sold Become a New Species' [1993] JBL 485

'Wrongful Trading: Has it Been a Failure?' (1993) 8 IL&P 134

'Directors' Liability for Management Errors' (1994) 110 LQR 390

Disqualification of Directors: No Hiding Place for the Unfit? ACCA Research Report No. 59 (London, 1998)

'Director Disqualification: Can It Deliver?' [2001] JBL 433

Hill, S., 'Company Voluntary Arrangements' (1990) 6 IL&P 47

Hitchens, L., 'Directorships: How Many Is Too Many?' [2000] CFILR 359

HM Treasury, *Economic Appraisal in Central Government* (1991)

Enterprise for All: The Challenge for the Next Parliament (June 2001)

Hoffmann, Lord, 'The Fourth Annual Leonard Sainer Lecture – The Rt Hon. Lord Hoffman' (1997) 18 Co. Law. 194

Hogan, A., 'Banks and Administration' (1996) 12 IL&P 90

'Receivers Revisited' (1996) 17 Co. Law. 226

Holderness, C., 'Liability Insurers as Corporate Monitors' (1990) 10 *International Review of Law and Economics* 115

Homan, M., *A Survey of Administration Under the 1986 Insolvency Act* (Institute of Chartered Accountants, London, 1989)

Hopt, K., 'Legal Elements and Policy Decisions in Regulating Groups of Companies' in C. Schmitthoff and F. Wooldridge (eds.), *Groups of Companies* (Sweet & Maxwell, London, 1991)

'Legal Issues and Questions of Policy in the Comparative Regulation of Groups' [1996] *I Gruppi di Societas* 45

Hopt, K. (ed.), *Groups of Companies in European Laws* (de Gruyter, Berlin, 1982)

Hoshi, T., A. Kashyap and D. Scharfstein, 'The Role of Banks in Reducing the Costs of Financial Distress in Japan' in J. S. Bhandari and L. A. Weiss (eds.), *Corporate Bankruptcy: Economic and Legal Perspectives* (Cambridge University Press, Cambridge, 1996)

Houston, K., 'Agreement to Share Fruits of Wrongful Trading Claim Void' (1997) 18 Co. Law. 297

Howells, G. and S. Weatherill, *Consumer Protection Law* (Dartmouth, Aldershot, 1995)

Huberman, G., D. Mayers and C. Smith, 'Optimal Insurance Policy Indemnity Schedules' (1983) 14 *Bell Journal of Economics* 415

Hudson, J., 'Characteristics of Liquidated Companies' (Mimeo, University of Bath, 1982)

'The Case Against Secured Lending' (1995) 15 *International Review of Law and Economics* 47

Hume, D., *A Treatise of Human Nature*, L. Selby-Bigge and P. Nidditch (eds.) (Oxford University Press, Oxford, 1978)

Humphries, M., E. Pavlopoulos and P. Winterborne, 'Insolvency, Mediation and ADR' (1999) *Insolvency Bulletin* 7

Hunter, M., 'The Nature and Functions of a Rescue Culture' [1999] JBL 491

Hutton, W., *The State We're In* (Vintage, London, 1996)

ICAEW, Statement, *Guidance for Auditors on the Implications of Goods Sold Subject to Reservation of Title* (1977)

    Guide to Professional Ethics, Statement on Insolvency Practice (September 1998)

    Memorandum TECH 13/99, *A Review of Company Rescue and Business Reconstruction Mechanisms* (1999)

Ife, L., 'Liability of Receivers and Banks in Selling and Managing Mortgaged Property' (2000) 13 *Insolvency Intelligence* 61

Insolvency Lawyers Association/AAG, 'The Liquidation Expenses Principle' [2000] Ins. Law. 126

Insolvency Regulation Working Party, *Insolvency Practitioner Regulation – Ten Years On* (DTI, 1998)

    A Review of Insolvency Practitioner Regulation (DTI, 1999)

Insolvency Service, *Framework Document 1990* (DTI, 1990)

    Company Voluntary Arrangements and Administration Orders: A Consultative Document (1993)

    Revised Proposals for a New Company Voluntary Arrangement Procedure (1995)

    A Review of Company Rescue and Business Reconstruction Mechanisms, Interim Report (DTI, September 1999)

    Bankruptcy: A Fresh Start (2000)

    A Review of Company Rescue and Business Reconstruction Mechanisms, Report by the Review Group (DTI, 2000)

Institute of Directors, *Professional Development of and for the Board* (January 1990)

    Sign of the Times (1998)

    Business Finance (1999)

Isaacs, B., 'The Hazards of Contested Administration Petitions' (2001) 14 *Insolvency Intelligence* 22

Jackson, D., 'Foreign Maritime Liens in English Courts: Principle and Policy' [1981] 3 LMCLQ 335

Jackson, T. H., 'Bankruptcy, Non-Bankruptcy Entitlements and the Creditors' Bargain' (1982) 92 Yale LJ 857

    The Logic and Limits of Bankruptcy Law (Harvard University Press, Cambridge, Mass., 1986)

Jackson, T. H. and A. T. Kronman, 'Secured Financing and Priorities Among Creditors' (1979) 88 Yale LJ 1143

Jackson, T. H. and R. Scott, 'On the Nature of Bankruptcy: An Essay on Bankruptcy Sharing and the Creditors' Bargain' (1989) 75 Va. L Rev. 155

James, R., *Private Ombudsmen and Public Law* (Ashgate, Dartmouth, 1997)

Jefferson, M., 'Directors, Controlling Shareholders, Employees and Rights on Insolvency' (1998) 19 Co. Law. 307

Jensen, M. C. and W. H. Meckling, 'Theory of the Firm: Managerial Behaviour, Agency Costs and Ownership Structure' (1976) 3 *Journal of Financial Economics* 305

Jeremie, J., 'Gone in an Instant: The Death of *"Scintilla Temporis"* and the Growth of Purchase Money Security Interests in Real Property Law' [1994] JBL 363

Johnston, B., 'Contractual Debt Subordination and Legislative Reform' [1991] JBL 225

Jones, L., 'Distinguishing Shadow Directors' (1994) Sol. Jo. 440 (6 May)

Jones, W. J., 'The Foundations of English Bankruptcy: Statutes and Commissions in the Early Modern Period' (1979) 69(3) *Transactions of American Philosophical Society* 69

Justice, *Bankruptcy* (Justice, London, 1975)

    Insolvency Law: An Agenda for Reform (Justice, London, 1994)

Kapper, D., 'Insolvency and the Human Rights Act 1998: Early Northern Ireland Perspectives' [2001] Ins. Law. 119

Katz, A. and M. Mumford, 'Should Investigating Accountants be Allowed to Become Receivers? The Question of Continuity', ICAEW Discussion Document (September 1999)

Keay, A., 'The Australian Voluntary Administration Regime' (1996) 9 *Insolvency Intelligence* 41

    Avoidance Provisions in Insolvency Law (LBC Information Services, Sydney, 1997)

    'Australian Insolvency Law: The Latest Developments' (1998) 11 *Insolvency Intelligence* 57

    'The Avoidance of Pre-Liquidation Transactions: Anglo-Australian Comparison' [1998] JBL 515

    'Preferences in Liquidation Law: A Time for Change' [1998] 2 CfiLR 198

    'Public Interest Petitions' (1999) 20 Co. Law. 296

    'Disputing Debts Relied on by Petitioning Creditors Seeking Winding Up Orders' (2000) 22 Co. Law. 40

    'The Duty of Directors to Take Account of Creditors' Interests: Has it Any Role to Play?', paper presented to SPTL Company Law Section, SPTL Annual Conference, September 2000

    'The Recovery of Voidable Preferences: Aspects of Restoration' [2000] 1 CFILR 1

Keay, A. and P. Walton, 'Preferential Debts: An Empirical Study' [1999] Ins. Law. 112

    'The Preferential Debts Regime in Liquidation Law: In the Public Interest?' [1999] CfiLR 84

Kelly, G. and J. Parkinson, 'The Conceptual Foundations of the Company' [1998] CfiLR 174

Kemp, K. and D. Harris, 'Debt to Equity Conversions: Relieving the Interest Burden' (1993) PLC 19

Kennedy, T., 'Rescue Culture: The Royal Bank of Scotland's Approach' (1997) *Insolvency Bulletin* (September)

Kent, P., 'The London Approach' (1993) 8 *Journal of International Banking Law* 81

    'The London Approach: Distressed Debt Trading' (1994) *Bank of England Quarterly Bulletin* 110

    'The London Approach: Lessons from Recent Years' (1994) *Insolvency Bulletin* 5 (February)

    'Corporate Workouts: A UK Perspective' (1997) 6 *International Insolvency Review* 165

Kilpi, J., *The Ethics of Bankruptcy* (Routledge, London, 1998)

Klein, B., 'Vertical Integration, Appropriable Rents and the Competitive Contracting Process' (1978) 21 *Journal of Law and Economics* 297

Knippenberg, S., 'The Unsecured Creditor's Bargain: An Essay in Reply, Reprisal or Support' (1994) 80 Va. L Rev. 1967

Korobkin, D. R., 'Rehabilitating Values: A Jurisprudence of Bankruptcy' (1991) 91 Colum. L Rev. 717

    'Contractarianism and the Normative Foundations of Bankruptcy Law' (1993) 71 Texas L Rev. 541

Kraakman, R. H., 'Corporate Liability Strategies and the Cost of Legal Controls' (1984) 93 Yale LJ 857

    'Gatekeepers: The Anatomy of a Third Party Enforcement Strategy' (1986) *Journal of Law, Economics and Organization* 53

Kripke, H., 'Law and Economics: Measuring the Economic Efficiency of Commercial Law in a Vacuum of Fact' (1985) 133 U Pa. L Rev. 929

Landers, J., 'A Unified Approach to Parent, Subsidiary and Affiliate Questions in Bankruptcy' (1975) 42 U Chic. L Rev. 589

'Another Word on Parents, Subsidiaries and Affiliates in Bankruptcy' (1976) 43 U Chic. L Rev. 527

Lavargna, C. S., 'Government-Sponsored Enterprises are "Too Big to Fail": Balancing Public and Private Interests' (1993) 44(5) Hastings LJ 991

Law Commission, Consultation Paper No. 142, *Shareholder Remedies* (1996)

Report No. 246, *Shareholder Remedies*, (Cm 3769, 1997)

Company Directors: Regulating Conflicts of Interests and Formulating a Statement of Duties, LCCP 153, SLCDP 105 (TSO, London, 1998) Part 111

Law Commission and Scottish Law Commission, *Company Directors: Regulating Conflicts of Interest and Formulating a Statement of Duties* (Law Commission Report No. 261, Scottish Law Commission Report No. 173, 1999)

Law Society Company Law Committee, *Comments on the Insolvency Bill*, March 2000, No. 396

LCD, Consultation Paper, *Access to Justice with Conditional Fees*, March 1998

Leebron, D., 'Limited Liability, Tort Victims and Creditors' (1991) 91 Colum. L Rev. 1565

Lester, V. M., *Victorian Insolvency* (Oxford University Press, Oxford, 1996)

Levmore, S., 'Monitors and Freeriders in Commercial and Corporate Settings' (1982) 92 Yale LJ 49

Lewis, N., 'The Citizens' Charter and Next Steps: A New Way of Governing?' (1993) *Political Quarterly* 316

Lickorish, A., 'Debt Rescheduling' (1990) 6 IL&P 38

Lightman, G., 'Voluntary Administration: The New Wave or the New Waif in Insolvency Law?' (1994) 2 *Insolvency Law Journal* 59

'The Challenges Ahead' [1996] JBL 113

'Office Holders: Evidence, Security and Independence' [1997] CfiLR 145

'Office Holders' Charges: Cost, Control and Transparency' (1998) 11 *Insolvency Intelligence* 1

Lightman, G. and G. Moss, *The Law of Receivers of Companies* (2nd edn, Sweet & Maxwell, London, 1994)

Lingard, J. R., *Corporate Rescues and Insolvencies* (2nd edn, Butterworths, London, 1989)

Litan, R. and C. Winston (eds.), *Liability: Perspectives and Policy* (The Brookings Institution, Washington D.C., 1988)

LoPucki, L., 'The Unsecured Creditor's Bargain' (1994) 80 Va. L Rev. 1887

LoPucki, L. and G. Triantis, 'A Systems Approach to Comparing US and Canadian Reorganization of Financially Distressed Companies' in J. Ziegel (ed.), *Current Developments in International and Comparative Corporate Insolvency Law* (Clarendon Press, Oxford, 1994)

LoPucki, L. and W. Whitford, 'Corporate Governance in the Bankruptcy Reorganisation of Large, Publicly Held Companies' (1993) 141 U Pa. L Rev. 669.

Loughlin, M., *Public Law and Political Theory* (Clarendon Press, Oxford, 1992)

Lower, M., 'Good Faith and the Partly Owned Subsidiary' [2000] JBL 232

Lowry, J. and Watson, L., *Company Law* (Butterworths, London, 2001)

Lynch, C., 'Insolvency Set-Off: A Review of Current Issues' (1994) 10 IL&P 161

MacNeil, J., 'Economic Analysis of Contractual Relations' in P. Burrows and C. Veljanovski (eds.), *The Economic Approach to Law* (Butterworths, London, 1981)

Mannolini, J., 'Creditors' Interests in the Corporate Contract' (1996) 6 *Australian Journal of Corporate Law* 1

Manolopoulos, L., 'Note – A Congressional Choice: The Question of Environmental Priority in Bankrupt Estates' (1990) 9 *UCLA Journal of Environmental Law and Policy* 73

Marantz, R., R. Chartrand and S. Golick, 'Canadian Bankruptcy and Insolvency Law Reform Continues: The 1996/97 Amendments' (1998) 14 IL& P 22

Mason, C. and R. Harrison, 'Public Policy and the Development of the Informal Venture Capital Market' in K. Cowling (ed.), *Industrial Policy in Europe: Theoretical Perspectives and Practical Proposals* (Routledge, London, 1999)

Mayers, D. and C. Smith, 'On the Corporate Demand for Insurance' (1982) 55 *Journal of Business* 281

Mayson, S. W., D. French and C. L. Ryan, *Mayson, French and Ryan on Company Law* (18th edn, Blackstone Press, London, 2001)

McCahery, J., S. Piccoitto and C. Scott (eds.), *Corporate Control and Accountability* (Oxford University Press, Oxford, 1993)

McCartney, P., 'Insolvency Procedures and a Landlord's Right of Peaceable Re-entry' (2000) 13 *Insolvency Intelligence* 73

McCormack, G., '*Pari Passu* Distribution and Construction Contracts' (1993) 8 IL&P 169
    Reservation of Title (2nd edn, Sweet & Maxwell, London, 1995)
    Proprietary Claims and Insolvency (Sweet & Maxwell, London, 1997)
    'Charge-Backs and Commercial Certainty in the House of Lords (*Re BCCI (No. 8)*)' [1998] CfiLR 111
    'Receiverships and the Rescue Culture' [2000] 2 CFILR 229
    'Retention of Title and the EC Late Payment Directive' [2001] 1 JCLS 501
    'Personal Property Security Law Reform in England and Canada' [2002] JBL 113
    'Security Interests in Deposit Accounts: The Anglo-American Perspective' [2002] Ins. Law. 7

McCraken, S., *The Banker's Remedy of Set Off* (2nd edn, Butterworths, London, 1998)

McIntosh, M., 'Insolvency Act 2000: Landlords' Right of Peaceable Re-entry' (2001) 17 IL&P 48

McKenzie Skene, D. and Y. Enoch, 'Petitions for Administration Orders – Where there is a Need for Interim Measures: A Comparative Study of the Approach of the Courts in Scotland and England' [2000] JBL 103

McLauchlan, D., 'Fixed Charges over Book Debts: *New Bullas* in New Zealand' (1999) 115 LQR 365

McMeel, G., 'Retention of Title: The Interface of Contract, Unjust Enrichment and Insolvency' in F. Rose (ed.), *Restitution and Insolvency* (Lloyd's of London Press, London, 2000)

McMullen, J., *Business Transfers and Employee Rights* (2nd edn, Butterworths, London, 1992)

MERA, *An Evaluation of the Loan Guarantee Scheme*, Department of Employment Research Paper No. 74 (1990)

Miller, M., 'Wealth Transfers in Bankruptcy: Some Illustrative Examples' (1977) 41 *Law and Contemporary Problems* 39

Miller, P. and M. Power, 'Calculating Corporate Failure' in Y. Dezalay and D. Sugarman (eds.), *Professional Competition and Professional Power: Lawyers, Accountants and the Social Construction of Markets* (Routledge, London, 1995)

Milman, D., 'Insolvency Act 1986' (1987) 8 Co. Law. 61

'Priority Rights on Corporate Insolvency' in A. Clarke (ed.), *Current Issues in Insolvency Law* (Stevens & Sons, London, 1991)

'Personal Liability and Disqualification of Directors: Something Old, Something New' [1992] 43 NILQ 1

'The Administration Order Regime and the Courts' in H. Rajak (ed.), *Insolvency Law: Theory and Practice* (Sweet & Maxwell, London, 1993)

'Wrongful Trading Actions: Smoke without Fire?' [1995] 8 *Palmer's In Company* 1

'Litigation: Funding and Procedural Difficulties' (1997) *Amicus Curiae* 27

'Security for Costs: Principles and Pragmatism in Corporate Litigation' in B. Rider (ed.), *The Realm of Company Law* (Kluwer, London, 1998)

'Groups of Companies: The Path towards Discrete Regulation' in D. Milman (ed.), *Regulating Enterprise* (Hart, Oxford, 1999)

'Landlords of Insolvency Companies' [1999] 6 *Palmer's In Company* 1

'The Ten Per Cent Fund' [1999] Ins. Law. 47

'Winding Up in the Public Interest' [1999] 3 *Palmer's In Company* 1

'Company Charges: Recent Developments' [2000] 7 *Palmer's In Company* 1

'Controlling Managerial Abuse: Current State of Play' [2000] Ins. Law. 193

'A Fresh Light on Shadow Directors' [2000] Ins. Law. 171

'Post Liquidation Tax as a Winding Up Expense' [2000] Ins. Law. 169

'A Question of Honour' [2000] Ins. Law. 247

'Remuneration: Researching the Fourth R' (2000) *Recovery* (August) 18

'Company Charges: A Return to Harsh Reality' [2001] Ins. Law. 135

'Company Law Review: Company Charges' [2001] Ins. Law. 180

'The Courts and the Administration Regime: Supporting Legislative Policy' [2001] Ins. Law. 208

'Firming Up Moratoria' [2001] 3 *Palmer's In Company* 1

'Insolvency Reform' [2001] Ins. Law. 153

'Schemes of Arrangement' [2001] 6 *Palmer's In Company* 1

'Schemes of Arrangement: Their Continuing Role' [2001] Ins. Law. 145

Milman, D. and F. Chittenden, *Corporate Rescue: CVAs and the Challenge of Small Companies*, ACCA Research Report 44 (ACCA, London, 1995)

Milman, D. and C. Durrant, *Corporate Insolvency: Law and Practice* (3rd edn, Sweet & Maxwell, London, 1999)

Milman, D. and D. Mond, *Security and Corporate Rescue* (Hodgsons, Manchester, 1999)

Milman, D. and R. Parry, *A Study of the Operation of Transactional Avoidance Mechanisms in Corporate Insolvency Practice*, Insolvency Lawyers' Association Research Report (1997)

Mistry, H., '*Hollicourt*: Bringing the Authorities Out of Disarray' (2001) 22 Co. Law. 278

Mithani, A. and S. Wheeler, *Disqualification of Company Directors* (Butterworths, London, 1996)

Moffat, G., *Trusts Law: Text and Materials* (3rd edn, Butterworths, London, 1999)

Moffat, M., 'Directors' Dilemma: An Economic Evaluation of Directors' Liability for Environmental Damages and Unpaid Wages' (1996) 54 U Toronto Fac. LR 293

Mokal, R., 'Resolving the *MS Fashions* "Paradox"' [1999] CfiLR 106

'An Agency Cost Analysis of the Wrongful Trading Provisions: Redistribution, Perverse Incentives and the Creditors' Bargain' [2000] 59 CLJ 335

'The Authentic Consent Model: Contractarianism, Creditors' Bargain and Corporate Liquidation' (2001) 21 *Legal Studies* 400

'Consideration, Characterisation, Evaluation: Transactions at Undervalue after *Phillips* v. *Brewin Dolphin*' [2001] JCLS 359

'Priority as Pathology: The *Pari Passu* Myth' [2001] CLJ 581

Morgan, R., 'Insolvency and the Rights of Employees' [1989] *Legal Action* 21

Morris, C. and M. Kirschner, 'Cross-border Rescues and Asset Recovery: Problems and Solutions' (1994) 10 IL&P 42

Morris, G., 'Transferring Liability for Employee Claims' [2000] JBL 188

Morris, R., *Early Warning Indicators of Corporate Failure* (Ashgate/ICCA, London, 1997)

Morse, G., 'Shadow Directors and De Facto Directors in the Context of Proceedings for Disqualification on the Grounds of Unfitness and Wrongful Trading' in B. Rider (ed.), *The Corporate Dimension: An Exploration of Developing Areas of Company and Commercial Law* (Jordans, Bristol, 1998)

Moss, G., 'Fixed Charges on Book Debts: Puzzles and Perils' (1995) 8 *Insolvency Intelligence* 25

'Comparative Bankruptcy Cultures: Rescue of Liquidations? Comparisons of Trends in National Law – England' (1997) 23 *Brooklyn Journal of International Law* 115

'Chapter 11: An English Lawyer's Critique' (1998) 11 *Insolvency Intelligence* 17

'Insurance Company Insolvency: A Step in the Right Direction' (1999) 12 *Insolvency Intelligence* 45

'The Chairman's View: A Look at Three Recent Cases' (2002) 15 *Insolvency Intelligence* 3

Moss, G. and N. Segal, 'Insolvency Proceedings: Contract and Financing: The Expenses Doctrine in Liquidation, Administration and Receiverships' [1997] 1 CfiLR 1

Mudd, P., 'The Insolvency Act 1994: *Paramount* Cured?' (1994) 10 IL&P 38

'*Paramount*: The House of Lords Decision – Is There Still Hope of Avoiding Some of Those Claims?' (1995) 11 IL&P 78

Mujih, E., 'Legitimising Charge-Backs' [2001] Ins. Law. 3

Myers, S., 'Determinants of Corporate Borrowing' (1977) 5 *Journal of Financial Economics* 147

Naccareto, J. and P. Street, '*Re New Bullas Trading Ltd*: Fixed Charges over Book Debts – Two into One Won't Go' [1994] JIBFL 109

Napier, C. and C. Noke, 'Premium and Pre-Acquisition Profits; the Legal and Accounting Professions and Business Combinations' (1991) 54 MLR 810

'Accounting and Law: An Historical Overview of an Uneasy Relationship' in M. Bromwich and A. G. Hopwood (eds.), *Accounting and the Law* (Institute of Chartered Accountants in England and Wales, London, 1992)

Narey, I. and P. Rubenstein, 'Separation of Book Debts and their Proceeds' [1994] CLJ 225

Newbegin, 'Disqualifying Directors', *The Lawyer*, 24 September 1991

Newton, R., 'Insolvency Bar Reaps Results at Royal Bank' (1994) *Accountancy Age*, 10 February

Nolan, R., '*Downsview Nominees Ltd* v. *First City Corporation Ltd* – Good News for Receivers – In General' (1994) 15 Co. Law. 28

'Less Equal than Others: *Maxwell* and Subordinated Unsecured Obligations' [1995] JBL 484

Nozick, R., *Anarchy, State and Utopia* (Blackwell, Oxford, 1974)

Philosophical Explanations (Clarendon Press, Oxford, 1981)

Oakley, A., 'Proprietary Claims and their Priority in Insolvency' [1995] CLJ 377

Obank, R., 'European Recovery Practice and Reform: Part I' [2000] Ins. Law. 149

Oditah, F., 'Wrongful Trading' [1990] LMCLQ 205

Legal Aspects of Receivables Financing (Sweet & Maxwell, London, 1991)

'Assets and the Treatment of Claims in Insolvency' (1992) 108 LQR 459

'Misfeasance Proceedings against Company Directors' [1992] LMCLQ 207

'Fixed Charges over Book Debts after *Brumark*' (2001) 14 *Insolvency Intelligence* 49

Oditah, F. and A. Zacaroli, 'Chattel Leases and Insolvency' [1997] CfiLR 29

O'Donovan, J., 'Group Therapies for Group Insolvencies' in M. Gillooly (ed.), *The Law Relating to Corporate Groups* (Butterworths, Sydney, 1993)

Offer, 'Influential Desire and Dominant Intention' (1990) 3 *Insolvency Intelligence* 42

Office of Fair Trading, *The Protection of Consumer Prepayments: A Discussion Paper* (1984)

Ogowewo, T., 'A Perfect Case for the Application of Section 423 of the Insolvency Act 1986: *Yukong Line of Korea v. Rendsburg Investments Corp. of Liberia (No. 2)*' [1999] Ins. Law. 106

Ogus, A. I., *Regulation: Legal Form and Economic Theory* (Oxford University Press, Oxford, 1994)

Ogus, A. and C. Rowley, *Prepayments and Insolvency* (OFT Occasional Paper, 1984)

Ogus, A. and C. Veljanovski, *Readings in the Economics of Law and Regulation* (Oxford University Press, Oxford, 1984)

Omar, P. J., 'The Future of Corporate Rescue Legislation in France, Part II: Survey and Analysis' [1997] ICCLR 171

'French Insolvency Laws: An Outline of Reform Proposals' [1999] Ins. Law. 132

'New Initiatives on Cross-Border Insolvency in Europe' [2000] Ins. Law. 211

'The Reform of Insolvency Law in France: The 1999 Orientation Document' [2000] Ins. Law. 263

'The Wider European Framework for Insolvency' (2001) 17 IL&P 135

Page, A. C., 'Self-Regulation: The Constitutional Dimension' (1986) 49 MLR 141

Painter, C., 'Note: Tort Creditor Priority in the Secured Credit System: Asbestos Times, the Worst of Times' (1984) 36 Stanford L Rev. 1045

Parkinson, J. E., *Corporate Power and Responsibility: Issues in the Theory of Company Law* (Clarendon Press, Oxford, 1993)

'The Contractual Theory of the Company and the Protection of Non-Shareholder Interests' in D. Feldman and F. Meisel (eds.), *Corporate and Commercial Law: Modern Developments* (Lloyd's of London Press, London, 1996)

Parry, R., 'Funding Litigation in Insolvency' [1998] 2 CfiLR 121

'Case Commentary' [2001] Ins. Law. 58

Parry, R. and D. Milman, 'Transaction Avoidance Provision in Corporate Insolvency: An Empirical Study' (1998) 14 IL&P 280

Pateman, C., *Participation and Democratic Theory* (Cambridge University Press, London, 1970)

Payne, J., 'Casting Light into the Shadows: *Secretary of State for Trade and Industry v. Deverell*' (2001) 22 Co. Law. 90

Pesse, J. and D. Wood, 'Issues in Assessing MDA Models of Corporate Failure: A Research Note' (1992) 24 *British Accounting Review* 33

Peterson, M. and R. Rajan, 'The Benefits of Lending Relationships: Evidence from Small Business Data' (1994) 49 *Journal of Finance* 3

Pettet, B., 'Limited Liability: A Principle for the 21st Century?' in M. Freeman and R. Halson (eds.), (1995) 48 *Current Legal Problems* 125

Phillips, M., *The Administration Procedure and Creditors' Voluntary Arrangements* (Centre for Commercial Law Studies, QMW, London, 1996)

Pickin, A., 'Getting Rid of Waste Management Licences' (1999) 13 *Insolvency Intelligence* 79

Pike, N., 'The Human Rights Act 1998 and its Impact on Insolvency Practitioners' [2001] Ins. Law. 25

Plainer, A., 'Challenging an Administrator' (1999) *Insolvency Bulletin* 5 (July/August)

'Administrators: When to Go to Court?' (2000) 2 *Finance and Credit Law* 1

Platt, H. D., *Why Companies Fail: Strategies for Detecting, Avoiding, and Profiting from Bankruptcy* (Lexington Books, Lexington, Mass., 1985)

Png, C.-A., 'Conflicting Obligations in Insolvency Cases' (2001) 22 Co. Law. 281

Pointon, F., 'London Approach: A Look at its Application and its Alternatives' (1994) *Insolvency Bulletin* 5 (March)

Polinsky, S. and S. Shavell, 'Should Employees be Subject to Fines and Imprisonment Given the Existence of Corporate Liability?' (1993) 13 *International Review of Law and Economics* 239

Pollard, D., *Corporate Insolvency: Employment and Pension Rights* (2nd edn, Butterworths, London, 2000)

Pope, T. and M. Woollard, 'The Balance of Power in the Expenses Regime: Part 1 – *Leyland Daf* ' (2001) 14 *Insolvency Intelligence* 9

'Part 2 – *Lewis* (2001)' 14 *Insolvency Intelligence* 20

Posner, R., 'The Rights of Creditors of Affiliated Corporations' (1976) 43 U Chic. L Rev. 499

Economic Analysis of Law (5th edn, Aspen Law and Business, New York, 1998)

'Utilitarianism, Economics and Legal Theory' (1979) 8 *Journal of Legal Studies* 103

Poutziouris, P., F. Chittenden and N. Michaelas, *The Financial Development of Smaller Private and Public SMEs* (Manchester Business School, Manchester, 1999)

Power, M., *The Audit Society* (Oxford University Press, Oxford, 1998)

Pratten, C. F., *Company Failure* (Institute of Chartered Accountants in England and Wales, London, 1991)

Prentice, D., 'The Effect of Insolvency on Pre-liquidation Transactions' in B. Pettet (ed.), *Company Law in Change* (Stevens & Sons, London, 1987)

'Creditors' Interest and Directors' Duties' (1990) 10 OJLS 265

'Directors, Creditors and Shareholders' in E. McKendrick (ed.), *Commercial Aspects of Trusts and Fiduciary Obligations* (Clarendon Press, Oxford, 1992)

'Contracts and Corporate Insolvency Proceedings', paper given at SPTL Seminar on Insolvency Proceedings, Oxford, September 1995

'Some Observations on the Law Relating to Preferences' in R. Cranston (ed.), *Making Commercial Law* (Clarendon Press, Oxford, 1997)

'Corporate Personality, Limited Liability and the Protection of Creditors' in R. Grantham and C. Rickett (eds.), *Corporate Personality in the Twentieth Century* (Hart, Oxford, 1998)

Prosser, T., *Law and the Regulators* (Oxford University Press, Oxford, 1997)

Pugh, C., 'Duties of Care Owed to Mortgagors and Guarantors: The Hidden Liability' (1995) 11 IL&P 143

'*Hollicourt* to Reduce Banks' Exposure under Section 127' (2001) 17 IL&P 53

R3, the Association of Business Recovery Professionals, 'The Moratorium Provisions for the Company Voluntary Arrangement Procedure in the Insolvency Bill 2000' (2000) 16 IL&P 77

Ninth Survey of Business Recovery in the UK (R3, London, 2001)

Ostrich's Guide to Business Survival (R3, London, 2001)

Rabin, R., 'Deterrence and the Tort System' in M. Friedman (ed.), *Sanctions and Rewards in the Legal System* (University of Toronto Press, Toronto, 1989)

Rajak, H., 'Company Rescue' (1993) 4 IL&P 111

    Insolvency Law: Theory and Practice (Sweet & Maxwell, London, 1993)

    'The Challenges of Commercial Reorganisation in Insolvency: Empirical Evidence from England' in J. S. Ziegel (ed.), *Current Developments in International and Comparative Corporate Insolvency Law* (Clarendon Press, Oxford, 1994)

    'Can a Receiver be Negligent?' in B. Rider (ed.), *The Corporate Dimension: An Exploration of Developing Areas of Company and Commercial Law* (Jordans, Bristol, 1998)

Rajani, S., 'Enforceability of Subordination of Debt in a Liquidation' (2000) 16 IL&P 58

    'Fixed Charges Over Company's Book Debts after *Brumark*' (2001) 17 IL&P 125

Ramsay, I., 'Corporate Governance, Shareholder Litigation and the Prospects for a Statutory Derivative Action' (1992) 15 UNSW LJ 149

Rasmussen, R., 'Debtor's Choice: A Menu Approach to Corporate Bankruptcy' (1992) 71 Texas L Rev. 51

    'An Essay on Optimal Bankruptcy Rules and Social Justice' (1994) U Illinois L Rev. 1

    'The Ex Ante Effects of Bankruptcy Reform on Investment Incentives' (1994) 72 Wash. ULQ 1159

Rawls, J., *A Theory of Justice* (Harvard University Press, Cambridge, Mass., 1971)

    The Liberal Theory of Justice: A Critical Examination of the Principal Doctrines in 'A Theory of Justice' (Clarendon Press, Oxford, 1973)

Report of the Commission on the Bankruptcy Laws of the US, Pt 1, HR Doc. No. 137, 93d Cong., 1st Sess. 85 (1973)

Report of the Committee on Consumer Credit (Lord Crowther, Chair) (Cmnd 4596, 1971)

Report of the Committee on the Enforcement of Judgement Debts (Payne Committee) (Cmnd 3909, 1969)

Report of the Committee on the Financial Aspects of Corporate Governance (Cadbury Committee) (December 1992)

Report of the Review Committee on Insolvency Law and Practice (Cmnd 8558, 1982) (Cork Report)

Report of the Study Committee on Bankruptcy and Insolvency Legislation (Canada, 1970)

Richardson, P., 'Consumer Protection and the Trust' [1985] JBL 456

Rickett, C., 'Different Views on the Scope of the *Quistclose* Analysis: English and Antipodean Insights' (1991) 107 LQR 608

    'Of Constructive Trusts and Insolvency' in F. Rose (ed.), *Restitution and Insolvency* (Lloyd's of London Press, London, 2000)

Ridgway, P., 'Corporation Tax in Insolvency: Part 3 – Equitable Set-Off and Crown Debts' (2000) 13 *Insolvency Intelligence* 9

Riley, C., 'Directors' Duties and the Interests of Creditors' (1989) 10 Co. Law. 87

    'The Company Director's Duty of Care and Skill: The Case for an Onerous but Subjective Standard' (1999) 62 MLR 697

Rinze, J., 'Konzernrecht: Law on Groups of Companies in Germany' (1993) 14 Co. Law. 143

Roberts, H., '*T & D Industries plc* Revisited: Further Guidance for Administrators in Disposing of Assets' (2000) 16 IL&P 61

Roe, M., 'Commentary on "On the Nature of Bankruptcy": Bankruptcy, Priority and Economics' (1989) 75 Va. L Rev. 219

Rosh, R., 'New York's Response to the "D & O" Insurance Crisis' (1989) 54 Brooklyn LR 1305

Rubin, G. R. and D. Sugarman (eds.), *Law, Economy and Society: Essays in the History of English Law* (Professional Books, Abingdon, 1984)

Samuels, J., F. Wilkes and R. Brayshaw, *Management of Company Finance* (6th edn, International Thompson Business Press, London, 1995)

Sandel, M. J., *Liberalism and the Limits of Justice* (Cambridge University Press, Cambridge, 1982)

Sappideen, R., 'Ownership of the Large Corporation: Why Clothe the Emperor?' (1996–7) 7 King's College LJ 27

Sargeant, M., 'An Amended Acquired Rights Directive' [1998] JBL 577

'Business Transfers and Corporate Insolvencies: The Effect of TUPE' (1998) 14 IL&P 8

'More Flexibility for Insolvent Transfers: The Amended Acquired Rights Directive' (1999) 15 IL&P 6

'Proposed Transfer Regulations and Insolvency' [2002] JBL 108

Schermer, B. S., 'Response to Professor Gross: Taking the Interests of the Community into Account in Bankruptcy' (1994) 72 Wash. ULQ 1049

Schmitthoff, C. M., 'A Consumers' Prepayment (Protection) Bill?' [1984] JBL 105

Schmitthoff, C. and F. Wooldridge (eds.), *Groups of Companies* (Sweet & Maxwell, London, 1991)

Schulte, R., 'Corporate Groups and the Equitable Subordination of Claims on Insolvency' (1997) 18 Co. Law. 2

Schwarcz, A., 'The Easy Case for the Priority of Secured Claims in Bankruptcy' (1997) 47 Duke LJ 425

Schwartz, A., 'Security Interests and Bankruptcy Priorities: A Review of Current Theories' (1981) 10 *Journal of Legal Studies* 1

'A Theory of Loan Priorities' (1989) 18 *Journal of Legal Studies* 209

'Taking the Analysis of Security Seriously' (1994) 80 Va. L Rev. 2073

Scott, C. and J. Black, *Cranston's Consumers and the Law* (3rd edn, Butterworths, London, 2000)

Scott, J., 'Bankruptcy, Secured Debt and Optimal Capital Structure' (1977) 32 *Journal of Financial Law* 2

Scott, R., 'A Relational Theory of Secured Financing' (1986) 86 Colum. L Rev. 901

Sealy, L. S., *Company Law and Commercial Reality* (Sweet & Maxwell, London, 1984)

'Directors' "Wider" Responsibilities: Problems, Conceptual, Practical and Procedural' (1987) 13 Monash LR 164

'Personal Liability of Directors and Officers for Debts of Insolvent Corporations: A Jurisdictional Perspective (England)' in J. Ziegel (ed.), *Current Developments in International and Comparative Corporate Insolvency Law* (Clarendon Press, Oxford, 1994)

'Corporate Rescue Procedures: Some Overseas Comparisons' in F. Macmillan (ed.), *Perspectives in Company Law* (Kluwer, London, 1995)

'Company Liquidations: When Should Post-petition Banking Transactions be Avoided?' (2000) 57 CCH Company Law Newsletter 1

Disqualification and Personal Liability of Directors: A Guide to the Changes made by the Insolvency Legislation of 1985 and 1986 (5th edn, CCH New Law, Kingston upon Thames, 2000)

'Mortgagees and Receivers: A Duty of Care Resurrected and Extended' [2000] CLJ 31

'Company Charges: *New Bullas* Overruled – But is This the End of the Story?' [2001] 76 CCH Company Law Newsletter 1

Sealy, L. S. and D. Milman, *Annotated Guide to the Insolvency Legislation* (5th edn, CCH, Bicester, 1999)

Segal, N., 'Rehabilitation and Approaches other than Formal Insolvency Procedures' in R. Cranston (ed.), *Banks and Remedies* (Oxford University Press, Oxford, 1992)

'An Overview of Recent Developments and Future Prospects in the UK' in J. Ziegel (ed.), *Current Developments in International and Comparative Corporate Insolvency Law* (Clarendon Press, Oxford, 1994)

'Corporate Recovery and Rescue: Mastering the Key Strategies Necessary for Successful Cross Border Workouts – Part I and Part II' (2000) 13 *Insolvency Intelligence* 17, 25

Selwyn, N., *Law of Employment* (11th edn, Butterworths, London, 2000)

Sen, A. and B. Williams (eds.), *Utilitarianism and Beyond* (Cambridge University Press, Cambridge, 1982)

Shanker, M., 'The Worthier Creditors (and a Cheer for the King)' (1975–6) 1 Canadian Bus. LJ 341

'The American Bankruptcy Preference Law: Perceptions of the Past, the Transition to the Present, and Ideas for the Future' in J. Ziegel (ed.), *Current Developments in International and Comparative Corporate Insolvency Law* (Clarendon Press, Oxford, 1994)

Shavell, S., 'On Liability and Insurance' (1982) 13 *Bell Journal of Economics* 120

'Liability for Harm Versus Regulation of Safety' (1984) 13 *Journal of Legal Studies* 357

Economic Analysis of Accident Law (Harvard University Press, Cambridge, Mass., 1987)

Shaw, P., 'Administrators: Peaceable Re-entry by a Landlord Revisited' [1999] Ins. Law. 254

Shrubsall, V., 'Competitive Tendering, Out-sourcing and the Acquired Rights Directive' (1998) 61 MLR 85

Shuchman, P., 'An Attempt at a "Philosophy of Bankruptcy"' (1973) 21 UCLA L Rev. 403

Shulte, S., 'Enforcing Wrongful Trading as a Standard of Conduct for Directors and a Remedy for Creditors: The Special Case for Corporate Insolvency' (1999) 20 Co. Law. 80

Shupack, P., 'Solving the Puzzle of Secured Transactions' (1989) 41 Rutgers L Rev. 1067

Sikka, P., 'Turkeys Don't Vote for Christmas, Do They?' (1999) *Insolvency Bulletin* 5 (June)

Simmons, M., 'Avoiding the *Pari Passu* Rule' (1996) 9 *Insolvency Intelligence* 9

'Wrongful Trading' (2001) 14 *Insolvency Intelligence* 12

Simmons, M. and T. Smith, 'The Human Rights Act 1998: The Practical Impact on Insolvency' (2000) 16 IL&P 167

Smith, A. and M. Neill, 'The Insolvency Act 2000' (2001) 17 IL&P 84

Smith, C. and J. Warner, 'On Financial Contracting: An Analysis of Bond Covenants' (1979) 7 *Journal of Financial Economics* 117

Smith, M., 'The London Approach', conference paper to Wilde Sapte Seminar, 1992

Snaith, I., with assistance of F. Cownie, *The Law of Corporate Insolvency* (Waterlow, London, 1990)

Society of Practitioners of Insolvency, Eighth Survey, *Company Insolvency in the United Kingdom* (SPI, London, 1999)

Response to the Consultation Paper of September 1999 (SPI, London, 12 November 1999)

Spahos, D., 'Lenders, Borrowing Groups of Companies and Corporate Guarantees: An Insolvency Perspective' [2001] JCLS 333

Spencer, J., 'The Commercial Realities of Reservation of Title Clauses' [1989] JBL 220

Stein, J., 'Rescue Operations in Business Crises' in K. J. Hopt and G. Teubner (eds.), *Corporate Governance and Directors' Liabilities: Legal, Economic, and Sociological Analyses on Corporate Social Responsibility* (De Gruyter, Berlin, 1985)

Steiner, M., 'Receivers v. Liquidators v. Preferential Creditors v. Unsecured Creditors: Practitioners Beware!' (2001) 17 IL&P 3

Stewart, G., 'No Remedial Trust in Insolvency' (1998) (August) *Insolvency Practitioner* 8

'Section 127 in the Court of Appeal' (2001) *Recovery* (February) 9

'Legal Update' (2001) *Recovery* (July) 8

'*Brumark*: The World Stops Spinning on its Axis?' (2001) *Recovery* (September) 6

'The British Eagle has Landed' (2001) *Recovery* (December) 7

Stewart, R. B., 'The Reformation of American Administrative Law' (1975) 99(2) Harv. L Rev. 1667

Stokes, M., 'Company Law and Legal Theory' in W. Twining (ed.), *Legal Theory and Common Law* (Blackwell, Oxford, 1986)

Stone, C. D., 'The Place of Enterprise Liability in the Control of Corporate Conduct' (1980) 90 Yale LJ 1

Stone, K. Van Wezel, 'Policing Employment Contracts Within the Nexus-of-Contracts Firm' (1993) 43 U Toronto LJ 353

Stulz, R. and H. Johnson, 'An Analysis of Secured Debt' (1985) 14 *Journal of Financial Economics* 501

Sugarman, D. and G. Teubner (eds.), *Regulating Corporate Groups in Europe* (Nomos, Baden-Baden, 1990)

Sugden, R., *The Economics of Rights, Cooperation and Welfare* (Blackwell, Oxford, 1986)

Sullivan, T. A., E. Warren and J. L. Westbrook, *As We Forgive Our Debtors: Bankruptcy and Consumer Credit in America* (Oxford University Press, New York, 1989)

Sutton, B. (ed.), *The Legitimate Corporation* (Blackwell, Oxford, 1993)

Swain, C., 'The Landlord's Claim: The *Park Air Services* Case' (1999) *Insolvency Bulletin* 6

Swain, V., 'Taking Care of Business' (1999) *Insolvency Bulletin* 9

Symes, C., 'The Protection of Wages When Insolvency Strikes' (1997) 5 *Insolvency Law Journal* 196

Symposium, 'Contractual Freedoms in Corporate Law' (1988) 89 Colum. L Rev. 1385

Taffler, R., 'Forecasting Company Failure in the UK Using Discriminant Analysis and Financial Ratio Data' (1982) *Journal of the Royal Statistical Society*, Series A, 342

Taffler, R. and D. Citron, Study (City University, 1995)

Tateossian, R., 'Briefing' (2000) 2 *Finance and Credit Law* 5

'The Future of Directors' Disqualification' [2000] *Insolvency Bulletin* 6

'The Scope of Section 166(5) Insolvency Act 1986: An Analysis' (2001) *Finance and Credit Law* 4

Telfer, T., 'Risk and Insolvent Trading' in R. Grantham and C. Rickett (eds.), *Corporate Personality in the Twentieth Century* (Hart, Oxford, 1998)

Tetley, W., *Maritime Liens and Claims: Chorley and Giles' Shipping Law* (7th edn, BLAIS, Montreal, 1989)

Theobold, K., 'The Ferris Report' (1998) 14 IL&P 300

Thomas, K., and C. Ryan, 'Section 459, Public Policy and Freedom of Contract' (2001) 22 Co. Law. 199

Trade and Industry Committee, Second Report from the Trade and Industry Committee (Session 1999–2000) Draft Insolvency Bill, HC 112

Fourth Special Report, *Government Observations on the First and Second Reports from the Trade and Industry Committee* (session 1999–2000) HC 237

Triantis, G., 'Mitigating the Collective Action Problem of Debt Enforcement through Bankruptcy Law: Bill C-22 and its Shadow' (1992) 20 Canadian Bus. LJ 242

'Secured Debt Under Conditions of Imperfect Information' (1992) 21 *Journal of Legal Studies* 225

'The Interplay between Liquidation and Reorganisation in Bankruptcy: The Role of Screens, Gatekeepers and Guillotines' (1996) 16 *International Review of Law and Economics* 101

Triantis, G. and R. Daniels, 'The Role of Debt in Interactive Corporate Governance' (1995) 83 Calif. L Rev. 1073

Trower, W., 'Bringing Human Rights Home to the Insolvency Practitioner' (2000) 13 *Insolvency Intelligence* 52

'Human Rights: Article 6 – The Reality and the Myth' [2001] Ins. Law. 48

Tunc, A., 'The Fiduciary Duties of a Dominant Shareholder' in C. Schmitthoff and F. Wooldridge (eds.), *Groups of Companies* (Sweet & Maxwell, London, 1991)

Ulph, J., 'Equitable Proprietary Rights in Insolvency: The Ebbing Tide?' [1996] JBL 482

'Sale and Lease-Back Agreements in a World of Title Relativity: *Michael Gerson (Leasing) Ltd v. Wilkinson and State Securities Ltd*' (2001) 64 MLR 481

Varollo, G. and J. Fukelstein, 'Fiduciary Obligations of Directors of the Financially Troubled Company' (1982) 48 *Business Lawyer* 239

Verrill, J., 'Attacking Antecedent Transactions' [1993] 12 JIBL 485

'*Brumark Investments* and Fixed Charges on Book Debts' (2001) 3 *Finance and Credit Law*, No. 2

Vetsuypens, M., 'Creditor Control in Financially Distressed Firms: Empirical Evidence' (1994) 72 Wash. ULQ 1005

Villiers, C., 'Employees as Creditors: A Challenge for Justice in Insolvency Law' (1999) 20 Co. Law. 222

Walters, A., 'Foreshortening the Shadow: Maintenance, Champerty and the Funding of Litigation in Corporate Insolvency' (1996) 17 Co. Law. 165

'A Modern Doctrine of Champerty?' (1996) 112 LQR 560

'*Re Oasis Merchandising Services Ltd* in the Court of Appeal' (1997) 18 Co. Law. 214

'Anonymous Funders and Abuse of Process' (1998) 114 LQR 207

'Enforcing Wrongful Trading: Substantive Problems and Practical Disincentives' in B. Rider (ed.), *The Corporate Dimension: An Exploration of Developing Areas of Company and Commercial Law* (Jordans, Bristol, 1998)

'Round Up: Corporate Finance and Receivership' (1999) 20 Co. Law. 324

'Directors' Disqualification' (2000) 21 Co. Law. 90

'Directors' Duties: The Impact of the Directors' Disqualification Act 1986' (2000) 21 Co. Law. 110

'Round Up: Corporate Insolvency' (2000) 21 Co. Law. 262

'Staying Proceedings on Grounds of Champerty' [2000] Ins. Law. 16

'Bare Undertakings in Directors' Disqualification Proceedings: The Insolvency Act 2000, *Blackspur* and Beyond' (2001) 22 Co. Law. 290

'Directors' Disqualification after the Insolvency Act 2000: The New Regime' [2001] Ins. Law. 86

'*Re Floor Fourteen Ltd* in the Court of Appeal' (2001) 22 Co. Law. 215

'Wrongful Trading: Two Recent Cases' [2001] Ins. Law. 211

Walton, P., 'The Landlord, his Distress, the Insolvent Tenant and the Stranger' (2000) 16 IL&P 47

Walzer, M., *Spheres of Justice* (Basil Blackwell, Oxford, 1995)

Warren, E., 'Bankruptcy Policy' (1987) 54 U Chic. L Rev. 775

'The Untenable Case for Repeal of Chapter 11' (1992) 102 Yale LJ 437

'Bankruptcy Policymaking in an Imperfect World' (1993) 92 Mich. L Rev. 336

Warren, E. and J. L. Westbrook, *The Law of Debtors and Creditors: Text, Cases and Problems* (Little, Brown, Boston, 1986)

Webb, D., 'An Economic Evaluation of Insolvency Processes in the UK: Does the 1986 Insolvency Act Satisfy the Creditors' Bargain?' (1991) *Oxford Economic Papers* 144

Wedderburn, K. W., *Company Law Reform* (Fabian Society, London, 1965)

'Multinationals and the Antiquities of Company Law' (1984) 47 MLR 87

'The Social Responsibility of Companies' (1985) 15 Mel. ULR 4

Westbrook, J. L., 'A Functional Analysis of Executory Contracts' (1989) 74 Minn. L Rev. 227

'A Comparison of Bankruptcy Reorganisation in the US with Administration Procedure in the UK' (1990) 6 IL&P 86

'Global Insolvencies in a World of Nation States' in A. Clarke (ed.), *Current Issues in Insolvency Law* (Stevens & Sons, London, 1991)

'Universal Participation in Transnational Bankruptcies' in R. Cranston (ed.), *Making Commercial Law: Essays in Honour of Roy Goode* (Clarendon Press, Oxford, 1997)

Weston, D., 'The London Rules and Debt Restructuring' (1992) Sol. Jo. 216

Wheeler, S., 'The Insolvency Act 1986 and ROTs' [1987] JBL 180

Reservation of Title Clauses (Oxford University Press, Oxford, 1991)

'Disqualification of Directors: A Broader View' in H. Rajak (ed.), *Insolvency Law: Theory and Practice* (Sweet & Maxwell, London, 1993)

'Capital Fractionalised: The Role of Insolvency Practitioners in Asset Distribution' in M. Cain and C. B. Harrington (eds.), *Lawyers in a Post Modern World: Translation and Transgression* (Open University Press, Buckingham, 1994)

'Empty Rhetoric and Empty Promises: The Creditors' Meeting' (1994) 21 *Journal of Law and Society* 350

'Directors' Disqualification: Insolvency Practitioners and the Decision-making Process' (1995) 15 *Legal Studies* 283

Wheeler, S. and G. Wilson, *Directors' Liabilities in the Context of Corporate Groups* (Insolvency Lawyers' Association, Oxfordshire, 1998)

White, M., 'Public Policy Toward Bankruptcy' (1980) 11 *Bell Journal of Economics* 550

'The Corporate Bankruptcy Decision' (1989) 3 *Journal of Economic Perspectives* 129

White, J., 'The Recent Erosion of the Secured Creditor's Rights Through Cases, Rules and Statutory Changes in Bankruptcy Law' (1983) 53 Miss. LJ 389

'Efficiency Justifications for Personal Property Security' (1984) 37 Vand. L Rev. 473

White Paper, *A Revised Framework for Insolvency Law* (Cmnd 9175, 1984)

Lifting the Burden (Cmnd 9571, 1985)

Building Business, Not Barriers (Cmnd 9794, 1986)

Releasing Enterprise (Cm 512, 1988)

Our Competitive Future: Building the Knowledge Driven Economy (Cm 4176, December 1998)

Enterprise, Skill and Innovation (2001)

Productivity and Enterprise: Insolvency – A Second Chance (Cm 5234, July 2001)

Wilding, J., 'Instructing Investigating Accountants' (1994) 7 *Insolvency Intelligence* 3

Wilkinson, A., A. Cohen and R. Sutherland, 'Creditors' Schemes of Arrangement and Company Voluntary Arrangements' in H. Rajak (ed.), *Insolvency Law: Theory and Practice* (Sweet & Maxwell, London, 1993)

Williams, C., 'Retention of Title: Some Recent Developments' (1991) 12 Co. Law. 54

Williams, C. and A. McGee, 'A Company Director's Liability for Wrongful Trading' *ACCA Research Report* (No. 30) (1992)

Wilson, J., *British Business History 1720–1994* (Manchester University Press, Manchester, 1995)

Winterborne, P., 'The Second Hand Cause of Action Market' (2001) 14 *Insolvency Intelligence* 65

Wishart, D., 'Models and Theories of Directors' Duties to Creditors' (1991) 14 NZULR 323 *Company Law in Context* (Oxford University Press, Auckland, 1994)

Withyman, T., 'Disclaimer: Practical Tips on the Consequences' (2000) *Insolvency Bulletin* 5

Wolff, R., *Understanding Rawls* (Princeton University Press, Princeton, N.J., 1977)

Wood, P., *English and International Set-Off* (Sweet & Maxwell, London, 1989)
Principles of International Insolvency (Sweet & Maxwell, London, 1995)
Allen & Overy Global Law Maps: World Financial Law (3rd edn, Allen & Overy, London, 1997)

Worthington, S., *Proprietary Interests in Commercial Transactions* (Clarendon Press, Oxford, 1996)

Wright, D., 'The Remedial Constructive Trust and Insolvency' in F. Rose (ed.), *Restitution and Insolvency* (Lloyd's of London Press, London, 2000)

Wruck, K., 'Financial Distress, Reorganisation and Organisational Efficiency' (1990) 27 *Journal of Financial Economics* 419

Zacoroli, A., 'Fixed Charges on Book Debts' (1997) 10 *Insolvency Intelligence* 41

Zalman, D., 'The Unpaid Employee as Creditor' (1980) 6 Dalhouse LJ 148

Ziegel, J. S., 'Creditors as Corporate Stakeholders' (1993) 43 U Toronto LJ 511
'The Privately Appointed Receiver and the Enforcement of Security Interests: Anomaly or Superior Solution?' in Ziegel (ed.), *Current Developments in International and Comparative Corporate Insolvency Law* (Clarendon Press, Oxford, 1994)

Index